D0721759

DELPHI PROGRAMMING EXPLORER

Jeff Duntemann

Jim Mischel

Don Taylor

 CORIOLIS GROUP BOOKS

USS LIBERTY MEMORIAL
PUBLIC LIBRARY

Publisher	*Keith Weiskamp*
Editor	*Jeff Duntemann*
Proofreader	*Diane Green Cook*
Cover Design	*Gary Smith*
Interior Design	*Bradley Grannis*
Layout Production	*Michelle Stroup*
Publicist	*Shannon Bounds*
Indexer	*Diane Green Cook*

Trademarks: All brand names and product names included in this book are trademarks, registered trademarks, or trade names of their respective holders.

Distributed to the book trade by IDG Books Worldwide, Inc.

Copyright © 1995 by The Coriolis Group, Inc.

All rights reserved.

Reproduction or translation of any part of this work beyond that permitted by section 107 or 108 of the 1976 United States Copyright Act without the written permission of the copyright owner is unlawful. Requests for permission or further information should be addressed to The Coriolis Group, 7339 E. Acoma Drive, Suite 7, Scottsdale, Arizona 85260.

Library of Congress Cataloging-in-Publication Data

Duntemann, Jeff
    Delphi Programming Explorer / Jeff Duntemann, Jim Mischel, Don Taylor
        p. cm.
    Includes Index
    ISBN 1-883577-25-X : $39.99

Printed in the United States of America

10 9 8 7 6 5 4 3 2 1

To Gretchen Duntemann Roper, who sets my words to music.

Jeff Duntemann

For Margaret L. Mischel, mother and friend. I can't repay you, mom—but I can sure as hell tell the world that you did a great job.

Jim Mischel

To the two most important women in my life—Doris, my mother, and Carol, my wife and best friend.

Don Taylor

CONTENTS

INTRODUCTION

Halfway into one of his very long comedy monologues (the one about Fat Albert, if I recall correctly) Bill Cosby pauses and says, "I told you that story so I could tell you *this* one." Only then did he get down to the real point of what he was saying.

I got the same sort of feeling the day I finally received the shrink-wrapped version of Delphi and installed it on my system. Installing a new version of Turbo Pascal is a sort of sacred ritual for me. I installed Turbo Pascal 1.0 in February 1984, and in its turn every version since then—and, as far as I'm concerned, Borland did everything they've done with Turbo Pascal since 1983 so that they could create Delphi. All of that was necessary research and practice, if you will. They created a compiler optimized for speed of development— what a thought! They created a windowed user interface and an ever-expanding suite of highly-integrated tools. They added necessary features to the feature-starved ISO Pascal language, and made it the equal of C. They added objects, and made a couple of stabs at object-oriented application frameworks. They enhanced Pascal to enable it to create Windows applications, something the estimable Charles Petzold told me he doubted could ever be done.

They did all of that so that they could do Delphi, and do it *right*.

The millennium starts here.

That being the case, we at The Coriolis Group decided to begin a new era as well. The book you're holding is as different from all my previous books as Delphi is from all previous versions of Pascal. The idea was to put together a presentation of Delphi that would get a new user up and running in as little time as possible—and make it a wild good time. I needed some help with that, especially if we were to make the book happen reasonably soon after Delphi's release. So I approached two good friends and formidable writers, Jim Mischel and Don Taylor, with an idea for a new sort of book. The idea, in a nutshell, was to do practice *first* and then theory. I wanted to have alternating chapters of fast-paced demonstrations of the Delphi process, followed by more methodical explanations of Object Pascal and Delphi's awesome toolset. Theory puts people to sleep, but worse, it doesn't *stick* without real-world context to hang it on. Taking you through a demonstration of Delphi's powers—deferring detailed explanations for the moment—we give you some experience to hang the theory on. Sitting down and bashing your way through a simple project will cause the lights to go on a lot faster when you read about the nature of what you've actually done. After all, I'll bet most of you work that way: You get a new compiler, and without even glancing at the doc, you try to bash out Hello World or yet another version of The Eternal Print Formatter. Only after you've bloodied your knuckles for an afternoon will you deign to Read Those Fabulous Manuals.

Would you keep on doing that if it didn't work? Don't be silly.

So we decided to be scientific about it, and maybe the knuckles wouldn't get quite as bloody in the process. We decided to make it fun, so that you wouldn't notice the pain.

One final thing: I want to take this space to give full credit to Don Taylor for his utterly indescribable series of chapters, beginning with Chapter 15 and going to the end. I simply suggested that he describe a complete application design and implementation scenario. He countered by suggesting a *story*, about this unemployed private detective who takes up non-traditional programming, and one day lays hands on a copy of Delphi....

I held the phone a little back from my head and grit my teeth. It was one of those totally gonzo ideas that would either crash and burn and take out half the county, or else head for orbit at Mach 17. No middle ground. Naturally, I told him to go for it. Don, if you recall, published the TUG Lines newsletter for Turbo User Group for over ten years. He has an impish sense of humor and dazzling skills with the written word. I don't think I'd have trusted anyone else with such a completely insane challenge. Did he pull it off? Ha. He didn't even break a sweat. (Well, maybe a little one.)

Once the smoke cleared, we realized we had something that was unlike any other book we'd ever written or you've ever read. It's only fitting to start the new programming millennium with a new way to learn programming. We had a riot writing it. We hope you have fun reading it. Please write and let me know what you think.

—Jeff Duntemann
Coriolis Group Books
7339 E. Acoma Drive, Suite 7
Scottsdale, Arizona, 85260

PART 1

Delphi's Home Turf

1

WAY RAD!

Jim Mischel

Rapid Application Development (RAD) is Delphi's purpose. Rapid? You want rapid? Check this out!

Welcome to the world of Delphi! You can bet we're talking about Delphi because you bought this book as a fully alert and literate human being, and since this is a hands-on sort of a book, we'll assume you've already installed Delphi itself. (There are excellent installation instructions in Borland's documentation. You don't need me to explain that.) So why waste time telling you up front what Delphi is? We'll tell you what it *is* by showing you what it *does*, right now and without any further waffling.

We're going to jump right in and develop a small example program. At this early stage, the program's not going to be very exciting, but it'll give you some idea of what Delphi programming is all about. To get you oriented, let me take a page or so to introduce the tools you'll be using for this and all your future Delphi projects.

PICKING UP DELPHI'S TOOLS

To start Delphi (assuming that you've already installed it on your system according to Borland's instructions), start Windows and bring up the Delphi program group. It should look something like Figure 1.1.

Double-click on the "Delphi" program item to start the Delphi application. After Delphi loads, you'll notice that it exists in several small windows that leave most of the underlying screen visible, allowing you to see the Program Manager and any other applications that you have running. I find this distracting, so I normally minimize Program Manager and minimize (or close) the other applications, leaving only the Delphi windows visible on my screen, as shown in Figure 1.2.

Figure 1.1   *The Delphi program group.*

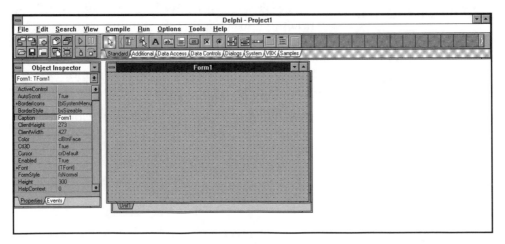

Figure 1.2   *Delphi's initial display.*

 **Clearing the Clutter Quickly**

The obvious way to minimize Program Manager after you run Delphi is to minimize Delphi, then minimize Program Manager, and finally maximize Delphi again. The *smart* way is to grab the extreme right-hand edge of Delphi's main window and size it toward the left just enough to expose Program Manager's minimize button. Press the button—and it's gone to the icon bar at the bottom of the screen!

When Delphi is first loaded, four windows are displayed on the screen:

- Delphi's main window, the title of which is "Delphi - Project1"
- The Object Inspector window
- The form window, labeled "Form1"
- The unit window, labeled UNIT1.PAS, which is mostly hidden by the form window when you start out

Main Window

Delphi's *main window*, which occupies the top of the screen, contains the menu, the speedbar, and the component palette. The *speedbar* is below the menu on the left side of the screen, and contains 14 buttons that perform a variety of actions. These buttons are shortcuts for menu functions.

The *component palette* is below the menu and to the right of the speedbar. You use this palette to select the components that you place on your forms.

Object Inspector Window

The *Object Inspector* window has a "Properties" page that displays information about the currently-selected object in the form window, and allows you to change many of the object's properties. It also has an "Events" page in which you define actions that the object is to perform when the object receives certain events. When you first start Delphi, the Object Inspector displays the properties for the current form. We'll get back to what properties actually *are* in a little bit.

Form Window

The *form window* is the window in which most of your design work will take place. You place controls on the form, and arrange them as desired (by moving and resizing) to create your application's window. There are some things in the form window (such as the grid lines and any non-visual components) that won't be visible at runtime, but for the most part Delphi is a WYSIWYG (What-You-See-Is-What-You-Get) programming environment. This means that what you see in your form at design time is very similar to what the program will look like when it runs.

There may be more than one form window in an application that is more advanced than the one we're about to build. A real world program may have several—or dozens.

Unit Window

The *unit window*, shown in Figure 1.3, is initially "under" the form window. This window contains a source code editor in which you write program source code for your Delphi application. Initially, this window contains only one page, which contains the source code for the new form that you're about to create. In later chapters, you'll see that we can edit other source files in this window as well.

The Role of Code in Delphi

The unit window is initially placed "under" the form window because code— hand-written user interface code—plays a small (albeit important) part in Delphi programs. There's still coding involved, but most of the user interface code is automatically generated by Delphi as you place components on the form. The only part that you have to write is the "glue" code that ties the

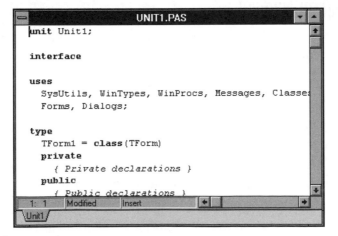

Figure 1.3   The unit window.

components together. This "glue" normally consists of a line or two of code that defines what action to take when a particular event is received. Jeff will have a lot more to say about the ideas behind this kind of programming (called event-driven programming) in the next chapter.

To be sure, Delphi doesn't entirely eliminate the necessity of coding. If you're building a mortgage calculator program, for example, you'll still need to write the "engine"—the procedures and functions that actually perform the mortgage calculations, as opposed to displaying them on the screen. What Delphi does, and does very well, is eliminate most of the common user interface and event-handler coding that has in the past made Windows programming so very difficult.

Lists in a Box

PROJECT As a first example, we're going to build a simple program in which you type names into an edit control and add the names to a list box. You also have the option of sorting or clearing the list box. When it's finished, the application will look similar to Figure 1.4.

We need to start with a fresh form, so if you've been doodling with Delphi's screens during our ongoing discussion, you should select the File | New Project menu item to erase your work and start with a blank form and a clear conscience.

As you can see in Figure 1.4, the ListBox application has an edit control, a list box, and three buttons. We need to add these components to our blank form. We'll start with the edit control.

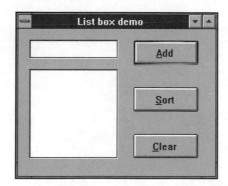

Figure 1.4 *The completed ListBox application.*

 **Controls and Components**

When you first get started with Delphi, some of the terminology can confuse you. One of the toughest to get
straight is the difference between a control and a component. A very simple rule is: *All
controls are components, but not all components are controls.*

For example, an edit control is actually an "edit control component." And a list box is
actually a "list box control component." Since everything that you place on your form is
a component, we will sometimes drop the word "component" or "control" when discussing the items that you place on your forms.

In later chapters, you'll see examples of components (such as timers, data dources,
and standard dialogs) that are *not* controls.

Dropping Components onto the Form

Move the mouse cursor to the edit control component on the component
palette and click the left mouse button. This selects the component for use.
Then, move the mouse to the upper left-hand corner of the form window and
click the left mouse button again. An edit control should now be visible on
the form, as shown in Figure 1.5.

Now, you may not know (though it's possible to guess) exactly which button
selects the edit control. Not a problem, and no need to guess—Delphi will tell
you. If you move the mouse cursor over one of the buttons and hesitate for a
second or two, a *pop-up hint* will appear as a small yellow box containing the
type of control selected by that button. Float the mouse cursor over a few of

Figure 1.5 *Placing the edit control on the form.*

the other buttons and see what the hints tell you. Delphi has a lot of buttons, but they nearly all have hints. Take them!

To add the list box to the form, select the list box component from the component palette, move the mouse cursor somewhere below the edit control on the form, and press and hold the left mouse button while dragging the mouse down and to the left. This places and sizes the list box on the form. When the list box is approximately the proper size, release the left mouse button. You should now have a list box on the form, as well as the edit control, and your form should look something like Figure 1.6.

The controls you drop on the form won't automatically "line up" when you drop them, and after you drop a few controls, things may begin to look a little jagged or random. Don't worry about aligning the controls on the form yet. We'll get to that after we've placed the buttons. Alignment is easier when everything that's going to be on the form is entered.

Dropping Multiple Components of the Same Type

Adding the buttons to the form is even easier than adding the edit control and the list box because Delphi lets us add multiple components of the same type without having to select the component from the component palette each time.

To add the three buttons, place the mouse cursor over the button component on the component palette, hold down the shift key on the keyboard, and click the left mouse button. This selects the button component, and tells Delphi that we're going to place more than one of them on the form. (Notice

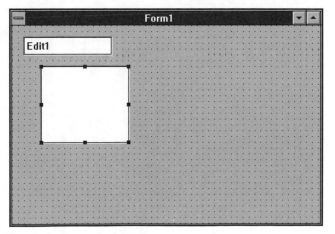

Figure 1.6 *Adding the list box to the form.*

that the button component's button stays down.) Release the shift key, move the mouse cursor to where you want the first button, and click the left mouse button. Move the mouse cursor down a bit to where you want the next button, and click the left mouse button again. Repeat for the third button.

After you've placed the third button on the form (again, don't worry about alignment, we'll get to that in a minute), move the mouse cursor to the arrow cursor bitmap that's on the left end of the component palette and click the left mouse button. This "deselects" the button component so that we won't be adding buttons to the form every time we click the left mouse button. This arrow cursor button is one of Delphi's few buttons that does *not* have a hint, since it is in fact selected most of the time.

Moving and Sizing Components

Unless you're more careful about placing your components than I am, your form probably looks similar to Figure 1.7. All of the components are there, but they're scattered around, and the list box probably isn't the exact size that you want it to be. This, too, is easy to fix, thanks to Delphi's alignment tools and the form window's grid lines.

To move a component, simply place the mouse cursor on the component that you want to move, and press and hold the left mouse button. Then, drag the component to its new position and release the left mouse button.

To size a component, place the mouse cursor over the component that you want to size, and click the left mouse button. This selects the component and

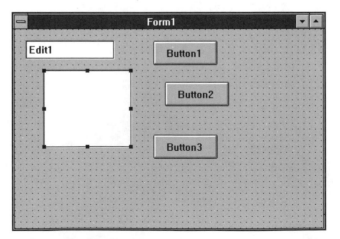

Figure 1.7 *The form with components in disarray.*

displays eight small black squares called *handles* on the component's outline. Then, place the mouse cursor over one of the handles, press and hold the left mouse button, and drag the mouse to enlarge or shrink the component. When the component is the size that you want, release the left mouse button.

The handles on the top, bottom, and sides of the component move that border of the component. The handles on the corners move the two borders that meet at that corner.

Aligning Components

The instructions above should be sufficient for moving and sizing the list box so that it's aligned with the edit control. You could use the same method for each of the three buttons, but Delphi's *alignment tool* makes aligning multiple components much quicker.

To align the buttons, move the mouse cursor to a point near the top of the form so that it's above the first button that you placed on the form, and a line drawn straight down the form would intersect all three buttons. Then, press and hold the left mouse button while moving the mouse cursor down and to the left, drawing a box around the three buttons on the form. Enlarge the box until it encloses all three buttons, and then release the left mouse button. Your display will now look similar to Figure 1.8, with dark gray handles on each corner of each of the three buttons. These gray handles indicate that the three buttons have now been selected as a group, to be acted on as a group.

To align the buttons, we use the alignment tool, which you can access by selecting Edit | Align from the main menu, or by clicking the right mouse

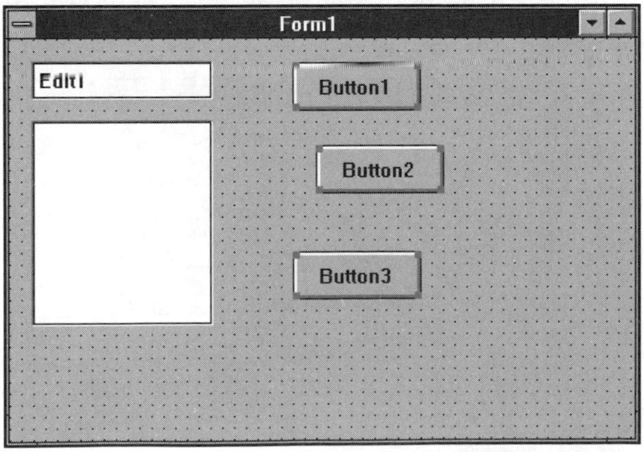

Figure 1.8   *Selecting multiple components for alignment.*

button while the pointer is inside the form (don't forget that!) and selecting "Align…" from the popup menu that appears. Delphi displays the Alignment dialog box, shown in Figure 1.9.

We want to align the left sides of the buttons, and space them equally in the vertical space that they occupy. So, in the Alignment dialog box under Horizontal, select "Left sides," and under Vertical, select "Space equally." Press the OK button, and Delphi will align the buttons as you instructed.

The three buttons should still be selected as a group, which is good—because now we want to move them to their proper position. Simply move the mouse cursor over one of the handles on one of the buttons, click and hold the left mouse button, and drag the controls to their new position. When you have them where you want them, release the left mouse button. Then, move the mouse cursor to the right so that it's not over any component, and click the left mouse button. This will release the controls so that they're no longer treated as a group.

Once you've placed the controls, move the mouse cursor to the bottom left corner of the form window's frame, press and hold the left mouse button, and size the form window so that it looks similar to Figure 1.10. In general, your forms should not be any larger than they have to be, and sizing the form is just a way of getting rid of unnecessary window real estate.

Saving Your Work

Before we go any further, you should save your work. There are actually two files to be saved—the unit source code and the project file.

Select File | Save Project from the main menu. Delphi will display a file save dialog box titled "Save Unit1 As." Type "listform.pas" in the edit box and press

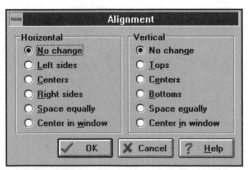

Figure 1.9   *The Alignment dialog box.*

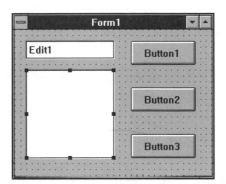

Figure 1.10 *The completed form.*

Enter. Delphi will save the unit file, and then display another file save dialog box, this one titled "Save Project1 As." Type "listdemo.dpr" in the edit box and press Enter. Delphi will save the project file and return to the form window.

Once you've done this the first time (so that Delphi knows what the names of all your files are), you can save the project at any point in the future simply by pressing the Save button on the Delphi toolbar. This is the button showing a file folder and an arrow pointing to a hard disk.

A Difference in Names

Don't make the mistake of applying your pet project name to the source code file (which you name first) and then trying to apply the same name to the project as a whole. It won't work! Delphi requires that the two be different.

Running the Program

Believe it or not, you have just created a working program without writing a single line of code! The program won't really *do* anything, but all the components work as expected. To test it, simply press F9 (or select Run | Run from the main menu). Delphi will compile and run your program. You can enter text in the edit control, tab from control to control, and click on the buttons to make them go up and down. As a program, it's not very exciting—but it's sure impressive when you consider how much code you had to write—like, none.

When you're finished playing with the program, press Alt+F4 to exit and return to Delphi.

CHANGING OBJECT PROPERTIES

Now that we have our user interface designed and working, we need to make the user interface actually *do* something. We also need to change the captions on the buttons and clear the edit control so that it's initially blank when the program is loaded. All these things are changed in the Object Inspector window.

So what's an object? That's a big question, and the answer is one existing on many levels. We'll have a lot more to say about objects later in this book. For now, think of an object as a form or any component placed on a form. This isn't the whole truth, but it's true nonetheless, and it will carry you until we can work a fuller explanation into the text.

Refining the Form

First, let's change the form's caption. "List box demo" is a much more descriptive name for the form than "Form1." To change the caption, move the mouse cursor to a blank spot on the form (not over any component, and not on the title bar) and click. This selects the form as the object we want to inspect. Then click on the Object Inspector window's title bar, to make the Object Inspector the active window. You will see the form's properties displayed in the Object Inspector window, as shown in Figure 1.11.

In the Object Inspector, the selected component's properties are listed on the left side of the window, and the properties' values are shown on the right. To change the form's caption, click on the **Caption** property in the Object In-

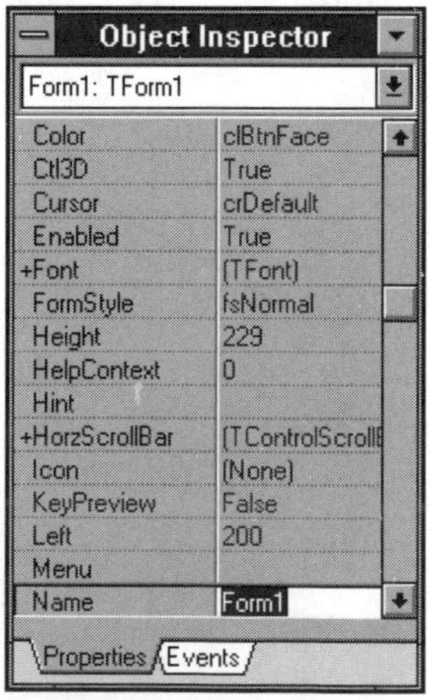

Object Inspector	
Form1: TForm1	
Color	clBtnFace
Ctl3D	True
Cursor	crDefault
Enabled	True
+Font	(TFont)
FormStyle	fsNormal
Height	229
HelpContext	0
Hint	
+HorzScrollBar	(TControlScroll)
Icon	(None)
KeyPreview	False
Left	200
Menu	
Name	Form1

Properties / Events

Figure 1.11   *The form's properties in the Object Inspector.*

spector window, and type "List box demo" in the value field. The text in the form window's title bar should change as you're typing.

To clear the edit control's text, click on the edit control in the form window to select it, and then click on the title bar of the Object Inspector window. The Object Inspector window will display the properties for the selected edit control. To change the text in the edit control, click on the **Text** property in the Object Inspector window. This will highlight the text, "Edit1," which is the current value of that property. Press the Delete key to clear the text. This also clears the edit control's text in the form window. That's the only change that we need to make to the edit control.

We don't need to make any changes to the list box component, but the three buttons do in fact need some work. Click on the first button, **Button1**, in the form window, and then click on the title bar of the Object Inspector window. The properties for the first button are displayed in the Properties page.

The first button is the Add button. Click on the **Caption** property, type, "&Add", and press Enter. The text on the first button in the form window should change as you're typing in the Object Inspector. The ampersand symbol causes Delphi to treat the "A" in "Add" specially—allowing the button to be "pressed" from the keyboard by pressing Alt+A. It also causes the A character to be underlined when the button is displayed.

We want the Add button to be the default push button on the form (that is, the one that gets pushed when we press Enter while working with the form), so we need to change the **Default** property from **False** to **True**. To do this, click on the **Default** property in the Object Inspector window, and then double-click on the highlighted **False**. This will change the value of the property to **True**. True/false properties can be *toggled* by double-clicking on them; that is, you can switch a true/false value to its opposite by double-clicking on the property. Notice that a heavy line appears around the button, to indicate visually that it is now the default button.

The second button is the Sort button. Click on the second button in the form window, and then click on the Object Inspector window. Change the **Caption** for this button to "&Sort". Repeat the process with the third button, changing the **Caption** to "&Clear". When you're finished, your form window will be in its finished state, and should look like Figure 1.12.

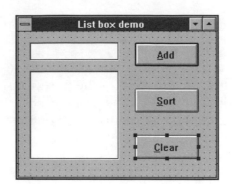

Figure 1.12 *The form in its finished state.*

Responding to Events

The user interface is completed now, and we're ready to make the program respond and actually do something when the buttons are pressed. In short, this is what our program is going to do: When the Add button is pressed, the program takes the text from the edit control, adds the text to the list box, and then clears the edit control. When the Sort button is pressed, the program sorts and re-displays the contents of the list box. When the Clear button is pressed, the list box is cleared. We have to actually write some code to make these things happen. Let's start with the Add button.

Click on the Add button in the form window, and then click on the Events tab at the bottom of the Object Inspector window. You should see a list of events to which this component can respond, as shown in Figure 1.13.

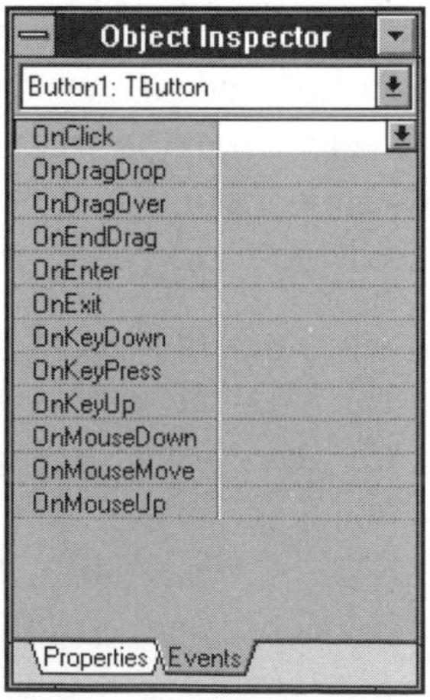

Figure 1.13 *The Events page of the Object Inspector window.*

For this example, we're only interested in the OnClick event—the function that is performed when the button is clicked. We'll discuss this and other events in more detail in later chapters.

Double-click in the value field to the right of the OnClick event in the Object Inspector window. This causes Delphi to bring the unit window (titled LISTFORM.PAS) to the top, over the form window. The unit window will look like Figure 1.14.

The vertical bar edit cursor should be positioned at the point where you should enter code to respond to the Add button's OnClick event. (Note that you won't see the actual cursor in Figure 1.14—cursors, like ghosts, are notoriously hard to capture!) Type the following two lines, exactly as shown, into the unit window between the **begin** and **end** words:

```
Listbox1.Items.Add(Edit1.Text);
Edit1.Text := '';
```

For the moment, you'll have to trust me that this code is going to do what we want. In later chapters we'll discuss exactly what code like this does, and describe the properties that we're changing. For now, accept that the first line adds an item to the list box, and the second line clears the edit control.

Click on the "Toggle Form/Unit" button on the speedbar (the fourth button from the left on the bottom row of the speedbar—check its hint!) to bring the form window to the top. Then, click on the Sort button in the form window to select it, and double-click in the OnClick event's value field in the Object

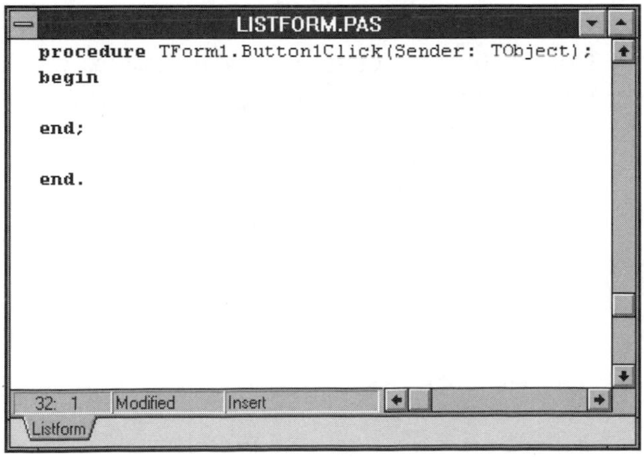

Figure 1.14 *The unit window.*

Inspector window. Again, this brings the Unit window to the top and positions the vertical bar cursor where you should insert the code for the button's OnClick event. (Each button has its own set of events, including its own OnClick event.) Enter this line of code in the Unit window:

```
Listbox1.Sorted := True;
```

Finally, to add the Clear button's OnClick event handler, bring the form window to the front again, click on the Clear button, and then double-click on the OnClick event's value field in the Object Inspector. Then insert these two lines of code in the Unit window:

```
Listbox1.Clear;
Listbox1.Sorted := False;
```

And that's all the coding involved! Bring the form window to the top again and then select File|Save Project to save your work. To run the program, press F9. The program should operate exactly we described at the beginning of this section. To exit the program, press Alt+F4.

SHAZAM! YOU'RE A PROGRAMMER!

As you've seen, developing user interface applications with Delphi is largely a design issue, with little actual programming involved. There *are* situations where programming is required, but the user interface isn't one of those places. Developing the user interface involves adding, moving, and sizing controls on the form. The small example program that we developed in this chapter gives you a good overview of the basic steps involved in building an application with Delphi. In later chapters, we'll explore more components and the different ways that they can be placed on the form.

Is This Really Programming?

Jeff Duntemann

The shape of Delphi differs radically from earlier types of programming, and you have to accept its underlying concepts before you can work well within it.

OK. We gave it a spin. Now, can we talk? Some of you are doubtless bewildered, while others caught on fast and are raring to go. (That crowd might as well press onward to Chapter 3.) What we're going to do here is take a break from exploring, and sit by the fire for a bit and speak of the things that we've seen. That'll be a pattern in this book, remember: We'll go exploring, and then we'll talk about what's going on, and fill in some of the background details. If you find this part boring, well, you can always jump ahead to the next chapter, in which Jim will begin another Delphi Programming project.

But first, some clues for the clueless.

THE SHAPE OF DELPHI

To someone with a totally open mind, there are no surprises. (This should explain why the world is such a surprising place.) As a nerdy 13-year-old reading the latest *Popular Mechanics*, I gasped in awe at the cutaway view of a Wankel Engine. It was a three-cylinder engine with two moving parts. It was weird. It was astonishing. It was impossible.

Come on, already. I knew how engines worked: Intake, compression, ignition, exhaust. Up and down, round and round. But try as I might, I could not get my mind around the Wankel, and I confess that I was in college (and had had some additional experience with mechanical gizmoids) before I genuinely understood how the guldurned thing worked.

From my prepubescent perspective, the Wankel's *shape* was all wrong.

I don't entirely mean the fact that the engine block was a fat cookie-shaped blob instead of a crisp V-8 shaped blob. I mean that the same physics that drove the engine in my 1968 Chevelle drove the Wankel in that *Popular Mechanics*, but those physical laws were used in two radically different ways. My Chevelle had nice round cylinders moving up and down in neat round chambers. The Wankel's blunt rotor lobes sort of made virtual cylinders out of bulges in the engine block wall as they passed by. Somehow or another, intake, compression, ignition, and exhaust were all going on in there, but yeek! Trying to grok the fullness of the process made my head hurt.

Does this start to sound familiar?

Most of us who come to Delphi from almost any other traditional language have the same problem, and that goes double if you're coming to Delphi from a older version of Pascal. (Yes, Delphi is in fact a version of Pascal, but the Pascal is pretty well hidden, no?) We have preconceived notions of how computer programming is supposed to work, and when confronted with Delphi's reality, we get a headache trying to hammer its perceptual shape into the familiar old shape of Turbo Pascal—or even of Turbo C. Somehow, code is getting executed in there, but getting an intuitive grasp of how it's accomplished takes a little interior rearrangement of some very old furniture.

Thinking about lines of code is actually half the problem. It's time to step back far enough so that we can't see the Pascal code at all any more, and look at Delphi's overall shape through the eyes of an architect—and not a code jockey.

ALL THINGS VISIBLE AND INVISIBLE

A Delphi program is, first of all, an *application framework*. An application framework is the "bones" of a functioning application, without anything at all specific sticking to those bones. The bones do work, strictly as given—as you'll discover if you select File | New Project and then run the blank form without adding any controls or making any changes. You'll get an empty window...but that window can be zoomed, moved, resized, or minimized. It has an icon to display when you minimize it. It has everything a Windows program needs that *all* Windows programs need—but not one line of code more.

That empty Delphi program is a lot like a newly-built factory that hasn't yet been sold to any particular manufacturing company. The walls, the heating vents, the power lines, the lights, the intercom and PA system, all of that is there and fully operational, but the building doesn't yet have any particular purpose. That is, it's not any particular *kind* of factory, and it's not set up to build anything. You still have to add the milling machines, punch presses, and assembly lines before you can point to it and say, Ah, of course, that's an *eggbeater* factory.

So an application framework is a way to get a serious leg up on programming an application, by providing you with everything that *all* applications share in common. There's no need to build your own keyboard or mouse handlers. There's no need to build a windowing package. Furthermore, there's no need even to integrate a ready-made mouse handler into a ready-made windowing package. It's all been done for you, and the application framework is already a finished, functioning application. It just doesn't "do" anything.

What's going on behind that empty window? The application framework is listening for input from the user: Mouse clicks and keystrokes. If you click the mouse on the blank frame, the application will know it. It "hears" you. But since you haven't told it to do anything upon hearing something, it hears—and ignores. It reacts only to mouse clicks or keyboard events that trigger actions fundamental to all Windows programs: Resizing, zooming, dragging, and the other commands that affect the size and position of the application on the Windows desktop. Inside the empty window, well, it literally has nothing to do.

I've heard it suggested that making Delphi's "empty" application a fully compilable and runnable program is a marketing gimmick, just a little bit of hacker goofiness in the long tradition for which Borland is famous. (The person

I heard this from apparently had not seen Visual Basic, which operates the same way and did it first.) There's no marketing issue here at all. The empty application is runnable because there is a very clear and sharp line in Delphi between what you start with (the empty application) and what you, the programmer, add.

There's a reason for this, and a damned good one. (If you've ever tried writing a Windows program the old way, you'll know exactly what I mean.) Internally, Windows is a nightmare, full of handles and brushes and contexts and callbacks and a multitude of other things that need remembering and managing and wholesale fooling around with. But since all of those things are present in *every* functioning Windows program, Delphi puts them behind a Romulan cloak of invisibility so that you're not tripping over them constantly. The only things that come through that cloak are the things that must.

As you'll discover in due course, that's remarkably little. Most of the monster can safely remain hidden.

Stimulus and Response

The key to understanding the operation of a Delphi program lies in the notion of stimulus and response. When the user stimulates a button on a Delphi form, program code that you have created as a response is executed. If you don't create a response, there is no response. The stimulus is called an *event*, and the response is called a *procedure*. (A special kind of procedure, actually, called an *event procedure*.) Delphi generates the events in response to things the user does (and to a couple of things unrelated to the user) and you generate the responses. The whole "programming" side of programming in Delphi (that is, things apart from dragging controls around on forms) consists of creating program code that responds, directly or indirectly, to events.

People who have programmed in the traditional fashion sometimes have a lot of trouble with this. They're used to being able to see code execution at every step of the way, from where it starts at the beginning of a program to where it stops at the end. (Never mind that they obligingly look the other way whenever execution dives into an operating system function or library call!) Delphi reminds them somewhat bewilderingly of that "Whack-a-Mole" carnival game in which a stuffed mole jumps up unpredictably from one of a dozen holes in the game field. If you're not there with a hammer to bonk it when it jumps, well, you lose. Delphi code execution seems to jump unpredictably up out of holes in the ground, to run in the light of day for a few lines before vanishing again into some unknowable Stygian deep.

This is true to an extent, but being bewildered is entirely the wrong reaction. (You want bewilderment, check out traditional SDK-style Windows programming. *Bewilderment* we'll give you!) Look at Figure 2.1, which lays out the "Whack-a-Mole" paradigm of programming. The application framework and Windows itself are givens. However, everything above the application framework is code that you write yourself, in relatively compact procedure blocks.

Each hole in the top of the framework is an event. When execution jumps out of one of the holes in the form of an event, it looks for a procedure that you have prepared specifically for that event. If you're there and ready with a procedure, execution will go through your procedure, doing something useful for your application. Notice that not all of the holes in Figure 2.1 have procedures associated with them. If you don't prepare a procedure for a given event, execution jumps out of that hole and simply jumps back in again, having done nothing at all. No harm done; no *nothing* done. This is the default state of affairs for events. Unless you prepare a procedure for an event, the event, when triggered, will return without doing anything.

Another point to be made here is that not all of the "given" code for a Delphi program (that is, the parts you don't write) is even in Delphi's application

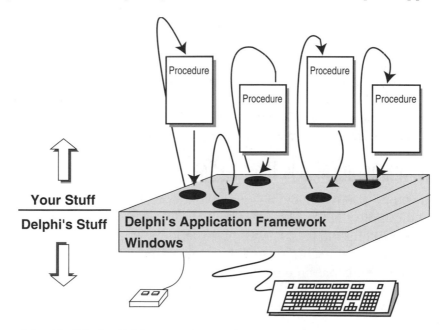

Figure 2.1   *The 'Whack-a-Mole' programming paradigm.*

framework. Quite a bit of it is actually a part of Windows. The line between your programs and Windows itself is much fuzzier than the line between your older programs and DOS. Code for things like the standard dialog boxes and standard buttons is all delivered with Windows. Delphi simply uses it by making the appropriate calls into the Windows DLLs that everybody who runs Windows already has installed. But because of Delphi's application framework design, you simply don't care where the code for the buttons and dialogs and other things is stored, nor how it's called. That's a few less (or several hundred less) things you have to worry about.

Your Own Code Libraries

Event procedures are almost always short and to the point. If an event has to do something ambitious, it's good practice to write that something ambitious in the form of a separate code library written in Object Pascal. This is easy to do, and we'll go into it a little more later on. In fact, if you've programmed in Turbo Pascal or Borland Pascal, what you'll find is that a Pascal unit works just as well in Delphi as it does in Borland or Turbo Pascal. (To top it all, I've found that most ordinary Pascal units created with Borland's Pascal compilers, even in the old days, will load and run without any changes at all in Delphi! It's not such an alien land after all, mole-whacking notwithstanding.)

Figure 2.2 shows this. The rightmost event procedure calls a procedure stored in a unit library. This allows that event procedure to do a lot more work without becoming ungainly in size. Better still, it allows the other procedures to make use of the code in the unit library as well. By not duplicating code in multiple event procedures, you can keep the size of your Delphi applications down and their speed up. Again, we'll explain all this in detail later on.

How Much Programming Is There to Do?

About this time you may have begun to wonder if Delphi programming consists of little more than bonking events with little Pascal procedures. You're probably expecting me to say, Well, it's a little more involved than that. In fact, it may be—or it may not. How much actual Pascal coding you yourself have to do depends on three general factors:

- *How ambitious your application is.* Obviously, all else being equal, you'll have to do more coding in a large, multi-featured application than in a small quick Windows utility.

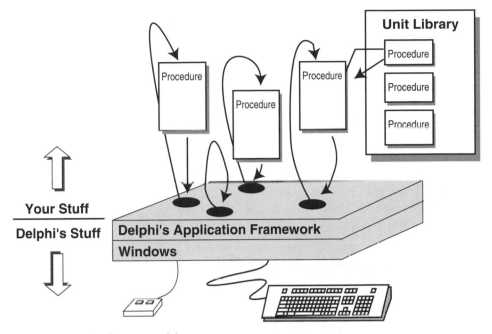

Unit Library

Procedure

Procedure

Procedure

Procedure

Procedure

Procedure

Your Stuff

Delphi's Stuff

Delphi's Application Framework

Windows

Figure 2.2   Code Libraries in Delphi.

- *What sort of application it is.* Delphi provides some tools specifically for database-oriented programming, which is in fact the most common type of programming there is. You can put together a relatively ambitious database program in Delphi with very little Pascal code. Delphi's database features are so completely awesome that you should keep them in mind for use in the sorts of non-database situations where you used to use simple Pascal files. They can save you a lot of coding.

- *What sort of components you can find and use.* The more components you can find that can be used in your program, the less of the program you'll have to write yourself. There is a host of VBX (Visual Basic-style) components already on the market, and more and more of the compact Delphi VCL (Visual Component Library) components are being released every day. If you keep abreast of the components that are available, you'll be able to make the best use of other people's programming talents, some of which (admit it now) just *might* be superior to your own.

Where you'll probably have to do most of your actual coding is in the portions of your application that are most specific to what your application is to do. For example, I wrote a Delphi program to calculate and display mortgage tables. The vast majority of the actual programming I had to do involved a unit library that performed the financial calculations required to generate a mortgage table. There's no component out there that calculates mortgages. (Yet!) So I had to do that work myself. However....

I already *had* a unit library in Borland Pascal that calculates mortgage tables. I wrote it years ago for a DOS-based mortgage program. When I attempted to use it with Delphi, I found that I *had to make no changes to it at all.* So if you have some "old" code in your archives that does the sort of work your new Delphi application is intended to do, fish it out and have a look at it. You may not always have it as easy as I did with my mortgage library, but you may be surprised at how little code surgery you'll have to perform to get old code to operate within a Delphi application.

Building Your Own Components in Delphi

What I just said applies to creating programs in Delphi the usual way. You have another option, one that you should use early and often and as soon as you manage to figure it out. That option is building your own components in Delphi, for use in your Delphi programs or those written by others.

As you work in Delphi you'll find that certain pieces of things you do keep turning up again and again. It's hard to say what those will be, but we all have a certain programming style, and most of us tend to work in certain areas like databases or graphics where the same kinds of problems come up regularly. Sooner or later you'll spot parts of your programs that really beg to be made into components. Special kinds of buttons, certain calculating engines (more on these later on), and other things should just plug into a tools palette for endless re-use. *Code it once, use it forever*—that motto should be first among equals in your motto collection.

Although you can incorporate existing components into new components, most of the work in creating components is in fact Pascal coding, so if you end up making components a lot, you'll be programming a lot more as well. It's a special sort of coding that we won't have the room to cover in this book, but once you've been through this book, I encourage you to study it and give it a try. (Coriolis Group Books will have a component writer's guide in print before the end of 1995. Watch for it!)

The Middlethink Approach to Pascal

If you're a Pascal person (as I am and have been for many years), you may wonder why Delphi isn't called Borland Pascal, or Borland Visual Pascal, or *some* kind of Pascal, sheesh. The cynical view holds that the C bigots have so slandered Pascal over the years as a "kiddie language" that the market doesn't take it seriously any more. There's a lot of truth to this, but that particular war's been lost and it's not worth stewing over. (Furthermore, the C guys are now finding that *their* beloved language is being tossed out of development shops right and left as simply too slow to create anything useful—and, to add humiliation to injury, it's often being replaced by Visual Basic!)

Borland's decision to give the product a new name makes a certain sense once you've used Delphi enough to understand that it really isn't Pascal any more, not the way most of us learned Pascal. You need a whole new way of looking at the programming process to use Delphi effectively, one as alien to Pascal as Pascal is alien to the assembly language culture that preceded Pascal and all higher-level languages. Call it a culture, call it a mindset, but it's different nonetheless. I call it *middlethink*, and it's a useful way to conceptualize the whole concept of visual software development.

Bigthink versus Littlethink

In the ancient days of wooden computers and iron programmers, creating a piece of software took two steps: 1) You designed it and 2) you wrote it. The design was usually a document of some sort with lots of pictures and flow-charts. The program you started at the top and worked your way through in a fairly linear fashion, documenting (one would hope) what you did as you went. The program was mostly linear too, consisting of one sizable procedure that called a multitude of other procedures, many of which called still other procedures, and so on. (That assumes that you didn't just start at the top and write one tremendous 20,000 line procedure, as Paleolithic programmers did in historical times, like when I worked at Xerox in the early 1980s.)

The folks who designed the program were not always the folks who wrote it. Larger programming shops had whole staffs of people who did nothing but design software for separate teams of people to write. (This works well when the designers are good programmers who have been promoted, and badly when the designers are mechanical engineers who bailed out of a cashiered copier design project and needed a job somewhere else in the company. Have I been there? Ha. Guess.) The design people were rightfully more concerned with the shape of the project and the logic that governed it than with the nature of the code that implemented the design. This is a culture I call *bigthink*, since it takes the big picture of the project and from there attempts to crystallize it into reality at levels of ever-increasing detail. At some point there is enough detail to hand it to the programmers.

The programmers, on the other hand, were playing a different game. They knew the quirks and limitations of the machines they wrote for and the tools they were forced to use. The quirks were often bizarre and the limitations often serious. (The PDP-8 was considered a minor miracle of its time, and it could address *4K* of physical memory. 4K. You can't write a business letter in that small a file any more.) Because programmers have to produce working code, they're traditionally obsessed with constraints, performance, capacity, and the ability to put one instruction ahead of another and make it all go. They're mindful of the big picture and they follow its dictates, but their job is to create a binary file that does what the spec says. So most of their truly inspired attention is focused on a window opening on, say, fifty lines of code. They think about the program in small chunks nearly all of the time, because when the chunks gets too big, the code starts to disappear in the distance. Hence their mindset, which I call *littlethink*.

There's no implied Great Chain of Being here. Bigthink is not better than littlethink, or vice versa, just as Cajun cooking is no better than Thai. Be it coding or cooking, you'll probably enjoy one over the other according to personal taste or aptitude, but both parts are necessary to make anything in terms of a program (or a thriving restaurant district) actually happen.

Middlethink and the Edges Issue

Code libraries have been with us almost since the beginning. The problem is that each code library took a different approach to the problems it solved, not only in terms of inner algorithms, but also in the ways its pieces connected to one another and to the operating platform in the large. Each library came with a whole set of assumptions that had to be learned from scratch. The individual procedures and functions may not have come with source code, but they were by no means "black boxes," because the programmer had to "psych out" their philosophy of interconnection. This wasn't the fault of the library vendors. They had no standards to follow. The operating systems of old (DOS, Unix, VMS, OS/360, whatever) basically spun the disks. Everything else was completely up in the air. The architecture of an application back then was basically anything a programmer could imagine that would compile and run. There were an infinite number of ways to connect the different elements that made up a given program. Programmers chose or invented one set of connection conventions each time they put a program together.

The result, of course, is that nothing one programmer invented would connect to anything another programmer invented without serious bloodshed. Software components remained just out of reach from each other.

Then Microsoft Windows happened. For the first time in computing history, a single operating platform won an installed base in the many tens of millions. Furthermore, Windows went far beyond the old-style operating systems in specifying the interior architecture of its applications. Standard drivers, DLLs, a standard help system, standard dialog boxes, consistent UI conventions, a strictly-enforced event management and messaging architecture—all of this was new on the mass market. And what few people noticed at the time is that these new features of Windows were virtually all concerned with the ways things came together. Understanding Windows is largely a matter of understanding a whole lot of edges. The stuff on either side of those edges is very much up to the individual programmer. But the edges themselves are defined and controlled by Windows.

With 80 million-odd Windows machines out there (and that's just a guess; nobody's really sure how many Windows systems there are in the world), programmers began to take those now-standard edges for granted, and in fact studied them almost as a separate discipline. Whole books have been written on individual Windows APIs (application program interfaces; in other words, edges) like DDE, OLE, and the GDI. This was the birth of middlethink: The science of how the elements of a standard platform come together and interact. Once those edges were well understood, development tools emerged that took the edges as a non-negotiable given, and hid their complexity inside black boxes that would, in fact, run on any Windows system—not only those subscribing to one tool vendor's idiosyncratic philosophies.

Here's the core point: *What makes middlethink possible is an operating platform that standardizes program structure sufficiently to allow software components to emerge.* In the PC world, we didn't have this until Microsoft Windows basically took over. As old as it is, Unix has only had it for a few years, since the workstation market standardized on architectures like X Window. The mainframe world isn't there yet and probably never will be. (Fortunately, with client/server architectures coming to the forefront, they don't need to be.)

Delphi as a Middlethink Environment

Delphi is very much a middlethink product. It allows littlethink-style line-by-line programming, of course, but the product as a whole is dominated by the ways things come together. The edges are the thing: The edges between components, and the edges between the application and Windows. If you keep that in mind, you'll have a lot less trouble understanding the best way to use Delphi. Remember this if you remember nothing else: *Get the edges right, and all the rest will fall into place.*

That's enough theory, and to the converted it might seem like I spent too many pages explaining the obvious. But like my long-delayed epiphany on the Wankel engine, it's only obvious after that *Aha! Insight!* has caught fire inside your head. Until then, darkness reigns. What I want to do now is spend a page or two giving you hints on how to approach your study of the Delphi development process. It's basically a summary of how to think (and program) in the middlethink way.

- *Learn by doing.* That is, don't curl up by the fire and try to read the Delphi manuals straight through. It won't stick. Trust me. Do what we're doing in this book: Build a little app, then look closely at how it works. Then build a slightly bigger app. And then a slightly bigger one. This is much easier than reading umpty-thousand pages of doc—and it's fun!

- *Don't try to be a Pascal wizard.* (At least, not for a while...) If you learn too much Pascal before you truly grok the fullness of Delphi in its middlethink glory, you'll be too tempted to use line-by-laborious-line Pascal to do things that Delphi can do for you essentially for free. It's not called Pascal any more. This is for a reason.

- *Learn one component at a time, and learn it wholly.* When you use a component for the first time, go into online help and cruise the summaries of all of its properties and methods. Know what it can do—all of it! A component's properties and methods are its edges, and much of what you do will involve gluing edges together. If you only read up on a couple of those edges, you may assume that a component can not be used to solve a given problem, and you'll either give up in disgust or make a horrible (and unnecessary) mess in Pascal.

- *Examine Borland's example applications.* Short, detached summaries of a component's methods and properties in Online Help is a good and necessary start, but you won't instantly perceive the myriad ways a component can connect and be used with other components just from summaries of its edges. To truly light that spark, it helps to see those edges in action. Go through every example app with a knife and a flashlight. You will learn a lot.

- *Exile the bulk of your Pascal code to separate units apart from your form units.* Don't create monster event procedures. My rule of thumb to stay out of trouble is that you should be able to see the entire event procedure on the screen at one time. More than that and you're probably duplicating code within multiple event procedures, or just trying to do too much in one place. Units are where Pascal code should live.

- *Don't try to create your own Delphi components before you completely understand how to use them.* Component writing isn't necessarily rocket science, but it's a very separate discipline from developing Delphi applications. Component creation is definitely a littlethink task with a middlethink goal, and doing it well requires that you be a very good middlethink developer *first*. My take on it? Do Delphi application development intensively for at least six months before you start hammering out components. The components you hammer out will be much better as a result.

- *Use your right brain.* Far more than either bigthink or littlethink, middlethink is a right-brain exercise. Pay attention to the gestalt of how a Delphi application is put together—then kick back in your chair and groove on the coolness of it. Listen to the suggestions your subconscious presents. Delphi isn't bricklaying. It's God's own game of Scrabble. Goofy little ideas and combinations of things that might seem strange at first could turn out to be the foundation genius upon which you build your empire. Middlethink development isn't always logical. But it's almost always cool.

YES, IT'S REALLY PROGRAMMING!

With that on the table, let's get this underway. From now on, there will be more and more gonzo programming and less and less hand holding. If something we say whizzes by you, jump back and read it again. If it means you need to light out on a short side trip of your own (by creating a quickie little app that tests the interaction of two components you perhaps don't fully understand), do it! Books are patient. (We'll be here when you get back!) And comprehension is why we're all here.

Components and Properties

CHAPTER 3

Jim Mischel

Properties define Delphi objects, and a little bit of "property management" can go a long way in helping you bring sense and speed to your development projects.

By now, you should have some feeling for the ideas behind Delphi—both from a quick run-through of the Delphi development process, and also from the conceptual overview in the previous chapter. In this chapter, we're going to take a closer look at component properties, how to change them, and how those changes affect our application's appearance. In addition, we'll see a few more components and how they are used in Delphi programs.

People coming to Delphi from more traditional programming practice often don't fully understand just how fundamental components are to Delphi development. Without components, the whole idea doesn't make sense, and the notion of an application framework becomes a hindrance rather than a help. (With all due respect to Borland, the Turbo Vision framework likely fell into that category.) Once Delphi gets some time in grade and a thriving third-party market in Delphi's VCL components develops, we'll all wonder how we ever got anything done the old, hard way.

UNDERSTANDING COMPONENT PROPERTIES

The key to understanding how a component works is to understand the component's properties. In Chapter 1 you changed just a few component properties, on my word that the changes would produce the desired result. But knowledge comes from understanding—not blind faith—so we need a better grasp on how changing a component's properties affects its behavior.

You already know that properties are the attributes that define how components are displayed and how they function in the running application. A form's **Caption** property, for example, defines the caption that's displayed in the form's title bar, and a list box's **Sorted** property determines whether or not the items in the ListBox are automatically kept sorted in alphabetical order.

The properties that you see in the Object Inspector window for a particular component are *design-time* properties. The values that you set for these properties are the values that will be used when that component is initially displayed. These properties may be changed while the program is running. There are also *run-time* properties that aren't displayed by the Object Inspector and can only be accessed while the program is running, and *read-only* properties that can be examined but not changed. We'll see examples of all three types of properties in this chapter.

Active and Passive Data

If you're familiar with Pascal or C programming, you might be tempted to think of properties as fields in a record or members of a structure. This analogy is correct, but incomplete. Properties are *active*, whereas record fields or structure members are passive. For example, changing a component's **Color** property has an immediate, visual effect on the way the component is displayed. To achieve a similar result in a C program would require that you change the field, and then call a function to effect the change.

With that brief explanation of component properties in mind, let's start touring the component palette and see what kinds of user interface elements Delphi provides, and how to change their properties to change the look of our applications.

THE FORM COMPONENT

Every Delphi application consists of at least one Form component—the "main window" of traditional Windows applications. There may be more than one form window in an application, and (as we'll show in later chapters) a form window can summon and display another form with a single line of code. When you create a new form, Delphi initializes it with a default size and sets the properties to reflect a fairly standard Windows window. From this point, you're free to change its properties to fit your application. Let's take a look at some of these properties and how to change them.

Changing the Form's Size and Position

The **Height**, **Width**, **Left**, and **Top** properties describe the position of the form on the desktop. Most often, you won't change these properties directly. Rather, you'll change the form's position and size by moving and resizing the form with the mouse. As you move and resize the form, the changes will be reflected in the Object Inspector window. If for some reason you need to set the form's size or position exactly and "by the numbers," you can click on the corresponding property in the Object Inspector window and enter the number manually, just as you entered the form's name in the ListBox program in Chapter 1.

Changing the Form's Border

Not all properties are changed by typing a parameter. If you click on the **BorderStyle** property, for example, a combo box containing a list of possible values appears to the right of the property name, as shown in Figure 3.1.

There are a number of ways to change this property. If you double-click on the property value, Delphi will cycle through the valid values. For example, if

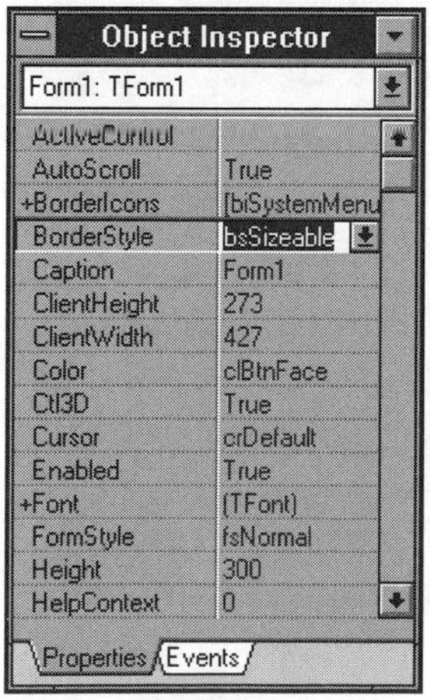

Figure 3.1   *The Form component's BorderStyle property.*

you double-click on the value **bsSizeable**, the property value will change to **bsDialog**. Double-clicking again will change the property to the next value.

Probably the most common way to change this type of property is to click on the combo box button (the button with the down-pointing arrow to the immediate right of the displayed property value) to display a list of the possible values for this property, as shown in Figure 3.2. From this list, you can click on the desired value to set the property.

The other way to change this property is to simply type in the value. If you know, for example, that you want to set the property to **bsDialog**, you can type that into the edit control portion of the combo box. The risk here, of course, is that you may not remember the precise spelling of the value you want, or may simply fumble the typing job. If you enter an invalid value, Delphi will display an "Invalid property value" message.

Note that changes you make to the **BorderStyle** property aren't reflected in the form at design time. So if you change the **BorderStyle** to **bsNone**, the form's border will still have a thick, sizable border. Once you compile and run the program, however, the form won't have a border. (If you try this, remember that pressing Alt+F4 will terminate the program and return you to Delphi.) Fortunately, there aren't many properties whose values aren't reflected at design time. The **BorderIcons** property, which we'll look at shortly, is another exception.

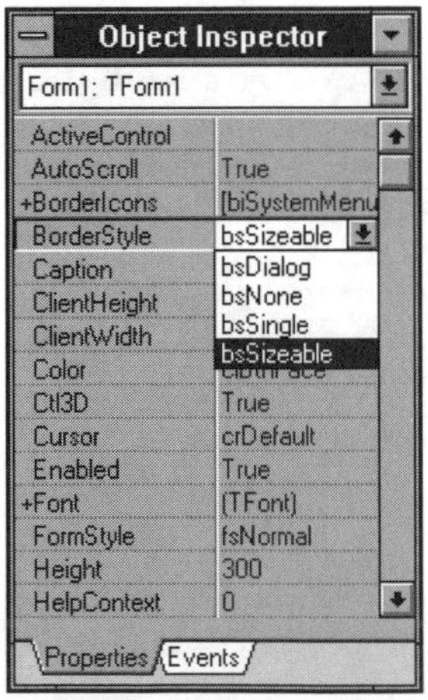

Figure 3.2 *The BorderStyle combo box with possible values.*

Changing Colors on the Fly

If you've done any traditional Windows programming, you've probably tried to change a window's background color. It's easy enough to define a different background color when the window is first created, but changing the color after the window is displayed is a more involved process, and darned confusing the first time you do it. Not so with Delphi.

The **Color** property is similar to the **BorderIcons** property in that it has a combo box in which you can either type the name of a color or select a color from a drop-down list. But, unlike **BorderIcons**, double-clicking on the property's value doesn't cycle through the color values. Instead, if you double-click on the color name in the combo box, Delphi displays a Color dialog box, shown in Figure 3.3, from which you can select a color or define a custom color. Selecting a color is as easy as clicking on one of the color blocks in the Basic Colors area of the dialog. Defining a new color is a little more involved, and to do it well you should understand some color theory that we don't have the room to explain here. You might launch ahead with some independent exploration some time and mix a few colors on your own, just to see how it happens.

If you select one of the colors, or define a custom color, and press OK, Delphi will set the Color property to a hexadecimal number that describes the color. When you change the color in the Object Inspector, the change is immediately reflected on the form. Try it and see. Changing the color while the program is running is equally simple. Here's a project to demonstrate this feature.

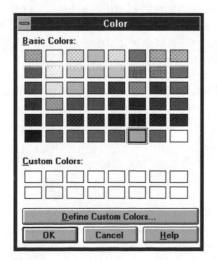

Figure 3.3 *The Color dialog box.*

 ### Changing Form Properties at Runtime

Most properties (with a few important exceptions) may be changed at runtime. We're going to create a simple form with one button, and the button will toggle the background color of the form between two colors by changing the **Color** property.

Select File | New Project to start a new project with default values. Then, select the button component from the tool bar and drop a button anywhere on the form. Double-click on the button in the form to create an OnClick event handler. The Unit window is displayed, ready for you to enter code for the button's event handler. Type these four lines in the window at the current caret position:

```
If Form1.Color <> clPurple Then
 Form1.Color := clPurple
Else
 Form1.Color := clSilver;
```

(If you're utterly new to Object Pascal and these lines are still obscure to you, hold on until Jeff describes simple Pascal coding in the next chapter.)

Save your work by selecting File | Save Project from Delphi's main menu. When prompted for the name of the unit, type "COLORFRM" and press Enter. When prompted for the name of the project, type "CLRXMPL" (color example) and press Enter.

Then press F9 to compile and run the program. When the program starts, the background should be light gray. (Delphi calls this color "clSilver"—but that may lean toward gilding the dandelion). If you click on the button, the form's color changes from gray..er...silver, to purple. Clicking again will change it back to silver. Press Alt+F4 to close the window.

This example, changing a window's background color with a single Pascal statement, was the first thing to really bring home to me the essence of Delphi programming. Rather than calling functions to change parameters, or sending a message to the control, you just set the control's property and be done with it. Finally, I don't have to know the entire Windows SDK in order to write a Windows program.

I know, of course, that at a lower level, in order to change the form's background color Delphi is making all of those function calls and sending a gazillion messages around the Windows message loop. But I don't care. What's better,

I don't *have to* care! Delphi takes care of it so I don't have to mess with it. The whole point is to get an application done quickly. Fooling around with Window arcana like handles, contexts, and pointers? Feh—that's what computers are for!

SETS AND OBJECTS AS PROPERTIES

Up to this point, all of the component properties that we've examined are single values. The Form component's **Color** property, for example, consists of a single value that describes the form's background color. Some properties, though, are not single values at all, but instead collections of other properties. Two such properties are **BorderIcons** and **Font**.

The BorderIcons Property

If you look closely at the Object Inspector window in Figure 3.1, you'll notice that the **BorderIcons** property (directly above the **BorderStyle** property) has a plus sign (+) directly to the left of the property name. This character indicates that the property has sub-properties that can be viewed by double-clicking on the property name. For example, if you double-click on **BorderIcons**, the Object Inspector expands the display to show the sub-properties, as shown in Figure 3.4.

Each of **BorderIcons**' sub-properties can be toggled from **True** or **False** by double-clicking on the value for that particular sub-property. The resulting changes are shown in the **BorderIcons** value field: If a sub-property is set to

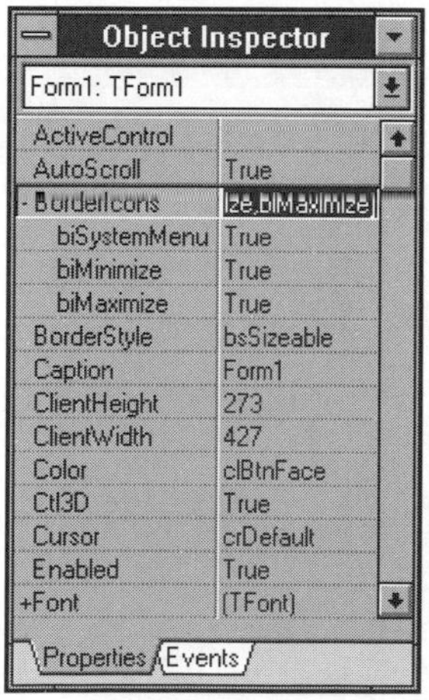

Figure 3.4   *Examining sub-properties of the BorderIcons property.*

True, then its corresponding value is included in the set that describes **BorderIcons**' value. For example, the default **BorderIcons** value is **[biSystemMenu, biMinimize, biMaximize]**. Named constant values enclosed in square brackets comprise a *set*, which is a Pascal data structure. In short, a value is either in the set or it isn't—the sense of the set shown in this paragraph is that the default value for **BorderIcons** has a system menu, and both a minimize and maximize button.

If you don't want the form to have minimize or maximize buttons, change the corresponding sub-properties **biMinimize** and **biMaximize** to **False**, and the resulting value in **BorderIcons** will be **[biSystemMenu]**. By setting **biMinimize** and **biMaximize** to **false**, you "take them out of the set"—and the buttons will no longer be present in the form.

The Font Property

Every component that displays (or can display) text has a **Font** property that describes the font Delphi is to use when it displays that component's text. In designing most forms, you'll likely change only the form's **Font** property and let the components on the form inherit the form's font by setting the component's **ParentFont** property to **True**, as described in the next section. However, you do have the ability to change the font for any given component.

As with **BorderIcons**, the **Font** property in the Object Inspector has a plus sign to the left of the property name. If you double-click on **Font**, the Object Inspector expands the property to show its sub-properties (see Figure 3.5).

Object Inspector	
Form1: TForm1	
Cursor	crDefault
Enabled	True
- Font	(TFont)
Color	clBlack
Height	-21
Name	Times New Ro
Pitch	fpDefault
Size	16
+Style	[fsBold]
FormStyle	fsNormal
Height	300
HelpContext	0
Hint	
+HorzScrollBar	(TControlScrollE
Icon	(None)
Properties / Events	

Figure 3.5 *Viewing the Font property's sub-properties.*

Of the **Font** property's sub-properties, the most commonly-changed are **Color**, **Name**, **Size**, and **Style**. **Color**, of course, changes the color of the text, and **Name** defines the font name: System, MS Serif, Arial, etc. **Style** is a set property that has four sub-properties: **fsBold**, **fsItalic**, **fsUnderline**, and **fsStrikeOut**. If you want the font to have one of these styles, set the corresponding **Style** sub-property to **True**.

The **Size** and **Height** sub-properties have a sort of inverse relationship. Both define the size, in points (a point is 1/72 inch), of the characters. If you enter a positive number for the **Size** property, then Delphi approximates the font's size when it is displayed. If you want to specify an absolute size (that is, if you don't want Delphi to approximate things), then specify a positive value for the **Height** property. In most cases, you'll want to specify the value for **Size**, and not worry about **Height**.

If you don't want to fiddle with the font's sub-properties in the Object Inspector, you can use the Font dialog box, shown in Figure 3.6, in which you can change almost all of the properties. To bring up the Font dialog box, click on the button to the right of the **Font** property's value (the button with three dots on it). Then, select the font name and other properties and press OK. The various sub-properties of **Font** will reflect the changes that you made.

If you want to experiment with different values for the **Font** property, select the **Label** component from the component palette (the button with the capital "A" on it) and click on the form to drop a label on it. The text of the label will read "Label1". Then, use the Object Inspector to change the label's font.

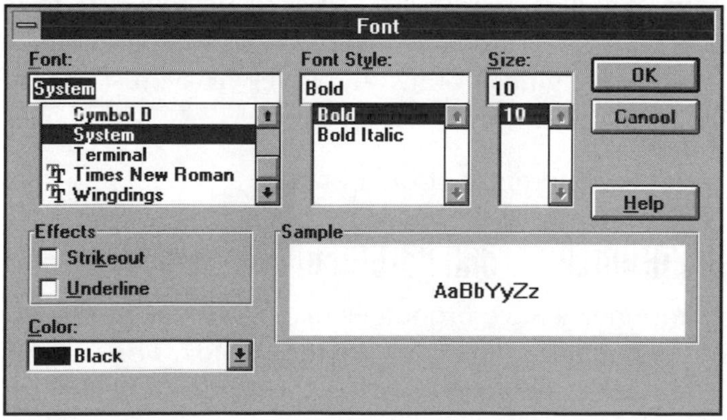

Figure 3.6   *The Font dialog box.*

 **Changing the Title Bar Font**

You're probably wondering why changing the form's **Font** property didn't change the font of the title bar text. The reason is that the title bar is drawn by the internal Windows machinery that draws the form's border. There's no easy way to hook into this machinery to change the font. It's not impossible, but requires an in-depth understanding of Delphi and Windows' inner workings that is beyond the scope of this book.

INHERITING PARENT PROPERTIES

If you changed the form's font and then added a label to the form, you probably noticed that the label component's font, rather than reflecting the system default, was the same as the font that you defined for the form. Why do you suppose *that* happened?

There are several properties that Delphi passes from the form (the *parent* control) to the components on the form (the *children*). Three of these properties are **Color**, **Font**, and **Ctl3D**. We've discussed the first two in the previous sections. **Ctl3D** tells Delphi whether or not you want forms to have the "3-Dimensional" look that has become popular over the last few years. This property is set to **True** by default. If you turn it off, the forms will have the standard Windows look that you define with the Control Panel—a boring white background.

Delphi assumes that if you change one of these properties for a parent control (the form), then you also want that change to be reflected in that parent's children. This is how things are done in most Windows programs, and Delphi's assumption makes changing a form's "look" very easy: Just change the form's font, color, or 3-D flag.

But what if I want a different font on a button?

ParentCtl3D, ParentColor, and ParentFont

Most visual components have properties that allow you to define whether or not you want the control to inherit its parent's **Color**, **Font**, and **Ctl3D** properties. These properties—**ParentFont**, **ParentFont**, and **ParentCtl3D**—are set to **True** by default, which causes the component to inherit the form's property: Delphi uses the parent's value for the corresponding property when drawing the component. If you set one of these properties to **False** for a particular component, then Delphi will use the component's—not the parent's—value when drawing that component.

If you want to change the font used to draw a button's text, you can simply change the button's **Font** property, and the **ParentFont** property will be changed to **False**. Similarly, if you change the value of **Color** or **Ctl3D** for a component, then the corresponding **ParentColor** or **ParentCtl3D** property is set to **False**. If you change one of the component's **ParentXXX** properties from **False** to **True**, then Delphi automatically copies the corresponding font, color or 3-D setting from the parent to the component, erasing any change you may have made to the property.

It's time for a demonstration to clarify this whole business.

Playing with Parent Properties

We're going to write a Delphi program that allows you to change the form's background and font colors. In addition to a Color Grid component that lets you select colors, the form will have a label and a check box. The label inherits the form's properties, and the check box will inherit the form's properties when it's checked, and will use its own properties when it's not checked.

If you've been experimenting while reading this chapter, select File|New Project from Delphi's main menu so we can start with a fresh form. In the Object Inspector, change the Form's **Caption** property to "Parent Properties Example."

Select the Label component from the component palette and place the label in the upper left-hand corner of the form. Once you've placed the label, if you want, you can use the Object Inspector to change the label's **Caption** property from "Label1" to whatever text you want displayed. I changed it to "This label always inherits the form's colors."

Next, select the CheckBox component (the white square with the "x" in it), and place the CheckBox component on the form. Don't worry about placement just yet—just make sure that the new check box component doesn't overwrite the existing label. In the Object Inspector, change the CheckBox's **Caption** property to "ParentColor", and change the **Checked** property to **True**. You may want to size the check box so that it's just big enough to hold the caption (that is, so there's no blank space to the right of the caption in the check box).

The last component we're going to add is a ColorGrid. This component is located on the Samples page of the component palette. To get to it, first click on the tab marked "Samples" on the component palette, and then use the fly-by hints to locate the ColorGrid component. (It's a large grid with 16 differently-colored cells.) Click on the ColorGrid component, and then click on the form to drop the component onto the form. Before going on, you might want to click on the tab marked "Standard" on the component palette in order to display the standard components again.

In the Object Inspector, change the ColorGrid's **BackgroundIndex** property to "5," and make sure that the **ForegroundIndex** property is set to "0." These settings correspond to a purple background with black text.

If you like, you can position the controls so that the form looks a little nicer. One possible arrangement is shown in Figure 3.7.

There's a little more actual programming here than there was before. We have to write Object Pascal code that:

1. Sets the form's **Color** and **Font.Color** properties to reflect the settings in the ColorGrid when the program starts up.
2. Changes the form's **Color** and **Font.Color** properties when the foreground or background colors are changed in the ColorGrid.
3. Changes the CheckBox's **ParentColor** and **ParentFont** properties when the CheckBox is checked or un-checked.

There's a notation here you may not have seen before: "**Font.Color**", which simply means the **Color** subproperty of the **Font** property. Think of the dot as indicating ownership of the right item by the left item. The form has a **Color** property, but so does the **Font** property. (Properties can and often do

Figure 3.7 *The Parent Properties Example form.*

have properties of their own.) If "**Font.**" weren't there in front of "**Color**", Delphi would assume that we were talking about the *form*'s **Color** property. We'll discuss such relationships in detail later in this book.

OnCreate: Setting Component Properties at Startup

When a form is first loaded, Delphi calls the form's **OnCreate** event procedure so that the form can initialize its startup values. Since we want the form's background and text colors to reflect the settings in the **ColorGrid**, we need to make sure that they're set correctly when the program begins running.

To add an **OnCreate** event handler, click on a blank space in the form to make sure that the Object Inspector is displaying the form's properties. Then click on "Events" to select the Events page, and double-click on the value field to the right of the **OnCreate** event. Delphi will display the Unit window, and the caret will be positioned for you to enter the code for the event between **begin** and **end**. Enter these two lines of code at the current caret position:

```
Color := ColorGrid1.BackgroundColor;
Font.Color := ColorGrid1.ForegroundColor;
```

The first line sets the form's background color (the **Color** property) to the color that corresponds to the ColorGrid's **BackgroundIndex** property, and the second line sets the form's **Font** property's **Color** sub-property to the color that corresponds to the ColorGrid's **ForegroundIndex** property.

Run-time and Read-only Properties

If you examine the Object Inspector's list of properties for the ColorGrid component, you'll notice that **BackgroundIndex** and **ForegroundIndex** are there, but there's no **BackgroundColor** or **ForegroundColor**. What's going on? A couple of things.

First, we can't write this code:

```
Color := ColorGrid1.BackgroundIndex;
```

to change the background color, because Windows defines colors by describing the intensities of red, green, and blue in the color. This color-definition scheme is called RGB (for red, green, blue). Using RGB, the color black has intensities of 0 for red, 0 for green, and 0 for blue, and is written (0, 0, 0). In a sense, black is the color with no color, or (more correctly) no light of any color. White has intensities of (255, 255, 255)—essentially red, green, and blue all cranked up as high as they can go. If we used the above line of code, then our background color would be 7, or, in RGB parlance, (0, 0, 7). The resulting color is very close to black.

What the ColorGrid component does is ask Windows for its standard system color palette, and maps those colors to its 16 grid squares. The **BackgroundIndex** and **ForegroundIndex** properties are indexes into the table in which the ColorGrid stores the RGB values for Windows' standard colors. **BackgroundColor** and **ForegroundColor** are run-time properties that return the actual RGB values that are indexed by the **BackgroundIndex** and **ForegroundIndex** properties. When you write:

```
Color := ColorGrid1.BackgroundColor;
```

what you're really telling Delphi is "give me the value in your color table that's addressed by the **BackgroundIndex** property." In a traditional programming language, this would take quite a few lines of code. The mechanism by which Delphi accomplishes this little bit of magic is pretty involved, and quite beyond the scope of this book.

Do note that **BackgroundColor** and **ForegroundColor** are read-only properties. If you were to write:

```
ColorGrid1.BackgroundColor := 0;
```

in one of the event handlers, Delphi would display the error message: "Error 174, Cannot assign to a read-only property" when you tried to compile the project. Read-only properties are just that: You can't write code to change them.

Where Do You Find This Stuff?

This book will give you a good introduction to, and many examples of working with, Delphi. But it won't even come close to covering the entire scope of the product and all the nuances of each component. Many of the components have properties that we won't cover (although we'll cover the major parts of most components), and there are more programming techniques than we could cover in a book of any reasonable size. If you want to do something that's not described in this book, you'll have to study the online help and the printed Reference Guide. It's also helpful to study other programmers' code.

If you have a modem and access to CompuServe, you can post questions on the Delphi forum (GO BDELPHI), where Borland's Technical Support staff is more than happy to help out.

Above all, *experiment*. Unlike working on cars (something I've given up), where mistakes are potentially dangerous or at least wasteful of paint, parts, and other metal, if you make a mistake tinkering with Delphi, the absolute worst thing you can do is crash your computer. It's annoying, but one push on the Reset button will get you back on your path.

Responding to Color Changes

The next bit of code that we have to write is the code that changes the form's colors when you change to the colors in the ColorGrid. Since Delphi calls the ColorGrid's OnChange event handler whenever you make a change to one of the ColorGrid's colors, we need to create an OnChange event handler for the ColorGrid component.

If the Form window is visible, click on its title bar to select it. If you can't see the Form window, either move the Unit window so that the Form window is visible, or click on the "Toggle Form/Unit" button on the speed bar (use the fly-by hints to locate the proper button). Once the Form window is selected, click on the ColorGrid component so we can change its properties.

In the Object Inspector, select the Events page, and double-click in the value field to the right of the OnChange event. The Unit window will be displayed again, with the edit cursor positioned where you can enter the code for the ColorGrid's OnChange event. Enter these two lines of code (yes, they *are* identical to the two lines you just entered for the Form's OnCreate event handler):

```
Color := ColorGrid1.BackgroundColor;
Font.Color := ColorGrid1.ForegroundColor;
```

Handling the CheckBox

As you probably know, a standard Windows check box can be in one of two states: checked or un-checked. This control normally is used to set a "true or false" program option, such as the Run Minimized check box in the Program Manager's Program Item Properties dialog box. Delphi's CheckBox control implements the functionality of a standard Windows check box.

In our program, the CheckBox component's state (checked or un-checked) defines whether or not the CheckBox should use the form's **Color** and **Font.Color** properties. If the CheckBox is checked (if the **Checked** property is set to **True**), then the CheckBox will be displayed using the form's colors. If the box is un-checked (the **Checked** property is **False**), then the CheckBox is displayed using its own colors.

We can add this behavior to the CheckBox control by changing the **ParentColor** and **ParentFont** properties to match the check box state. Delphi calls the CheckBox's **OnClick** event handler whenever the mouse is clicked on the CheckBox, so all we have to do is add an OnClick event handler. With the form visible, click on the CheckBox component, make sure the Events page is visible in the Object Inspector, and double-click on the value field to the right of the OnClick event handler. When the Unit window is displayed, enter these two lines of code:

```
CheckBox1.ParentColor := CheckBox1.Checked;
CheckBox1.ParentFont := CheckBox1.Checked;
```

Saving and Running the Program

Before you test the program, you should save your work. Select File|Save Project from Delphi's main menu and when prompted, name the unit PARNTFRM.PAS, and the project PARENT.DPR. Once you've named the two files, you can save the entire project by pressing the Save Project button on the toolbar. It's the top middle button in the leftmost group of six, showing a file folder with an arrow pointing down to a hard disk. Be sure which button it is by holding the mouse cursor over it until the fly-by hint pops up, reading "Save project."

Once you've saved your work, you can compile and run the program by selecting Run|Run from the menu, or by pressing the shortcut key: F9. (The "green triangle" button on the toolbar will also run the program, compiling it first if you've made any changes since the last compile.) If you get a compiler error, ensure that you've entered the lines exactly as shown in the text above. A miss is as good as a mile! You can make changes by selecting the Unit window and editing the code as you would with any text editor. Be sure to save your work again before you try to run the program. It's as easy as pushing the Save project button.

When you run the program, the form's background will initially be purple, and the text will be displayed in black. To change the foreground color, position the mouse cursor over the desired color in the **ColorGrid** component and click on the left mouse button. To change the background color, position the mouse on the desired color and click the *right* mouse button.

If you don't want the CheckBox component to use the same colors as the form, click on the CheckBox so that the box is cleared (that is, so that there's no "x" in the box). This won't have any immediate effect on the CheckBox's colors, as the **Color** and Font.Color properties were already set to reflect the parent's. If you now change the parent's colors by clicking on the ColorGrid, the CheckBox's colors won't change. Note that the Label component's colors always reflect the Form's setting because the Label's **ParentColor** and **ParentFont** properties are always **True**.

If you click on the CheckBox again, the CheckBox's colors will immediately change to reflect the Form's colors.

So, as you see, changing **ParentColor**, **ParentFont**, or **ParentCtl3D** from **True** to **False** has no immediate effect on how a component is changed because the component's properties were already set to the parent's. But the component's properties stop following the parent's once **ParentXXX** is set to **False**. Conversely, changing a **ParentXXX** property from **False** to **True** causes the component to immediately inherit the parent's corresponding property, and to follow the parent property's changes from that point on.

PROPERTY MANAGEMENT

As you continue to experiment with Delphi, remember that the key to understanding components is the components' properties. If you know what properties a component has, and understand how changing those properties affects the component's appearance or behavior, then you've won most of the battle.

In the next chapter, we're going to begin our discussion of Object Pascal code with an introduction to data and its role in Delphi programs. After that, we'll go back to exploring the component palette.

All of Your Stuff—and Buckets to Put It In

CHAPTER 4

Jeff Duntemann

If you're new to Object Pascal, here's a gentle introduction, emphasizing data and what you can do with it.

In our little two-and-a-half acres of desert paradise, at least, 1994 was definitely the Year of the Bucket. Early that year I bought a house, and in the first month of ownership I was billed for 22,000 gallons of water.

The trouble is, no one was living there at the time. That is what we might call a bad sign.

After spending a couple of months making sure there was no administrative mistake behind it, we called in Glen the Plumber and his assistant Vernon, who spent most of the summer digging tunnels under the house, searching for leaking pipe joints. They found a bunch of them. In fact, if they found a joint that *didn't* leak, I for one didn't hear about it.

Come mid-July several *tons* of dirt had come up through a little hole in the concrete slab, and my laundry room was beginning to look like a sound stage for *Escape from Stalag 17*. Every handful of that dirt came up out of the hole in buckets. When the job was over, the dirt went back in the same way. Tools went down the hole and back up in buckets. Mr. Byte sat on his little doggie bed (he is, after all, 14 years old now) and watched the process with a jaundiced eye. I hid upstairs and tried not to cry.

Buckets. Thank God for buckets—or my stupid house would still be weeping a river into the desert soil.

VARIABLES: BUCKETS FOR DATA

I've got a new appreciation of containers with handles—that is to say, buckets—as used in plumbing and other pursuits. And it occurred to me, in pondering the best way to present Pascal as Pascal is used in entry-level Delphi programming, that the bucket metaphor would be a good place to start. For I discovered in writing simple Delphi programs that a lot of what those very few lines of necessary Pascal code actually did was carry data from component to component, or hold a piece of data while something was done to it.

So we're going to start in on Pascal from that perspective: The buckets that carry data around, and the implements used to stir, slice, dice, fold, spindle, and recombobulate the data in the bottom of the buckets. The buckets, of course, are Pascal variables, and the implements are the operators and functions that act on those variables. Master the sense of Pascal's use of variables, operators, and functions, and you've got most of what you need for simple Delphi programming in your hip pocket.

Variables and Their Types

In Pascal as in life, there are different kinds of buckets for carrying different kinds of things. You can carry water in a plastic bucket, but you can't carry molten lead—or bowling balls. And while a colander might serve for carrying meatballs, it's less than optimal for carting orange juice from the kitchen to the table. Pascal variables have their specialties as well. A numeric variable contains numbers—not letters or true/false Boolean values.

You have to keep this matter of variable types straight in your head, because Delphi is fairly fussy about it. You can't just load a number into a Boolean—true/false—variable. If you try, you'll get the following error message in the status bar at the bottom of the source code window you're working in:

```
Error 26: Type mismatch
```

Delphi could, of course, just let the matter slide. But think about it: What does it mean to place a number—say, 6—into a variable that is supposed to indicate whether something is true or false? It makes no sense, and, hey, programming is hard enough without deliberately inserting nonsense into code.

This is why every Delphi variable has a type, and why there are rules about what you can do with a variable based on its type. I'll go over most of the more common types in this chapter, and explain what those rules are.

Building Buckets

Nearly all of the work you'll be doing with Delphi variables will be done inside relatively short procedures and functions, which are the "nuggets of work" that are executed in order to get something done. A typical Delphi procedure looks like this:

```
procedure TForm1.Button1Click(Sender: TObject);

VAR Counter : Integer;

begin
 Counter := Counter + 1;
end;
```

I won't explain everything you see here right now—we'll get to all of it in time. The short explanation is that everything that is "done"—that is, statements of executable code—must fall between the **begin** and **end** words. Above **begin** is bucket territory. If your procedure is going to build any buckets for itself, this is where it's done.

Here, we've got a variable named **Counter**. We know it's a variable because it's preceded by the **VAR** word. After "Counter" is a colon, followed by the word **Integer**. "Integer" is the *type* of the variable we're calling **Counter**. The sense of the statement is rather like tersely scrawling "Clinton : loser" on the back of somebody's garage. You've made a statement with no wasted effort, and people reading that statement will know *exactly* what you mean.

Reserved Words

As you look at your own code (and also code written by Delphi) you'll notice some boldface words in the code, made bold by the code editor. These words are recognized by the editor as special and placed in bold so that you know what they are and can spot them from ten steps back.

These words are called *reserved words*, and they are the "framing members" of an Object Pascal procedure. There aren't very many of them (a little less than 60), but they have a crucial task in telling Delphi's built-in Object Pascal compiler where procedures begin (with the reserved word **procedure**, natch), where variable declarations happen (with **VAR**), and lots of other important things. Reserved words are "reserved" in that you cannot use them for anything else in a Delphi program. You can't create a variable named **begin**, for example, or **procedure**. The compiler will call you on it; it reserves those words for its own use.

This can sometimes be annoying; I tried once to create variables for each of the states in the U.S. using the standard Post Office state abbreviations. No go—the compiler demanded sole ownership of **OR** (Oregon) and **IN** (Indiana) and forced me to create new, non-standard abbreviations. Gakkh. However, this prevents a whole host of nasty bugs from happening, and allows the compiler to be *certain* what the individual parts of your code really mean. Reserved words are the solid ground on which the entire remainder of your Object Pascal code is written, so in general, they are very good to have. To get a list of the reserved words in Object Pascal, do a topic search for "Reserved Words" in Delphi Help.

Once you give a type to a variable, certain rules come into play regarding that variable. The **Integer** type is a numeric type. The first rule it imposes is that *only* numeric values can be placed in variables of type **Integer**. (In the generic, we just call such variables and their values "integers.") Trying to put other types of data in a numeric variable makes no sense.

The second rule involves the range of numeric values that may be placed in variables of type **Integer**. There are several different numeric types in Delphi, and each of them has a range of legal values which variables of their types can hold. An integer, for example, can contain numeric values from -32768 to 32767. It's "against the rules" for you to try to load a value of 46,721 into an integer. Attempting to do so will land you a *range error*, which can occur either at compile-time or at runtime, depending on what you're trying to do.

Filling Buckets

Applying a name and a type to a variable within a procedure or a unit is called *declaring* the variable. Once it's declared, the variable exists and may be used. The first thing you have to do with it, realistically speaking, is load some value into it. A newly-declared variable is not automatically set to blanks, 0, or 1, or anything else. Until you load a value into a new variable, that variable may contain a random out-of-a-hat value that may be *anything at all*—so we say its value is *undefined*.

Filling a variable can be done in a number of ways, but the commonest is what we call an *assignment statement*. Such a statement, in its simplest form, would look like this:

```
Counter := 0;
```

All this does is take the value 0 and drop it into variable **Counter**. From this point on, until something else affects **Counter**, **Counter** has the value 0. The symbol ":=" is known as the *assignment operator*. It's one of a whole class of such symbols in Object Pascal called *operators* that specify a relationship or action between two items.

Notice the semicolon after the assignment statement. This signals to the compiler that the statement ends there. There's some trickiness to semicolon placement in Pascal, and it stems from the role of semicolons as statement separators. For the near term, simply remember to put a colon at the *end* of every Pascal statement you write. Strictly speaking, some Pascal statements don't require a semicolon at the end, but you can nearly always put one there without the compiler complaining. Where things get tricky is inside complex statements with several parts—but let's set that aside for now.

Literal Constants

The single digit "0" in the assignment statement shown just above is what we call a *literal constant*. A literal constant is a "naked value" that doesn't have a name. 0, 15, 246, -47, and 105562 are all numeric literal constants. Literal constants are useful for loading initial values into variables within assignment statements and in other places. There are literal constants for most simple data types, including characters and strings.

It's pretty obvious from the sense of things, but remember that you can't put a literal constant on the left side of an assignment statement. A literal constant *is* a value; you can't assign another value to it.

Named Constants

Sometimes it's handy to take a literal constant and give a name to it. Object Pascal allows you to create *named constants*, which are much like variables in the sense that they are a named container with a value in it. Unlike variables, however, constants cannot be changed in assignment statements or any other Object Pascal construct. You fill 'em and then they're sealed and can't

be opened again, although you can read from the constant's value at any time. It's a little like immersing a preserved dragonfly in a cube of acrylic resin. You can look at it through the resin, but you can't do anything to the dragonfly.

Declaring a named constant is a lot like declaring a variable. It's done in the same place inside a procedure (or inside a unit, as you'll see in a later chapter) and ends with a semicolon. You use a different reserved word, **CONST**, and an equal sign instead of a colon:

```
procedure TForm1.Button1Click(Sender: TObject);

CONST BaseCount = 255;
VAR   Counter : Integer;

begin
 Counter := BaseCount + Counter + 1;
end;
```

Here, we've got a named constant called **BaseCount** with a value of 255. Anywhere we use the name **BaseCount** in a program, Delphi's compiler will substitute the value 255.

So why bother? Well, in a sizeable program, we may need to apply a base count to calculations in dozens or hundreds of different places. We could write the number 255 in every one of those places, and it would work. But suppose later on we wanted to change the base count value to 127? We'd have to hunt down *every last place* we wrote in 255, delete it, and replace it with 127—and as sure as it rains in Oregon all the damned time, we'd miss a few.

However, if you declare a named constant at the top of a program, you can change the value of that constant at the point where it's declared, and that change will automatically be made to every place in the program where you used the constant, missing none.

You're unlikely to need to use your own named constants before you begin writing substantial programs. You need to know what they are, however, because Delphi uses a fair number of named constants that it defines, and you should be aware that they exist.

OTHER NUMERIC TYPES

The **Integer** type has a cousin called **Word**. **Word** is, like **Integer**, a numeric type that can contain only numeric values. It has a different range and it slightly different set of rules. A **Word** may contain values from 0 to 65,535. It differs from **Integer** primarily in that it may *not* contain negative values. If you know that a numeric value will never need to be negative (many situations calling for a counter are like that, since you can't count fewer than 0 things) you can declare it as a **Word** and get twice the range on the high end. Negative values are outside the range for the **Word** type, so if you try to assign a negative value to a **Word** variable, you'll get a range error.

Declaring **Word** variables is done just as with integers:

```
VAR MyWord : Word;
```

Long Integers

Another standard Object Pascal type is the *long integer*. The type identifier for long integers is **LongInt**. They are declared just as any variable is declared:

```
VAR BigCounter : LongInt;
```

Long integers, as the name suggests, can hold numbers larger than ordinary integers. The range for long integers is -2147483648 to 2147483647. I'd put commas in there, but Object Pascal doesn't accept commas in its literal constants, so it's a bad habit to get into. Just keep the range in your head as (roughly) negative two billion to positive two billion. This used to be an unthinkably large number in programming circles, but now that multi-gigabyte hard disk drives are common and relatively cheap, it's gotten downright scary to think we soon won't have an integer type that can count all the bytes we might possibly be able to store. Suppose you had a 3 GB hard drive and wanted to write a program in Delphi that reported how much space was left? You couldn't use a long integer, that's for sure. As useful as it would be, there is no "LongWord" type to take us from 0 to four billion in a positive direction. (Perhaps if we all ask Borland for it, a future release of Delphi will have one.) And the alternative to long integers isn't the best, as we'll see in the next section.

Floating Point Values

There are two sorts of numbers in the programming world: Integer values (which we've just discussed) and floating point values. Integer values are just whole numbers. They may be positive or negative, but they have no fractional part. So what if you need to express a fractional part? For that you need floating point numbers.

A floating point number is a number with a fractional part, and a decimal point to set off the fractional part from the whole number part. 6.77 is a floating point value, as is 0.0038. Why "floating?" The decimal point can move around inside the number, as required. There is no "set" number of decimal places to the right of the decimal point. 6.77 has only two places to the right of the decimal point, but 0.0038 has 4 places—and in the other direction.

Delphi has several different data types to support floating point values. The most useful is called **Real**, hearkening back to the real numbers you learned about in high school. The others are **Single**, **Double**, and **Extended**. These are odd names for numeric types, perhaps, but if you do any serious programming that involves "real word" values or anything requiring decimal places, you'd do yourself a favor to become familiar with them. Table 4.1 summarizes Delphi's floating point types.

As with the integer types, each floating point type has a range, which is the breadth of values the type may contain. But there's something new here: Significant figures. In integer types, values have absolute accuracy. If you're counting cats, 7 cats is *exactly* 7 cats, no more and no less. In floating point values, on the other hand, you're not *counting* cats anymore—you're *measuring* them.

Take your high-accuracy steel rule and measure how long that cat is. You'll get something like 17.2 inches, nose to tail. Does that means that the cat is exactly 17.2 inches long? No. It means that *as best your measuring implements can tell*, the cat is 17.2 inches long. If you had a better steel rule (and if the cat would sit still a little more) you might read off 17.25 inches long. I doubt you'd do better than that with a live cat. (I've had cats. I don't have them anymore.) If your cat was a bronze statue of a cat and you brought out your king-size high-accuracy micrometer, you could conceivably call it as close as 17.2537 inches long, depending on how much dirt there was on the statue.

The point I'm trying to make here is that a floating point value can express a very large value (the **Extended** type can express a value out to 10 with 4,932

Table 4.1   *Delphi's Floating Point Types*

Type	Range	Significant Figures of Accuracy
Real	2.9×10^{-39} to 1.7×10^{38}	1-12
Single	1.5×10^{-45} to 3.4×10^{38}	7-8
Double	5.0×10^{-324} to 1.7×10^{308}	15-16
Extended	3.4×10^{-4932} to 1.1×10^{4932}	19-20

zeroes after it!) but that doesn't mean that every last one of those digits is precise. If you're measuring something like the diameter of the solar system, you can express its diameter in feet, perhaps—but you won't be able to say with a straight face that the solar system is *exactly* that many feet in diameter.

Extended has a huge range—but it only has 19 or 20 figures of accuracy. Here's a big number:

```
4276615267751428491000000000000000000000000000000
```

You could load this number into a variable of type **Extended**. No sweat. Here's the same big number with a greater number of significant figures:

```
4276615267751428491589278687123455670000000000000
```

This number cannot be expressed in type **Extended**. Not because of how big it is (it's not significantly larger than the first number) but simply because it contains more significant figures than type **Extended** can express.

Given its tremendous capacity, shouldn't you use **Extended** for all your floating-point work? No. There's a safety issue here and in fact, I recommend against using **Extended** at all, unless you know *exactly* what you're doing. Sometimes in doing an arithmetical calculation, the compiler will need to keep an intermediate value in a corner somewhere. **Extended** is the largest and most accurate numeric format Delphi understands. If you multiply two **Extended** values and then intend to divide them by 100, you might run out of "room" at the point where you multiply the two values. There's simply no larger place to tuck the intermediate value.

Type **Real** has a lot of range, and the fewest potential hassles. Use it unless you have an excellent reason to have something else hold floating point values.

ARITHMETIC OPERATORS

Delphi can do math with the best of them, by manipulating variables of integer or floating point types with its suite of arithmetic operators. Operators are symbols or short words placed between two numeric variables or constants, to specify some sort of action to be taken upon those two variables or constants. Using an operator can be as simple as this:

```
Counter := Counter + 1;
```

This statement uses the addition operator + to specify that the current value of variable **Counter** is to be added to 1, and the sum placed back in **Counter**. Thus during this statement **Counter** is "bumped up" by 1.

Subtraction works the same way, using the - symbol as its operator:

```
Counter := Counter - 1;
```

Here, 1 is subtracted from the current value of **Counter**, and the difference is placed back in **Counter**.

Multiplication suffers from the lack of an × symbol in the ASCII character set, so the asterisk character * is used for multiplication instead, as in this example:

```
Counter := Counter * 6;
```

Here, the current value of **Counter** is multiplied by 6, and the product is placed back into **Counter**.

EXPRESSIONS

You can perform more than one calculation within a single assignment statement. Object Pascal handles arithmetic very intuitively, and by using parentheses you can combine operators in one assignment statement without wondering what's going on. Here's an example:

```
Counter := (Counter * ScaleFactor) + 1;
```

If you know your arithmetic, you should be able to understand this statement. That portion of the above assignment statement to the right of the assignment operator is called an *expression*. The Delphi compiler evaluates expressions pretty much the way you would on paper: In the example above, it first multiplies **Counter** by **ScaleFactor**, and then adds 1 to the product. The resulting sum is called the *value* of the expression, and that value is finally placed in **Counter**, replacing whatever was in **Counter** before.

Whatever is within parentheses is evaluated first, and if parentheses are nested, the innermost subexpression is evaluated first. Evaluation works outward from the innermost parentheses until the entire expression has been evaluated.

Mixing Integer and Floating Point Values

If the values on both sides of an operator are of the same type, you would expect that the resulting value of the expression would be of that same type. Add an integer to an integer and what you get is an integer. It gets more interesting when you mix numeric types within an expression. You can add a floating point number to an integer, or subtract a floating point number from an integer. Mixing floats (as insiders often call them) and integers in an expression, however, forces the ultimate value of the expression to a floating point type. So if you add a float to an integer, you must assign the sum to a float, and so on.

Division

Division is more of a problem. When you divide one integer by another, the quotient is not necessarily an integer. 13 divided by 4 is 3.25—and "3.25" is definitely not an integer. It's tough to tell in advance which numbers "go into" another evenly, so the rule in Object Pascal is that the quotient of two numbers—any two numbers, whether integer or floating point—must be assigned to a floating point variable. The division operator is the forward slash character / with the dividend on the left and the divisor on the right:

```
Speed := Distance / Time;
```

Here, it doesn't matter whether **Distance** and **Time** are of type **Integer** or **Real**—the variable **Speed** must be type **Real** (or one of the other floating point types) because the quotient of **Distance** and **Time** will *always* be a floating point value. If **Time** divides **Distance** evenly, the quotient will have a 0 decimal part, but it will still be a floating point value.

Integer Division with Mod and Div

Returning a quotient as a floating point value is sometimes inconvenient. Object Pascal has a trick for integer division, though, that hearkens back to the way you initially learned division in fourth grade: the "gazinta" method. Faced with the need to divide 75 by 8, grade schoolers ponder how many times 8 "goes into" 75. There are 9 8's inside 75—but there are also leftovers. So the complete statement of the problem and its solution is that 75 divided by 8 is 9, remainder 3. That is, 8 goes into 75 9 times, with 3 left over.

Object Pascal has two operators that do division as you did it in fourth grade. The **DIV** operator divides two integers—and returns an integer quotient. **DIV** gives you the number of times the divisor is present in the dividend, as an integer value. As with the floating point division operator, the dividend is on the left and the divisor on the right:

```
Pages := Lines DIV LinesPerPage
```

DIV does nothing with the remainder, however—for that you need to perform an entirely separate calculation with **DIV**'s sister operator, **MOD**. If you wanted to perform the same calculation as above but want to find out how many lines would be on the last (partially filled) page, you'd use **MOD** to get the remainder:

```
LinesOnLastPage := Lines MOD LinesPerPage
```

DIV and **MOD** are for use only with integer types. Trying to use them with floating point types will generate a compile-time error.

Comp: The Weird Numeric Type

Long integers aren't nearly as long as they used to be, sadly. They run as high as two billion and change, but two billion isn't a lot these days, when 3 gigabyte (3 billion byte) hard drives are approaching $1000, their prices dropping like stones. Furthermore, if you try to do financial calculations with long integers, you'll need to count in pennies (because there is no decimal point in any integer type) which means that the most money you can express with a long integer is $21,474,836.47. This wouldn't even keep IBM in doughnuts for six months.

Delphi has one more trick in terms of numeric types, and it's slightly odd. Type **Comp** has considerable range, from -9.2×10^{18} to 9.2×10^{18}. Better still, it has absolute whole number precision, meaning that through its entire range, there is no "fuzz." You can count with it accurately. You can express money values up to ten quadrillion dollars, which should keep IBM in doughnuts for at least a couple of years. (No bets on doughnuts for the Federal Government, however....)

So what's weird about **Comp**? It's technically a floating point type. It has no decimal point, however, and if you use it to express money, you have to express money in pennies. Still, decimal or no decimal, you cannot use **DIV** or **MOD** with **Comp**. You must use the floating point division operator /. There are several other integer-like things that **Comp** cannot do either, like index arrays (which is unfortunate) or work with the **Pred** or **Succ** standard functions.

CHARACTERS

Object Pascal has a type specifically designed for holding individual letters, digits, and other symbols that are part of the extended ASCII character set. There are 256 different characters in the extended set. The first 127 contain all the familiar letters of the alphabet, numeric digits, and punctuation marks like commas, periods, semicolons, and so on. In its release of the IBM PC in 1981, IBM extended the ASCII set with a number of foreign language characters (letters with accents, umlauts and other dojiggers over and under them), math symbols, and "line drawing" characters that were widely used when text screens ruled the PC world.

Type **Char** was meant to contain individual symbols from this character set. A **Char** variable may contain *one* character. (For multiple characters in the form of words or phrases, you need to use type **String**, which we'll discuss shortly.) You can assign values to a **Char** variable by using character literal constants, which are simply character symbols enclosed in single quotes:

```
StartingChar := 'A';
```

This will do well for all the familiar letters and numbers. But there are still 255 characters in the full extended ASCII character set, and not all of them can be ready-typed from the keyboard. A few of the characters, in fact, are not displayable characters at all, but are "control characters" inherited from the ancient days of mechanical Teletype machines. There is an ASCII character called BEL whose job it was to ring the Teletype printer's bell when it was received. This character is still with us, and some communications software still uses it to signal a beep. (I'm old enough to remember Teletype printers, and I sort of miss their polite, refined little "ding!") There are other "invisible" characters as well, including carriage return (we call this CR) and line feed (LF) that are used as "end of line" markers in many text files. In your programming efforts, you may need to load such invisible characters into **Char** variables and manipulate them. What to do?

Ordinal Types

The secret is simple: The ASCII characters can be identified by number as well as by symbol. The ASCII set appears in a set order, from 0 to 255, with symbols assigned to most characters, and names (at least) assigned to the invisible ones. But visible or invisible, every ASCII character has a number, and those numbers (as you would expect of numbers) always appear in the same order.

The letter "A", for example, is ASCII character number 65. The exclamation point character is number 33. Invisible (but occasionally audible) BEL is number 7.

This is a powerful concept, and it's used elsewhere in Object Pascal. Type **Char** is what we call an *ordinal type*, because it has a limited number of values that exist in a set and unvarying order. You can define your own ordinal types, as I'll describe a little later. Delphi defines quite a few ordinal types, mostly as sets of possible values for component properties.

STANDARD FUNCTIONS

For every ASCII character there is a numeric value, and for every numeric value from 0 to 255 there is an ASCII character. This trait of ordinal types allows you to convert from numeric values to character values and back, using two of Object Pascal's standard functions. A *function* is a named routine that returns a value of some kind when you execute it. This returned value can then be assigned to a variable of the appropriate type. A *standard function* is simply one of the suite of functions that are predefined within Object Pascal. (You can write your own specialty functions, as we'll show later in this book.)

As I said earlier, the ordinal value of the capital A character is 65. Your programs can extract the ordinal value (also called the *ordinality*) of any ordinal type (like **Char** and **Boolean**) using the **Ord** standard function. The **Ord** function takes a character value as its *operand*, which is a variable, constant, or expression enclosed in parentheses. The returned value can be assigned to any integer type:

```
AnyInteger := Ord('B'); { AnyInteger would be given the value 66 }
AnyInteger := Ord(MyCharVariable); { Ord returns the ordinality of whatever's in
MyCharVariable }
```

There's a standard function that goes the other way as well: **Chr**. Pass a number from 0 to 255 to **Chr**, and it will return the character having the ordinality of that number:

```
MyGrade := Chr(65);   { Give yourself an A! }
ControlChar := Chr(7);   { Variable ControlChar now contains the BEL character }
```

Functions are rather like procedures, with the major difference that you cannot just call a function by itself as a statement. In other words, this is *not* legal:

```
Chr(175);  {Will generate a compile-time error!}
```

A function always returns a value of some kind and must "give" its return value to something. This is often as simple as putting a function on the right side of an assignment statement, but functions can also be elements of expressions, as in the following example:

```
CharacterIndex := Ord(InputCharacter) + 32;
```

Here, the value returned by the **Ord** standard function is added to 32 before the sum is assigned to the numeric variable **CharacterIndex**.

There are quite a few other standard functions in Object Pascal, and they all work more or less the same way. We'll be using quite a few more of them in this book, and we'll point them out as we encounter them.

COMMENTS

If you've done any programming at all, I'm sure you know that reading someone else's code is a lot harder than reading code you've written yourself. What you may not realize going in is that reading your own code six or eight months down the road is sometimes just as hard as reading code written by somebody else. This is why most people place *comments* in their Object Pascal code, to amplify what the code is doing, and amplify it in plain English.

I've been using comments informally in this chapter for several pages. A comment is just some text enclosed in a pair of "curly" brackets { }. It can be anything at all; whatever falls between the curly brackets (which are known more formally as *comment delimiters*) is simply ignored by Delphi's compiler.

There are actually two distinct sets of comment delimiters in Object Pascal. The commonest one is the pair of curly brackets mentioned earlier, but you can also use the pair of compound symbols (* and *). They work exactly the same way.

Comments can enclose line ends. That is, you can start a comment on one line and continue it down several lines before adding the closing delimiter. Things like this are perfectly legal:

```
{ JLABEL 2.0 by Jeff Duntemann
 (c) 1995 by The Coriolis Group, Inc.
 All Rights Reserved }
```

A key thing to remember about comments is that if you open 'em, ya gotta close 'em. Leaving a comment open is one of the oldest errors in Pascal programming. Delphi makes this error much easier to spot, because comments are distinctively formatted in Delphi's code editor windows. If you open a comment, all code after the opening delimiter "looks funny"—a dead giveaway.

STRINGS

Individual characters are often useful in programming, but what really comes in handy is the ability to pour whole words, phrases, or sentences into variables. Variables that may contain text like this are called *strings*. Strings are among the most useful of all data buckets you'll find in Object Pascal.

You'll find strings in almost every Delphi component, in the form of the **Caption** property. The Label component is in some respects a machine for displaying string data; whatever string you load into its **Caption** property will be displayed on the form where the Label has been dropped. String variables are useful for manipulating data for display in the **Caption** property of a Label, or for use in other string properties in any of several standard Delphi components.

You declare a string variable this way:

```
VAR TextData : String;
```

Then you can fill it with text data by assigning a string literal, which is text enclosed within single quote marks:

```
TextData := 'I am an American, Chicago-born.';
```

You can assign string variables to string properties in components:

```
Label1.Caption := TextData;
```

It's often useful to be able to construct phrases or messages out of separate string variables. You can do this by linking strings together, using the string concatenation operator +. The strings are glued onto one another nose-to-tail. This example should make it all clear:

```
City := 'Scottsdale';
State := 'AZ';
ZIP := '85260';
FullAddress := City + ', ' + State + ' ' + ZIP;
```

The string variable **FullAddress** now contains the string "Scottsdale, AZ 85260". If you're concatenating words that must be read somewhere, don't leave out the spaces! As you'll notice, Object Pascal makes multiple use of certain symbols. We think of the + operator for numeric addition, but it serves nicely for string concatenation as well.

It's also possible to concatenate characters onto strings. The character is, in a sense, a string with only one element, so it makes sense:

```
TextData := 'Error Message #'+Chr(ErrNumber + 48);
```

In this case, if you had a value of 6 in integer variable **ErrNumber**, you could make a character out of the 6 value with the **Chr** standard function, and concatenate it onto the text string "Error Message #" yielding a string for display on a form reading "Error Message #6".

There's a handy standard function that returns the number of characters in a string, considered the string's length. The **Length** function is used this way:

```
MessageSize := Length(TextData);
```

If the string data in **TextData** is "Error Message #6" then **Length(TextData)** would return the value 16. Don't forget that spaces are characters just as surely as letters and numbers are!

 **Keeping an Eye on String Values**

If you simply want to see what a string value is doing during the course of program execution, you don't necessarily have to go into Delphi's integrated debugger and open a watch window. That's the high road, of course, and the correct way to do such things, but there's a simpler way: Drop an extra Label component onto your form, tuck it into a corner where it doesn't get severely in the way of the "real stuff" on your form, and assign the string in question to the Label's **Caption** property at critical points in the program. This is Delphi's equivalent to the ancient Pascal technique of performing a **WriteIn** to the screen or printer with the string as **WriteIn**'s parameter.

BOOLEANS: TRUE OR FALSE?

Should I or shouldn't I? That's a question that comes up a lot in programming. To make decisions you sometimes have to determine whether something is, or is not. A variable may contain a 0—or it may contain something other than 0. A string may be within a size limit—or it may be over that size limit. The logic of a program may depend completely on being able to express the truth or falsehood of a statement.

That's what Object Pascal's type **Boolean** is for. (When speaking generically we call them "Booleans" and retain the capitalization because they are named for the mathematician George Boole, who developed a system of logic now called Boolean Algebra.) A variable of type **Boolean** may have one of only two states: **True** or **False**. Now, **True** and **False** are *values*, not variables. They are the literal constants of the **Boolean** type. Once you declare a Boolean variable, you may assign a value of either **True** or **False** to it:

```
ValueIsZero := True;
```

This emphatically does *not* mean that **ValueIsZero** contains the text string "True" in it somewhere. **True** is an abstraction, and the Object Pascal compiler encodes it compactly within the Boolean variable. In truth, **Boolean** is an ordinal type just like **Char**, but instead of 256 different values, **Boolean** has only two. The order of **Boolean**'s values is **False**, **True**. The ordinality of **False** is 0, and the ordinality of **True** is 1.

Boolean Values and Relational Operators

So, apart from assigning one of the constants **True** or **False**, where do Boolean values come from? Primarily from Boolean expressions making use of *relational operators*. A relational operator is essentially a test for some relation between two values. (These values are, in the technical jargon, called *operands*.) For example, the equal symbol = is a relational operator testing whether the values on either side of it are equal. If the two values are equal, the expression as a whole returns a Boolean value of **True**. The values themselves may be constants, variables, or expressions. Here's an example:

```
VAR  AllDone : Boolean;
     Counter : Integer;
.
.
.

AllDone := False; { The default condition for AllDone is False  }
AllDone := Counter = 63;{ If Counter contains 63, AllDone becomes True }
```

There is a whole raft of other relational operators in Object Pascal. The ones you're likely to use are shown below in Table 4.2. Some of the data types in Table 4.2 haven't been covered in this book yet, but we'll get to them in time.

The operators should be almost self-explanatory. In general, an operator expresses a relationship between its operands. If this relationship exists, the expression containing the operator returns the Boolean value **True**. Otherwise it returns **False**. For example, if the two operands of the inequality operator <> are unequal, the expression returns **True**, otherwise **False**.

Relational expressions read from left to right with respect to the operator. In other words, the expression **ValueX < ValueY** tests for the relationship that **ValueX** is less than **ValueY**. If this is the case, the expression returns **True**.

The two operators >= and <= are portmanteau operators, in that they simultaneously test for two different relationships, and if *either* relationship is found, the expression returns **True**. As an example, the >= operator tests to see if its left operand is greater than its right operand. It also tests to see if the two are equal. If either the left operand is greater than the right or the two are equal, the expression returns **True**, otherwise it returns **False**.

Table 4.2 Simple Relational Operators

Operator	Symbol	Operand types
Equality	=	Numeric, ordinal, set, string
Inequality	<>	Numeric, ordinal, set, string, record
Less Than	<	Numeric, ordinal, string
Greater Than	>	Numeric, ordinal, string
Less Than or Equal	<=	Numeric, ordinal, string
Greater Than or Equal	>=	Numeric, ordinal, string

Boolean Values and IF Statements

But what are Boolean values and variables *for?* In truth, Booleans wouldn't be worth much without another Object Pascal feature: the **IF..THEN..ELSE** statement. (We generally shorten this to "the **IF** statement.") This is how Object Pascal makes decisions to go one way with program logic or another.

The **ELSE** portion of the statement is optional. In its simplest form, the **IF** statement looks like this:

```
IF <Boolean expression> THEN <statement>
```

When Delphi encounters an **IF** statement like this, it first evaluates the Boolean expression to one of the two Boolean values, **True** or **False**. If the resulting value is **True**, Delphi executes the program statement after **THEN**. If the resulting value is **False**, Delphi simply "falls through" to the next program statement without doing anything. Like so:

```
IF Counter >= Limit THEN Label1.Caption := 'Operation is complete!';
```

This **IF** statement tests a counter against a value stored in the constant **Limit**. Once **Counter** meets or exceeds **Limit**, a string message is loaded into a Label for display on the form.

Adding an **ELSE** clause to the **IF** statement requires adding a second path for program execution to take. Like so:

```
IF Counter >= Limit THEN Label1.Caption := 'Operation is complete!'
 ELSE Label1.Caption := 'Operation underway...';
```

Here, one of two different messages is displayed on the form, depending on the state of **Counter**. Execution cannot simply fall through; it *must* pass through either one assignment statement or the other.

Something very important to note here: *There is no semicolon after the first assignment statement!* Inside an **IF** statement, there is never a semicolon immediately before the word **ELSE**. Semicolons separate statements, and the **IF** statement shown above is one single statement. There is nothing to separate, and Delphi's compiler will give you an error message if you try.

Compound Statements

What happens when one path within an **IF** statement needs to execute more than one statement? That's where *compound statements* come in. You can combine multiple statements into one single compound statement and execute them as a block. Doing this is as simple as bracketing the statements to be executed together between the **BEGIN** and **END** reserved words:

```
IF Counter >= Limit THEN
 BEGIN
  Label1.Caption := 'Operation is complete!';
  Counter := 0;
 END
ELSE Label1.Caption := 'Operation underway...';
```

Here, Delphi executes two statements as a compound statement when **Counter** meets or exceeds **Limit**. One statement in the compound statement displays a message, and the other resets **Counter** to 0, ready for another go-round.

Making a Good Case

Delphi is case-insensitive. That means that **BEGIN** and **begin** mean exactly the same thing to Delphi's compiler; Delphi cannot tell the difference. Character case is stripped out of program code before the compiler even sees it.

So what should you use? From a correctness standpoint (that is, from the standpoint of getting the compiler to accept your code) you can do whatever you like. But there's a readability issue here as well. Some people (I first among them) feel that reserved words should stand out like beacons in your code, since they alone define the shape of the code that you hand to Delphi for compilation. Therefore, when I type in a reserved word, I type it in upper case, as BEGIN, END, VAR, and so on. This lets me see my procedures' "framing members" from ten steps back.

You'll probably notice that when Delphi creates an event procedure for you, it uses lower case for reserved words like **procedure**, **begin**, and **end**. That's fine. In fact, I like it that way, because I can tell at a glance what code Delphi wrote and what code I wrote. This is a new problem in programming; in the old days the programmer wrote everything. Now the programmer and the environment are partners in producing code, and it sometimes helps to be able to tell who wrote what.

So I let Delphi use lower case for reserved words, and I use upper case.

THE FOUNDATIONS OF OBJECT PASCAL

What you've just been through is a bare minimum tour of the Object Pascal language. Most of it is a matter of understanding Pascal's simple data types and what they're for within the language. Understand data, and you have most of what you need. The old emphasis on program structure passes away with Delphi, because Delphi defines the program structure and hides most of it from you. Nearly all of what you'll do as a Delphi programmer involves writing procedures that manipulate data.

There's more to writing procedures than what I've explained here. We'll return to the details of the Object Pascal language in Chapter 6.

VISUAL AND NON-VISUAL COMPONENTS

Jim Mischel

The core of Delphi programming consists of knowing what components are available and how to use them well—whether they're visible or working behind the scenes within your application.

One of my former coworkers used to be fond of dividing the world into "two different kinds of people" for purposes of his philosophical pontificating. It didn't seem to bother him that if you eliminated his artificially-created (sometimes wildly so) categories, there was absolutely no logic to his arguments. When I got tired of his ravings, I started making up categories of my own: "You know," I'd say, "the world is divided into two kinds of people: those named Jim, and everybody else." And then I'd climb up on my soap box (usually an old crate) and begin extolling the virtues of those fortunate individuals who share my given name. I guess when you're moving furniture for a living, anything out of the ordinary is funny.

You can divide Delphi's component palette into two groups: visual components—those that have a visible on-screen presence when the program is executing—and non-visual components, which aren't visible on the form at runtime. Forms, labels, buttons, and the other components that we've been working with up to this point are obvious

examples of visual components. Non-visual components include timers, menus, common dialog boxes, and data-access controls.

Unfortunately, like my former coworker's artificial categories, the dividing line between visual and non-visual components isn't crystal clear. Dialogs, for example, aren't visible on the form when the program starts, but they do have a visual presence at some point when the program is running. And menus are visible at runtime, although their appearance at runtime is somewhat different from their appearance at design-time. Finally, regardless of their appearance or non-appearance, as the case may be, we manipulate all components in the same manner—by changing their properties.

In this chapter, we're going to explore the Timer component, and then take a brief look at menus and standard dialogs, to which we'll return in later chapters. We'll be writing a bit more actual program code here than in previous chapters, but nothing that you can't handle. There is programming involved in creating a Delphi application, but it's hardly the kind of brain-bending stuff that's normally associated with Windows programming.

THE TIMER

I'm forever writing programs that need to either delay for a set period of time or determine the duration of a particular task. For example, you may want your program to display a two-second screen message. Or consider Delphi's fly-by hints: If you move the mouse pointer to the component palette or the speed bar and leave it motionless for about half a second, a hint box pops up.

Delphi's Timer component is a simple little timekeeper that sits in the background, and at regular intervals "wakes up" and sends a message to your application by calling the OnTimer event handler. You can turn a timer on and off by changing its **Enabled** property, and you can adjust the speed of a timer (that is, how often it "ticks") by changing its **Interval** property.

Setting the Interval

The Timer's **Interval** property defines the number of milliseconds (thousandths of a second) between OnTimer events (ticks). That is, if **Interval** is set to 1000, then the timer will issue an OnTimer event every 1,000 milliseconds (in other words, once per second). To determine the proper value for **Interval**, divide 1,000 by the number of ticks you want to occur per second. So, if you want 10 timer ticks per second (one tick every tenth of a second), you should set **Interval** to 100 (1000/10=100). If the desired interval between ticks is more than one second, then just multiply the desired interval by 1000. For example, if you want the timer to tick once every 2.5 seconds, then set the Timer's **Interval** property to 2500 (2.5*1000=2500). Setting **Interval** to 0 is the same as turning the timer off. The maximum **Interval** setting is 32767, which would result in one timer tick every 32.767 seconds.

Although Delphi's Timers are capable of generating 1,000 ticks per second, you should be careful in programming your program's response to a timer tick. If your program spends more than **Interval** milliseconds processing the timer tick, you're going to miss OnTimer events. For example, if you set a timer to generate 100 ticks per second (one tick every 10 milliseconds), and it takes 12 milliseconds for your program to process the timer tick, you'll to miss every other timer tick because the program will be processing when the next tick comes through. If you run into this problem, you can either increase the interval between ticks, or reduce the amount of work your program does every tick.

Note also that other Windows programs can affect whether or not timer ticks are generated. If you have a processor-hungry application running in the background, then it's doubtful that your program will get all of its timer ticks if **Interval** is set to generate 100 ticks per second.

The Stopwatch Program

Let's introduce the timer by writing a stopwatch program that acts just like a very simple hand-held digital stopwatch. This program will have two displays: Total Time and Lap Time, and three buttons: Start/Stop, Lap, and Reset. The completed form is shown in Figure 5.1.

Dropping Components

Start with a new form by selecting File | New Project from Delphi's main menu. Change the Form's **Caption** property to "Stopwatch" so you know what it is

Figure 5.1 *The completed Stopwatch form.*

you're working on. (Nothing's dumber than showing off your new master-piece, which reads "Form1" in the title bar....)

Click on the Label component on the component palette and drop the label onto your form. In the Object Inspector, change the label's **Caption** property to "Total Time". Create another label and change its **Caption** to "Lap Time". Position these labels as shown in Figure 5.1.

Although the two time displays look like Edit components, they're actually Memos. The reason I used the Memo component is that it has an **Alignment** property that allows us to display text right-justified. The Edit component lacks this property. To add the display for Total Time, select the Memo component from the component palette and place the memo on your form to the right of the "Total Time" label. You'll have to resize the component so that it fits correctly, as Memos are usually more than one line in height. In the Object Inspector, set the component's properties as shown in Table 5.1.

We set **Enabled** and **TabStop** to **False** so that the Memo can't be selected with the mouse or tabbed to with the keyboard. Our program will display information in this field, not accept input, leaving no reason for the user to select it. That's also why we changed **ReadOnly** to **True**: It keeps the user from changing the Memo text, but doesn't prevent the program from changing it.

Component Copy and Paste

Since the Lap Time display will have the same properties as the Total Time display (with the exception of the **Name** property), you can save yourself some time creating the Lap Time display by using Delphi's component copy and paste facility. Click on the **TotalTime** Memo, and then select Edit|Copy

---

Table 5.1 *Property Changes for the Total Time Display*

Property	Change to
BorderIcons.Maximize	False
BorderStyle	bsSingle
Enabled	False
Name	TotalTime
ReadOnly	True
TabStop	False
Text	0.0

from Delphi's main menu. Then select Edit | Paste, and a new Memo component will be displayed, overlaying the first Memo and offset slightly to the right and down. This new Memo component has all the properties of the **TotalTime** Memo, except that the name and position have changed. Grab it with the mouse and move it to the right of the "Lap Time" label, and then use the Object Inspector to change its name to "LapTime."

 **Naming Components**

When you drop a component onto your form, Delphi automatically gives it a name: **ComponentX**, where **Component** is the type of component and **X** is a number. If you drop two buttons on your form, for example, they'll be called **Button1** and **Button2**.

Button1 doesn't tell you much about what the button is or does, so it's a good idea to change the **Name** property to something more descriptive: **AddButton**, for example, if the button is going to be used to add an item. The same goes for most other components. Sure, if there's only one of a particular type of component on a form (like the Timer in the Stopwatch program), it's perfectly fine to leave its **Name** as **Timer1**. In general, though, you'll find it much clearer to name the components according to the function they perform or data they display.

Keeping Time

Select the Timer component (the one that looks like a clock) from the System page of the component palette, and place it on your form to the right of the two time display Memos. In the Object Inspector, set the Timer's **Enabled** property to **True**, and set **Interval** to 100, which will give us ten ticks per second. Then, switch to the Events page in the Object Inspector and double-click to the right of OnTimer to create an event handler for the Timer's ticks. Edit the **Timer1Timer** procedure in the Unit window to look like Listing 5.1.

LISTING 5.1   The Stopwatch OnTimer event handler

```
procedure TForm1.Timer1Timer(Sender: TObject);
Var
 s : String;
 Seconds : Real;
begin
 TickCounter := TickCounter + 1;
 Seconds := TickCounter / 10;
 Str (Seconds:10:1, s);
 TotalTime.Text := s;
end;
```

Before we get into a discussion of what this code does, we need to do one more thing. Move to the beginning of the file in the Unit window and locate the **private** section of the **TForm1** class definition. Insert these variable declarations right below the comment that reads "Private declarations":

```
TickCounter : Longint;
LapCounter : Longint;
```

When you finish, your Unit window should look like Figure 5.2.

The first variable, **TickCounter**, counts ticks—it's our program's way of keeping time. A Timer component generates ticks however often you tell it to. The Timer doesn't keep track of its ticks, so if you want to know how long the timer's been running, you have to define a variable to hold the tick count, and your OnTimer event handler has to update this variable every timer tick.

The second variable, **LapCounter**, will be used to calculate the elapsed lap time when the Lap button is pressed. We'll discuss this in more detail when we add the Lap button and its event handler.

The OnTimer event handler, **TForm1.Timer1Timer**, is the procedure that's called whenever the timer generates a tick. The first line of code increments the **TickCounter** variable by 1, indicating that the timer ticked. The second line converts the number of ticks (tenths of a second) to seconds by dividing the **TickCounter** by 10. The result is stored in the **Seconds** variable.

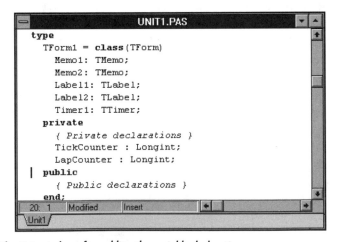

Figure 5.2 *The Unit window after adding the variable declarations.*

The third line of code in the OnTimer event handler uses Object Pascal's **Str** procedure to convert the value stored in the **Seconds** variable into a formatted string, which is stored in the locally-declared string, **s**. **Str** is a versatile function that can convert any number to a string, and format the string several different ways.

The final line of code changes the **Text** property of the **TotalTime** Memo component, setting it to reflect the new elapsed time. It is this statement (more correctly, Delphi's handling of the statement) that actually changes the text that's displayed in the Memo component.

Initializing the Tick Counter

There's one last detail that I almost forgot. We need to make sure that the **TickCounter** and **LapCounter** variables are set to 0 when the program first starts. If we don't initialize these variables, then their values will correspond to whatever random values were in memory at the time the program was started. I know that some programming languages, Delphi included, automatically initialize variables to 0, but not all do. It's good programming practice to initialize all of your variables, even if the language you're working with automatically initializes them to 0. It's a good habit to get in to, so that you remember to do it when you need to initialize your variables to something other than 0. (Even Delphi won't do that without your telling it to!)

When a Form is created, an OnCreate event is triggered. It's in the handler for this event that you want to initialize the Form's local variables. To add an OnCreate event handler, select the Form component by clicking on a blank spot in the Form's client area, and from the Events page of the Object Inspector, double-click next to OnCreate. Add these two lines to the **TForm1.FormCreate** procedure:

```
TickCounter := 0;
LapCounter := 0;
```

Testing the Form

We're not done with Stopwatch yet, but now is a good time to stop and make sure that you've got things right up to this point. Select File | Save Project (or click on the Save Project button on the speed bar), and name the unit

TIMERFRM.PAS, and the project STOPWTCH.DPR. Once you've saved your work, press F9 to compile and run the program. If you get compiler errors, go back and make sure that you've entered all of the code correctly, save your work, and then press F9 to try it again.

The program should start updating the **TotalTime** Memo component immediately, and will continue for as long as you let it. If your computer is swapping things in and out of memory (the disk light will be on), it's possible that you could lose some timer ticks and the **TotalTime** value won't reflect the actual elapsed time. In the next section, we'll add the Start/Stop and other buttons so that we can control the stopwatch.

When you're tired of watching the time go by, press Alt+F4 to terminate the program.

STOPWATCH, MARK II

As it is, Stopwatch is a mildly interesting example program, but it doesn't really do anything useful. To use the stopwatch, you need the ability to control it. It's time to add those controls: the Start/Stop, Lap, and Reset buttons.

Before doing anything else, select the Timer component and change its **Enabled** property to **False**, as we want the stopwatch to be off when we start the program. Then, select the Button component from the tools palette and drop three buttons onto the form below the time displays. Use the alignment and sizing tools to place the buttons where you want them.

Starting and Stopping the Timer

Click on the first button, labeled "Button1," and then use the Object Inspector to change its **Name** property to **StartBtn**, and its **Caption** property to "&Start". Then, from the Events page, select the OnClick event and double-click to the right of it to create an OnClick event handler. Edit the code in the Unit window so that it looks like Listing 5.2.

LISTING 5.2   The Start button's OnClick event handler

```
procedure TForm1.StartBtnClick(Sender: TObject);
begin
 If Timer1.Enabled Then Begin
  Timer1.Enabled := False;
  StartBtn.Caption := '&Start';
 End
 Else Begin
```

```
   Timer1.Enabled := True;
   StartBtn.Caption := '&Stop';
 End;
end;
```

The event handler in Listing 5.2 simulates the start/stop button on a real stopwatch by toggling the timer on and off. If the stopwatch is running (that is, the Timer's **Enabled** property is **True**), then the event handler turns the timer off and changes the button's **Caption** to "Start". If the stopwatch isn't running, then this code starts the Timer by setting its **Enabled** property to **True**, and changes the button's Caption to "Stop".

If you like, you can press F9 at this point and experiment with starting and stopping the stopwatch.

Counting Laps

To count laps, we need to know the current elapsed time, and also the time at the end of the previous lap. For example, if you're keeping quarter-mile lap times for somebody running a mile, your results would look similar to those in Table 5.2.

Of course, if you were timing *me* running a mile those times would be somewhat different, but we'll save that particular discussion for another day.

Each lap time is the difference between the current elapsed time and the elapsed time at the end of the previous lap. Our lap timer, then, has to keep track of the elapsed time at the end of the previous lap so that it can compute the current lap time.

To add this ability to Stopwatch, click on the second button that you dropped onto the form, change its **Name** property to "LapBtn", and change its **Caption** property to "&Lap". Then, create an OnClick event handler for this button and edit it so that it looks like Listing 5.3.

Table 5.2   *Sample Quarter-Mile Lap Times for a Mile Runner*

Lap	Elapsed Time	Lap Time
1	65.2	65.2
2	138.9	73.7
3	214.0	74.1
4	278.3	64.3

LISTING 5.3 The Lap button's OnClick event handler

```
procedure TForm1.LapBtnClick(Sender: TObject);
Var
 s : String;
 Temp : Longint;
begin
 Temp := TickCounter - LapCounter;
 LapCounter := TickCounter;
 Str ((Temp/10):0:1, s);
 LapTime.Text := s;
end;
```

The first line of code in Listing 5.3 computes the current lap time by subtracting the tick count at the end of the previous lap from the current tick count. This value is stored in temporary variable **Temp**. We then update the **LapCounter** variable so that it now holds the tick count at the end of this lap so we'll be able to compute the next lap time. Finally, we use **Str** to format the lap time in **Temp**, and then set **LapTimer**'s **Text** property to reflect the new lap time.

Clearing the Clock

Resetting the timer is a simple matter of setting the **TickCounter** and **LapCounter** variables to 0, and setting the time display's **Text** properties back to 0. The code that does this is very simple. Change the third button's **Name** property to **ResetBtn**, its **Caption** property to "&Reset", and after creating an OnClick event handler for this button, edit the code so that it looks like Listing 5.4.

LISTING 5.4 The Reset button's OnClick event handler

```
procedure TForm1.ResetBtnClick(Sender: TObject);
begin
 TickCounter := 0;
 LapCounter := 0;
 LapTime.Text:= '0.0';
 TotalTime.Text := '0.0';
end;
```

The Final Product

When you finish making those changes, you have a fully-functional stopwatch program! Save your work and then press F9 to compile and run it. "Nifty," as my wife likes to say, and all in a couple-dozen lines of fairly simple Pascal code.

MENUS

What's a Windows program without a menu? True, Stopwatch doesn't have a menu, but it's hardly more than a toy. Any full-featured Windows application simply must have a menu.

Traditional Windows development systems usually include a resource editor program in which you can define menus graphically, which is preferable to creating menus at runtime. However, writing the code that actually responds to the menu is a bit of a convoluted process. And it's way too easy to get your code out of sync with the menu resource, resulting in a very big mess and a program that doesn't work as expected.

One of Delphi's handy tools is the Menu Designer—a mini-application that makes designing and responding to menus much easier than with other Windows programming tools.

Building Menus with Menu Designer

Delphi provides two different menu components: MainMenu and PopupMenu. A MainMenu is the standard menu bar that almost all Windows applications contain. A PopupMenu is a menu box—normally a local menu—like the menu that pops up when you right-click on a form in Delphi. The Menu Designer works for both types of menus. In this section, we'll introduce Menu Designer by building a MainMenu. In the next section we'll use a PopupMenu to illustrate the use of common dialog boxes.

Starting with a new form, select the MainMenu component from the Standard page of the component palette, and drop the component onto your form. Then, double-click on the new component in order to bring up the Menu Designer window, shown in Figure 5.3.

The Menu Designer works in concert with the Object Inspector to help you build menus. Some programmers like to define each menu item and all of its properties before moving on to the next item. I find it much easier to create the menu display first, and then go back and add functionality to each menu item. This way, I can get the menu just right before I start writing code to implement the menu's functions.

The menu I've chosen for this demonstration is pretty simple, although it does include features that go into most Windows applications. The completed menu is shown in Figure 5.4.

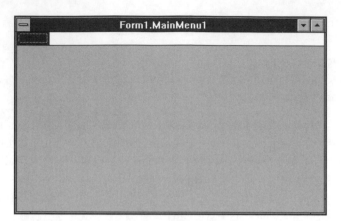

Figure 5.3 *The Menu Designer tool.*

I don't want to get bogged down in implementation details here, so our example application is going to have a menu, but those menu items won't do anything but display a "Function not implemented" message box. In Chapter 7, I'll show you how to create a real application with a more complete menu.

Adding Menu Items

As Glenda the Good Witch says, it's always best to start at the beginning. This is as true of menus as it is of roads of any color—so let's start by creating the File menu and its items.

With the highlight bar positioned in the far left corner of the menu in Menu Designer (see Figure 5.3), type "&File" (without the quotes) and press Enter.

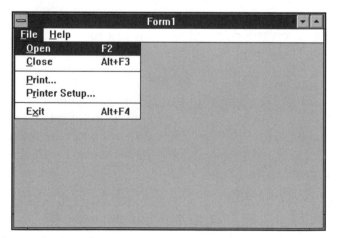

Figure 5.4 *The completed sample menu.*

This creates the File menu, and then moves the highlight bar down so that you can enter the first item in the File menu. The Menu Designer window should look like Figure 5.5.

You probably noticed that the Object Inspector window changed when you began typing the menu caption. In addition to the main menu itself, each menu item is also a component with its own properties and events. As you create new menu items, the properties for those items are displayed in the Object Inspector window. You'll notice that the **Caption** and **Name** properties change as you enter the menu items in the Menu Designer. For now, don't worry about the menu items' properties—we'll come back to them after we've entered all of the menu items.

To create the first item on the File menu, type "&Open..." and press Enter. Don't worry about the shortcut key F2 for now—we'll come back to that after we've added all of the menu items.

The Open menu item should be displayed below the File menu and the highlight bar will move down to the next insertion spot. Repeat this process—enter the menu item text and press Enter—for each of the remaining items on the File menu: "&Close", "&Print...", "P&rinter Setup...", and "E&xit". We'll go back and add the menu separators next, so just skip them for now. When you're done, your Menu Designer window should look like Figure 5.6.

Inserting and Deleting Menu Items

Invariably, once you've got things just right, somebody comes up with a suggestion (or demand) that you change it. The File menu we just created

Figure 5.5 *Creating the File menu.*

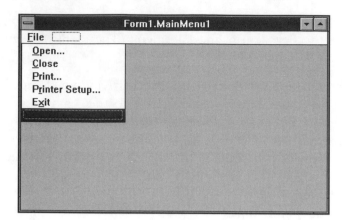

Figure 5.6 *Adding items to the File menu.*

needs a couple of menu separators so that the items are grouped visually a little better. Fortunately, inserting menu separators is really easy.

Using the up and down arrow keys, position the highlight bar over the Print menu item and press the Insert button. If you prefer to use the mouse, click on the Print menu item, click the right mouse button to bring up the Menu Designer's local menu, and select Insert from there. You can also display the local menu by pressing Alt+F10. However you do it, the Menu Designer will create a "blank spot" in the menu by moving the Print item and all of the items below it down one line.

To create a menu separator, just type "-" (the minus key) and press Enter. The Menu Designer knows that a single "-" in the item name specifies a separator, and will draw a horizontal line for that menu item. This doesn't prevent you from creating menu items that begin with "-", though. If you enter anything after the "-", then the entire text that you enter will be displayed for that item.

If you want to delete a menu item, simply position the highlight bar over the menu item that you want to delete, and then press the Delete key. Or, you can bring up the local menu (right click, or Alt+F10), and select Delete from there. When you delete an item from the menu, all of the menu's sub-items are deleted as well. For example, if you were to click on the File menu and press Delete, the entire File menu and all of its menu items would be deleted.

Before we move on, be sure to add the second separator to the File menu. Select the Exit menu item, press Insert, and then type "-" and hit Enter.

To add the Help menu and its single item, just press the right arrow key to move the highlight bar to the blank spot to the right of the File menu, and then type "&Help" and press Enter. The highlight bar will move down one line, where you can enter "&About" and press Enter in order to create the Help menu's About menu item.

Adding Shortcut Keys

Once all the menu items are added, it's time to go back and add any shortcut keys, and also the event handlers for each menu item. In the Menu Designer window, click on the File menu, and then on the Open menu item. This will select the menu item, and its properties will be displayed in the Object Inspector. We want a shortcut key of F2 for this menu item, so in the Object Inspector, click on the **ShortCut** property, and then on the drop-down arrow. The Object Inspector will display a list of shortcut keys similar to Figure 5.7.

Using the mouse or the arrow keys, select the entry for F2. The edit portion of the **ShortCut** combo box will display your selected shortcut key, and it will also be displayed to the right of the menu item in the Menu Designer window.

Once you've added the shortcut key for the File|Open menu item, you can add the other shortcut keys by simply selecting the menu item in the Menu Designer window, and then typing the text of the shortcut key. For example, to add the shortcut key for the File|Close menu item, click on that item in the Menu Designer window, type "Alt+F3", and press Enter. As long as the **ShortCut** property is highlighted in the Object Inspector, you can repeat this process for each menu item that requires a shortcut key.

Before going on, add the "Alt+F4" shortcut key for the File|Exit menu item.

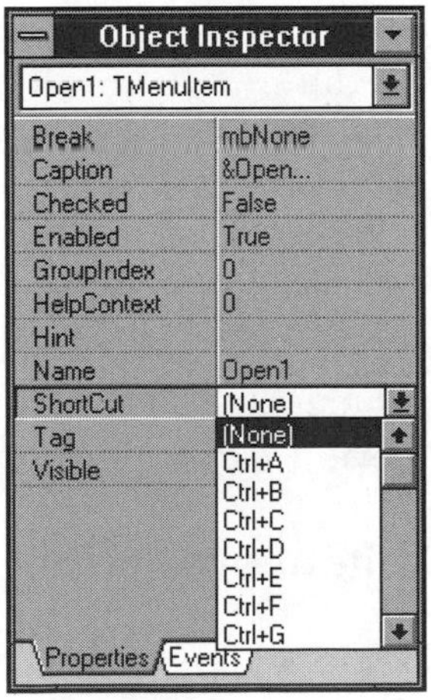

Figure 5.7   *Displaying menu shortcut keys in the Object Inspector.*

Making the Menu Work

Once you've entered all of the menu items and added their shortcut keys, you're ready to assign actions to the individual menu items. As with Buttons, we do this by creating OnClick event handlers. With the exception of File | Exit, which will close the form, our menu items will just display a message that says that the particular option is not implemented.

The Menu Designer gives us an easy shortcut to adding event procedures for menu items—just double-click on the menu item and Delphi automatically opens the Unit window and positions the caret at the point where you should enter code for the event procedure. This is far easier than selecting each menu item in Menu Designer, and then using the Object Inspector to create an OnClick handler.

In the Menu Designer, double-click on the File | Exit menu item, and when the Unit window is displayed, enter the following line of code in the **TForm1.Exit1Click** event handler:

```
Close;
```

The Form's **Close** procedure closes the form, and here also terminates the application, because the form is the application's main window. In an application with multiple forms, closing a form won't necessarily close the application.

In this example, the other menu items's functions aren't implemented, so we'll make each one of them call the **ShowMessage** procedure to display a message. To add the event procedure for the File | Open menu item, double-click on the File | Open menu item in the Menu Designer, and then enter this line of code in the event procedure:

```
ShowMessage ('File|Open not implemented');
```

Repeat this procedure for each of the menu items: Double-clicking on the menu item in the Menu Designer, and then inserting a **ShowMessage** call to display the "not implemented" message. Listing 5.5 shows the complete code for each of the menu items's event handlers.

LISTING 5.5   The menu item event handlers

```
procedure TForm1.Open1Click(Sender: TObject);
begin
 ShowMessage ('File|Open not implemented');
end;
```

```
procedure TForm1.Close1Click(Sender: TObject);
begin
 ShowMessage ('File|Close not implemented');
end;

procedure TForm1.Print1Click(Sender: TObject);
begin
 ShowMessage ('File|Print not implemented');
end;

procedure TForm1.PrinterSetup1Click(Sender: TObject);
begin
 ShowMessage ('File|Printer setup not implemented');
end;

procedure TForm1.Exit1Click(Sender: TObject);
begin
 Close;
end;

procedure TForm1.About1Click(Sender: TObject);
begin
 ShowMessage ('Help|About not implemented');
end;
```

Running the Program

After you've created event handlers for all of the menu items, save the unit as MENUFORM.PAS and the project as MENUTEST.DPR. Press F9 to compile and run the project.

To see if your menu is working, select a menu item. If you select anything other than File|Exit (which should exit the program), you should see a message box similar to Figure 5.8.

Remember also that you've defined shortcut keys for three of the menu items. Pressing F2 should perform the same function as selecting File|Open, and pressing Alt+F3 should do the same as File|Close. Pressing Alt+F4 will exit the program.

Figure 5.8 *A "Not Implemented" message.*

More Menus Later

We're by no means done with menus, but we've covered the basics. In the next section we'll create a popup menu, but that's pretty much the same as a main menu. In Chapter 7, we'll use the Menu Designer to create the menu for a simple file viewer, and we'll discuss menu item properties (including adding and removing menu items at runtime) in more detail then. To learn more about menus, menu items, and the other options on the Menu Designer's local menu, see the appropriate entries in Delphi's online help.

COMMON DIALOG BOXES

Common dialog boxes are standard dialog boxes that a large number of Windows programs use, such as the Font, Color, and File Open dialog boxes. In order to give Windows programs a more common "look and feel," Microsoft added a dynamic link library (COMMDLG.DLL) to Windows that implements these standard dialog boxes. Windows programs can call the routines in this DLL in order to provide common services, relieving the programmer of writing yet another File Save dialog box—and not incidentally allowing all File Save dialog boxes to look alike. (Users, at the very least, should be abundantly glad for this.) This DLL does reduce the amount of programming required to use one of the standard dialog boxes, but it still involves quite a bit of programming if you're using traditional Windows programming tools. Delphi encapsulates the common dialogs into components that you can place on a form and then execute with just a few lines of code.

The Delphi components that encapsulate the common dialogs are all located on the Dialogs page of the component palette. These components are: OpenDialog, SaveDialog, FontDialog, ColorDialog, PrintDialog, PrinterSetupDialog, FindDialog, and ReplaceDialog. If you've been following along this far, you've already seen OpenDialog, SaveDialog, ColorDialog, and FontDialog, as they're all used by Delphi itself (Borland makes no secret that Delphi was written in Delphi—allowing Delphi to demonstrate its own capabilities better than any canned demo program ever could). Before we continue our discussion of the common dialog boxes, let's take a few minutes to create the form and popup menu that we will use to illustrate their use.

 **The Font and Color Dialog Boxes**

PROJECT In this section, we're going to write a small program with a popup menu that uses the Font and Color dialog boxes. This will give you an understanding of how dialog boxes work, without getting into the details of working with files. We'll leave that to Chapter 9, where we'll create a few dialog boxes of our own.

Popup Menus

Popup menus are in many ways similar to application main menus, but they normally serve a more limited purpose. Typically, an application will have a single main menu, and each window in the application will have its own local menu, normally implemented as a popup menu. This menu is traditionally accessed with a right mouse click, or by pressing Alt+F10. Creating a popup menu in Delphi involves the same general tasks as creating a main menu.

Select File | New Project from Delphi's main menu to start with a fresh canvas. Then, select a PopupMenu component from the Standard page of the component palette, and drop it onto your form in the upper left-hand corner. Double-click on the component on your form to bring up the Menu Designer.

Our popup menu will have two items: Font and Color. In the Menu Designer, you can add these menu items by entering the menu item text ("&Font" or "&Color"), and then pressing Enter. After you've created these two items, close the Menu Designer window. We'll come back to it shortly.

Add a Label component to your form, and change its **Caption** property to "Click the right mouse button to activate the popup menu". Position this label so that it's centered horizontally in the Form, right below the PopupMenu component.

Click on a blank spot on your form to select it, and then in the Object Inspector, change the Form's **PopupMenu** property to "PopupMenu1". You can type this value into the **PopupMenu** property's edit box, or select it from the drop-down list.

Save your work, calling the Unit DLGFORM.PAS, and the Project DLGXMPL.DPR. Then press F9 to compile and run the program. When the program is executing, place the mouse cursor inside the client area of the form and click the right mouse button. The menu should pop up, creating a display similar to Figure 5.9.

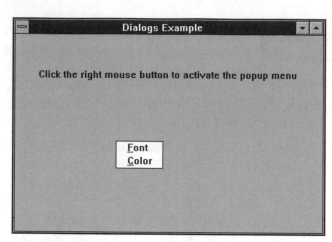

Figure 5.9 *Activating the popup menu.*

Since we haven't added any event handlers for the menu items, selecting one of them won't do anything. Once you're satisfied that everything is working the way it should, press Alt+F4 to close the application.

Using Common Dialogs

To use one of Delphi's common dialog box components in a program, you must place the component on your form, and then provide an event procedure that accesses the dialog box component. The event procedure must:

1. Set the dialog box component's initial values.
2. Execute the dialog box.
3. Read the dialog box's values and set your program's options appropriately.

A dialog box's **Execute** method will normally return **True** if the user selected OK, indicating that the program is to apply any changes that were made in the dialog box. If **Execute** returns **False**, then the program should ignore the dialog box's values.

The FontDialog Component

In Chapter 3, you used the FontDialog component to change a Form's **Font** property at design-time. Your programs can use this same dialog box at runtime to change the font of any component. Let's see how.

Using the form that we just designed, select a Memo component and place it on your form below the instruction label. Go ahead and size and position the Memo however you like. Then, select a FontDialog component from the Dialogs page of the component palette, and drop it on the form next to the PopupMenu. We'll also be using a ColorDialog in this example, so you might as well grab one of those from the component palette and drop it onto the form beside the FontDialog component. When you're done, your form should look like Figure 5.10.

We need something to activate our FontDialog component. Double-click on the PopupMenu component to bring up the Menu Designer, and then double-click on the Font menu item to create an event handler. Enter the code shown in Listing 5.6.

LISTING 5.6   The Font menu item's OnClick event handler

```
procedure TForm1.Font1Click(Sender: TObject);
begin
 FontDialog1.Font := Memo1.Font;
 If FontDialog1.Execute Then
  Memo1.Font := FontDialog1.Font;
end;
```

I said it was going to be simple. Save your work and press F9 to compile and test the program. Click the right mouse button anywhere on the client area of the form, and then select the Font item from the popup menu. The Font dialog should display and allow you to change the Form's font. If you press OK, then the font of the text in the Memo will change.

So what does the code do? The first line sets the FontDialog component's **Font** property to match the Memo component's **Font**. The next line calls the

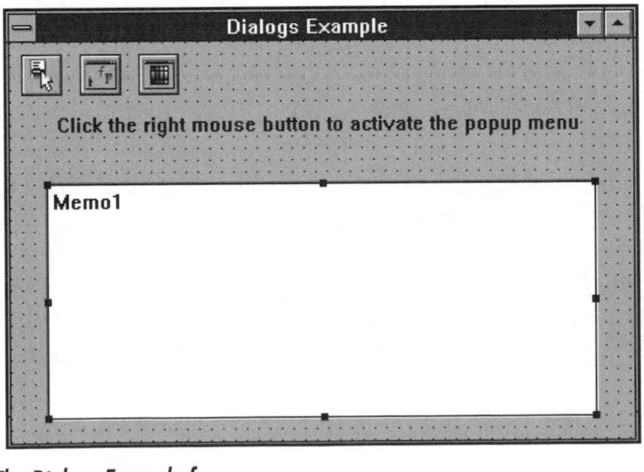

Figure 5.10   *The Dialogs Example form.*

FontDialog's **Execute** method, which displays the dialog box and allows you to set the options. If you close the Font dialog by pressing the OK button, then **Execute** returns **True**. If you close the Font dialog box any other way (that is, by pressing Cancel or by double-clicking on the control-menu box), then **Execute** returns **False**.

The last line in the event handler simply sets the Memo's **Font** property to reflect the changes that you made in the Font dialog box. This code is executed only if **FontDialog1.Execute** returns **True**.

FontDialog Properties

The FontDialog component is pretty simple. It only has a handful of properties, and just one event. Other than **Font**, the only property you're likely to change often is **Options**, which describes the options and types of fonts that should be displayed in the Font dialog box when it's displayed. **Options** is a set property, and double-clicking on it will display all of its sub-properties. Most of these sub-properties specify what types of fonts should be displayed in the dialog box. If you set **fdWysiwyg** to **True**, for example, then only those fonts that are available to both the printer and the screen will be displayed in the dialog box.

If **fdEffects** is set to **False**, then the Effects check boxes and Color combo boxes aren't displayed in the Font dialog box. If **fdShowHelp** is set to **True**, then a Help button will be shown in the dialog box. The other options determine whether or not a value is highlighted (selected) in a particular combo box. For more information about these sub-properties, see the online help for the FontDialog component.

FontDialog Events

The FontDialog has one event: OnApply. If you create an event handler for this event, then the Font dialog box will display an Apply button. Pressing this Apply button activates the OnApply event handler. You can use this handler to effect the changes in the Font dialog box without closing the dialog.

In your form, click on the FontDialog component to select it, and then from the Events page of the Object Inspector, double-click next to the OnApply event to create an event handler. In the Unit window, enter the code shown in Listing 5.7.

LISTING 5.7 The FontDialog's OnApply event handler

```
procedure TForm1.FontDialog1Apply(Sender: TObject);
begin
 Memo1.Font := FontDialog1.Font;
end;
```

This code simply sets the Memo's font to match the settings in the Font dialog box. If you run the program, bring up the Font dialog box, change the font and then press the Apply button, the font in the Memo component will change, but the Font dialog box will remain on the screen.

The ColorDialog Component

In Chapter 3, we used the ColorGrid component to change a form's **Color** and **Font.Color** properties. ColorGrid is pretty handy, but it only allows you to choose from Windows' 16 standard colors. ColorDialog, on the other hand, allows you to select from 48 different colors, or you can define custom colors that take full advantage of your video display's capabilities. Using the ColorDialog component is very similar to using a FontDialog.

We've already got a ColorDialog component on our form, and a menu item to control it. All we need to do is attach the two.

Double-click on the PopupMenu component to bring up the Menu Designer, double-click on the Color menu item to create the event procedure, and then enter the code shown in Listing 5.8.

LISTING 5.8 The Color menu item's OnClick event handler

```
procedure TForm1.Color1Click(Sender: TObject);
begin
 ColorDialog1.Color := Memo1.Color;
 If ColorDialog1.Execute Then
  Memo1.Color := ColorDialog1.Color;
end;
```

Just like that. Save your work, and press F9 to test the program. When you select Color from the popup menu, the Color dialog appears and allows you to select a color or define a custom color. When you press OK, the new Memo component's background changes to reflect your new color selection.

ColorDialog Properties

Like FontDialog, the ColorDialog component doesn't have many properties. And it doesn't have any events. The **Options** property, another set property, consists of three options that determine how the Color dialog box should be displayed. The **cdFullOpen** sub-property is set to **False** by default, which instructs the dialog box to display only the standard colors when it's first displayed. If this is set to **True**, then the custom colors part of the dialog box (the right half) is also visible when the dialog box is first displayed.

If you set **cdPreventFullOpen** to **True**, then the Define Custom Colors button in the Colors dialog box will be disabled. If **cdShowHelp** is set to **True**, then a Help button will be displayed in the dialog box. Again, to learn more about the ColorDialog component, see the online help.

PLACING NON-VISUAL COMPONENTS

From a form-design standpoint, non-visual components are inconvenient to work with. They're handy, don't get me wrong, but on a pretty full form there's just no place to put the darned things. In our Dialogs Example form, we left blank space at the top of the form for the three non-visual components. This is hardly an optimum solution, as it makes for an odd-looking form at runtime. In many cases, you will have blank space on a form in which to place the non-visual components. But if you don't, you have to get creative.

One way to handle it is to place the non-visual component between two visual components so that it partially overlaps both. If you have a big enough visual component, like the Memo component in the last example, you can put the non-visual components on top of it. I'm not particularly fond of either solution, because both of them make my form look funny at design-time.

Another way to handle the problem is to make your form just a little larger than it has to be to fit all of the visual components, place the non-visual components on a panel at the left or bottom of the form—away from the visual components—and then resize the form at runtime in the **OnCreate** event procedure. This method has the advantage of grouping all of the non-visual components in one spot, and doesn't detract too much from the form's appearance at design-time.

Next Steps

We covered a lot of ground in this chapter. You created your first "real" Delphi application—the Stopwatch—and you saw how to use menus and dialog boxes, which are the building blocks of all but the simplest Windows programs. We're not done with menus or dialogs—not by a long shot. We haven't even touched on changing menu items while the program's running, and you haven't yet seen how to create your own dialog boxes. We'll come back to both of these components in later chapters.

In the last chapter, you received your first lesson in Object Pascal programming. The next chapter will build on that knowledge with an introduction to complex data types and how they're created—along with more of Object Pascal's standard procedures, functions, and statements. In Chapter 7, we'll start concentrating more on building Windows applications, and much less on dragging components around the form. There are plenty of other Delphi components left to explore, and we'll tackle quite a few of them in the chapters that follow

Data, Data, Everywhere

CHAPTER 6

Jeff Duntemann

Object Pascal data types can be as simple or as complex as you need them to be to get the job done—once you learn the skills you need to roll your own.

Well, there are buckets and there are buckets. Back in Chapter 4, I described Object Pascal variables as buckets into which you can throw data for carrying around between manipulations, or between other buckets. The metaphor works pretty well, as long as you understand that if you consider a bucket a device for carrying something, there are lots of different kinds of buckets, some of which look nothing at all like the venerable tin pail with a handle.

I bought an Erector set for my nephew Brian a year or so ago. It came in a longish box, within which was an injection-molded plastic tray. The tray had twenty-odd little depressions molded into it, each of which carried a part or a little pile of parts. There was a gear-shaped depression, a bracket-shaped depression, numerous girder-shaped depressions, several square plate-shaped depressions, and a nondescript depression full of nuts and bolts. That tray was a bucket—a bucket of Erector set parts, though we usually don't think of it that way.

A dozen eggs come home from Safeway by way of an egg carton, which has a dozen little egg-sized bins arranged in two neat rows of six. It's a bucket for carrying eggs, obviously.

The point I'm making here is that data comes in a lot of shapes, sizes, and (especially) complexities. Object Pascal can handle them all—even the ones that don't exist until you think them up. That's one of the abilities of Object Pascal that we'll confront in this chapter: The creation of your own custom data types and new buckets to put them in.

DEFINING YOUR OWN DATA TYPES

Like almost everything else in Object Pascal, your custom data type definitions occur in statements. A type definition statement begins with the reserved word **TYPE**, a new identifier to act as the name for your type, an equal sign (not a colon!) and then the definition of your type. Some (but by no means all) type definitions must be closed with the reserved word **END**.

Delphi automatically defines a new type for you whenever you begin a new project or a new form. If you create a new project and bring up the code window in the code file UNIT1.PAS, you'll see the following statement:

```
type
  TForm1 = class(TForm)
  private
    { Private declarations }
  public
    { Public declarations }
  end;
```

This is a type definition, and more specifically, an object definition, which is the most advanced and versatile—and certainly the single most important—sort of type definition. I'll explain these in Chapter 8. For the time being, note that it begins with the reserved word **type** (in lowercase here, since Delphi generated it) followed by the name of the type, which is **TForm1**. As a convention in Object Pascal, the names of new types (that is, types beyond the fundamental Pascal types and especially types that you define for your own use) begin with a capital T. Nothing enforces this—it's strictly a convention. You can name your type anything that isn't already spoken for in the Delphi environment. But prefixing a type's name with a "T" ensures that you'll always know at a glance that it's a type, and not a variable or constant. When you're up to your you-know-what in alligators, it's helpful not to be totally bamboozled by your own Pascal identifiers.

The example above is advanced type definition, and I won't explain right here what the word **class** is for, nor the business of public and private declarations. We'll get back to that, if not in this chapter, then in Chapter 8.

Enumerated Types

Just about the simplest sort of type definition is the creation of an *enumerated type*. Delphi uses a lot of these, and you'll see them almost everywhere you go. An enumerated type is an ordered sequence of identifiers to which you assign some symbolic significance. All enumerated types are ordinal types.

The best way to explain how an enumerated type is defined is simply to show you one used regularly in Delphi. Here's one that's easy to understand:

```
TYPE
  TFormBorderStyle = (bsNone, bsSingle, bsSizeable, bsDialog);
```

An enumerated type is defined by enclosing a list of symbolic constants in parentheses. The order of the list as you define it is significant; just as surely as "B" comes after "A," in **TFormBorderStyle**, **bsSingle** comes after **bsNone**, and **bsSizeable** comes after **bsSingle**.

Once your type is declared, you can define variables of that type, and assign values to the variables. These values must be chosen from the constants in the definition list:

```
VAR
  MyBorder : TFormBorderStyle;

  MyBorder := bsSingle;
```

Here, variable **MyBorder** of type **TFormBorderStyle** has value **bsSingle**.

But What Are Enumerated Types For?

Enumerated types (called *enumerations* in some circles) are not as blatantly useful as the fundamental Object Pascal types like **Char**, **Integer**, and **Real**. So what are they good for? Most of the time, you define enumerated types for their symbolic value, and as mnemonic devices—that is, symbols with names that help you remember something or keep it straight in your head.

Delphi supports four border styles for forms. They could have coded them as border style 0, 1, 2, and 3. In the property window for a form, you would then see the **BorderStyle** property have a default value of 2. What does "2" tell you about a border style? Absolutely nothing. Having a sequence of symbolic constants to represent border styles helps you remember what a given border style actually is. Although the ordinality of constant **bsSizeable** is in fact 2 (which is what the **Ord** standard function would give you if you were to pass it **bsSizeable**), a constant like **bsSizeable** tells you a lot more than a naked numeric literal. Most of the enumerated types you'll find in Delphi (and there are scads of them) exist for that reason.

Enumerated types can be tested for equality. You can check to see what's in a variable of an enumerated type with an **IF** statement:

```
IF MyBorder = bsSizeable THEN ...
```

Because there is an implied order to the constants that comprise any enumerated type, the other relational operators also work. Whereas logically it may sound a little odd, it's perfectly true that **bsSizeable** > **bsNone** and **bsSingle** < **bsDialog**. The order runs from left to right, where the leftmost constant in the definition is the "smallest" in the order, and they get "bigger" from there.

Subranges and Closed Intervals

Once a type is defined, you can define other new types in terms of that type. Types like this are called *derived types*. The most common sort of derived type is a *subrange*.

A subrange is a subset of an existing ordinal type (which may be an enumerated type) and consists of some contiguous sequence of the values in the existing type. Here's an example of a subrange from Delphi that you'll see, of the enumerated type **TFormBorderStyle**:

```
TYPE
  TBorderStyle = bsNone..bsSingle;
```

Bring up the property window for a Memo component, and you'll see that it has a **BorderStyle** property. Not all controls have this property, but those that allow you to set the border style will. Controls can have only two types of borders: a single line, or none at all. Because symbolic constants for those two styles are already defined in the **TFormBorderStyle** enumerated type, it's easy to make the first two constants (which describe the border styles legal for controls) into a subrange type. This is what was done above.

The notation is significant. When you want to express a run of constants from any ordinal type, you can express it as the starting value and the ending value, with two dots in between. This notation specifies those two values and all the values (if any) that lie between them. This notation describes a *closed interval*. **TBorderStyle** is a type defined as a closed interval of the values originally defined in the declaration of the **TFormBorderStyle** type.

Closed intervals may be constructed from any ordinal type, which includes characters and integers as well as enumerations. (Floating point values, remember, are not ordinal types!) You can easily create closed intervals of characters and integers, for example:

```
TYPE
  Grades = 'A'..'F';
  MonthNumbers = 1..12;
```

Both of these subrange types are declared in terms of a closed interval of some existing type. You might wonder whether a subrange of integers is especially useful. It can be—in a way having nothing to do with the symbolic value of any of the numbers in the subrange. Delphi can check to see whether you're assigning a value to a subrange that falls outside its legal range—which would really make no logical sense, no more than it makes sense to suppose a month value of 13. Such an error is called a *range error,* and I'll be discussing them a little later in this chapter. As your Delphi applications become more complex, you'll gleefully grasp at any tool that'll help you home in on program bugs.

INC, DEC, AND ITERATION

One of the most valuable attributes of ordinal and integer types is that they consist of some number of values in a set and unchanging order. That is, 2 comes before 3—now and always—and "A" comes before "B" every time you check. Delphi gives you ways to move along a series of ordered values like this that can be very useful in your "behind the scenes" processing.

It's easy enough to take an integer variable and "bump" it to its next value: You simply add 1 to it. But what do you do if you want to bump a **Char** variable to its next value? Adding 1 to the letter G doesn't make a whole lot of sense, so Object Pascal doesn't allow it. But suppose you've processed all the words beginning with G and want to move on to the H's? That's what the **Inc** (for "increment") standard procedure can do.

Inc takes one operand, which can be a variable of any ordinal or integer type. It forces the value of that variable to the next in its sequence. Note that **Inc**

isn't a function, and doesn't return a value. Instead, like any other procedure, it stands alone as an independent statement:

```
TYPE
  NameLetter = 'A'..'Z';   { Subrange of type Char }

VAR
  NameGroup : NameLetter;

NameGroup := 'G';          { Put a "G" in NameGroup }
Inc(NameGroup);            { NameGroup now contains "H"}
```

Here, the variable **NameGroup** is a subrange of **Char**, containing only the upper-case alphabetic characters. You can assign a letter to it, and then increment that letter to the next one in the **Char** sequence with the **Inc** procedure. This is as close to "adding 1 to G" as you'll need to come, since it does what the sense of "adding 1" implies: Moving something to the next value in an ordered sequence.

Inc has its opposite number: **Dec** (for "decrement"). What **Dec** does is "subtract 1" from a value in an ordered sequence, and force a variable to the *previous* value in the ordered sequence. Given "G" in a **Char** variable, executing **Dec** on that variable will force the variable to "F."

Inc and **Dec** can be used on any ordinal type, including any enumerated type or subrange type. It may not be especially useful to be able to increment and decrement types like **TFormBorderStyle**, but it can be done. The "value added" of enumerated types like **TFormBorderStyle** is their symbolic meaning more than the order that they exist in. However, numbers and characters are often used to encode a sequence (months, grades, and so on) where the order of the elements is the "value added" in the variable.

Succ and Pred

The richness of the Delphi environment and the Object Pascal language often gives you more than one way (and sometimes many ways) of doing one thing. As I've been describing, you use **Inc** to increment an ordinal type, and **Dec** to decrement one. There is another pair of standard routines that do the same thing: **Succ** (for "successor") and **Pred** (for "predecessor"). The main difference is that **Succ** and **Pred** are functions and not procedures. This means that they must be used as "value generators" that must be used within an expression. They cannot stand alone as procedures. The following two statements both take a character subrange variable and increment it to the next legal value in the character subrange:

```
NameGroup := 'G';              { Put a "G" in NameGroup }
Inc(NameGroup);                { NameGroup now contains "H"}
NameGroup := Succ(NameGroup);  { NameGroup now contains "I"}
```

There is another, more subtle difference between the two pairs of routines. **Inc** and **Dec** are highly optimized. What this means is that when the Delphi compiler generates machine code to implement your program, it translates **Inc** and **Dec** into extraordinarily fast machine code. The code it generates for **Succ** and **Pred** isn't quite as fast. This probably won't be a significant issue for you until you start writing some seriously advanced projects, but it's something to keep in mind. You should also keep in mind that there's a price to be paid for this extra speed: **Inc** and **Dec** are *not* part of Delphi's range-checking machinery. In other words, they're fast, but they're a little heedless. Because Delphi isn't as careful when you use **Inc** and **Dec**, *you* need to be. And if you don't really need the speed, it might be better to use **Succ** and **Pred** instead.

You may not have encountered range checking before. In that case, it's worth a little discussion.

Beware Premature Optimization

Sometimes when beginning programmers read of procedures like **Inc** and **Dec** being "highly optimized," they begin to think that **Pred** and **Succ** and other not-so-highly-optimized Object Pascal features are spoiled goods, to be avoided whenever possible. That's dumb; optimization is nothing if not rocket science, and until you learn the whole of the language and grok the fullness of it all, optimization is a trap. If most of your program runs slowly, making two or three lines run quickly won't help you at all, and if your "fast" routines have a cost (like a lack of range checking) you may be better off with "slow" code. And the joker in all of this is that Delphi's compiler is very, very good at generating fast code—probably way better than you, until you have a year or two "in grade" and know what all the issues are. Make it work—*then* make it fast. And trust me, making it work will be a full-time job for your first year as a Delphi programmer. (And this is not because Delphi is difficult, but simply because there is a *lot* of Delphi!)

Range Errors and Range Checking

Delphi has a feature called *range checking* that monitors the values you assign to variables. If a variable has a limited legal range of values according to its type, attempting to assign a value outside of its legal range at runtime will generate a *range error*. This will tell you that something's wrong with your code, and make it easier to find and correct the problem.

For example, if you use the integers from 1 to 12 to encode months as shown earlier in this chapter, a range error would be triggered if your code tried to assign a value of 0 or less, or 13 or greater, to a variable of type **MonthNumbers**. If Delphi's compiler can plainly identify a range error at compile time, you'll see a compile time error #76, as shown in Figure 6.1. This is normally limited to assigning an out-of-range literal or named constant to a variable. Beyond that the compiler has trouble knowing what you're up to.

So it's important to note that not all range errors can be detected at compile time. If you're adding to a variable with the addition operator and you increment it beyond the limits of its range, you'll get a runtime range error like the one shown in Figure 6.2. (Remember, some standard functions like **Inc** and **Dec** are *not* subject to range checking—so be careful when you use them!) The compiler can't know from your code whether or not you'll stop incrementing in time to prevent the error, so it doesn't try to second guess you. Only at runtime, when an invalid value actually makes it into a variable, will you see a runtime range error.

Compile-time range error testing is done all the time. However, runtime range checking is not enabled by default; you have to go into the Compiler tab of the Options | Projects dialog to set it. (See Figure 6.3; this is the default state of the dialog, and the Range Checking box is not checked.) Check the Range Checking box in the Runtime Errors pane and then recompile your project. After recompilation, the code will be checked for range errors as it runs.

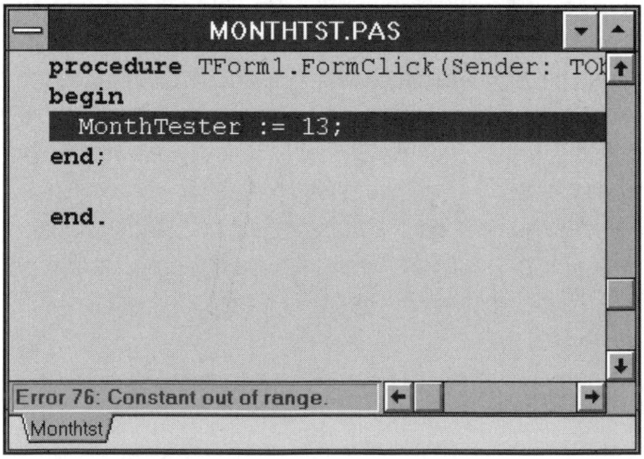

Figure 6.1   *A range error detected at compile time.*

Figure 6.2 *A runtime range error message box.*

FOR Statements

The notion of stepping through an ordered series of things, performing some task with or on the elements of that series, is called *iteration.* If you were told, "Figure out the square roots of all the numbers from 1 to 100," that would be an iterative task. You'd start with 1, calculate its square root, go on to 2, calculate its square root, go on to 3, and continue in that way until reaching 100. This sort of thing is done a lot in programming—so much so that Object Pascal has a kind of statement specifically designed to iterate. It's a ***FOR*** *statement,* or (informally) a ***FOR** loop,* since it's as a kind of "go through the steps over and over" construct, implying a loop of statement execution.

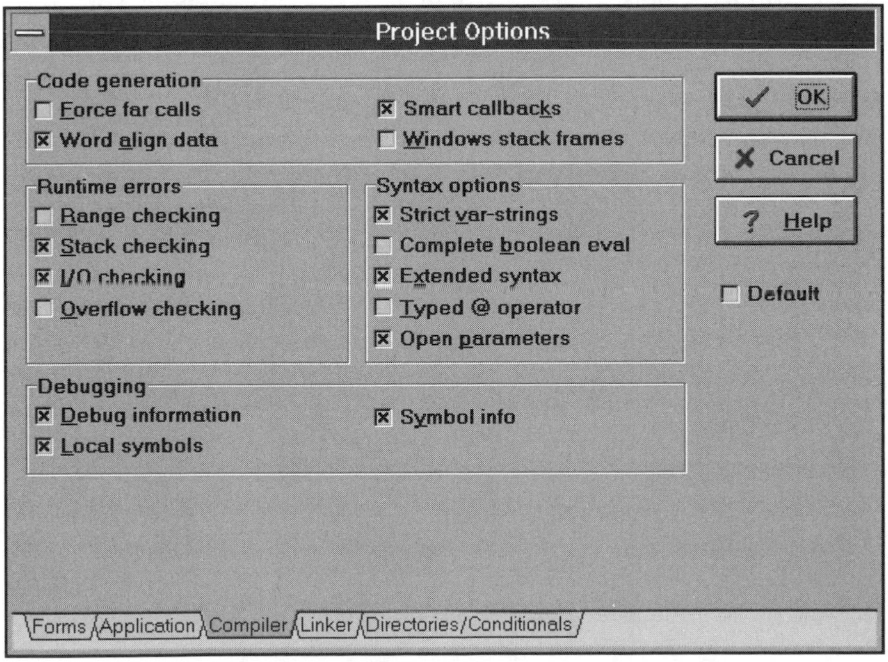

Figure 6.3 *Enabling range checking at runtime.*

The structure of a **FOR** statement looks like this:

```
FOR <control variable> := <lower limit> TO <upper limit> DO <statement>
```

This is a relatively complicated item, compared to what we've seen in Object Pascal so far. From a height, a **FOR** statement's purpose is to assign an initial value to an ordinary variable, which acts (within the **FOR** statement) as a *control variable*. The control variable is then iterated between two limits. At each iteration, a statement is executed. This statement may be a compound statement consisting of several statements between the **BEGIN..END** pair. The control variable may be referenced inside the statement or compound statement. This allows the control variable to control some process within the statement.

Like a lot of things, **FOR** statements show better than they tell. There's a project on the listings disk for this chapter named ROOTDEMO.DPR. Load it, run it, and take a look at what it displays: A scrollable table of square roots, for the integers from 1 to 100. This very simple display is shown in Figure 6.4.

There's not much to the program. The form contains a single ListBox, and a button that will end the appplication when pressed. The table is built inside the ListBox component. A ListBox is a simple way to display a number of character strings. Simply load the strings into the box with its **Add** method, and the box displays what you've loaded. Scroll bars are built in and appear when it contains more strings than can be displayed at once. You can scroll through the strings stored in the box, displaying whichever ones you like.

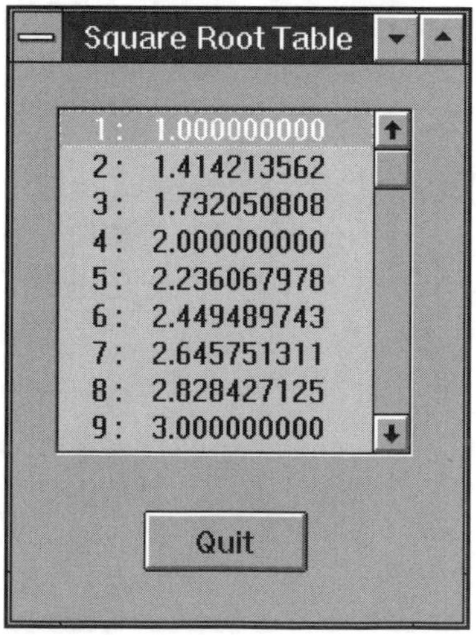

![Square Root Table window showing values 1:1.000000000 through 9:3.000000000 with a Quit button]

Figure 6.4 *A simple scrollable square root table.*

 *Closing a Delphi Application*

One thing that puzzled me very early about Delphi (in fact, within about fifteen minutes of trying it out for the first time) was how to terminate an application's execution and return control to Windows. It's not the least bit obvious. Of course, as with all Windows applications, you can double-click on the close box in the upper left corner of the main form. For naive users, however, it's better to put some explicit means of terminating the application on the form.

Doing so is no more difficult than executing the main form's **Close** method from within a button's **OnClick** event handler. **Close** closes the form, and when the main form closes, a Delphi application's execution is terminated. Here's an example, from the square root demonstration program ROOTDEMO.DPR on the listings diskette for Chapter 6:

Listing 6.1   Closing a single-form Delphi application

```
procedure TForm1.Button1Click(Sender: TObject);
begin
  Close;
end;
```

The ListBox component starts out empty. It's loaded in an event procedure that responds to the form's OnCreate event. When the application's form is created, the OnCreate event is triggered, and the following event handler for OnCreate fills the ListBox component with the square root table data, as shown in Listing 6.2.

Listing 6.2   Creating a square root table

```
procedure TForm1.FormCreate(Sender: TObject);

VAR
  I : Integer;
  R : Real;
  RealText,IntText : String;

begin
  FOR I := 1 TO 100 DO
    BEGIN
      R := Sqrt(I);
      Str(R:14:9,RealText);
      Str(I:5,IntText);
      ListBox1.Items.Add(IntText+' : '+ RealText);
    END;
end;
```

The whole event procedure shown here is essentially a single **FOR** statement. The control variable is **I**, and the limits are 1 and 100. What happens is that when the **FOR** statement is first entered, **I** is given the value 1. The compound statement then executes, and the square root of 1 is calculated in the statement **R := Sqrt(I)**. The next two lines convert both **I** and **R** (a variable of type **Real** that holds the calculated square root value) to string equivalents, because the ListBox component can *only* display strings, not numeric types of any kind. The string values are concatenated into a single string, which is then placed in the ListBox through the ListBox's **Items** property, which in fact owns the **Add** method.

The **FOR** statement then begins once more at the top. This time, however, **I** has been incremented to 2. The compound statement executes again, calculating the square root of 2 and then placing a string representation of the two figures into the ListBox. The compound statement is executed 100 times, once for each count from the lower limit to the upper limit.

One very convenient thing about using a **FOR** statement is that you can usually change the limit values without changing anything else. If you wanted to calculate the square roots of the numbers from 1 to 1000, you'd need only change the upper limit to 1000. The count doesn't have to begin at 1; you could as easily calculate roots from 1000 to 2000, or any other legal range of integer values.

There is a variation of the **FOR** statement that replaces the **TO** reserved word with **DOWNTO**. As you might guess, with **DOWNTO** the **FOR** statement operates with limit values running from higher to lower. You could do a square root table that started with 100 and counted down to 1, simply by replacing **TO** with **DOWNTO** and reversing the limit values. Try it!

Our example has been with a numeric control variable, but a **FOR** statement can in fact iterate over the range of any ordinal type. These are both valid **FOR** statements:

```
VAR
  Initials : Char;
  Border : TFormBorderStyle;

FOR Initials := 'A' TO 'Z' DO...
FOR Border := bsNone TO bsDialog DO...
```

Some odd notes on **FOR**: If the upper limit is *lower* than the lower limit, the statement will not execute at all. If the limit values are identical, the statement will execute only once. Within the statement or compound statement controlled by the **FOR** statement, *consider the control variable read-only*. Don't try to modify it—that defeats the purpose of the statement, and may give rise to bugs that are difficult to figure out. Finally, don't assume that the final value of the control variable is retained after the **FOR** statement runs to completion and stops. It may—or it may not. Technically, the value of the control variable becomes undefined once the **FOR** statement finishes and execution passes on to the next statement in line.

DISPLAY FORMATTING

Once you make a few attempts to display floating point values in a ListBox or even a Label, you'll discover it's not a simple business. You can't simply assign a numeric value to the **Caption** property of a label. You must first convert the numeric value to a string with the **Str** procedure. **Str** is extremely useful for this reason, and for another we'll address shortly. **Str** takes two parameters. The first is a numeric value, and the second is a string variable into which **Str** will place the string equivalent of the numeric value:

```
Str(<numeric value>,<string variable>);
```

This isn't tricky in itself, but the results may not be what you really want. Suppose you've calculated the square root of 17, and need to display it. You create a string equivalent with **Str** and place it in **String** variable **RealString**:

```
Str(Sqrt(17),RealString);
```

Now you assign **RealString** to the **Caption** property of a Label—and what you see looks like Figure 6.5. Yikes!

This is full-blown scientific notation, and whereas it might look good in a NASA research paper on the creation of galaxies, it will make your square

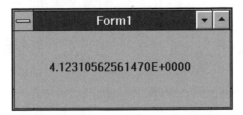

Figure 6.5 *Default formatting of a value of type Real.*

root table nearly impossible to read. The way out of this bind is to use Object Pascal's display formatting feature for strings, which is built into the **Str** procedure that converts numeric values to strings.

That's what the colon business was for in the **Str** procedure calls in ROOTDEMO.DPR. You can use colons as format specifiers to specify two things when converting a number to a string:

- How wide a string space to place the number in
- For floating point values, how many decimal places should be displayed

Formatting values are placed after the numeric value or expression passed to **Str**, and separated from it by a colon. The first value specifies the width of the string field within which to place the numeric representation. The representation is right-justified within the field. The string returned by **Str** will have a length equal to that first formatting value—*unless the value converted becomes a string longer than the specified field width*. In that case, the length of the string expands to become the length of the generated string representation. In other words, if you specify 17353:2, you will not create a string of length 2, but a string of length 5.

The second value, separated from the first by a colon, indicates how many decimal places to display in the formatted string. Here are some examples:

```
17:4 {Formats the value 17 right-justified in a 4-character wide string field }
17.005:10:4   {Formats the value 17.005 right-justified in a 10-character wide
              field with 4 decimal places }
```

Note that it's illegal to use the second format specifier for integer types, because they don't have decimal parts to display.

Rounding for Display

Display formatting is a little bit more than just "writing the value" to a string. There is the possibility of numeric rounding of floating point values during display formatting. **Str** will round off the value if you have significant figures that fall outside the specified number of decimal places. The statement **Str(17.005:5:2,MyString)** will place the value "17.01" in **MyString**. Why? You've allowed for two decimal places in the formatting, but there are three decimal places of significant figures in the value being converted.

Rounding, when it occurs, rounds up to the next significant figure that will fit in the display space allotted for decimal places. Remember that there is *no* corresponding truncation for the whole number part of a numeric representation. If you format a value with too many whole number figures to fit in the field width allotted, the string will simply grow to accommodate all whole number figures, the decimal point, and the number of specified decimal places.

ARRAYS

The **FOR** statement in Object Pascal has a partner in data: the *array*. Arrays are fundamentally different from the data types we've talked about so far in that they are types that are composed of other types, like a wall is made of bricks. An array cannot exist unless it is an array of *something;* and that something has to be a previously defined data type.

I provided a metaphor for Object Pascal arrays at the beginning of this chapter: the humble egg carton, which has 12 little compartments, in each of which you can place an egg. An egg by itself is useful; you can at least make an omelette out of it. On the other hand, the egg carton—absent eggs—is scrap cardboard and has no particular value.

An array is basically a row of numbered compartments for data. The type of all items that can be placed in the compartments (formally called *elements*) in an array must be identical. If it's an array of integers, every element in the array is an integer. If it's an array of **Char**, every element in the array must be a character. (Not the *same* integer or character, of course.)

To define an array type, you have to specify three things:

- The name of the array type;
- The *base type* of the array type, which is the data type of the array's elements;
- The *bounds* of the array type, which is the numbering scheme for the array's elements.

The declaration of a simple array type is shown below:

```
TYPE
  Chars1D = ARRAY[0..11] OF Char;
```

As with all type definitions, "Chars1D" is the name of the type. "ARRAY" indicates that it's an array type that we're defining. The bounds of the array are specified in brackets; here, "[0..11]." If that notation looks familiar, it should: 0..11 is a closed interval, no different from the ones we looked at earlier in this chapter. The bounds of an array must be in the form of a closed interval, either an explicit one like the one shown here (where both bounds of the array are given as literal constants), or a named subrange type that specifies a closed interval.

Array Bounds and Array Access

If you can picture an array as a row of identical boxes with numbers on them, the array's bounds are the first and last of the numbers on the boxes. In the type **Chars1D** shown above, I gave the bounds as **[0..11]**. This means that the first box in the array is box 0, and the last box in the array is box 11, for a total of 12 boxes in all. The "number" on a box in the array is that box's *index*, and specifies the position of the element within the array as a whole. Indexes don't have to be numbers; they can be values from any ordinal type. You can index an array with characters, or Booleans (a small array of two elements), or even enumerated types. Indexes have to be values with a fixed and unchanging order, which is a cornerstone attribute of all ordinal types. "Ordinal" and "order," after all, have the same root.

The first of the two bounds doesn't have to be 0. The **Chars1D** type could have had as its bounds [1..12], or even [22..33], although that's edging toward the weird side of things. In fact, an array's bounds don't have to be numeric at all, as I mentioned above, as long as they're members of an ordinal type.

To access an array element, you must use its index, in brackets. You can assign to an array element, or assign from it as you wish:

```
VAR
  Array1D : Chars1D;          { Declare an array of type Chars1D }

  Array1D[4] := 'Q';          { Stick a 'Q' in element 4 }
  Array1D[2] := Array1D[4];   { Copy the 'Q' to element 2 }
```

Here, recall that type **Chars1D** is an array of 12 characters. To place a specific character into element 4, you specify that element number (its index) between brackets.

In this example I've used numeric literal constants as indexes, but a variable can index an array as well, and in most cases you will be indexing an array with a variable. This allows the index variable to change, and "step through" the array, one element at a time. You may be a little ahead of me already—that's a major use of **FOR** loops in Object Pascal.

Let me show you. Let's load the first 12 letters of the alphabet into the **Array1D** array defined above. It's this simple:

```
VAR I : Integer;

FOR I := 0 TO 11 DO
  Array1D[I] := Chr(65+I);
```

Not much to it, really. The **FOR** statement causes its assignment statement to be executed 12 times. Each time, the next element of **Array1D** is assigned a character. The only tricky thing in the statement is this **Chr(65+1)** business. **Chr** is another Object Pascal standard function. You pass it a value from 0-255, and it returns the Extended ASCII character that corresponds to that number. In a sense, **Chr** is a means of converting an array index—that is, **I**—into an ASCII character. The **65+I** expression passed to **Chr** is there because capital A is character 65 in the ASCII sequence. So to place the correct character into the array, you must start with character 65 and go up from there. On the first run through the **FOR** loop, adding 0 to 65 gives you character 65 ("A"), and on the next loop through, adding 1 to 65 gives you character 66 ("B"), and so on.

Adding a Dimension

The simple array we just looked at is a *one-dimensional* array. We call it that because it consists of one, and only one, row of bins. The bins are addressed by a single sequence of array index values. That's what the vast majority of arrays are, but you don't have to stop there. Object Pascal allows you to add additional dimensions to an array if you want them. (Whether or not you want them is a separate—and important—issue by itself.)

Adding a second dimension to our array of characters is simple enough. We add a second closed interval to the type definition, separated from the first by a comma:

```
TYPE
  Chars2D = ARRAY[0..11,0..3] OF Char;
```

The array is no longer a single row of bins of 12 characters. It's now four rows of bins of 12 characters, side by side. Specifying a single character within a *two-dimensional* array like this requires two indexes: One to select a single row from the four in the array, and a second to specify the individual character within that single row. I've drawn this out in Figure 6.6 to make it a little easier to grasp, and I've shown a one-dimensional array for contrast.

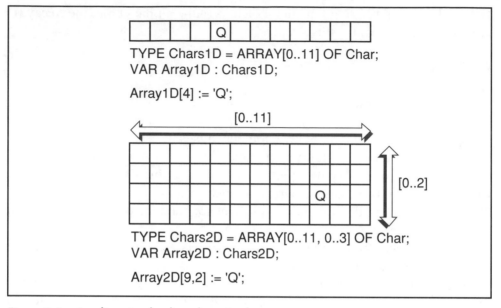

TYPE Chars1D = ARRAY[0..11] OF Char;
VAR Array1D : Chars1D;

Array1D[4] := 'Q';

[0..11]

TYPE Chars2D = ARRAY[0..11, 0..3] OF Char;
VAR Array2D : Chars2D;

Array2D[9,2] := 'Q';

[0..2]

Figure 6.6 *One-dimensional and two-dimensional arrays.*

There's no arbitrary limit to the number of dimensions an array can have. I personally have never used more than two dimensions in an array, and using more than three is rare indeed. There are both theoretical and practical reasons for this. The theoretical reason is that multidimensional arrays beyond two or (perhaps) three are very hard to visualize and hence understand. We generally map array dimensions to spatial dimensions in our minds when we picture an array. Two dimensions, no problem—it's like a grid on a piece of paper. Three dimensions, perhaps a pile of bricks or a Rubik's Cube. Four dimensions? I get stuck here. Keeping sense in your programs is hard enough without trying to cope with the Fourth Dimension.

The purely practical reason to keep your dimension count down is that the more dimensions an array has, the more likely it is that large portions of the array are either empty or contain duplicate data. (Explaining *why* this should be so would be difficult in an entry-level book, but trust me—I learned it the hard way, before I ever read a book on data structures.) Arrays take up space, and wasting space isn't something you want to do if you can avoid it. If the solution to a programming problem suggests a five-dimensional array, think it through again—my guess is that the problem can be attacked in far more straightforward and less obscure ways.

RECORDS

As I just explained, an Object Pascal array is a way of gathering together some number of items of a single data type as an aggregate data item, with each individual element having its own unique sequential label. The elements of an array are "numbered," even though they can be numbered with things (like characters) that aren't exactly numbers.

There's another aggregate data type in Object Pascal, which takes a different tack. A *record* is a data type that gathers together some number of items of *different* types—and identifies each by a unique name. The different items should be related to one another in some logical way, or else the whole business of binding them together in a record makes very little sense.

Think of the different attributes that describe you as an individual. You have a name, a birth date, a sex (hey, people have sex; nouns have genders), an address, a Social Security number, and loads of other things. What they have in common is that they all apply to you—and hence storing them within a single bin called a record makes logical sense.

At the beginning of this chapter I described the plastic bin containing the parts comprising my nephew's Erector set. In a single plastic tray were a dozen or so bins, each with an injection-molded shape conforming to the shape of one of the Erector set parts. There was a bin for each of three sizes of girders, a bin for metal shafts, a bin for brackets, a bin for nuts and bolts...you get the picture. Taken together, all the parts belong to a single aggregate thingie—the Erector set. Yet each had a distinct place within the plastic tray.

The Erector set tray is a good metaphor for the Pascal record idea. You define a record type by giving the type a unique name (ideally beginning with "T"), the reserved word **RECORD** to tell the compiler what we're up to, and then a list of the different items that make up the record. Each of these must have a name and type, just as in a variable declaration. A record is, after all, an aggregate variable. Here's the syntax:

```
TYPE
  TGirder = RECORD
            PartNumber  : Integer;
            Length      : Real;
            HoleCount   : Integer;
            Finish      : Tcolor;
            Description : String;
          END;
```

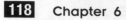

If we wanted to be able to catalog the different kinds of Erector Set girders, we might create a record type to do so. The record would be a gathering-together of all the different attributes of a girder: Its length in inches, the number of holes, what color it's painted, and its replacement part number. We might also add a brief text description. Each attribute becomes what we call a *field* of the record type. Each field has a unique name.

In a sense, a record is a compound variable in the same way that a group of statements gathered between **BEGIN** and **END** are a compound statement. You can treat the record as a unit for certain things (like writing it out to a disk file, for example) and treat the individual fields separately for other things, such as editing.

Once a record type has been declared, record variables are declared just as any other Object Pascal variable:

```
VAR
  Girder1 : TGirder;
```

Record Qualifiers and WITH

There are certainly fields inside record type **TGirder**, but how do you get at them? The answer (as with much of the details of Object Pascal) is hierarchical in nature. You first name the record, and then you name the field within the record. The name of the field that narrows down the scope of the reference to one field within a particular record containing several fields is called a *record qualifier*. The two names are separated by a period character. We could load a girder record with the number of holes in the girder like this:

```
VAR
  Girder1 : TGirder;

  Girder1.HoleCount := 25;
```

This implies that we just need to run down the list, tossing a value in each of the fields with the help of the record's name and the "dot" (as programmers generally call the period character) like so:

```
Girder1.PartNumber  := 1;
Girder1.Length      := 12.5;
Girder1.HoleCount   := 25;
Girder1.Finish      := clGreen;
Girder1.Description := 'Standard green part #1';
```

This works just fine. But there's another way that's a little more within the spirit of Object Pascal. A special kind of compound statement takes a single record name and applies it to all statements it controls. This is known as a **WITH** *statement,* and we can re-cast the above sequence of assignment statements into a **WITH** statement very simply:

```
WITH Girder1 DO
  BEGIN
    PartNumber  := 1;
    Length      := 12.5;
    HoleCount   := 25;
    Finish      := clGreen;
    Description := 'Standard green part #1';
  END;
```

What this **WITH** statement means is that within the **BEGIN..END** pair, the use of "Girder1." is implied for any access to a field name present in the **TGirder** type definition. Ordinarily, if you simply used the identifier **HoleCount**, Delphi's compiler wouldn't recognize it by itself, since it was defined as part of **TGirder**. But within this **WITH** statement, using the identifier **HoleCount** is the same as using the fully qualified identifier **Girder1.HoleCount**.

Any time we need to reference **Girder1.HoleCount** within the **WITH** compound statement, we need only say **HoleCount**. This applies to assignment statements, expressions, and procedure parameter lists, along with anyplace else where referencing a variable would be legal.

So what does this buy us, apart from a few saved text characters? As with much in Pascal, it's a sense thing. Looking at the **WITH** statement shown above gives us the sense that the assignment statements belong together, which they do. The assignment statements are part of a family, just as surely as the field identifiers within the **TGirder** type are part of a family. Being able to see such associations at a glance are part of what makes Object Pascal code so easy to read.

MODELLING COMPLEX DATA

Virtually any data type can be a part of a record definition, including other record types. There's nothing tricky about the syntax; you just name a record type as one of the fields in the larger record. As usual, this is easier shown than told, so let's come up with a scenario a little more real-world than cataloging Erector set parts, and in the process begin building a useful utility in Delphi.

The issue is mortage payments. When buying a house these days, if you don't first shop for a mortgage, you're likely to end up paying *lots* more for the loan *over the life of the loan,* than you would if you spent just a little time comparing rates and payments. Seemingly insignificant differences can add up to big bucks over thirty years!

How do you decide the way to represent something like a mortgage in a Delphi program? It's no different from deciding how to model *anything* in software: You look carefully at the data that defines what you're modelling, and from that determine its structure. "Structure" is Pascal's middle name; if you can dope out a structure within a concept, Pascal can model it.

A mortgage as a whole has a number of different attributes. There is a mortgage vendor; that is, the bank or other firm offering the loan to you, the consumer. There are a number of financial parameters like the length of the mortgage in payments, the percentage rate, the principal, and so on. Finally, there is a long string of payments, each of which has a unique set of values including the principal paid this payment, the interest paid this payment, the principal balance remaining, cumulative totals for interest and principal paid so far, and so on.

Modelling by Successive Refinement

We'll use a simple modelling concept called *successive refinement.* Simply described, successive refinement means first describing the data succinctly, and then gradually refining the description to include more and more detail. At each stage, you look hard at what you have and ask whether there are more details hiding within the "broad strokes" you've already put down.

Let's take a stab at an initial statement of the mortgage model. A mortgage, in simplest terms, could be described something like this:

```
TMortgage =
  RECORD
    Lender;              { Who the lender is (optional) }
    Loan Parameters;     { Interest rate, periods, principal, etc. }
    Payments;            { One description for each payment }
  END;
```

What we have here is the identity of the lender, the parameters of the loan as a whole, and then a separate description of each payment in the loan. The identity of the lender is optional because when loan shopping, you can compare monthly payments without necessarily knowing who will offer the loan. The other information, however, is required for the description to be useful.

The identity of the lender contains details including the lender's name, address, and phone number. These items need to be expanded and included in the record. Now, these can easily be expressed in record form, and because records may contain other records, creating a new **LenderData** record type would certainly work. But is it a good idea? I think so, for this reason: In a financial program of some sort, it might be useful to have a description of financial institutions quite apart from tracking mortgages. Banks do lots of different things—and there are many sorts of "banks."

Let's do it:

```
TLender =
  RECORD
    LenderID      : Integer;
    LenderName    : String;
    LenderAddress : String;
    LenderCity    : String;
    LenderState   : String;
    LenderZIP     : String;
    LenderPhone   : String;
  END;
```

The loan parameters are also easy to describe; things like interest rate, periods, and so on are simple numbers dictated by traditional financial practice. These, too, could be stored in their own record type, but in this case that might not be desirable. There are only a few such values, and they don't have much meaning outside of the context of a mortgage loan. So we'll leave them as fields of the **TMortgage** record. The next refinement of the record would look like this:

```
TMortgage =
  RECORD
    Lender        : TLender;   { Who the lender is (optional) }
    Periods       : Integer;   { Number of payments in loan schedule }
    PeriodsPerYear : Integer;  { Number of payments in a year }
    Principal     : Real;      { Amount of initial principal loaned, in cents }
    Interest      : Real;      { Percentage of interest per *YEAR* }
    MonthlyPI     : Real;      { Monthly payment in cents }
    Payments;                  { One description for each payment }
  END;
```

Every payment of a mortgage loan is different, and needs a separate description. Nearly all lenders allow borrowers to apply extra principal to a loan payment, and this needs to be tracked, as well as values like the balance due and cumulative interest and principal already paid. Now, although every payment is different in terms of these values, all payments store the same number

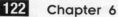

and types of values, so all payments can be described by a single data type. The whole run of payments suggests an array of a new payment type...so let's define that payment type:

```
TYPE
TPayment =
  RECORD    { One element in the amortization table. }
    PaymentNumber  : Integer; { Which payment this is }
    PayPrincipal   : Real;    { Principal (in cents) paid this payment }
    PayInterest    : Real;    { Interest (in cents) paid this payment }
    PrincipalSoFar : Real;    { How much principal has been paid off so far }
    InterestSoFar  : Real;    { How much interest has been paid in so far }
    ExtraPrincipal : Real;    { Extra principal (if any) paid this period }
    Balance        : Real;    { How much of the loan remains AFTER this payment }
  END;
```

This describes each payment pretty thoroughly, and I honestly don't think there's any more detail hiding here. An array of **TPayment** records at least as large as the largest number of periods expected in a common loan will complete the **TMortgage** record type. So let's expand our definition to its next— and near-final—level of refinement:

```
TMortgage =
  RECORD
    Lender         : TLender;   { Who the lender is (optional) }
    Periods        : Integer;   { Number of payments in loan schedule }
    PeriodsPerYear : Integer;   { Number of payments in a year }
    Principal      : Real;      { Amount of initial principal loaned, in cents }
    Interest       : Real;      { Percentage of interest per *YEAR* }
    MonthlyPI      : Real;      { Monthly payment in cents }
    Payments       : ARRAY[1..600] OF TPayment; { One record for each payment }
  END;
```

It doesn't look like there's much in the line of undiscovered detail lurking inside any of these items within the record. We may find later on that data may be *missing;* but there doesn't appear to be any "fuzz" in the fields we've defined. Once the fuzz is gone, you can begin to design the computation that has to be done on or with the data in the record. I'd start in on that task here...but there's a problem. I said "*near*-final" for a reason.

The Capacity Problem

The **TMortgage** record type I just presented will correctly describe any mortgage up to 600 payments in size. That's a *big* mortgage; 50 years of monthly payments is a long time. On the other hand, I've heard of at least one 100-year mortgage, so it may not be big enough to handle all possible mortgages. But it's way oversize to handle your everyday average 30-year monthly mortgage.

Is this really a problem? In practical terms, probably not, in these salad days of gigabyte hard drives and 32MB RAM installations. Ten years ago it would definitely have been a consideration. Each variable of type **TMortgage** is about 25Kb in size, but of that 25Kb, about 11Kb is nearly always wasted. Few mortgages have more than 360 payments, so the last 240 array elements in **Payments** will almost always lie empty. A smaller, but still considerable waste of space lies in the **TLender** record, which consists of six fields of type **String**. One downside to the **String** type is that each variable of type **String** is 256 bytes in size, regardless of how much actual string data is contained in the variable. Place a 2-letter state code in **TLender.LenderState**, and you have 253 bytes of wasted space that nothing else can ever use. The other fields in **TLender** waste space as well.

Besides, mortgages beyond 600 payments are simply out of reach.

Although we could use these definitions without getting in too much trouble, there's something about all that wasted space that should bother a programmer. Delphi provides solutions to both the wasted string space problem and the wasted payment record space problem. The first one is easy. The second one is, well, subtle. Easy first....

Derived String Types

Type **String** is Delphi's standard string type, and as I said earlier, each instance of a **String** variable is 256 bytes in size. It would be handy to have a smaller **String** type to contain strings that you know will never go beyond a certain size. Such smaller strings are yours for the defining.

All you need to do is define a new string type with a specified maximum size. The maximum size figure is placed in square brackets after the **String** reserved word. I recommend defining a number of such types in various sizes as you're likely to need, and building the size of the string into the new string type's name. Here are a few I have used:

```
TYPE
   String2 : String[2];    { Handy for state codes }
   String10 : String[10]; { Handy for 9-digit ZIP codes }
   String25 : String[25];
   String40 : String[40];
   String80 : String[80];
```

I've known programmers who have defined a separate string type for every possible length of string from 1 to 255. This might be a little compulsive, but they make the valid point that *type definitions take no space at all in your programs.* Variables *do* take space, in memory and on disk, but types themselves are like blueprints for the creation of variables—blueprints printed on infinitely thin paper, if you will.

The size of these derived string types is the number in the brackets, plus one additional byte where Delphi stores the current length of the data stored inside the string. If we recast the **TLender** record to use these derived string types, we can save almost 1400 bytes of space:

```
TLender =
  RECORD
    LenderID       = Integer;
    LenderName     = String40;
    LenderAddress  = String40;
    LenderCity     = String25;
    LenderState    = String2;
    LenderZIP      = String10;
    LenderPhone    = String25;
  END;
```

Not bad for a quick trick, huh?

The problem of wasted space in the **Payments** array is a lot harder to approach. What we want is a **Payments** array that takes up no more space than it needs. In a 360-period mortgage, we want only 360 elements in the **Payments** array, no more. In a 180-period loan, we'd like 180 **Payments** elements, period. Can we do that in Object Pascal?

Yes, we can. But to do it we need objects. Objects are the final frontier in our study of data and data types. In Chapter 8 I'll return to the **TMortgage** type, and once I explain what objects are and how they work, I'll show you how to express **TPayments** such that no more space is used than you need to store the payments themselves.

They don't call it Object Pascal for nothing.

PART 2

TRAVELING FURTHER AFIELD

FORMS AND UNITS

CHAPTER

7

Jim Mischel

It's time to pull together what we've learned, and create a real, functioning MDI application that actually does something useful.

Up to this point, we've been exploring the component palette and experimenting with some pretty simple programs. With the exception of the StopWatch program in Chapter 5, all of our programs so far have been examples that don't really do much. Now that you've got a better understanding of what user interface programming in Delphi is all about, it's time to start writing more complex programs that require some significant behind-the-scenes processing in order to work.

In this chapter, we're going to develop a simple file viewer program that will display text or picture files. In the process, you'll see how menus, common dialogs, and other components go together to create a real, working program. You're also going to see how to create an MDI (Multiple Document Interface) application with Delphi.

In the process, we're going to begin using Object Pascal's *units*, which are separate little packages of program code that allow you to "seal off" some processing within a reusable module. Units aren't new with Delphi, and in fact they go way back with Borland's Turbo Pascal, to UCSD Pascal before Turbo Pascal. Units incorporate some of the ideas of object-oriented programming, and so we're also going to look a little more closely at using and modifying Delphi's objects in this chapter. For a fuller (if somewhat more theoretical) explanation of both objects and units, make sure you read Chapter 8 carefully.

The FileView Application

FileView is a simple MDI application that allows you to view and print text and picture files. As simple as it is, FileView has all of the features of a "real" Windows program, with the exception of context-sensitive help.

Figure 7.1 shows FileView with two windows open: a text file and a bitmap file. (Yes, that *is* me standing next to an unreasonable cardboard facsimile of Marilyn Monroe!)

The Multiple Document Interface

The Windows Multiple Document Interface is a specification that describes a user interface and window structure for programs that work with multiple documents in a single application. MDI is like a miniature Windows. Just as Windows can handle multiple application windows on the screen, MDI applications maintain multiple document windows within a single window's client area. The Windows Program Manager is a good example of an MDI application.

In an MDI application, the main window looks like a normal application window, with a title bar, menu, sizeable border, and other characteristics. The client area, though, isn't used for program output. Rather, the client area is a "workspace" in which document windows (or, more properly, *child windows*) display information.

Child windows also look like regular windows, except that they don't have menus. Only the application window has a menu, but those menu items can be applied to the child windows as well. Although many child windows can be simultaneously displayed, only one of them can be *active* at a time. All child windows are clipped so that they never appear outside of the MDI window.

The MDI specification defines what happens when child windows are manipulated (opened, closed, moved, sized, minimized, maximized), and what special keystrokes are used to manipulate child windows. There are also suggested standard menu layouts and many other details defined in the specification. Most of this special behavior is handled internally by Windows when

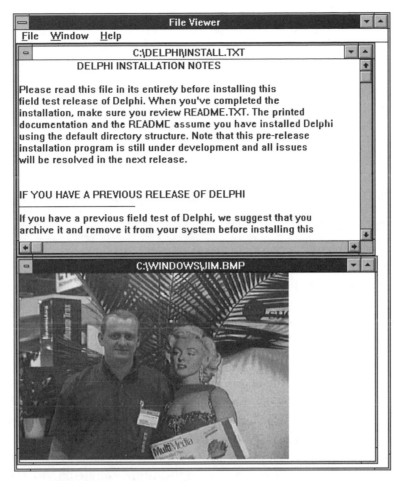

Figure 7.1   *The FileView application.*

you create an MDI application. With traditional Windows programming tools, you have to jump through a number of hoops to get MDI applications to respond correctly. Not so with Delphi. Delphi handles all of the MDI-specific details automatically, leaving you free to concentrate on those things that are specific to your application.

Creating the Application's Main Form

FileView is quite a bit more involved than anything we've done so far. But putting it together is very straightforward. We're going to start by creating the main form and the text file viewer form. Then we'll write the code that connects those two pieces. Once we've got the program working with text files, we'll add the picture file viewer.

Table 7.1 *Property Changes for the FileView Application's Main Form*

Field	Value
Caption	"File Viewer"
Ctl3D	False
FormStyle	fsMDIForm
Name	"MDIFileViewer"
Position	poDefault

Select File | New Project from Delphi's main menu, and in the Object Inspector change the Form's properties as shown in Table 7.1.

Changing the **FormStyle** property to **fsMDIForm** tells Delphi to make the main form an MDI application, and changing the **Position** property to **poDefault** causes the application to get its initial size and position from Windows. For more information on these properties, consult the online help.

Adding the Menu

MDI application menus usually adjust to reflect the options that are available in whichever child window is currently active. Normally, the only options on the application's main window menu are those active when no windows are open. For example, the File menu of an MDI text editor's main window would contain New, Open, and Exit items only. There would be no Save or Print options because these menu items are only active when windows are open. Other menu items are added to the application's menu bar to reflect the actions that can be performed on the currently-active child window.

In Delphi, you define the application's menu with the bare minimum number of menu items. You then create a menu for each child window, which reflects the options that affect that child window as well as the application's main window. Delphi automatically merges the child window menu with the application's main menu by examining the individual menu items's **GroupIndex** properties. We'll discuss this in more detail when we create the individual child window menus.

The application's menu bar has two items: File and Help. To create this menu, drop a MainMenu component onto the form and then double-click on it to bring up the Menu Designer. In the Menu Designer, add the menu items shown in Table 7.2.

Table 7.2 *The FileView Application's Main Menu*

Menu	Caption	GroupIndex	ShortCut
	&File	1	
File	&Open	0	F3
File	- (separator)	0	
File	E&xit	0	Alt+F4
	&Help	10	
Help	&About	0	

Finally, create an event procedure for the File|Exit menu option. All this event procedure has to do is close the application window. Edit your event procedure so that it looks like Listing 7.1.

LISTING 7.1   The File|Exit event handler

```
procedure TMDIFileViewer.Exit1Click(Sender: TObject);
begin
 Close;
end;
```

Before we continue, save your work, calling the unit VIEWMAIN.PAS, and the project FILEVIEW.DPR.

Using the OpenDialog Component

In order to get the name of the file that we want to view, we're going to use an OpenDialog component. This is a standard dialog component that is used in much the same way as the FontDialog and ColorDialog components that we discussed in Chapter 5. From the Dialogs page of the component palette, select an OpenDialog and drop the component onto your form. In the Object Inspector, change the component's properties as shown in Table 7.3.

Table 7.3 *Property Changes for the Main Form's OpenDialog Component*

Property	Value
Filter	All Files|*.*|Picture Files|*.bmp;*.ico;*.wmf|Text Files|*.txt
Name	"FileOpenDialog"
Options.ofFileMustExist	True

Figure 7.2 *The Filter Editor dialog box.*

You can change the **Filter** property by typing the text as shown, or you can use the special Filter property editor, shown in Figure 7.2.

Tie **FileOpenDialog** to the menu by creating an event handler for the File|Open menu option and adding the code shown in Listing 7.2.

LISTING 7.2   The File|Open event handler

```
procedure TMDIFileViewer.Open1Click(Sender: TObject);
begin
 If FileOpenDialog.Execute Then Begin
 End;
end;
```

As you can see, this event handler doesn't do anything with the data returned by **FileOpenDialog**, but the infrastructure is there. We'll add the code that actually opens the files after we've created the text file viewer.

Save your work again and then compile and run the program. You should be able to select File|Open and see the OpenFile dialog come up, and selecting File|Exit should exit the program.

VIEWING TEXT FILES

The next step in creating our MDI file viewer is to create a form that will display text files, and add that form to the project. When we create the form, we'll set **FormStyle** to **fsMDIChild** so that the form will act like an MDI child window. After the form is created, we'll go back to the main form and add the code that creates and displays this new child window.

Before we continue with creating the new form, let's make sure that your Delphi options are set so that you can follow along with the next discussion. Select Options|Environment from Delphi's main menu, and on the Preferences page make sure that "Use on New Form" check box in the bottom right of the dialog is checked, as shown in Figure 7.3.

Setting this option will cause Delphi to display the Browse Gallery dialog box whenever you select File|New Form from the main menu. After making that change, press the OK button to save the options. Now we're ready to go on.

The Gallery

Select File|New Form from the main menu. Delphi will display the Browse Gallery dialog box, shown in Figure 7.4.

The Browse Gallery dialog box lets you select a form from a group of standard form types that have been previously defined. This can be a great time saver if you're creating a number of forms that have substantially the same layout. You simply create the basic form once and add it to the Gallery. Then, whenever you need a similar form, you choose it from the Gallery and make whatever minor changes you need to fit the form into your application. You can also set up Delphi to display the Browse Gallery dialog box when you

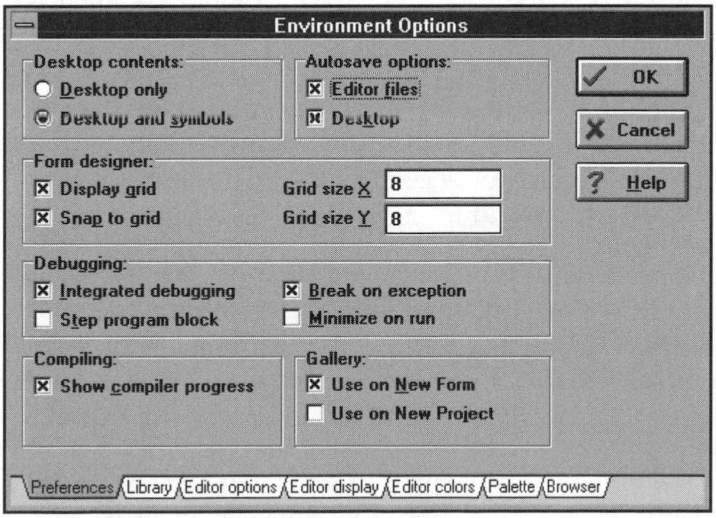

Figure 7.3   *Setting Delphi's options.*

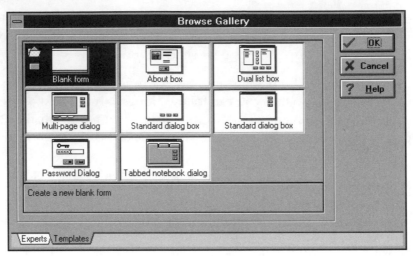

Figure 7.4   The Browse Gallery.

create a new project. For more information about adding new project and form templates to the Gallery, select Options|Gallery from Delphi's main menu, and then view the online help for the Gallery Options dialog box.

Our new form is pretty simple, so we're just going to use the Blank form template. Double-click on the Blank form template in the Browse Gallery dialog box, and Delphi will create a new blank form for you to work with.

Forms and Units

When you add a new form to your project, Delphi automatically creates a new Form window for that form, and also creates a new unit file to hold the source code belonging to that form. The new form window is placed on your desktop in front of all of the other windows, and a new page that holds the form's source code is added to the Unit window. This is Delphi's way of helping you manage your projects. Since each form has its own Form and Unit file, it's very easy to add forms to, or remove forms from, your project.

When you compile your program, Delphi compiles the project source file and each of the unit source files, combines them with the form files, and links them all together to create the executable program. What actually goes on when Delphi is compiling a program is a bit more involved than that simple description implies, but this view is detailed enough for our purposes.

Delphi knows what units to include by examining the **uses** statement in the project and unit files. We'll discuss the **uses** statement in the next chapter when we take a more detailed look at units.

Note that, whereas every form has an associated unit source file, not all unit source files are associated with forms. Units can contain any kind of code—from complex calculations and special device interfaces to general-purpose "helper" functions that you've found are useful in a large number of programs. In a later chapter, we'll work with some units that aren't associated with any specific forms.

Before we continue, select File | Save Project from the menu, and call the new unit TEXTVIEW.PAS.

Building the Text Viewer Form

The only thing special about our text viewer form is that it's an MDI child window rather than a standard form. Make sure the new form is selected, and then in the Object Inspector, change its properties as shown in Table 7.4.

For the first working version of our text viewer, we're just going to add a single component: a Memo that displays the text of the file. Drop a Memo component onto the Text Viewer form, and change its properties as shown in Table 7.5.

Setting the **Align** property to **alClient** causes the memo box to occupy the form's entire client area. It also ensures that the Memo component is automatically resized when the Form window is resized. **ReadOnly** is set to **True** because this is a file *viewer*; we don't want users changing the text. **WordWrap** is set to **False** so that the Memo won't automatically wrap the text to fit within the window. We want each line of the file to occupy a single line in the Memo component.

Gluing it Together

We now have a main form, and a child form that will display a text file. All we have to do now is write the few lines of code that allow the main form to create and display a text viewer form.

Table 7.4 *Property changes for the Text Viewer Child Form*

Property	Value
Caption	"Text Viewer"
Ctl3D	False
FormStyle	fsMDIChild
Name	"TextViewer"

Table 7.5 *Property Changes for the TextViewer Form's Memo Component*

Property	Value
Align	alClient
BorderStyle	bsNone
ReadOnly	True
ScrollBars	ssBoth
WordWrap	False

In the Unit window, select the tab marked Textview to display the unit source for the TextViewer form. In the definition of the **TTextViewer** class, add a **Filename** variable in the **private** section, and an **Open** procedure declaration in the **public** section, as shown in Listing 7.3.

LISTING 7.3   The edited TTextViewer class

```
TTextViewer = class(TForm)
 Memo1: TMemo;
private
 { Private declarations }
 Filename : String;
public
 { Public declarations }
 Procedure Open (Const AFilename : String);
end;
```

Then add the **Open** function in the **implementation** part of your unit source file so that it looks like Listing 7.4. Don't worry about the details of classes, nor the meaning of the **implementation** section just yet—we'll get to objects and units in the next chapter.

LISTING 7.4   The TTextViewer.Open procedure

```
implementation

{$R *.DFM}

Procedure TTextViewer.Open (Const AFilename : String);
Begin
 Filename := AFilename;
 Memo1.Lines.LoadFromFile (Filename);
 Caption := Filename;
End;
end.
```

This code saves the name of the file that's being loaded, and then loads the file into the Memo component. Finally, the form's **Caption** property is set to reflect the name of the file that's being displayed.

The code that creates and displays a text viewer form is simple, too. Click on the Viewmain tab in the Unit window to display the source for the main form. Locate the **TMDIFileViewer.Open1Click** procedure, and edit it so that it looks like Listing 7.5.

LISTING 7.5   Creating and displaying a text viewer window

```
procedure TMDIFileViewer.Open1Click(Sender: TObject);
Var
 TextViewer : TTextViewer;
begin
 If FileOpenDialog.Execute Then Begin
  TextViewer := TTextViewer.Create (Self);
  TextViewer.Open (FileOpenDialog.Filename);
  TextViewer.Visible := True;
  TextViewer.SetFocus;
 End;
end;
```

The code in Listing 7.5 executes the Open dialog box, which returns **True** if you select a file and press OK indicating that you want to open that file. If **FileOpenDialog** returns **True**, then this code creates a new **TextViewer** form and tells it to open the file specified by **FileOpenDialog.Filename**. After the file is loaded, we make the new form visible and set the keyboard focus to that window.

There's one last detail that we have to take care of before we can test the program. Locate the beginning of the **implementation** section in VIEWMAIN.PAS and add a **uses** statement so that the first few statements look like Listing 7.6.

LISTING 7.6   Adding a uses statement to VIEWMAIN.PAS

```
implementation

uses TextView;

{$R *.DFM}
```

The **uses** statement just tells Delphi that it needs to get information from the TEXTVIEW.PAS unit in order to compile VIEWMAIN. We'll discuss **implementation** and **uses** in detail in the next chapter.

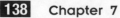

After you've made those changes, save your work and press F9 to compile and test the program. The first thing you'll notice is that you automatically have a TextViewer form displayed, with the text "Memo1" in the window. I'll show you how to get rid of this window in a moment.

You should be able to select File | Open from the menu and select a text file to view. If there aren't any files with the extension .TXT displayed in the Open dialog, try the Windows directory, or just select a .PAS or .DPR file. In any case, FileView will display the selected file in a window. You can display as many files as you like, each in a separate window. You can move, size, minimize, maximize, or close the individual windows independently of the others. Press Alt+F4 to close the application.

Closing Child Windows

You probably noticed that when you double-clicked on a child window's control menu box to close it, the window was minimized rather than closed. This is default behavior for MDI child windows. We can make close really *mean* close by adding an **OnClose** event handler to the form. On the Events page of the Object Inspector, double-click on the **OnClose** event to create an event handler, and then insert the code shown in Listing 7.7.

LISTING 7.7   The child window's OnClose event handler

```
procedure TTextViewer.FormClose(Sender: TObject; var Action: TCloseAction);
begin
 Action := caFree;
end;
```

Modifying the Project Source

The reason that initial TextViewer window is displayed has to do with the way Delphi generates code. When you create a new form, Delphi automatically creates a global variable for the new form in the form's unit file, and also adds a line to the project source file that initializes an instance of that form. For most forms, this isn't a problem, as they're initially hidden. But you can't hide an MDI Child form, so when Delphi creates one, it's automatically displayed for you. I don't think this is correct behavior, but heck, I don't make the rules.

To get around this, you need to open the project source file and remove a line of code. Select View | Project Source from Delphi's main menu, and delete the line of code (towards the end of the file) that reads:

```
Application.CreateForm(TTextViewer, TextViewer);
```

Save and execute your program, and notice that the initial text window no longer appears when the program starts up.

CHILD WINDOW MENUS

Some operations aren't applicable unless at least one file is being displayed by the application. While it's possible to include those items on the menu as disabled menu items when there aren't any files being displayed, it's preferable to have them not appear at all unless they're applicable. This allows us to have different menu options for each type of window that will be displayed by the application. Fortunately, Delphi's support of MDI applications makes it very easy to define and merge child window menus.

Merging Menus

In FileView, we want to add three new items (Close, Print, and Printer Setup) to the File menu whenever a text window is open, and we want a Window menu that will allow us to cascade or tile the child windows within the application's client area.

Make sure that the TextViewer form is the active form, and then select a MainMenu component from the component palette and drop it onto the form. Because the Memo component is occupying the entire client area of the form, you'll have to place the MainMenu component within the boundaries of the Memo component. This may look a bit strange at design time, but you won't see it at run time.

Double-click on the MainMenu component to bring up the Menu Designer. Within Menu Designer, add the menu items shown in Table 7.6.

After you've made these changes, press F9 to compile and run the program. Then, open a file and notice that the menu has changed. The three new items and the separator have been added to the File menu, and the Window menu is now visible between the File and Help menus on the menu bar.

The menu item's **GroupIndex** property controls how child window menus are merged with the application's (the main form's) main menu. Simply put, if the **GroupIndex** value for a top-level menu item in a child window menu is the same as the **GroupIndex** value for one of the application menu's top-level items, then the child window menu item replaces the corresponding

Table 7.6 *The TextViewer Form's Menu*

Menu	Caption	GroupIndex	ShortCut
	&File	1	
File	&Open	0	F3
File	&Close	0	Alt+F3
File	- (separator)	0	
File	&Print	0	
File	P&rint Setup...	0	
File	- (separator)	0	
File	E&xit	0	Alt+F4
	&Window	5	
	Window &Tile	0	
	Window &Cascade	0	
	Window Close &all	0	

top-level item in the application's menu bar. If the **GroupIndex** property for a top-level menu item in the child window menu doesn't correspond to the **GroupIndex** value in any of the application's top-level menu items, then the child window menu item is inserted into the application's menu bar.

In this case, the child window's File menu replaces the application's File menu because both **GroupIndex** values are 1. The child window's Window menu, which has a **GroupIndex** value of 5, is inserted between the File menu (**GroupIndex** 1) and the Help menu (**GroupIndex** 10). Notice that the child window's menu doesn't have a Help menu, because the Help window doesn't have to change when a child window is displayed.

The GroupIndex Property

The **GroupIndex** property affects *only* top-level menu items—those items that appear on the menu bar. Don't try to use the **GroupIndex** property to just insert items into the File menu. It won't work. If your child window has to insert items into one of the existing top-level menu items, then you must specify the entire contents of that menu.

Calling the Parent Form

Since we've replaced the File menu, none of the main form's menu event procedures will work when a child window is open, because the events are being directed to the child window rather than the application's main window. So if you run the program and press F3 to open a file, everything works as expected. But after that, none of the items on the File menu will work. We obviously don't want to duplicate the code for each of the application's menu options in every child form, so we need a way to call event handlers in the main form. As you probably expect by now, it's very easy.

In the **interface** section of the VIEWMAIN.PAS unit, there's a global variable called **MDIFileViewer** that defines the main form. This variable is automatically created by Delphi when you create the form, and it's initialized when the FileView program begins executing. Since the variable is in the unit's **interface** section, it's visible to any unit that uses the VIEWMAIN unit. (That's what the **interface** section is for: To allow other programs to "interface" to our unit without having to show them everything that the unit contains. What's in the **interface** section is what they get; everything else is for the unit's internal use alone. More on this in the next chapter.) So all we have to do to call the main form's procedures is to use that unit.

Add the line:

```
uses ViewMain;
```

at the beginning of the **implementation** section in TEXTVIEW.PAS, and then create event handlers for the File|Open, File|Close, File|Exit, Window|Tile, Window|Cascade, and Window|Close all menu options. We'll cover the File|Print and File|Print Setup items in the next section. The code for the individual event handlers is shown in Listing 7.8.

LISTING 7.8   The child window menu item event handlers

```
procedure TTextViewer.Open1Click(Sender: TObject);
begin
 MDIFileViewer.Open1Click (Sender);
end;

procedure TTextViewer.Close1Click(Sender: TObject);
begin
 Close;
end;
```

```
procedure TTextViewer.Exit1Click(Sender: TObject);
begin
 MDIFileViewer.Exit1Click (Sender);
end;

procedure TTextViewer.Tile1Click(Sender: TObject);
begin
 MDIFileViewer.Tile;
end;

procedure TTextViewer.Cascade1Click(Sender: TObject);
begin
 MDIFileViewer.Cascade;
end;

procedure TTextViewer.Closeall1Click(Sender: TObject);
begin
 MDIFileViewer.CloseAllChildren;
end;
```

Before you try to compile the program, add the **CloseAllChildren** procedure shown in Listing 7.9 to VIEWMAIN.PAS. Be sure to include this procedure declaration:

```
procedure CloseAllChildren;
```

in the **public** section of the **TMDIFileViewer** class.

LISTING 7.9   The CloseAllChildren procedure

```
procedure TMDIFileViewer.CloseAllChildren;
Var
 i : Integer;
Begin
 For i := 0 To MDIChildCount - 1 Do
  MDIChildren[i].Close
End;
```

PRINTING TEXT

In the past, printing *anything* from a Windows program was a major undertaking that involved a considerable amount of code and generally a lot of headscratching and hairpulling. Not so with Delphi. Printing text from a Delphi program is almost as easy as printing from a DOS program. All you have to do is get the print parameters, open the printer device for output, and then send each line of text. It's really that simple.

Getting Ready to Print

Most Windows programs that print allow you to choose the printer to which the output should go, and a number of other options that affect the output. These options are selected from the Printer Setup dialog box and the Print dialog box.

From the Additional page of the component palette, select a PrintDialog component and drop it onto the TextViewer form next to the MainMenu component. Then select a PrinterSetupDialog and drop it next to the PrintDialog. Finally, add event handlers for the File|Print and File|Printer Setup menu items. The code for these event handlers is shown in Listing 7.10.

LISTING 7.10   The TTextViewer form's printer event handlers

```
procedure TTextViewer.PrintSetup1Click(Sender: TObject);
begin
 PrinterSetupDialog1.Execute;
end;

procedure TTextViewer.Print1Click(Sender: TObject);
var
 Line: Integer;
 PrintText: System.Text;
begin
 if PrintDialog1.Execute then begin
  AssignPrn(PrintText);
  Rewrite(PrintText);
  Printer.Canvas.Font := Memo1.Font;
  for Line := 0 to Memo1.Lines.Count - 1 do
   Writeln(PrintText, Memo1.Lines[Line]);
  System.Close(PrintText);
 end;
end;
```

The **PrintSetup1Click** event handler in Listing 7.10 is very simple; all it does is execute the Printer Setup dialog, which allows you to select the printer that you want output to go to.

The **Print1Click** event handler is more complex, but hardly rocket science. This procedure executes the Print dialog, allowing you to set your printer options. It then calls **AssignPrn** to assign a file of type **Text** (which is a simple ASCII text file) to the printer device, and **Rewrite**, which opens the assigned file for output. Finally, we set the font for the printer's canvas and send each line of output to the printer file. We haven't discussed the canvas yet—it's Delphi's encapsulation of the Windows Graphic Device Interface (GDI). In Chapter 12, we'll discuss the canvas in detail, for both forms and printers.

If you've done any Pascal programming at all, you're probably familiar with text files. They work the same way in Delphi as they do in previous versions of Borland Pascal. If you're not familiar with Pascal text files, don't be too concerned for now—we'll come back to them in a later chapter.

Before you try to compile the program, be sure to add Printers to the list of units in the **TextView** unit's **uses** statement. The Printers unit contains **AssignPrn** and other procedures that let you use the printer. Your **uses** statement should look like this:

```
uses ViewMain, Printers;
```

VIEWING PICTURES

The picture viewer form is almost identical to the text file viewer form. The only changes are in the component that's used to display the pictures, and the code that prints them. In addition, we'll have to make a few minor changes to the main form's **Open1Click** procedure.

The Picture Viewer Form

To create the picture viewer form, select File | New Form from Delphi's main menu, and select Blank form from the gallery. With the Object Inspector, change the Form's properties as shown in Table 7.7.

The Image Component

The Image component is to picture files what the Memo component is to text files. With an Image component you can load and display bitmaps, icons, and Windows metafiles. The internal workings of the Image component are smart enough to figure out what kind of image is loaded, and take care of all of the futzing around with display contexts, palettes, and everything else associated

Table 7.7   *Property Changes for the PictureViewer Form*

Property	Value
Caption	"Picture Viewer"
Ctl3D	False
FormStyle	fsMDIChild
Name	"PictureViewer"

with displaying pictures in a Windows program. With Delphi, displaying a picture is as easy as displaying a text file.

Select an Image component from the Additional page of the component palette, and drop it onto your form. Change the Image component's **Align** property to **alClient**.

As with the TextViewer form, we'll add an **Open** procedure to the bitmap viewer. Add the **Filename** variable declaration and the **Open** procedure declaration to the **TPictureViewer** class so that the class looks like Listing 7.11.

LISTING 7.11 The edited TPictureViewer class

```
TPictureViewer = class(TForm)
 Image1: TImage;
private
 { Private declarations }
 Filename : String;
public
 { Public declarations }
 procedure Open (Const AFilename : String);
end;
```

Then, add the **Open** procedure shown in Listing 7.12.

LISTING 7.12 The TPictureViewer.Open procedure

```
Procedure TPictureViewer.Open (Const AFilename : String);
Begin
 Filename := AFilename;
 Image1.Picture.LoadFromFile (Filename);
 Caption := Filename;
End;
```

Before we continue, press F2 to save the file. Call the new unit PICVIEW.PAS.

Modifying the Main Form

We have to make a few additions to the main form's code in order to accommodate displaying pictures. First, change the **uses** statement in the **implementation** section of the unit, as shown here:

```
uses TextView, PicView;
```

so that the main form can access forms of type **TPictureViewer**.

Then, change the **TMDIFileViewer.Open1Click** procedure, as in Listing 7.13.

LISTING 7.13 The modified TMDIFileViewer.Open1Click method

```
procedure TMDIFileViewer.Open1Click(Sender: TObject);
Var
 TextViewer : TTextViewer;
 PicViewer : TPictureViewer;
 FileExt : String[4];
begin
 If FileOpenDialog.Execute Then Begin
  FileExt := ExtractFileExt (FileOpenDialog.Filename);
  If (FileExt = '.BMP') or (FileExt = '.ICO') or
    (FileExt = '.WMF') Then Begin
   PicViewer := TPictureViewer.Create (Self);
   PicViewer.Open (FileOpenDialog.Filename);
   PicViewer.Visible := True;
   PicViewer.SetFocus;
  End
  Else Begin
   TextViewer := TTextViewer.Create (Self);
   TextViewer.Open (FileOpenDialog.Filename);
   TextViewer.Visible := True;
   TextViewer.SetFocus;
  End;
 End;
end;
```

The procedure in Listing 7.13 uses the **ExtractFileExt** function to get the extension of the file that is to be loaded. If the file is a picture file (extension of .BMP, .ICO, or .WMF), then the program initializes and displays a **TPictureViewer** form. Otherwise, the program assumes that the file is a text file, and so creates and displays a **TTextViewer** form.

Don't forget to edit the project source file and remove the line of code that automatically (and erroneously!) creates and displays a **TPictureViewer** form. You should also create an OnClose event handler for the new form, and copy the **TTextViewer.FormClose** code shown in Listing 7.7.

After you've made all of those changes, save your work and press F9 to compile and run the program. Try loading a few text files and a few different types of picture files. You should be able to find plenty of bitmap and icon files in your \WINDOWS directory.

Picture Viewer Menus

The bitmap viewer has the same menu items as the text file viewer. You can save yourself some time creating the bitmap viewer's menu by using Delphi's copy and paste facility to copy the menu. Simply follow these steps:

1. Click on the "Select form from list" button on the tool bar.
2. Select the TextViewer form from the View Form dialog box.
3. Click on the MainMenu component in the displayed form to select it.
4. Select Edit | Copy from Delphi's main menu.
5. Click on the "Select form from list" button again, and select the Picture Viewer form.
6. Select Edit | Paste from Delphi's main menu to copy the menu onto the new form.

This copies the MainMenu component and all of its properties from the TextViewer form to the PictureViewer form. It doesn't copy the event handlers, though, so you'll have to use the Menu Designer to create event handlers for each of the menu items. With the exception of the **Print1Click** procedure, which will have to be modified to print pictures rather than text, the event handlers for the bitmap viewer form are the same as the text viewer's event handlers. Create event procedures for each of the bitmap viewer's menu items, and copy the code from the event procedures in Listings 7.8 and 7.10, *except* the **Print1Click** procedure in Listing 7.10.

Be sure to add this **uses** statement:

```
uses ViewMain, Printers;
```

at the beginning of the **implementation** section of PICVIEW.PAS.

Before we continue, be sure to drop a PrintDialog and a PrinterSetupDialog component onto your form. Then save your work and test the program. With the exception of printing, which we'll discuss next, the BitmapViewer form should work exactly like the TextViewer form.

PRINTING PICTURES

In its most basic form, copying a picture to the printer is even easier than printing text. Simply tell the **Printer** object to begin printing, copy the picture to the printer, and then tell the **Printer** object to stop printing. Three lines of code is all it takes, as shown in Listing 7.14.

LISTING 7.14   Copying a picture to the printer

```
procedure TPictureViewer.Print1Click(Sender: TObject);
begin
 if PrintDialog1.Execute Then Begin
```

```
With Printer Do Begin
  BeginDoc;
  Canvas.Draw (0, 0, Image1.Picture.Graphic);
  EndDoc;
 end;
 end;
end;
```

Create an event handler for the Picture Viewer form's File|Print menu item, and enter the code shown in Listing 7.14. Compile the program, load a picture file, and select File|Print to create a hard copy of the picture.

Unless you selected a fairly large picture, the results will likely be a bit disappointing. The picture is positioned at the upper left-hand corner of the page, and printed using the printer's resolution; resulting in a very small picture. It'd be nice if the program would automatically stretch and position the picture so that it's larger and centered on the page. That's a little more involved, but not overly so, as you can see from Listing 7.15.

LISTING 7.15 Sizing the picture to fit the paper

```
procedure TPictureViewer.Print1Click(Sender: TObject);

Var
 StretchRect : TRect;
 TempHeight,
 TempWidth : Integer;

begin
 if PrintDialog1.Execute Then Begin
  {
   Stretch the picture so that it takes up about 1/2
   of the printed page.
  }
  TempHeight := Image1.Picture.Height;
  TempWidth := Image1.Picture.Width;
  While (TempHeight < Printer.PageHeight div 2) and
     (TempWidth < Printer.PageWidth div 2) Do Begin
   TempHeight := TempHeight + TempHeight;
   TempWidth := TempWidth + TempWidth;
  End;

  { Position the picture so that it prints centered }
  With StretchRect Do Begin
   Left := (Printer.PageWidth - TempWidth) div 2;
   Top := (Printer.PageHeight - TempHeight) div 2;
   Right := Left + TempWidth;
   Bottom := Top + TempHeight;
  End;
```

```
 { And copy it to the printer }
 With Printer Do Begin
  BeginDoc;
  Canvas.StretchDraw (StretchRect, Image1.Picture.Graphic);
  EndDoc;
 End;
 end;
end;
```

The code in Listing 7.15 performs three steps. First, it repeatedly doubles the picture's size until the picture's height or width is larger than the printer canvas' corresponding dimension. Then, it positions the picture in the center of the printer's canvas. Finally, it initializes the printer and calls **StretchDraw**, which stretches the picture so that it fits into the rectangle that we calculated. When **StretchDraw** is finished, we call **EndDoc** to close the printer device.

FURTHER STUDY

Many of the most popular Windows programs are MDI applications, and if you're doing any serious Windows programming, you'll most likely be required to write an MDI application at some point. In this chapter, we've examined the very basics of the Multiple Document Interface. There are many other features of MDI that you can incorporate into your programs. The MDI Application template in the Browse Gallery dialog box (displayed when you select File | New Project, if you have enabled that option on the Preferences page of the Environment Options dialog box) creates the shell for a complete MDI application that includes a much more detailed menu, a tool bar, and other options that are not discussed in this chapter. In addition, the TextEdit demo application (found in the \DELPHI\DEMOS\DOC\TEXTEDIT directory) provides a good working sample.

There's much more to printing, too. We got a little ahead of ourselves with the **canvas** property, and we still haven't discussed **uses**, **implementation**, **interface**, and all of the other details about units, but that's the nature of programming—sometimes you have to use something before you fully understand how it works. The three of us writing this book happen to feel that if you've already seen an idea like Object Pascal units at work in a simple project, it'll stick to you better when you finally sit down and study it in detail. At that point you'll have some *context* to hang your new knowledge on—which is very much the heart of the idea of the Explorer series.

We'll talk more about Delphi printing in Chapter 12, when we discuss drawing pictures on the **canvas** property of both forms and printers.

In the next chapter, we're going to take a detailed look at objects and units and how they make your code easier to maintain and reuse. You've learned a lot so far, and the pace is about to pick up quite a bit. Hang on!

UNITS AND OBJECTS

Jeff Duntemann

Object-oriented programming is the foundation on which all of Delphi is built. Objects are the natural extensions of both records and units. It's time to meet them in detail.

Way back in the Sixties, some gasoline company made a lot of noise on national TV about their new blend of gas, which was fortified with M_2PG. What sounded like super gas was in fact hot air—since M_2PG stands not for some exotic chemical additive, but More Miles Per Gallon.

We like to think of ourselves, silicon-fortified geeks that we are, as a little too smart to fall for that sort of thing. I dare to point out that it's happened again and again and again, every time things get boring enough so that the latest buzzword begins to stand apart from the general ennui.

Back in 1986 and 1987 it was AI. Artificial Intelligence. Never mind that the machines of the time were barely powerful enough to recalculate a bowling scores list in realtime. Every time a product upgrade appeared, the vendor would yell, "Now, with AI!" Nobody ever quite knew what "AI" really stood for, and when argued into a corner, the AI partisans all but admitted that it was a fancy name for pattern-matching—if not a total fraud to begin with.

We got stung again in 1989, only this time it was Objects. A great many people made a very big fuss about Object Oriented Programming (OOP) and how it would overturn all current paradigms (please note that no one except for Michael Swaine still uses that word, since he's one of the few who ever understood it to begin with) and completely revolutionize everything, for reasons that were never made especially clear. I confess, I was one of them. I've had a while to think it through, however, and after a fair number of years of working with them, I'd say at this point that I understand objects. I know how they're done. I know what they're good for.

It's time to go after objects and (although I almost dread saying so) object-oriented programming. You may or may not be surprised to know that we've been doing object-oriented programming from the beginning in this book, or at any rate programming with objects. If it's revolutionary, it's not for the objects themselves, but for the shape and the power of the tools that manipulate them. Furthermore, objects don't fit in well with traditional methods of programming and program design. Being a little object oriented is way worse than being a little pregnant—it's more like being a little catatonic.

That is the source of the Big OOP Gotcha: *Unless the entire development environment is object-oriented, objects create far more trouble than they're worth.* This is why the old object-oriented Smalltalk systems I saw at Xerox back in the 1970s worked—and this is why current C++ and Object Pascal systems don't work. Delphi is completely object-oriented, and boy oh boy, does it work!

It's time to explore the reasons why.

THE GREAT DICHOTOMY

I am a child of the liberal arts; this is one reason I get in so much trouble. Way back at DePaul University in 1973, I was sitting in one Core Curriculum course or another (forgive me if I've totally forgotten which one or what it was about) when an earnest young woman made a point that included something about the "female species." I tried to swallow a giggle and failed, but wonder of wonders, our professor (who was a woman) rose to the occasion and with much qualification and apology tried to insist that there is no "female species" and we are all part of the same human race. This may have been the last time this point was ever made in academia, but I was most impressed.

A similar and no less phony dichotomy rules in the world of programming: That code and data are two very separate things, to be treated apart and independently from one another. This may be true at the very lowest level of things, where the actual silicon is by necessity divided into memory (data) and microcode (code) but there is no reason that this distinction has to extend all the way out to the syntax of our languages and the architecture of our tools. Neither code nor data is useful alone. We are not, after all, pursuing either code or data but *computation*. To make it happen, we need to think of code and data as equal and intimately related elements of computation, welded at the hip and pumping the same blood.

What silicon has divided, let common sense join together. What we have here, in fact, is nothing worse than a packaging problem.

Packages of Computation

If I were to suggest that there are "packages of computation," what you'd think of almost immediately are procedures and functions. This is true to an extent, since within a procedure you'll certainly find code and usually some data too, tidily tied off in one box:

```
procedure TMDIFileViewer.Open1Click(Sender: Tobject);

Var
  TextViewer : TTextViewer;
  PicViewer : TPictureViewer;
  FileExt : String[4];

begin
  If FileOpenDialog.Execute Then Begin
    FileExt := ExtractFileExt (FileOpenDialog.Filename);
    If (FileExt = '.BMP') or (FileExt = '.ICO') or
       (FileExt = '.WMF') Then Begin
      PicViewer := TPictureViewer.Create (Self);
      PicViewer.Open (FileOpenDialog.Filename);
      PicViewer.Visible := True;
      PicViewer.SetFocus;
    End
    Else Begin
      TextViewer := TTextViewer.Create (Self);
      TextViewer.Open (FileOpenDialog.Filename);
      TextViewer.Visible := True;
      TextViewer.SetFocus;
    End;
  End;
end;
```

(This is Listing 7.13 from the previous chapter; I reprint it here only as an example of a fairly typical procedure, of the sort you'll see in Delphi a *lot*.)

There are three local variables after the **Var** reserved word, and code statements between **begin** and **end**. The procedure header provides a sort of "front door," in that the only way to execute this little bundle of computation is to call it by using its name and parameter list.

The three variables declared inside the procedure are called *local* because they belong to this procedure alone. Another procedure cannot "reach in" to this procedure and access **FileExt**, for example. It simply can't be done. The main reason it can't be done is that except when a procedure is actually executing, *its local variables literally do not exist.* When a procedure is executed, the first thing it does is lay out its local variables in memory, just as you'd lay out a line of tools on your workbench before you begin dismantling an engine block.

And when the procedure runs to its conclusion, the last thing it does is release the memory occupied by its local variables, so that the memory may be used by other procedures for their own local variables. The first procedure's local variables thus "go away" and no longer exist, either logically or physically. When we say (as we will, from this point on) that variables are "created" or "destroyed," this is what we mean: To create a variable is to lay it out somewhere in memory, and to destroy a variable is to abandon that memory to some other use, which overlays and thus (literally!) destroys that variable.

So a procedure is a pretty good example of a package of computation, in which the code and the data are inseparable parts of one unified whole. The code can't run (or even compile) without the variables, and the variables do not exist except through the intercession of the code. If that isn't welded at the hip, well, I don't know what would be.

Let's try our best, right now, to stop thinking of the "code species" and the "data species."

Units: Packages of Packages

As packages of computation, procedures and functions are a good start, but they're nowhere near enough. Data has to exist in some form outside of procedures, so it can be passed among different procedures for processing. Besides, data is in most cases the end result of computation. What we want out of a word processor isn't the word processing itself but a document, which is data.

This is why variables can exist independently of procedures, and to some extent how we got into trouble in the first place. What we lack is a package that can embrace procedures and variables that both exist at the same time, and still give us this same sense of connectedness. Packages like this exist in most modern programming languages, with the highly notable exceptions of C and C++, the two "high-level" languages that supposedly rule our world. In the Ada programming language they're even called "packages." In Modula-2 they're called modules. In Object Pascal they're called *units*.

One way to think of units is as boxes with packing slips. I order things through the mail a lot, and when my treasures arrive, they're usually in small brown boxes with a computer-printed form slapped onto the side in a clear plastic pocket. On that form is a list of what's inside the box.

A unit is a little like that. From a height, a unit has a name, a packing list, and a box for the goods. The packing list is called the *interface section*, and the goods box is the *implementation section*. I've drawn this out in Figure 8.1.

TOOLS TO BE USED

First and foremost, an Object Pascal unit is a package. It's a way of associating data types and variables with the code that works with them, just as a plastic case for a socket wrench set associates the various-sized sockets with the handles they mount on. If you want to use any of the sockets and handles in any combination, you reach for the socket wrench case and open it up. Then you choose the proper combination of items stored in the box. You don't have to go hunting through the garage for each individual socket or handle component (at least not if you keep them in the box they came in!) and you know that the sockets in the box will fit the handles from the same box.

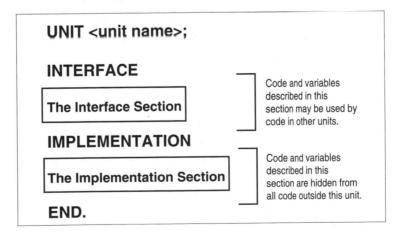

Figure 8.1   *The idea of a unit.*

If you create data types and procedures that act on those data types, a unit helps keep everything together in one comprehensible bundle. The fact that a unit is also a physical file makes it a reusable module. You don't have to yank it out of an existing program by the roots.

You can define constants, types, variables, procedures, and functions in a unit. The unit is stored as a disk file, and the items it contains and makes public (I'll come back to that point later) may be used by other units in your programs. You've probably seen the **uses** statement at the top of the main unit in the projects presented in this book so far:

```
uses
  SysUtils, WinTypes, WinProcs, Messages, Classes, Graphics, Controls,
  Forms, Dialogs, StdCtrls, Grids;
```

This is just a laundry list of units that your program needs to use. All of these units are standard units shipped with Delphi, and contain the components that you use to build your programs. When you define a form with components on it, Delphi knows what units the components are stored in, and adds the appropriate units to the list. You can add the names of your own units to the list as well. We'll be doing that shortly in this chapter.

A Mortgage Calculation Engine in Unit Form

We're going to take the record type definitions I presented at the end of Chapter 6 and place them in a unit, along with new procedures and functions that perform the actual calculations required in generating an amortization table for a mortgage. The unit will become a "mortgage engine" that can be used to calculate and store mortgage tables as a service to a Delphi program that provides visible controls and tables that display mortgages. Separating calculation from presentation is a common practice in Delphi programming, and a good habit to get into.

Probably the best way to explain the structure of a unit is simply to show you one and go over its various elements in detail. Listing 8.1 is a simple mortgage calculation "engine" in unit form. It stores not only the data model of a mortgage presented at the end of Chapter 6, but also the procedures and functions that perform the calculations necessary to fill the amortization table with correct values. The calculations are nothing special, and don't require more than grade school arithmetic—with the exception of one "magic" function. The Object Pascal code itself, though it may seem advanced at first glance, is very simple and contains nothing that we haven't already addressed in this book.

Listing 8.1   The MORTUNIT.PAS Mortgage Engine

```
{————————————————————————————————}
{                    MORTUNIT                    }
{              By Jeff Duntemann KG7JF           }
{                                                }
{ A mortgage calculation "engine" for Delphi.    }
{ Written for *Delphi Programming Explorer*      }
{ Copyright (c) 1995 The Coriolis Group, Inc.    }
{                                                }
{ Adapted loosely from code originally published }
{ in DDJ for October 1991 — Last Updated 2/26/95 }
{————————————————————————————————}

UNIT MortUnit;

INTERFACE

TYPE
  String2  = String[2];    { Handy for state codes }
  String10 = String[10];   { Handy for 9-digit ZIP codes }
  String15 = String[15];
  String25 = String[25];
  String40 = String[40];
  String80 = String[80];

  TLender =
    RECORD
      LenderID      : Integer;
      LenderName    : String40;
      LenderAddress : String40;
      LenderCity    : String25;
      LenderState   : String2;
      LenderZIP     : String10;
      LenderPhone   : String25;
    END;

  TPayment =
    RECORD        { One element in the amortization table. }
      PaymentNum    : Integer;
      PayPrincipal  : Real;
      PayInterest   : Real;
      PrincipalSoFar : Real;
      InterestSoFar : Real;
      ExtraPrincipal : Real;
      Balance       : Real;
    END;

  PaymentArray = ARRAY[1..600] OF TPayment;

  TMortgage =
    RECORD
      Lender      : TLender;  { Lender information on a loan    }
      Periods     : Integer;  { Number of periods in mortgage   }
```

```
      PeriodsPerYear : Integer;   { Number of periods in a year    }
      Principal      : Real;      { Amount of principal in cents   }
      Interest       : Real;      { Percentage of interest per *YEAR*}
      MonthlyPI      : Real;      { Monthly payment in cents       }
      Payments       : PaymentArray; { Array of payment records    }
    END;

PROCEDURE InitMortgage(VAR ThisMortgage      : TMortgage;
                           StartPrincipal    : Real;
                           StartInterest     : Real;
                           StartPeriods      : Integer;
                           StartPeriodsPerYear : Integer);

PROCEDURE SetNewInterestRate(VAR ThisMortgage : TMortgage;
                                 NewRate       : Real);

PROCEDURE Recalc(VAR ThisMortgage : TMortgage);

PROCEDURE ApplyExtraPrincipal(VAR ThisMortgage  : TMortgage;
                                  PaymentNumber  : Integer;
                                  Extra          : Real);

PROCEDURE RangeExtraPrincipal(VAR ThisMortgage : TMortgage;
                                  StartPayment,
                                  EndPayment    : Integer;
                                  Extra         : Real);

PROCEDURE MultipleExtraPrincipal(VAR ThisMortgage : TMortgage;
                                     StartPayment : Integer;
                                     Extra        : Real);

PROCEDURE RemoveExtraPrincipal(VAR ThisMortgage  : TMortgage;
                                   PaymentNumber  : Integer);

PROCEDURE RemoveAllExtraPrincipal(VAR ThisMortgage : TMortgage);


IMPLEMENTATION


FUNCTION CalcPayment(Principal,InterestPerPeriod : Real;
                     NumberOfPeriods : Integer) : Real;
VAR
  Factor : Real;

BEGIN
  Factor := EXP(-NumberOfPeriods * LN(1.0 + InterestPerPeriod));
  CalcPayment := Principal * InterestPerPeriod / (1.0 - Factor)
END;


PROCEDURE InitMortgage(VAR ThisMortgage      : TMortgage;
                           StartPrincipal    : Real;
                           StartInterest     : Real;
```

```
                              StartPeriods        : Integer;
                              StartPeriodsPerYear : Integer);

VAR
  I : Integer;
  InterestPerPeriod  : Real;

BEGIN
  WITH ThisMortgage DO
    BEGIN
      { Set up all the initial state values in the TMortgage object: }
      Principal      := StartPrincipal;
      Interest       := StartInterest;
      Periods        := StartPeriods;
      PeriodsPerYear := StartPeriodsPerYear;
    END;
  Recalc(ThisMortgage);   { Build the mortgage table }
END;


PROCEDURE SetNewInterestRate(VAR ThisMortgage : TMortgage;
                                 NewRate       : Real);

BEGIN
  ThisMortgage.Interest := NewRate;
  Recalc(ThisMortgage); { Re-amortize the mortgage and rebuild the table }
END;


{ This routine calculates the amortization table for the mortgage.   }

PROCEDURE Recalc(VAR ThisMortgage : TMortgage);

VAR
  RemainingPrincipal   : Real;
  PayNum               : Integer;
  InterestThisPeriod   : Real;
  InterestPerPeriod    : Real;
  HypotheticalPrincipal : Real;

BEGIN
  WITH ThisMortgage DO
    BEGIN
      InterestPerPeriod := Interest/PeriodsPerYear;
      MonthlyPI := CalcPayment(Principal,
                               InterestPerPeriod,
                               Periods);
      { Round the monthly to cents: }
      MonthlyPI := int(MonthlyPI * 100.0 + 0.5) / 100.0;

      { Now generate the amortization table: }
      RemainingPrincipal := Principal;
      { Do this for each period (that is, payment) in the loan: }
      FOR PayNum := 1 TO Periods DO
```

```
            BEGIN
                { Calculate the interest this period and round it to cents:  }
                InterestThisPeriod :=
                Int((RemainingPrincipal * InterestPerPeriod) * 100 + 0.5)
                    / 100.0;
                { Store values into current payment record in payment array: }
                WITH Payments[PayNum] DO
                  BEGIN
                    PaymentNum := PayNum;          { The payment number, from 1 }
                    IF RemainingPrincipal = 0 THEN   { Loan's been paid off! }
                      BEGIN
                        PayInterest := 0;
                        PayPrincipal := 0;
                        Balance := 0;
                      END
                    ELSE      { There's still principal to repay }
                      BEGIN
                        HypotheticalPrincipal :=
                        MonthlyPI - InterestThisPeriod + ExtraPrincipal;
                        IF HypotheticalPrincipal > RemainingPrincipal THEN
                          PayPrincipal := RemainingPrincipal
                        ELSE
                          PayPrincipal := HypotheticalPrincipal;
                        PayInterest  := InterestThisPeriod;
                        { Update running balance: }
                        RemainingPrincipal :=
                          RemainingPrincipal - PayPrincipal;
                        Balance := RemainingPrincipal;
                      END;
                    { Update the cumulative interest and principal fields: }
                    IF PayNum <= 1 THEN { First payment; so cumulative values }
                      BEGIN                  { are simply the current values }
                        PrincipalSoFar := PayPrincipal;
                        InterestSoFar  := PayInterest;
                      END
                    ELSE     { We're not at first payment, so we must reach back to}
                      BEGIN { previous payment to calculate cumulative totals:    }
                        PrincipalSoFar :=
                          Payments[PayNum-1].PrincipalSoFar + PayPrincipal;
                        InterestSoFar  :=
                          Payments[PayNum-1].InterestSoFar + PayInterest;
                      END;
                  END; { WITH Payments[PayNum] }
              END;      { FOR PayNum := 1 TO Periods }
          END;        { WITH ThisMortgage }
      END;            { Recalc }


PROCEDURE ApplyExtraPrincipal(VAR ThisMortgage  : TMortgage;
                                  PaymentNumber : Integer;
                                  Extra         : Real);

BEGIN
  ThisMortgage.Payments[PaymentNumber].ExtraPrincipal := Extra;
```

```
    Recalc(ThisMortgage); { Re-amortize the mortgage and rebuild the table }
END;


PROCEDURE RemoveExtraPrincipal(VAR ThisMortgage  : TMortgage;
                                  PaymentNumber : Integer);

BEGIN
  ThisMortgage.Payments[PaymentNumber].ExtraPrincipal := 0.0;
  Recalc(ThisMortgage); { Re-amortize the mortgage and rebuild the table }
END;


PROCEDURE RemoveAllExtraPrincipal(VAR ThisMortgage : TMortgage);

VAR
  I : Integer;

BEGIN
  WITH ThisMortgage DO
    FOR I := 0 TO Periods DO
      Payments[I].ExtraPrincipal := 0.0;
  Recalc(ThisMortgage); { Re-amortize the mortgage and rebuild the table }
END;


PROCEDURE MultipleExtraPrincipal(VAR ThisMortgage : TMortgage;
                                     StartPayment : Integer;
                                     Extra        : Real);

VAR
  I : Integer;

BEGIN
  WITH ThisMortgage DO
    BEGIN
      FOR I := StartPayment TO Periods DO
        Payments[I].ExtraPrincipal := Extra;
      Recalc(ThisMortgage); { Re-amortize the mortgage and rebuild the table }
      { Here, we clear out any unnecessary extra principal values: }
      FOR I := 1 TO Periods DO
        BEGIN
          IF (Payments[I].Balance <= 0.00) OR
             (Payments[I].Balance < Extra)
          THEN Payments[I].ExtraPrincipal := 0.00;
        END; { FOR I := 1 TO Periods }
    END;     { WITH ThisMortgage }
END;         { MultipleExtraPrincipal }


PROCEDURE RangeExtraPrincipal(VAR ThisMortgage : TMortgage;
                                  StartPayment,
                                  EndPayment : Integer;
                                  Extra      : Real);
```

```
VAR
  I : Integer;

BEGIN
  WITH ThisMortgage DO
    BEGIN
      FOR I := StartPayment TO EndPayment DO;
        Payments[I].ExtraPrincipal := Extra;
      Recalc(ThisMortgage); { Re-amortize the mortgage & rebuild the table }
      { Here, we clear out any unnecessary extra principal values: }
      FOR I := 1 TO Periods DO
        BEGIN
          IF (Payments[I].Balance <= 0.00) OR
             (Payments[I].Balance < Extra)
          THEN Payments[I].ExtraPrincipal := 0.00;
        END;   { FOR I := 1 TO Periods }
    END;       { WITH ThisMortgage      }
END;           { RangeExtraPrincipal    }

END.  { MORTUNIT }
```

The Interface Section

The *interface section* of a unit consists of everything between the reserved word **INTERFACE** and the reserved word **IMPLEMENTATION**. The interface section is for definitions only. This includes the obvious things like constant, type, and variable definitions—but it also includes definitions of procedures and functions.

Note in Listing 8.1 that after the type definitions is a series of procedure headers (that is, the names and parameter lists of procedures) without any procedure *bodies*. These disembodied (as it were) procedures are the most that Object Pascal will allow. You can't put actual Pascal code in the interface section of a unit. On the other hand, the procedure headers are all we need to actually use the procedures themselves from outside the unit. To call a procedure, we need only its name and its parameter list:

```
InitMortgage(MyMortgage,100000.0,0.085,360,12);
```

So in terms of definition, all we need is the name and the list of parameters with their types:

```
PROCEDURE InitMortgage(VAR ThisMortgage       : TMortgage;
                           StartPrincipal      : Real;
                           StartInterest       : Real;
                           StartPeriods        : Integer;
                           StartPeriodsPerYear : Integer);
```

This is all we need to know about a procedure to call it—assuming someone has told us exactly what it is that the procedure does. That's a documentation issue. (Or it should be, in any event.) So if we're doing up a packing list of all the procedures and functions stored in a unit, listing their headers as shown here is all we really need to do.

Using Code and Data Stored in Units

If you have a unit and want to use some of the things it contains, you must first include the name of the unit in the **USES** statement of the unit from which you'll access the first unit's types, variables, or code. Here's an example, which is a peek ahead at the **USES** statement from Listing 8.3:

```
uses
  SysUtils, WinTypes, WinProcs, Messages, Classes, Graphics, Controls,
  Forms, Dialogs, StdCtrls, Grids,           { Borland's standard units }
  { Units listed below are non-Borland: }
  MortUnit;                                  { Our mortgage engine unit }
```

Separating Your Units from Borland's

A large and involved programming project might use a dozen of Borland's units and perhaps as many of your own. It's good practice not to intermix the unit names within the **USES** statement. I recommend keeping the two groups of units separate, even though they're part of the same project. All you need to do is break the **USES** statement at the comma after the last Borland unit, and begin the list of *your* units on the next line.

In general, placing your units after Borland's in the list is the proper way to do things. The reason is simple: A routine in a unit can reference code and data in a unit named *before* it in the **USES** statement, but not one named *after* it. Realistically, your units will need to use Borland's—and the reverse will almost never be the case.

Once you've named a unit in the **USES** statement of another unit that you're working on, you can reference anything in the named unit's interface section. You can create variables of types defined in the unit, read and write variables defined in the unit, and call the unit's functions and procedures. It's as though you've added the identifiers in the **USE**d unit's interface section to the unit you're working on.

Which brings up the inevitable question: What happens if you **USE** a unit and an identifier in that unit is the same as one in the code you're working on? You will *not* get a compile error...but one of the two will not be "visible" to references from code. You might have the option to change the conflicting identifier in your own code...or you might not. Knowing what's in your units will help you avoid conflicts like this, but sooner or later something's going to collide. The way out is simply to use the same "dotting" notation used with records. You can fully qualify one of the identifiers by preceding it by the name of the unit in which it resides, and of course the dot:

```
MortUnit.Recalc;
```

Even if there's another **Recalc** procedure somewhere else in your application, you can be sure to call the one that recalculates mortgages by specifying **MortUnit.Recalc**.

Finally, there's the question: If two identical identifiers collide, which one will be visible? The answer is that the one whose unit was cited *later* in the **USES** statement is the visible one. The reasoning is fairly simple: As Delphi's compiler scans the **USES** statement, it builds a table in memory of the identifiers it finds in the interface sections of all the units cited in the **USES** statement. If the same identifier appears a second time, the second meaning of the identifier overlays the first in the table. This doesn't mean that the first identifier is completely inaccessible. You must simply qualify it with its unit's name and a period character, as described above.

The Implementation Section

Everything from the reserved word **IMPLEMENTATION** down to the closing **END**. (don't forget the period!) is considered the *implementation section* of a unit. Two general groups of things are defined in the implementation section of the unit: Function and procedure bodies implementing the headers defined in the interface section, and definitions private to the unit as a whole.

The procedure bodies are easy to understand: You define them in the interface section, and you implement them (that is, fully create them in every detail) in the implementation section, which is how the section got its name. What takes a little more thought is the notion of private definitions that exist for the use of the unit alone.

In Listing 8.1, notice the procedure **CalcPayment**, which is right after the **IMPLEMENTATION** reserved word. There is no procedure header for **CalcPayment** in the interface section of the unit. **CalcPayment**, in other words, is not on the packing list—but it still exists inside the box. **CalcPayment** is in the unit to serve the other procedures and functions within the unit; that is, the ones that *are* on the packing list. Because there is no **CalcPayment** procedure header in the interface section, there is no way that a procedure in another unit can call **CalcPayment**. It is very definitely for the private use of the other procedures in the unit, and their use alone.

Although I haven't defined any data types or variables in the implementation section of Listing 8.1, you very definitely have that power. Constants, types, and variables may all be defined in the implementation section. When they are, they serve the unit, and not the outside world. Think of it like the guy who repairs stereos in the back room of the stereo store. You never talk to him directly. The counter clerks take broken stereos from customers, log them in, and then carry them back to the back room and hand them to the repair tech. If you're a customer, you may not know the repair tech's name— you may not, in fact, be entirely sure that he's back there at all. (I've had this suspicion on more than one occasion.) The store might justifiably ship repair work down to some central office, where expensive test equipment can serve all the stores in the stereo store chain. All they promise you, as a customer, (and from their perspective a member of the "outside world") is that your broken stereo is going to get fixed. How it actually happens, well, they really don't have to say.

IMPLEMENTING A MORTGAGE ENGINE

Back in Chapter 6 we developed a number of data types that allowed us to "model" a mortgage, where *model* simply means to represent it as structures of data values that an Object Pascal program can understand and manipulate. In a sense, we built an elaborate box that can contain all the details of what we call a mortgage. The box, however, isn't enough. We need machinery to fill it with correct values.

This is something that code rather than data has to do. Listing 8.1 contains a number of procedures to perform the necessary calculations. Before mentioning any of the procedures explicitly, notice that every last one of them has as its first parameter something called **ThisMortgage**. This is your way of telling each procedure which particular **TMortgage** record they're to work on. You can have more than one **TMortgage** record in memory at the same time, perhaps to compare the payments on two similar but not identical mortgages. In order to get a procedure to work on the correct mortgage, you must pass the name of that mortgage to the procedure in **ThisMortgage**.

When you declare a variable of type **TMortgage**, it's all there but empty. Filling it initially with values representing a mortgage amortization table starts with a procedure called **Init**. The **Init** procedure takes several initial values such as principal, interest, the number of periods (that is, payments) across which the loan will be amortized, and the number of periods occurring in a year. **Init** first stores those values into the proper fields of the **TMortgage** record. It then calculates the **TPayment** records in the **Payments** array by calling another procedure, **Recalc**.

Why does **Init** farm out this critical calculation to another procedure? Quite simply, **Init** isn't the only thing that has to calculate the amortization table. If you change any aspect of the mortgage along the way, (most commonly, by adding additional principal to a payment) the whole amortization table must be recalculated. So **Recalc** is a procedure in its own right, and may be called by any of the other procedures that manipulate the **TMortgage** record type.

Factoring out recalculation makes **Init** so simple that you might reasonably ask why it exists at all. You could just as easily plug the starting values into the record's fields and call **Recalc**. True enough—but having a single procedure that "fills" a mortgage table *with one operation* is a good thing. That way, you're quite sure that you won't forget one part of the operation, like applying a value to the **PeriodsPerYear** field. Once you make sure that you have the initialization of a mortgage done correctly, you can "seal it off" in a procedure, and be sure that from now on and for all time, you need only call **Init** to kick off a mortgage correctly.

Recalc

The **Recalc** procedure is by far and away the most important single procedure in **MortUnit**. It takes the current values in the **TMortgage** record, calculates a per-period payment value, and then uses that payment value to distribute the payment of the loan across a table with one entry for each of the specified number of periods. You must call **Recalc** when setting up a mortgage for the first time, and also any time you change any of the mortgage's parameters. This includes changing the amount paid for any single payment or group of payments, as people often do to shorten the term of a mortgage and avoid payment of some of the interest that would ordinarily go to the lender.

In fact, if you look at the rest of the procedures in **MortUnit**, you'll see that they nearly all involve adding or removing extra principal somewhere in the amortization table of a mortgage. Because changing even a single payment in a mortgage requires recalculating the entire table from the changed payment on, nearly all of the other procedures call **Recalc** as well.

This is a major reason for using procedures: If we had every procedure in **MortUnit** do its own recalculation, there would be a huge amount of duplicated code in the unit, making the unit far larger than it had to be. But that's a minor issue compared to the danger of not doing all the recalculation the same way. As you'll see in glancing at **Recalc**'s innards, it's not a simple process. Leave out a step somewhere, and the calculation might be subtly in error. By forcing all the routines in **MortUnit** to call **Recalc** to do their calculation, we only need to ensure that **Recalc** works correctly—not the recalculation code within six or seven different procedures.

Two Magical Functions: EXP and LN

If any part of **MortUnit** is tricky to understand, it'll be the **CalcPayment** function, which exists completely only in the implementation section of the unit, and is thus for the sole and private use of the other routines in the unit. **CalcPayment** takes the initial values for a mortgage and returns the amount to be paid for each payment. The formula is standard financial practice, and if you know your money science you'll at least recognize it. To do its work, it uses two Object Pascal mathematical standard functions, **EXP** and **LN**.

The **EXP** function is the Pascal implementation of the *exponential function*, which returns the value that is *e* raised to the power of **EXP**'s single parameter. The constant *e* is the base of the natural logarithms, and to several decimal places is 2.718282. Explaining where *e* came from is way beyond the charter of this book, and I really don't have the space to explain in detail how the **EXP** function is used. Just as in the case where if you have to ask the price, you can't afford the car, if you have to ask what natural logarithms are, you're unlikely to be able to use **EXP**. On the flipside, if you're mathematically literate enough to understand natural logs, **EXP** will be obvious.

The same is true of **LN**, which returns the natural logarithm of its single parameter. The natural logarithm of an arbitrary value X is the logarithm of X in base *e*. **EXP** and **LN** are in one sense opposites of one another, and are often used together. Their most common application lies in filling a hole in the Object Pascal language spec: Exponentiation. Pascal has no built-in X-to-the-power-of-Y function or operator, as does FORTRAN, its close cousin. In FORTRAN, the expression **X**Y** raises X to the power of Y. In Pascal you have to (as they say) fake it.

Faking it isn't too tough, given **EXP** and **LN**. Here's a function that raises X to the power of Y:

Listing 8.2 An exponentiation function

```
FUNCTION Power(X,Y : Real) : Real;
BEGIN
  Power := Exp(Ln(X)*Y);
END;
```

How this works lies in the nature of **EXP** and **LN**, and would take most of a chapter to explain if I also explained the math behind them. But it works, as long as you do not pass a zero or negative number in X, the mantissa value. **LN(X)** is undefined for X <= 0.

Visible and Hidden

Providing a convenient package of data types, variables, and procedures is the obvious job of a unit. Managing the parts of a package of computation to be revealed to the public at large (that is, to other units in your programs) and the parts to remain the secrets of the unit itself, is the subtle job of a unit. Some things are visible, and some things are hidden. By and large, what is defined in the implementation section of a unit remains hidden, and everything else (being part of the interface section) is visible to any unit that uses your unit. See Figure 8.2.

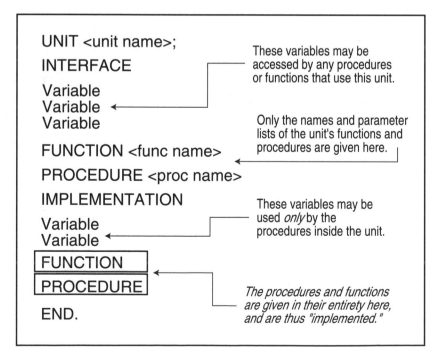

Figure 8.2 Object Pascal unit structure.

The unit can enforce that sort of hiding with ease. How you decide what to reveal and what to hide is a different matter, and something you'll have to learn from experience. Most experienced Object Pascal programmers will recommend that you hide everything you can, and only reveal what is absolutely necessary to get the job done. If you discover along the way that getting the job done is difficult without revealing a little more of the unit, move that little more from the implementation section to the interface section.

The **MortUnit** unit provides a small lesson or two in what to hide and what to reveal. As I mentioned earlier, the **CalcPayment** function is private to the unit, and hidden from all references outside the unit. The reason was relatively simple. I asked myself: Would any code that made use of the mortgage engine need to calculate a payment on its own? I couldn't think of a circumstance, so I didn't define **CalcPayment** in the interface portion of the unit.

That was what they call a no-brainer. A trickier question is this: Why should **Recalc** be visible outside the unit? As you can see in Listing 8.1, **Recalc** is defined in the interface section, and is thus callable from outside the unit. Why is this useful?

I reasoned that any change at all to the mortgage table required a recalculation of the table—even changes that I might not anticipate in the suite of procedures I created to process mortgage information. To take my unit and do something to a mortgage table that I hadn't anticipated, the programmer would still have to re-amortize the mortgage table, which is what **Recalc** does. Without **Recalc**, nothing can be done to a **TMortgage** variable that isn't already defined in the existing procedures in **MortUnit**. If I exposed **Recalc** to the outside world, programmers who wanted to use **MortUnit** could extend it in their programs, even if I didn't distribute the source code to the unit.

Recalc is the heart of **MortUnit**. Without **Recalc**, nothing useful happens within the unit, and all of the procedures that manipulate a mortgage in some way are dependent on it. Making **Recalc** visible allows other programmers to create additional procedures that manipulate mortgages modeled with **TMortgage**. It's the difference between a closed-ended engine and an open-ended engine. Maybe in some cases you want to limit the extendibility of a unit. In this case, well, limiting its usefulness would be a nuisance. Remember, unless you give source code for a unit, another programmer can't change the routines in the unit, visible or not. **Recalc** works and is correct...so making it callable makes it less likely that a programmer will try to write a **Recalc**, and blow it.

Nobody said these decisions are easy or obvious. The more you think questions like this through, however, the better at it you'll become.

Attaching a User Interface to a Unit-Based Engine

Listing 8.1 is a completely functional mortgage calculation engine, including just about anything you'd need to create and maintain a mortgage amortization table in memory. That doesn't do you much good, however—since you can't readily look into memory to see what's in the table. (You can in fact inspect the mortgage table in memory with the Delphi Integrated Debugger, but that's certainly the hard way!) To make the mortgage engine or *any* engine really useful, you need to give it a user interface.

If you've been reading this book through from the beginning, by now you ought to have a reasonable idea of how a user interface is created: Basically, you drop components like buttons and memo boxes onto a form, and "wire them up" with code that responds to Delphi's events. But until now we've done all our coding within the event-handler procedures themselves. Our mortgage engine exists in a separate unit, outside of all event handling routines. Let's take a look at how the engine might be "wired in" to a Delphi form-based user interface.

The simplest possible user interface for the mortgage engine is a table control—called a *string grid* in Delphi jargon—and a button that quits the program. To make it a truly professional-quality mortgage calculator utility, you'll have to spend considerably more effort with dialog boxes and data-entry controls—but I'll let Jim handle that in the next chapter. For the purposes of attaching a user interface to the mortgage engine, all we really need is that string grid. The final results don't look half bad, either, as shown in Figure 8.3.

MortUnit Test Form						
Payment #	Principal	Interest	Prin. So Far	Int. So Far	Extra Prin.	Balance
102	147.49	517.81	11380.27	56480.33	0.00	88619.73
103	148.35	516.95	11528.62	56997.28	0.00	88471.38
104	149.22	516.08	11677.84	57513.36	0.00	88322.16
105	150.09	515.21	11827.93	58028.57	0.00	88172.07
106	150.96	514.34	11978.89	58542.91	0.00	88021.11
107	151.84	513.46	12130.73	59056.37	0.00	87869.27
108	152.73	512.57	12283.46	59568.94	0.00	87716.54

Quit

Figure 8.3 *An extremely simple mortgage calculator.*

The challenge is knowing when to create the mortgage table in memory, and when (and how!) to get that table displayed inside a string grid component. Since the string grid dominates the form, (and the form has no other controls on it, or any other real purpose) the proper time to create the mortgage table is when the form itself is created. There's an event for precisely that purpose, too: The form's OnCreate event. Inside an event handler for OnCreate, you should create the mortgage table by using the mortgage engine, and then load that table into the form's StringGrid component.

The type definition **TMortgage** is available for your use in the **MortUnit** unit. All you need to do to create a mortgage in memory is to declare a variable of type **TMortgage**. Voila! Your mortgage, Sir. Unfortunately, just declaring the variable does nothing to calculate the table proper, and a table full of zeroes is no mortgage at all. For that I've provided the **InitMortgage** procedure. Call **InitMortgage** from within the OnCreate event handler, with all the appropriate initial values filled in, and the name of the new mortgage passed as the first parameter. The new mortgage variable will then have a completed mortgage amortization table inside it, ready for display.

Displaying the mortgage table is actually the challenging part of this particular exercise. I've done the work for you, and the resulting form unit is shown in Listing 8.3. **UnitTest** is a good example of how to use data and procedures stored in units, and how to load data into a string grid. Read over the code in Listing 8.3, and we'll go over it in detail.

Note that all we're doing is *displaying* a mortgage table. The parameters for the mortgage are "hard wired" into the code that creates the mortgage, to simplify matters. The greater part of an application is often simply getting values from the user—and so it is here. By notto request initial values from the user, the code to display a mortgage table is *very* simple. About all the form does is create a mortgage and load it into a string grid component.

Listing 8.3　A user interface for the mortgage engine

```
{ This is the unit-based version of the }
{ example program shown as Listing 8.5  }

unit UnitTest;

interface

uses
  SysUtils, WinTypes, WinProcs, Messages, Classes, Graphics, Controls,
```

```
    Forms, Dialogs, StdCtrls, Grids,  { Borland's standard units }
    MortUnit;              { The unit-based mortgage engine unit }

type
  TUnitTestForm = class(TForm)
    Button1: TButton;
    UnitTestGrid: TStringGrid;
    procedure Button1Click(Sender: TObject);
    procedure FormCreate(Sender: TObject);
  private
    { Private declarations }
  public
    { Public declarations }
  end;

var
  UnitTestForm: TUnitTestForm; { Delphi plugged in this declaration   }
  Mortgage : TMortgage;        { This one you have to put in yourself }

implementation

{$R *.DFM}

procedure TUnitTestForm.Button1Click(Sender: TObject);
begin
  Close;  { Shut down the form and hence the program }
end;



{When the form is created on program startup, all this happens: }
procedure TUnitTestForm.FormCreate(Sender: TObject);

VAR
  I          : Integer;
  TempString : String15;

begin
  InitMortgage(Mortgage,
               100000.00, { Initial principal }
               0.07,      { Interest rate as decimal fraction, NOT %! }
               360,       { Periods in loan }
               12);       { Periods per year }

    WITH UnitTestGrid DO
      BEGIN
        { We need one row per payment plus a header row at the top: }
        RowCount := Mortgage.Periods+1;
        { Fill in the header row with the column caption strings: }
        Cells[0,0] := 'Payment #';
        Cells[1,0] := 'Principal';
        Cells[2,0] := 'Interest';
        Cells[3,0] := 'Prin. So Far';
        Cells[4,0] := 'Int. So Far';
```

```
      Cells[5,0] := 'Extra Prin.';
      Cells[6,0] := 'Balance';
    END;

  { Next we transfer the data from the mortgage record to the }
  { string grid on the form: }
  WITH Mortgage DO FOR I := 1 TO Periods DO
    BEGIN
      { To put the mortgage table into the string grid we must }
      { convert the numeric values in the mortgage table to    }
      { to strings.  That's what this messiness is for:         }
      WITH Payments[I] DO WITH UnitTestGrid DO
        BEGIN
          Str(I:5,TempString);
          Cells[0,I] := TempString;
          Str(PayPrincipal:12:2,TempString);
          Cells[1,I] := TempString;
          Str(PayInterest:12:2,TempString);
          Cells[2,I] := TempString;
          Str(PrincipalSoFar:12:2,TempString);
          Cells[3,I] := TempString;
          Str(InterestSoFar:12:2,TempString);
          Cells[4,I] := TempString;
          Str(ExtraPrincipal:12:2,TempString);
          Cells[5,I] := TempString;
          Str(Balance:12:2,TempString);
          Cells[6,I] := TempString;
        END;
    END;
end;

end.
```

Using the StringGrid Component

Delphi's StringGrid component is the display portion of a simple spreadsheet. There's no calculation behind it—all it does is display a grid of cells, within which you place string data. There's a highlighted cell that you can steer around the spreadsheet grid with the arrow keys, or else with the mouse. When more than the visible number of rows and columns have been loaded with string data, the StringGrid automatically brings up scroll bars, with no involvement on your part.

That's about it in terms of what a StringGrid can do—but that's about all we need in this application. To use a StringGrid to display a mortgage table, you're going to have to deal with a few design-time properties, and a few runtime properties. But from ten steps back there's remarkably little to it.

The first thing you have to do to configure the StringGrid you drop on a form is set up a fixed row and a fixed column for row numbers and titles. It's not as obvious in black and white as it would be in color, but in Figure 8.3, the top row and the leftmost column are a different color than the cells that contain numeric data. These different colored cells are the fixed row and column. If you have more data in the StringGrid than will display at one time, you can scroll the data...but the fixed row and column do *not* scroll, and remain on display to provide labelling information. I set the **FixedCols** and **FixedRows** properties both to 1, giving me one fixed row and one fixed column. The **FixedColor** property I set to **clBtnFace**. This makes the fixed row and column take on the same color as the face of the standard Delphi button component. You have your choice of a lot of different colors, both explicit (like *clTeal* and its cousins) and colors that take on the hue of standard Windows elements, like active scroll bars, inactive scroll bars, and so on. This is what *clBtnFace* is. You can change such colors from the Windows Control Panel utility—but gray is a good color and the Windows default.

The second design-time property you need to set is **Align**, the first property in the property window. Notice that in Figure 8.3, the StringGrid is as wide as the form, but not as tall, and that it seems to touch the top edge of the form's client area. A single property value sets this behavior: **alTop**. The **alTop** value tells the StringGrid to occupy the full width of the form, and place its top edge at the top of the client area. The bottom edge you can pull up or down to suit your form's design. Here, I placed a Quit button near the bottom edge of the form and didn't want the StringGrid to cover it, so **alTop** was a logical choice.

However, if you had used a pull-down menu instead of a Quit button (which is actually better practice but more complexity than I wanted in this simple example) you could set the **Align** property to **alClient**, which directs the StringGrid to occupy the entire client area, starting beneath the menu bar. Other available values allow you to align the StringGrid to the bottom edge of the form, or to the left or right edge of the form (while filling it top to bottom.) You can also set the **Align** property to **alNone**, which simply leaves the StringGrid in the size you made it when laying out the form. If the user resizes or zooms the form, however, the StringGrid will not "follow along." Some sort of alignment is usually a good idea, and a professional-quality spreadsheet-type application would have a pull-down menu bar and a grid that occupied the full client area.

You can set the number of rows and columns that a StringGrid will display at either design-time or runtime. In fact, my example program does some of both. The **ColCount** property is set to 7 at design time, and that's where it stays. There are seven columns of information to be displayed, no more, no less, and that doesn't change. The **RowCount** property is set to 360 at design-time, simply because the vast majority of mortgages are set up for 30 years of monthly payments, which is 360 payments total. However, nothing prevents you from displaying a 500-payment mortgage, or a 180-payment mortgage, or any other value. When the **TUnitTestForm.FormCreate** event handler procedure sets up the grid, it looks at the mortgage to see how many payments are in fact in the actual mortgage being displayed, and updates the **RowCount** property accordingly:

```
{ Need 1 row per payment plus a header row at the top: }
RowCount := Mortgage.Periods+1;
```

The number of payments in a mortgage is actually the number of periods, which is stored in the **TMortgage.Periods** field. We add one to it because we need to display that number of rows plus an additional row at the top for the column captions. Many if not all Delphi component properties that can be set at design time can also be set at runtime.

Loading the Cells in a StringGrid

The StringGrid component has other design-time properties you could tweak for different effects, and I encourage you to try them out to see what happens. (That's the main way you'll learn the nuances of Delphi—there's no way anyone can summarize the full range of its possibilities in anything less than a shelfload of books!) The single most important property of a StringGrid is in fact its **Cells** property, which can only be accessed at runtime. The **Cells** property is where the StringGrid stores the string data it displays when your application runs.

Cells is set up as a two-dimensional array, which I introduced briefly back in Chapter 6. You can look at it as a simple matrix of strings with two indexes: The first for columns, and the second for rows. Both indexes begin at 0. The easiest way to show how this two-dimensional addressing works is to show you the code that loads the top line of captions in the fixed row. (Look back to Figure 8.3 while you read this code):

```
WITH UnitTestGrid DO
    BEGIN
      { Need 1 row per payment plus a header row at the top: }
      RowCount := Mortgage.Periods+1;
      { Put the header strings in the grid: }
      Cells[0,0] := 'Payment #';
```

```
      Cells[1,0] := 'Principal';
      Cells[2,0] := 'Interest';
      Cells[3,0] := 'Prin. So Far';
      Cells[4,0] := 'Int. So Far';
      Cells[5,0] := 'Extra Prin.';
      Cells[6,0] := 'Balance';
   END;
```

The upper left corner of the grid is addressed as **Cells[0,0]**. As you move to the right in that top row, the first index increases by one for each column, while the second index (which specifies the row being addressed) remains at 0. Each cell is assigned a string literal in a simple assignment statement.

The rows are filled using a **FOR** loop, which runs from 1 to the number of periods in the mortgage, which may change from mortgage to mortgage. The control variable of the **FOR** loop selects one of the **TPayment** records in the **Payments** array of such records, and the string equivalents of the values in that **TPayment** record are loaded into the **Cells** array. Keep in mind that **Cells** can only hold strings; if you want to display numeric values (as we do here) you must convert them to strings with the **Str** standard procedure.

In terms of the addressing of the **Cells** array, notice in the code below that for loading the cells, the row is not held to 0 (as above), but to the value of the current payment record being loaded into the array. The columns are indexed from 0 through 6 using numeric literals to specify the column.

```
WITH Mortgage DO FOR I := 1 TO Periods DO
    BEGIN
      { To put the mortgage table into the string grid we must }
      { convert the numeric values in the mortgage table to    }
      { to strings.  That's what this messiness is for:        }
      WITH Payments[I] DO WITH UnitTestGrid DO
        BEGIN
          Str(I:5,TempString);
          Cells[0,I] := TempString;
          Str(PayPrincipal:12:2,TempString);
          Cells[1,I] := TempString;
          Str(PayInterest:12:2,TempString);
          Cells[2,I] := TempString;
          Str(PrincipalSoFar:12:2,TempString);
          Cells[3,I] := TempString;
          Str(InterestSoFar:12:2,TempString);
          Cells[4,I] := TempString;
          Str(ExtraPrincipal:12:2,TempString);
          Cells[5,I] := TempString;
          Str(Balance:12:2,TempString);
          Cells[6,I] := TempString;
        END;
    END;
```

Once the rows have been loaded with the mortgage data, the StringGrid has everything it needs to show your mortgage to the world. Load the MORTGAGE.DPR project and run it. There's not a great deal to it—most of the work is done for you in the StringGrid component.

FROM RECORDS TO OBJECTS

We've gotten a fair way along in this chapter, and we haven't really dealt with objects yet. That's a natural consequence of what objects are; just as the history of houses is the history of bricks, the history of objects is the history of both records and units. If you don't understand both records and units, your understanding of objects will be pretty superficial.

An object is a data structure, just as a record is. At the simplest possible level, you could look at objects as records to which procedure and function definitions have been added. That's far from the whole story—objects have at least two additional major tricks that Delphi uses in some pretty amazing ways—but welding code and data together is the foundation task given to objects. In an object, code and data are indeed two different sexes belonging to the same indivisible species.

Furthermore, an object is a package—just as a unit is. Objects and units are amazingly similar, and their fundamental difference is subtle: A unit is a *physical* package, existing as a disk file; whereas an object is a *logical* package, which exists in memory and takes part in far more of the "life" of a Delphi application than a unit can. Units and objects are both packages, but objects are far more than just packages. Most of what we'll talk about for the rest of this chapter is the role of objects as packages. To treat the "far more," I'll need additional space to run, and will have to hold off until Chapter 10.

Code and Data Welded at the Hip

Converting the simple record-oriented mortgage engine we developed earlier in this chapter to an object-oriented version is a good way to see the relationship between records and objects. The record type **TPayment**, for example, lines up to be an excellent object. Here's the type definition:

```
TPayment = CLASS(TObject)      { One element in the amortization table. }
              PaymentNum    : Integer;
              PayPrincipal  : Real;
              PayInterest   : Real;
              PrincipalSoFar : Real;
              InterestSoFar  : Real;
```

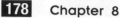

```
                ExtraPrincipal : Real;
                Balance        : Real;
                PROCEDURE GetStringForm(VAR StrPayNum,
                                            StrPayPrin,
                                            StrPayInt,
                                            StrPrinSoFar,
                                            StrIntSoFar,
                                            StrExtraPrin,
                                            StrBalance : String15);
            END;
```

There are really only two changes here. One is that instead of a record, **TPayment** is now defined as a *class*. A class is an object type. In Borland's earlier versions of Object Pascal, in fact, objects were defined with the reserved word **OBJECT** rather than **CLASS**. In moving to the word "class," Borland is aligning its thinking with older object-oriented languages like Smalltalk, as well as C++, which is the most widely-used object-oriented language today. The type of an object is its class. Delphi uses the class definition to create an instance of the class in memory at runtime. This instance is what is most properly called an object. It's important to keep this difference straight in your head, especially while you're first exploring object-oriented programming: A class is just a definition; a plan, if you will, for the construction of an *instance* of the class, which is the actual object. The class exists in your source code; the object exists in memory at runtime. The class is sheet music; the object is a song drifting in on the evening air.

The "TObject" in parentheses after **CLASS** indicates that our **TPayment** class builds upon an existing Delphi class called **TObject**. **TPayment** is in fact an extension of **TObject** and contains **TObject**, just as a floral arrangement could be considered an extension of an empty vase, and contains the vase. Delphi provides **TObject** as a kind of "foundation slab" for building objects upon, and I'll return to what that means shortly.

The second change is more obvious: **TPayment** now includes a procedure header for a new procedure, **GetStringForm**, that is not present in the record-based mortgage engine unit. Everything we would need to call **GetStringForm** is there in the class definition: The name of the procedure, and the names, types, and order of all of its parameters. A procedure or function defined as part of an object in this way is called a *method*. We've used that term in this book before, in speaking of the components Delphi provides for building applications. Delphi components are objects too—with some special features, true, but objects no less. Calling a procedure or function a method indicates that it's a part of an object somewhere, and has a specific mission for a specific data structure.

That mission is the answer to an obvious question: Why put a procedure header in a data structure, anyway? The whole idea is to associate data with the code that manipulates that data. What **GetStringForm** actually does (as we'll see when I show you the procedure's implementation) is convert the several numeric values stored in **TPayment** to string equivalents, and pass those string equivalents back to the caller in **TPayment**'s parameters. Its job is intimately connected with **TPayment**'s data, so building the procedure "into" the data structure makes a lot of sense. We no longer have to wonder which data structure **GetStringForm** works with. It works with **TPayment**. That is now obvious from its definition.

The **TMortgage** record becomes an object with equal ease. Again, your task is mainly to build the procedures that act on **TMortgage** into **TMortgage** itself, clearly associating code with the data it acts on. Here's the new class definition:

```
TMortgage =
   CLASS(TObject)
      Periods          : Integer;   { Number of periods in mortgage    }
      PeriodsPerYear   : Integer;   { Number of periods in a year      }
      Principal        : Real;      { Amount of principal in cents     }
      Interest         : Real;      { Percentage of interest per *YEAR*}

      MonthlyPI        : Real;      { Monthly payment in cents         }
      Payments         : TList;     { List object holding payments     }

      CONSTRUCTOR Init(StartPrincipal     : Real;
                       StartInterest      : Real;
                       StartPeriods       : Integer;
                       StartPeriodsPerYear : Integer);
      PROCEDURE SetNewInterestRate(NewRate : Real);
      PROCEDURE Recalc;
      FUNCTION  GetPayment(PaymentNumber   : Integer) : TPayment;
      PROCEDURE ApplyExtraPrincipal(PaymentNumber : Integer;
                          Extra         : Real);
      PROCEDURE RangeExtraPrincipal(StartPayment,
                          EndPayment : Integer;
                          Extra      : Real);
      PROCEDURE MultipleExtraPrincipal(StartPayment : Integer;
                          Extra        : Real);
      PROCEDURE RemoveExtraPrincipal(PaymentNumber : Integer);
      PROCEDURE RemoveAllExtraPrincipal;
   END;
```

Most of the procedure headers built into the **TMortgage** class were present in **MortUnit** as well. We've just married them to the data structure they serve. The procedure bodies themselves are, as before, defined in the implementation section of the unit that the class is defined in. (Classes are always defined in units.) We'll come back to that issue as well.

Active Data

The people who created object-oriented programming in the 1970s had an interesting perspective on objects, thinking of them as "active data." Prior to object-oriented programming, programmers considered data raw material or "dumb stuff" that program code beat on like a cook with a meat tenderizer. But if you build data manipulation code right into the data, it is no longer a passive slab of meat. It becomes a willing servant. When the job needs doing, you instruct the servant to go off and do it. You might tell such a servant "Go comb your hair!" The servant knows how to do this, and has the comb in his pocket. The servant, his comb, and his hair are all part of the same package.

The philosophy in creating objects is to define both the data and the machinery to manipulate it in one package. A mortgage object created this way carries all the machinery with it to calculate a loan amortization table, add extra principle to a payment or range of payments, and so on. Calling the **Recalc** method in **TMortgage** is tantamount to instructing the mortgage object, "Go regenerate your amortization table." Once you add the **Recalc** method to **TMortgage**, all **TMortgage** objects "know how" to regenerate that table. They're active data now. They can do it themselves.

UNITS AND OBJECTS

Like all other data types, classes are created within units. Assuming you want the class to be visible outside of the unit, place the class definition within the interface section of the unit. The implementations of all of the methods called out in the class definition must be in the implementation section of the unit.

When you implement a method in a unit, you must prefix the name of the class to which the method belongs to the name of the method itself:

```
PROCEDURE TMortgage.RemoveAllExtraPrincipal;

VAR
  I : Integer;
  TempPayment : TPayment;

BEGIN
  FOR I := 0 TO Payments.Count-1 DO
    BEGIN
      TempPayment := Payments.Items[I];
      TempPayment.ExtraPrincipal := 0.0;
    END;
  Recalc;   { Re-amortize the mortgage and rebuild the table }
END;
```

The qualified identifier **TMortgage.RemoveAllExtraPrincipal** pins down precisely which class the method serves. Apart from that, object methods are syntactically identical to any procedure or function that might be defined in a unit.

Note that in the method shown above, the **Recalc** method is called without any qualifier prefix indicating which class **Recalc** belongs to. That's OK—the compiler knows that **Recalc** belongs to **TMortgage** because the **Recalc** header was defined within the **TMortgage** class definition. Any object method can call any other method belonging to the same class without qualification.

Visibility in Units and Objects

Sharp readers will notice a significant difference in this routine that I haven't mentioned yet: There is no **ThisMortgage** parameter, as there is in the corresponding **RemoveAllExtraPrincipal** routine in **MortUnit**. Nothing is passed to the method to indicate which object it belongs to. How, then, does the method know which data to act upon?

Perhaps this question didn't occur to you, so let me emphasize that it's crucial. Recall that there is only one class definition for any given object—but that the class definition works as an "object factory" and can create any number of objects at runtime. Each object is a separate and independent instance of the object's class. So at runtime you can have several different instances of a class kicking around, each one with its own separate data values.

Perhaps this doesn't seem like a problem to you. When you call a method at runtime, after all, you prefix it with the name of the object instance you're working on:

```
ScottsdaleBankMortgage.Recalc;
```

No ambiguity here. But what about any methods that **Recalc** might call from inside itself? How do those methods know which object to act on? The compiler takes care of this for you by means of an invisible parameter passed to **Recalc**, which **Recalc** passes, in turn, to any methods that it calls. This invisible parameter tells the code which individual object instance to act upon.

If you look back to **MortUnit** (seen in Listing 8.1), you'll observe that its **RemoveAllExtraPrincipal** procedure relies completely on the **ThisMortgage** parameter to reference fields in the correct **TMortgage** record. In our initial unit-based mortgage engine, **ThisMortgage** is necessary with every single procedure or function that acts upon the **TMortgage** record. That being the case, Delphi "factors it out" and makes it an automatic mechanism once we change **TMortgage** to an object class instead.

To sum up: When *you* call an object method, you must specify which object instance that method call works with. However, the method you called "knows" which instance it's acting on, and it passes that instance invisibly to any methods that it calls.

INHERITING CREATION

Quite apart from this business of welding code and data together at the hip, objects have two additional tricks up their sleeves. One is called inheritance; the other polymorphism. Inheritance I'll deal with here; polymorphism is a lot more subtle, and I'll speak further of it in Chapter 10.

Inheritance is a feature of object-oriented programming whereby a class can be defined as an extension of an existing class. If you'll recall, when you define a new class, you have the option of including the name of an existing class in the definition statement. This existing class is the new class's *parent class*. The new class contains everything its parent class contains, plus all the additional things you might build into it. The first line of the **TPayment** class definition shows this. (I haven't included the details of the class definition.)

```
TPayment = CLASS(TObject)    { One element in the amortization table. }
```

Here, new class **TPayment** is built on Delphi's class **TObject**. **TObject** is **TPayment**'s parent class. Everything within **TObject** is automatically present in **TPayment**. You don't see it in your definition, but it's there.

So how do you find out what's actually inside **TObject**? Your best bet is to look up **TObject** (or any other Delphi-provided class you may be curious about) in Delphi Help. For nearly any class you might wish to use as a parent class, Delphi provides a detailed description of what that potential parent class contains. Figure 8.4 shows the Help page for **TObject**, listing its methods. Unlike most classes, **TObject** has no data fields. When you look up a class having fields, Delphi Help will list them. If you click on the name of any method, you'll bring up a brief description of that method. (Most of the methods of **TObject**, however, aren't likely to be of much interest to you until you begin delving *very* deep into Delphi's object-oriented powers.)

```
┌──────────────────────────────────────────────────────────────────────┐
│ ═                          Component Writer's Help                ▼│▲│ │
│ File  Edit  Bookmark  Help                                             │
│ Contents│ Search │ Back │  History │Search all│  <<  │   >>   │ Delphi │ API │
│ TObject Object                                                         │
│                                                                        │
│ Unit                                                                   │
│ System                                                                 │
│ The TObject object type is the ultimate ancestor of every object (and therefore, every component) in Delphi. │
│                                                                        │
│ Methods                                                                │
│ ClassInfo        DefaultHandler    Free             InstanceSize       │
│ ClassName        Destroy           FreeInstance     MethodAddress      │
│ ClassParent      Dispatch          InheritsFrom     MethodName         │
│ ClassType        FieldAddress      InitInstance     NewInstance        │
│ Create                                                                 │
│                                                                        │
└──────────────────────────────────────────────────────────────────────┘
```

Figure 8.4   *Delphi Help for the TObject class.*

Everything's At Least a TObject

Although in my example programs in this chapter I explicitly declare my objects as children of **TObject**, (so that I remind myself, and you, that this is the case) in fact *all* classes declared without an explicit parent class are child classes of **TObject**. Since all standard classes provided with Delphi descend from **TObject**, this guarantees that every single object class declared by you in Delphi will at minimum be a child class of **TObject**. This enforces a standard method of creating and destroying objects across all Delphi objects, (as I'll explain below) and also makes polymorphism possible across all objects, as I'll explain in Chapter 10.

Creating Objects

Only two of **TObject**'s methods are of any conceivable use to the beginning Delphi programmer. The more important of the two is **Create**. The **Create** method is how you create an instance of an object class. *Don't* make the common mistake of assuming that all you need to do to create an object is simply to declare a variable whose type is the object class:

```
VAR
  MyObjectInstance : ItsClass;  { This isn't enough! }
```

Don't get me wrong here: You *do* need to do this—as you can see in Listing 8.5 a little later in this chapter—but declaring a variable of an object's class isn't enough. Objects are special underneath the skin in a number of ways that I can't explain just yet, and they come to be in a two-step process. First you must declare a variable of an object's class, as shown above. Then you must create that object using its **Create** method:

```
MyObjectInstance.Create;
```

Keep in mind that you didn't build a **Create** method into class **ItsClass** when you wrote it. The **Create** method is part of the **TObject** class definition, and every class defined under Delphi has as its uttermost foundation the **TObject** class. So regardless of what class you define or what parent class it's based upon, at the bottom you'll find all of **TObject**'s methods, including **Create**.

What **Create** does involves an area of memory called the *heap*, which we won't be explaining in detail in this book. The heap is also known as *dynamic memory*, and it's called that because Delphi's underlying code can create and destroy variables there as it needs them. There is something called static memory where ordinary variables are created, but static memory is just that—unchanging during the time that an application executes—and ordinary variables take up space in static memory all the time a program runs. Variables in dynamic memory, however, can come and go as needed, and this makes much more effective use of your precious system RAM.

Objects can exist *only* in dynamic memory. The **Create** method lays them out on the heap and informs the hidden Delphi machinery that manages dynamic memory that the object exists, and says where it is. The static variable you might declare with an object's class is like a stake driven into the ground, holding the string of an airborn kite. The stake needs to be there, or the kite would fly away and be lost—but the stake without a kite is just a stake. Using the **Create** method is like launching the kite and tying its string to the stake.

The fact that all Delphi classes are child classes of **TObject** gives all Delphi object the same code for the **Create** method. This allows all objects to be created in an identical fashion. In a sense, the **TObject** parent class is a "broadcasting station" that distributes its code into all Delphi objects. We'll return to this notion of classes as distributors of functionality in Chapter 10.

Destroying Objects

Create has its opposite number in the **Destroy** method, which, like **Create**, is distributed to all Delphi objects through the **TObject** parent class. When you call the **Destroy** method for a specific object instance, that instance is removed from the heap so that whatever memory it had occupied becomes available for the use of new objects:

```
MyObjectInstance.Destroy;
```

This is the metaphorical equivalent of pulling in the kite string and putting away the kite. The stake (assuming your object was declared as a static variable) remains in the ground—but the kite is no longer flying.

Although it is absolutely essential to call the **Create** method for every object that you declare, you don't always need to call **Destroy**. When your Delphi application ceases running, all the memory that it uses is carefully recycled to Windows for re-use, whether you call **Destroy** on your objects or not. When **Destroy** comes in handy is in cases where your application creates multiple instances of an object at the user's request, and then allows the user to "close" the object or otherwise make it go away.

AN OBJECT-ORIENTED MORTGAGE ENGINE

With all that in mind, it's time to present an object-oriented version of the mortgage engine shown in Listing 8.1. The vast majority of the code is pretty much the same, and functionally it works the same way, with only one significant exception that will turn out to be an excellent example of the power of objects in action.

 **PROJECT**

An Object-Oriented Mortgage Engine and Simple Mortgage Calculator

We're going to build on the unit-based mortgage engine shown in Listing 8.1, and make use of Delphi's object-oriented technology. Instead of records we'll use objects, and convert all the procedures and functions associated with the mortgage objects into methods. We'll use Delphi's **TList** standard object to store the array of **TPayment** objects that describe a mortgage's payments.

USS LIBERTY MEMORIAL
PUBLIC LIBRARY

The object-oriented mortgage engine is shown in Listing 8.4. Notice that it's still stored physically in a unit. All classes are defined in units; for that matter, any and all Pascal code you might write for Delphi is stored in a unit. Units are how Delphi packages its Object Pascal code, and a Delphi application is simply a collection of units that relate to one another in well-defined ways through their **USES** statements and a central project file.

Listing 8.4   MORTLIB.PAS, an Object-Oriented Mortgage Engine

```
{————————————————————————————————}
{                    MORTLIB                         }
{              By Jeff Duntemann KG7JF               }
{                                                    }
{ A mortgage calculation "engine" for Delphi, with }
{ full use of the new Delphi VCL class libraries.   }
{ Written for *Delphi Programming Explorer*         }
{ Copyright (c) 1995 The Coriolis Group, Inc.       }
{                                                    }
{ Adapted loosely from code originally published    }
{ in DDJ for October 1991 — Last Updated 3/7/95     }
{————————————————————————————————}

UNIT MortLib;

INTERFACE

USES Classes;

TYPE
  String2  = String[2];    { Handy for state codes }
  String10 = String[10];   { Handy for 9-digit ZIP codes }
  String15 = String[15];
  String25 = String[25];
  String40 = String[40];
  String80 = String[80];

  TLender =
    RECORD
      LenderID      : Integer;
      LenderName    : String40;
      LenderAddress : String40;
      LenderCity    : String25;
      LenderState   : String2;
      LenderZIP     : String10;
      LenderPhone   : String25;
    END;

  TPayment = CLASS(TObject)    { One element in the amortization table. }
                PaymentNum    : Integer;
                PayPrincipal  : Real;
                PayInterest   : Real;
                PrincipalSoFar : Real;
```

```
             InterestSoFar   : Real;
             ExtraPrincipal  : Real;
             Balance         : Real;
             PROCEDURE GetStringForm(VAR StrPayNum,
                                         StrPayPrin,
                                         StrPayInt,
                                         StrPrinSoFar,
                                         StrIntSoFar,
                                         StrExtraPrin,
                                         StrBalance : String15);
          END;

  TMortgage =
    CLASS(TObject)
      Periods        : Integer;  { Number of periods in mortgage  }
      PeriodsPerYear : Integer;  { Number of periods in a year    }
      Principal      : Real;     { Amount of principal in cents   }
      Interest       : Real;     { Percentage of interest per *YEAR*}

      MonthlyPI      : Real;     { Monthly payment in cents       }
      Payments       : TList;    { List object holding payments   }

      CONSTRUCTOR Init(StartPrincipal      : Real;
                       StartInterest       : Real;
                       StartPeriods        : Integer;
                       StartPeriodsPerYear : Integer);
      PROCEDURE SetNewInterestRate(NewRate : Real);
      PROCEDURE Recalc;
      FUNCTION  GetPayment(PaymentNumber   : Integer) : TPayment;
      PROCEDURE ApplyExtraPrincipal(PaymentNumber : Integer;
                                    Extra         : Real);
      PROCEDURE RangeExtraPrincipal(StartPayment,
                                    EndPayment : Integer;
                                    Extra      : Real);
      PROCEDURE MultipleExtraPrincipal(StartPayment : Integer;
                                       Extra        : Real);
      PROCEDURE RemoveExtraPrincipal(PaymentNumber : Integer);
      PROCEDURE RemoveAllExtraPrincipal;
    END;


IMPLEMENTATION

{ This is not a method, but simply a "utility" function private }
{ to this unit.  It calculates a monthly payment.               } .

FUNCTION CalcPayment(Principal,InterestPerPeriod : Real;
                     NumberOfPeriods  : Integer) : Real;
VAR
  Factor : Real;

BEGIN
  Factor := EXP(-NumberOfPeriods * LN(1.0 + InterestPerPeriod));
  CalcPayment := Principal * InterestPerPeriod / (1.0 - Factor)
END;
```

```
{ This method exists to convert the numeric values inside the   }
{ TPayment Object to string forms for display in a TStringGrid. }

PROCEDURE TPayment.GetStringForm(VAR StrPayNum,
                                    StrPayPrin,
                                    StrPayInt,
                                    StrPrinSoFar,
                                    StrIntSoFar,
                                    StrExtraPrin,
                                    StrBalance : String15);


BEGIN
  Str(PaymentNum:5,StrPayNum);
  Str(PayPrincipal:12:2,StrPayPrin);
  Str(PayInterest:12:2,StrPayInt);
  Str(PrincipalSoFar:12:2,StrPrinSoFar);
  Str(InterestSoFar:12:2,StrIntSoFar);
  Str(ExtraPrincipal:12:2,StrExtraPrin);
  Str(Balance:12:2,StrBalance);
END;



CONSTRUCTOR TMortgage.Init(StartPrincipal      : Real;
                           StartInterest       : Real;
                           StartPeriods        : Integer;
                           StartPeriodsPerYear : Integer);

VAR
  I : Integer;
  InterestPerPeriod  : Real;

BEGIN
  { Set up all the initial state values in the TMortgage object: }
  Principal      := StartPrincipal;
  Interest       := StartInterest;
  Periods        := StartPeriods;
  PeriodsPerYear := StartPeriodsPerYear;

  Payments := TList.Create; {All objects must be created via Create }

  { We configure the Payments TList to expand to the exact size we need: }
  Payments.Capacity := Periods;

  { Create & add Period empty payment objects to TList: }
  FOR I := 1 TO Periods DO
    BEGIN
      Payments.Add(TPayment.Create);
    END;

  Recalc;   { Build the mortgage table }
END;
```

```
PROCEDURE TMortgage.SetNewInterestRate(NewRate : Real);

BEGIN
  Interest := NewRate;
  Recalc;   { Re-amortize the mortgage and rebuild the table }
END;


{ This method calculates the amortization table for the mortgage. }
{ The table is stored as the Items array inside Payments' TList.  }

PROCEDURE TMortgage.Recalc;

VAR
  I : Integer;
  RemainingPrincipal       : Real;
  PayNum                   : Integer;
  InterestThisPeriod       : Real;
  InterestPerPeriod        : Real;
  HypotheticalPrincipal    : Real;
  TempPayment, LastPayment : TPayment;

BEGIN
  InterestPerPeriod := Interest/PeriodsPerYear;
  MonthlyPI := CalcPayment(Principal,
                           InterestPerPeriod,
                           Periods);
  { Round the monthly to cents: }
  MonthlyPI := int(MonthlyPI * 100.0 + 0.5) / 100.0;

  { Now generate the amortization table: }
  RemainingPrincipal := Principal;
  FOR PayNum := 0 TO (Payments.Count-1) DO
    BEGIN
      { We must assign here because Payments doesn't "know" what  }
      { object type it contains.  The assignment gives "form" to  }
      { the object stored at Payment.Items[PaymentNum]. This will }
      { be the case throughout this unit.  You cannot use the items }
      { stored in TList directly, but must assign them to one of  }
      { the same type that you originally stored into the TList.  }
      TempPayment := Payments.Items[PayNum];
      { Calculate the interest this period and round it to cents:  }
      InterestThisPeriod :=
        Int((RemainingPrincipal * InterestPerPeriod) * 100 + 0.5) / 100.0;
      { Store values into payment object: }
      WITH TempPayment DO
        BEGIN
          PaymentNum := PayNum+1; { The payment number, counting from 1 }
          IF RemainingPrincipal = 0 THEN   { Loan's been paid off! }
            BEGIN
              PayInterest := 0;
              PayPrincipal := 0;
              Balance := 0;
            END
```

```
              ELSE    { There's still principal to repay }
                BEGIN
                  HypotheticalPrincipal :=
                  MonthlyPI - InterestThisPeriod + ExtraPrincipal;
                  IF HypotheticalPrincipal > RemainingPrincipal THEN
                    PayPrincipal := RemainingPrincipal
                  ELSE
                    PayPrincipal := HypotheticalPrincipal;
                  PayInterest  := InterestThisPeriod;
                  RemainingPrincipal :=
                    RemainingPrincipal - PayPrincipal; { Update running balance }
                  Balance := RemainingPrincipal;
                END;
              { Update the cumulative interest and principal fields: }
              IF PayNum <= 0 THEN { First payment; so cumulative values }
                BEGIN        { are simply the current values }
                  PrincipalSoFar := PayPrincipal;
                  InterestSoFar  := PayInterest;
                END
            ELSE      { We're not at first payment, so we must then reach back }
                BEGIN  { to previous payment to calculate cumulative totals:   }
                  LastPayment := Payments.Items[PayNum-1];
                  PrincipalSoFar :=
                    LastPayment.PrincipalSoFar + PayPrincipal;
                  InterestSoFar  :=
                    LastPayment.InterestSoFar + PayInterest;
                END;
          END;  { WITH }
      END;      { FOR }
END;            { TMortgage.Recalc }


FUNCTION TMortgage.GetPayment(PaymentNumber : Integer) : TPayment;

BEGIN
  GetPayment := Payments.Items[PaymentNumber];
END;


PROCEDURE TMortgage.ApplyExtraPrincipal(PaymentNumber : Integer;
                                        Extra         : Real);
VAR
  TempPayment : TPayment;

BEGIN
  TempPayment := Payments.Items[PaymentNumber];
  TempPayment.ExtraPrincipal := Extra;
  Recalc;   { Re-amortize the mortgage and rebuild the table }
END;


PROCEDURE TMortgage.RemoveExtraPrincipal(PaymentNumber : Integer);

VAR
  TempPayment : TPayment;
```

```
BEGIN
  TempPayment := Payments.Items[PaymentNumber];
  TempPayment.ExtraPrincipal := 0.0;
  Recalc;   { Re-amortize the mortgage and rebuild the table }
END;


PROCEDURE TMortgage.RemoveAllExtraPrincipal;

VAR
  I : Integer;
  TempPayment : TPayment;

BEGIN
  FOR I := 0 TO Payments.Count-1 DO
    BEGIN
      TempPayment := Payments.Items[I];
      TempPayment.ExtraPrincipal := 0.0;
    END;
  Recalc;   { Re-amortize the mortgage and rebuild the table }
END;


PROCEDURE TMortgage.MultipleExtraPrincipal(StartPayment : Integer;
                                           Extra        : Real);

VAR
  I : Integer;
  TempPayment : TPayment;

BEGIN
  I := StartPayment;
  REPEAT
    TempPayment := Payments.Items[I];
    TempPayment.ExtraPrincipal := Extra;
    Inc(I);
  UNTIL I > Periods;
  Recalc;  { Re-amortize the mortgage and rebuild the table }
  { Here, we clear out any unnecessary extra principal values. }
  FOR I := 1 TO Periods DO
    BEGIN
      TempPayment := Payments.Items[I];
      IF (TempPayment.Balance <= 0.00) OR
         (TempPayment.Balance < Extra)
      THEN TempPayment.ExtraPrincipal := 0.00;
    END;
END;


PROCEDURE TMortgage.RangeExtraPrincipal(StartPayment,
                                        EndPayment : Integer;
                                        Extra      : Real);
VAR
  I : Integer;
  TempPayment : TPayment;
```

```
BEGIN
  I := StartPayment;
  REPEAT
    TempPayment := Payments.Items[I];
    TempPayment.ExtraPrincipal := Extra;
    Inc(I);
  UNTIL (I > EndPayment);
  Recalc;      { Re-amortize the mortgage and rebuild the table }
  { Here, we clear out any unnecessary extra principal values: }
  FOR I := 1 TO Periods DO
    BEGIN
      TempPayment := Payments.Items[I];
      IF (TempPayment.Balance <= 0.00) OR
         (TempPayment.Balance < Extra)
      THEN TempPayment.ExtraPrincipal := 0.00;
    END;
END;


END.  { MORTLIB }
```

Apart from the syntax that declares the classes at the top, you'll see two significant differences between **MortLib** here and **MortUnit**, which was Listing 8.1. Every procedure and function that worked on the **TMortgage** record type in **MortUnit** had a **ThisMortgage** parameter of type **TMortgage**. That's gone now; the methods all know that they work with the **TMortgage** class.

Using Delphi's TList Object

The more significant difference lies in the way **MortLib** handles the array of payment objects of class **TPayment**. In Listing 8.2, the payments were a simple Object Pascal array of **TPayment** records. The difficulty with that is that the **Payments** array had to be declared to carry as many **TPayment** records as any mortgage would ever conceivably have. So although most mortgages have 30 years of monthly payments, and hence 360 payments, there is an occasional 50-year mortgage having 600 payments. Maybe 1 percent of all mortgages are 50-year mortgages, yet we need to take up all that extra room in the **Payments** array (which is considerable) in *every* mortgage record, against the odd chance of needing to express such an uncommon mortgage.

That's an awesome waste of memory.

Delphi gives us something to address this problem, and express as many **TPayment** objects as we need for any given mortgage, without wasting a single byte of memory. It's a predefined object class called **TList**, and it turns out to be a truly wonderful thing.

TList is not a visual component like the StringGrid. You don't pull it down from a tool palette to use it. It's present in one of Delphi's standard units called out in your main **USES** statement. All you need to do is declare a variable or field of class **TList**, and then create the **TList** using its **Create** method at an appropriate place in the program.

In the **MortLib** mortgage engine, I've replaced the **Payments** array in **TMortgage** with a **TList** called **Payments**. You can think of **TList** as a little machine that can do what an array does, and more, with tremendous flexibility. For example, the **Payments TList** doesn't need to be any larger than the mortgage it contains would require. After you create the **TList**, you can set one of its properties to the number of payments in the mortgage you're setting up. Here's the code, drawn from Listing 8.4:

```
Payments := TList.Create; {All objects must be created via Create }

{ We configure the Payments TList to expand to the exact size we need: }
Payments.Capacity := Periods;
```

The **Capacity** property tells the **TList** object how many **TPayment** objects it will need to contain. Sharp readers might object that it seems strange to define the size of the **TList** *after* it's created on the heap. Good point—but you must understand that when created, the **TList** doesn't reserve space for any **TPayment** obejcts at all. It just sets aside a little room for its core machinery. Every time you add a **TPayment** object to the **TList**, **TList** reserves just enough room on the heap for that payment. The **Capacity** property simply sets a upper limit to the amount of space that the **TList** is going to need.

Payment objects are stored into the **TList** using the **TList**'s **Add** property. It's done in the **TMortgage.Init** method, and I'll extract the code that does the adding here:

```
{ Create & add Period empty payment objects to TList: }
  FOR I := 1 TO Periods DO
    BEGIN
      Payments.Add(TPayment.Create);
    END;
```

This syntax may cause you a little headscratching. It's a special way of calling **Create** that you haven't seen before. What does it mean to pass a method call to another method? How can you pass "TPayment.Create" to **Payments.Add**? The secret is that the **Create** method can act as a function under certain

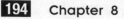

circumstances. As with any function, when you call it, it returns a value. The value returned by **Create** is in fact an instance of the object class name that precedes the call to **Create**.

This may seem a little peculiar. **TPayment** is a *class*, not an instance, and I warned you earlier about not confusing an object class with an object instance...so what do we get when we call **TPayment.Create**? *We get an object instance without a name.*

Names, Pointers, and Object Instances

The obvious way to create an instance of a class is to declare a static variable of the class, and then call **Create** on that variable:

```
VAR
  MyInstance : ItsClass;

MyInstance.Create;
```

You'll recall a little earlier that I compared this process to pounding a stake in the ground (where the stake is the static variable), launching a kite, and then tying the kite string to the stake. The static variable isn't the kite; it's just a way of anchoring the kite to a name that we can reference when we need to.

Well, the kite exists and it flies even before it's tied to a stake. You can stand there and hold the string if you want, for as long as you want. You can hand the kite string to someone else to hold, and walk away. After all, the kite's the thing, not the stake.

It's possible to create an object instance that has no direct connection to a static variable. The way to do this is to call the **Create** method, not on a particular instance of a class, *but on the class itself.* When done that way, **Create** becomes a function that returns a value, and that value is an instance of the class on which you call **Create**. The instance generated in this way has no name and is not associated with any static variable. It's the metaphorical equivalent of launching a kite with no intention of tying the string to a stake.

Pascal programmers from olden tymes will recognize this mechanism. The **Create** method in fact creates an object instance on the heap and returns a *pointer* to that object. This is the "string" by which we are connected to our kite. We can hand this pointer around, assign it to a static object variable if we want, or (as we do here) pass it to a method of another object. Delphi objects are manipulated solely through pointers. They are not explicit pointers, in that you don't have to declare a pointer type to handle an object, as you did in earlier Object Pascal implementations like Borland Pascal 7.0. With Delphi, the pointer references have all gone underground. You should be aware that they're there, however, and especially be aware of their limitations. (I'll be taking up the issue of those limitations in Chapter 10.)

Now, *something* has to be done with the nameless instance we generate with the class name and **Create**. It can't just sit there on the heap without any connection to the rest of your program. We can pass the instance along to a method of another object as a parameter, which is what is going on in the little excerpt of **TMortgage.Init** that I showed above:

```
Payments.Add(TPayment.Create);
```

Here, we're creating a nameless instance of **TPayment** and passing it as a parameter to a method belonging to the **TList** class; in this case an instance of **TList** called **Payments**. The **TList.Add** method adds the object to its internal array. This array is referenced by index, so there's no need at all to ever give a name to any of the **TPayment** objects that represent the payments of a mortgage.

We can read back or modify and update the objects from the **TList.Items** property, which is an array that can be indexed by the number of the loan payment we want to read or write.

This is majorly cool in my view, but it's not even close to stretching the capabilities of the **TList** class. Unlike an Object Pascal array, you don't have to tell **TList** what object class you're going to store in it. Furthermore, all the objects you store don't have to be of the same class. You could store any mixture you choose of **TPayment** objects and other objects of whatever class. With a little more complexity (actually, with explicit pointers) you can store non-objects in a **TList** as well.

Because only the objects we need to hold our loan table are created on the heap, we waste no memory on "extra" and unnecessary **TPayment** objects. There is some small use of memory for the **TList**'s overhead, but it's a small thing (a few hundred bytes) compared to the thousands of bytes we would waste in declaring a catch-all 600-payment array.

There's very little more to understanding the object-oriented mortgage engine. We can create a simple user interface around it, just as we did in Listing 8.2. The object-oriented user interface is shown in Listing 8.5.

Listing 8.5   OBJTEST.PAS, a Simple Object-Oriented Mortgage Calculator

```
{ This is the object-oriented version of the }
{ example program shown as Listing 8.3.      }

unit Objtest;

interface

uses
  SysUtils, WinTypes, WinProcs, Messages, Classes, Graphics, Controls,
  Forms, Dialogs, StdCtrls, Grids,   { Borland's standard units }
  MortLib;              { The object-oriented mortgage engine unit }

type
  TForm1 = class(TForm)
    MortgageGrid: TStringGrid;
    Button1: TButton;
    procedure Button1Click(Sender: TObject);
    procedure FormCreate(Sender: TObject);
  private
    { Private declarations }
  public
    { Public declarations }
  end;

var
  Form1: TForm1; { Delphi plugged in this declaration automatically }
  Mortgage : TMortgage;     { This one you have to put in yourself }

implementation

{$R *.DFM}

procedure TForm1.Button1Click(Sender: TObject);
begin
  Close; { Shuts down the form and hence the program }
end;

{ When the form is created on program startup, all this happens: }
procedure TForm1.FormCreate(Sender: TObject);

VAR
  I : Integer;
  TempPayment : TPayment;
  TempPayNum,TempPayPrin,TempPayInt,TempPrinSoFar,TempIntSoFar,
  TempExtraPrin,TempBalance : String15;

begin
  { Before we do anything else, we create a mortgage and fill it: }
  Mortgage := TMortgage.Create;
  Mortgage.Init(100000.00, { Initial principal }
```

```
            0.07,       { Interest rate as decimal fraction, NOT %! }
            360,        { Periods in loan }
            12);        { Periods per year }

  { Here we load the column captions into the StringGrid's header: }
  WITH MortgageGrid DO
    BEGIN
      { We need one row for each payment plus a header row at top: }
      RowCount := Mortgage.Payments.Count + 1;
      { Fill the header row with column caption strings: }
      Cells[0,0] := 'Payment #';
      Cells[1,0] := 'Principal';
      Cells[2,0] := 'Interest';
      Cells[3,0] := 'Prin. So Far';
      Cells[4,0] := 'Int. So Far';
      Cells[5,0] := 'Extra Prin.';
      Cells[6,0] := 'Balance';
    END;

  { Next we transfer the data from the mortgage object to the }
  { string grid on the form : }
  FOR I := 1 TO Mortgage.Periods DO { Once for each period }
    BEGIN
      { Remember here that Payments.Items indexes from *0*: }
      TempPayment := Mortgage.Payments.Items[I-1];
      TempPayment.GetStringForm(TempPayNum,
                                TempPayPrin,
                                TempPayInt,
                                TempPrinSoFar,
                                TempIntSoFar,
                                TempExtraPrin,
                                TempBalance);
      WITH MortgageGrid DO
        BEGIN
          Cells[0,I] := TempPayNum;
          Cells[1,I] := TempPayPrin;
          Cells[2,I] := TempPayInt;
          Cells[3,I] := TempPrinSoFar;
          Cells[4,I] := TempIntSoFar;
          Cells[5,I] := TempExtraPrin;
          Cells[6,I] := TempBalance;
        END;
    END;


end;

end.
```

Everything of interest here happens in the **OnCreate** event handler for the form. When the form is created, we create a **TMortgage** object and fill it with the specific parameters for a particular mortgage loan. Once the loan has been created and initialized via the **Init** method, we read the values back from the **TList.Items** array for loading into the StringGrid:

```
TempPayment := Mortgage.Payments.Items[I-1];
```

The **Items** property of the **Payments TList** is indexed just as any one-dimensional array would be.

THE EXPERIENCE OF OBJECTS

It isn't necessary to know all of Delphi to use a lot or even most of it. Similarly, you can use objects in simple programs without knowing anything more about them that I've been able to present in this chapter. That doesn't mean that this is all there is. Inheritance and polymorphism are extremely powerful abilities in the object idea, and if you understand them all the way down to the bottom, you will able to handle absolutely everything and anything that Delphi can throw at you.

I'll be coming back to object theory in Chapter 10, specifically to explain the "big picture" of objects and how they work in the abstract. Ordinarily I would have given you that explanation before the material in this chapter. But I had this hunch that the big picture of objects would go down a lot easier (and stick around a lot longer) if you had first seen objects at work, under your own hand, in a program that did something real and possibly even useful.

Let this all stew in your subconscious for a chapter, while Jim takes the object-oriented mortgage engine we worked out in this chapter, and turns it into a real, generalized mortgage calculator utility that you could use to shop for houses.

DELPHI AND THE DIALOGS

Jim Mischel

Most of the time, obtaining input from the user is done through dialog boxes, which Delphi makes easier than ever before.

As I write this, Debra is making lists, finding boxes, and trying to organize things for our upcoming move. I've accepted a new job, and in less than a month we pack all of our belongings into a U-Haul truck, put the dog and cat in the back, and leave sunny Arizona for new digs in Austin, Texas. It's going to be an interesting 30 days.

When we first started contemplating our move, it seemed overwhelming. We've been in the same house for over five years, and have accumulated an amazing amount of *stuff*. Just thinking about how many boxes it will take to pack all of our books is enough to make me shudder. And when we start thinking about the services we'll have to cancel, people we'll have to tell, friends we have to say goodbye to...what a nightmare!

It wasn't until we started making a list of all of the things we have to do, and then breaking those lists into other lists, that we realized that we just might be able to make this move without going insane. The process of compartmentalizing tasks—grouping related tasks together and thinking about them apart from other things that we have to do—helped us to get a handle on this huge project.

PROGRAMMING IN BOXES

All but the simplest Windows programs have *dialog boxes*—special windows that display information about the program and its current state, and allow you to change program parameters. Dialog boxes vary in complexity from the simple "About" dialog box common to most all Windows programs to multi-page options dialog boxes like Delphi's "Environment Options" dialog box.

By breaking a large program into smaller stand-alone pieces, it is easier to keep the program's overall structure in your head while at the same time allowing you to concentrate on the smaller details. The result is a reduction in program complexity—both internally *and* externally—which results in an easier-to-maintain and easier-to-use program. You keep the program's overall structure in your head, and pack away the implementation details into separate boxes. Then, all you have to worry about at any given time is how a particular box affects the main program.

In Delphi, dialog boxes are just forms to which you add some special machinery so that your program can display and interact with them. They're easy to create and even easier to use.

A Useful Mortgage Calculator

In Chapter 8, Jeff used the shell of a mortgage calculator application to test his mortgage calculation engine. In this chapter, we'll create a useful, working mortgage calculator based on that same engine, that allows you to change the mortgage parameters. Along the way, we'll explore a few more of Delphi's standard components, and see how to create and use dialog boxes. The completed mortgage calculator application is shown in Figure 9.1.

Main Form

We're going to completely re-do the main form from the one shown in Chapter 8, although we will retain the StringGrid component that actually displays the calculated amortization schedule. StringGrid is a nearly perfect vehicle for displaying this kind of tabular data.

Start with a new form and change the Object Inspector's properties as shown in Table 9.1.

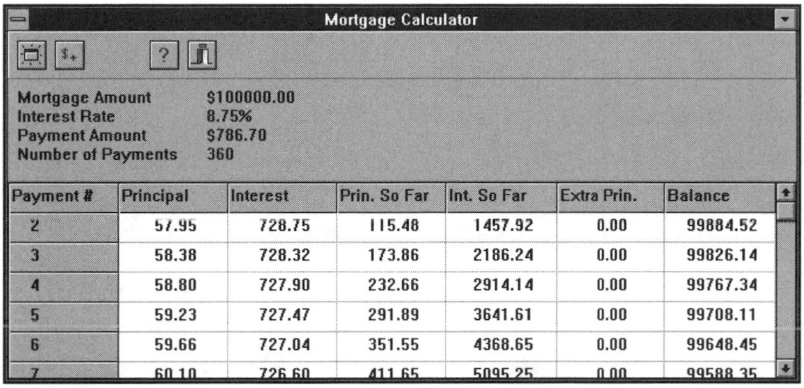

Figure 9.1   *The mortgage calculator application.*

If you like, you can change the **Height** and **Width** properties. I chose these numbers after a bit of experimentation: A **Width** of 677 is just big enough to accommodate the StringGrid component, and a **Height** of 390 allows us to display 5 payments without having to scroll.

Once you've set all those properties, save your work, calling the unit MORTFORM.PAS and the project MORTCALC.DPR.

Panel Component

If you look closely at Figure 9.1, you'll notice that there are four speed buttons arranged on a tool bar at the top of the form. These buttons reside on a Panel component, which is aligned with the top of the window.

Panels are very useful objects in that they can be used to group other components on your form. Components that are placed on a panel are positioned relative to the panel, which means that if the panel moves, so do the components on it. This makes it much faster to arrange control groupings on a form while keeping them aligned with one another.

Table 9.1   *Property Changes for the Mortgage Calculator's Main Form*

Field	Value
BorderIcons.biMaximize	False
Caption	"Mortgage Calculator"
Height	390
Name	"MortgageForm"
Width	677

Panels can also be aligned with the top, left, right, or bottom border of the window, so that when the window is resized, the Panel remains in the same position relative to the border. And since the Panel's components are positioned relative to the Panel itself, they move right along with it. Panels also have built-in support for fly-by hints, and a **Caption** property that lets you display text on the panel. All in all, the Panel component is an excellent choice as a foundation for a tool bar, tool palette, or status bar.

Select the Panel component from the component palette (it's way over on the right side of the Standard page), and drop it onto your form. Change its **Align** property to **alTop**, and set **ShowHint** to **True**. **ShowHint** is the "hook" that lets us add fly-by hints to the Panel's components. Blank out the **Caption** property, as the Panel won't be displaying any text. When you've finished, the Panel component should be positioned at the top of the form, and stretched across its entire width.

All by itself, this particular Panel isn't especially exciting. We need to put something on it to make it dance.

Speed Buttons

If your program only has a few options, why take the time to build a boring old menu when a tool bar can do the job just as well, and look better in the bargain? Speed buttons, implemented with Delphi's SpeedButton component, are special-purpose buttons that were designed specifically to be used on a tool bar or tool palette. The SpeedButton is similar to a standard Button component, but includes special internal machinery that allows it to interact with other SpeedButtons, and also with the Panel that contains it. It also lets you put a picture, rather than just text, onto the button's face.

To add the speed buttons to your panel, select the Additional page on the component palette, hold down the Shift key, and click on the SpeedButton component. Drop four buttons onto the panel, and be sure to click on the component palette's arrow cursor when you're done so that you de-select the SpeedButton component.

After you've added the SpeedButtons to your form, change their **Glyph**, **Hint**, and **Name** properties as shown in Table 9.2.

You'll have to use the Picture Editor dialog box, shown in Figure 9.2, in order to modify the **Glyph** properties. The bitmaps mentioned in Table 9.2 are located on the code disk for this book. If you don't want to add pictures to the

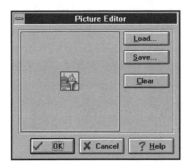

Figure 9.2   *The Picture Editor dialog box.*

Table 9.2   *Property Changes for the Tool Bar Speed Buttons*

Name	Hint	Glyph
btnNew	"New Mortgage"	"new.bmp"
btnExtra	"Extra Principal"	"extra.bmp"
btnAbout	"About"	"about.bmp"
btnQuit	"Quit"	"quit.bmp"

speed buttons, you can leave the **Glyph** properties set to "(None)", and edit the buttons' **Caption** properties so that there will be *something* on the button faces.

After you've added the buttons and changed their properties, save your work and press F9 to compile and run the program. Move the mouse over one of the speed buttons and leave it there for about a second so that the fly-by hint pops up. If you don't see any hints popping up, be sure that the Panel's **ShowHint** property is set to **True**, and each SpeedButton's **ParentShowHint** property is also set to **True**.

Finishing the Form

We only have a few more things to add to the main form. Select the Label component from the component palette's Standard page, drop four of them on your form, and change their **Caption** properties to "Mortgage Amount", "Interest Rate", "Payment Amount", and "Number of Payments". Arrange them in a column at the left side of the form just below the speed bar.

Next, select the Label component again and put four more labels onto the form, in a column to the right of the labels that you just added. These four

Table 9.3 *Property Changes for the Information Labels*

Name	Caption
lblMortgageAmt	"$0.00"
lblIRate	"0.00%"
lblPaymentAmt	"$0.00"
lblNumPmts	"0"

labels will display the actual information; that is, the parameters of the mortgage being displayed. Change their properties as shown in Table 9.3.

The last component to add is the StringGrid that will display the amortization schedule. Select the StringGrid from the Additional page of the component palette, and drop it onto your form just below the "Number of Payments" label. Change its properties as shown in Table 9.4.

ColCount gives us seven columns—one for each field the mortgage calculator displays for each payment. The **DefaultColWidth** of 92 pixels provides enough room to display a pretty big number, and a **Width** of 669—obtained by trial-and-error—is just the right size to hold seven columns and a vertical scroll bar. Setting **goThumbTracking** to **True** makes the contents of the grid scroll while the scroll bar thumb is being moved. When set to **False**, the grid's display doesn't change until the thumb is released. **Visible** is set to **False** so that the grid isn't displayed when the program starts up. You'll notice that we didn't set the StringGrid's **Height** property. We're going to have the program change that automatically when it starts, and whenever the form is resized.

Table 9.4 *Property Changes for the StringGrid Component*

Field	Value
ColCount	7
DefaultColWidth	92
Left	0
Name	"MortgageGrid"
Options.goThumbTracking	True
ScrollBars	ssVertical
Visible	False
Width	669

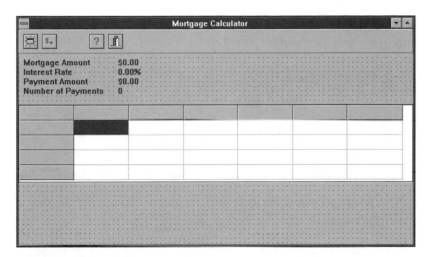

Figure 9.3   *The completed mortgage calculator form.*

When you've made those changes, your mortgage calculator form should look similar to Figure 9.3.

Startup and Exit

Now that we've got the main form designed, we can start adding features. The first thing to do is make the Quit button actually exit the program. Double-click on the Quit SpeedButton button to automatically create an OnClick event handler. Add this single line:

```
Close;
```

between the **begin** and **end** reserved words in the event handler. That'll take care of exiting the program when you click on the Quit button.

We also need to add a **TMortgage** variable to the form so that we have something to display in the StringGrid. In the Unit window add this line:

```
Mortgage : TMortgage;
```

in the **private** section of the form's **class** definition. Also, add MortLib to the list of units in the **uses** statement at the beginning of the program. Finally, create an OnCreate event handler for the form, and add this line:

```
Mortgage := TMortgage.Create;
```

to the event procedure. This will correctly create the **Mortgage** object so that the mortgage calculator can work with it.

ADDING A PROGRAM ICON

Before we start talking about dialog boxes, let's take a short intermission and add a program icon to the project. This is the icon that the Program Manager will display if you add the mortgage calculator application to a program group, and also the icon that we'll use when we construct the program's About box.

The program icon, shown in Figure 9.4, is located on the listings diskette in a file named MORTGAGE.ICO.

I created this icon using Delphi's Image editor. I'm no artist, so you can go ahead and laugh at this little icon if you like—I certainly did. The point of this exercise is more to show you how to attach the icon to the application than to display my artistic prowess.

To make this the program icon, select Options | Project from Delphi's main menu, and then select the "Application" page in the Project Options dialog box. Your display will look like Figure 9.5.

Figure 9.4 *The mortgage calculator icon.*

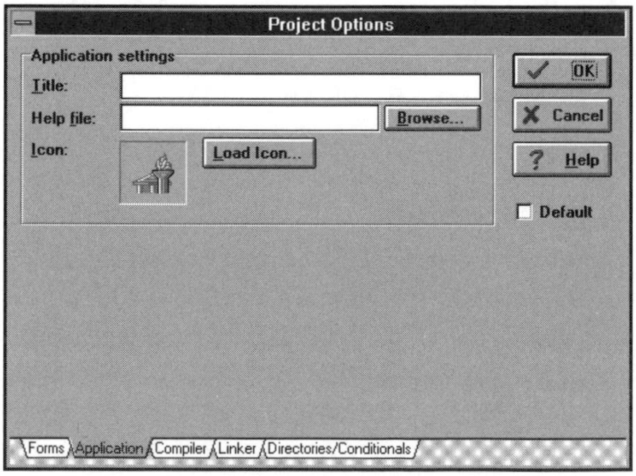

Figure 9.5 *The Application page of the Project Options dialog box.*

Just press the Load Icon button, and select MORTGAGE.ICO from the list of icons in the Application Icon dialog box. Then, press the OK button to close the Project Options dialog box.

The program's infrastructure is now in place. Press the Save Project button to save your work. We'll start our exploration of dialog boxes with a simple About dialog box.

DIALOG BOX BASICS

Dialog boxes are just forms. Really. The only thing that makes a dialog special is that it's not the main form. You create dialog boxes the same way that you create main forms: with the form designer, Object Inspector, Menu Designer, and all of Delphi's other tools.

Dialog boxes behave differently at run-time, based on the way that your main program tells them to appear. A dialog box can be modal or modeless. When a dialog box is *modal*, the user must close it before working on any other form. Any attempt to click outside the dialog or enter text outside the dialog triggers an error sound. A *modeless* dialog box, on the other hand, can remain active while the user works in other forms or other parts of the screen. You've already seen an example of a modal dialog box: In Chapter 5, we used the **ShowMessage** function to display a modal message box.

To create and use a dialog box in your program, you must perform the following steps:

1. Create the dialog box's form and event handlers.
2. Add the unit that contains the dialog box to your **uses** statement.
3. Create an instance of the dialog box in your program.
4. Write code to display the dialog box in response to some action by the user.

A Simple "About" Dialog Box

To see just how easy it is to create and display a dialog box, let's make a very simple About dialog box and attach it to the About button on our mortgage calculator, so that the dialog box is displayed when the About button is clicked.

Select File | New Form (or click on the New Form speed button) to create a new form. Select Blank form from the Gallery. (Yes, there *is* an About box template, but we'll discuss it a little later.) When the new Form window is displayed, go into the Object Inspector and change the form's **Caption** property to "About Mortgage Calculator" and the **Name** property to "Aboutbox1". Press F2 to save your work, calling the unit ABOUT1.PAS. Then, go back to the main form. Double-click on the About button to create an event handler, and add this line of code in the event procedure:

```
Aboutbox1.ShowModal;
```

Finally, add a **uses** statement to the **interface** section of the main form's unit, listing ABOUT1, like this:

```
uses About1;
```

Save your work, and press F9 to run the program. When the main form is displayed, click on the About button and your new About dialog box should appear.

Yes, it's really that easy. Of course, the About box we just designed isn't especially exciting, but it's *easy* to add a nice look. In the wide world of Windows programming, it's traditionally been easy to *design* dialog boxes, but something else entirely to display and manipulate them. Even something as simple as our minimal About dialog box would require a couple dozen lines of C or pre-Delphi Pascal code, and a fairly detailed understanding of things like instance handles and callback functions. (No, not in *this* book you don't!) With Delphi, we wrote 2 lines of code to get our About box, and we don't have to care at all about Windows' internal workings.

The About dialog box is modal. If it's on your screen, you can't switch back to the application that spawned it. You *must* close the dialog box before you can continue working in your application. If you want to make the dialog modeless, all you have to do is change a single line of code in your program. Just change the line in **TMortgageForm.btnAboutClick** to read:

```
Aboutbox1.Show;
```

and then re-run the program. The dialog box is now modeless, and you can switch between it and the main mortgage calculator form at will.

 **Following Windows Traditions**
You can create a modal or modeless dialog box as you choose, and in Delphi one is no more difficult than the other. You should begin to consider, however, that in Windows work there are certain traditions, and users have come to expect certain parts of programs to work in certain

ways. Dialog boxes are usually modal, and require a button-click or some other signal from the user to put them away. If you make your About box modeless, a user could forget to close the box, and the box would hang around, perhaps hidden behind the main form or some other window. This would cause no real harm (apart from using some memory needlessly) but if the user suddenly discovers an unsummoned About box beneath the File Manager window, it could trigger a pointless tech support call. Take the time to make sure you understand what "standard practice" is in Windows programming, to make sure your users understand how your programs work and aren't surprised at what they do.

Making a Better About Box

Now that you've seen how easy it is to display a dialog box from within your program, we can pretty up the About dialog box. First, select File|Remove File from Delphi's main menu, and select the Aboutbox1 form from the Remove From Project dialog box to remove our minimal About box from the project.

Select File|New Form, and select the About box form template from the Browse Gallery dialog box. Delphi will load the template and create a new Form window that looks like Figure 9.6.

The About box template form has everything you need for a simple About dialog box: an Image field where you can put your program's icon; Label fields for the product name, version number, copyright message, and comments; and an OK button. The template also sets some of the Form's properties for you to reflect the most common usage of an About dialog box. The **BorderStyle** property, for example, is pre-set to **bsDialog**, and the **Width** and **Height** properties are already set as required.

All you have to do is change the Form's **Caption** property, fill in the blanks with your program's specific information (and perhaps its program icon), and you have a customized About dialog box. No coding is required.

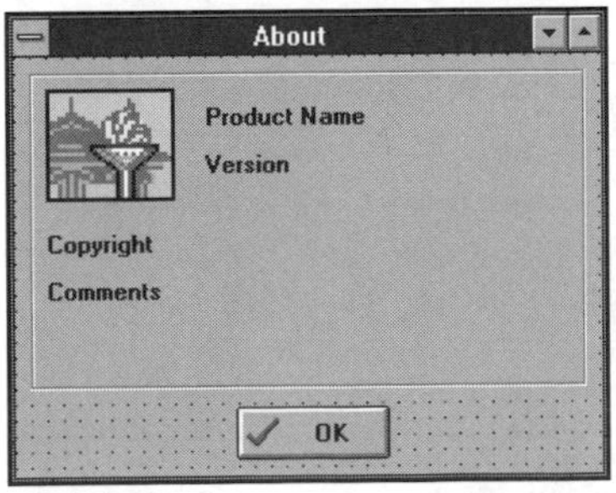

Figure 9.6 *The About box form template.*

You can change the information in the Label fields by modifying their **Caption** properties. With the exception of the Comments field, they all have their **AutoSize** properties set to **True**, so that when you change the **Caption**, the field will automatically size to fit the new text. If you're going to change the Comments field, you should set its **AutoSize** property to **True** first.

To change the picture that's displayed in the **ProgramIcon** Image component, simply double-click on its **Picture** property in the Object Inspector, and use the Picture Editor dialog box to load the icon, bitmap, or metafile that you want displayed here. If you like, you can use the MORTGAGE.ICO icon for the About dialog box, as well as for the program's icon.

The completed About box form is shown in Figure 9.7.

Before you continue, change the Form's **Name** property to "Aboutbox2" and press F2 to save the modified form. Call it ABOUT2.PAS.

Closing Modal Dialog Boxes

When a modal dialog box is closed, it returns a value to the program that displayed it. This return value is normally used to indicate how the dialog box was closed. For example, if you display a dialog box that has two buttons: OK and Cancel, you will almost certainly want to know which of those buttons was used to close the dialog box.

A modal dialog box has a **ModalResult** property that is used to return this information. Actually *all* forms have this property, but it's only used if the form is modal. This property is set to **mrNone** when you call **ShowModal** to display the dialog box, and the dialog box will remain active until you change **ModalResult** to a value other than **mrNone**. If you search for **ModalResult** in the online help, you'll see a list of eight possible values for this property. These are the possible return values for a dialog box.

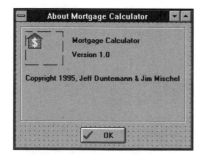

Figure 9.7 *The completed About box form.*

There are two ways to set the **ModalResult** property. The most obvious is to write a line of code that sets it in response to some event. For example, you could create an OnClick event handler for the About box's OK button that contains this line of code:

```
ModalResult := mrOk;
```

That would certainly do the trick, but it's one more line of code than you need. Since buttons are commonly used to close dialog boxes, Delphi buttons have a **ModalResult** property of their own, and you can change its value at design time. Setting a button's **ModalResult** property to **mrOk**, for example, tells that button to set its form's **ModalResult** property to **mrOk** when the button is pressed. This is the method our About box uses. If you examine the Ok button's **ModalResult** property in the Object Inspector, you'll see that it is pre-set to **mrOk**.

Buttons and BitBtns

You probably noticed that the About dialog box's OK button has a picture on it. This button is actually a BitBtn component—which is nothing more than a button that allows you to place a picture on it, as well as text. A BitBtn component has all of the properties of a standard button, plus some additional properties such as **Glyph**, **Kind**, and **Layout** that are used to define the button's picture and appearance.

The **Kind** property allows you to specify a standard button type—like **bkOk**, **bkYes**, **bkRetry**, and the like—for the button. If you set **Kind** to anything other than **bkCustom**, you don't have to specify a **Glyph** because Delphi already has built-in pictures for each of the standard button types. This is really handy, because it allows you to create a common look for all of your standard buttons with minimum effort. If you do specify **bkCustom** for this property, you'll have to use the Picture Editor to load a picture for your button.

The **Layout** property allows you to specify where you want the picture to appear on the button. Possible values for **Layout** are **blGlyphBottom**, **blGlyphLeft**, **blGlyphRight**, and **blGlyphTop**. The default is **blGlyphLeft**.

Displaying the New About Dialog Box

Before we move on, we need to make a couple of changes to our main form's code so that it references the new About dialog box, rather than the old one. We already removed the old About dialog box from our project, but that didn't change the code that we wrote to reference it. You need to make two changes:

- Change the reference to About1 in the **implementation** section's **uses** statement to "About2".
- Change the line in **TMortgageForm.btnAboutClick** so that it reads:

```
Aboutbox2.ShowModal;
```

Save your work and run the program. When you click on the About button, you should see the new About dialog box.

THE "NEW MORTGAGE" DIALOG BOX

The About dialog box is really just an information box. It doesn't accept any user input other than a mouse click that closes the dialog box. Information boxes like that make up only a very small portion of the dialog boxes that Windows programs use. Our mortgage calculator, for example, needs a way to get information from the user so that it can display an amortization schedule. The New Mortgage dialog box is the vehicle we'll use to obtain this information. The completed dialog box is shown in Figure 9.8.

Creating the Dialog's Form

Select File | New Form from Delphi's main menu, and then select the Standard Dialog template (the one with the buttons on the bottom of the form) from the Browse Gallery. When Delphi displays the new form, click on the Help button and press the Delete key to remove this button, and change the form's properties as shown in Table 9.5.

This dialog box will have three input fields: Mortgage Amount, Interest Rate, and Number of Payments. We'll need three Label components to hold the descriptions, and three Edit components to accept the input.

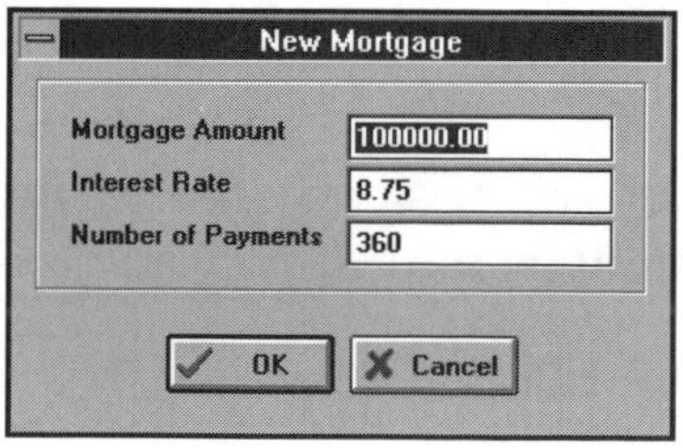

Figure 9.8   *The New Mortgage dialog box.*

Table 9.5 *Property changes for the New Mortgage dialog box*

Field	Value
Caption	"New Mortgage"
BorderIcons.biMaximize	False
Name	"NewMortDlg"

Select the Label component and drop three of them onto the panel in a column along the left side, and then use the alignment tools to line up the three components. Adjust the labels' **Caption** properties to those shown in Figure 9.8.

Then, select the Edit component and drop three of them onto the panel to the right of the Label components. Align them, blank their **Text** properties, and change their **Name** properties to "editMortAmt", "editIRate", and "editNumPmts", respectively.

Finally, change the Form's **ActiveControl** property to "editMortAmt" and make sure that the OK button's **Default** property is set to **True**. After you've made these changes, resize the panel, move the buttons, and resize the form so that it looks like Figure 9.8. Press F2 to save the form, calling it NEWMORT.PAS.

Making it Work

We need to add some initialization code, and an **Execute** method that will allow the mortgage calculator to access our new form. But first, we need to add some declarations to the form's **class** definition. In the Unit window, find the **TNewMortDlg**'s **class** definition, and add these lines to its **public** section:

```
{ Public declarations }
PrincipalBalance : Real;
InterestRate : Real;
NumberOfPayments : Integer;
Function Execute : Boolean;
```

These three fields are used to pass information back to the mortgage calculator, and the **Execute** function is the method that the mortgage calculator will use to display the dialog box.

Click on the form to select it, and in the Object Inspector double-click next to the OnCreate event to create an event handler. Enter these three lines of code in the event procedure:

```
MortgageAmount := 100000.00;
InterestRate := 0.0875;
NumberOfPayments := 360;
```

This will initialize the variables so that the edit fields will have some reasonable values the first time the form is displayed. Add the **Execute** function, shown in Listing 9.1, to the **implementation** section of NEWMORT.PAS.

Listing 9.1   The New Mortgage dialog's Execute function

```
Function TNewMortDlg.Execute : Boolean;
Var
  Temp : String[15];
  i : Integer;
Begin
  { set the edit fields' Text properties }
  Str (MortgageAmount:0:2, Temp);
  editMortAmt.Text := Temp;
  Str ((InterestRate*100):0:2, Temp);
  editIRate.Text := Temp;
  editNumPmts.Text := IntToStr (NumberOfPayments);
  ActiveControl := editMortAmt;

  { show the dialog box and check the return value }
  If ShowModal = mrOk Then Begin
    { if OK was pressed, get the new values }
    Val (editMortAmt.Text, MortgageAmount, i);
    Val (editIRate.Text, InterestRate, i);
    InterestRate := InterestRate/100;
    NumberOfPayments := StrToInt (editNumPmts.Text);
    Result := True;
  End
  Else
    Result := False;
End;
```

The **Execute** function is called by the mortgage calculator to display the New Mortgage dialog box. This function sets up the edit fields, shows the dialog box, and then sets the object's variables to reflect the entered information if the user closes the dialog box by pressing the OK button. If the dialog box is closed by pressing the OK button, **Execute** returns **True**. If any other method is used to close the dialog box (pressing the Cancel button or double-clicking on the control menu box), **Execute** returns **False**.

Before we continue, be sure to press F2 to save your work.

Always Execute

It's a good idea to add an **Execute** function to all of your dialog boxes. That way, your programs have a standard means by which they can display a dialog box and obtain its return value. It also allows you to hide dialog-specific implementation issues from the program. If we hadn't created the **Execute** function, then any program that wanted to use the New Mortgage dialog box would have to contain all of the code that's in the **Execute** function.

Including an **Execute** function also makes it much easier to change the dialog box in the future. If we add a field to the New Mortgage dialog box, we'll have to change the **Execute** function so that it will set up and retrieve the information from the new field. We'll also have to change a line or two of code in any program that wants to access the new field. But if we didn't have the **Execute** function, we'd have to add the setup and retrieval code to every program that uses the dialog box.

Why duplicate effort? Always include an **Execute** function. It'll save you time, and make things *much* easier when it comes time to change the dialog box's behavior.

Accessing the New Mortgage Dialog Box

Now that the New Mortgage dialog is finished, all we have to do is create an event handler for the mortgage calculator's New Mortgage button. This event handler will execute the New Mortgage dialog box, and display the new amortization schedule.

Select the mortgage calculator's form, and double-click on the New Mortgage button to create an OnClick event handler. When the Unit window appears, enter the code shown in Listing 9.2.

Listing 9.2   Executing the New Mortgage dialog and displaying the results

```
procedure TMortgageForm.btnNewClick(Sender: TObject);
begin
  With NewMortDlg Do
    { Execute the New Mortgage dialog box }
    If Execute Then Begin
      { calculate the mortgage }
      Mortgage.Init (MortgageAmount,
                     InterestRate,
                     NumberOfPayments,
                     12);
      { and display the results }
      InitMortgageDisplay;
    End;
end;
```

```
Procedure TMortgageForm.InitMortgageDisplay;
Var
  I : Integer;
  TempPayNum,TempPayPrin,TempPayInt,TempPrinSoFar,TempIntSoFar,
  TempExtraPrin,TempBalance, Temp : String15;
  TempPayment : TPayment;

Begin
  { initialize labels }

  Str ((Mortgage.Principal):0:2, Temp);
  lblMortgageAmt.Caption := '$'+Temp;

  Str ((Mortgage.Interest*100):0:2, Temp);
  lblIRate.Caption := Temp + '%';

  Str ((Mortgage.MonthlyPI):0:2, Temp);
  lblPaymentAmt.Caption := '$' + Temp;

  lblNumPmts.Caption := IntToStr (Mortgage.Periods);

{ Now initialize the mortgage grid }
  WITH MortgageGrid DO
    BEGIN
      RowCount := Mortgage.Payments.Count + 1;
      Cells[0,0] := 'Payment #';
      Cells[1,0] := 'Principal';
      Cells[2,0] := 'Interest';
      Cells[3,0] := 'Prin. So Far';
      Cells[4,0] := 'Int. So Far';
      Cells[5,0] := 'Extra Prin.';
      Cells[6,0] := 'Balance';
    END;

  { Next we transfer the data from the mortgage object to the }
  { string grid on the form : }
  FOR I := 0 TO Mortgage.Periods - 1 DO
    BEGIN
      TempPayment := Mortgage.Payments.Items[I];
      TempPayment.GetStringForm(TempPayNum,
                                TempPayPrin,
                                TempPayInt,
                                TempPrinSoFar,
                                TempIntSoFar,
                                TempExtraPrin,
                                TempBalance);
        WITH MortgageGrid DO
          BEGIN
            Cells[0,I+1] := TempPayNum;
            Cells[1,I+1] := TempPayPrin;
            Cells[2,I+1] := TempPayInt;
            Cells[3,I+1] := TempPrinSoFar;
            Cells[4,I+1] := TempIntSoFar;
```

```
        Cells[5,I+1] := TempExtraPrin;
        Cells[6,I+1] := TempBalance;
      END;
   END;
  { and make the mortgage grid visible }
  MortgageGrid.Visible := True;
End;
```

The **btnNewClick** event procedure in Listing 9.2 executes the New Mortgage dialog box. If **Execute** returns **True**, then the program calculates a new mortgage by calling the **Mortgage.Init** procedure in MORTLIB.PAS. After the mortgage is recalculated, **InitMortgageDisplay** is called to set up the labels that show the mortgage parameters and to fill the string grid with the payment information. The last thing that **InitMortgageDisplay** does is set the string grid's **Visible** property to **True** so that the grid will be displayed.

After you've entered Listing 9.2, add NewMort to the list of units referenced in the **implementation** section's **uses** statement, and add SysUtils to the **interface** section's **uses** statement. NewMort, of course, is the unit that contains the New Mortgage dialog box. SysUtils is a standard unit that is shipped with Delphi. It contains a number of useful objects, types, variables, and functions, **IntToStr**, which converts an integer to a string representation, among them.

Finally, be sure to add this line:

```
Procedure InitMortgageDisplay;
```

to the **private** section of the **TMortgageForm class** definition.

After you've made those changes, save your work and press F9 to compile and run the program. Click on the New Mortgage button to test the new dialog box.

RESIZING THE MORTGAGE GRID

Back when we created the string grid component on the mortgage calculator form, we left it at the default height. Now that we're actually displaying information in the grid, it'd be nice to have it automatically change its height so that it fills the form. This will allow us to enlarge the form in order to display more payments at once. And it's *easy* to do. All we have to do is create an **OnResize** event handler that computes and sets the string grid's size based on the form's new size.

Select the mortgage calculator's Form component, and in the Events page of the Object Inspector, double-click next to the OnResize event to create an event handler. The new **FormResize** event procedure is shown in Listing 9.3.

Listing 9.3 Resizing the string grid to fit the window

```
procedure TMortgageForm.FormResize(Sender: TObject);
var
  Temp : Integer;
begin
  Temp := Self.ClientHeight - MortgageGrid.Top;
  If (Temp < 100) Then
    Temp := 100;
  MortgageGrid.Height := Temp;
end;
```

EXTRA PRINCIPAL

Jeff's mortgage calculation engine was designed to let you enter extra principal payments for one or more payments, and then re-calculate the amortization schedule based on the new information. This lets you play "what if" to find out how much money you'd save (and how much sooner you could burn that mortgage!) if you paid an extra $20 per month on top of your regular house payment. Since the mortgage engine is all set up to handle extra principal payments, we might as well add a dialog box that lets us use the feature.

There are three ways to add extra principal: to a single payment, to a range of payments, or to all payments. If you just want to add extra principal to a single payment, then you only need two input fields: one for the payment amount and one to tell which payment number gets the extra principal. But if you're entering extra principal for a range of payments, then you need to enter the starting and ending payments, plus the payment amount. And if you're entering extra principal for all payments, you don't need to enter a starting or ending payment number at all. Probably the easiest way to handle this is to create a dialog box that changes its look depending on which of three radio buttons is pressed. The Extra Principal dialog box shown in Figure 9.9 works that way.

You've probably got the sequence of events down by now. First we design the dialog box's form. Then we write the code that makes the form work internally. Finally, we write the code in the mortgage calculator that executes the dialog and processes the results.

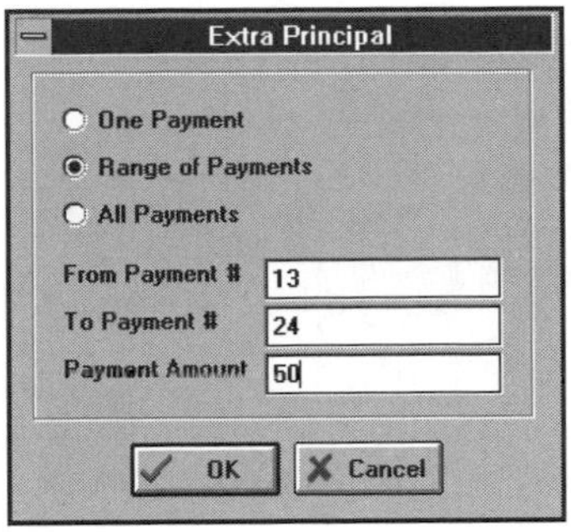

Figure 9.9   *The Extra Principal dialog box.*

Extra Principal Form

Create a new form using the Standard dialog box template from the Browse Gallery, delete the Help button, and set the form's properties as shown in Table 9.6.

Next, select the RadioButton component from the component palette and drop three of them onto the form. Set their **Caption** properties as shown in Figure 9.9, and change their **Name** properties to "rbOnePmt", "rbRangePmts", and "rbAllPmts", respectively. Set the **Checked** property on the "rbRangePmts" button to **True**, and set the other two's **Checked** properties to **False**.

We need three labels and three edit controls. First, select the Label component and drop three of them onto the form. Name them "lblFromPmt", "lblToPmt", and "lblExtraAmt". Then drop three Edit components onto the form, blank out their **Text** properties, and change their **Name** properties to "edFromPmt," "edToPmt", and "edExtraAmt".

After you've made those changes, use the alignment and sizing tools to arrange the components as you like them. When you're done, your form should look similar to Figure 9.10.

Before we continue, save the new unit as EXTRA.PAS.

Table 9.6   *Property Changes for the Extra Principal Dialog Box*

Field	Value
Caption	"Extra Principal"
BorderIcons.biMaximize	False
Name	"ExtraPrinDlg"

Figure 9.10 The completed Extra Principal form.

Reconfiguring a Dialog "On the Fly" in Response to Input

The only tricky part about this dialog box is how to handle the three different cases. What we're going to do is hide or display the first two labels and edit boxes based on which of the three radio buttons is checked. If the "One Payment" radio button is checked, then the first label and edit box will be displayed, and the label's **Caption** will be changed to "Payment #". If the "Range of Payments" radio button is checked, both labels and edit boxes will be displayed, and the labels' **Caption** properties will be as shown in Figure 9.10. And if the "All Payments" radio button is checked, neither of the boxes will be displayed. The Payment Amount edit box is always displayed.

It's not as much work as the above description makes it sound, and Delphi makes the job almost trivial. All we have to do is create an OnClick event handler for each of the three radio buttons, and enter the code shown in Listing 9.4.

Listing 9.4   The radio buttons' OnClick event procedures

```
procedure TExtraPrinDlg.rbOnePmtClick(Sender: TObject);
begin
  { Set the caption on the first label }
  lblFromPmt.Caption := 'Payment #';
  { make the first label and edit box visible }
  lblFromPmt.Visible := True;
  edFromPmt.Visible := True;
  { hide the second label and edit box }
  lblToPmt.Visible := False;
  edToPmt.Visible := False;
end;

procedure TExtraPrinDlg.rbRangePmtsClick(Sender: TObject);
begin
  { set the caption on the second label }
  lblFromPmt.Caption := 'From Payment #';
```

```
  { and make both labels and edit boxes visible }
  lblFromPmt.Visible := True;
  edFromPmt.Visible := True;
  lblToPmt.Visible := True;
  edToPmt.Visible := True;
end;

procedure TExtraPrinDlg.rbAllPmtsClick(Sender: TObject);
begin
  { hide both labels and edit boxes }
  lblFromPmt.Visible := False;
  edFromPmt.Visible := False;
  lblToPmt.Visible := False;
  edToPmt.Visible := False;
end;
```

You might want to take a moment to study how those three procedures correspond to the above description of the dialog box's behavior.

Execute Function

The Extra Principal's **Execute** function is similar to the New Mortgage dialog's. We need to set **public** variables that correspond to the three data entry fields, and an additional variable that indicates which of the radio buttons was pressed.

First, add these statements to the **public** section of the **TExtraPrinDlg**'s **class** definition:

```
{ Public declarations }
FromPayment : Integer;
ToPayment : Integer;
ExtraAmount : Real;
WhichButton : TExtraPaymentType;
function Execute : Boolean;
```

TExtraPmtType is an enumerated type that can take on one of three values: **eptOne**, **eptRange**, or **eptAll**. These three values correspond to the three radio buttons on the Extra Principal dialog. You need to define this type right before the **TExtraPrinDlg class** definition. Add the following line right after the **type** statement in EXTRA.PAS:

```
TExtraPaymentType = (eptOne, eptRange, eptAll);
```

Now all we have to do is write the code that initializes the dialog box's fields from the **public** variables, displays it, and sets the **public** variables based on the user's input. This code, implemented in the **TExtraPrinDlg.Execute** function, is shown in Listing 9.5.

Listing 9.5 The Extra Principal dialog's Execute function

```
function TExtraPrinDlg.Execute : boolean;
var
  Temp : String[15];
  i : Integer;
begin
  { set the radio buttons according to the value of WhichButton}
  rbOnePmt.Checked := (WhichButton = eptOne);
  rbRangePmts.Checked := (WhichButton = eptRange);
  rbAllPmts.Checked := (WhichButton = eptAll);
  { change the caption on lblFromPmt, if required }
  if (rbOnePmt.Checked) then
    lblFromPmt.Caption := 'Payment #'
  else if (rbRangePmts.Checked) then
    lblFromPmt.Caption := 'From Payment #';

  { set the label and edit components' Visible properties }
  lblFromPmt.Visible := Not rbAllPmts.Checked;
  lblToPmt.Visible := rbRangePmts.Checked;
  edFromPmt.Visible := lblFromPmt.Visible;
  edToPmt.Visible := lblToPmt.Visible;

  edFromPmt.Text := IntToStr (FromPayment);
  edToPmt.Text := IntToStr (ToPayment);

  Str (ExtraAmount:0:2, Temp);
  edExtraAmt.Text := Temp;

  { show the dialog box }
  if ShowModal = mrOk then begin
    { set variables as required }
    if (rbOnePmt.Checked) then begin
      WhichButton := eptOne;
      FromPayment := StrToInt (edFromPmt.Text);
    end
    else if (rbRangePmts.Checked) then begin
      WhichButton := eptRange;
      FromPayment := StrToInt (edFromPmt.Text);
      ToPayment := StrToInt (edToPmt.Text);
    end
    else    { rbAllPmts.Checked}
      WhichButton := eptAll;
    Val (edExtraAmt.Text, ExtraAmount, i);
    Result := True;
  end
  else
    Result := False;
end;
```

True, that's a bit of code—almost 50 lines. But it's pretty straightforward if you take it a bite at a time. The first part sets the dialog box's fields based on the values in the **WhichButton**, **FromPayment**, **ToPayment**, and **ExtraAmount** variables. Then the dialog box is executed, and if it returns **mrOk**, the variables are set from the input fields. There is a bit of code duplication here in that some of the functions that are performed by the **Execute** function are also performed by the individual radio buttons' **OnClick** event handlers. Code duplication is a good thing to eliminate whenever possible, and we'll eliminate ours after we tie everything together.

Before we continue, be sure to add SysUtils to the list of units in the **interface** section's **uses** statement.

Applying Extra Principal

Once you've added the Extra Principal dialog's **Execute** function, save your work and switch back to the mortgage calculator form. Then, double-click on the Extra Principal button to create an OnClick event handler and enter the event procedure code shown in Listing 9.6.

Listing 9.6   The Extra Principal dialog's OnClick event procedure

```
procedure TMortgageForm.btnExtraClick(Sender: TObject);
begin
  { don't display dialog box if no mortgage is displayed }
  if (not MortgageGrid.Visible) then Exit;

  with ExtraPrinDlg do begin
    if Execute then begin
      case WhichButton of
        eptOne :
          Mortgage.ApplyExtraPrincipal (FromPayment,
                                        ExtraAmount);
        eptRange :
          Mortgage.RangeExtraPrincipal (FromPayment,
                                        ToPayment,
                                        ExtraAmount);
        eptAll :
          Mortgage.MultipleExtraPrincipal (1,
                                           ExtraAmount);
      end;
      { and display the results }
      InitMortgageDisplay;
    end
  end
end;
```

Before I go into an explanation of how this code works, let's make sure it works. Add Extra to the list of units in the **interface** section's **uses** statement, save your work, and press F9 to test the program.

First, create a new mortgage. If you click on the Extra Principal button when there's no mortgage displayed, the OnClick event handler will return without doing anything. After you've displayed the new mortgage, click on the Extra Principal button, select one, range, or all, and enter the other values in the dialog box. When you press the OK button, the extra principal will be applied, and the mortgage recalculated and redisplayed.

EXIT AND CASE

There are two constructs in **TMortgageForm.btnExtraClick** that you haven't seen before: the **Exit** procedure and the **case** statement.

Exit isn't difficult to understand. The first executable line of code in this event procedure:

```
if (not MortgageGrid.Visible) then Exit;
```

simply checks to see if a mortgage is currently being displayed. If no mortgage is being displayed, then the **Exit** standard procedure is called. **Exit** immediately exits the procedure containing it, without executing any more code in that procedure. The program continues executing with the statement *after* the one that called the procedure—just as if the procedure was exited normally. **Exit** is a good way to get around excessive nesting inside of a procedure. For example, sooner or later you'll end up writing a procedure that resembles this pseudo-code:

```
if (some condition is true) then begin
  { do something }
  if (some other condition is true) then begin
    { do some more stuff }
    if (yet another condition is true) then begin
      { do more stuff }
      { if .... ad infinitum }
    end
  end
end
```

Writing this kind of code gets tiresome in a hurry, and excessive nesting of this sort is hard to keep straight, especially six months after you write it. The **Exit** procedure lets us change the sense of our tests and short-circuit all of that nesting, like this:

```
if (some condition is false) then Exit
{ do something }
```

```
if (some other condition is false) then Exit
{ do some more stuff }
if (yet another condition is false) then Exit
{ do more stuff }
{ ad infinitum }
```

Code that uses **Exit** in this manner is, to me, much easier to read and under-stand than is the nested **if** construct in the previous example. Structured pro-gramming purists don't like the **Exit** procedure because it breaks the cardinal rule that each procedure should have one, and *only* one, exit point. But I'm not a purist: I'm more interested in writing code that I can easily read, under-stand, and modify six months (or more!) down the road. If I have to break a few silly rules from time to time in order to make the procedure simpler, then that's the way it goes. Fortunately, the Structured Programming Police haven't confiscated my computer yet....

The case Statement

The **case** statement is another, more general way of eliminating excessive cascading **if** statements. In **TMortgageForm.btnExtraClick**, we have the following code, which is executed if the Extra Principal dialog's **Execute** function returns **True**:

```
case WhichButton of
   eptOne :
     Mortgage.ApplyExtraPrincipal (FromPayment,
                                   ExtraAmount);
   eptRange :
     Mortgage.RangeExtraPrincipal (FromPayment,
                                   ToPayment,
                                   ExtraAmount);
   eptAll :
     Mortgage.MultipleExtraPrincipal (1,
                                      ExtraAmount);
end;
```

This code is simply testing the value of **ExtraPrinDlg.WhichButton**, and executing a different function based on that value. Written using the standard cascading **if** construct, this code would be:

```
if WhichButton = eptOne then
  Mortgage.ApplyExtraPrincipal (FromPayment,
                                ExtraAmount)
else if WhichButton = eptRange then
  Mortgage.RangeExtraPrincipal (FromPayment,
                                ToPayment,
                                ExtraAmount)
```

```
else if WhichButton = eptAll then
  Mortgage.MultipleExtraPrincipal (1,
                                    ExtraAmount);
```

The advantage of the **case** statement is in the information that it provides. When you see the first line of a **case** statement:

```
case SomeVariable of
```

you know immediately that the program is branching to different conditions based on the value of **SomeVariable**. With the cascaded **if** construct, you'd have to examine each separate **if** statement to determine what is being tested. Both methods of testing a value are equally valid, but the **case** statement provides more information at a glance, and is bit easier to type.

There's also a performance issue involved in that the compiler can generate much smaller and more efficient code for a **case** statement than for a cascaded **if** statement. The performance gain won't be noticed in this particular context, but in some applications where performance and code size are an issue, replacing cascading **if** statements with a **case** statement will provide a dramatic increase in speed and reduction in code size.

The **case** statement can have an (optional) **else** clause, which is executed if none of the other cases match. For example, you could write this code fragment:

```
type
  PetType = (dog, cat, tiger, wolf);
var
  MyPet : PetType
begin
  MyPet := GetPetType;
  case PetType of
    dog : ShowMessage ('Nice doggie');
    cat : ShowMessage ('Here kitty, kitty!');
    else  ShowMessage ('You have an exotic pet!');
  end;
end;
```

In this code, if the **MyPet** variable is **dog** or **cat**, then the message for that specific pet is displayed. If **MyPet** is something else, then the code in the **else** clause is executed.

You can also have multiple cases execute the same code, like this:

```
case PetType of
  cat,
```

```
    tiger :
      ShowMessage ('Your pet is a type of cat');
    dog,
    wolf :
      ShowMessage ('Your pet is a type of dog');
  end;
```

In all, the **case** statement is a very useful tool to have around. The **if** statement is more commonly used, as it can test for multiple conditions and conditions other than equality, but **case** is the statement of choice if you have to select among many different values for a particular variable.

ELIMINATING CODE DUPLICATION

When I presented the Extra Principal dialog's **Execute** function, I mentioned that much of the code that it contains is duplicated by the event handlers for the dialog box's radio buttons. Indeed, each of the radio button's event handlers duplicates some of the code in the other event handlers. It's a good idea to eliminate code duplication wherever possible by encapsulating the duplicated code into a single procedure. That way, if you change the way things work, you only have to change the code in one place. It also makes for a smaller and more easily understood program. With that in mind, let's see how we can consolidate some of the code in the Extra Principal dialog box.

Identifying and Encapsulating Duplicate Code

The first step in removing duplicated code is identifying it. If you took the time to type in the code listings, you probably identified the duplicated portions in a hurry. In each of the radio button's event handlers, we're setting the **Visible** properties of the various components based on which radio button is currently selected. And in the **Execute** function, we do the same thing based on the value of the **WhichButton** variable. If you sit back and think about it for a moment, an obvious solution comes to mind: Why not create a procedure that does all this work, and pass it a parameter telling it which button is selected? The **TExtraPrinDlg.SetFieldsVisible** procedure, shown in Listing 9.7, does exactly that.

Listing 9.7   A procedure to serve several buttons

```
procedure TExtraPrinDlg.SetFieldsVisible (btn : TExtraPaymentType);
begin
  { change the caption on lblFromPmt, if required }
  if (btn = eptOne) then
    lblFromPmt.Caption := 'Payment #'
```

```
  else if (btn = eptRange) then
    lblFromPmt.Caption := 'From Payment #';

  { set the label and edit components' Visible properties }
  lblFromPmt.Visible := not (btn = eptAll);
  lblToPmt.Visible := (btn = eptRange);

  { if the label's not visible, neither is the edit box }
  edFromPmt.Visible := lblFromPmt.Visible;
  edToPmt.Visible := lblToPmt.Visible;
end;
```

This code does exactly what the code at the beginning of the original **TExtraPrinDlg.Execute** does. We've simply encapsulated it in a procedure so that it can be called by others. With this new procedure, we cut ten lines of code out of our **Execute** function, and the individual radio buttons' OnClick event procedures become one-liners, as shown in Listing 9.8.

Listing 9.8 The modified Execute function and OnClick event procedures

```
procedure TExtraPrinDlg.rbOnePmtClick(Sender: TObject);
begin
  SetFieldsVisible (eptOne);
end;

procedure TExtraPrinDlg.rbRangePmtsClick(Sender: TObject);
begin
  SetFieldsVisible (eptRange);
end;

procedure TExtraPrinDlg.rbAllPmtsClick(Sender: TObject);
begin
  SetFieldsVisible (eptAll);
end;

function TExtraPrinDlg.Execute : boolean;
var
  Temp : String[15];
  i : Integer;
begin
  { set the radio buttons according to the value of WhichButton}
  rbOnePmt.Checked := (WhichButton = eptOne);
  rbRangePmts.Checked := (WhichButton = eptRange);
  rbAllPmts.Checked := (WhichButton = eptAll);

  SetFieldsVisible (WhichButton);

  { Initialize field values }
  edFromPmt.Text := IntToStr (FromPayment);
  edToPmt.Text := IntToStr (ToPayment);
```

```
    Str (ExtraAmount:0:2, Temp);
    edExtraAmt.Text := Temp;

    { show the dialog box }
    if ShowModal = mrOk then begin
      { set variables as required }
      if (rbOnePmt.Checked) then begin
        WhichButton := eptOne;
        FromPayment := StrToInt (edFromPmt.Text);
      end
      else if (rbRangePmts.Checked) then begin
        WhichButton := eptRange;
        FromPayment := StrToInt (edFromPmt.Text);
        ToPayment := StrToInt (edToPmt.Text);
      end
      else   { rbAllPmts.Checked}
        WhichButton := eptAll;
      Val (edExtraAmt.Text, ExtraAmount, i);
      Result := True;
    end
    else
      Result := False;
end;
```

That's a significant decrease in code size, and the program's much more readable in the bargain. And this is just a simple example. When you write larger programs with many more options, the difference can be dramatic. It's always a good idea to sit back and *think* about what you're doing before you start banging away on the keyboard. You might also consider looking for ways to encapsulate duplicated code after you've gotten your program working. You've got nothing to lose but a little time, and the potential benefits—decreased code size and program complexity—are well worth the effort.

MODAL OR MODELESS?

Modeless dialog boxes do have their uses—probably the most common being status dialog boxes that display ongoing information about a long process. In addition to status dialog boxes, modeless dialog boxes can also be used for tool palettes, or for separate windows in a multiple-window program.

Whereas displaying a modal dialog box stops execution of the procedure that displayed the dialog box, displaying a modeless dialog box adds the new dialog box to the list of active windows. Since the procedure that shows a modeless dialog box continues to execute while the dialog box is displayed, modeless dialog boxes don't normally return information to the procedures that display them.

More so than modal dialog boxes, modeless dialog boxes are "just forms." They're created in the same way that other forms are created, and their function usually doesn't affect the functioning of the rest of your program.

MOVING ON

We touched on a lot of new subjects in this chapter: panels, speed buttons, icons, dialog boxes, and **case** statements, to name a few. We also created a useful little program that's seeing some pretty heavy use here as Debra and I contemplate the purchase of our new house in Austin.

Dialog boxes can do *anything* your program's main form can do. They are forms, after all, and as such have all of the rights and privileges of other forms. You'll want to experiment with dialog boxes to see all of the things you can do with them. As a first experiment, you might try adding a "Clear all extra principal" radio button to the mortgage calculator's Extra Principal dialog box. This exercise will give you some experience in adding features to an existing program, and is a pretty useful option to boot. The mortgage calculating engine in MORTLIB.PAS already has routines, **RemoveExtraPrincipal** and **RemoveAllExtraPrincipal**, which will do this—all you have to do is figure out how to instruct them to do it.

Our Object All Sublime

Jeff Duntemann

Our object all sublime, which shall be seen in time, is to create a Grand Design— a Delphi Grand Design!

In the fall of 1974 I was out of school, had a job fixing Xerox machines, and my poor 1968 Chevelle was crumbling into rust. So I did the obvious: I bought a new car. A new car—a brand new Honda Civic—and (without giving it much thought) a whole new way of driving. The Honda was a stick shift. I had never driven a stick shift before. How hard could it be?

The day the car was ready to go, my friend Art drove me down to Hejhal Oldsmobile in the western suburbs of Chicago, and dropped me off. My new toy and I were on our own. Like I said, how tough could it be to drive stick?

Well, maybe a little tougher than it looked.

We got home alive, Tigger (as I named the car) and I, though not without a significant amount of growling and grinding of gears—not to mention howls from the driver's seat. I suspect I killed the engine no more times than could be expressed in a standard integer, assuming you ignore that road sign bit.

But by the next day, hey, mon, no sweat. I even went to the airport to pick up Carol, and parked in one of those concrete garages with a very steep circular ramp. And after that little adventure, stick was a breeze. Almost. More or less.

Like Uncle Louie said more than once: One or two good scary projects'll learn ya.

LEARNING AND UNLEARNING

On the other hand, stick a kid in a five-speed with no previous experience, and they're off with a roar. My trouble was I already knew how to drive, had been driving since I was 16, and had burned the whole process into my synapses. For me it was automatic, and to have to actually *think* about driving again was almost more than I could bear. I had to unlearn everything I knew, down to a very deep, almost instinctual level, before I could drive quite as automatically as I drove Shakespeare (my first Chevelle) all the years I had him.

Something like this happens when people confront objects for the first time. If you've never programmed before, well, you're off with a roar. If you take the time to read the book and think it over, no sweat. One or two good scary projects'll learn ya.

The people who have trouble are the people who have been doing it The Other Way for years 'n' years. The better you know something, the tougher it is to unlearn it.

In Chapter 8, I approached objects from a hands-on perspective. An object is something like a record with code welded on, and something like a unit. With that taken on faith, I led you through the rest, and *showed* you what Delphi objects could do, more than I *told* you. If there's a problem here, it's because I couldn't tell you the whole story. If you're new to objects, you're probably way ahead of me. If you don't already know how to program, objects make sense almost immediately and become second nature in a day and a half. But if you're an old-school structured programmer with 572 years in grade, you're probably still in trouble.

The purpose of this chapter is to help you experienced programmers do a little un-learning. Newcomers should read this chapter too, because I'm going to hand you the rest of the story, piece by piece, so that the entire edifice stands before you, bathed in (sheesh, I hope!) the golden light of clarity.

So let's begin by reviewing a little bit of what I covered in Chapter 8.

ENCAPSULATION REDUX

The fundamental thing to understand about objects is that both code and data are bound up into a single structure. (I suppose an object is a "data structure," but I hate to use that term because an object is more than just data.) This aspect of objects is called *encapsulation*, a word that in a Delphi context implies way more than it delivers, and thereby confuses people some.

"Encapsulation" as it's used in the world at large implies that something is buried or hidden inside something else. And in the beginning, that's how it really was: The first rigorous object-oriented language, Xerox's Smalltalk, embedded an object's fields inside the object to the extent that you couldn't read from or write to the fields from outside the object. Not at all! That's encapsulation, fersure. The key was that you had to "get at" an object's fields by way of its methods and *only* its methods.

In practice, this meant that most fields inside an object had two associated methods: One to set a value into the field, and another to return a value to a program calling the method. If we were writing in Smalltalk, the **TMortgage** type would have to have a lot more methods than it does. These two would be necessary, for example:

```
PROCEDURE TMortgage.SetPeriods(NewPeriodsValue : Integer);
BEGIN
   Periods := NewPeriodsValue;
END;
FUNCTION TMortgage.GetPeriods : Integer;
BEGIN
   GetPeriods := Periods;
END;
```

(And there would be a lot more very similar to this.) Now, a method belonging to a class can read and write the class's fields (otherwise the fields wouldn't be very useful), so the method acts as a middleman between the class's fields and the code that uses the class somehow.

The Smalltalk people were rather fundamentalists about this privacy of a class's fields to the class itself. They had their reasons, some of which were good and some of which were, well, good reasons if you were a fundamentalist who sat in a beanbag chair thinking deep thoughts for a living and never had to create code that sold on the open market to pay the bills. For example: If you don't know much about the nature of the fields inside an object, you won't make assumptions about those fields when you write code that uses the object. This also allows the creators of the object to change the internal representation of the data in the object without causing havoc with code that uses the object. If for some reason you wanted to express the number of mortgage periods internally as a string rather than an integer, you could do so—and convert between string and integer values within the methods.

This makes sense in certain applications, and if you anticipate that the nature of the data in a class might need to change in the future, you can "insulate" it from the outside world by allowing access only through a suite of methods. The downside is that every method call takes a little bit of time and a little bit of space, and in a major application that overhead can add up. So Delphi compromises, and allows you to be only as paranoid as you want to be in creating your own object classes. You can make a class's data seriously private if you wish, or you can do as I did in **TMortgage** and just let anyone who wants to reference the fields directly.

This same philosophy is taken by most modern mainstream object-oriented languages, including C++ and Delphi's Object Pascal. Encapsulation today means that code and data are present *together* in the same structure. You can build walls around the data if you choose, walls breachable only through the class's methods. But it's your choice. The walls are only possible because code and data belong to the same structure.

Data in the Active Voice

Encapsulation makes possible the first "object weirdness" that trips up people accustomed to programming in the old way. In what we call "structured programming" (a term that today carries just a hint of scorn about it), code and data were two very distinct sorts of things, and code was definitely what got all the press and most of the attention. You defined data items like records, and then you defined procedures and functions to act upon and manipulate those records. The meatgrinder metaphor sums it up in a gross sort of a way: Data was something you fed into the hopper while you turned the crank on the code. Transformed data came out the other side, and if you wrote the meatgrinder correctly, what you got was out of it was what you wanted.

This notion of code as the transforming machinery and data as the raw materials is one possible functional model for programming. It was a way of thinking about the whole business of computing, and a general plan-of-plans for creating programs. Such a functional model is often called a *paradigm*. "Paradigm" is a much-abused term I avoid these days, but you should be aware of it.

What structured programming certainly is is a *mindset*. Structured programs tend to have a beginning and an end and operate in a fairly linear fashion: input, processing, output, done. A more subtle consequence of the structured programming mindset is that the way a program operated was pretty rigid. There was a preset plan, and the user had to follow that plan, because that was the only path through the program.

When you combine code and data into objects, this whole mindset gets turned on its ear. It's no longer quite appropriate to think of feeding the data into the meatgrinder, *because the data is now part of the meatgrinder.* This is where a lot of object-oriented headaches begin. You must unlearn the meatgrinder mindset; you have to start putting data more stage-center, and begin thinking of data in the active voice. In an object, the data has the power to act. The data "knows" how to manipulate itself.

Data, Center Stage

I guess where we went wrong the first time is that we started having way too much fun building meatgrinders. It's a natural human tendency, I think: We're attracted to the stuff that moves and buzzes and lights up and makes noise. But we have to keep reminding ourselves that *data* is what we're doing this for. The document is what we hand the boss, not the word processor. The cash flow statement is what guides us through the daily operations of our business; once the spreadsheet program spits it out, the spreadsheet program is quickly (if temporarily) forgotten about.

Object-oriented programming allows us to return to this real-world mindset. If a mortgage table is what we want, then we should build a mortgage table. Give it the power to recalculate its amortization schedule, change its interest rate, add extra principal to one or more of its payments. Then, when we want the amortization schedule recalculated, we call a method that says, in a metaphorical sense, "Go recalculate your table for me."

A mistake would be to begin with a mindset that says, "Now, how do we calculate a payment for a mortgage?" Stop right there; if not the gates to hell, that sort of thinking is certainly the gates to the La Brea tar pits. The *first* thing to do is model the mortgage in data, and then determine what "powers" that data needs to become useful to us. Only after we have a complete data model of the mortgage should we begin casting about for payment calculation algorithms. (I stepped through the development of such a data model for mortgages back in Chapter 8, which you should read if you haven't already.) Yes, you need the payment algorithm in either event—but by going after payment calculations first, you distort your whole view of what a mortgage *is*.

That's the goal of data modeling: To create a complete, workable representation of some real-world idea. Object-oriented thinking requires that we define that model first, before creating any code to manipulate the model. You have to know what the object is before you can divine what it does.

The Question of Scale

Readers who have used Delphi a little might throw in an objection here. Many of the Delphi objects look more like meatgrinders than data models of anything useful. The Edit component, for example, sure looks like something you grind string data with. You load a string value into a **TEdit**'s **Text** property for editing, and you can read it out when you're done.

This is true. But what you have to remember is that **TEdit** *always* contains a string value in its **Text** property. You can copy a different value in for editing, but you can also think of an Edit component as a string that "wears" its editing machinery like a carpenter carries tools on a leather belt. The string value, after all, is the point of having an Edit component, no?

But the larger conceptual problem here is that Delphi's components (all components are objects) are not the end results of the software development process. They are pieces of many potential applications that you might create, use, and distribute. At that small scale—a minor component in a much larger work—the object-oriented mindset changes a little. An Edit component is certainly code and data encapsulated together—but rather than being an active data model of some larger idea, it is a "standard part" with which you create such a data model. Objects can be and almost invariably are used as parts in building larger objects.

And at the very bottom of the scale are data items that are too small to be objects at all. Theorists have suggested that *everything* should be an object, right down to the individual number and ASCII character—and some erstwhile programmers did things that way—but at that atomic scale, the advantages of object orientation cannot outweigh the burden of object overhead. To make our programs run quickly and not be massively oversize, atoms simply have to be atoms.

INHERITING CREATION

If all you're going to do is use Delphi's "canned" objects to create simple applications, you don't need to know a great deal more about objects than what I've discussed so far. If you think that you've begun to catch the whiff of a Grand Design, however, you're right—and that Grand Design has two other major elements that you'll need to understand if you intend to go further.

The more important of the two—and perhaps the linchpin of all ambitious object-oriented systems—is *inheritance*.

The term "inheritance" is much more evocative of its meaning than "encapsulation." Inheritance is that aspect of object-oriented programming whereby you can define a new object class as a *descendant* of an existing class. The new class inherits everything that the existing class is. Every field and every method in the ancestor (or parent) class exists in the descendent (or child) class, before you add a single new thing to your new class. The parent class is almost literally a foundation slab upon which you build your new class.

If you recall, when we created a new **TPayment** class in Chapter 8, we defined it as a descendant of an existing class called **TObject**:

```
TPayment = CLASS(TObject)    { One element in the amortization table. }
      PaymentNum      : Integer;
      PayPrincipal    : Real;
      PayInterest     : Real;
      PrincipalSoFar  : Real;
      InterestSoFar   : Real;
      ExtraPrincipal  : Real;
      Balance         : Real;
      PROCEDURE GetStringForm(VAR StrPayNum,
            StrPayPrin,
            StrPayInt,
            StrPrinSoFar,
            StrIntSoFar,
            StrExtraPrin,
            StrBalance : String15);
      END;
```

Because the **TPayment** class inherits from **TObject**, it has within it everything that **TObject** has. You don't see any of that in its class definition shown above, but every last little piece of **TObject** is right in there with the fields like **PaymentNum**, **Balance**, and so on.

Great, you say—I inherit the Invisible Man. How do you know what's inside **TObject**, and how to use it? To a degree that's a good question, but to a

greater degree it may be the *wrong* question. Only a couple of things inside **TObject** are of direct use to you, the Delphi programmer—especially the beginning Delphi programmer. Those uses are documented in Delphi's manuals, and I'll explain them here as well. There is a general method of looking at your objects to see all of the things that are inside them (Delphi's Object Browser), but that's a more advanced topic that I can't explain in detail in this small book. However, when I say that the question, "How do I use the power of **TObject** in my programs?" is the wrong question, what I mean is that inheriting from **TObject** isn't done for *your* benefit. It's done for Delphi's—or perhaps for the benefit of that Grand Design you may be starting to sense.

Common and Uncommon Ancestors

A far better question here would be the following: "What does it *mean* to inherit everything that **TObject** is into my classes?" That question may seem philosophical, but it *is* philosophical, and strikes at the heart of what we're doing with object-oriented programming. We are modeling things—creating representations of larger ideas—and in doing that we begin to move away from simpler questions like, "Will this compile?" A far more important question is simply what an object actually *is*.

In this case, the answer is that a **TPayment** object is a model of a mortgage payment. But because it inherits from **TObject**, it is also a **TObject**. And because it is a **TObject**, it is now a part of Delphi's Grand Design.

All classes in Delphi are descended from **TObject**, and only **TObject** descends from nothing earlier. **TObject** is thus the *root class* in Delphi's *class hierarchy*. It is the common ancestor of all Delphi classes, and is the common thread tying all Delphi classes into the Grand Design.

The framework of the Grand Design is a hierarchy of object classes, with **TObject** at the top and all other classes descending from it. The **TPayment** and **TMortgage** classes descend directly from **TObject**. Most predefined Delphi classes are part of whole families of classes, descending down from **TObject** in layer after layer. From **TObject** descends **TPersistent**, and from **TPersistent** descends **TControl** (and others as well). From **TControl** descends **TWinControl**, from which descends **TButtonControl**, from which (finally!) descends **TButton**, that handy little guy you probably drop on your forms more than anything else. At every layer in the hierarchy is a layer of functionality that all objects descending through that layer share. At every layer is a new opportunity for a new class to "split off" from the existing hierarchy and be somehow different from every class down to that point.

There's your Grand Design! Don't you see it? No? Not even a little? Then I guess I'd better be a trifle more specific.

THE GRAND DESIGN

Every year about October they begin to arrive in the arts 'n' crafts stores: White Styrofoam cones of various sizes. Middle-class mothers with children buy them by the cartload to make Christmas decorations in the shape of little Christmas trees. This is an enduring Christmas tradition if ever there were one; shall we say it was well-entrenched in 1959 and was still going strong at the end of 1994.

Back in 1959, my mother bought the usual collection of Christmas cones, and she and my little sister painted the cones and glued macaroni noodles, beads, sequins, and other thingies to them to add a festive touch. I got a cone too, but I made *my* cone into a spaceship. This involved a different configuration of macaroni noodles and a different color of paint, but when I was done, nobody would mistake what I had made for a Christmas tree.

Those styrofoam cones were, in a sense, abstract Christmas tree decorations. They were everything that *all* Christmas tree-shaped decorations should be, but there was nothing specific about them. They were a shape, and that was all. We had to take them and add color, spangles, and Creamettes "ornaments" to make them into real Christmas tree-shaped decorations. I would guess that of the tens of thousands of cones that went home with middle-class mothers in the fall of 1959, no two ended up looking exactly alike—but they all started out with the identical styrofoam cone. The fact that any 7-year-old could also turn them into perfectly serviceable spaceships lent credence to my contention that there was nothing specifically Christmas tree-ish about them. They were abstractions; mere cone shapes, not especially useful as they came off the store shelf. They were places to start. They made it unnecessary for us to gash ourselves up whittling cone-shaped forms out of wood or (God help us) wreck the kitchen molding them out of papier mache. That was certainly (from the perspective of millions of middle-class mothers) a big plus.

What if this were possible with software?

It is. Borland did it. You can too.

From the Abstract to the Specific

The obvious thing that Delphi does to make developing applications easy is to provide a suite of useful program parts: Buttons, forms, edit controls, labels, scroll bars, database data sources, and so on, Erector-set style. That's a cool idea but hardly a brilliant one; after all, we've had Erector sets (albeit ones made of metal and not software) since the turn of the century.

The brilliance in Delphi's approach to standard parts for programmers comes in the way the parts were laid out and created. Rather than simply drawing up a list of useful software components and then turning a team of crack programmers loose to create them, Borland did some serious thinking about what all those parts on the list actually *were*, (philosophy again, sheesh!) how they were similar, and how they were different.

They looked hard at what the components had in common. They asked a lot of hard questions like, What makes a button a button and not a check box? What makes an edit box an edit box and not a label? They created charts on which component functionality was shown in layers. Relatively abstract features shared by a lot of different kinds of components was migrated up the chart toward the top. The most specific features, those that made single components unique apart from all others, sank to the bottom.

I've created a chart of this sort for Figure 10.1. Read it carefully, and see if you get the feeling for the nature of the top-to-bottom continuum. It's a scale from the abstract at the top to the specific at the bottom.

Now, programming is a results-oriented craft that emphasizes the useful. A lot of people therefore have trouble conceptualizing what an "abstract component" might be. Think back to those naked white styrofoam cones that we made into Christmas trees (or spaceships) in 1959. Now consider Delphi's object class **TPersistent**. An object of class **TPersistent** is a sort of rolling chassis. It has the machinery, if you will, that allows it to be brought in from its place in the .EXE file on disk at the time a program starts running. *It has nothing else.*

So what good is that? By itself, not much. You would never actually create an *instance* of class **TPersistent**. But if you wanted to create a new class that had the ability to be brought in from disk at program startup, that much of the work is already done for you. The naked styrofoam cone is available, and you add to it whatever makes your class unique.

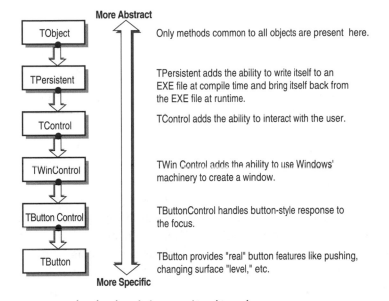

More Abstract

TObject — Only methods common to all objects are present here.

TPersistent — TPersistent adds the ability to write itself to an EXE file at compile time and bring itself back from the EXE file at runtime.

TControl — TControl adds the ability to interact with the user.

TWinControl — TWin Control adds the ability to use Windows' machinery to create a window.

TButton Control — TButtonControl handles button-style response to the focus.

TButton — TButton provides "real" button features like pushing, changing surface "level," etc.

More Specific

Figure 10.1   *Functionality distributed along an object hierarchy.*

The "what is it?" question occurs here. What *is* an object of class **TPersistent**? Because it's a child class of **TObject**, it's a **TObject**, meaning that it's an integral part of the Delphi Grand Design. But it is also a *persistent object*. A persistent object is one that can be written out to disk and brought back again, with all its methods and fields intact. When you create a new form and save it to disk, it can happen because the form "knows how" to write itself out to the application's .EXE file, and bring itself back again when the application runs. Your form can do this because it descends from **TPersistent**. That's where it got the machinery by which it writes itself to the .EXE file and reads itself back again. The same is true of all the components that you drop onto your form. The buttons, the panels, the edit boxes, the labels, all of them are descendants of **TPersistent**. When your application runs, they too know how to bring themselves in off disk. All of those components are different, and may not have much else in common. However, they all have in common the power to write themselves to your application's .EXE file at compile time, and to read themselves from your application's .EXE file at runtime.

Abstract Classes as Points of Departure

TPersistent is an *abstract class*. It exists to act as a "functionality repository" that new classes can draw on if they need that functionality. In this case, it contains the functionality allowing classes to read themselves from and write themselves to the application EXE file. Many, if not most of the classes in the Delphi Grand Design are abstract classes. If you look back to Figure 10.1, every class I listed there *except* the bottommost one is an abstract class.

Each class coming down from the top is a little less abstract and contains a little more functionality than the one above it. Each class grows a little closer to usefulness and a little further from total generality.

So why so many steps? The difference between **TControl** and **TWinControl** seems fairly slight. Why draw any distinction between the two at all? This is a very key point: The more abstract the classes that exist, the more distinctions can be drawn between new classes that descend from them. Each of the abstract classes shown in Figure 10.1 is a "branching point" that allows creators of new classes to begin precisely where their new classes differ from all other classes. Each time a programmer designs a new class, he or she has to think about where to make that "hard right turn" away from the existing Delphi class hierarchy.

Here's an example of such a decision: Class **TControl** and its children know how to interact with the user of an application. That's what a "control" is— something by which the user controls operation of an application. If you wanted to create a class that was a displayable bitmap, you wouldn't need to interact with the user. A bitmap is just art on the wall; it has no buttons to push and nothing for the end user to interact with. So what is a bitmap? Well, one thing it *isn't* is a control. That means a bitmap class would not descend from **TControl**. It would branch off of the class hierarchy above **TControl**— probably at **TPersistent**.

But perhaps not. The smart class designer studies the Delphi class hierarchy looking for possible "points of departure." What you want is an abstract class that comes as close as possible to what your desired new class must do, but doesn't go so far as to limit what your new class can do. Sometimes that takes a little thought, and at times it's a tough decision to make. But making such decisions is part of being a programmer in an object-oriented context.

In fact, the right place for a **TBitmap** class is beneath the **TGraphic** class. **TGraphic** has everything a display graphics class ought to have, without the graphics itself. It's like a general-purpose art frame, which might contain an oil, an acrylic, batik, or a collage—but until you add the art, it's simply an empty frame. If you didn't notice the presence of **TGraphic**, you might have gone to a lot of trouble duplicating in your **TBitmap** class what **TGraphic** had already implemented. By defining your **TBitmap** class as a child of **TGraphic**, you do two important things: You avoid duplicating effort by not re-implementing functionality already implemented in **TGraphic**; and you ensure that your new class operates as much in harmony with Delphi's other classes as it's possible to be.

I've drawn a portion of the Delphi class hierarchy in Figure 10.2. It's not all there—in fact, what I've shown is just one tiny corner of a class hierarchy that contains over a hundred classes in all. What's important to understand from Figure 10.2 is that an object hierarchy is not just one line from abstract to specific, but a line that branches and sub-branches again and again. Each class can have many child classes. **TPersistent** has a great many, of which I've only shown a few.

Your Classes Are the Most Specific of All

You might wonder what this has to do with you, since if you're just starting out, it may be a while before you begin defining your own classes beyond the simplest, like the **TMortgage** or **TPayment** classes I discussed in Chapter 8. But the truth is, you've defined new classes since the very first program you

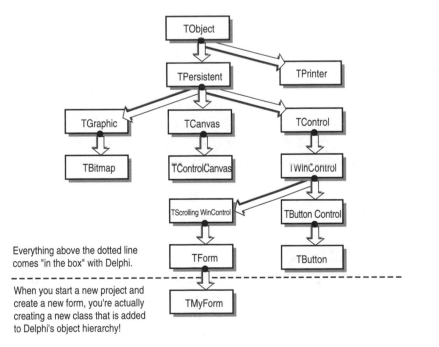

Figure 10.2   A portion of Delphi's object hierarchy.

wrote in Delphi. When you pull down a new form and begin dropping components on it, *you are creating a new class.* It's totally visual creation, but after completing a project, if you look at the Object Pascal code file created with the project, you'll see a definition something like this:

```
type
   TForml = class(TForm)
      MortgageGrid: TStringGrid;
      Button1: TButton;
      procedure Button1Click(Sender: TObject);
      procedure FormCreate(Sender: TObject);
   private
   { Private declarations }
public
   { Public declarations }
end;
```

You created this class—Delphi simply wrote it down for you, in the Object Pascal code file for your project. This particular class definition is for the form used for the simple mortgage calculator presented in Chapter 8, and can be seen in Listing 8.5—but the ones for the forms you create will look very similar.

In creating a new form, you begin with an abstract class—**TForm**—and quite literally begin building on it. When you drop a component on a form, Delphi goes behind the scenes and adds a field to the new form class that you're creating. (This is another "weirdness" that has nothing to do with objects: A compiler that writes part of your source code for you! Hey, gang, we're in the future!) When you double-click on an event and create a new event handler procedure, Delphi adds the procedure body to the same Object Pascal code file, and allows you to fill in the guts of that event handler procedure. You're starting with an abstract form class that is very general, and has everything that *all* forms need, but not one whit more. You make it a specific kind of form, one that does the work that you need done. Your form classes are thus the most specific of all Delphi's many classes, since they are specific to you alone, apart from all the other hundreds of thousands of Delphi users.

Behold the Grand Design!

Now do you see what Borland's up to? With Delphi's object hierarchy, Borland has not only implemented a large, powerful set of software components from which you can build new applications, they've "spread out" the functionality of those components into a class hierarchy, and made the components *and* the hierarchy available to you. At many points in the hierarchy, there are abstract classes that encapsulate some set of functionality that you can build upon.

The process of choosing just where in the hierarchy a new class should go is largely one of starting at the most abstract class in the hierarchy, and moving class-by-class toward the specific. At each class you stop and ask whether the class you wish to create "is" of that class. If it is, you continue on down the hierarchy to the next most specific class. If the answer is no, you've reached the point at which you must depart from the existing hierarchy and add your new class. (This process is actually a little more involved than that, because the hierarchy is not a single line but a *tree*—and what you're in fact doing is searching a tree, branch by branch, looking for the proper branch from which to sprout a leaf.)

If you choose your "point of departure" carefully, your new class will duplicate nothing that already exists in the hierarchy, and by using everything in the hierarchy that you can, you'll ensure that your classes are as much in harmony with the Delphi Grand Design as they can be.

The Grand Design is made all the grander by the fact that Delphi is built from the same components it offers you—in fact, Delphi is written in itself, and compiled with itself. It is object-oriented from top to bottom.

That's what Delphi's Grand Design *is*. How it works depends on some additional new concepts. Let's take a look.

OVERRIDING NECESSITY

I could cook down all my advice about creating new object classes to two simple statements: *Inherit everything you can. Add or change only what you must.* Adding to an abstract class is pretty obvious, and we did it in creating the mortgage model objects in Chapter 8. All we did was declare the **TMortgage** class to be a child class of **TObject**, and we were adding things to what **TObject** already gave us.

The question will arise once you begin doing any but the simplest objects in Delphi: What if what I inherit isn't quite what I want? What if I have to *change* what I inherit? Changing a field that you inherit is tough—but changing methods is easy, and by changing methods you can often get the same results as changing a field.

The way it's done is simple: You create a new method with exactly the same name as the method you need to change. When the compiler processes a method call to that method name, your new method gets the call—the old method does not. The new method is said to *override* the old method.

A simple example is the **Create** method that I explained in Chapter 8. **TObject** contains a **Create** method that must be called to properly set up an instance of a class in memory. This **Create** method is good enough for all simple classes like **TPayment** and **TMortgage**, which you create "manually" after the program begins running.

Delphi's drop-in components are objects too, and like the simple objects you create as Delphi newcomers, they need to be created properly before they're used. But a Delphi component is a much more complex machine than a **TPayment** object, and creating it is considerably more involved. Components may be attached to other components and therefore "own" them, and when the owning component is disposed of, the owned components must go too. Connections like that must be put in place when the objects are created. There are other issues as well that I can't explain in an entry-level book, but the truth is that the simple **Create** method inherited from **TObject** won't quite handle the job any more. So the **TComponent** abstract class overrides the **Create** method present in **TObject** with a more powerful **Create** that can properly create a Delphi component.

Overriding a method doesn't necessarily mean completely duplicating everything the overridden method does. If all you need to do is add a little something to what the overridden method does, you can create a new method that overrides the old method, and within that method call the old method *first*—and then do whatever additional things that need doing.

People who have accidentally crashed themselves by calling the procedure they're writing from within that procedure might properly ask, How can you call the old method from within a method of the same name? Simple: You qualify the old method name with the name of the class in which it is defined. Within a new **Create** method we might do this:

```
BEGIN
   TObject.Create;
   DoSomething;
   DoSomethingElse;
END;
```

As long as we say *which* **Create** we're calling, the compiler is happy, and the original **Create** method is completely accessible. Overriding a method is not the same as shooting it in the head and burying it forever. Similarly, you can *precede* a call to the "old" method with statements that perhaps change some initial conditions expected by the old method—and then call the old method.

The syntactic mechanism by which you override methods is limited to methods. You can override any method you inherit from any class further up the hierarchy tree. Fields, however, *cannot* be overridden, and once a field of a certain name is defined in a class, no field in any class that inherits from that class may have the exact same name. Changing the way a field is used is something that takes considerable cleverness, and until you're a crackshot object-oriented programmer I advise against it.

Obviously, before you do any overriding of existing methods, you had better be very sure you understand *completely* what those methods do. There's a lot more to be said about the implications of inheritance and the ability to override inherited methods. I'm not going to go into it much further in this book, because to be useful it must be done within the context of the Delphi class hierarchy, and there is a great deal more to be learned about the Delphi classes than I can possibly describe here. I mostly want you to understand that inheritance exists and to some extent, know what it means. And to do that, we'll need to take a conceptual look at one final major trick that objects have up their sleeves: Polymorphism.

POLYMORPHISM: DOING IT YOUR OWN WAY

At the core of this whole notion of objects as "active data" is the truth that telling somebody to do something isn't the same as telling them *how* to do it. The goal in defining objects is to create a sort of software robot that both contains data and knows how to manipulate it. This is very helpful in setting up useful data models of a real-world computing problem, as we discovered when we put together a mortgage object toward the end of Chapter 8.

If active data "knows how" to do something, you don't have to tell the active data how to do its work. But there is another consequence of active data that isn't really as obvious: If objects as active data know how to do their work, you don't even have to know what *type* of object is out there to get it to do something useful. *Generalized instructions can produce specific results*—that's the subtle half of the Delphi Grand Design, and the flipside of the power of inheritance.

It's also a very tricky concept. To get started, I'd better fall back on what was once called a "homey metaphor."

"Harvest Your Crops Now!"

It's mid-September in the American heartland, and it's been a warm, peaceful growing season. It's a strong economy, exports are at their strongest ever, record crops are in the fields, and in Cuyadasco County farmers go to sleep at night with visions of record profits (what a thought!) dancing in their heads.

County Agent Hank O'Cord is paid to help out the farmers of the Cuyadasco country. He provides advice on bugs, crop diseases, spot shortages and over-supplies, new and changing government programs, and simple things like satellite weather forecasts. Hank is an agent of the 90s—he has his own Pentium machine, a satellite downlink from the National Weather Service, and years of experience and education on all things agricultural and environmental.

So on the morning of September 20, Hank checks out the satellite downlink from the NWS, and notices with horror that a massive front of arctic cold has unexpectedly begun marching south out of northern Canada. Temperatures are falling drastically all through Manitoba and Saskatchewan, with killing frosts and isolated violent thunderstorms bringing freezing rain and hail. He's had plenty of experience watching fronts move their way south from the Arctic—but one this early, moving this fast, is unusual. It'll be over Cuyadasco County in thirty-six hours, and that means major trouble.

Moving fast, Hank cuts and pastes the NWS weather warning into a Windows word processor document, and below it types a simple message in 24-point type: "Killer frost and violent storms in thirty-six hours. *Harvest your crops now!*" He brings up WinFaxMaster and tells his Pentium to begin FAXing the 1-page document to the database list of all of the farmers in Cuyadasco County— and then hops in his truck to go beat some sense into irascible old "Veggies" Montini, who grows organic produce and is so self-righteously convinced that electricity causes lettuce rot that he refuses to even have a phone installed.

Notice what's going on here: Hank does *not* call each farmer individually and tell each one how to go out into the fields and harvest their crops. His clients know how to do that better than he or anyone else. He issues a single, gener-alized instruction to all the farmers, and each farmer then goes out with his own equipment to harvest his crops as those crops require.

Hank doesn't even know the number of farmers in the county, who they are, what they grow, or who is signed up for his CropAlert service. Lila, his assistant, opens the mail and types in new applications to the Pentium. Hank knows they're out there, and how to issue his bulletins. Beyond that, well, it's up to the farmers to do what they do best—with a little manual help for loons like Montini.

With enormous efficiency of effort, Hank has in effect saved the majority of his farmer clients from financial catastrophe—without even knowing who most of them are. And without thinking of it in quite those terms, he got Cuyadasco's bumper crop harvested polymorphically.

Generalized Instructions, Specific Results

Polymorphism is from the Greek for "many shapes." In an object-oriented programming context, polymorphism means that a general kind of action can be done in many specific ways, depending on what object class is doing the acting. "To harvest" is a very general verb, but it's something that all farmers do. A farmer who grows sweet corn does his harvesting a certain way with a certain machine. Another farmer who grows potatoes harvests his crops in a very different way, with a completely different machine. And Montini yanks his lettuce up by hand.

The easiest example of polymorphism in Delphi lies in a method defined in the **TControl** class. **TControl** is an abstract class that with only a few exceptions includes all components that have a visual presence on a form at runtime. **TControl** has a method called **Repaint**, which when called regenerates the visible presence of the control on the screen.

TControl is an abstract class, containing only those things that *every* control must have—but nothing more. Not all controls draw themselves on the screen the same way, so the question you might have is this: If abstract class **TControl** defines the **Repaint** method, how does it know how to repaint all the many different kinds of controls that descend from it? Of course, it *doesn't*. All of the control child classes that descend from **TControl** override **TControl**'s **Repaint** method with a new, specific **Repaint** method of their own.

In a sense, **TControl**'s **Repaint** method is a placeholder. It may be empty or contain only some setup code that applies to all repaint operations for whatever type of control. What it actually does is provide a specific place in Delphi's object hierarchy where general "repaint yourself" commands may be sent. These general commands are then handled by each individual control's specific **Repaint** method, which does that control's physical repainting of the screen.

Ideas and Their Implementations

Another way of thinking of polymorphism is this: There are ideas, and then there are implementations. "Repainting a control" is an *idea*; a concept that underlies the way certain things work in Delphi. An idea represents the *what* but not necessarily the *how*. You can understand the fact that a control needs to be repainted without necessarily knowing how that repainting is accomplished. A **TControl** object is an idea object, which in Delphi's Grand Design represents the idea of a control, without all the ugly little details that define a particular control that works a particular way.

Polymorphism is a means of separating an idea from its implementation within an object class hierarchy. Inheritance is the means by which such a system is laid out; polymorphism is how it functions. The machinery through which polymorphism is made to work is a little advanced for a first book on Delphi, but I'll explain it in simple terms so that you can fill in the last gaps in your picture of the Grand Design.

Pointers and Masks

If you think back to my story of County Agent Hank O'Cord, consider that Hank doesn't really know all of the farmers in Cuyadasco County personally. He's met a lot of them, but hardly all of them. He interacts with them through a FAX/Modem board, and a list of phone numbers stored on his Pentium. The one thing he does know about all of them, however, is that they're all farmers. They have that much, at least, in common. When he sends them a FAX, it is as farmers, not corn farmers, or potato farmers, or misguided lettuce farmers.

When you want to send the command "repaint yourselves" to a group of components, you must do it at a level that all the components have in common. The only thing all components have in common is that they all descend from **TComponent**. So when you're addressing all the components on a form, for example, you must treat them all as **TComponent** objects, not labels or StringGrids or buttons. In a sense you must put a mask over the face of each component on the form, so that they all look alike—and all look like **TComponent**s.

The way to put a mask over objects is with something called a typecast—and in Object Pascal it can be done most easily using the operator **AS**. The **AS** operator treats one class "as" another. The **AS** operator's left operand must be an object instance, and its right operator must be an object class. Delphi then treats the object instance on the left as though it were of the class shown on the right:

```
(MyButton AS TControl).ShowHint := True;
```

Here, we have the object instance **MyButton**, which is a **TButton**, being typecast to a **TControl** through the use of the **AS** operator. There are subtleties to the **AS** operator that I can't completely explain here, but I simply want to give you a flavor for how **AS** is used. For example, it's generally a good idea to place **AS** expressions in parentheses to avoid precedence problems, and on that you're simply going to have to take my word for it. (But ask yourself: Without the parentheses, would the compiler attempt to evaluate **MyButton.ShowHint** or **TControl.ShowHint**?)

The line of code shown just above, while legal and compilable, isn't especially useful. All it does is place a **TControl** "mask" on a **TButton** object. To show you how this mechanism operates in polymorphism, well, we need "many shapes"—or at least more than one. And for that a simple project is called for.

A Typecast with AS

Typecasts are behind all polymorphism. It's possible to see a typecast in action with a simple program that channels all program clicks through a single **OnClick** event handler, which then sets a property common to all controls via a polymorphic reference. This is the project POLYTEST.DPR on the listings disk. The main form is shown in Figure 10.3.

The form in the project POLYTEST.DPR has several typical controls on it: A label, a TEdit, a button, and a panel. All of them have "fly-by" hints enabled through setting their **ShowHint** properties to **True**. Each has a "personalized" fly-by hint indicating what sort of control it is. If you run the program and linger the mouse pointer over the button, a yellow hint reading "I'm a button!" will appear over the button. The label will say, "I'm a label!" and so on.

The program has been set up in a way we haven't discussed in this book. There is a single **OnClick** event handler procedure, and it serves the form

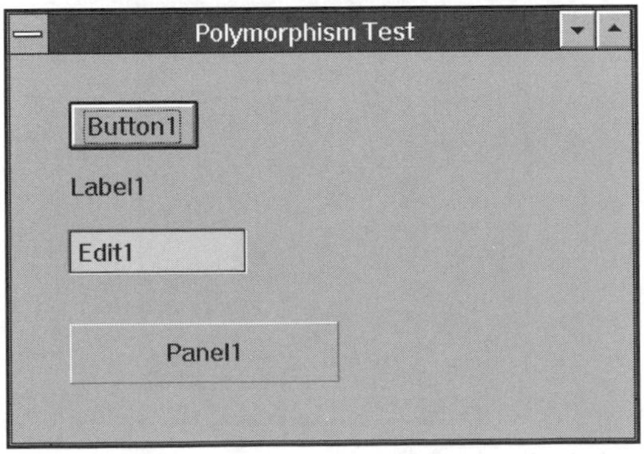

Figure 10.3   *The typecast test form.*

and all four of the controls. Normally, each control has its own event handler for each event, but there's nothing sacred about that. You can route all events through a single handler to ensure common processing, or for other reasons. It's not done often, but it certainly can be done. The called-in-common OnClick event handler is shown in Listing 10.1.

Listing 10.1 A single OnClick event handler for an entire program

```
procedure TForm1.FormClick(Sender: TObject);
begin
   (Sender AS TControl).Hint := 'I''m hosed!';
end;
```

This procedure was created by double-clicking on the OnClick event line for the project's main form, in the usual fashion. Then, however, the OnClick event for each of the four controls on the form was manually set to **TForm1.FormClick**. This can be easily done by clicking once to the right of the OnClick line in the Object Inspector window, and then clicking on the down arrow that appears on the right-hand end of the line. You'll see the names of any OnClick event procedures currently defined, as shown in Figure 10.4.

By clicking on the name of an event handler you see in the drop-down list, you can attach that event handler to the OnClick event of the object you're currently inspecting in the Object Inspector window. (In our case, as you can see in Figure 10.4, it's the button.) In creating the POLYTEST.DPR project, I set the OnClick events for all four of the controls to the form's OnClick event

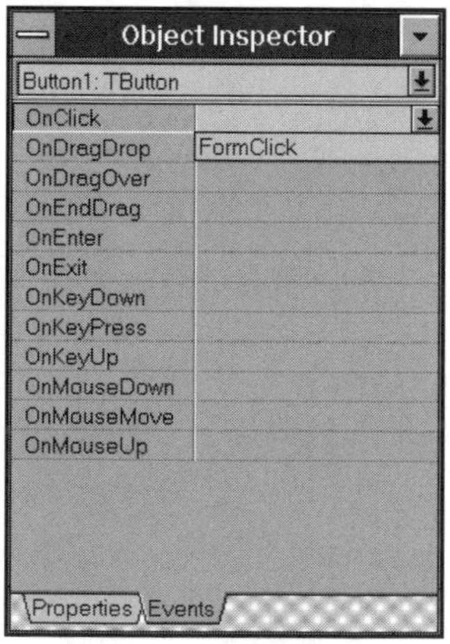

Figure 10.4 Selecting an OnClick event handler for a button.

handler. That way, each time *any* control on the form is clicked, the procedure in Listing 10.1 is executed. The trick is to figure out what it does, and how.

The Sender Parameter

You've probably noticed the **Sender** parameter present in all Delphi event handler procedures, and you may have wondered what it was for. When an event with an associated event handler happens, the event handler receives a reference to the object that generated the event. This reference is transferred into the event handler through the **Sender** parameter. Essentially, when an event handler is called, **Sender** contains the object that generated the event. In this case, when **TForm1.FormClick** from Listing 10.1 is called, **Sender** contains the object that the user clicked on. Because the event handler is shared by the form and four controls, it can be useful to know what control was actually clicked. **Sender** tells us.

Sender, however, is declared in the procedure header as a **TObject**. It's a **TObject** no matter what class is passed into the procedure in **Sender**.

Huh?

Polymorphic Assignment

This sort of thing gives traditional Pascal programmers the willies. In the old way of doing things, if a procedure parameter is type **Integer**, you can only pass **Integer** values in it. If it's not an integer, you can't. Object-oriented principles change things a little: An instance of any class descended from **TObject** can be assigned to a variable or parameter of type **TObject**. Read that again. Nay, read it two or three more times. It's important, and it tends to go down sideways if you've ever done any traditional Pascal programming at all.

But think about it: All Delphi objects are descended from **TObject**, which is very much the Father (or Mother) of All Classes. So quite truthfully, all objects are **TObject**s as well as whatever else they might be, like models of mortgage payments or StringGrids. Because deep down inside all objects are also **TObject**s, you can assign an object of any class to an object or parameter of type **TObject**. We call this sort of thing *polymorphic assignment*.

In a way, **Sender** is a mask, and the control that triggers an event enters the event handler procedure wearing the **Sender** mask. (It's more than a mask; it's closer to a bag over the head. When an object comes into a procedure in the **Sender** mask, you can't tell much of anything at all about it!) It's actually a way to allow *any class of object at all* to be passed into the event handler procedure.

What we want to do in Listing 10.1 is change the value of a property belonging to the control that triggered the event. Couldn't we just do this:

```
Sender.Hint := 'I''m hosed!';
```

No! Sender is a **TObject**, and class **TObject** has no **Hint** property. What we're trying to do here is talk to the mask itself, which is pointless. What we need to do is either talk to the object behind the mask—or find a better mask.

Which brings us to the **AS** expression **Sender AS TControl**. The class **TControl** is the closest class all four controls on the form have in common. **TControl** *does* have a **Hint** property; in fact, all controls inherit their **Hint** properties from **TControl**. So if we use the mask **TControl** rather than **Sender**, we can access the **Hint** property of any control that may enter the procedure in the guise of **Sender**.

Because we know that any object coming in as **Sender** will at least be a **TControl**, we can treat **Sender** as a **TControl** in this example. So regardless of whether the actual object passed in through **Sender** is a **TButton**, a **TEdit**, a **TLabel**, or a **TPanel**, because they're all **TControl**s, we can treat them all the same way and assign a new string to their **Hint** property. If you run the POLYTEST.DPR program and click on any of the four controls, the **Hint** for that control will be changed to the string "I'm hosed!" by way of a typecast and a polymorphic assignment. Many shapes—one assignment statement, and somehow the correct object (the one that generated the **OnClick** event) gets the new data.

Polymorphic Execution

That's polymorphic assignment. But what I was describing earlier in leading up to this was actually polymorphic *execution*. The mechanisms are much the same, and the reason I created POLYTEST.DPR as I did is that it's much easier to demonstrate polymorphic assignment than polymorphic execution. No, scratch that. Polymorphic execution is easy enough to demonstrate...it's just hard to *see*.

Here's how to do it. Go into the **TForm1.FormClick** procedure (the one I show in Listing 10.1) and delete the one line of code it contains, replacing it with this even simpler line:

```
(Sender AS TControl).Repaint;
```

Now when you run the program, clicking on any of the four controls will repaint the control on which you click, through polymorphic execution. It really is happening, but you won't see any change in any of the controls.

What the above line does is call the **Repaint** method for the control that triggered the OnClick event. Each control has a different **Repaint** method, because each control draws itself to the screen in a different way—after all, if they all did it the same way, they'd all look alike. So we treat all four controls as the **TControl** objects they all are, and tell them to redraw themselves as best they know how. They all do it, too. The problem is that they didn't *need* redrawing, and having them draw themselves again when they're already perfectly drawn on the screen doesn't look like anything happening at all.

POLYMORPHISM AND THE GRAND DESIGN

If after all this you find yourself completely bewildered, don't feel bad about it. From a beginner's perspective, polymorphism is a bit of a black art, but its compensating virtue is that it isn't often confronted directly. You as an application programmer will rarely have to set up polymorphic situations on your own. You'll be *using* polymorphism all the time—but you won't always know it's there. Delphi hides its inevitable complexity very well.

What inheritance (through the "spreading out" of components into a hierarchy) makes possible, polymorphism accomplishes. Polymorphism allows objects to be treated similarly at the object hierarchy level where they are similar. In an application divided into objects with specific tasks, polymorphism allows the application's high-level design to deal with *ideas* (the creation of new objects, re-display of objects on the screen, and other abstract descriptions of program operations) while leaving the implementation details (how and where objects are created, how objects are redrawn, and so on) to the objects that best know how to handle them.

Thinking of an application in these terms is tough if you learned programming in earlier and simpler structured ways. I had that problem, and about all I can say is, It comes to you over time. To accelerate your understanding of object-oriented programming, emphasize these important points in your explorations:

- Objects are active data. Think of them as data structures wearing a belt of tools; that is, data that can *do* things.

- Objects can inherit both data (fields) and code (methods) from existing objects. You can extend an existing class by inheriting from it and adding your extensions to the new child class.

- Polymorphic assignment and execution allow you to work on objects of different and unpredictable classes farther up the object hierarchy, where they have a common ancestor class containing common fields and methods.

As a creator of applications you'll be working mostly on the outermost leaves of Delphi's object hierarchy, using its provided software components in a straightforward way. Where you'll need to really be sure you understand object-oriented programming in all its detail is when you become a component programmer, and begin creating drop-in Delphi components on your own. But that's another level of difficulty (and another book) entirely.

Files and File Types

Jim Mischel

Before I accepted my new job (which, by the way, has me writing games for Windows), I worked for an alarm monitoring center where I helped maintain and enhance the monitoring software. One of my projects was to write a program that keeps track of the number and types of signals that we receive and respond to. Every 15 minutes, the program writes a totals record, which contains all of the information for the previous 15-minute period, out to a file. The file itself contains information for an entire week.

It sounds like busy work, but it's really quite necessary. The boss would use the information to determine how many operators she should have available at any given time, and in the back room we'd use the information to determine equipment needs and off-peak hours when we could schedule tests (usually about 3:00 AM on Sunday). Our business manager used the information to create a graph comparing the current month's totals with the previous month's (and year's) showing how the business had grown.

Long before there were databases, there were disk files. Delphi's file handling can help you accomplish things that databases simply can't do.

Getting the information from the alarm monitoring software into the file every 15 minutes was the easy part. The tough part came when we had to *do* something with the information. You see, when my program stored the information, it was in a special format that made it easy to find and update a particular 15-minute record, and we backroom types had a few utility programs that let us examine and massage the data. But my boss and the business manager had spreadsheet programs into which they wanted to import the data, and our file's format was definitely not something that a spreadsheet would understand. And thus was born the conversion program to turn my special file format into a spreadsheet-readable format.

Object Pascal has two file types: **Text**, which is simply a file that contains one or more lines of (usually) human-readable text; and **File**, which encompasses "everything else;" files with fixed- or variable-length records of binary data. Each type of file has its own strengths and weaknesses. We'll look at both of them in this chapter and see how to convert data from one format to another.

Delphi also supports database files, but that support is built into components, *not* into the Object Pascal language. We're not going to cover database files in this chapter. Database programming is a separate topic, covered in detail in Chapters 13 and after.

TEXT FILES

As far as Object Pascal is concerned, a text file is made up of lines, and each line can be further broken down into words or characters, depending on how you look at it. Each line in a text file is terminated with an end-of-line marker, which in the Windows world is a carriage-return and line feed. This type of file is known by many different names, "ASCII file" and "DOS text file" being the most common. Windows' Notepad accessory, the text file viewer developed in Chapter 7, and Delphi's code editor all read and/or write this type of file.

Text files are *sequential*: in order to read information at the end of the file, you must first read all of the information ahead of it in the file. When reading, think of a text file as a cassette tape in a player with a Rewind button that always rewinds all the way to the beginning. You can fast forward through the file to get to a particular line in the file, but if you want to see a previously-read line, you have to rewind to the beginning of the file and start reading again. There is no way to jump back and forth in the file to read lines at random.

Writing to a text file is also a sequential process. You have the choice of starting a new file and writing information from beginning to end; opening an existing file and overwriting any data that's in it; or opening an existing file and adding text to it starting at the end of any previously-written data. You *do not*, however, have the option of writing information somewhere in the middle of an existing file. When writing, think of the text file as a cassette tape in a recorder whose Rewind button always goes to the beginning, and whose Fast Forward button always goes to the end of the most recent recording. You can either press Rewind and start recording at the beginning, or press Fast Forward and start recording at the end.

Finally, a text file can be opened for reading or writing, but not both at the same time.

In order to access a text file, you need a variable of type **Text**, which is a standard Object Pascal data type. You declare this variable in your program just as you would any other variable, like this:

```
var
  MyTextFile : Text;
```

Opening Text Files

Before you can access data in, or write data to, a text file, you have to open it for reading or writing. Opening the file requires two steps: You associate the file variable with a file name, and then you initialize the reading or writing.

- To associate the file variable with a file, you call the **Assign** standard procedure. For example, to associate **MyTextFile** with the file "MYFILE.TXT", you would write:

  ```
  Assign (MyTextFile, 'MYFILE.TXT');
  ```

- You can pass full path names to **Assign**, as in:

  ```
  Assign (MyTextFile, 'c:\alarms\stats.dat');
  ```

  and the file name string can be uppercase, lowercase, or mixed case.

- **Assign** doesn't check to see that the file actually exists. All it does is tell Delphi that you want all operations on **MyTextFile** to affect the particular named file.

- After you've assigned the variable a file name, you open the file. You have three options:

  - **Reset** opens the file for reading and positions the file pointer at the beginning of the file so that the first read operation will access the first line in the file. If you try to **Reset** a non-existent file, you will receive an error and your program will stop.

- **Rewrite** creates a new file, opens it for writing, and positions the file pointer at the beginning of the file so that the data from the first write operation appears at the beginning of the file. If you **Rewrite** an existing file, all of the existing data in that file will be lost.

- **Append** opens an existing file for writing and positions the file pointer at the end of the file so that data is written after any existing data in the file. If you try to **Append** to a non-existent file, you will receive an error and your program will stop.

Closing Text Files

When you're done with a text file (that is, you've finished reading from or writing to it), you should close it. Closing the file ensures that any data that was buffered by Delphi's (or the operating system's) internal machinery is actually written to the disk, which prevents the file system from becoming corrupted. To close a file, whether it's been opened for reading or writing, you simply call the **Close** procedure, like this:

```
Close(MyTextFile);
```

And here's where we run into unit scope problems, which Jeff touched upon briefly in Chapter 8. If you recall, the **TForm** object has a **Close** procedure, which is called to close the form and, in single-form applications, end execution. Since the form's **Close** procedure is defined *after* the standard file-specific **Close** procedure, **TForm**'s **Close** is "in scope" and visible by default, without any additional qualification. (The *last* definition with a given name is the one visible by default—and this allows you to alter existing identifiers by replacing them with your own.) For this reason, you'll get a compile-time error if you write the above line of code anywhere in a form's procedure, because the compiler thinks you're calling **TForm.Close**, which does not take a parameter. The solution is to use the *unit.procedure* "dotting" notation to fully qualify the reference by specifying precisely *which* **Close** you want to call. Since **Close** is defined in the System unit, you'd write:

```
System.Close (MyTextFile);
```

According to the documentation, Delphi automatically closes all open files during its exit processing. That's nice of Delphi to do that, but depending on the language you're using to close files automatically is sloppy programming. It's also an invitation to disaster if you ever try to port code to another platform that *doesn't* automatically close open files. If you do it yourself, you're at least sure that it gets done.

A bigger issue is *file handles*—file pointers that are internal to Windows. Depending on your particular boot-time setup, when your Delphi program starts up, it is given somewhere between 15 and 20 file handles to work with. (There are ways to get more file handles—up to 255—but that's a subject for a more advanced book.) Every open file requires a single file handle, which means that you have a limit to the number of files that you can have open at any particular time. If you keep opening files and don't close them when you're done with them, your program's going to run out of file handles in short order. But if you close a file when you're done with it, that frees up a file handle that can then be reused when you open another file.

Writing Text Files

There are two write operations that you can perform on text files: **Write** and **WriteLn**. **Write** sends the data that you specify out to the file. **WriteLn** does the same thing as **Write**, but also adds an end-of-line marker to the file after the data is written. The data that you can output using these procedures is restricted to just a handful of data types: **Char**, **String**, **Integer**, **Word**, **Longint**, **Byte**, **Real**, or **Boolean**.

To output a string to a text file, then, you would write:

```
Write (MyTextFile, 'Hello, world');
```

If the string was in a variable, like this:

```
var
  HelloString : String;
begin
  HelloString := 'Hello, world';
```

then to output it, you would write:

```
Write (MyTextFile, HelloString);
```

Write and **WriteLn** are odd procedures in that they accept a *variable* number of parameters—something you almost never see in Object Pascal. The first parameter must always be the name of the file that you want to output to, but the rest of the parameters (if any) can be any number of the types described above. For example, to output a **String** and an integer, you would write:

```
Write (MyTextFile, HelloString, MyInteger);
```

Assuming that **MyInteger** was assigned a value of 25, the output file would contain:

```
Hello, world 25
```

Specifying Field Width

Many times you'll want to output things in columns (in a printed report, for example), and you'll want to specify the width of a particular output field. Any parameter to **Write** can have an optional width specifier tacked onto it by placing a colon and the field width after the parameter. For example, to output a row of four numbers that are equally-spaced at 10-character intervals, you would write:

```
WriteLn (MyTextFile, Number1:10, Number2:10, Number3:10, Number4:10);
```

If the variables had values of 100, 200, 300, 400, respectively, you'd end up with:

```
    100       200       300       400
```

Write right-justifies values to fit the specified column width, which makes building tables a snap. For example, if you were to write:

```
WriteLn (100:10, 200:10, 300:10, 400:10);
WriteLn (1234:10, 5678:10, 1:10, 15:10);
```

Your output would look like this:

```
       100       200       300       400
      1234      5678         1        15
```

The :*width* specifier defines the *minimum* width of the output field. **Write** will not truncate a number to fit in the specified width. In the above example, if you had specified 2, rather than 10, for the width, you'd end up with all the output piled together in a row, with no spacing between the distinct values:

```
100200300400
```

You can also use the :*width* specifier for **String** types, but they will be right-justified, which I find a bit odd. So if you were to output a column of names using a *width* of 10, you would end up with this:

```
      Jeff
       Jim
     Diane
       Don
  Michelle
```

This is unfortunate, as it's more common to left-justify string data. It's still possible to create left-justified columns of strings, but you have to do some additional work to make it look right.

Specifying Decimal Places

When you write a **Real** variable, the output will likely surprise you. Unlike **Integer** types, which are output as you would expect, **Real** numbers are output using scientific notation. For example, if you were to write:

```
Write (MyTextFile, 25.1);
```

the contents of the text file would be:

```
2.5100000000E+01
```

This notation is just another representation of 25.1. This notation says "multiply 2.5100000000 by 10 to the first power." Since "10 to the first power" works out to 10, we end up with 2.51 times 10, or 25.1. All of which is well and good, but your boss probably doesn't want to know that last week's receipts were 5.6892700000E+03 dollars.

Fortunately, you can get Delphi to output **Real** values in a more standard notation, so that 25.1 is actually output as 25.1. You do this by specifying a width and the number of decimal places to output. For example, if you want 25.1 to be output with 2 decimal places in a column that's 10 digits wide, you would write:

```
Write (25.1:10:2);
```

All of this might look familiar—it's the same formatting mechanism used with the **Str** procedure, as Jeff described in Chapter 6.

Reading Text Files

Reading information from text files is pretty simple, although it gets a little weird at times with strings. Two standard procedures, **Read** and **ReadLn**, perform most of the work, and the standard functions **Eoln** (end of line) and **Eof** (end of file) help out. The data types that can be read with **Read** and **ReadLn** are the same as those that can be written with **Write** and **WriteLn**.

The easiest type of information to read from a text file is numbers: integer or real types. For example, if you have a text file that contains three numbers on a single line, like this:

```
100   200   300
```

you can read them with a single statement, like this:

```
Read (MyTextFile, Number1, Number2, Number3);
```

or with three separate **Read**s, like this:

```
Read (MyTextFile, Number1);
Read (MyTextFile, Number2);
Read (MyTextFile, Number3);
```

In either case, assuming that the three variables are numeric types, they will contain 100, 200, and 300, respectively.

Read and **ReadLn** assume that numbers to be read from a text are separated by one or more spaces, not by commas, semicolons, or any other characters. If they encounter any other character while they're looking for a number, they stop reading and issue a runtime error. So, if you had this data:

```
100   200,   300
```

in your file, **Read** would get the first number, 100, but would get an error when it tried to convert "200," (including the comma) into a number.

As I said, reading strings is a bit weird. **Read** doesn't support the concept of a field separator when it comes to strings, so separating two strings in the file with one or more spaces doesn't guarantee that **Read** will read them back as two separate strings. For example, if you have this line of text in your file:

```
hello world
```

and try to read it as two separate strings as in this program fragment:

```
var
  s1,s2 : string;
  MyTextFile : Text;

begin
  Assign (MyTextFile, 'MYFILE.TXT');
  Reset (MyTextFile);
  Read (MyTextFile, s1, s2);
```

You're going to end up with **s1** containing the string 'hello world', and **s2** containing nothing at all.

The trick is that **Read** reads as many characters as will fit into the string, or up to the end-of-line marker, whichever is less. So if you're reading formatted string data from a text file, all you have to do is declare strings to match the width of the columns. For example, to read from a file that has two columns of data; 10 and 12 characters wide, respectively, you would declare these two strings:

```
var
  String1 : String[10];
  String2 : String[12];
```

If you want to read individual words from a text file, you have to read each line of the file into a string and parse the string for individual words, or read the file a character at a time and perform the tests that determine the word breaks after each character. Yes, Delphi does leave some "real programming" for us to do.

End of Line and End of File

Two standard procedures, **Eoln** and **Eof**, let you determine if you've reached the end of a line or the end of the file when reading a text file. **Eoln** returns **True** if the next read operation will encounter the end of a line, and **Eof** returns **True** if the next read operation will encounter the end of the file. **Eof** is used by just about any program that reads text files.

Eoln isn't used as often as **Eof**, because most programs that read text files read the data into strings a line at a time, so they don't care too much about end-of-line markers. However, there are times when **Eoln** comes in very handy. If you are reading a text file that contains many lines of one or more numbers each, you can use **Eoln** in a counting loop to figure out how many numbers are on that line. For example, if your file lists miles driven per day each week, and you don't make an entry if you don't drive on a particular day, your file might look like this:

```
15 132 12
20 20 100 97 36 48 79
620 540
```

This means that the first week you drove three days, the second week you drove every day, and the third week you drove only two days. To compute an average number of miles driven per week (or per day), you need to read each number and keep track of how many numbers you read for each line. A Pascal procedure that does this is shown in Listing 11.1.

Listing 11.1 Pascal procedure to compute average mileage per day

```
Procedure ComputeAverageMiles;
var
  TotalMiles : Real;
  WeekTotal : Real;
  DayMiles : Real;
  DaysThisWeek : Integer;
  TotalDays : Integer;
  NumberOfWeeks : Integer;
  MileFile : Text;
  OutputFile : Text;
Begin
  { open the input file }
  Assign (MileFile, 'miles.txt');
  Reset (MileFile);

  { create the output file }
  Assign (OutputFile, 'miles.out');
  Rewrite (OutputFile);

  { initialize totals }
  TotalMiles := 0;
  TotalDays := 0;
  NumberOfWeeks := 0;
  While not Eof (MileFile) Do Begin
    { initialize week totals }
    WeekTotal := 0;
    DaysThisWeek := 0;
    While Not Eoln (MileFile) Do Begin
      Read (MileFile, DayMiles);
      WeekTotal := WeekTotal + DayMiles;
      DaysThisWeek := DaysThisWeek + 1;
```

```
  End;
  { read the end-of-line marker }
  ReadLn (MileFile);

  NumberOfWeeks := NumberOfWeeks + 1;

  { output information }
  Write (OutputFile, 'Week #',NumberOfWeeks);
  Write (OutputFile, WeekTotal:10:2, ' miles in ',
    DaysThisWeek, ' days.');
  WriteLn (OutputFile, (WeekTotal/DaysThisWeek):10:2,
    ' average miles per day.');

  { add to totals }
  TotalMiles := TotalMiles + WeekTotal;
  TotalDays := TotalDays + DaysThisWeek;
End;

{ The entire file has been read, now write the totals }
WriteLn (OutputFile);  { blank line }

WriteLn (OutputFile, 'Total of ', NumberOfWeeks, ' weeks:');
WriteLn (OutputFile, TotalMiles:0:2, ' miles in ',
  TotalDays, ' days.');
WriteLn (OutputFile, (TotalMiles/NumberOfWeeks):0:2,
  ' average miles per week.');
WriteLn (OutputFile, (TotalMiles/TotalDays):0:2,
  ' average miles per day.');
Close (MileFile);
Close (OutputFile);
End;
```

WHAT'S THIS "WHILE" THING?

CAM.PAS (Listing 11.1) is pretty straightforward code. It opens the input and output files, initializes the fields to hold the totals, and starts processing the file, computing each week's totals and averages and adding the week totals to **TotalMiles** and **TotalDays** variables. It's mostly bookkeeping, but there's an Object Pascal construct in there that you haven't seen yet: **while** *condition* **do**.

The **while** *condition* **do** construct is just another looping construct like the **for** loop. But, whereas **for** is a counting loop that continues executing until the index variable reaches a particular value, the **while** loop continues executing as long as *condition* evaluates to **True**. You can make a **while** loop act like a **for** loop by breaking the **for** loop's implicit "initialize, test, increment, loop" action into separate statements. For example, this **for** construct:

```
for Counter := 1 to 100 do begin
  ...
end;
```

can be recast as a **while** loop like this:

```
Counter := 1;  { initializatize }
while Counter <= 100 do begin { test }
  ...
  Counter := Counter + 1;  { increment }
end; { loop }
```

Obviously, if you're going to do loops that count up or down by one, **for** is the construct of choice. But if you want to count by 2, 3, or 86, **for** isn't going to help you and it's time to reach for a **while** loop.

The **while** loop's strengths extend far beyond counting loops. *Any* expression that resolves to a **True** or **False** value can be used as the *condition* in a **while** loop. In Listing 11.1, for example, you see this statement:

```
while not eof (MilesFile) do begin
```

Eof returns **True** if we've reached the end of the file, or **False** otherwise. Translated into English, this statement reads: "While we haven't reached the end of the Miles file, do this stuff."

Any condition that you put in an **if** statement can be used as the *condition* for a **while** statement, including expressions that use the Boolean operators. For example, if you wanted to limit the number of weeks tested by the procedure in Listing 11.1 to 10, you would write something like this:

```
while (not eof (MilesFile)) and (NumberOfWeeks <= 10) do begin
```

which would terminate the loop after 10 weeks, or if the end of the file was reached before 10 weeks' worth of data was read.

TEXT FILES SUMMARY

If you're generating a report to the printer, you have to learn how to use **Write** and **WriteLn**—there's simply no other way to get data to the printer short of using ReportSmith (see Chapter 21). In Chapter 7, you saw how to associate a text file with the printer.

When reading, text files are most often treated as files of *lines*, and the program parses out the individual fields in each line internally after reading a line from the file. This requires a bit more work than reading the fields directly from the file, but it allows for error recovery when the file contains bad data, and also allows you to read data types that can't be read directly by **Read** and **ReadLn**.

Text files are great for outputting reports, for reading text-based information, and for converting data from one system to another (as we'll see later in this chapter). And because text files contain human-readable data, it's easy to edit and view them with a text editor. They have some drawbacks, though; the biggest being that you can't update a record in a text file, and you can't randomly hop from one record to another. Both of these are necessary features, but beyond the capability of text files. For record hopping, we need a file type uniquely suited to contain Object Pascal records.

FILES OF RECORDS

Pascal's other file type, **File**, is used to define random-access files of fixed-length records. You can also use **File** to define untyped files, but such files are beyond the scope of this book. With a file of records, you obtain the ability to randomly access any record in the file, to update any record, and to have a file open for reading and writing at the same time. This flexibility comes at a cost, though: The files now contain *binary* data and aren't easily modified with a text editor or any other program that doesn't understand the unique format of the records in the file.

If you think of a text file as a cassette tape that can be read or written sequentially, you might want to think of a file of records as an audio Compact Disk. With a CD, you can randomly play any particular portion of the disk without having to fast-forward through the rest of the songs, as you do with a cassette tape. The same is true of files of records: You can position to any record and read or write it at will, without affecting the rest of the file.

Before you can declare a file of records, you have to define the record that the file is going to contain. I've created a much-simplified version of the alarm data record that my alarm statistics program has to deal with. This simplified record structure is shown in Listing 11.2

Listing 11.2   The AlarmStatsRecord record definition

```
{ statistics record for each one-hour period }
  AlarmStatsRecord = record
    Day : String[3];
    Time : String[5];
    NumberOfSignals : Integer;
    OperatorSignals : Integer;
    AlarmSignals : Integer;
    TroubleSignals : Integer;
  end;
```

This record simply stores the total number of signals received by the monitoring center from subscribers' alarms during each one-hour reporting period, and further breaks that total down into alarm signals (burglar, fire, medical emergency, etc.), trouble signals (low battery, lost power, etc.), and signals that required an operator's intervention. There are other types of signals (test, for example), so **AlarmSignals** plus **TroubleSignals** won't always add up to **NumberOfSignals**. All alarm signals require operator intervention, as do some trouble signals and other types of signals. The full record used by the real software is quite a bit more involved, with information about how many signals each of the 10 alarm receivers processed during that period, and even further breakdowns of signal types.

The original program wrote one record to the file for each 15-minute period in the week, and our reporting program would consolidate the records into a more manageable one-record-per-hour format. I've chosen the one-record-per-hour format for this example simply to save space. Our alarm statistics file contains one of these records for each one-hour period in the week, with the first record containing the information from midnight on Saturday until 1:00 AM on Sunday morning, and the last record containing the information from 11:00 PM until midnight the following Saturday.

To tell Delphi that you have a file full of these records, you simply declare a **file** of **AlarmStatsRecord**, like this:

```
var
  StatsFile : file of AlarmStatsRecord;
```

Opening and Closing Files of Records

As with text files, the **Assign**, **Reset**, and **Rewrite** standard procedures are used to open files of records; and the **Close** standard procedure closes the file. You can't use **Append** to open a file of records—**Append** is strictly for text files.

After you call **Assign** to associate a file name with a given file variable, you call **Reset** or **Rewrite** to open the file. **Reset** opens the file for reading and/ or writing, and **Rewrite** creates a new file (or overwrites an existing one) and opens it for reading and/or writing. If you try to **Reset** a non-existent file, you will receive a runtime error.

Closing files is, if that were possible, even more important with files of records than it is with text files. If you fail to close a text file that you've been writing to, the worst that can happen is that the file will be truncated—the last few lines of data that you wrote to the file might not actually be written to the disk. This can cause some trouble, but it's normally pretty easy to fix. With files of records, though, you can corrupt the entire file by forgetting to close it after you're through modifying and adding records. *Always* close a file when you're done with it—preferably as soon as you've finished working with that file, but in any case before you exit the program.

The FileMode Variable

When used to open files of records, the **Reset** standard procedure by default opens the files for reading and writing. This is normally the mode that you'll want to use, as it lets you read, add, and update records in the file at will. However, sometimes it might be necessary to access a file on a network to which your program only has read access. If you try to **Reset** a file that's protected in this way, you're going to get a runtime error.

The **FileMode** variable, defined in the **System** unit, allows you to specify the mode in which the file should be opened. The default value is 2, which means that the file will be opened for reading and writing. There are two other values for **FileMode**: 0 (read only) and 1 (write only). So, to open a file of records for reading only, you'd write this code:

```
FileMode := 0;
Reset (MyFileOfRecords);
```

FileMode is a global variable, and its value affects the operation of *all* **Reset** operations. If you're going to change it, it's a good idea to restore its value after you've opened your file. If you don't, then every **Reset** operation that you perform after the initial one is going to open the file in the new mode. So the above code, in order to be friendly to the rest of your program, really should look more like this:

```
Var
  OldFileMode : Byte;

Begin
  { assign file }
  OldFileMode := FileMode; { save current FileMode value }
  FileMode := 0;           { 0 = read only }
  Reset (MyFileOfRecords); { open the file }
  FileMode := OldFileMode; { restore FileMode }
```

Writing and Reading Records

To write a record into a file of records, you simply call **Write** and pass it a file variable and one or more records. For example, the following code writes the contents of the **StatsRecord** variable to the **StatsFile**:

```
Write(StatsFile, StatsRecord);
```

If you have more than one record that you want to write, you can call **Write** twice, or just specify both records in a single **Write** statement, like this:

```
Write(StatsFile, StatsRecord1, StatsRecord2);
```

Similarly, to read a record from a random access file, you simply call **Read** with a file variable and record variable, like this:

```
Read(StatsFile, StatsRecord);
```

As with **Write**, **Read** can read multiple records with a single call. If you try to **Read** beyond the end of a file, you will receive a runtime error.

The File Pointer and Record Numbers

It's useful to think of a file having an invisible pointer that points to the record that's going to be affected by the next **Read** or **Write** operation. Whenever a file is opened, either by **Reset** or **Rewrite**, this invisible pointer is positioned at the beginning of the file. Each **Read** or **Write** operation moves the file pointer ahead by one record so that it points to the next record beyond the last one that was affected.

If you **Read** or **Write** multiple records, the file pointer is moved ahead once for each record that's read or written. So, if your code reads two records, like this:

```
Read(StatsFile, StatsRecord1, StatsRecord2);
```

the file pointer will be positioned to the record after the one read into the **StatsRecord2** variable.

Records in a file of records are numbered sequentially, starting at 0. So the first record in a file is record 0, and the last record in a file of 12 records would be record number 11.

If you want to find out how many records are in a file, call the **FileSize** standard function. I'll discuss **FileSize** in detail in the next section.

Moving and Examining the File Pointer

The mechanism that makes it possible to randomly access records is the ability to move and examine the file pointer's position. These capabilities are implemented in the **Seek** procedure and **FilePos** function. **Seek** moves the file pointer to the specified record in the file, and **FilePos** tells you to which record the file pointer is currently pointing.

So, to locate and read the fifth record in a file of records, you would write:

```
Seek(StatsFile, 4);              { seek to the 5th record counting from 0 }
Read(StatsFile, StatsRecord);    { and read the record }
```

Similarly, if you want to update the fifth record in the file with new information, you'd seek to that position and **Write** the record.

And here's where you have to be careful. If you want to read a record, change it, and then write the new information over the top of the old information, you have to **Seek** back to the record before writing. For example, the following code reads, changes, and updates a record in a file:

```
Seek(StatsFile, 4);              { seek to 5th record }
Read(StatsFile, StatsRecord);    { read the record }
StatsRecord.NumberOfSignals := 100;
Seek(StatsFile, 4);              { move the file pointer back to the 5th record }
Write(StatsFile, StatsRecord);   { and update the record }
```

If you forget that second **Seek**, you'll end up overwriting the *sixth* record in the file with the updated information. This is a fairly common error that trips up beginners and experienced programmers alike.

If you want to add records to the end of an existing file, you have to **Seek** to a position that's one record beyond the current end of file before you start writing. The easiest way to do this is to use **FileSize** to obtain the number of records in the file, and use *that* number as a parameter to **Seek**, like this:

```
{ seek to the end of the file before appending records }
Seek(StatsFile, FileSize(StatsFile));
```

Since records are numbered starting at 0, the last record in a file of 12 records would be record number 11. **FileSize** returns the number of records in a file—*not* the number of the last record! In the case of a file containing 12 records, **FileSize** returns 12, which just happens to be the number that's one more than the last record in the file. (Almost like they planned it that way, huh?)

 **Handling I/O Errors**

As I've mentioned, if your program tries to do something illegal like open a non-existent file for reading, or read beyond the end of a file, you'll end up with a run time error and the program will stop. This is the default mode of operation, and occurs when you have I/O error checking turned on. This mode also allows you to use *exceptions* to trap and respond to I/O errors. Exceptions allow you to trap many different types of program errors.

You can also turn I/O checking off if you like, and use the **IoResult** standard function to trap and respond to I/O errors. **IoResult** is included in Delphi to maintain compatibility with older versions of Pascal. It's the "bad old way" of handling I/O errors, and not something that I recommend for new programs. As such, we're not going to cover it in this book, and I suggest that you leave I/O checking on at all times.

For now, understand that Delphi will halt with an error message if your program tries to do something illegal, and know that it *is* possible for your program to detect these error conditions and respond accordingly without crashing.

 **Creating and Modifying a File of Records**

After the preceding discussion of files and file types, you're probably itching to see how to use these files in a working program. We're going to create a small application called STATS that will read a text file of alarm statistics and create a file of **AlarmStatsRecord** records. The program will allow you to examine and modify any record in the file, and also allow you to print reports. The main form of the completed application is shown in Figure 11.1.

Figure 11.1 *The Stats application.*

THE MAIN FORM

We're going to move through the design of this form fairly quickly, because by now you're familiar with most of the components that we're going to be using. We're going to use a separate unit to do the file I/O in order to keep the main form independent from the file structure. This is a useful approach in that it allows us to change the way the file is handled without having to change anything in the main form.

Start a new project, and change the main form's properties as shown in Table 11.1. Then save your work, calling the Unit STATFORM.PAS, and the project STATS.DPR.

ComboBoxes

The first two components we're going to put on the form are ComboBoxes, which you haven't seen before. It's best to think of a ComboBox as an Edit control and ListBox that have been joined at the hip. The top part of a ComboBox is an Edit control in which you can (sometimes) enter text. A ComboBox also has a drop-down ListBox that can contain strings or any other type of information that can be stuck in a ListBox. ComboBoxes are useful when you want the user to select from one of a wide range of choices.

The ComboBox's **Items** property allows you to enter a list of strings that is to be displayed by the drop down ListBox portion of the component. You can build this list of strings into the ComboBox at design-time, and you can also modify the list at runtime.

A ComboBox has a **Style** property that you can set to change the way that the ComboBox behaves. We're going to use the **csDropDownList** style for our ComboBoxes, which prevents the user from entering text in the Edit portion of the combo box, forcing them to select from the list. This prevents the user from entering bad data in the field. Two other **Style** values: **csDropDown** and **csSimple** can be used if you want the user to be able to enter text into

---

Table 11.1 *Property Changes for the Alarm Stats Main Form*

Field	Value
BorderStyle	bsSingle
Caption	"Alarm Statistics"
Name	"AlarmStats"

the Edit portion. For more information about these and the rest of the ComboBox styles, see the online help.

Select the ComboBox component, drop two of them onto your form, and position them as shown in Figure 11.1. Change both of their **Style** properties to **csDropDownList**, and change their **Name**s to "DayList" and "HourList", respectively. Then, double-click on the **Items** property of the first ComboBox to bring up the String list editor and enter the day names as shown in Figure 11.2.

After you've entered the day names, as shown, press OK and then select the second ComboBox. Bring up the String list editor and enter these 24 time strings, one per line, in order (that is, 00:00, 01:00, 02:00 ... 23:00):

```
00:00    04:00    08:00    12:00    16:00    20:00
01:00    05:00    09:00    13:00    17:00    21:00
02:00    06:00    10:00    14:00    18:00    22:00
03:00    07:00    11:00    15:00    19:00    23:00
```

Completing the Form

Select the Label component, drop four Labels onto your form, and change their **Caption** properties as shown in Figure 11.1. Then drop four Edit components onto your form, clear their **Text** properties, and change their **Name** properties to "TotalSigs", "AlarmSigs", "TroubleSigs", and "OperatorSigs", respectively.

To add the buttons, select the Button component and drop six buttons onto the form at the right side, as shown. Change their **Caption** properties to reflect Figure 11.1, and their **Name** properties to "btnImport", "btnLookup", "btnUpdate", "btnPrint", "btnExport", and "btnQuit". Finally, add OnClick event handlers for each and enter the event procedures shown in Listing 11.3.

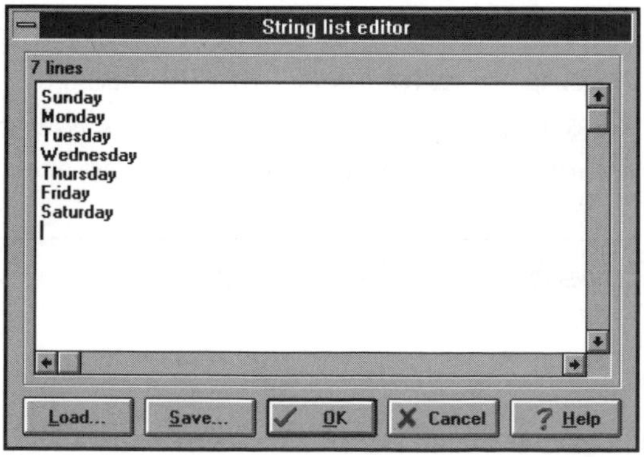

Figure 11.2   Entering the day names in the String list editor.

Listing 11.3   OnClick event procedures for the Stats program

```
procedure TAlarmStats.btnImportClick(Sender: TObject);
begin
  CloseTheFile;
  { import the data }
  Almstats.Import (TextFilename, StatsFilename);
  { and read the first record }
  DayList.ItemIndex := 0;
  HourList.ItemIndex := 0;
  btnLookupClick (Sender);
end;

procedure TAlarmStats.btnLookupClick(Sender: TObject);
Var
  Rec : Almstats.AlarmStatsRecord;
begin
  OpenTheFile;
  Almstats.Lookup (AlarmFile,
                   DayList.ItemIndex,
                   HourList.ItemIndex,
                   Rec);
  TotalSigs.Text := IntToStr (Rec.NumberOfSignals);
  AlarmSigs.Text := IntToStr (Rec.AlarmSignals);
  TroubleSigs.Text := IntToStr (Rec.TroubleSignals);
  OperatorSigs.Text := IntToStr (Rec.OperatorSignals);
end;

procedure TAlarmStats.btnUpdateClick(Sender: TObject);
Var
  Rec : Almstats.AlarmStatsRecord;
begin
  if Not FileIsOpen then
    exit;
  With Rec Do Begin
    Day := Copy (DayList.Items[DayList.ItemIndex], 1, 3);
    Time := HourList.Items[HourList.ItemIndex];
    NumberOfSignals := StrToInt (TotalSigs.Text);
    AlarmSignals := StrtoInt (AlarmSigs.Text);
    TroubleSignals := StrToInt (TroubleSigs.Text);
    OperatorSignals := StrToInt (OperatorSigs.Text);
  End;
  Almstats.Update (AlarmFile,
                   DayList.ItemIndex,
                   HourList.ItemIndex,
                   Rec);
end;

procedure TAlarmStats.btnPrintClick(Sender: TObject);
Var
  Day,
  Hour : Integer;
  Rec,
```

```
    DayRec,
    WeekRec : Almstats.AlarmStatsRecord;
    PrintText : System.Text;
begin
  OpenTheFile;
  { Initialize the printer }
  AssignPrn (PrintText);
  Rewrite (PrintText);
  { use a fixed-pitch font so things line up }
  Printer.Canvas.Font.Name := 'Courier';
  Printer.Canvas.Font.Pitch := fpFixed;
  { clear week totals }
  with WeekRec do begin
    NumberOfSignals := 0;
    OperatorSignals := 0;
    AlarmSignals := 0;
    TroubleSignals := 0;
  end;
  { for each day }
  for Day := 0 to 6 do begin
    { clear the day totals }
    with DayRec do begin
      NumberOfSignals := 0;
      OperatorSignals := 0;
      AlarmSignals := 0;
      TroubleSignals := 0;
    end;
    WriteLn (PrintText, DayList.Items[Day]);
    { and for each hour in the day }
    for Hour := 0 to 23 do begin
      { get the record }
      Almstats.Lookup (AlarmFile, Day, Hour, Rec);
      with Rec do begin
        { print the record }
        WriteLn (PrintText,
          Time:11, ' ',
          NumberOfSignals:10,
          OperatorSignals:10,
          AlarmSignals:10,
          TroubleSignals:10);
        { and update the day totals }
        DayRec.NumberOfSignals :=
          DayRec.NumberOfSignals + NumberOfSignals;
        DayRec.OperatorSignals :=
          DayRec.OperatorSignals + OperatorSignals;
        DayRec.AlarmSignals :=
          DayRec.AlarmSignals + AlarmSignals;
        DayRec.TroubleSignals :=
          DayRec.TroubleSignals + TroubleSignals;
      end;
    end;
    with DayRec do begin
      { print the day's totals }
```

```
      WriteLn (PrintText,
        'Day Totals':11, ' ',
         NumberOfSignals:10,
         OperatorSignals:10,
         AlarmSignals:10,
         TroubleSignals:10);
      { and add to week's totals }
      WeekRec.NumberOfSignals :=
        WeekRec.NumberOfSignals + NumberOfSignals;
      WeekRec.OperatorSignals :=
        WeekRec.OperatorSignals + OperatorSignals;
      WeekRec.AlarmSignals :=
        WeekRec.AlarmSignals + AlarmSignals;
      WeekRec.TroubleSignals :=
        WeekRec.TroubleSignals + TroubleSignals;
    end;
    WriteLn (PrintText);  { blank line between days }
  end;

  WriteLn (PrintText);  { extra blank line before grand totals }
  { print the week totals }
  with WeekRec do
    WriteLn (PrintText,
      'Week Totals':11, ' ',
       NumberOfSignals:10,
       OperatorSignals:10,
       AlarmSignals:10,
       TroubleSignals:10);
  System.Close (PrintText);
end;

procedure TAlarmStats.btnExportClick(Sender: TObject);
Var
  Rec : Almstats.AlarmStatsRecord;
  Day,
  Hour : Integer;
  OutputFile : System.Text;
begin
  OpenTheFile;
  { create the output file }
  System.Assign (OutputFile, OutputFileName);
  Rewrite (OutputFile);
  { for each day }
  for Day := 0 to 6 do begin
    { and each hour }
    for Hour := 0 to 23 do begin
      { get the record }
      Almstats.Lookup (AlarmFile, Day, Hour, Rec);
      with Rec do
        { and output it in comma-separated values format }
        WriteLn (OutputFile,
          '"',Day,'",',
          '"',Time,'",',
```

```
            '"',NumberOfSignals,'"',',
            '"',AlarmSignals,'"',',
            '"',TroubleSignals,'"',',
            '"',OperatorSignals,'"');
      end;
    end;
    System.Close (OutputFile);
end;

procedure TAlarmStats.btnQuitClick(Sender: TObject);
begin
  Close;
end;
```

Before we begin our discussion of that code, we've got a couple more items to add to the form's code. First, add these declarations:

```
{ Private declarations }
AlarmFile : AlarmFiletype;
FileIsOpen : Boolean;
procedure OpenTheFile;
procedure CloseTheFile;
```

to the **private** section of the **TAlarmStats class** definition. Then, add these constant definitions right above the form's **class** definition:

```
const
  TextFilename = 'ALMSTATS.TXT';
  OutputFilename = 'ALMSTATS.CSV';
  StatsFilename = 'ALMSTATS.DAT';
```

Finally, create OnCreate and OnClose event handlers for the form and enter the code in Listing 11.4.

Listing 11.4   The Stats program's OnCreate, OnClose, and file-handling procedures

```
procedure TAlarmStats.FormCreate(Sender: TObject);
begin
  FileIsOpen := False;
end;

procedure TAlarmStats.FormClose(Sender: TObject; var Action: TCloseAction);
begin
  CloseTheFile;
end;

procedure TAlarmStats.OpenTheFile;
begin
```

```
  if not FileIsOpen then begin
    Almstats.OpenAlarmFile (AlarmFile, StatsFilename);
    FileIsOpen := True;
  end;
end;

procedure TAlarmStats.CloseTheFile;
begin
  if FileIsOpen then begin
    Almstats.CloseAlarmFile (AlarmFile);
    FileIsOpen := False;
  end;
end;
```

Just one more thing: Add Printers and Almstats to the list of units in the form's **uses** statement, and then press F2 to save your work. *Now* we can talk about the program. Don't try to compile the program, as you'll get an error when it tries to find the Almstats unit.

How it Works

The first thing that you'll notice about the program in Listings 11.3 and 11.4 is that it never accesses a file! All file access is done through routines in the Almstats unit, which we haven't written yet. We know what we want the Almstats unit to do, though: We want it to encapsulate all file manipulation.

Almstats contains the **AlarmStatsRecord** structure, a **type** definition called **AlarmFileType**, and the following procedures:

- **OpenAlarmFile** opens a named file
- **CloseAlarmFile** closes a file
- **Lookup** reads the specified record from an open file
- **Update** updates the specified record in an open file
- **Import** reads a text file containing alarm information, and creates a file of **AlarmStatsRecord**

We'll discuss the implementation of these procedures in the **Almstats** unit in the next section. Let's concentrate on the main form's code for the moment.

When the program first starts, the OnCreate event procedure sets the **FileOpen** variable to **False**, indicating that no file has been opened yet. Each of the procedures that reads the file calls **OpenTheFile** to make sure the file is open before proceeding. The reason the file isn't opened when the program starts is that it might not be there. If the file didn't exist and we tried to open it when the program started, we'd get an I/O error and the program would stop.

The form's OnClose event procedure calls **CloseTheFile** to ensure that the file is closed before the program exits.

The event procedures for the **Lookup** and **Update** buttons are pretty straightforward. **Lookup** simply obtains the **Day** and **Hour** values from the combo boxes and calls **Almstats.Lookup** to obtain the record. After getting the record, it sets the edit fields to reflect the information just read.

Update is the opposite of **Lookup**. It gets the **Day** and **Hour** values from the combo boxes, sets the **Rec** variable's fields from the information in the edit fields, and then calls **Almstats.Update** to write the new information to the file.

The Import button's processing simply calls **Almstats.Import** to read new information into the alarm statistics file, and then calls the **Lookup** routine to obtain and display the first record in the file.

The Print button processing in Listing 11.3 is similar to the **ComputeAverageMiles** procedure shown in Listing 11.1, except that we're reading from a file of records instead of a text file. The processing techniques are the same, though, and are best described by this pseudo-code:

```
clear the week's totals
for each day
  clear the day's totals
  for each hourly record
    print the information
    add the information to the day's totals
  end of hourly record
  print the day's totals
  add day's totals to week's totals
end of each day's processing
print week's totals
```

That's really all there is to it. This type of processing makes up a very large part of day-to-day business programming. Today's automated tools (like Borland's ReportSmith product) help eliminate most of the drudgery, but those tools are normally designed to work on database files—not simple text files and files of records. Automated tools also handle things like column headings, page breaks, and page numbers—things that I didn't include in this program.

Comma-Separated Values

The last of the event procedures, **TAlarmStats.btnExportClick**, reads the alarm statistics file and creates a special kind of text file that contains *comma-separated values*. A typical record in this kind of file would look like this:

```
"WED","13:00","287","65","24","84"
```

Each field in the record is enclosed in quotation marks, and the fields are separated by commas. Most database and spreadsheet programs are able to read this type of file, which makes it the natural choice for moving data from one program to another. This is the file format that I used to transfer the alarm statistics information at work to my boss' and the business manager's spreadsheet programs.

As you can see by the Export button's event procedure, creating a file of comma-separated values is fairly simple. *Reading* this type of file is a little more difficult. In order to do so, you have to read each line of text into a **String** variable, and then parse out each individual field. It's not an impossible task, but it's beyond the scope of this book.

The Almstats Unit

The only thing missing from our program now is the Almstats unit that implements all of the file I/O. To add this unit to your project, select File | New Unit, and enter the code shown in Listing 11.5.

Listing 11.5   The Almstats unit

```
{ alarm statistics unit }
unit AlmStats;

interface

type
  { statistics record for each 15-minute period }
  AlarmStatsRecord = record
    Day : String[3];
    Time : String[5];
    NumberOfSignals : Integer;
    OperatorSignals : Integer;
    AlarmSignals : Integer;
    TroubleSignals : Integer;
  end;

  AlarmFileType = File of AlarmStatsRecord;

procedure OpenAlarmFile (var f : AlarmFileType;
  Const AlarmFilename : String);
procedure CloseAlarmFile (var f : AlarmFileType);
procedure Lookup (var f : AlarmFileType;
  Day, Hour : Integer; var Rec : AlarmStatsRecord);
procedure Update (var f : AlarmFileType;
  Day, Hour : Integer; var Rec : AlarmStatsRecord);
```

```
procedure Import (Const InputFilename, AlarmFilename : String);

implementation

procedure OpenAlarmFile (var f : AlarmFileType;
  Const AlarmFilename : String);
begin
  Assign (f, AlarmFilename);
  Reset (f);
end;

procedure CloseAlarmFile (var f : AlarmFileType);
begin
  Close (f);
end;

procedure Lookup (var f : AlarmFileType;
  Day, Hour : Integer; var Rec : AlarmStatsRecord);
var
  RecordNo : Integer;
begin
  RecordNo := (Day * 24) + Hour;
  Seek (f, RecordNo);
  Read (f, Rec);
end;

procedure Update (var f : AlarmFileType;
  Day, Hour : Integer; var Rec : AlarmStatsRecord);
var
  RecordNo : Integer;
begin
  RecordNo := (Day * 24) + Hour;
  Seek (f, RecordNo);
  Write (f, Rec);
end;

procedure Import (Const InputFilename, AlarmFilename : String);
Var
  f : AlarmFileType;
  t : Text;
  Rec : AlarmStatsRecord;
  c : Char;
begin
  { open the input file }
  Assign (t, InputFilename);
  Reset (t);
  { create the output file }
  Assign (f, AlarmFilename);
  Rewrite (f);
  { now read all of the records }
  while not Eof (t) do begin
    with Rec do
      ReadLn (t,
        Day,
```

```
       c,     { trash the extra space }
       Time,
       AlarmSignals,
       TroubleSignals,
       NumberOfSignals,
       OperatorSignals);
   Write (f, Rec);
  end;
  Close (f);
  Close (t);
end;

end.
```

After you enter this code, press F2 to save the file, calling it ALMSTATS.PAS.

There really isn't any magic in Almstats: It's all pretty straightforward file handling. There are two things that might trip you up.

The **Lookup** and **Update** procedures compute the record number by multiplying the **Day** parameter by 24, then adding the **Hour** parameter. This corresponds to the format of the file: 24 records per day. Remember that days and hours are numbered starting at 0—not at 1—which makes this approach work.

The other thing that might trip you up is in the **Import** procedure, where I have this **Read** statement:

```
ReadLn(t,
       Day,
       c,     { trash the extra space }
       Time,
       AlarmSignals,
       TroubleSignals,
       NumberOfSignals,
       OperatorSignals);
```

which is simply reading a record from the text file into an **AlarmStatsRecord**. A typical record in the input file looks like this:

```
SUN 00:00 56 11 329 57
```

Since **Read** doesn't understand the concept of field separators when it's reading **String** variables, we need to read the space character between the day and time (the first two fields in the record) into a temporary variable. If we didn't do this, then **Read** would be off by one character when it tried to read the first number (56 in this example), and we'd get an "Invalid numeric format" runtime I/O error.

After you've entered the Almstats unit and saved your work, you can go ahead and press F9 to start the program. The first thing you should do is click on the Import button to create the alarm statistics file from the ALMSTATS.TXT file on the listings diskette. Then, try looking up and updating some records, printing, and exporting the file.

END OF FILE

There's another kind of file that we didn't discuss, the *untyped file*, which allows you to read and write files that contain variable-length records. Untyped files are the common ancestor of both text files and typed files, but accessing an untyped file directly is a fairly advanced programming technique, and the subject for another time. If you're interested in learning about untyped files, consult the online help for the **BlockRead** and **BlockWrite** functions.

The file types that we did discuss—text files and files of records—should allow you to implement simple flat-file database programs. For more advanced database applications, you'll want to use Delphi's database components, which we'll be talking about in Chapters 13 and after.

Points of Light, Spots on Paper

Jeff Duntemann

Graphics on the screen or on paper—it's the same thing, really, if you use the Delphi canvas graphics architecture.

Back at the Dawn of Real Time (say, 1980 or thereabouts) I was sitting in Todd Johnson's basement apartment in Chicago's western suburbs, admiring a strange device on his battered dining room table. It was eerily reminiscent of the original Macintosh computer: A smallish cabinet dominated by a monochrome screen and little else. It was called a Vectrix, and in fact it was a video game, but one based on *vector* graphics technology rather than raster graphics technology. In vector graphics, a specially-designed display draws individual lines at arbitrary positions and angles, rather than scanning the full screen from top to bottom. Back when computer power was mostly a dream (as in 1980) this allowed very fast computer graphics, because the computer only had to draw a few lines...not cover an entire screen with them.

Todd was fascinated by the device, and was intent on figuring out how to get behind the Vectrix's video game facade and actually program it. Another onlooker (whose name, perhaps mercifully for him, has been forgotten) cynically commented, "Some computer you'll have—all it'll do is graphics."

At that point my good friend William Skeffington Higgins, (a celebrated Fermilab physicist who plays pocket billiards with subatomic particles) stepped in and said, "Hey, hold on a second—graphics are what computers are *for.*"

Bill was right, as he usually is about things. When people go to a computer show, what do they gather around and gape at? Accounting packages? Personnel management systems? Or *Doom II?* I've actually seen a Pac Man knock-off running in *text mode*, for crying out loud. Shall we say it lacks something.

In a sense, all Delphi programming is graphics, because Delphi applications are Windows applications. But by "graphics" most people mean putting points of light on the screen, or points of dirt (hey, be honest now) on paper, in interesting patterns, with extra credit when they move around. (On the screen, at least.) So we're going to talk a bit about Delphi's abilities with points, lines, and simple figures. Remarkably enough, drawing to the screen and drawing to paper are pretty much the same task, as I'll show you shortly.

Graphics is a big topic, and this is not a big book, so I won't be able to explain everything you'll ever need to know about graphics. But as is my usual goal, I'll try my best to explain enough so that you can figure the rest out on your own.

A CARTESIAN CANVAS

There was this old French guy named Descartes, see, and he got into the history books for inventing graph paper...well, that's not entirely the case, but I could understand how a seventh-grader might think so, having tried to confront the reality of a Cartesian grid. (And no, Descartes did not invent the Cartesian Well either, since there is no such thing as a Cartesian Well.) But what you probably would call an x,y coordinate system was very much what Descartes invented, and the fact that most such systems have historically been drawn on graph paper is incidental.

The true Cartesian grid is shown in Figure 12.1. It's actually two number lines at right angles to one another, both going off to infinity, or at least to the edge of the graph paper. The point where the two number lines cross is called the *origin*. Other points on the grid are represented by pairs of numbers indicating their distance from the origin along the two number lines. The origin itself

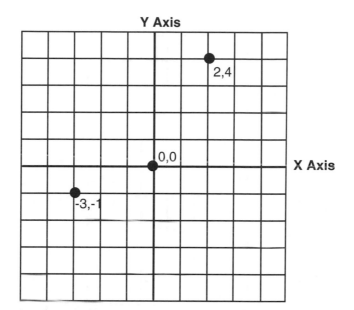

Figure 12.1 *The Cartesian grid.*

has the coordinates 0,0. By convention, the first number is the distance from the origin along the x number line (that's the horizontal one) and the second number is the distance from the origin along the y number line, which is vertical. In Figure 12.1, there is a point located at 2,4 on the grid.

Accentuate the Positive, But With a Twist

Because number lines go off to infinity in both positive and negative directions, there may be negative coordinates on a Cartesian grid. That's why there's a point with the coordinates -3,-1 in Figure 12.1. If you limit yourself solely to positive coordinates, you'll only be able to plot points in the upper right quadrant of the Cartesian grid. In a sense, that's how Delphi handles things. When you draw graphics in Delphi, you'll be working on a Cartesian coordinate system, but one in which the number lines grow only in a positive direction away from the origin.

There's a twist, though: Delphi puts the origin at the upper left corner of your drawing area (called a *canvas*) rather than at the lower left. The y axis goes down as it gets more positive, rather than up, but points get themselves plotted just as well. This is a convention in most computer graphics: The origin is placed at the upper left corner of the drawing area. I'm honestly not sure why this is so (and it's not universal; the OS/2 operating system goes back to the

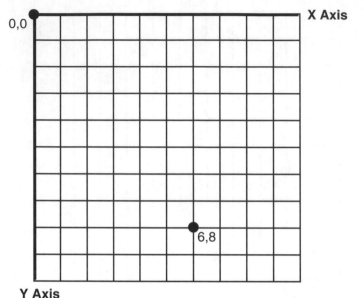

Figure 12.2 *A Delphi canvas.*

Cartesian convention of the y axis going up in a positive direction) but we're stuck with it. Figure 12.2 shows a Delphi canvas and its coordinate system.

THE CANVAS AS OBJECT

You can think of a Delphi canvas as a piece of programmable graph paper without the lines. (Since it's programmable, who needs lines?) A canvas is actually an object of class **TCanvas**, and like all objects, has its properties and methods. Canvases aren't usually used alone, however. In most cases, a canvas will be an object belonging to another object, and serves as the drawing surface for that "owner" object. Think of it as a sheet of paper in a clipboard; it's tough to hold a piece of paper in mid-air and draw on it, so you attach the paper to a clipboard to stiffen it up and give yourself a way to hold it.

So a canvas has properties; in most cases a canvas *is* a property—of other more complex objects like forms and printers. Because it's really the same canvas regardless of what object owns it—form, printer, whatever—you'll find that drawing graphics is basically the same kettle of fish, irrespective of what you're drawing on. This allows you to use a lot of the same Object Pascal code to do your drawing, no matter where the final patterns will appear.

The Canvas.Pixels Array

The easiest way to see a canvas in action is simply to draw on the canvas owned by every form. When you drop controls onto a form, you're actually dropping them on the form's canvas. You can draw on that canvas as well—in fact, you can draw anywhere on a form where the form isn't covered up by controls.

The way it's done is to think of the canvas as a Cartesian grid, as shown in Figure 12.2—but a Cartesian grid implemented as a two-dimensional array called **Pixels**, each element of which is a dot on the canvas that can be set to any of numerous colors. This array is actually a property of the canvas itself, and you can assign to it and read from it just as you would any Pascal two-dimensional array. The left dimension is the x value, and the right dimension is the y value. The syntax for reading and setting values in the **Pixels** array is pretty much what you'd expect:

```
VAR
  TestColor : TColor;
  X,Y : Integer;

Canvas.Pixels[X,Y] := clWhite;
TestColor := Canvas.Pixels[X,Y];
```

There's no distinction between foreground and background colors here. The **Pixels** array is simply an array of dots with colors. When you instantiate a form, all of the dots in its **Pixels** array will be set to the color held by the form in its **Color** property, which you can see in the Object Inspector. You can change them all to another color, either at design time or runtime, simply by assigning one of the other legal **TColor** values to the **Color** property.

Setting dots individually using the **Pixels** array isn't done very often, because to make any visible effect on the screen you have to set a *lot* of dots—and that's slow work done one-by-one.

DRAWING LINES

Drawing lines on a canvas in Delphi is done in almost exactly the same way it was done in the Borland Graphics Interface (BGI) in earlier versions of Turbo and Borland Pascal. There's some jargon-wrestling to be done, alas. What the BGI called the *current pointer* is called the *pen position* for Delphi.

The word "pen" is more in keeping with Windows notation, because Windows itself defines logical entities called *pens* that are used for drawing. The pen position should be thought of as where the invisible pen is *now*; when you draw a line, the pen position will be the first end of the line. The other end, obviously, is where the pen ends up when you finish drawing the line.

When you instantiate a form, the pen position defaults to 0,0—which is the upper left corner of the canvas. As you draw things, the pen position moves around on the canvas. You can't see the pen position directly, but you can query it with the **TCanvas.PenPos** property. Consider **PenPos** read-only—don't try to move the pen position by writing to it! (That's what **MoveTo** is for.)

As in the BGI, lines are drawn with the **MoveTo** and **LineTo** routines. **MoveTo** places the pen position somewhere on the canvas. **LineTo** draws a line from the pen position to the x,y coordinate you pass as the parameters to **LineTo**. This is easier to show than to tell you, so let's just do it.

X Marks the Spot

This only slightly brain-dead project draws a Big X with **LineTo** and **MoveTo**. In the process you'll see how canvas graphics work, along with the relationship between the form's canvas and any controls you might place on it.

Start a new project with a blank form. Drop a button on the form; although it doesn't matter where, see if you can place it bang-on in the center of the form. There's a reason for that which I'll come to shortly. For the **OnClick** event for the button, set up the following procedure:

Listing 12.1   OnClick event handler from XMAKER.PAS

```
procedure TForm1.Button1Click(Sender: TObject);
begin
  WITH Canvas DO
    BEGIN
      MoveTo(0,0);
      LineTo(ClientWidth,ClientHeight);
      MoveTo(ClientWidth,0);
      LineTo(0,ClientHeight);
    END;
end;
```

That's all the code you need to write for the time being. Save the project as BIGX and the unit file as XMAKER.PAS. Run it. Press the button—and there's your X!

No, it's not rocket science, but it teaches a couple of lessons. Make sure you fully understand what both **LineTo** and **MoveTo** do here. I'll admit that the first **MoveTo** is not really necessary, because the default pen position for a new form is 0,0. But if you wanted to start your X somewhere else, you'd need to move the pen position first. After the first **LineTo**, the pen position moves to coordinates **ClientWidth,ClientHeight**—which is the lower right corner of the client area of the form. And since in our simple form the canvas covers the entire client area, that means the lower right corner of the canvas. **ClientWidth** and **ClientHeight** are both properties of **TForm**, and they always contain the size of the client area of the form. They can be mighty handy for adjusting form-based graphics to the size of the form. (Hint: the **OnResize** event happens whenever the user changes the size of the form.)

There's another lesson that you'll learn if you placed the button anywhere in the path of the two lines making the Big X: Graphics drawn with **LineTo** fall *behind* any controls on the form. This is a general rule: When you drop controls onto a form, they are really "on top of" the form, and therefore on top of the canvas. And while one control may be on top of another control, all controls are *always* on top of (and therefore hide) the canvas of the form they're placed on. There's nothing easy that you can do to draw on top of controls like buttons. Buttons, in fact, are creatures owned by Windows and controlled by Windows, and even changing the color of a standard Windows button is non-trivial.

Clearing a Canvas

The better half of knowing how to make a mess is knowing how to clean up after your mess. Clearing a canvas back to a single color is easy—so easy, in fact, that I'm not even going to make a project out of it. Here's all you do: Drop a second button anywhere on the Big X form, and create an event procedure for its OnClick event. As the single solitary line of code in that event procedure put the method **Refresh**. That's all!

When you execute the **Canvas.Refresh** method, all the pixels in the **Pixels** array are set back to the color specified in the form's **Color** property.

The form with both of the buttons (and the X) is shown in Figure 12.3.

Fooling Around with Line Widths and Styles

That invisible pen that you track with the pen position is itself an object of type **TPen**, and a property of the canvas. On a new form the pen draws a

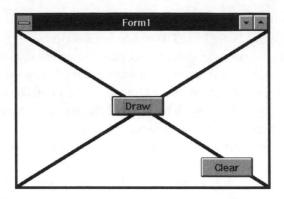

Figure 12.3 *The Big X.*

solid black line one pixel wide, but you can change all of those aspects by changing the properties of the **Pen** property. **Pen.Width** specifies the width of the line. It can be any reasonable integer value; I've used up to 120 without a burp from Delphi. **Pen.Color** can be any of the legal **TColor** values like **clBlue**, **clWhite**, **clSilver**, and so on.

Pen.Style may be set to any of the values in Table 12.1. Most are self-explanatory, which means that if you try using them they will explain themselves. Inside the **OnClick** event procedure for the Draw button in Big X, set **Pen.Width** or **Pen.Style** to a few different values and see what happens.

The **psClear** style allows you to draw some lines without actually marking the canvas. This can also be done by using **MoveTo** instead of **LineTo**, but you might be drawing lines by iterating through a loop of some sort, and simply changing the style of the pen to **psClear** might be simpler than branching between the **MoveTo** and **LineTo** methods. This is especially true if you are reading a complex polygon from a table, and only need to draw some of the strokes, as when rendering a stroke font.

SIMPLE FIGURES

Every canvas has built-in methods for drawing several types of simple figures. These include rectangles, rounded rectangles, ellipses, pie slices, arcs, and chords. The general class of ellipses also includes circles. Closed figures may be filled with colors. Beyond simple figures are polylines and polygons, which we'll discuss in the next section.

Table 12.1   *Style Values for the TPen Object*

Pen Styles	Style Description
psSolid	Solid line
psDash	Dashed line
psDot	Dotted line
psDashDot	Pattern in which dashes and dots alternate
psDashDotDot	Pattern composed of dash-dot-dot sequences
psClear	"Transparent" style; that is, nothing visible drawn
psInsideFrame	Line drawn within a bounding rectangle only

Bounding Rectangles

Specifying certain simple figures in Delphi is done by specifying a bounding rectangle, which is simply a rectangle within which the figure just barely fits. For rectangular figures, (which includes rectangles and squares) the bounding rectangle *is* the rectangle; for some other figures like ellipses and rounded rectangles, the figure fits inside and just touches the bounding rectangle.

A bounding rectangle is specified as four values comprising two coordinate sets. Think of the first pair as the x,y of the upper left corner of the rectangle, and the second pair as the lower right corner. All four of the coordinate figures are integers. The coordinates are *absolute coordinates*, which means that they specify actual positions on the canvas measured from the canvas's origin at its upper left corner, and not positions relative to the current pen position or some other point.

The best way to make this stick, as usual, is simply to show it in action. Load the FIGURES project from the companion disk and run it. There's not a lot of action involved, but you'll see a number of figures drawn within their bounding rectangles. I'll be referring back to Figure 12.4 as I discuss several different kinds of figures over the next several pages. Listing 12.2 shows the actual drawing code that generated the graphics shown in Figure 12.4. As you can see, there's not a whole lot to it.

Listing 12.2   OnPaint event handler from FIGMAKER.PAS

```
procedure TForm1.FormPaint(Sender: TObject);
begin
  Width  := 490;
  Height := 310;
```

```
WITH Canvas DO
  BEGIN
    {First we draw an ordinary rectangle, which is }
    {congruent to its bounding rectangle:           }
    Rectangle(10,10,170,80);
    {Next we'll draw the same size bounding rectangle   }
    {shifted down a ways, but with an ellipse inside it:}
    Rectangle(10,100,170,170);  {Bounding rectangle      }
    Ellipse(10,100,170,170);     {Ellipse within it       }
    {For good measure, here's the ellipse by itself:  }
    Ellipse(10,190,170,260);
    {Now we'll draw the bounding rectangle of a rounded }
    {rectangle, and then the rounded rectangle itself:  }
    Rectangle(200,10,370,80);
    RoundRect(200,10,370,80,20,20);
    {The rounded rectangle looks bad with its bounding }
    {rectangle around it, so let's draw one alone:      }
    RoundRect(200,100,370,170,20,20);
    {One draws a circle by drawing an ellipse within a }
    {bounding rectangle that is in fact a square:       }
    Rectangle(400,10,470,80);   { This is a square       }
    Ellipse(400,10,470,80);      { This is a circle       }
    {And now the circle all by itself:                 }
    Ellipse(400,100,470,170);
    {The two rounded corner parameters to RoundRect do }
    {not have to be the same. Here's another rectangle }
    { with asymmetrical rounded corners:                }
    RoundRect(200,190,370,260,50,20);
  END;

end;
```

Rounded Rectangles

The **RoundRect** method takes two additional parameters beyond the coordinates for the bounding rectangle. These two parameters indicate how the

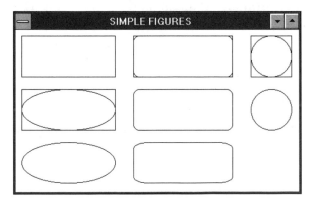

Figure 12.4 *Simple figures and their bounding rectangles.*

corners are to be rounded. It's an interesting system that you have to try a few times to truly get a knack for. The trick is that the rounded corners are each quarter segments of an ellipse, as shown in Figure 12.5. The first of the two corner parameters specifies the width of the ellipse. The second of the two corner parameters specifies the height of the ellipse. If the two values are the same, the corners will be quarters of circles, since a circle is an ellipse with identical width and height. The middle rounded rectangle in Figure 12.4 has such symmetrical corners.

Compare the corners of the final rounded rectangle (which have different corner parameters) with the corners of the rounded rectangle in the center of the form, in which the rounded corners are symmetrical, with both corner parameters at 20.

Ellipses

If you've got a bounding rectangle defined, you've also defined an ellipse. If you think of a deformed circle residing inside a rectangle such that the deformed circle touches the inside of the rectangle at four points, then that circle is an ellipse as Delphi would draw it. If you have a bounding *square* instead of a rectangle (with four equal sides), then the ellipse it defines is in fact a circle. There are both an ellipse and a circle drawn within their respective bounding rectangles in Figure 12.4, and this whole business of ellipses can be explained better by looking at that one figure than I could describe in a whole afternoon.

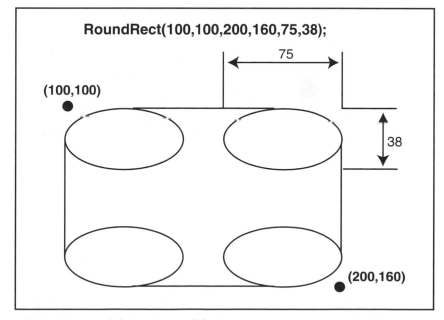

Figure 12.5 *How rounded rectangles are defined.*

To draw an ellipse or a circle, you simply pass the corner coordinates of its bounding rectangle to the canvas's **Ellipse** method:

```
Canvas.Ellipse(10,100,170,170);
```

Polylines and Polygons

Most people think of *polygons* as figures like squares, triangles, pentagons, and the like. These are actually *regular polygons*, which have the requirement that all the sides are of equal length and all the angles between the sides are equal as well. But a polygon is actually any closed figure consisting of three lines or more.

If a polygon isn't closed (that is, if the line that encloses it has two ends that don't meet), what you have isn't a polygon at all but a *polyline*. A polyline is simply a series of lines joined together that don't come together at the "loose ends." The classic yellow folding 6' rule (which may or may not exist any-more, in this age of cheap tape measures) is a good example of a polyline in real life. It consist of six one-foot rulers hinged together at their ends.

Both polylines and polygons can be drawn in Delphi using canvas-oriented graphics. The **TCanvas** type has two methods, **Polyline** and **Polygon**, to do the job. Both methods are called precisely the same way, and take the same (somewhat peculiar) parameter described in the next section.

Open Array Parameters

This peculiar parameter is something called an *open array parameter*, and it allows you to pass arrays of various sizes to a procedure or function. In the case of **Polyline** and **Polygon**, this means an array of elements that are of type **TPoint**. **TPoint** is a simple record, predefined in Delphi, that expresses a coordinate pair:

```
TYPE
  TPoint =
    RECORD
      X : Integer;
      Y : Integer;
    END;
```

If you were to define an array of **TPoint** records, you could express a line, since a line (whether open, as in a polyline, or closed, as in a polygon) is nothing more than a string of points connected between them. The first point in the array is the starting point of the polyline or polygon, and the second point defines the end of the first line segment. The third point defines the end of the second line segment, and so on.

The parameter you pass to either **Polyline** or **Polygon** is an *open* array because you do not have to pass the same number of array elements every time you call the function. *Any* array of **TPoint** records may be passed to **Polyline** or **Polygon** as its sole parameter. You can define an array and fill it via assignment statements. Or you could do something a little bit different and pass an *array constant*, consisting of numeric literals as coordinate pairs in sequence. We won't be covering array constants in detail in this book. You can get additional information by looking up "Array-type constants" in Delphi Help.

The easiest way to put together an array constant of **TPoint** records for **Polyline** and **Polygon** is to use one of Delphi's built-in functions called **Point**. **Point** takes an x and a y integer value and returns as its result type a record of type **TPoint**. You can string calls to the **Point** function together in sequence, like this, to form an array of **TPoint** records

```
[Point(x,y),Point(x,y),Point(x,y)..Point(x,y)]
```

This is nothing more than a series of function calls to **Point**, separated by commas, with the whole shebang enclosed in square brackets. There can be as many of these function calls in the array as you like.

The main difference between the **Polyline** and **Polygon** methods is that the **Polygon** method always closes the lines it draws into a polygon, whereas **Polyline** leaves the figure open. **Polygon** automatically draws one additional line between the endpoint that you draw and the point where you started. **Polyline** doesn't draw that final line. Compare the syntax of the two methods as used in Listing 12.3.

Listing 12.3   Drawing figures with Polyline and Polygon

```
procedure TForm1.FormPaint(Sender: TObject);
begin
  WITH Canvas DO
    BEGIN
      Brush.Color := clYellow;
      Polygon(
        [Point(150,20),
         Point(260,100),
         Point(220,220),
         Point(80,220),
```

```
        Point(40,100)]); { The last line is from this point }
                         { back to the first point!         }

      PolyLine(
        [Point(110,160),
         Point(110,100),
         Point(150,160),
         Point(190,100),
         Point(190,160)]);
    END;
end;
```

The output generated by Listing 12.3 is shown in Figure 12.6. A passable (if not entirely regular) pentagon drawn by **Polygon** has within it a passable letter "M" drawn with **Polyline**.

PRINTING GRAPHICS

The marvelous thing about printing graphics in Delphi is that it's basically the same as printing to the screen. All of Delphi's graphics output primitives are canvas-based. The **TCanvas** class provides that "clean sheet" to draw on—and it's left to the object that owns the canvas to implement that clean sheet in the real world. A canvas owned by a **TForm** draws on the screen, within a clipping rectangle represented by the bounds of the form's window. On the other hand, a canvas owned by a **TPrinter** class does its drawing on an actual physical clean sheet of paper that comes out of your printer. Essentially all of the drawing methods you've encountered in drawing to the screen can be used to draw to paper.

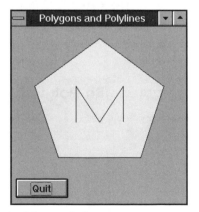

Figure 12.6 *The Polygon and Polyline methods.*

The drawing methods work the same way, and assume a Cartesian grid with its origin in the upper left corner of the sheet of paper. There are typically a lot more pixels on a **TPrinter**'s canvas as compared with a **TForm**'s canvas, which is their major difference. If you draw a figure of a reasonable size on a form, it'll show up in the same shape on a printer—only tiny. If you have a high-resolution laser printer, that could mean *very* tiny.

To print graphics, you have to include the **Printers** unit in the **uses** statement of your main project unit; that is, the one that defines your main form. This allows you to use objects of the **TPrinter** class. There is an object of class **TPrinter** automatically declared for you within the **Printers** unit: **Printer**. This object represents the currently selected Windows printer, and in most cases you won't have to fuss with declaring your own **TPrinter** objects.

The Mechanics of Printing

Printing graphics on a printer page is different from printing graphics on a form in another important way: When you print graphics on a form, your graphics patterns simply show up on the form. When you print graphics to a printer, you have to tell the printer when to kick out a piece of paper with your graphics on it.

So to place graphics on a piece of paper, you have to bracket your actual calls to the drawing methods between two other methods of **TPrinter**: **BeginDoc** and **EndDoc**. What **BeginDoc** does is set up the necessary memory buffers to support the generally high resolution of current printers, especially the newer laser printers, which may have 600 dots per inch of resolution. After **Printer.BeginDoc** executes, you can execute the canvas-oriented drawing methods of the **Printer** object, like **LineTo**, **Rectangle**, **Polyline**, and so on. When you're done drawing to the printer canvas and want to print what you've drawn, call **Printer.EndDoc**. This kicks the current paper out of the printer with your graphics on it, and disposes of the memory buffers involved in printing, so that the memory can be used for other things.

Which Printer and How Big Is Its Canvas?

Under Windows, you can define several printers as being present on the system, but only one of them is considered the *default printer*. The default Windows printer is the printer to which you can print through the **Printer** object that is instantiated when you put the **Printers** unit in your **uses** statement. In general Windows terms, it's the printer to which print output is sent, absent any other specific instructions about which printer to print to.

You can choose which of the installed printers is the default printer by selecting the Printer Setup menu option in Windows 3.1 Print Manager, highlighting the printer of your choice in the list shown in the dialog box, and then pressing the Set as Default Printer button. Windows for Workgroups has a more powerful Print Manager, and there is a single button on the toolbar that allows you to choose the default printer. Read up on the matter in Windows Help if this isn't entirely clear.

You can perform this same choice from within a Delphi application by using the Printer Setup dialog box component, which is available in the Dialogs section of the component palette. This is one of the easiest of the standard dialog components to use, because it speaks directly to Windows. (In fact, the whole dialog is part of Windows, and the component is only an encapsulation of the Windows API call that brings up the dialog.) Basically, all you have to do is drop it on your form and then execute it, which is done with the following statement:

```
PrinterDialogSetup1.Execute;
```

For simple applications, you might add a button or a menu item that (when selected) executes this statement. The dialog shows which printers have been installed under Windows and allows you to select which one is to become the default printer. You don't have to process the user input entered through the dialog; all input goes right to Windows, which knows how to handle it.

Unlike the size of a form's canvas, which changes any time the form is resized, the printer canvas is fixed in size by the definition of the default Windows printer. The size of the printer canvas is contained in two properties: **Printer.PageWidth** and **Printer.PageHeight**. You can read them at any time (assuming **Printers** was in your **uses** statement) and they will not change during the run of a program.

Portrait or Landscape?

Most modern printers allow you to select the orientation of the graphics on the paper. The *portrait* orientation is the "tall" way—like a person's portrait. The *landscape* orientation is the "wide" way—like a painting of Mount Rushmore. You can read the orientation of the **Printer** canvas through the **Printer.Orientation** property. There are only two possible values: **PoPortrait** and **PoLandscape**. They are the two defined values in the enumerated type **TPrinterOrientation**. The orientation of the printer determines the corner in which you'll find the origin point, as shown in Figure 12.7.

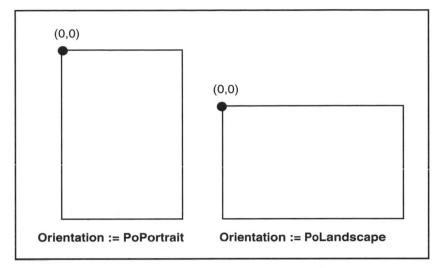

Figure 12.7   *How printer orientation determines the location of point 0,0.*

Orientation is a runtime read-only property. It won't appear on any property sheet. You can't simply assign to it to change the printer orientation; that must be done from Windows Print Manager, or else through the Printer Setup dialog box, as I'll show in the SpiroMania program that concludes this chapter. If you try assigning to **Orientation**, the compiler will let you by, but your program will raise an exception at runtime and you'll see an error box when you try to run the app.

Printing Multiple Sheets

If you only need to print one sheet of paper, bracketing your drawing statements between **BeginDoc** and **EndDoc** will take care of it. However, you may want to print a number of sheets before calling **EndDoc**, which deallocates the memory used for the **Printer.Canvas** buffer and essentially shuts down Delphi's printer machinery until the next **BeginDoc**. To print the current canvas and gain a clean canvas, simply call the **Printer.NewPage** method. **NewPage** will print whatever is on the current canvas, clear the canvas, and set the canvas's pen to 0,0. Only when you're done printing and could use the canvas's buffer memory elsewhere should you call **EndDoc**.

GRAPHICS DEMO: CYCLOID CURVES

To close out this chapter, let me present the umpty-umph descendant of a program I originally presented in *Complete Turbo Pascal, Second Edition* almost ten years ago. It's a software implementation of a marvelous plastic toy I had as a child called a SpiroGraph, which is doubtless someone's trademark, though I'm sure I don't know whose. What the SpiroGraph consisted of was a number of small plastic gears that ran around on the inner edge of a much larger internal gear. There were pencil holes in the small gears, and if you placed a pencil through one of the holes and ran the gear around the inside of the larger internal gear, the pencil would draw elaborate patterns on a sheet of paper beneath the whole assembly.

The sort of curves drawn by a SpiroGraph are called *cycloid curves*, which are easily modeled in software. The gears go away, but the patterns remain, and because you have your choice of a near-infinite number of "pencil holes," the patterns can become elaborate indeed.

SpiroMania!

I'll tie up most of the elements I've explained in this chapter through a Delphi implementation of my poor defunct plastic SpiroGraph. As with our mortgage calculator projects, the cycloid generator is an "engine" in its own separate unit. But unlike the mortgage calculator, the cycloid engine does in fact access the screen, through the **TargetCanvas** parameter of the **SpinWheels** procedure. Since **TargetCanvas** can accept any Delphi canvas, the cycloid engine can draw to either a form canvas or a printer canvas. Buttons are included to allow you to clear the form, draw the curve, set the Windows printer parameters, and quit the program.

Load SPIRO.DPR from the companion disk, compile, and run it. You'll see a display like that shown in Figure 12.8. You don't have to enter any values to generate a pattern; there are default values for all variables in the program, and a pattern will come up as soon as you execute it.

The nature of the curve displayed is governed by three values, A, B, and D. Each of these three values has a SpinEdit control associated with it on the left side of the window. You can either type a new value for any of the three or run the existing values up or down by clicking on the up/down arrows on the SpinEdit controls. Once you change any of the values, click on the Spin button to re-draw the cycloid according to the new values. Clicking on the Clear button clears the display in the window. Drawing a pattern does not automatically clear the display; this allows you to overlay one pattern atop another if you choose. This can be especially effective for patterns laid down in contrasting colors.

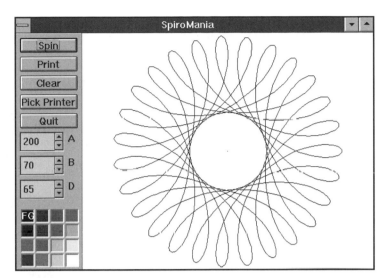

Figure 12.8 *The SpiroMania screen form.*

The Color Select control dictates in which color the next pattern displayed will appear. (Note that Color Select doesn't affect the printed color, even if you have a color printer. Adding support for color printers would be a good research project, if you're one of the fortunate few with a color printer.) Whatever color block has the "FG" (foreground) marker in it will be the next color displayed; to move it, simply click on another color block.

Clicking on the Print button prints the same pattern you see in the window to the default Windows printer. The printed pattern will be at a much higher resolution than the displayed pattern, especially on a laser printer. When you print a pattern, the three governing values A, B, and D will be printed beneath the pattern, so that if you get a nice one, you will know how to re-create it.

Listing 12.5 is the main form unit for SpiroMania. Again, the main form unit implements the user interface. The code that actually generates the cycloid curves is in Listing 12.4, and is called by the user interface routines in Listing 12.5.

Listing 12.4 SPINNER.PAS, the Cycloid Curve Generator

```
{————————————————————————————}
{                SpiroMania                    }
{    SPINNER.PAS : Cycloid Curve Generator     }
{          By Jeff Duntemann KG7JF             }
{                                              }
{ The cycloid curve generator shown here generates }
{ patterns similarly to the old SpiroGraph toy.    }
```

```
{ Written for *The Delphi Programming Explorer*    }
{ Copyright (c) 1995 The Coriolis Group, Inc.      }
{              Last Updated 3/9/95                 }
{————————————————————————————————————————————————}

UNIT Spinner;

INTERFACE

USES SysUtils, WinTypes, WinProcs, Messages, Classes, Graphics, Controls,
Forms, Dialogs, StdCtrls;

PROCEDURE SpinWheels(TargetCanvas : TCanvas;
                     A,B,D,
                     CenterX,CenterY : Integer;
                     DrawColor : TColor);

IMPLEMENTATION

VAR
  A,B,D,I : Integer;
  Quit    : Boolean;


FUNCTION HighestCommonFactor(A,B : Integer) : Integer;

VAR
  I,J,HCF : Integer;

BEGIN               { Euclid's algorithm for finding the HCF }
  IF A < B THEN     { of two integers A and B. }
    BEGIN
      HCF := A;
      I   := B
    END
  ELSE
    BEGIN
      HCF := B;
      I   := A
    END;
  REPEAT
    J := I MOD HCF;
    IF J <> 0 THEN
      BEGIN
        I := HCF;
        HCF := J
      END
  UNTIL J = 0;
  HighestCommonFactor := HCF
END;


PROCEDURE SpinWheels(TargetCanvas : TCanvas;
                     A,B,D,
```

```
                            CenterX,CenterY : Integer;
                            DrawColor : TColor);

VAR
  Rab,Lines,I : Integer;
  Alpha,Beta,ADif,AoverB : Real;
  XPT,YPT : Real;                    { Line endpoint coordinates }

BEGIN
  RAB := A-B; Alpha := 0.0;
  { The constants 100 and 200 here control the smoothness of }
  { the displayed or printed curve. The larger value must be }
  { twice the value that divides PI.  Larger values make for }
  { smoother curves but longer draw times since there are    }
  { more line segments in the drawn curve.                   }
  ADif := PI/100.0; AoverB := A/B;
  Lines := 200 * (B DIV HighestCommonFactor(A,B));
  TargetCanvas.Pen.Color := DrawColor;
  TargetCanvas.MoveTo((Round(RAB+D)+CenterX),CenterY);
  FOR I := 1 TO Lines DO
    BEGIN
      Alpha := Alpha + Adif;
      Beta := Alpha * AoverB;
      XPT := RAB * COS(Alpha) + D * COS(Beta);
      YPT := RAB * SIN(Alpha) - D * SIN(Beta);
      TargetCanvas.LineTo((Round(XPT)+CenterX),Round(YPT)+CenterY);
    END
END;

END. {Spinner}
```

Spinning the Cycloids

Only one routine is made available in the interface section of the **Spinner** unit: **SpinWheels**, which is the routine that actually draws the pattern on the canvas, received as a parameter. This canvas can be either a form canvas or a printer canvas—**SpinWheels** literally can't tell the difference, and doesn't care.

How **SpinWheels** works involves some tricky geometry that I don't have the room to describe in detail here. You might as well take my word for it—it does work. One place in the **SpinWheels** routine where you can apply some leverage is in a pair of literal numeric constants that controls how "smooth" the generated cycloid curve is. In the version published here, I've used 100 and 200, but you can play around with almost any pair of values as long as the second is exactly twice the first. The larger these values are, the smoother the curve will be. Make them very small, and you'll still get a cycloid curve, but it will be somewhat angular and deco-looking. Make them very large, and you'll get a smooth curve indeed, but the time to draw the curve will increase greatly. If you intend to draw patterns on a high-resolution laser printer (600 X 600 DPI or greater), you might try doubling the two constants to 200 and 400.

All this is due to the fact that the cycloid curve is drawn entirely with straight lines! They're short lines, true, but lines nonetheless. The larger the two constants are, the more lines are actually drawn to make up the curve and the shorter the lines are, hence the smoother the curve.

Listing 12.5 SPINFORM.PAS, The SpiroMania Main Form

```
{──────────────────────────────────────────────}
{                  SpiroMania                    }
{          SPINFORM.PAS : Main Form Unit         }
{              By Jeff Duntemann KG7JF           }
{                                                }
{ The main form unit for a cycloid curve generator }
{ functionally similar to the old SpiroGraph toy. }
{ Written for *The Delphi Programming Explorer*  }
{ Copyright (c) 1995 The Coriolis Group, Inc.    }
{              Last Updated 3/9/95               }
{──────────────────────────────────────────────}

unit Spinform;

interface

uses
  SysUtils, WinTypes, WinProcs, Messages, Classes, Graphics, Controls,
  Forms, Dialogs, StdCtrls, Printers,
  Spinner, Buttons, ColorGrd, Spin, ExtCtrls;

type
  TForm1 = class(TForm)
    ButtonPanel: TPanel;
    ClearButton: TButton;
    SpinButton: TButton;
    PrintButton: TButton;
    QuitButton: TButton;
    ColorGrid1: TColorGrid;
    SpinA: TSpinEdit;
    SpinB: TSpinEdit;
    SpinD: TSpinEdit;
    SpinALabel: TLabel;
    SpinBLabel: TLabel;
    SpinDLabel: TLabel;
    PickPrinterButton: TButton;
    PrinterSetupDialog1: TPrinterSetupDialog;
    procedure QuitButtonClick(Sender: TObject);
    procedure SpinButtonClick(Sender: TObject);
```

```
      procedure ClearButtonClick(Sender: TObject);
      procedure PrintButtonClick(Sender: TObject);
      procedure FormCreate(Sender: TObject);
      procedure FormPaint(Sender: TObject);
      procedure PickPrinterButtonClick(Sender: TObject);
    private
      { Private declarations }
    public
      { Public declarations }
    end;

var
  Form1: TForm1;

implementation

var
  CanvasIsClear : Boolean;    { Flags when pattern needs to be regenned }
                              { from within the Paint method.           }

{$R *.DFM}

procedure TForm1.QuitButtonClick(Sender: TObject);
begin
  Close;
end;

procedure TForm1.SpinButtonClick(Sender: TObject);

VAR
  CenterX,CenterY : Integer;

begin
  CanvasIsClear := False;
  CenterY := ClientHeight DIV 2;
  CenterX := (ClientWidth DIV 2) + (ButtonPanel.Width DIV 2);
  Canvas.Pixels[CenterX,CenterY] := CLBlack;
  SpinWheels(Canvas,SpinA.Value,SpinB.Value,SpinD.Value,
             CenterX,CenterY,ColorGrid1.ForegroundColor);
end;

procedure TForm1.ClearButtonClick(Sender: TObject);

begin
  CanvasIsClear := True; { Canvas is clear; don't repaint pattern on Paint }
  Refresh;
end;

{ Printing may seem complex, but it's really only a matter of using  }
{ a scaling factor with SpinWheels and passing the printer canvas    }
{ to SpinWheels as a parameter.  SpinWheels is executed between the   }
{ BeginDoc/EndDoc pair...and that's it!                              }
procedure TForm1.PrintButtonClick(Sender: TObject);
```

```
VAR
  CenterX,CenterY : Integer;
  ScaleFactor    : Integer;
  SpinAText,SpinBText,SpinDText,LabelText : String;

begin
  WITH Printer DO
    BEGIN
      { Calculates a scale factor, which is the ratio of the shortest }
      { dimension of the printed page to the shortest dimension of    }
      { the displayed form canvas: }
      ScaleFactor := PageWidth DIV ClientHeight;
      CenterX := PageWidth DIV 2;
      CenterY := PageHeight DIV 2;
      BeginDoc;
      { We spin the wheels again on the printer canvas, generating   }
      { the same pattern shown on the form, only scaled to fill the  }
      { same portion of the printer canvas: }
      SpinWheels(Printer.Canvas,
                 SpinA.Value*ScaleFactor,
                 SpinB.Value*ScaleFactor,
                 SpinD.Value*ScaleFactor,
                 CenterX,CenterY,ClBlack);
      { Create the label for the printed sheet: }
      LabelText := 'A='+IntToStr(SpinA.Value)+
                 '  B='+IntToStr(SpinB.Value)+
                 '  D='+IntToStr(SpinD.Value);
      { We're re-using CenterX and CenterY here to position the label }
      { that displays the spin parameters on the printed sheet:       }
      CenterY := Trunc(PageHeight - (PageHeight * 0.07));
      CenterX := (PageWidth - Canvas.TextWidth(LabelText)) DIV 2;
      Canvas.TextOut(CenterX,CenterY,LabelText);
      EndDoc;
    END;
end;


{ We only need to set the default values once for the cycloid pattern, }
{ so this is done when the form is created:                            }
procedure TForm1.FormCreate(Sender: TObject);
begin
  SpinA.Value := 200;
  SpinB.Value := 70;
  SpinD.Value := 65
end;


{ All the real action happens when the form is redrawn.  Each time that }
{ happens, the pattern is regenerated using SpinWheels:                 }
procedure TForm1.FormPaint(Sender: TObject);

VAR
  CenterX,CenterY : Integer;

begin
  IF NOT CanvasIsClear THEN
```

```
    BEGIN
      CenterY := ClientHeight DIV 2;
      CenterX := (ClientWidth DIV 2) + (ButtonPanel.Width DIV 2);
      Canvas.Pixels[CenterX,CenterY] := CLBlack;
      SpinWheels(Canvas,SpinA.Value,SpinB.Value,SpinD.Value,
                 CenterX,CenterY,ColorGrid1.ForegroundColor);
    END;
end;

{ This is all it takes to run the Printer Setup dialog box.  It's really }
{ all done by Windows:                                                   }
procedure TForm1.PickPrinterButtonClick(Sender: TObject);
begin
  PrinterSetupDialog1.Execute;
end;

end.
```

The code in Listing 12.5 consists of event handler procedures for user interface events. Many of these are button clicks: There are buttons to draw the pattern, to clear the form, to choose a printer via the Printer Setup dialog box, and to quit the program.

A set of default parameters for the pattern is set up when the form is created, within the **FormCreate** procedure that handles the **OnCreate** event. These values have to be set sometime, and form create time is a good time to do it. In a sense you could have set them at design time by building named constants into your code, but I did it this way to point out that whatever values need to be initialized can be initialized when the form is created.

Printing Text

One trick SpiroMania performs that I didn't explain earlier in this chapter is text printing. You can place text on a canvas as easily as graphics. It's done with the **Canvas.TextOut** method, which operates to either a form canvas or a printer canvas:

```
Canvas.TextOut(X,Y,SomeText);
```

All you need to do is pass the x,y coordinates for the upper left corner of the rectangular box enclosing the text you want to display or print, and the text itself as a string literal or variable. The text is drawn in whatever font is called out in the canvas's **Font** property.

The **Font** property is itself an object with properties, and **Font** has a property called **Color** that allows you to specify the color of the text you're displaying.

(Needless to say, this requires a color printer for printed color output.) Assign a new color to **Canvas.Font.Color** before you display your text, and it will appear in the color that you set.

You can change the font to any Windows font you have installed by changing the font name held in the **Canvas.Font.Name** property. Simply assign a string containing the name of the font you want to the **Name** property:

```
MyCanvas.Font.Name := 'Courier New';
```

Font has additional properties that you can set, including **Style** (for things like italic, underline, strikeout) and **Size** (to specify font height in points.) Play around with them and you'll learn them as easily as I can explain them to you; the important thing (as with much in an environment as rich and deep as Delphi) is simply knowing that they're there.

One final caution on displaying text on a screen canvas: Make sure the text is redrawn every time the form itself is redrawn. This applies to graphics as well as text; *anything* you draw to a canvas must be redrawn when the form is redrawn.

This is one of those wonderful Windows weirdnesses that you never had to fuss with back in those bad ol' DOS days. But that was then, this is now, and fuss we must.

DRAWING AND REDRAWING

There's a problem with drawing in a Windows environment that might not occur to you immediately: At any point, another window may overlay your drawing window partially or completely, obliterating your graphics. When that interfering window goes away...what happens?

Bad news: You have to draw everything again.

The same is true when you minimize a window with graphics in it down to the icon bar, and then double click on the icon to bring back the original window. The form reappears, along with any controls you might have placed on that form. But if you've drawn any graphics or text on the form's canvas, the graphics and text are gone, and you have to draw them again.

So who draws the form and the controls? Either Windows (which draws the windows and some of the standard controls, like the common buttons) or

Delphi's runtime library. How does it know when to draw them? When a form is suddenly uncovered on the screen or changed in size with the minimize or maximize buttons, or if you bring a form up from an icon, Windows is aware of it, and sends a *message* to the form whose status is changing. A message is a special kind of function call, and the Windows messaging system knits together all of Windows' far-flung mechanisms into one (more or less) organized whole. The message Windows sends to the form instructs it to redraw itself.

Shades of object-oriented active data!

The form can redraw itself, and it sends messages in turn to each of the controls placed upon it, so that they can redraw themselves. But that leaves your graphics out in the cold.

Well, not quite. There is an event associated with every form called the **OnPaint** event, and this event is triggered whenever the form receives the Redraw message from Windows. If you build an event handler for **OnPaint** that handles the event, you can redraw your graphics at the same time that the rest of the form and controls are redrawing themselves.

The **FormPaint** procedure in Listing 12.5 handles the form's **OnPaint** event. Whenever the form is repainted (that is, redrawn on the screen for whatever reason), that event occurs and the pattern is redrawn on the form canvas. This happens automatically... so automatically that we have to be careful that it doesn't happen when we don't want it to happen. The obvious case is if we clear the form, pending the drawing of a new cycloid pattern. If you clear the form and then minimize the program to an icon, it would ordinarily redraw the pattern as soon as you double click on the icon to bring the program to its normal windowed state. But you don't want it to be redrawn if the drawing area is supposed to be cleared. This is why I had to use the Boolean variable **CanvasIsClear** in Listing 12.5 to govern whether the pattern is redrawn within the **FormPaint** procedure. If **CanvasIsClear** is **True** when the **OnPaint** event occurs, the pattern is *not* redrawn.

As a general rule, any text or graphics your code draws to a form canvas must be somehow easily *re*drawable, ideally with a single function call. It's best to gather any calls to **TextOut**, **Polyline**, **Rectangle**, **Ellipse**, and so on, into a single procedure that you can call from the procedure handler that executes when the **OnPaint** event occurs. Study how SpiroMania handles this. For a good lesson, comment out the code in **FormPaint** that calls **SpinWheels**, compile the program, and then either overlap and expose it, or iconize and redisplay it. Your pattern will go away until you press the Spin button once again.

ENHANCEMENTS FOR SPIROMANIA

I kept SpiroMania as simple as possible so it would be easy to understand, but once you understand it, there are a host of cool enhancements you might want to add to it. Most significantly, it has the weakness that although it can display multiple patterns overlaid upon one another, it cannot redraw multiple patterns. That is, if you overlay two or more patterns on the form and then overlay the form with another window, only the most recent of the patterns will be redrawn when SpiroMania is exposed again.

The right way to handle this is to create a simple object that defines the state of a pattern: Its A, B, and D values, as well as its color and perhaps its line weight. Then create a **TList** object to store one such cycloid object for each pattern you draw, and read them back, one by one, from the **TList** each time you redraw the form. When you clear the form, empty out the **TList**.

Adding a control allowing entry of line weight would be another interesting thing to do, although I prefer the thinner lines in every case.

The first time I wrote a cycloid generator in Turbo Pascal (almost ten years ago now, yikes!) the machines of the time were so slow that you could actually watch the line looping the loop as it drew to the screen. Nowadays the pattern seems to flash into place almost instantaneously, but there was something a little bit fun watching it draw slowly enough to follow. Try putting a time delay between each line that **SpinWheels** draws. How? Use a Delphi Timer object. That's your hint...

...the rest I leave to your ingenuity.

CHAPTER 13

CREATING SIMPLE DATABASE APPLICATIONS

Jim Mischel

There's so much power in Delphi's built-in database machinery that you can create a useful flat file or master-detail database without writing any Object Pascal code at all!

High school chemistry was a snap. (Actually, it was a *bang*—but that's another story...) The instructor would lecture in class for an hour about an upcoming experiment, and then take us into the lab where we'd perform the experiment and come up with the figures that he'd put on the board in the previous hour. And if you goofed on the lab experiment (or did something else entirely), it was pretty easy to fudge the numbers so that it looked like you performed the experiment and your results were within a reasonable margin of error. With a good memory and a natural knack for (and love of) number crunching, I didn't have to strain to achieve a good grade in high school chemistry.

College chemistry was something else entirely. There, the instructor would explain concepts, give us cautions about handling certain hazardous materials (I still don't remember if you're supposed to pour the water into the acid, or the acid into the water), and then take us into the lab where we would put our understanding of the concepts to the test by performing an experiment. The trick was that, unless I'd *studied* the material (perish the thought) in preparation for the class, I didn't know what the results of the experiment were supposed to be, so there was no way to fudge my figures.

Throughout this book, we've tried to maintain an "explore, then explain" structure in which we illustrate how something works, and then explain the theory behind it. I suspect that you've had to pay attention in order to follow along, but we've tried to minimize the brain strain by telling you what something's going to do before you see it in action. This approach works well when we can explore and explain small chunks of information, but becomes more difficult to pull off when the subject being explored is as wide and as deep as Delphi's database support.

Rather than deviate from the structure of the book and place this exploration chapter *after* the explanation chapter, I'm going to tell you up front that if you're fairly new to programming, or if you're completely unfamiliar with database programming concepts, you may find yourself taking an awful lot of things in this chapter "on faith." I've tried to make this exploration chapter as simple as possible, but the learning curve for Delphi's database features looks more like a cliff than a slope—you have to know *lots* of stuff before you can get anything useful done. So if you find this chapter hard going and want to lay a little groundwork first, skip ahead to Chapter 14 and come back here after you've got a better handle on database concepts and terminology.

FLAT FILE DATABASES THE EASY WAY

We're going to cheat here and forego the explanation of how to actually create a database file (or, in database parlance, a *table*) with Delphi. In the next chapter, Jeff will explain the Database Desktop program, which allows you to create tables, and add and delete fields and indexes. In this chapter, we're going to assume that the table is already created, and concentrate instead on how to add, delete, display, and modify records with a minimum of coding—like, none.

This approach really isn't cheating. In the overall scheme of building an application, the creation of the application's tables is a fairly minor task. Proper *design* of the tables is something else entirely. For simple applications, a little thought and some paper sketches may do you, as Don will demonstrate in his section later in the book. For more involved applications, where you'll have to confront many-to-many relationships, data duplication, referential integrity, and other bugbears, you'll need to read up on more advanced relational database theory. Creating the tables once they're designed is purely mechanical work that's easily handled by Database Desktop, and we're not too concerned right now with how the table gets where it is—we just want to access it.

In this chapter we'll be dealing with a miniature database of amateur (ham) radio authors and articles that they've written. This database consists of two tables: AUTHORS.DB, a table of author information; and ARTICLES.DB, a list of articles written by these authors. The tables exist in the listings disk subdirectory for this chapter.

 ### Viewing a Table

PROJECT   We're going to create a very simple application called Authors that displays the contents of AUTHORS.DB in a DBGrid component. This is what we call a flat file database, and it's the simplest sort of database application that Delphi can create. The completed application is shown in Figure 13.1.

Three Components, No Code

Creating a form that displays a table's contents is amazingly simple with Delphi. All it takes is (you guessed it) three components. There is no coding involved. None at all! Everything is connected via properties, and what events occur are handled "behind the scenes."

Start a new project, and change the Form's **Caption** property to "Authors", and change the **Name** property to "AuthorsForm". Then, from the Data Access page of the Component Palette, select and place a DataSource compo-

AUTHOR ID	AUTHOR LAST NAME	AUTHOR FIRS
1	Stockton	John
2	Trauffer	Art
3	Hutchens	Walt
4	White	James B.
5	Green	Charles
6	McCoy	Lewis G.
7	Blakeslee	Douglas A.
8	Math	Irwin

Figure 13.1   *The Authors demo program.*

nent and a Table component (they're the first two components on this page of the palette) on your form in the upper left-hand corner. These are non-visual components, so all you'll see on your form are the components' icons.

Before we start changing component properties, let's add the grid. From the Data Controls page of the Component Palette, select a DBGrid component and drop it onto the form below the other two. When you're done, your form should look like Figure 13.2.

Setting the Properties

We have to change just a handful of properties in order to make this program display the author data from the table in the DBGrid. These changes are shown in Table 13.1.

There's a possible snag here: You'll have to fill in the **Table1.DatabaseName** property with the pathname of the subdirectory where you actually place the tables on your hard disk. The value shown in Figure 13.1. was where the files

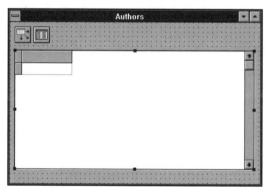

Figure 13.2   *Placing components on the Authors form.*

Table 13.1   *Property Changes for the Authors Program*

Field	Value
DataSource1.AutoEdit	False
DataSource1.DataSet	Table1
Table1.DatabaseName	"d:\delphi\chap13"
Table1.TableName	AUTHORS.DB
Table1.Active	True
DBGrid1.DataSource	DataSource1

existed on my machine, but you may choose to put it somewhere else. In Delphi, a "database" is actually a directory where your table files exist; don't get confused by the need to put a pathname here.

The **DataSource1.DataSet**, **Table1.TableName**, and **DBGrid1.DataSource** properties all have drop-down list boxes that allow you to select their values from a list of possible values, which makes it much easier to ensure that you get everything right when you're building your application.

DataSource1.AutoEdit is set to **False** in order to prevent you from making changes to the data. We'll talk about this in a little more detail in the discussion that follows.

Order Counts!

Dealing with databases is one of the few places in Delphi where the *order* in which you set property values at design time is important. When you set the **TTable.Active** property to **True** at design time, Delphi actually attempts to open the table specified by **TTable.TableName**. If that table doesn't exist (or if there's nothing in **TTable.TableName**), Delphi will pop up an error message and **TTable.Active** will remain **False**. Also, once **TTable.Active** is set to **True**, there are certain properties you can't change, **TTable.DatabaseName** and **TTable.TableName** among them. To change these, you must first re-set **TTable.Active** to **False**.

You'll almost certainly get it wrong at least once. In the course of your explorations, you'll likely see Delphi pop up an error box with a message that reads "Cannot perform this operation on an open database." When you see this error, simply set **TTable.Active** to **False**, make the desired change, and then set **TTable.Active** back to **True**

When you set the value of **DBGrid1.DataSource**, Delphi will fill the DBGrid component with the values from the AUTHORS.DB table. The program is almost completely functional at design time, and you'll be able to use the scroll bars in the DBGrid to view all the records in the table—without even running the application!

Running the Program

Save your work, calling the unit AUTHFORM.PAS, and the project AUTHORS.DPR. Then press F9 to compile and run the program. When the program starts up, you can use the scroll bars and keypad movement keys to move from field to field and from record to record. You can't modify the data because we set the **DataSource1.AutoEdit** property to **False** in order to prevent unintentional changes.

Each of the three components in our Authors program serves a very specific purpose, and the components are interconnected to produce the final program. The **TTable** component serves as an interface between the physical table on the disk and the rest of the application. **TTable** has methods that open and close, read, update, and otherwise manipulate disk files. In any Delphi database application, the **TTable** component is the real workhorse, and is kept (to paraphrase a particularly colorful Texasism) busier than the proverbial one-legged man.

The **TDataSource** component is an interface layer between the **TTable** and any data-aware components, such as a **TDBGrid** component. Most of the data-aware components are simply extensions to standard components that know how to get information from a **TDataSource** component. Others, such as **TDBGrid**, have more significant changes that make them *much* more useful than their standard non-database counterparts. An illustration of the relationship among these three components is shown in Figure 13.3.

The nice thing about the DBGrid component is that it knows how to ask for the next record or previous record in a table, and does so when you navigate through the records using the scroll bars or the cursor movement keys. All of

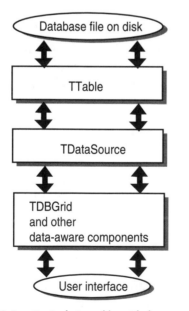

TTable reads and writes the database files on disk.

TDataSource instructs TTable to read and write records.

TDBGrid and other data-aware components obtain records from and pass changes to the table through a TDataSource component.

Figure 13.3   Manipulating tables with data-aware components.

the code that you would have written in order to make this happen with a string grid and a data access unit similar to the one we developed in Chapter 11 is already built into the DBGrid component.

DBGrid also knows how to add, delete, and modify records. If you want to be able to modify records with the Authors program, just set the **DataSource1.AutoEdit** property to **True** and then recompile and run the program. Using the movement keys, position the highlight bar in the DBGrid over one of the AUTHOR NOTES fields, and begin typing. The text that was in the field is replaced by the new text that you enter, and when you move to another record, the information that you entered is automatically written to the table. If you want to abandon the changes that you made, simply press the Escape key before leaving the field.

To add a new record at the end of the grid, position the highlight bar to the blank record at the bottom of the grid and begin entering information. If you want to insert a record in the middle of the grid, just press the Insert key. A blank record will be inserted after the current record, and you can begin entering information immediately.

To delete a record, position to any field within the record that you want to delete, and press Ctrl+Delete. There are some protections here; you will be asked to confirm that you do indeed wish to delete that record.

The DBGrid component gives you full control over whether or not records may be edited, added, or deleted. If you want to prevent all modification of the table, set the DBGrid's **ReadOnly** property to **True**, and set **Options.dgEditing** to **False**. (This will give you a read-only table browser rather than a database—which implies the ability to add, edit, and delete records.) Various combinations of these and other **Options** properties allow you to fine-tune the feature set that is made available to the user.

The DBGrid component is a handy thing to have if you want to display and edit records using a spreadsheet-like interface. But that's not the most user-friendly kind of interface available. If you want a more polished look, you have to use separate components to display the individual fields, and a DBNavigator component to control access to the table.

Building an Access Program with a DBNavigator

Let's refine our Authors program so that it displays the author information one record at a time in a dialog box, similar to the Alarm Statistics program of Chapter 11. A DBNavigator component will control

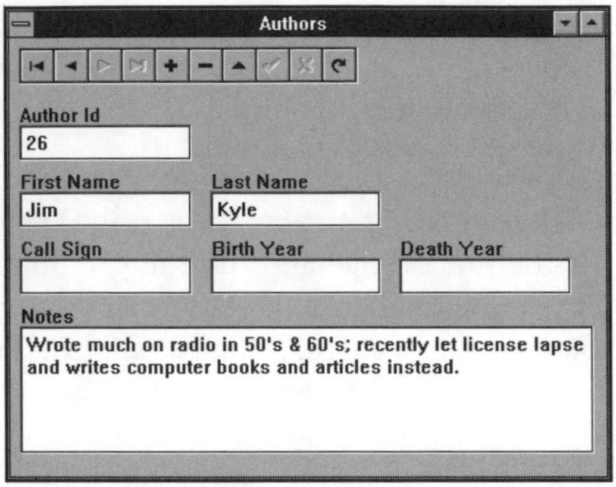

Figure 13.4 *The enhanced Authors program.*

record access—allowing us to select a record to display or edit, and also to add and delete records. The completed application is shown in Figure 13.4.

Building the Form

Let's move fairly quickly through building the form, as I suspect that you're familiar with the mechanics by this time. We'll place all of the components onto the form first, and then change their properties.

Start a new project, and set the Form's **Name** property to "AuthorForm2", and its **Caption** property to "Authors", Then, from the Data Access page of the Component Palette, select a DataSource and a Table component, and place them on the form in the upper right-hand corner. From the Data Controls page, select the DBNavigator component and place it in the upper left-hand corner.

The rest of the components on the form shown in Figure 13.4 are DBEdits and Labels, with the exception of the box underneath the "Notes" label, which is a DBMemo component. Create and place the components as shown in Figure 13.4, naming the DBEdit components "EditAUTHORID", "EditAUTHORFIRSTNAME", "EditAUTHORLASTNAME", "EditAUTHORCALL", "EditBIRTHYEAR", and "EditDEATHYEAR", respectively. Name the DBMemo component "MemoAUTHORNOTES".

Now, we need to link the Table and the DataSource, and then link all of the data-aware components to the DataSource. Change the Table's and DataSource's properties as shown in Table 13.2, and then change the **DataSource** property on the DBNavigator, the DBEdits, and the DBMemo to "DataSource1". For this

Table 13.2 *Property changes to the Table and DataSource components*

Field	Value
Table1.DatabaseName	"d:\delphi\chap13"
Table1.TableName	"AUTHORS.DB"
Table1.Active	True
DataSource1.AutoEdit	False
DataSource1.DataSet	"Table1"

project, at least, it's important to change the properties in the order shown in Table 13.2, starting at the top and working downward.

The last thing we have to do is link the individual components on the form to their corresponding fields in the table. We do this by changing the components's **DataField** property. For example, to link the DBEdit component named "EditAUTHORID" to the "AUTHOR ID" field in the table, follow these steps:

- Select the **EditAUTHORID** component in the form window.
- In the Object Inspector, click on the arrow to the right of the **DataField** property.
- Select the AUTHOR ID field name from the drop-down list.

Perform those steps for the other DBEdit components and the DBMemo field on the form and then save your work, calling the unit AUTHFRM2.PAS and the project AUTHORS2.DPR.

MOVING AROUND WITH THE DBNAVIGATOR

When you run the program, the first record in the file is displayed. You can use the Tab key to move from field to field, but you aren't able to edit the fields because we set the **Table1.AutoEdit** property to **False** in order to prevent accidental changes. To edit fields, insert or delete records, or display another record, you need to press one of the buttons on the DBNavigator component. The DBNavigator buttons and their functions are shown in Figure 13.5.

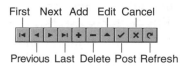

Figure 13.5 *The DBNavigator buttons.*

Most of the functions of the DBNavigator component are self-explanatory. What's really nice is that the DBNavigator knows about things like whether the current record pointer is at the beginning of the table or at the end of the table. If you're currently viewing the first record in a table, the "First" and "Previous" buttons on the DBNavigator will be "grayed out" and disabled. Similarly, if you're viewing the last record in the table, the "Next" and "Last" buttons are disabled. For a more detailed description of any individual buttons's actions, see online help.

To change a record once you've located it, click on the DBNavigator's "Edit" button, and then make whatever changes you need to make. After you've made all of your changes, click on the "Post" button to update the record in the table. (Updating a changed record to a physical table is called *posting* the record, in database jargon.) If you want to cancel the changes you've made, click on the "Cancel" button.

The "Cancel" button will only undo changes that were made to the record since the last time you posted changes to the table. That is, if you were to change the "Last Name" field and post the change, then change the "First Name" field and press "Cancel," the only change that will be undone is the change that you made to the "First Name" field. There's no way to "unpost" a change once it's been written to the table—you have to go back in and re-edit.

That said, be forewarned: *DBNavigator automatically posts changes when you move to another record.* If you change the "Call Sign" field in a record, for example, and then move to the next record without first pressing the "Post" button to update the table, the change will be automatically written to the table. Paradox, Access, and many other database packages work this way, so it's not an unheard-of new feature in database applications. It is possible to program around this and pop up a confirmation box asking the user if the changes should be saved before moving to the next record—but it takes a little code to do that.

Customizing the DBNavigator Component

Figure 13.5 is a handy illustration for us developers, but it doesn't help the casual user of your program. Fortunately, the DBNavigator component has a **ShowHint** property, and built-in fly-by hints for the individual buttons. If you set **ShowHint** to **True**, then fly-by hints are displayed when the mouse cursor lingers for a second or so over the buttons on the DBNavigator component. The DBNavigator's **Hints** property allows you to define custom hints for the individual buttons if you don't want to use the built-in hints.

There are a lot of buttons in a DBNavigator, not all of which are needed for every database application, particularly those that disallow changes to the table, or allow changes only under very close control. Fortunately, it's not an all-buttons-or-none proposition. The DBNavigator's **VisibleButtons** property is a set property in which you can define *which* buttons you want displayed by the DBNavigator. Each of the component's buttons may be turned on or off by setting its corresponding **nbxxx** property. For example, if you don't want the user to be able to update records in the table, then you wouldn't need the "Add," "Delete," "Post," "Cancel," or "Refresh" buttons, so you could set their corresponding **VisibleButtons** sub-properties to **False**.

When the **ConfirmDelete** property is set to **True** (the default), then your program will pop up a confirmation box whenever you click on the "Delete" button to delete a record. If you don't want this confirmation box to appear when the "Delete" button is pressed, set **ConfirmDelete** to **False**.

There are a few other properties that allow you to customize the appearance and behavior of the DBNavigator component. For more information about them see online help.

A Note about Database Errors

If you tried adding a record, or if you changed the "AUTHOR ID" field in one of the existing records, you may have encountered an error message similar to that shown in Figure 13.6.

This error occurs when you try to save a record whose "AUTHOR ID" field matches one that already exists in the table. The reason that this error occurs is that the "AUTHOR ID" field is the *primary key field* in the table, and primary keys must be unique—no two records may have the same primary key value. Jeff will talk more about primary keys, secondary indexes, and other such database topics in the next chapter—you don't have to completely understand what they are right now.

Figure 13.6   *A database error message.*

Delphi's built-in database support provides an *exception handler* that traps these errors and displays a message box similar to the one in Figure 13.6 if an error occurs. When you're building database programs without writing code, there's no easy way to tap into the error handler, so you have to trust Delphi to handle the error for you. In the next chapter, Jeff will talk briefly about exception handlers, but not in much detail. To learn more about exceptions and how to handle them, consult the online help and the Delphi User's Guide.

MASTER-DETAIL DATABASES

Flat file databases are adequate for many different applications: Christmas card lists and collection catalogs are two that come immediately to mind. But they're hardly powerful enough to handle all database applications. Flat file databases are great for keeping lists of things, but if you want to relate the items in the list to those in other lists, you're out of luck. For that, you need a *master-detail* database.

In a master-detail database, one table serves as the primary (or master) table in which summary information is stored, and other tables contain detail information that's related to the primary table. For example, our AUTHORS.DB file contains information on authors who have written articles about ham radio, and is the primary table. The ARTICLES.DB file contains information about individual articles, and can serve as a detail table. This is made possible by automatically searching the ARTICLES.DB file on the author number (the "AUTHOR ID" field in the AUTHORS table) and retrieving any records from ARTICLES.DB with the author ID code of a given author.

A master-detail database is the simplest form of a *relational* database—meaning that separate tables have logical relationships with one another based on values in fields they have in common. Here, the AUTHORS.DB and ARTICLES.DB have a field in common: AUTHOR ID. Given the author number, we can look up and display all of the ARTICLES.DB entries that were written by that author. It's actually not quite fair to say that *we* have to do the looking-up. Delphi's database engine code does it for us, behind the scenes, without so much as a single line of Object Pascal to tell it what to do.

One-To-Many Relationships

The two tables have what is called a *one-to-many* relationship. This means that for each author in AUTHORS.DB there may be many articles in ARTICLES.DB. The reverse is not true; each article has only *one* author.

The one-to-many relationship is a very common one. Even something as simple as a name/address database has one-to-many relations. Consider that one person can have more than one address: A home address, a work address, and perhaps a summer home; or that one person typically has multiple phone numbers these days. (Voice, FAX, and mobile, with maybe a "teenager" line or a separate data line...) So you would give a separate record in an separate addresses table to each address, and give each address record a NAME ID field containing the ID number of the person who "owns" that address.

The way to spot such relations is to ask yourself: In any given collection of data items, *which items are separately countable?* That is, when I count names, am I also counting addresses? Or is the number of addresses entirely or mostly independent from the number of names? In general, each independently countable data item should be stored in its own table, and related to other tables via "ID" values in common fields.

We're doing that here. Each author record has an AUTHOR ID field, and each article also has an AUTHOR ID field, containing the ID code of the author who wrote that article. The relationship between the AUTHORS.DB table and ARTICLES.DB table is maintained through that common field.

If you were to do a name and address database, each name record should have a unique NAME ID field. (Don't use even a first+last name combo; there are thousands of Mike Smiths in the world, and I know several of them!) Each address record in the ADDRESS.DB table should also have a NAME ID field, holding the ID value of the person whose address it contains.

Showing an Author's Articles

As an example of a master-detail database, we're going to extend the Authors program so that it will display all of an author's article entries in a DBGrid whenever the author is displayed. And we're going to do it without writing any code. The completed application is shown in Figure 13.7.

We're not going to build a new project here—just add on to the existing project that we created in the last section. In order to display the article citations in the DBGrid at the bottom of the form, we need to add another Table and DataSource, and also a DBGrid component. It's *really* easy to do.

Adding the Articles Grid

First, grab the bottom border of the form and pull it down in order to enlarge the form and make room for the DBGrid. Then, select the DBGrid component

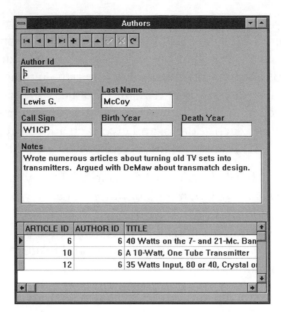

Figure 13.7   *The Authors program with article data display.*

from the palette and drop it onto your form below the "Notes" field. Leave enough space to put a separator between the author information above and the article citations below. We'll have to return to the DBGrid in a moment to change its **DataSource** property, but we have to create the new DataSource first.

The Bevel Component

Take another look at the form in Figure 13.7 and notice the raised "bump" between the "Notes" field and the DBGrid that displays the article citations. This is a Bevel component, whose sole purpose is to provide some visual separation between author information and article information. That's all a Bevel component is good for, really—to serve as a separator. It just has a handful of properties, and no events at all, so it can't respond to anything.

You can change the look of a Bevel by changing its **Shape** and **Style** properties, as well as its size. A Bevel's **Shape** can be a solid box, a frame (box outline), or a horizontal or vertical line. The style can be **bsRaised** (a "bump" as in Figure 13.7) or **bsLowered** (a "dip").

The Bevel can be found on the Additional page of the component palette. Grab one and place it on the form below the "Notes" field. Change its properties as shown in Table 13.3.

Table 13.3 *Property Changes for the Bevel Component*

Field	Value
Height	2
Left	0
Shape	bsTopLine
Style	bsRaised
Width	same as Form.ClientWidth

Hooking Up the Tables

In order to access the ARTICLES.DB file, we need another Table and another DataSource. Grab one of each from the Data Access page of the Component Palette, and drop them onto your form right below the two that are already there. Then, change their properties (and the DBGrid component's as well) as shown in Table 13.4.

By setting the **MasterSource**, **MasterFields**, and **IndexName** properties of **Table2**, we're telling Delphi that we want **Table2** to make just a subset of its information available at any given time. The subset of information to be made available is those article citations whose "AUTHOR ID" field matches the "AUTHOR ID" field in the current record of **DataSource1**—in other words, just the articles for the author whose information is currently displayed in the top portion of the form.

Table 13.4 *Property Changes for Other Components*

Field	Value
Table2.Active	True
Table2.DataBaseName	"d:\delphi\chap13"
Table2.IndexName	"AUTHOR INDEX"
Table2.MasterFields	"AUTHOR ID"
Table2.MasterSource	"DataSource1"
Table2.TableName	"ARTICLES.DB"
DataSource2.AutoEdit	True
DataSource2.DataSet	"Table2"
DBGrid1.DataSource	"DataSource2"

Running the Program

After you've made those few changes, press F9 to compile and run the program. When the first author record is displayed, the article citations for that author are displayed as well. Many of the authors have only one citation, and some don't have any, so don't be too concerned if the DBGrid is empty at times. Cursor or click your way down through the list of authors to see what articles each has written.

Possible Enhancements

And that's master-detail for you, in a nutshell. There are plenty of things you could do to make the program a little more useable. One possibility would be to remove the DBGrid component and create separate data-entry fields for each of the fields in the record, just as we did with the author information. If you do this, you'll have to add a DBNavigator component for the article citations.

NO-CODE DATABASES

More than anything else, the purpose of this chapter is to show you that it's possible to write some fairly involved database programs without writing a single line of code. These applications won't be commercial-quality, as they lack good error handling and other features that are expected of commercial-quality software. But they *are* good for prototyping and in-house utilities.

The beauty of the no-code database (and Delphi in general) is that non-programmers can create a working "first draft" application to prove a concept or just get the program design straight, without having to involve you in the early stages. Once they have the concept working "pretty much" the way they like, they can bring it to a programmer who adds the features that make the difference between a prototype and a production program.

TABLES ON THE RECORD

CHAPTER 14

Jeff Duntemann

Visual database access is terrific—but it's not the whole story. To make the most of Delphi's power, you have to write real code that reads, writes, and maneuvers data tables.

Until very recently, there were two distinct worlds in which software was developed. One was the traditional world of programming languages like C, Pascal, and BASIC. These languages and the industry that surrounded them were concerned with things like algorithms, data structures, and (more recently) object-oriented techniques. The other world grew out of extensions to popular database management packages, which sprouted rudimentary macro capabilities that over time evolved into simple but truly programmable command interpreters. Back in 1982 I helped another programmer at Xerox implement a system written in CP/M dBase II. The "programming language" wasn't much of a language, but that was okay. The "hard stuff" was done for us, and worked so well that it seemed almost miraculous. (In retrospect, that anything worked at all under CP/M seems something close to miraculous.) What we were doing was managing record-oriented data. What we needed to accomplish was to get a system working as quickly and as cheaply as possible, damn the frills.

We damned the frills. And we got our system.

Over the past fifteen years or so, evolution on both sides of the wall has been fast and furious, but, remarkably, there's been very little mixing of metaphors. The dBase language became XBase, acquired some good native-code compilers, and became a very serious programming system. Paradox begat PAL, which under Windows became ObjectPAL. ObjectPAL is a very significant programming system, but it's unlike anything else out there, and hasn't become outrageously popular, for all its trouble. Clipper became a distinct dialect of XBase, Clarion drew on COBOL, and most other significant database managers had their own languages, none of which were especially similar to any of the others.

If you wanted to do traditional, algorithmic programming in a database language, you did the best you could with what you had, which generally wasn't a lot. If you wanted to do database programming in a traditional language, you used a database "engine" in a linkable library, and did the best you could with what it gave you, which was mostly headaches. I've worked both sides of the fence, and have thought more than once that if we could somehow combine the best of these two worlds, we would finally have arrived.

With Delphi, I think we've arrived. It combines the best current traditional programming language, Object Pascal, with some of the most powerful database features I have ever seen. The synergy is seamless—and for what it does, is remarkably easy to understand.

I should qualify that just a little. Understanding Delphi's database power is your biggest single task in learning Delphi, not because it's difficult so much as because it's so *big*. I would venture to guess that about half of Delphi's complexity lies in its database and client/server machinery. Needless to say, we can't cover more than a small fraction of what it can do in this book. So what I want to do is cover the basics, and encourage you to try out those features that we don't explicitly explain. Delphi online help is very good, and you should read it closely whenever questions arise.

RECORDS ON STEROIDS

Back in Chapter 6, I explained Object Pascal's record data structure, and in Chapter 11, Jim explained how to create files of records to store multiple records out to disk. A record is a group of variables of various data types, bound together in a single bundle with a distinct name:

```
TYPE PartRec =
   RECORD
      PartID : Integer;
      PartNum : String15;
      PartDesc : String128;
      PartCost : Comp;
      PartSRP : Comp;
      PartMfrID : Integer;
   END;
```

Taken together, the fields in this record describe one part that a manufacturer of copy machines or other complex devices might maintain on hand for spares. Because it takes a lot of parts to make a copy machine (trust me on that), a file describing all the parts maintained as spares by a manufacturer would take hundreds or (more likely) thousands of such records.

To be useful, this file would need associated code for searching, appending records, updating records, deleting records, and—perhaps most important—a coherent method for allowing users to perform these tasks quickly and easily.

You can do all of this stuff in Object Pascal, using nothing more than files of records. But there's a major catch: To change the structure of the record that you store in a file (that is, to change the number of fields in the record, their sizes, or their types) you must re-compile your entire application, and probably make wholesale followon changes to the code. The minor catch, obviously, is that this is all a great deal of work for something that represents the core application of computing in the world today.

It is for these two reasons that database management as a separate field appeared. Delphi's database management machinery allows a lot more flexibility in creating and maintaining files of records without having to recompile the whole application for each small change. (Major changes will still require recompilation.) Also, the bulk of the work is done for you, and is provided in the form of Delphi components that handle routine data management tasks.

DATABASE JARGON

What to call things is a common problem in programming, and nowhere more than in database work, since it's a world only recently joined to what we might call traditional programming. Let me do a quick runthrough of some of the key terms in database work, so that I can use them in my mainstream discussion without leaving you face-down in the dirt.

A *database* is nothing more than one or more files of record-oriented data with a common purpose and often logical relationships between the files. By "logical relationships" I mean that there will be a file of parts manufacturers—and in the parts file a code for each part indicating a specific record inside that file of parts manufacturers. These sorts of logical relationships are the reason we call such systems *relational databases*.

The records stored in Delphi database files are not the familiar record data types I introduced in Chapter 6. They're much more sophisticated entities, true objects with enormous flexibility. Similarly, the files in which these super-records are stored are not ordinary Object Pascal files, but special files specially organized to handle the work that databases must do. We call them *tables* rather than files, and that's how I'll refer to them from now on.

In some database systems, those tables are bound together into a single disk file. Microsoft Access works that way. *Everything* connected with a particular database is bound up into one Titanic file—which can be a problem once the file gets to be a few megabytes in size. And if you corrupt that one file, you've lost it all—rather like *The Titanic*.

Borland's databases are generally not bound up in a single disk file, but in many files, each with a specific purpose. In Delphi, the database is a *place*—typically a subdirectory—where all those various files are stored. You can specify this place as a hard-coded directory path, or as something else called an *alias*. An alias is a name for a database that indicates where the files are stored, without calling out a physical directory path. At one place in the database—typically where the Borland database engine is installed—the alias is equated to a directory path specific to that machine alone. Your database code can refer to the alias rather than to a particular hard disk directory structure. This allows your database application to be independent of any particular disk drive or subdirectory name.

A *table* is one file containing records of a given structure. A record is one "slice" of that file, containing a group of values that typically pertain to a single instance of a group of identical entities. A parts table will contain one record for each part; in a customer table there will be one record for each customer, and so on. I've drawn a diagram showing the relationship of the various parts of a Delphi database table in Figure 14.1.

You can see that the records in a table act as "slices" of that table, each slice being structurally identical but containing different data values. Furthermore,

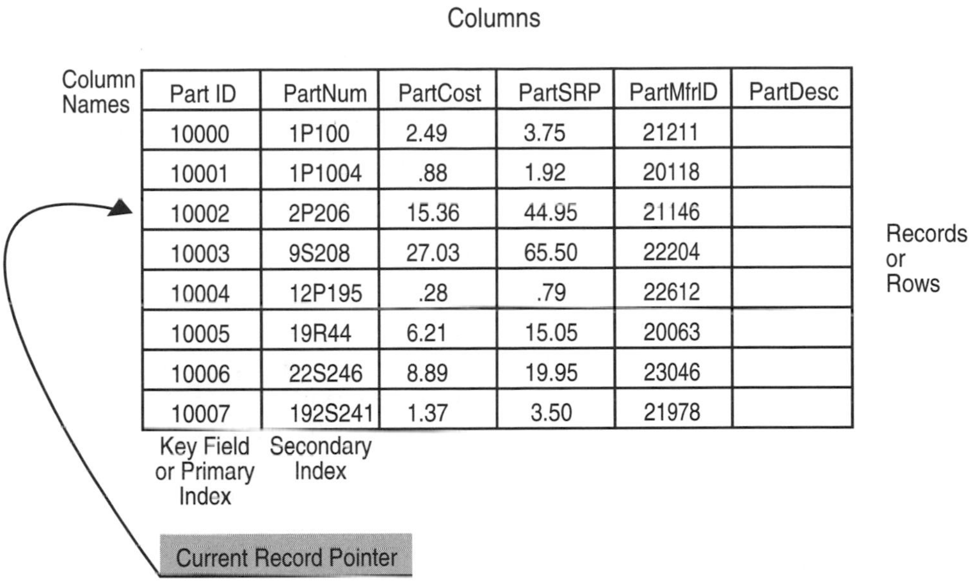

Columns

Column Names	Part ID	PartNum	PartCost	PartSRP	PartMfrID	PartDesc
	10000	1P100	2.49	3.75	21211	
	10001	1P1004	.88	1.92	20118	
	10002	2P206	15.36	44.95	21146	
	10003	9S208	27.03	65.50	22204	
	10004	12P195	.28	.79	22612	
	10005	19R44	6.21	15.05	20063	
	10006	22S246	8.89	19.95	23046	
	10007	192S241	1.37	3.50	21978	

Records or Rows

Key Field or Primary Index   Secondary Index

Current Record Pointer

Figure 14.1 *The anatomy of a Delphi table.*

the different fields in the records of a table all line up vertically, to the extent that we can refer to all instances of a given field as a *column* in a table. In Figure 14.1, all of the PART ID fields in the table line up vertically and form the PART ID column of the table. The columns take the names of the fields that define them.

Every table contains a pointer or marker that points to one of the records in the table as the *current record.* The pointer, not surprisingly, is called the *current record pointer.* Typically, this is the first record in the table until you move the pointer somehow to another record.

Different Database Formats

It would be mighty handy if every database program could understand the tables maintained by every other database program. Balancing the Federal Budget would be nice, too, but not even the Republicans seem to be able to pull that one off. And so in the database world we have a Babel situation in which Access can't really handle Paradox or Revelation tables, and Delphi can't easily read Access tables, and you can plug in almost any other permutation of formats with similar comments. Maybe it can be done—depending on how you define "done." Elaborate systems have been created to standardize database table formats, but they are complex and (in my view) prone to problems. Microsoft has such a system called ODBC (Open Database Connectivity) and Borland has a competing system called IDAPI. (Remarkably enough, Borland does not expand the acronym in Delphi's documentation or online help!) Delphi does its best with both ODBC and IDAPI to bridge the gap among the greatest possible number of database formats, but that mechanism is pretty complex, and deserves a book to itself. We can't go into it here.

For simplicity's sake, I'm going to limit my discussion to the Paradox for Windows 5.0 database format in this chapter. Most of what I describe also applies to dBase files as well, and Don will be showing you a real example of a dBase-oriented application in his chapters that conclude this book. Once you have the rudiments of database management under your belt, by all means explore the more elaborate database access machinery Delphi brings to the feast.

So, where to start, if you're coming to Delphi database management absolutely green? The answer is to get out of Delphi entirely—and become familiar with Borland's Database Desktop.

DATABASE DESKTOP

Bundled with every copy of Delphi is a substantial utility program called Database Desktop (DBD for short) which looks to be a stripped-down version of Paradox for Windows. It doesn't print, and it doesn't do any sort of output reporting, but it can load, edit, and change (we say, "restructure") tables created for use with Delphi. Think of it as a text editor for database tables.

In the Delphi way of doing things, you use DBD to create new tables and (if you like) enter data into them. This prevents you from having to "futz up" special-purpose one-shot utilities to do that sort of thing. Alas, DBD doesn't do everything it should—perhaps to prevent it from competing with and eating sales of Paradox or dBase. You can't edit *memo* fields—that is, large text blocks—in DBD, nor BLOBs. A *BLOB* is a wonderful coinage for Binary Large Object—basically, any data chunk that can't be interpreted as any particular data type. BLOBs are usually used to store pictures in databases. To edit memos or BLOBs, you *do* need to futz up special utilities—as Don will later demonstrate.

DBD is an excellent way to stake out a table for dissection. Let's do it.

Using DBD for Table Maintenance

Run DBD, and using the Files|Open|Table dialog, load the AUTHORS.DB table from the Chapter 13 directory of the companion disk. You can make the loading process a little easier by setting yourself a working subdirectory in which all your project tables exist. This is done by running the Database Desktop Local Configuration utility, which is essentially a single dialog, as shown in Figure 14.2.

In the top edit field, enter the full disk pathname of the directory in which all your database tables are going to be. Then, when you go to open a table in DBD, DBD will bring up the list of tables in your working directory without forcing you to enter the full path every time.

What you'll see in DBD will look a lot like what I show in Figure 14.3.

In any table displayed by DBD, the leftmost column is a little bogus. It's actually nothing more than record numbering for the table. Note that the column header is just the name of the table being displayed. You can't edit that leftmost column, and at best it's a way of showing you which record is the current record, through the use of a record number highlight. The other columns take their names from the fields that fall into those columns. Fields don't need to have any values in them and they can remain blank if desired. You can display columns that run off the right edge of the window using the scroll bars at the bottom of the window.

By default, tables displayed in DBD are displayed in *view mode*, meaning that you can look but not touch. To change the values in any displayed field, you must press F9 to go into *edit mode*, in which the contents of any database field may be changed from the keyboard. F9 actually toggles back and forth between edit mode and view mode; press it from either mode and you go into the other.

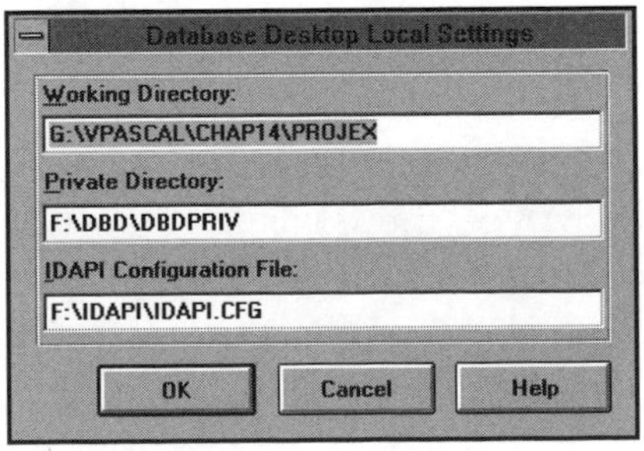

Figure 14.2   DBD's Local Configuration dialog.

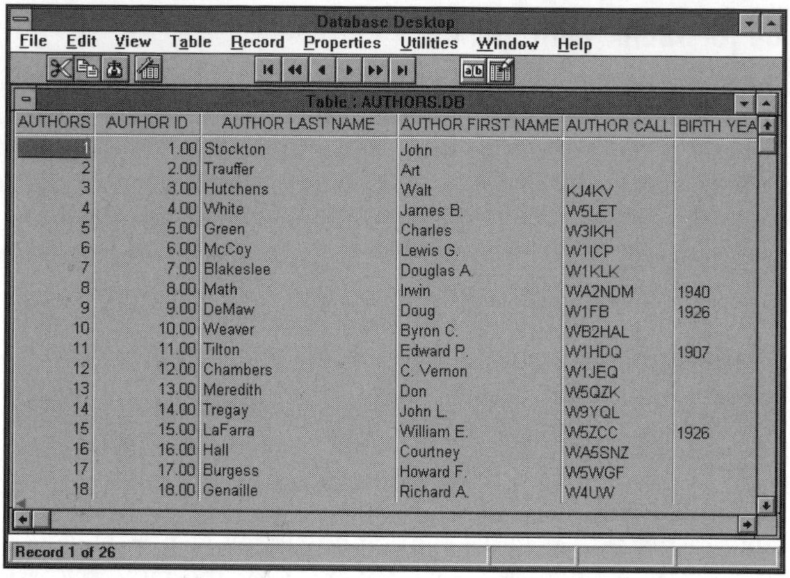

AUTHORS	AUTHOR ID	AUTHOR LAST NAME	AUTHOR FIRST NAME	AUTHOR CALL	BIRTH YEA
1	1.00	Stockton	John		
2	2.00	Trauffer	Art		
3	3.00	Hutchens	Walt	KJ4KV	
4	4.00	White	James B.	W5LET	
5	5.00	Green	Charles	W3IKH	
6	6.00	McCoy	Lewis G.	W1ICP	
7	7.00	Blakeslee	Douglas A.	W1KLK	
8	8.00	Math	Irwin	WA2NDM	1940
9	9.00	DeMaw	Doug	W1FB	1926
10	10.00	Weaver	Byron C.	WB2HAL	
11	11.00	Tilton	Edward P.	W1HDQ	1907
12	12.00	Chambers	C. Vernon	W1JEQ	
13	13.00	Meredith	Don	W5QZK	
14	14.00	Tregay	John L.	W9YQL	
15	15.00	LaFarra	William E.	W5ZCC	1926
16	16.00	Hall	Courtney	WA5SNZ	
17	17.00	Burgess	Howard F.	W5WGF	
18	18.00	Genaille	Richard A.	W4UW	

***Figure 14.3** Displaying a table in DBD.*

You can get from record to record by hammering on the arrow keys; you can also use the VCR-style navigator in the toolbar at the top of the DBD window. Whatever field is the current field in the current record will be highlighted, and that's the field that'll be edited if you go into edit mode and begin typing.

Structure and Restructuring

DBD's most obvious use is showing you what's actually in a table and allowing you to edit it; however, a far more important use lies in allowing you to change the *structure* of the table—the number, type, and order of the fields in each record. Most important of all, DBD allows you to specify keys and create indexes for tables (please forgive me for not saying "indices;" I'm following the usage in Delphi's documentation), a subject of tremendous importance that I'll come back to a little later.

You can display the structure of a table by selecting the Table | Info Structure menu item. DBD will show you the fields in order (leftmost at the top), and the type and size of each field. A display of the structure for the AUTHORS.DB table (which you'll find in the Chapter 13 directory of the listings disk) is shown in Figure 14.4.

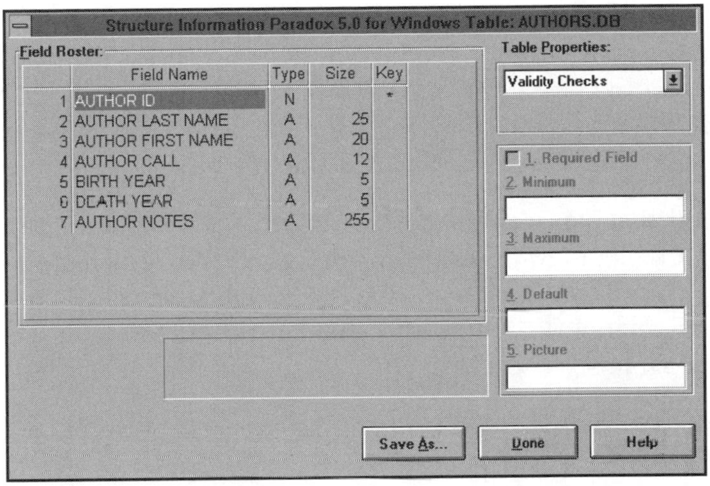

Figure 14.4   *DBD's table structure display.*

The AUTHORS.DB table only uses two different field types, but there are quite a few types that you can use, including a date type; a time type; a money type for financial formatting; a logical type that is a database Boolean field, and may take either **True** or **False** as values; and several others of interest to more advanced programmers. (There's a little variation of available field types depending on what database format you choose when you create the table. All the tables discussed in this chapter are Paradox for Windows 5.0 tables.) Most of the time you'll use the Alpha field type, which is basically a container for string data. The Alpha field may be set to any length you choose, up to 255 characters.

If you need to restructure a table, you can select Table | Restructure. The display will be very similar to that shown in Figure 14.1, except that you can remove existing fields; enter new fields—either at the end or insert them somewhere in the middle; move fields in the lineup to change their order; or alter the type or length of an existing field. Keep in mind that if you change the size or type of an existing field (or, obviously, remove a field from a table), you stand the chance of losing data. Make sure you know what you're doing—or that you're really sure you want to do it.

Using DBD for table restructuring is pretty intuitive for the most part. Some things are less than intuitive. Changing the *order* of the fields requires that you put the mouse cursor on the field number to be moved, then hold down the left mouse button while you drag the field to its new position in the lineup. To insert a new field into an existing field lineup, highlight the existing field that you wish to fall *after* the new field, and press the Ins key. A new, empty field line will be inserted ahead of the highlighted field. When you need to enter the type of a field, pressing the space bar or the right mouse button will bring up a menu of the available file types.

I recommend that you display the structure of a few tables, and alter the structure of a table a few times before you go ahead and create a new table. I've provided a separate copy of the AUTHORS.DB table called PRACTICE.DB, which you can mangle to your heart's content without losing data required for any demo programs.

CREATING NEW TABLES

Before you begin writing a database application, you should take the time necessary to think through the matter of what your tables must contain, and (if you're going so far as to create a multitable application) how the various fields relate to one another. If you don't know what your data's going to look like, it'll be tough to know what your application will look like. It's a good bet you'll have to go back and tweak your table structure a few times while the application is under construction, but you should move heaven and Earth to get within striking distance of your final table layout before you create your first form.

Assuming you have some notes on the record layout you need, you create your tables within DBD. Select the File | New | Table menu item. DBD will present you with a dialog allowing you to select the database format you want to use for your new table. The default is Paradox for Windows 5.0, but you can drop the list of possible formats and click on any of the others. See Figure 14.5.

Once a format has been selected, DBD will present you with a form for the actual definition of the table's fields, key fields, and indexes. Filling it out is straightforward. You start with the leftmost column in your proposed table, and fill in the field name, field type, field size (if applicable) and whether or

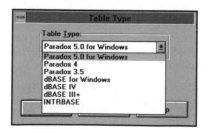

Figure 14.5 *Selecting a database format.*

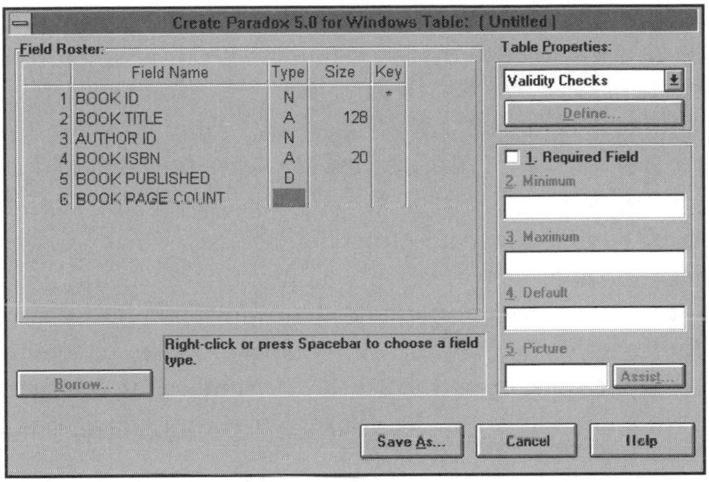

Figure 14.6 *Creating a new table's field lineup.*

not the field is a key field. (I'll further discuss key fields shortly.) A screen shot of a stage in this process is shown in Figure 14.6.

It may seem strange to a traditional programmer, but field names do *not* always have to be a single contiguous identifier without embedded spaces. Paradox for Windows field names may be several words separated by spaces, as in BOOK PAGE COUNT. I put field names in uppercase, as one little reminder to myself that they are in fact field names (this is a common practice among database grunts) but you may use any combination of upper and lower case.

Have a Field Naming System

Naming consistency pays off big when you have a complicated database application consisting of perhaps dozens of tables and hundreds of different fields. My system is simple and works well:

- Place field names entirely in capitals. Like I said, this works for me. Yeah, I know, if you're a former C programmer this makes you gag. Herbal tea may help.

- Key field names should end in "ID" as in BOOK ID, AUTHOR ID, PART ID, and so on. This tells you right away that an ID field is a key field and that all values are unique within a single table.

- Build the table name into field names that don't have to match the names of fields in other tables. (Database guys would say, "Don't build the table name into the names of fields acting as foreign keys.") In the table under construction in Figure 14.6, there's a field called AUTHOR ID. This field has to match a field named AUTHOR ID in a table containing author information. None of the other fields has such a job, so I put "BOOK" in each of them so that I know instantly what table they belong to. When you have a dozen tables and over a hundred field names, this can save a *huge* amount of confusion.

In deciding how large to make an Alpha field, consider that you can generally *enlarge* a field through restructuring a table without losing any data. The reverse isn't true; if you make a field too large and then find you need to cut the size of the field to save disk space, you're bound to have at least a few records (and maybe quite a few) that will be "trimmed" (as we gently say) of excess data, which is simply lost. Be conservative with your Alpha field sizes.

Key Fields

If you look back to Figure 14.6, you'll see an asterisk (*) in the Key area of the top field line. The asterisk indicates that the BOOK ID field is a key field, and is the only key field in the record lineup.

A *key field* is a field that is treated specially by Delphi's database engine, for rapid search and relational linkage. Values in key fields are guaranteed to be unique; that is, if one record in the BOOKS table has a BOOK ID field with a value of 42, no other record in that table may have its BOOK ID field set to 42. The value in a key field thus uniquely identifies a record, since no other record has exactly the same key field value.

This isn't always fully appreciated by beginning database programmers. No two books have the same title, right? Well, I can think of more than a few. There have been at least three books with the title *Mastering Turbo Pascal*, not counting different editions of Tom Swan's classic text. It's a good idea to create a completely synthetic ID value for your key fields inside your applications, even if you *think* one of your externally-generated fields is always unique. A part number is supposedly unique—but what happens when the same part comes in a blue and a yellow finish, and has the same part number? (This actually happened to me once while cataloging Erector Set girders.) If you create the ID value inside your application, *you* have control over whether the value is unique, and no outside screwup will ever paralyze your system.

Delphi's database machinery can seek to a specific key value *enormously* more quickly than searching for a specific non-key value. This alone is reason enough to put a key field in any table you might need to create.

To specify a key field during table creation, double click on the Key part of the field definition line. One caution: Key fields must be the *first* fields in the lineup. You can't specify a field in the middle of the record as the key field. It has to be the first field. You can have multiple keys in a record (though the need for this is a lot less common) but all key fields must come before any non-key fields in the record.

Key fields have a vital use in database work: When you relate one table to another in a one-to-many fashion, the fields that relate the two tables are typically key fields. I'll be talking more about this later on.

SECONDARY INDEXES

Once you've defined all your fields and chosen which (if any) is to be the key field, there are other things you can do before giving your new table a name and committing it to disk. The most important of these is the creation of *secondary indexes*

A secondary index (sometimes called a *secondary key*) is a lookup table that imposes a logical order on the records in the physical table on disk. You can index a table on a field like a last name field, and in doing so create a way to step through the table in alphabetical order by last name, even though the names may have been entered into the physical table in totally random order. By accessing a table through one of its indexes, you can "see" the records in a different order from the order in which they exist in the physical table. Having multiple indexes is therefore a means of having your table "sorted" in more than one way at the same time.

A secondary index is a little like a key field, but there's a critical difference: Values in secondary indexes do *not* have to be unique! In case a secondary index contains two records with identical values, the identical values are placed in index order by their physical order in the table.

Secondary indexes are especially important if you're using dBase or Paradox format tables. With those formats, the search methods available in the **TTable** component work *only* on fields for which a secondary index exists. If you want to search a table on a field for which no index exists, you must perform the search manually; that is, you must step through the table record-by-record, testing the field's value at each record for the desired relationship to the search key. This is a bother from a coding standpoint, and way worse, it's *slow*. If you expect to have to do any searching at all on a field, create a secondary index on that field. It doesn't cost much disk space and it's easy to do. Furthermore, once you've created a secondary index and told Delphi to maintain it, you can forget about the index. It literally updates itself as data is entered into the table.

Secondary indexes are created when you create a new table. You can also add secondary indexes to an existing table by using the Table | Restructure Table window in DBD, so don't panic if you don't anticipate every field to be indexed at table creation time.

Adding a New Secondary Index

This is one of those many things in Delphi that shows better than it tells. We're going to create a new secondary index on the PRACTICE.DB table included on the companion disk. PRACTICE.DB is a duplicate of the AUTHORS.DB table also provided, and I created PRACTICE to give you a table you can perform surgery on without fear of "messing up" something you might need to run one of the demos. What we'll do is index on the AUTHOR CALL field, which will allow us to search the author database by ham radio callsign.

Bring up DBD and open the PRACTICE.DB table. Select Table | Restructure Table. Notice the combo box in the upper right-hand corner of the Restructure Table window. It reads "Validity Checks" but that's only the first on its list of things it can do. Drop down the list, where you'll find (among other options) one called "Secondary Indexes." Select it. Notice that beneath the Define.. button is now a list of all currently defined secondary indexes.

The Define.. button (which was grayed out) will "get real," and become selectable. Click on it, and the Define Secondary Index window will appear. On the left pane of the window is a list of all the fields present in the PRACTICE.DB table. Click on the AUTHOR CALL field to select it. Then go to the pair of arrows shown between the two panes, and click on the arrow pointing to the right. This will move the AUTHOR CALL field from the left pane to the right pane. This situation is shown in Figure 14.7.

The right pane is a list of fields to be present in the secondary index that you're creating. In this case (and in most secondary indexes) the index will be on only a single field. There are times when multiple fields must be present in an index (most notably when you've separated last name and first name data into separate fields and yet want to index on the full name) but this isn't one of them. We're creating an index on AUTHOR CALL and the callsign is the only data that must be present in the index.

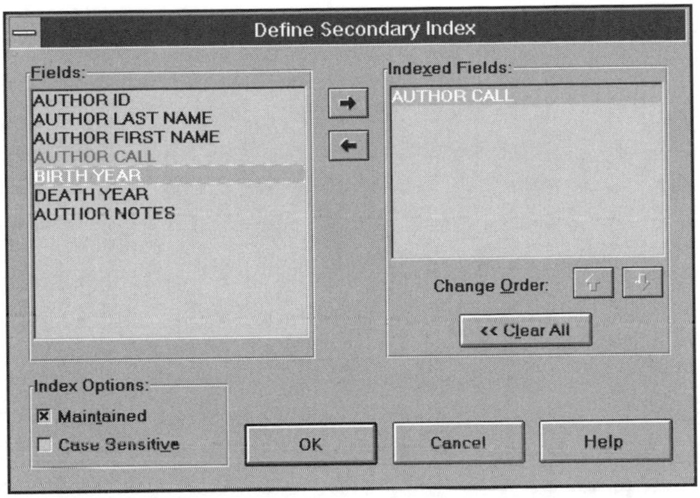

Figure 14.7 *Defining a secondary index.*

As the left-pointing arrow indicates, you can change your mind and move a field back out of the right pane if you feel you chose it in error. And if you simply want to start over again, you can clear the right pane completely by checking the Clear All button.

In our case, we've done all there is to do. Press OK, and the Save Index As window will appear. The new index needs a name. *Don't simply give it the name of the field present in the index!* That's asking for gross confusion, and there's confusion enough in this world. My system is simple: The name of an index is the name of the field in the index followed by the word INDEX. If you have multiple fields in an index, use all of the field names and follow them with INDEX. LAST NAME FIRST NAME INDEX may sound clunky—but you will never have to scratch your head wondering what it is.

Enter the name AUTHOR CALL INDEX (see Figure 14.8) and press OK. Your index will be saved under that name. When the Restructure Table window

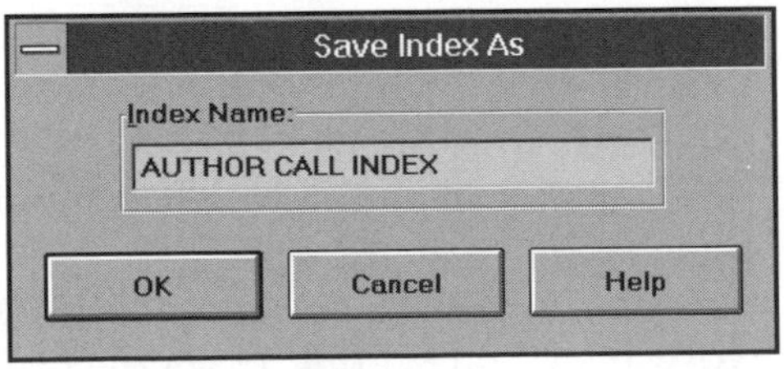

Figure 14.8 *Giving the new index a descriptive name.*

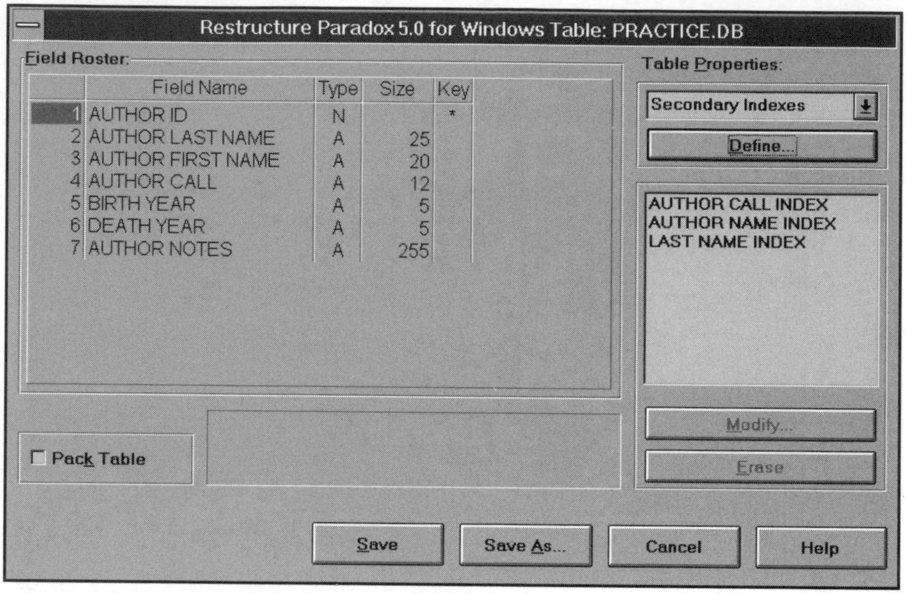

Figure 14.9   *The Restructure Table window with the new index shown.*

returns to the front, you'll see a list of secondary indexes that now includes AUTHOR CALL INDEX. See Figure 14.9.

To complete the operation, click on the Save button at the bottom of the Restructure Table window. It's done!

There's a great deal more you can do using Database Desktop, but that's the basics—and all we'll have room for in this book. Don will discuss aliases and their definition using DBD later on. The online help system is very good, and I encourage you to cruise its database topics whenever you get the chance. There are a *lot* of topics.

DELPHI'S DATABASE MACHINERY

That's a good grounding in what Delphi tables *are*. The next and obvious topic is how to use them. There are whole books to be written on this topic, but it doesn't take whole books to get you started. As Jim demonstrated in the last chapter, you can do some amazing things with Delphi's database machinery without writing any database-specific code at all.

There are basically two ways (representing two conceptual levels) to work with Delphi databases. The first way is almost purely visual: The creation of flat-file and master-detail database applications by the visual arrangement and connection of components on a form. This is easy to do and (because it's visual) easy to catch on to and understand. At the second level you're working with Delphi's database components at an Object Pascal code level, and almost literally anything can be done, including the resolution of nasty database design challenges like the dreaded many-to-many relationship.

What I'm going to attempt to do in this chapter is get you familiar enough with code-oriented access to Delphi tables that you can figure out the rest by experimentation. A good place to start would be that ever-so-essential view from a height.

Delphi's Master Plan for Desktop Databases

Before you try to do *anything* with Delphi database components, you should have it clear in your mind how all the pieces connect to one another from a height. Keep in mind that in this discussion (and in this book as well) we're simply leaving the whole universe of client/server database development aside. You have to walk before you run, and client/server is on the order of a four-minute mile. Not impossible, but you have to work up to it. What we're talking about in this chapter applies to database applications that run on one single machine, using either Paradox for Windows or dBase tables. Once you get into Interbase or remote servers, you're in a whole new universe with its own systems full of Klingons to contend with. You'll get there—take it step by step.

Delphi's database-oriented components fall into two categories: Data access components and data-aware controls. *Data access components* are your gateways to the database tables on disk. They represent tables and queries on your Delphi forms. *Data aware controls* are your viewports through those gateways, by which you actually see and change the data stored in your tables. They resemble many "ordinary" components, but have the additional ability to take data from your tables and display and edit that data. There is a data-aware edit box called DBEdit that looks and acts a lot like the ordinary Edit control that we met several chapters ago. Similarly, there is a DBText component that looks just like a Label component, except it displays data from tables in a read-only mode.

Other than their additional hooks into database tables, all the database components operate like the other components you've already seen. You drop them on forms, set their design-time properties in the Object Inspector, and define event handler procedures to take action when their various events are triggered.

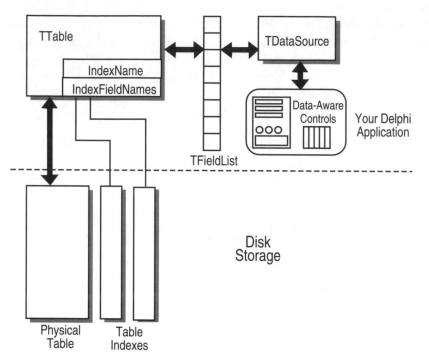

Figure 14.10   Delphi's database machinery.

I've drawn a schematic plan of how the various database elements go together in a Delphi application in Figure 14.10.

Table: The Linchpin Component

In your Delphi database work, everything revolves around the Table component, which is the logical representation of a database table in your application. Without a Table on your form, nothing else can happen. There is typically one Table component on your form for each database table used by that form in some way. However, there can be more than one Table component connected to a single table on disk, allowing you two different views of the same table.

Table's job is to mediate access to the database table on disk. It has a partner on your forms called DataSource, also on the Data Access tool palette. To make any use of data-aware controls, you must drop a DataSource onto your form. The DataSource component "talks" to Table, and makes data acquired from Table available to the data-aware controls on the form that display and edit the data.

One crucial role of Table is to hold the name of the current index or index field by which some operation on the database table on disk is to be done. Simple display of data from a table may be done without special consideration to indexes or key fields, but as soon as you wish to search a table or perform any significant edits to the table, you have to take indexes or key fields into account.

The pipeline runs this way: Data from the database tables on disk are accessed by the Table component, which hands them to the DataSource, filtered through a list of objects called Fields. (More on this in a moment.) The DataSource hands the data to any data-aware components on your form. If the user makes any changes to the data through the controls on the form, DataSource hands these changes back to Table, which passes them on to the tables on disk.

Fields: The Invisible Army

Table has as one of its properties a list of objects called Fields, of type **TField**. This list of Field objects is perhaps the single most perplexing part of Delphi database work, and you should make an extra effort to come to understand it. Fields are part of Tables. They are *not* separate components you select and drop onto forms. Worse, they have no visible representation at all, not at design time nor at runtime. Even getting them into the Object Inspector for a look-see is major pain in the hindquarters.

I don't have a whole lot of quibbles with Delphi, but I'll be very honest and say that I do *not* like the way Fields were implemented in Delphi's first release, particularly the ways fields are handled by Delphi's various tools. So if you have problems understanding or using Fields, feel a little less bad in knowing that it's probably the knottiest single area of desktop database programming to understand. This is made all the worse by the fact that it may also be one of the most important.

Just as the Table component is the representation of a disk-based table on your forms, the Field object (it is not strictly speaking a component) is the representation of table *columns* on your forms. Field objects control whether or not data from a column is displayed, and in what format. Fields are very much the gatekeepers between the Table's data and the data-aware controls that display it.

By default, one Field object is added to a Table's Fields list for every column present in the disk-based table to which the Table component is attached.

The list of Fields is created dynamically when a disk-based table is opened, and goes away when the table is closed. You also have the option of creating a persistent list of Field objects that Delphi will use instead of the list created on the fly. This is done with a Fields Editor, and Delphi takes your field object declarations and inserts them into your Form's type definition. The field spec is thus saved with the application, and remains even if you change the underlying structure of the table. (Obviously, if you change the structure such that a column you originally referenced no longer exists, Delphi will hand you an error.)

Using the Fields Editor for more than inspecting field objects is complex and awkward, and I won't be covering it in this book.

Because the fields in a database record may be of different data types, there is a separate **TField** class for each of the possible data types a field in a record might be: **TBooleanField**, **TCurrencyField**, **TStringField**, **TIntegerField**, **TBLOBField**, and so on. Most of the time you're likely to be using **TStringField** and **TIntegerField**. The various Field classes are very much the same from a programming standpoint, and you rarely need to be concerned about what type a Field object actually is. Their main difference, as you might expect, is the type of the data they maintain internally and transfer to and from the database table to which they're attached.

DataSources and Data-Aware Components

The last major player in the database game is the DataSource component. DataSources act as data pipes from the list of Fields maintained by Table out to any data-aware components you may have dropped on your form. DataSources are fairly simple, and there's not much to be done with them, either visually or programatically. Mostly they're there for the benefit of your data-aware components. You do not, in fact, need a DataSource on your form at all unless you intend to use data-aware components. You can access data in the list of Fields from your Object Pascal code and then plug the data into ordinary non-database components, and in that case you don't need a DataSource. Why do more work than you must?

There is one good reason to have a DataSource attached to every table you use on a form, however: **TDataSource** has the event that tells you when the the current record in a Table changes. This can be seriously useful. Keep it in mind.

SETTING UP FOR DATA ACCESS

Jim covered the fundamentals of purely visual database access back in Chapter 13. I'll recap the process before I get into the issue of programmatic database access.

There are two fundamental properties in a Table that must be set to perform any database access at all. First you must set the **Database** property. When using Paradox for Windows databases, the name of the database is actually the *location* of the database. This can be an explicit DOS pathname (like D:\DELPHI\PROJEX\) or it can be an alias, which is actually a symbolic name given to a pathname, so that you can change the location of your data tables without having to hunt through an entire application for hard-coded references to D:\DELPHI\PROJEX\. Aliases are maintained in one place in one of the Delphi subdirectories, and you define and edit them from Database Desktop.

Once you have the **Database** property filled in, you must select a table from whatever tables exist in that database and plug its name into the **TableName** property. You don't have to memorize all your table names. The **TableName** property is a combo box, and you can drop its list by clicking on its arrow to select one of the tables displayed.

If you're only going to access one table in a flat-file fashion, that's all you really need to do to the Table component. If you change the state of the Table's **Active** property, you'll be able to see "real" data in your data-aware components at design time. That's purely an option for your convenience at design time; when you run your application, **Active** becomes **True** automatically.

If you're going to use any data-aware components at all, you must drop a DataSource component on your form as well. DataSource components don't take much futzing. Simply set their **DataSet** property to an existing Table component, and you're ready to rock. If you set up your Table components first, clicking on the arrow on the DataSource's combo box for the **DataSet** property will show you a list of existing tables and allow you to choose one.

It's pretty awesome that you can create a complete, record-oriented table browser for a Delphi table by dropping a DBGrid component on your form and filling in some properties. Jim demonstrated this aspect of Delphi very well back in Chapter 13, and if for some reason you haven't read that chapter yet, get back there and soak it up now. On the other hand, you're going to get restless with this sort of code-less database hacking in a big hurry. So let's start talking about how you can manipulate databases from your Object Pascal code.

PROGRAMMATIC DATABASE ACCESS

Without writing a whole lot of Delphi code, you can create fairly sophisticated browsers and editors for database tables. This is true not only for single-table "flat file" databases, but also for master-detail databases where one record in a master table "owns" or is somehow otherwise related to multiple records in one or more detail databases. That's a lot—but that's about as far as it goes. To go further requires code in Object Pascal.

Moving From Record to Record

As Jim demonstrated in Chapter 13, you can move around in a Table by using the DBNavigator component on your forms. The DBNavigator is just a collection of buttons, and when you click the buttons, the DBNavigator calls methods that belong to the Table associated with it. You can also navigate a Table from your program code by calling methods of your Table components yourself.

The methods by which you maneuver through a table are very easy to understand. The current pointer for the table (also called the *cursor*) is what is actually being moved. I've summarized the methods in Table 14.1.

These should be pretty close to self-explanatory. The **First** method "rewinds" the table so that the current record is the first record again. Similarly, **Last** sends the cursor to the end of the table. **Next** and **Prior** move the pointer forward and backward by one record, respectively. **MoveBy** takes a count value, and it moves the number of records specified in the count value. The count can be negative, in which case the pointer moves toward the beginning of the table.

Table 14.1 *Delphi's Table Navigation Methods*

Method Name	What It Does
First	Moves the current pointer to the first record in the table
Last	Moves the current pointer to the last record in the table
Next	Bumps the current pointer one record toward the end of the table
Prior	Bumps the current pointer one record toward the beginning of the table
MoveBy(<count>)	Moves the current pointer by <count> records. Positive values move toward the end of the table, negative toward the beginning of the table

---

Table objects have a pair of properties that indicate when the pointer is at the first or last record in the table. The **BOF** property is **True** only when the pointer is at the first record in the table. The **EOF** property is **True** only when the pointer is at the last record in the table. In an empty table, both **EOF** and **BOF** are **True** at the same time.

Fields By Name or By Number

Fields are problematic because they are invisible at both design time and runtime, and also because by default (since they are created dynamically at runtime) they have no names of their own. So working with fields is a little like chasing stray black cats around a coal bin at midnight—there's some clawing and scrambling and screeching, and (if you're not careful) a little bloodshed.

Objects of type **TField** have properties, methods, and events, some (but by no means all) of which I'll discuss in this chapter. A Field object models a specific column in a specific database table. The data a given field object contains at any given time is the data from its column for the current record in the table. (The current record, if you recall, is indicated by the current pointer built into every table.) By default, when a table is opened, this is the first record in the table according to its primary key. Lacking a key field, the current record on opening is the first record in physical order.

Manipulating **TField** objects is easy, once you know which one you want. Fields have no names, unfortunately, unless you create persistent fields with names, which is difficult and not something I'll go into here. They exist as elements in a list called **Fields**, which is a property of the Table component. The Fields in the list have index numbers like elements in an array, and you can access them by that index number as though the **TTable.Fields** property were an array of **TField** objects. The index numbers are assigned at runtime, and begin with 0, taking the leftmost column in the table as index 0, the one to its right as 1, and so on. The syntax for accessing properties is done as with any object:

```
AuthorTable.Fields[0].DisplayLabel := 'ID';
```

Here, we're accessing the **DisplayLabel** property of Field 0 in a table, which is the leftmost column in that table. **DisplayLabel** dictates what the column label will be if that column is displayed in a DBGrid component.

Accessing fields in the **Fields** property by index number can be extremely useful if you need to iterate over a number of columns using a **FOR** loop. In most simple applications, however, it makes more sense and for more readable code to access fields by the names of the columns they represent. This can't be done directly, because the field has no name of its own, but **TTable** has a method called **FieldByName** that allows you to look up a Field object by the name of its column and use the reference that the lookup method returns. This sounds tougher than it is. For example, we could do the same thing as the line of code above this way:

```
AuthorTable.FieldByName('AUTHOR ID').DisplayLabel := 'ID';
```

Do understand that AUTHOR ID is the name of the field's column in the database table. It is *not* the text in the **DisplayLabel** property.

Inspecting Fields

There's only one way to look at properties of a Field at design time, and that is to bring up the Fields editor, which then makes Field properties available in the Object Inspector window. The mechanism is a little lame, but you need to learn it because it's all there is.

First, bring up the Field Editor. This is done by double-clicking on the Table component whose fields you wish to inspect. A list of the columns present in the Table is shown in the Field Editor's list window. (The Field Editor is shown on the right-hand side of Figure 14.11.) Click once on any of the column names, and the Field representing that column will be placed in the Object Inspector window for inspection. The Object Inspector window with a Field on display is shown on the left side of Figure 14.11. I widened both the windows in Figure 14.11 a little bit to better show the names, some of which are pretty long.

The Object Inspector synthesizes a name for each field by concatenating the name of the Table object with the name of the Table column represented by that field. If there are embedded spaces within the column name (which are legal) the Object Inspector omits them so that the final name of the Field will be one continuous string. Thus, the **AuthorTable** field representing the AUTHOR LAST NAME column will be named **AuthorTableAUTHORLASTNAME**, as you can see in Figure 14.11.

You can change Field properties in the Object Inspector, and the changes will be made to the Field in question each time Delphi creates the field list, at

Object Inspector	
AuthorTableAUTHORLASTNAME: TStringField	
Alignment	taLeftJustify
Calculated	False
DisplayLabel	AUTHOR LAST NAME
DisplayWidth	25
EditMask	
FieldName	AUTHOR LAST NAME
Index	1
Name	AuthorTableAUTHORLASTNAME
ReadOnly	False
Required	False
Size	25
Tag	0
Transliterate	True
Visible	True

Properties / Events /

Form1.AuthorTable Fields

Fields

AUTHOR ID
AUTHOR LAST NAME
AUTHOR FIRST NAME
AUTHOR CALL
BIRTH YEAR
DEATH YEAR
AUTHOR NOTES

Add...
Define...
Remove
Clear all

Figure 14.11 *Inspecting Field properties at design time.*

either design time or runtime. When you finish inspecting Fields, close the Field Editor window. The last field you selected will remain in the Object Inspector, but (obviously) you won't be able to switch to inspecting a different Field.

Looking Up Values in a Table

To demonstrate some of the simpler programmatic access techniques for Delphi tables, let's set up a simple form that allows a user to search the AUTHORS.DB table by name or by key. This can't be done using simple visual techniques. The project is called SEEKTEST.DPR, and a shot of its main form is shown in Figure 14.12. The view shown is at design time, and demonstrates how "invisible" components like Tables and DataSources "float" to the foreground at design time over any other control. This gives you easy access to such controls without requiring that you "leave a hole" in your form to contain invisible components. Since invisible component icons are quite small, it's rare that they will completely cover a "foreground" component and make it inaccessible at design time.

Setting Up Fields at Runtime

There are a lot of configurable properties in Field objects. If you're going to set them up at all, I suggest setting them up all at once in the same place. The obvious time to do this is when the form is created, and the obvious place is inside the form's OnCreate event handler. Here's the Form's OnCreate event handler from the SEEKTEST.DPR project:

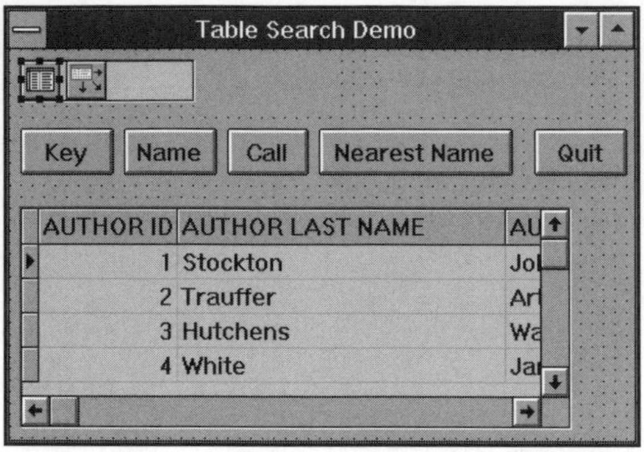

Figure 14.12 *The Table Search Demo main form at design time.*

Listing 14.1 Setting up fields in the form's OnCreate event handler

```
procedure TForm1.FormCreate(Sender: TObject);
begin
   WITH AuthorTable DO
      BEGIN
         { You can access fields by their index into the fields list. }
         { That's what I'm doing here, just to demonstrate it: }
         Fields[0].DisplayLabel := 'ID';
         { In most cases, it makes more sense to access fields by name: }
         FieldByName('AUTHOR ID').DisplayWidth := 4;
         FieldByName('AUTHOR ID').ReadOnly := True;
         FieldByName('AUTHOR LAST NAME').DisplayLabel := 'LAST NAME';
         FieldByName('AUTHOR LAST NAME').DisplayWidth := 12;
         FieldByName('AUTHOR FIRST NAME').DisplayLabel := 'FIRST NAME';
         FieldByName('AUTHOR FIRST NAME').DisplayWidth := 10;
         FieldByName('AUTHOR CALL').DisplayLabel := 'CALL';
         FieldByName('AUTHOR CALL').DisplayWidth := 10;
         FieldByName('BIRTH YEAR').Visible := False;
         FieldByName('DEATH YEAR').Visible := False;
      END;
end;
```

All of what's being done here is for the sake of the DBGrid component that displays information from the AUTHORS.DB table. We're changing the column display text and the width of each column, enabling us to show more of the table in a fairly small space.

Columns' Display Names and Display Width

I haven't seen this called out in Delphi's documentation, but so far I've been unable to set a field's **DisplayWidth** property to a value narrower than the width of the column's display label. If you want a narrow column in a DBGrid, you had better come up with a narrow column display label. "AUTHOR ID" is a fairly wide label for a column that only needs to be four or five characters wide, but until you change the label to "ID" you won't be able to reduce the column's display width to an appropriate value.

If you don't want a table column to appear in the DBGrid display for the table, you must set the **Visible** property for the Field object corresponding to that column to **False**. I've done this in Listing 14.1 for two columns in the AUTHORS.DB table. As you'll see if you run SEEKTEST.DPR, these two fields are simply not present in the DBGrid.

Another useful Field property is **ReadOnly**. If you don't want the user to be able to edit a column from a table, set that column's Field's **ReadOnly** property to **True**. It will display, but Delphi will refuse any attempt to change the data in a column with **ReadOnly** set to **True**.

There are a lot of other properties in **TField**, and I encourage you to read up on them in Delphi Help.

SEARCHING A TABLE

I guess it's not surprising that for anything as important as searching a table, there's more than one way to do it. The SEEKTEST.DPR project presents three of those ways, and they're the three ways you'll need most of the time.

If you wish to search a table, first be sure that the field you want to search on is either a key field of the table, or else a secondary index. If you're using either Paradox or dBase tables, this is your only option, at least until you've digested SQL and learned a great deal more of Delphi's database complexity. If a field doesn't have such an index, you can add one at any time through Database Desktop, as I described earlier in this chapter.

In broad terms, there are two major ways to search a table: The *goto* method, and the *find* method. The two are very similar, and differ almost entirely in how you specify the key value for which to search. In both methods, you search for a record containing a specified value in a specified column, and if the value is found in the table, the current pointer of the table moves to that record. You can then access any of the fields in the found record.

In the goto method, you must perform several steps:

1. Make sure the field you're searching on is a key field or has a secondary index defined for it—and make sure the key field name or secondary index name is present in **TTable**'s property list. More on this below.
2. Place the Table being searched into search mode by calling its **SetKey** method.
3. Assign the value you want to search for into the search buffer for the Field you're searching on. This assignment is made possible by the call to **SetKey**.
4. Call the Table's **GotoKey** method, and test its return value to see if the search succeeded or failed.

If the search succeeds, **GotoKey** (which is a function) returns **True**, and the current pointer of the Table moves to the found record. If the search fails, **GotoKey** returns **False**, and the current pointer does not change.

Two tricky things here. Getting the key field or secondary index right proved a major hangup to me while I was first learning Delphi, and the documentation does a very bad job of explaining this. I'll come back to it very shortly.

The other tricky thing is how you assign a value into a Field's search buffer. Fields, once again, are slightly spooky objects without their own names. Most of the time, you'll use the Table's **FieldByName** method to look up the Field in the Fields list and allow it to be assigned to. There's no name to the buffer; if the Table is in search mode, you simply assign the search value to the Field's **AsString** property.

AsString is more than it might appear. It's a *conversion property*, and any string assigned to a Field's **AsString** property will be converted to the Field's "native" data type. (Note that **AsString** cannot be used with certain of the more arcane field types, including BLOB, Bytes, Memo, and Graphic. You typically don't search for values of these types anyway.)

Below is an example of how such a search would work. Listing 14.2 was lifted from SEEKTEST.DPR. When the user enters a search value for an author last name into the **EntryEdit** component and clicks on the Name button, the search for the name in the Table is executed. If the search succeeds, the message "Entry Found!" is displayed in a label, and the callsign of the author found is displayed in another label. The current pointer will move to the found author's record in the table, and this will be reflected in the highlight on the DBGrid component.

Listing 14.2   Searching a Table using GotoKey

```
procedure TForm1.SeekButtonClick(Sender: TObject);
begin
   WITH AuthorTable DO
      BEGIN
         CallLabel.Caption := '';
         IndexName := 'LAST NAME INDEX';
         SetKey;
         FieldByName('AUTHOR LAST NAME').AsString := EntryEdit.Text;
         IF GotoKey THEN
            BEGIN
               StatusLabel.Caption := 'Entry Found!';
               CallLabel.Caption := FieldByName('AUTHOR CALL').Text;
            END
         ELSE StatusLabel.Caption := 'Entry Not Found!';
      END;
end;
```

Key and Index Values for Searches

The way this works should be pretty plain, but if you're like me, you may have had a lot of trouble getting a search to work the first time. Delphi's documentation does warn that for Paradox and dBase tables you may search *only* on a key field or a field for which a secondary index has been defined. Cool so far—but they neglect to say that the name of the key field or of the index must be present in one of two **TTable** properties for the Table being searched.

In Listing 14.2, you'll notice that I assign the name of a secondary index to the Table's **IndexName** property. LAST NAME INDEX is the name of a secondary index I defined in Database Desktop, and it's an index on the field the code will be searching. Without this property setting, the code throws an exception on the **FieldByName** assignment statement, stating that the field is not indexed and cannot be modified.

Boy, did I grind my teeth over *this* one.

You can place the name of the secondary index you'll be searching into the Object Inspector's line for the **IndexName** property, but I recommend assigning an index to **IndexName** immediately before a search will be done. If you'll be searching on more than field within a given form, you'll have to change it eventually anyway, and an explicit assignment close to where the search is actually performed will make your code easier to understand.

If you're searching on a key field, the search will be a little bit different, as shown in Listing 14.3.

Listing 14.3   Searching a Table on a key field rather than an index

```
procedure TForm1.KeySearchButtonClick(Sender: TObject);
begin
   WITH AuthorTable DO
     BEGIN
        CallLabel.Caption := '';
        IndexFieldNames := 'AUTHOR ID';
        SetKey;
        FieldByName('AUTHOR ID').AsString := EntryEdit.Text;
        IF GotoKey THEN
          BEGIN
             StatusLabel.Caption := 'Entry Found!';
             CallLabel.Caption := FieldByName('AUTHOR CALL').Text;
          END
        ELSE StatusLabel.Caption := 'Entry Not Found!';
     END;
end;
```

This code is almost the same as that in Listing 14.2. AUTHOR ID is the key field for the AUTHORS.DB table, rather than a secondary index. To specify a key field, you must place the name in the **IndexFieldNames** property of the Table being searched. If your table has multiple key fields, you can place more than one field name in the **IndexFieldNames** property. Separate them with semicolons.

It's also possible to place the name of a table field on which there is a secondary index in the **IndexFieldNames** property. In other words, in Listing 14.2, we could have replaced this line:

```
IndexName := 'LAST NAME INDEX';
```

with this line:

```
IndexFieldNames := 'AUTHOR LAST NAME';
```

and the search would have worked identically.

This probably seems grossly confusing. Think of it this way: **IndexName** is for named secondary *indexes*, like those I showed you how to create in Database Desktop earlier in this chapter. **IndexFieldNames** is for the names of *fields* which are either key fields, or fields on which secondary indexes have been defined.

In practice, use **IndexName** for named secondary indexes and **IndexFieldNames** for key fields. When you define a secondary index, you have to give it a distinct name anyway, so you might as well use **IndexName**.

Using Find for Searches

The goto method for table searches works well, but Delphi provides a slightly easier way in the find method. Find is a lot like goto, but it builds the same machinery into fewer statements—hence I had to explain goto before explaining find. I've written a third search into SEEKTEST.DPR, and it uses the find method. Here's the code:

Listing 14.4 Using FindKey to perform a table search

```
procedure TForm1.FindCallButtonClick(Sender: TObject);

VAR
   SeekValue : String;

begin
   WITH AuthorTable DO
      BEGIN
         IndexFieldNames := 'AUTHOR CALL';
         SeekValue := EntryEdit.Text;
         IF FindKey([SeekValue]) THEN StatusLabel.Caption := 'Entry Found!'
            ELSE StatusLabel.Caption := 'Entry Not Found!';
      END;
end;
```

The fundamental difference between the find and goto methods of searching tables is that the search value is passed to **FindKey** in its parameter list. **GotoKey**, if you recall, takes no parameters. It assumes that you have assigned the search value to the search buffer of the field representing the column you want to search.

FindKey takes a parameter that is a comma-delimited array of values, enclosed in square brackets. Each value in the array is a search value intended for a particular column—and by allowing multiple search values in the parameter, **FindKey** lets you search more than one column at a time. The **FindKey** invocation in Listing 14.4 passes only one search value in the variable **SeekValue**, and searches only one index, which (in this case) is passed by the name of the field, AUTHOR CALL. There is a named secondary index on the AUTHOR CALL field, named AUTHOR CALL INDEX. If you prefer, you can assign "AUTHOR CALL INDEX" to **AuthorTable**'s **IndexName** property instead, and the search will work the same way.

If you want to search more than one index, you must place the names of all indexed fields to be searched in the **IndexFieldNames** property, separated by semicolons, and then place one search value in **FindKey**'s parameter array for each index.

Inexact Searches with GotoNearest and FindNearest

The searches we've discussed so far either succeed or fail, because we've been looking for an exact match to a given search value. Delphi supports a different kind of search, one that never fails—which doesn't mean it always finds what you ask for. The **GotoNearest** and **FindNearest** routines look for the closest possible match to a search value. If they find the full value, terrific—and if they don't find it, they'll take you to the record that comes as close as possible to the search value you've specified.

In terms of how they're called, **GotoNearest** works identically to **GotoKey**, and **FindNearest** works identically to **FindKey**. **FindNearest** takes the same parameter array as **FindKey**, and search values are assigned to a field's search buffer for **GotoNearest** just as they are for **GotoKey**. The difference lies in the way the search values are interpreted. For the "nearest" search routines, the search value can be a full or partial value. In other words, if you wanted to perform an inexact search on "Duntemann" you could use "Duntemann," "Dun," or "Du" as search values, and the search would take you as close as possible to the search value.

Where an exact match to the search value is not found, the search overshoots and stops at the first record that *cannot* match the search value. If you searched for "Duntemann" and nothing close could be found, the search might stop at "Dunwoody" or even "Evans." On the other hand, if you search for "Dun" the search could stop at "Duncan" or "Dunn," long before it got to "Duntemann." (Of course, if someone in your table is named "Dun," the search stops there.)

GotoNearest and **FindNearest** return no Boolean values to indicate success or failure. They always succeed, in that they always move the table's current pointer *somewhere*. Keep that in mind—it's important.

The SEEKTEST.DPR project contains a search for an inexact match. To try it out, enter a partial search value in the edit box and the press the Nearest

Name button. Watch what comes up as the current record after such a search. Try it a few times, and you'll catch the gist of how it works.

The code is nearly identical to the code used for an exact search, except that you don't have to test to see whether the search succeeded or failed.

Listing 14.5 Performing an inexact search

```
procedure TForm1.FindNearestButtonClick(Sender: TObject);
begin
   WITH AuthorTable DO
      BEGIN
         IndexName := 'LAST NAME INDEX';
         SetKey;
         FieldByName('AUTHOR LAST NAMF').AsString := EntryEdit.Text;
         GotoNearest;
         CallLabel.Caption := FieldByName('AUTHOR CALL').Text;
      END;
end;
```

CHANGING DATA IN EXISTING RECORDS

After spotting a record of interest in a table, you may want to change something in that record and then write the changed record back to the table. This is fairly easy, at least once you've mastered the notion of Field objects and how to manipulate them. In broad terms, here's what you have to do:

1. Move the current pointer to the record you want to change.
2. Place the Table in Edit mode by calling its **Edit** method.
3. Change the Field or Fields that need to be changed.
4. Write the changes to the Table by calling its **Post** method.

That's the big picture. There are some important details that have to be tended to, however, and I've put another little demo application together to show you how things all fit together.

Changing All Records in a Table Programmatically

PROJECT The CASETEST.DPR project shows how you write a program that reads through all records in a table and makes a modification to only one field in each of the records. There's no user involvement other than in pressing a button to kick off the process. The controls on the form are disabled while the update operation is taking place, and a simple exception block makes sure that the controls are re-enabled even if an exception happens during the update. The screen of the program in operation is shown in Figure 14.13.

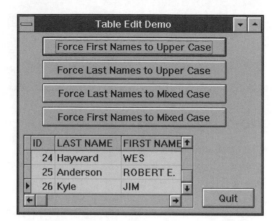

Figure 14.13   The Table Edit Demo form.

The Edit and Post Methods

In order for you to make changes programatically to any record in a Table, the Table must be in Edit mode. (Data-aware controls have special powers in this area; they handle the switch in modes automatically.) Most of the time, a table is open in Browse mode, which means that its Fields can be read from but not updated. The **Edit** method puts the Table in Edit mode, and any changes made to the record at the current pointer will be accepted. However, the changes will not be written out to the physical table on disk until you call the Table's **Post** method. **Post** forces any changed fields to write their new data out to the physical table.

In general terms, your code for scanning an entire table and making some change to a field in each record will look like this:

```
WITH SomeTable DO
  BEGIN
    DisableControls;   { Turn off display of data during update }
    First;                { Start at the top of the table }
    WHILE NOT EOF DO   { Do until end of table is encountered }
      BEGIN
        <Read a value from a Field into a temporary variable>
        <Make some change to the variable>
        Edit;                { Put table in edit mode }
        <Write the changed value back into the Field>
        Post;                { Write changes to table }
        Next;                { Bump to next record down }
      END;
    EnableControls;  { Turn display of data back on again }
  END;
```

There are a *lot* of references to the Table component in a sequence like this, so it makes abundant sense to use a **WITH** statement to avoid dotting yourself dotty. Notice the two methods, **DisableControls** and **EnableControls**. **DisableControls** turns off the connection between your Table and its DataSource while you're scanning and updating the Table. Otherwise, the DataSource would attempt to update the displays on all data-aware components on the form after every change to the Table. This will slow down the process tremendously and is completely wasted time. **EnableControls** remakes the connection and causes all data-aware components to be updated.

Notice the **First** method call. This ensures that the scan of the Table begins at the first record. The **Next** method call bumps the current pointer to the next record after each record update. Don't forget **Next**—without it, you've got an endless loop here.

TRY..FINALLY for Exception Protection

There is a danger here. It's possible that for some reason the update of the Table cannot go through to completion. If the code tries to execute **Post** to write changes back to disk, and the disk for some reason isn't ready, an exception will happen. An exception will pause the application with an error box, but once the user clicks the error box, execution will continue...somewhere. It won't necessarily be where you expect, and keep in mind that when the **Post** is attempted, *all controls are disconnected from the Table*. So you might find that a relatively innocuous exception can leave your form incommunicado with the database.

Object Pascal provides an out in the form of the **TRY..FINALLY** statement, which was introduced with Delphi. In a sense, a **TRY..FINALLY** statement gathers two groups of statements together. The **TRY** block of statements contains any code subject to exceptions. The **FINALLY** block contains any statement or statements that *must* be executed, *even if an exception occurs*.

In our case, that would be the **EnableControls** method call. We can recast the almost-code shown above to incorporate a **TRY..FINALLY** statement:

```
WITH SomeTable DO
   BEGIN
      DisableControls;       { Turn off display of data during update }
      TRY
         First;              { Start at the top of the table }
        WHILE NOT EOF DO    { Do until end of table is encountered }
           BEGIN
```

```
            <Read a value from a Field into a temporary variable>
            <Make some change to the variable>
            Edit;              { Put table in edit mode }
            <Write the changed value back into the Field>
            Post;              { Write changes to table }
            Next;              { Bump to next record down }
         END;
      FINALLY  { Anything from here to next END *WILL* be executed }
         EnableControls;  { Turn display of data back on again }
      END;        { Of the TRY..FINALLY statement }
   END;
```

Notice that all code that moves the current pointer or manipulates Table data lies between the reserved words **TRY** and **FINALLY**. This is the block of statements that might generate an exception. In such an event, we want to be sure that **EnableControls** is executed. The call to **EnableControls** is placed between **FINALLY** and the **END** word that ends the statement.

Don't confuse **TRY..FINALLY** with **TRY..EXCEPT**. If you want to actually take some sort of specific action to address the exception when an exception happens, use **TRY..EXCEPT**. If you simply want some protection against an exception disrupting the flow of necessary statements in your program, use **TRY..FINALLY**. **TRY..EXCEPT** is exception *handling*. **TRY..FINALLY** is exception *protection*.

With that in mind, I'll present some working code from the CASETEST.DPR project that pulls all of this together. Unlike the previous demo program, I'm going to present the full code listing here, because there are some interesting techniques I haven't demonstrated before.

Listing 14.6   The Table Edit Demo file, CASEUNIT.PAS

```
unit Caseunit;

interface

uses
   SysUtils, WinTypes, WinProcs, Messages, Classes, Graphics, Controls,
   Forms, Dialogs, Grids, DBGrids, StdCtrls, DB, DBTables;

type
   TEditDemoForm = class(TForm)
      AuthorTable: TTable;
      AuthorSource: TDataSource;
      UpperCaseLastNameButton: TButton;
      UpperCaseFirstNameButton: TButton;
      AuthorGrid: TDBGrid;
```

```
        QuitButton: TButton;
        MixedCaseLastNameButton: TButton;
        MixedCaseFirstNameButton: TButton;
        procedure QuitButtonClick(Sender: TObject);
        procedure FormCreate(Sender: TObject);
        {The following procedure is NOT an event handler! }
        PROCEDURE ForceCase(TargetField : String; ToUpper : Boolean);
        procedure UpperCaseFirstNameButtonClick(Sender: TObject);
        procedure MixedCaseFirstNameButtonClick(Sender: TObject);
        procedure UpperCaseLastNameButtonClick(Sender: TObject);
        procedure MixedCaseLastNameButtonClick(Sender: TObject);
    private
        { Private declarations }
    public
        { Public declarations }
    end;

var
    EditDemoForm: TEditDemoForm;

implementation

CONST
    Upper = True;
    Mixed = False;

{$R *.DFM}

FUNCTION IsUpper(Ch : Char) : Boolean;

BEGIN
    IF (Ch >= 'A') AND (Ch <= 'Z') THEN
        IsUpper := True
    ELSE
        IsUpper := False;
END;

PROCEDURE TEditDemoForm.ForceCase(TargetField : String;
                                              ToUpper : Boolean);

VAR
    WorkBuffer : String;
    I          : Integer;

BEGIN
    WITH AuthorTable DO
        BEGIN
            DisableControls;
            TRY
                First;    { Start at the top of the table }
                WHILE NOT EOF DO   { Do until end of table }
                    BEGIN
                        WorkBuffer := FieldByName(TargetField).AsString;
```

```
                    IF ToUpper THEN
                      FOR I := 1 TO Length(WorkBuffer) DO
                        WorkBuffer[I] := UpCase(WorkBuffer[I])
                    ELSE
                      BEGIN
                        FOR I := 1 TO Length(WorkBuffer) DO
                          IF IsUpper(WorkBuffer[I]) THEN
                            WorkBuffer[I] := Chr(Ord(WorkBuffer[I])+32);
                        WorkBuffer[1] := UpCase(WorkBuffer[1]);
                      END;
                    {This is the only place we actually write to the table: }
                    Edit;              { Put table in edit mode }
                    FieldByName(TargetField).AsString := WorkBuffer;
                    Post;              { Write changes to table }
                    Next;              { Bump to next record down }
                END;
          FINALLY
             EnableControls;
          END;
      END;
END;


procedure TEditDemoForm.QuitButtonClick(Sender: TObject);
begin
   Close;
end;

procedure TEditDemoForm.FormCreate(Sender: TObject);
begin
   WITH AuthorTable DO
      BEGIN
         { You can access fields by their index into the fields list. }
         { That's what I'm doing here, just to demonstrate it: }
         Fields[0].DisplayLabel := 'ID';
         { In most cases, it makes more sense to access fields by name: }
         FieldByName('AUTHOR ID').DisplayWidth := 4;
         FieldByName('AUTHOR ID').ReadOnly := True;
         FieldByName('AUTHOR LAST NAME').DisplayLabel := 'LAST NAME';
         FieldByName('AUTHOR LAST NAME').DisplayWidth := 12;
         FieldByName('AUTHOR FIRST NAME').DisplayLabel := 'FIRST NAME';
         FieldByName('AUTHOR FIRST NAME').DisplayWidth := 10;
         FieldByName('AUTHOR CALL').DisplayLabel := 'CALL';
         FieldByName('AUTHOR CALL').DisplayWidth := 10;
         FieldByName('BIRTH YEAR').Visible := False;
         FieldByName('DEATH YEAR').Visible := False;
      END;
end;

procedure TEditDemoForm.UpperCaseFirstNameButtonClick(Sender: TObject);
begin
   ForceCase('AUTHOR FIRST NAME',Upper);
end;
```

```
procedure TEditDemoForm.MixedCaseFirstNameButtonClick(
   Sender: TObject);
begin
   ForceCase('AUTHOR FIRST NAME',Mixed);
end;

procedure TEditDemoForm.UpperCaseLastNameButtonClick(Sender: TObject);
begin
   ForceCase('AUTHOR LAST NAME',Upper);
end;

procedure TEditDemoForm.MixedCaseLastNameButtonClick(Sender: TObject);
begin
   ForceCase('AUTHOR LAST NAME',Mixed);
end;

end.
```

Methods That Are Not Event Handlers

Before you start digesting what the crucial procedure **ForceCase** actually does, consider what it *is*: An object method that is not an event handler. By and large, the methods that you add to Form objects will be event handlers, and Delphi creates them automatically when you double-click on a blank event line in the Object Inspector's Events pane. Sometimes, though, it will be useful to have a method that isn't itself an event handler but is called by event handlers.

That's the case with **ForceCase**. Each of four buttons on the form has to do the same thing in slightly different ways when clicked. Rather than duplicate functionality in four OnClick event handlers, I factored out the duplicate code into a single procedure that could be called, with different parameters, from each of the four button OnClick handlers.

I made the new procedure a method of the Form object, rather than just tucking it off into a separate unit as a fully independent procedure. Why? There are a lot of references to Form object fields within **ForceCase**. Building it into the Form object makes it "part of the gang" and able to reference items within the Form object without any special fuss.

Make sure if you define such a method that you incorporate the name of the method in the implementation of the procedure. That is, when you write the full body of the method, the name of the method must include the name of the object to which it belongs:

```
PROCEDURE TEditDemoForm.ForceCase(TargetField : String;
                                  ToUpper : Boolean);
```

If you don't prefix "ForceCase" with "TEditDemoForm," Delphi will not know for sure that the procedure belongs to the **TEditDemoForm** object. Compilers don't make assumptions. (Good compilers, anyway...)

ForceCase is "generalized" by passing the field to be manipulated as a parameter, as well as a Boolean flag indicating whether the specified field is to be forced to upper case, or forced to mixed case. Notice, just below the reserved word **implementation**, these two definitions:

```
CONST
  Upper = True;
  Mixed = False;
```

These symbolic constants give us self-explanatory ways to pass a flag to **ForceCase**. **Upper** means we force it to upper case; **Mixed** means we force it to mixed case. These are just different names for our old friends **True** and **False**, but they make it obvious what **True** or **False** mean *in this context*. Making things obvious is something you should always do if you can. Constant substitutions like this happen at compile-time and impose no computational burden at all.

The rest of the meat of **ForceCase**, beyond what we've discussed about **Edit** and **Post**, simply takes a string value and either forces it to upper case, or to mixed case with an initial cap. I've covered all the machinery used here, and you should be able to read it and understand it without a whole lot more explanation. Run and experiment with CASETEST.DPR. It changes the case of one of two fields in the AUTHORS.DB table at the push of a button—all under program control.

INSERTING AND DELETING RECORDS

You can always add records to and delete records from tables using Database Desktop, but most database applications of any consequence need to do the same sorts of things at the end user's behest. Again, as with changing existing records, adding new records is easy if you understand fields and how they work. And deleting records—well, it's almost *too* easy.

Deleting records, in fact, is as easy as calling a Table's **Delete** method. The record at the current pointer will be deleted. You don't have to be in Edit mode first. All records below the deleted record are "pulled up" and the current pointer moves to the record that followed the deleted record. No confirmation is generated automatically, so be careful, and if you're creating a user application, it's probably a good idea to post a confirmation message box to ensure that the user did not select the deletion by accident.

Inserting a new record isn't a great deal more bother. Delphi gives you two general ways to insert a new record into a table: After the current pointer position or at the end of the table. There's a catch, though: *A record added to an indexed table will be written to its position in index order, regardless of whether you added the record with **Insert** or **Append***. What this means is that, for indexed tables, **Insert** and **Append** operate identically. In practical terms, then, **Append** is useful only for tables without indexes, which are not very useful and aren't often created. In nearly every case you'll be adding records to Tables with **Insert**.

Piecemeal Insertion

You can perform an insertion in two general ways: Piecemeal, creating an empty record, filling it, and posting it as three separate operations; or all at once, with a single **InsertRecord** method call. Let's speak of the piecemeal approach first.

The piecemeal approach happens in three distinct steps. Calling the Table's **Insert** method creates a new, empty record in the Table. You fill the Field objects in the empty record with new values, and finally use **Post** to write the new record to the physical Table file on disk. It's pointless to wonder where the inserted record goes in the Table until you fill it with values and post it. Assuming the Table has an index, **Post** will insert the new record at its correct position in index order. If there is no index in the Table, the new record will be written at the position following the current pointer.

So adding a new record in the piecemeal way would look something like this:

```
WITH DeviceTable DO
   BEGIN
     Insert;
     FieldByName('DEVICE NAME').AsString := '12AD6';
     FieldByName('DEVICE DESCRIPTION').AsString :=
        '12V space charge pentagrid converter';
     Post;
   END;
```

For Tables without indexes, you can replace **Insert** with **Append** and put the inserted record at the end of the Table.

Inserting a Record With a Single Statement

There will doubtless be occasions when you'll want to insert new records the piecemeal way, but for simple applications Delphi allows you to insert and post a new record, with a new value for as many fields as you choose, in a single slam. The **TTable.InsertRecord** method incorporates **Insert**, the assigning of values to Fields, and **Post** in a single statement.

InsertRecord takes an array of values as its sole parameter. You can provide one value in the array for each Field in the Table, or fill as many Fields contiguously from the leftmost column as you like. What this means is that you can start from the leftmost column in the Table and pass **InsertRecord** a value for the first however many columns in the table, up to the full number of fields. You can leave off values for fields at the end of the lineup, and **InsertRecord** will fill those remaining fields with null (that is, empty) values.

You also have the option of passing the reserved word **NIL** for any fields you would explicitly like to fill with null values.

The DEVICES.DB table is a good example. The equivalent to the piecemeal record insertion shown above would look like this:

```
InsertRecord([NIL,'12AD6','12V space charge pentagrid converter']);
```

In the code above, we only filled two Fields: DEVICE NAME and DEVICE DESCRIPTION. But if you go into Database Desktop and look at the structure of DEVICES.DB, you'll see that to the left of either of those fields is a field called DEVICE ID. DEVICE ID is an *autoincrement* field, meaning that whenever a new record is inserted into the Table, the next number in line is plugged into that field. Each record in the table thus gets a unique ascending ID code. You can't fill an autoincrement field; you can't write to it at all. It's filled with the proper ascending value when its record is created; after that, it's considered read-only.

So we use the reserved word **NIL** as a placeholder in the values list we pass to **InsertRecord**, so that the two string values get written to the correct fields. If we had for whatever reason wanted to leave the DEVICE NAME field blank, we could have used this statement:

```
InsertRecord([NIL,NIL,'12V space charge pentagrid converter']);
```

Or if (which is closer to reality) we wanted to insert a record with a device name but no description, we could simply have left off the last field entirely, and used this statement:

```
InsertRecord([NIL,'12AD6']);
```

You'll get an error if you try to pass more values in the array than there are Fields in the field lineup.

Inserting and Deleting Whole Records

To close out this chapter, let's take a look at a short program that allows you to insert new records in a file, or else delete existing records, all using programmatic techniques rather than data-aware controls. There's a DBGrid here, but it's been marked as read-only, and acts solely as a window into the Table to see the results of insertions and deletions. The form for the program is shown in Figure 14.14, and the full source code in Listing 14.7.

Listing 14.7   The Insert/Delete Demo program

```
unit Addunit;

interface

uses
   SysUtils, WinTypes, WinProcs, Messages, Classes, Graphics, Controls,
   Forms, Dialogs, StdCtrls, DB, DBTables, Grids, DBGrids;

type
   TInsertDeleteForm = class(TForm)
      DeviceTable: TTable;
      DataSource1: TDataSource;
      DeviceNameEdit: TEdit;
      QuitButton: TButton;
      DeviceDescriptionEdit: TEdit;
      DeviceNameLabel: TLabel;
      DeviceDescriptionLabel: TLabel;
      CreateNewRecordButton: TButton;
      DeviceGrid: TDBGrid;
      DeleteButton: TButton;
      procedure QuitButtonClick(Sender: TObject);
      procedure CreateNewRecordButtonClick(Sender: TObject);
      procedure FormCreate(Sender: TObject);
      procedure DeleteButtonClick(Sender: TObject);
   private
      { Private declarations }
   public
      { Public declarations }
   end;
```

```
var
   InsertDeleteForm: TInsertDeleteForm;

implementation

{$R *.DFM}

procedure TInsertDeleteForm.QuitButtonClick(Sender: TObject);
begin
   Close;
end;

procedure TInsertDeleteForm.CreateNewRecordButtonClick(Sender: TObject);
begin
   IF (Length(DeviceNameEdit.Text) = 0) AND
      (Length(DeviceDescriptionEdit.Text) = 0)
   THEN
      MessageDlg('No data has been entered!', mtError, [mbCancel], 0)
   ELSE
      WITH DeviceTable DO
         BEGIN
            IndexFieldNames := 'DEVICE NAME';
            IF FindKey([DeviceNameEdit.Text]) THEN
               MessageDlg('That device already exists!', mtError, [mbCancel], 0)
            ELSE
               InsertRecord([nil,DeviceNameEdit.Text,DeviceDescriptionEdit.Text]);
            DeviceNameEdit.Text := '';
            DeviceDescriptionEdit.Text := '';
         END;
end;

procedure TInsertDeleteForm.FormCreate(Sender: TObject);
begin
   WITH DeviceTable DO
      BEGIN
         Fields[0].Visible := False;
         FieldByName('DEVICE NAME').DisplayLabel := 'NAME';
         FieldByName('DEVICE NAME').DisplayWidth := 10;
         FieldByName('DEVICE DESCRIPTION').DisplayLabel := 'DESCRIPTION';
      END;
end;

procedure TInsertDeleteForm.DeleteButtonClick(Sender: TObject);
begin
   IF (Length(DeviceNameEdit.Text) = 0) AND
      (Length(DeviceDescriptionEdit.Text) = 0)
   THEN
      MessageDlg('No data has been entered!', mtError, [mbCancel], 0)
   ELSE
      WITH DeviceTable DO
         BEGIN
            { We first have to make sure the entered device is in the table: }
            IndexFieldNames := 'DEVICE NAME';
            IF FindKey([DeviceNameEdit.Text]) THEN
```

```
        BEGIN{ If it is, we must confirm the deletion: }
            IF MessageDlg('Are you sure you want to delete this record?',
                        mtConfirmation, [mbYes,mbNo], 0)
              = mrYes THEN Delete; { Deletes the current record }
        END
      ELSE { If it's not found, display an error box: }
        MessageDlg('That device is not in the table!',
                  mtError, [mbCancel],0);
      { Finally, clear the edit boxes: }
      DeviceNameEdit.Text := '';
      DeviceDescriptionEdit.Text := '';
    END;

end;

end.
```

If you take a close look at the code, you'll see that the deleting proper is the least part of the job of deleting a record. Housekeeping, as usual, takes most of your energy. You first have to make sure that the device entered into the edit line exists in the table, and that requires a search. Assuming the search is successful and the device is found, the current pointer will be pointing to the record that matches the device name entered into the **DeviceNameEdit** edit box. It's polite and good practice to display a confirmation box that allows the users to back out if they entered the wrong device or simply changed their mind. But once the user clicks the Yes button on the confirmation box, it's one call to **Delete** and *poof!* The record's gone.

If the search fails, you need to let the users know that they can't delete something that isn't already there, hence the error box.

Insertion works much the same way, in that the housekeeping is very similar. When the user enters a new device name, you must first check to see if the

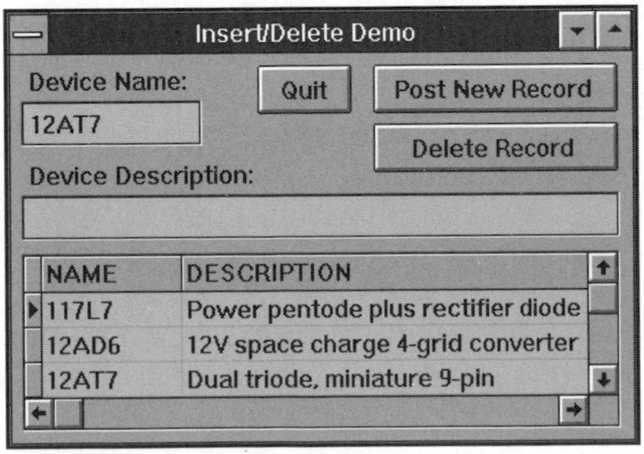

Figure 14.14   *The Insert/Delete Demo form.*

device is already in the table; you don't want to add a duplicate record. But assuming that the device entered is not already there, one call to **InsertRecord** places the new record in the table.

As an extra feature to avoid posting totally empty records, if both edit controls are empty, the record insertion is refused, and another error box is displayed.

Give the program a try. Enter a few new devices (even if you make them up off the top of your head) and then see if they appear in the DBGrid. Nuke a few for good practice. This will be especially satisfying if for some reason you hate tubes. Me, well, I have boxes full of them out in the garage. I got many of them the summer I met my wife, and if I'd liked tubes back then a little more than I did, I might *not* have met my wife—but that's a story for another day.

YOU'RE NOT DONE YET!

Is that all there is to Delphi database programming? Ha! I could have filled two books this size with nothing *but* database material, and I'm not sure I'd have nailed it even then. This very large chapter has barely scratched the surface, and if it enables you to figure out the rest by hammering on it yourself, then I'll feel like it's done the job.

I haven't mentioned queries, or God help us, SQL. I've said nothing about Interbase, or bookmarks, or ODBC. There are several nifty data-aware controls I badly wanted to explain, but space simply didn't allow. That doesn't let you off the hook. Go back in there and figure 'em out. Data without management is simply noise. Data with management is information. And information plus insight is as close to wisdom as we can come on this Earth.

With this end of this chapter, Jim and I bid you adios for the moment. The show isn't over, however—in fact, the show itself is only beginning. For the remainder of this book, Don Taylor will attempt to pull it all together by showing you, step by step, how to create an entire useful database application in Delphi. He'll recap some of the things Jim and I have been explaining, and introduce a few new concepts.

He will also make you laugh until your nose runs.

Now matter how you've managed to learn programming in the past, I can almost guarantee you that you've never learned it quite *this* way...

So stay tuned.

Ace Breakpoint's Database Adventure

PART 3

Programming Is My Business

CHAPTER 15

Don Taylor

Ace Breakpoint begins his great adventure in non-traditional programming, by getting an early impression of the scope of the project.

Okay. You've had a taste of the power Delphi has placed at your fingertips. You've seen how you can create simple Windows applications without having to write a single line of code. You've learned the fundamentals of programming with Object Pascal, and how adding code to your Delphi application can give you complete control of its operation.

Now it's time for the next step in your exploration.

You're probably expecting a detailed, step-by-step tutorial where you go at breakneck speed through the construction of an invoicing application. The word "boring" immediately comes to mind. If that's what floats your boat, I apologize in advance, because that's *not* what you're going to get.

My first engineering professor was a man named Ron. He taught me a lesson that has stuck with me throughout the years: It's more important to learn *how to solve a problem* than to get the right answer. That's especially true in design, where there is frequently a wide range of "correct" answers.

You are about to participate in an *experience,* as different from other tutorials as using Delphi is from programming with traditional development tools. In fact, we won't even call it a tutorial, because it's really an *adventure*—an adventure in which you can choose your own level of personal involvement.

You will be reading a fictional story about a programming consultant using Delphi for the first time. Through the story, you will be privy to his innermost thought processes, and you will follow his every move, from the definition of the problem through the design and implementation of an application and the database supporting it. You can simply read through the story and pick up some specific Delphi problem-solving techniques. If you are the type of person who learns more by getting involved, you can build the application described in the story, right along with the main character. Or if you're a total dweeb, you can just lie down on the couch, open a bag of potato chips, and read some bad fiction. The choice is yours.

Oh, yes—although the story is fictional, two things are true.

First, the client is a real company. (See the sidebar, *Boxlight Shines in Pacific Northwest Community.*) The information and specifications for Boxlight's products as told in the story describe a subset of their actual product line, and that information was accurate at the time this book went to press. We thank Boxlight Corporation for their cooperation—and courage—in making this "real world" example possible.

Second, Poulsbo (pronounced "PAULS-bo") is a real town, situated about 15 miles (as the crow swims) west of Seattle, Washington. At its inception, it was a fishing village, founded by a hardy group of Norwegian immigrants. Today it is largely a tourist town, with marinas and a winding street full of quaint shops and restaurants. (You don't want to move there, though. It's too crowded already. And it rains nearly all the time. Honest.)

Beyond these few details, very little in the story has any connection with reality. Information that might be sensitive to Boxlight, including vendor, customer, and pricing data has been entirely replaced with fabricated information. Locations mentioned are most likely fictional, as are most of the businesses. Characters in the story are purely fictional, and are not meant to represent any person, living or dead.

THE PLOT THICKENS

Against this background we present our drama. The hero: Ace Breakpoint, hard-hitting fictional Private Investigator-turned-programmer.

As a boy growing up in Hackensack, Ace dreamed of becoming a P.I., just like his heroes in the classic 1940 movies—Phil Marlowe, Sam Spade, and Ellery Queen. But after years of study and hard work learning investigative techniques and snappy dialog, Ace discovered there was little demand for a 1940-style P.I. in today's world.

Undaunted, Ace decided to make a serious career change. This time, Ace would choose a profession that would be in demand for a *lifetime*—he would become a Windows programmer. But even more important than becoming today's professional, he wanted to become today's *person*; he would shed his tough, no-nonsense demeanor to become a person of the 90s. Caring. Sensitive. Open. In touch with his environment.

He moved to Poulsbo, and for two long years he attended night classes in computer programming at the Suquamish School of Art. On graduation day, he was awarded an Associate of Arts in Programming Appropriateness. He promptly rented an office and hung out his shingle.

As with most heroes, Ace has his minor faults. In spite of all his formal education, he is still a little rough around the edges. He still carries a lot of baggage from the years he spent training to become a tough-minded private investigator. There are times when sensitivity hangs on him like a cheap suit. He frequently makes mistakes. But he has a tenacious quality about him, and you've got to love him for that. When faced with problems, he will doggedly track them down until he solves them—and that includes the challenges he faces in his first encounter with Delphi. As Ace himself puts it, "Hey—if *I* can do this Delphi thing, I guess just about *anybody* can."

Well said, Ace. As you read through the following story taken from an entry in Ace's casebook, we encourage you to work right along with Ace—to experience the process of envisioning and developing a complete application with Delphi. You'll find the sample files on the disk accompanying this book.

As you've already seen, Jeff, Jim, and I believe that learning to apply something new doesn't have to be dull and boring. In fact, it can be—and should be—downright *fun!*

So don't touch that dial! Grab some popcorn, turn down the lights, slide up close to your screen, and prepare yourself for the adventure I call...

Ace Breakpoint in...
"The Case of the Duplicitous Demo!"

BOXLIGHT SHINES IN PACIFIC NORTHWEST COMMUNITY

When Herb and Sloan Myers started selling computer projection panels from their home, they never dreamed it would become such a thriving business. But in less than 10 years, Boxlight Corporation has grown from its humble beginnings as a home-based business into one of the recognized leaders in the projection display industry.

In 1985, Liquid Crystal Display (LCD) panels were just appearing on the market. Because of their extensive backgrounds in management, the Myers were acutely aware of the advantages of computer-based presentations. "We saw a window of opportunity, and took advantage of it," Herb says.

From their home office in Marin County, California where they had sold the third LCD projection panel ever made, the husband and wife team moved to Poulsbo, Washington in November of 1989. From their offices on the pier overlooking Liberty Bay, their staff has grown to more than 40 in 5 short years, and their 1994 sales topped $10 million. Boxlight's product line has expanded to more than 50 models of projection devices alone. Their customer base has grown to include every Fortune 500 company, and most major universities and government institutions— names like Disney Corporation, AT&T, IBM, Ford Motor Company, Microsoft and Harvard University. They've even sold products to the President of the United States.

In 1994 Boxlight was named one of *Inc. Magazine*'s 500 fastest-growing privately held companies, boasting a 5-year growth rate of 642 percent. That same year they were ranked by *Washington CEO* magazine as one of the fastest-growing high-tech companies in the state.

What is the secret of their success? In addition to keeping up with the ever-increasing demands of technology, the Myers quickly point to their reputation for outstanding service. "We hire talented, highly-knowledgeable people," says Sloan. "Then we give them the power to do whatever it takes to service the customer—even if it means 'over-nighting' a replacement part or helping in other unique, service-oriented ways." Boxlight also prides itself on promptness, guaranteeing shipment within 24 hours of an order.

The Myers' consuming desire is for their company to be the best always at what it does. As Herb says, "In this kind of high-tech market, you're either in the game for all you're worth, or you're out. There's no in between."

With that kind of attitude, Boxlight's future looks very bright indeed.

I closed my copy of *Delphi Programming Explorer* and tossed it on top of the large mountain of papers occupying the middle of my desk. Part I had been pretty instructive, and I had learned a lot about programming for Windows. But when I began reading Part II, everything started sounding all too familiar. Little did I know how soon I would be putting what I had learned to a serious test.

The monotonous staccato of raindrops hitting the window had an almost hypnotic effect on me, effectively neutralizing the two cups of Colombian Supreme I'd drunk an hour earlier. I had been staring off into space and contemplating the use of buttons in dialogs for several minutes, when I suddenly realized the phone was ringing.

With my left hand I grabbed the candlestick phone on my desk, deftly pitching it upward, so the receiver flew into my right hand. I pulled the mouthpiece close to my lips.

"This is Ace Breakpoint. How may I empower you?"

It was only when the phone continued to ring that I realized in my stupor I had mistakenly grabbed the candlestick phone *bank* my nephew, Rodney, had given me Christmas before last. I dropped the bank on the desk, as I reached around Paper Mountain to hit the Talk button on my speaker phone.

"Breakpoint. What can I do for ya?"

There was a momentary hesitation at the other end. Then a man's voice came on the line.

"Is this Ace Breakpoint, the consultant?"

"Sure is. How can I help you?"

"Mr. Breakpoint, My name is Dave Carson. I'm the Operations Manager for Boxlight Corporation here in town. Perhaps you've heard of us?"

"Sure have." Anyone would have to be a hearing, speaking, and visually challenged youth to have missed their full-color advertising in all the trade journals. And my nickname definitely wasn't "Tommy."

"We've been experiencing steady growth over the last couple of years, and it appears our sales will double again in the next 12 months. The off-the-shelf applications we've been using to manage the company just aren't doing the job we want them to, and we're considering funding the development of some custom software."

"That's fairly typical in a situation like yours," I said. "It may also be possible to create some simple applications that would tie together the data from your existing software, and produce the reports you need."

"So I understand. I would like to discuss the situation in more detail. Could you be in my office at two o'clock this afternoon?"

"Count on it."

"Good. Our offices are in the marina, at the location of the old Marine Science Center. See you at two." Click.

I hung up the speaker phone. This was a real break, I thought to myself. The chance of a lifetime. Nothing could go wrong this time. But I was about to find out otherwise.

The time display on my car radio read 1:56 when I pulled into the parking lot at the marina. My luck was holding out, because I got a spot right up front. Before getting out of the car I fastened the top button on my trenchcoat and tugged downward on the brim of my Fedora, to make sure it was on tight. I grabbed my briefcase and ran down the pier toward the Boxlight office, vainly attempting to dodge the raindrops that pelted my face. After what seemed like an eternity, I reached the office door and slipped inside.

"May I help you?" a feminine voice asked. I turned to answer the receptionist, only to find myself totally speechless.

Her name was Rhonda Skuttnik. She had long blond hair and legs to match, with calves that went halfway to her knees. Her wire-rimmed glasses encircled deep, brown eyes that stared uncaringly into my own. I tried my best to review my favorite opening lines in my head, but all I could hear was low, pulsating saxophone music. Temporarily stymied, I decided to try my last resort—the truth.

"Ace Breakpoint. I'm here to see Dave Carson."

"Oh, yes," she said, laying down the copy of *Receptionism Weekly* she had been reading. "Mr. Carson is expecting you. Will you follow me, please."

I would have followed her over a cliff. I hadn't heard from Helen for nearly two weeks, and suddenly I didn't even care. As we walked down the carpeted hallway past the mailing center and the lunchroom, Rhonda and I chatted about the weather. I couldn't help thinking to myself that this wasn't an ordinary woman—merely someone a man would want to marry and raise a family with. No, I thought, this was a *person*. A person with a *brain*. All too soon, we reached the doorway that marked the entrance to the Operations Manager's office.

"Mr. Carson, Mr. Breakpoint is here to see you." Rhonda turned and headed back the way we had come, the rubber soles of her pin-striped sneakers brushing softly against the carpet with each step. I stood motionless for several seconds, staring down the hall as the water dripping from my coat painted a wet ring around my feet. Dave Carson finally interrupted my alpha state.

"Please call me Dave," he said, offering his hand. I shook it firmly. "Have a seat. Can I get you a cup of coffee?"

Although I had almost been in a trance while Rhonda was escorting me to Carson's office, I had noticed they were serving Belcher's Restaurant Blend in the lunchroom. I chose to decline.

"Nothing for me, thanks. And call me Ace." I sensed a slight discomfort on Carson's part, so I decided a little small talk was in order. I motioned to the window, where the wind was driving the rain into the glass in large droplets, which ran down the panes in small, vertical rivulets. "Nice view of the rain."

"Thanks, we like it," he replied, giving me a sidelong glance. As I reached to unfasten my top button, he hesitantly revealed what had been troubling him. "When I contacted you, I assumed I was calling a programming consultant. But, uh, your outfit is more that of a detective. Are you a P.I.?"

"No, I'm an N.T.P." I handed him my business card:

Ace Breakpoint

Non-Traditional Programmer.
Applications realized.

555-1010

I didn't let on that I had been a private investigator before I had gone into the programming racket. But once a P.I., always a P.I., and I couldn't help noticing things around me—little things that would probably not be obvious to the ordinary citizen. Like the fact that Dave Carson secretly suffered from a case of dry scalp. I knew, because I caught him scratching his head as he read my card.

"Let's talk," he said, slipping my card into his shirt pocket. And for the next 45 minutes, that's exactly what we did.

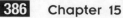

Carson explained that Boxlight was interested in developing a demo application that would give them an idea of how they might benefit from custom software. If the demo was able to provide them with the kind of information they needed, they would consider funding a complete suite of custom applications.

The demo was to use live product data taken from the data sheets in their catalog, along with data gleaned from their accounting and contact management systems. Because much of this data was proprietary to the company, all accounting and contact data would be fabricated for the demo.

The demo would address two specific needs, relative to support and repair of equipment sold to Boxlight's corporate customers. I scribbled some information in my spiral notebook:

1. Basic product support is presently handled by the Marketing Group. When a customer calls with an equipment problem, a salesperson takes the call and attempts to diagnose and handle the straightforward problems, like poor power connections, minor adjustments, etc.

2. When a problem is non-standard, it is handed over to the Repair Group, where technical personnel attempt to diagnose the problem over the phone. If the problem cannot be solved, an RMA (Return Material Authorization) is issued. An RMA includes several pieces of information used to track the repair, including a sequential RMA number, the date the RMA was issued, the number of the original invoice on which the equipment was shipped, a short description of the problem, and the failed equipment's stock number and serial number. The customer ships the equipment back to Boxlight, making sure to write the RMA number on the outside of the shipping container. Boxlight does not open boxes containing returned materials unless there is an RMA number listed on the outside of the box and unless that RMA number appears on an approved list. Once opened, an RMA-marked box is routed directly to the Repair Group. They check the RMA to determine the symptoms for troubleshooting, and also to determine if the work will be in-warranty repair, or will be billed to the customer.

"So what we're looking for," Carson concluded, "is a demo—a 'rough draft' of a custom Windows-based application that satisfies both of these needs for us. It doesn't have to be complete, just a demo that will show us you understand us, and that you know what you're doing." He leaned over and looked me straight in the eye. "Can you do it?"

I had long since graduated from the School of Hard Knocks, with a master's degree in Fake It Until You Make It. Besides, if anything ever sounded like a perfect match with Delphi's capabilities, this was it.

"Count on it," I said. Now I was ready to go in for the kill. To play the Big Trump Card that would assure me the job. "You know, this demo will also serve another very important purpose for *both of us.*"

"What's that?"

"It will be used as the premise of this book in which we're appearing," I explained. "The Author is using the demo as the underlying motivation for this scene. Without it, neither my character nor yours has reason for existence."

Carson looked unconvinced. "Whatever works for you, Ace. Personally, I'm a Methodist. Tell you what, though—create a demo application like I've just described, and we'll issue you a check for $1,000. How does that sound?"

"When do I start?"

"Today, if you like." He handed me a sheaf of papers and a couple of floppy disks. "You'll find everything you need here—data on five of the nearly 100 products we offer, including digitized photo files, and a list of the pertinent information available from our accounting and contact management systems. Of course, you'll have to fabricate data for items that would be proprietary for us, like customers, vendors, and pricing."

He escorted me to his door. "Oh, yes—just one more thing. To ensure we get the best product possible, we've decided to make this a competitive situation. You'll be competing with a Mr. Bohacker. The first one to complete the demo will win the contract to develop the real application, if we decide to go ahead with it." He shook my hand. "Thanks for stopping by. And be sure to let me know if you have any questions."

I suddenly felt my heart slide into my stomach. I turned and trudged back down the hall for what seemed like a mile or more. *Melvin Bohacker,* I thought to myself. Not again! I could have gone all week without hearing that name. Bohacker was an overly tall, pencil-necked geek with the uncanny ability to create powerful applications by writing low-level code and using extensive routines libraries. He had beaten me out of every competitive assignment I'd gone after, and now the stage was set for him to do it again.

The incessantly damp weather had given me a runny nose, and now I began to feel a little sick to my stomach. I plodded past Rhonda's desk, without giving her so much as a nod. All I wanted was to go home and crawl into a hole. I managed to push open the outside door and was attempting to walk through it, when I found my nose flattened against an all-too-familiar vinyl pocket protector.

"Well, who have we here?" wheezed Bohacker in his characteristically adenoi-dal voice. "One thing's for sure. It's a very *short* person."

Before pulling away, I took the opportunity to surreptitiously wipe my nose on the front of his jacket. "Short is relative," I retorted. "And I'm glad you're no relative of mine."

"Well, as I live and breathe—it's Ace Breakpoint. I was going to call you today. Whaddya doing here, Breakpoint?"

He was living and breathing, all right. And his breath was permeated with the unmistakably sweet odor of Twinkies. (I was never certain whether it was the sponge cake or the creme filling that gave them their unique scent. Then again, I was never sure exactly what "creme" was.)

"Just trying to earn an honest living," I shot back.

"Don't tell me you're here for the demo competition!" He began to laugh. "You don't have a chance, Breakpoint. Give it up. Why don't you just go home and do something you're *really* good at—like baking a soufflé?" His laugh had now turned into an almost uncontrollable cackle. He pushed past me and headed for Rhonda's desk.

Now outside, I began to review the situation. *What a dweeb,* I thought. *He's the kind of guy whose voice mail is returned to you, postage due.* As I stood in the downpour, the rain filled the brim of my Fedora and then began to spill over the edge like a miniature waterfall. I thought back to all the times Bohacker had beaten me. I caught myself starting to feel defeated, depressed. Then suddenly, I realized something. Something that both enabled and empowered me. I set my jaw, and a wry smile began to steal its way across my face. Yes, he had defeated me on countless occasions. That was in the past. But this was the present. And this time, I had Delphi.

This time it was going to be different.

EXAMINING THE BODY

Don Taylor

Ace catches fire on the Boxlight demo, and cooks up a suite of database tables and data management utilities in record time.

I gently removed the spinach souffle from the oven, sliding it onto the cooling rack I had placed on the breadboard. In the kitchenette in the corner of my office, I turned and leaned against the counter, attempting to think.

Clearly, I needed a strategy if I was to beat Bohacker to the punch—even with Delphi as my weapon. For the past three hours I had gone over the example data, vainly trying to formulate an approach. Finally, something—just a need for a mental break from frustration, perhaps—had compelled me to bake something. I carefully sliced off a chunk of soufflé and laid it beside the veggie burger already on my plate. I headed for my desk, stopping long enough at the refrigerator to grab a bottle of Purely Poulsbo Norwegian mineral water.

I pushed aside some of the papers to make room for my plate. As I sat down to eat, I began to think about the whole situation in earnest. Obviously, my greatest advantage with Delphi was the time it would save me in developing the demo application. Even so, if I was to maximize my chances of winning this competition, I would have to work through the night. But where should I start? Should I design some screens? Try some menu layouts?

Then I remembered what Professor Carruthers had taught us in Virtual Programming 202: "The underlying inspiration for any application lies in its data. If you can visualize your data, manifest it, capture it in your imagination, breathe into it and make it come alive—only then will you achieve the maximum potential for your application." I still didn't understand a word he had said, but I did get the distinct impression the solution to my problem lay in the analysis and structuring of the data.

I had gone over that data perhaps a hundred times. I was reminded of Dashiell Hammett, a former role model of mine and the author of the Sam Spade detective stories. Before becoming a writer, Hammett was a real-life detective. He once said, "The chief difference between the exceptionally knotty problem confronting the detective in fiction and that facing the real detective is that in the former there is usually a paucity of clues, and in the latter altogether too many."

I knew how he felt. It this case, there appeared to be altogether *too much data*. Information from invoices. Vendor names, addresses and part number cross-references. Employee data. Product specifications. Generic and product-specific usage and troubleshooting information. All this stuff was unrelated and coming from a collection of applications unaware of one another's existence. How in the world could I tie it all together into an integrated database?

I found myself daydreaming, using my fork to make lazy figure-eights in the pesto sauce on my veggie patty. I was jolted back to reality by the bell on my phone. I picked up the receiver.

"Ace Breakpoint. How may I empower you?"

"Ace, this is your old friend, uh, Bruiser."

It was good to hear a familiar voice. "Bruiser...! I haven't heard from you in ages. What've you been doing?"

"That's what I need to talk to you about. In fact, there's something very important I have to tell you. Could you meet me right away?"

"Listen, Bruiser, I'm in the middle of a really hot project. How about some time later in the week?"

"It can't wait that long. Ace, it's *critical.* I've got to see you *now.* Meet me at Lute's. Fifteen minutes." Click.

It sounded like Life and Death. I grabbed my keys and headed for my Honda.

PUTTING THE CARDS ON THE TABLE

Bruiser was one member of a close-knit group of friends who attended art school together. The group also included myself, Biff Murphy, Muffy Katz, and Helen Highwater, my long-time girlfriend. Herman "Bruiser" Buckendorf-Rabinowicz was a 6-foot-4, 320-pound mountain of a man who came to art school on a football scholarship. After graduation he was drafted as an offensive tackle by one of the new pro expansion teams with a non-violent, non-disparaging name—the Kansas City Kumquats. He was mysteriously let go after only six weeks. The official press release said it was because they couldn't fit his last name on his jersey, but I never bought that explanation. I hadn't seen him since graduation, nearly two years ago.

At The House of Lutefisk

I got to the House of Lutefisk ahead of Bruiser, and I chose a more-or-less secluded booth near the back of the joint. "Lute's," as we locals fondly refer to it, is one of those typical ethnic Norwegian restaurants. They specialize in Lutefisk, a specialty food prepared by taking a hunk of cod fish and soaking it in a solution of lye. After several days, when it has become the consistency of gelatin, the mixture is washed and poached in water, and then served swimming in butter. (The non-Norwegians call it "The piece of cod that passes all understanding.") At Lute's, every main dish comes with a large serving of Lutefisk on the side. I ordered coffee and a cinnamon roll instead.

I looked at my watch for the third time. It was 6:37, and Bruiser was now 10 minutes late. Hearing the clicking of hard heels on the linoleum floor, I looked up, expecting to see the waitress. What I saw dumbfounded me.

It was Bruiser. At least I *thought* it was Bruiser. He was wearing a gold lamé turban with matching high-heeled shoes, a pink-and-white striped silk blouse, and a brown and pink plaid wool jacket with a matching skirt. It was the single most disgusting thing I had ever seen. Everyone knows stripes and plaids don't mix.

He slid into the booth, facing me.

"Thank you for coming, Ace. I have several things to tell you. I suppose you have one or two questions you'd like to ask me, too."

"Oh, not at all. Say, Bruiser, nice earrings."

"There's something you need to know right off," he said. "My name's not 'Herman' anymore. I've had it legally changed to 'Mellow.' It more closely depicts the personality I want to emanate—calm, open, and non-violent."

His hands were folded in front of him on the table. They looked like two medium-sized hams covered with fur. I guessed he had taken one too many shots to the head during a pass rush, and I wasn't about to cross him in any way.

"Whatever you say, Bru—er, *Mellow*."

"Ace, I've embarked on a life-long journey of self-discovery. I'm going to find out who I really am."

At that point he began a long discourse on the correctness of preserving and celebrating our ethnic differences. I faded out, and I had nearly fallen asleep when I heard something that caught my attention.

"Wait a second, Mellow. What was that you just said?"

"I was talking about relationships. I merely said that our power lies in our network of relationships. As individuals, we are all composed of a number of characteristics unique unto ourselves. Each of us must be able to stand alone, completely integrated. But as each of us shares a portion of ourselves with others through relationships, we become connected together at a fundamental level. That's how we achieve our true power as a society. The whole is greater than the sum of its parts."

An explosion went off in my brain. "Bingo!" I nearly shouted.

"What's that?" he asked, taken aback.

"Just an expression," I said, sliding my game card and place markers into my briefcase. "Listen, I've got to go. We'll have to finish this conversation later." I grabbed a paper napkin from the dispenser and began to scribble some hurried notes on it.

"But Ace," Mellow complained, "I'm just getting to the part I have to talk to you about. It concerns personal relationships and our future—yours, mine, Helen's, and...."

"Sorry, old buddy," I interrupted. I stuffed the napkin in my coat pocket, and I handed him one of my business cards. "Here, stick this in your purse. Call me and we'll talk again, Real Soon Now."

"But Ace..."

I was all the way to the cash register before he could finish his rejoinder. I hesitated for just a moment, wondering if I should stick him with the bill. Then I walked out into the downpour. After all, he had requested this little clambake. Now he could be the one to shell out for it. Right now, I had bigger fish to fry.

THE TABLES TURN

I arrived back at the office at 8:23. I immediately took the napkin out of my coat and spread it out on my desk. The persistent rain had found its way into my pocket and had caused the ink to run, but I could still just make out most of the words:

- A database consists of one or more individual tables containing data.
- Each table must be independent and able to stand alone, to the maximum extent.
- Each table must be an integration of information unique to its purpose.
- The true power of a database lies in the relationships between its tables.
- Some animals are more equal than others. (I wasn't sure about this last one. The ink was really smeared.)

As near as I could tell, I would need at least eight tables to hold the pertinent information:

1. A Customers table;
2. A Vendors table;
3. An Employees table;
4. A Generic Tips table;
5. A Products table;
6. An Invoices table;
7. An Invoice Items table; and
8. An RMA table.

The first three tables would hold information about Boxlight's people and who they work with. The next two tables would contain information related to Boxlight's products. The following two tables would consist of all the information on invoices generated by the sales people. The remaining table would hold all the information specific to each RMA.

I would need some sort of data dictionary for each of the tables. I grabbed my keyboard and started punching in some notes.

Table 1: The Customers Table

The table that would hold all the pertinent customer data would be derived entirely from data in Boxlight's contact management system. This task would eventually be performed by a utility, but for the demo I would have to fake some information about customers. I decided to use dBASE file formats for all the tables, and I would name the file for this table CUSTOMER.DBF. The data structure I settled on appears in Table 16.1.

For each table, I would prefix the field name with an abbreviation that related to the table. (I suspected that later on down the line I would be juggling table fields as carefully as porcupines, and I wanted to be able to easily identify which field name went with which table.)

CST_ID would be the unique identification code given to each Boxlight customer. The length of the entry could vary from customer to customer, but there could be no duplicates. (Otherwise, confusion would arise as to which customer actually bought a particular item.) Also, this would have to be an

Table 16.1 *Structure of the Customers Table*

Name	Size/Type	Source	Comments
*CST_ID	12 Characters	CM System	Unique ID for each customer
*CST_COMPNM	30 Characters	CM System	Customer's company name
CST_ADDR1	30 Characters	CM System	Customer's first address line
CST_ADDR2	30 Characters	CM System	Customer's second address line
CST_CITY	20 Characters	CM System	Customer's city
CST_STATE	2 Characters	CM System	Customer's state
CST_ZIP	5 Characters	CM System	Customer's ZIP Code
CST_CONTAC	20 Characters	CM System	Name of contact person
CST_VPHONE	20 Characters	CM System	Voice phone number, incl. extension
CST_FAXNUM	20 Characters	CM System	Fax phone number

*Indicates the indexed field(s). Values in indexed fields must be unique.

indexed field, so it could be used for rapid lookup: If, for instance, I was examining an invoice and I grabbed the customer code listed on it, searching for that code in the CST_ID field would very quickly get me to the associated record in the Customers table.

CST_COMPNM would be the field that would hold the full name of the company. I also decided to use this field as an index, in case I later wanted to rapidly find something by name. Again, this would have to be a unique index.

CST_ADDR1 would hold the customer's first address line. This could be a street address, post office box, or even an attention (Attn:) line. No need at all to index on this field.

CST_ADDR2 would be identical to CST_ADDR1, except it would hold the remainder of the address. This might be an "in care of " line. No indexing needed.

CST_CITY is self-explanatory. No reason to index on the name of the city.

CST_STATE needed no explanation. No indexing, either.

CST_ZIP would hold the 5-digit ZIP code. No need for indexing this.

CST_CONTAC is where I would store the name of the contact person at the customer company. No reason whatsoever to index on this info.

CST_VPHONE would be for the company's voice phone number. It requires no indexing.

CST_FAXNUM would hold the customer's fax phone number. Again, no indexing required.

Table 2: The Vendors Table

This baby, which I would call VENDORS.DBF, would contain all necessary information about Boxlight's product vendors. As with the Customers table, the information for this table would come from the contact management system, and would be periodically generated with a utility. I would once again have to fabricate data for the demo application. The fields and their contents would be analogous to those of the Customers table, so I gave them similar names. In a real-world situation, this table would probably contain additional information such as Boxlight's customer number, credit limits, and such. For the demo, I came up with the simple structure in Table 16.2.

Table 16.2 *Structure of the Vendors Table*

Name	Size/Type	Source	Comments
*VEN_ID	12 Characters	CM System	Unique ID for each vendor
*VEN_COMPNM	30 Characters	CM System	Vendor's company name
VEN_ADDR1	30 Characters	CM System	Vendor's first address line
VEN_ADDR2	30 Characters	CM System	Vendor's second address line
VEN_CITY	20 Characters	CM System	Vendor's city
VEN_STATE	2 Characters	CM System	Vendor's state
VEN_ZIP	5 Characters	CM System	Vendor's ZIP Code
VEN_CONTAC	20 Characters	CM System	Name of contact person
VEN_VPHONE	20 Characters	CM System	Voice phone number, incl. extension
VEN_FAXNUM	20 Characters	CM System	Fax phone number

Indicates the indexed field(s). Values in indexed fields must be unique.

Table 3: The Employees Table

This table would contain minimal information about Boxlight's employees. The purpose of the table is to allow the application to track the name of the salesperson who wrote an invoice or the technician who initiated an RMA. In a real-world situation, such tracking might likely be done with the employee's identification number (probably the Social Security Number, or *SSN*). Since employee data is among the most sensitive a company deals with, I decided to stay away from including any additional data in this table. Once again, this table would be created as an entity separate from the personnel system. I would call the file EMPLOYEES.DBF. The structure is shown in Table 16.3.

EMP_ID would hold the identification code assigned to the employee by Boxlight. This would probably be an SSN. For this example I would just

Table 16.3 *Structure of the Employees Table*

Name	Size/Type	Source	Comments
*EMP_ID	12 Characters	Personnel System	Unique ID for each employee
*EMP_INITS	3 Characters	Personnel System	Employee's initials
EMP_LNAME	20 Characters	Personnel System	Employee's last name
EMP_FNAME	20 Characters	Personnel System	Employee's first name

Indicates the indexed field(s). Values in indexed fields must be unique.

combine portions of the employees' last and first names to come up with a unique ID for each person. Because I might want to look up the name by using the ID, I would make this an indexed field. Since no two employees should ever have the same ID, the index must be unique.

EMP_INITS would contain the three initials of each employee's name. Once again, this would be required for rapid lookup, so it had to be indexed. And since it was used to identify an individual employee, it had to be unique.

EMP_LNAME would hold the last name of the employee. I didn't foresee any reason to use this as an index, since the person was already uniquely identified either by the ID or initials.

EMP_FNAME was for the employee's first name. The same logic for the last name applied. No indexing.

I grabbed my plate and set it on top of the papers I was working on. The veggie patty, which had been invitingly warm before leaving for my impromptu meeting with Mellow, was now as cold as ice. I thought about nuking it, but instead decided to grab my fork and nibble on the remnants of the soufflé.

I had managed to design the three tables that described Boxlight's employees, and the customers and vendors they did business with. It was now time to develop the two tables that would describe Boxlight's products.

Table 4: The Generic Tips Table

Each product was to include a description of both general and specific troubleshooting tips for use by the salespeople. Although all of the products specified for the demo were of the same type—computer projection and display products—they weren't the only kind of products that Boxlight sold (and there was a good chance Boxlight would be adding new product lines in the future). Keeping the information specific to each product as part of that product's data seemed the natural thing to do. But what was I going to do with the more general information? It would be a waste of space to add it to every product it applied to.

I decided to create a separate data table that would contain one memo field that would describe the general information. For now, there would be only one record—the record containing the basic troubleshooting measures for any projection device. This information would come after thrashing through Boxlight's data sheets and technical support documents. I would call the table GENTIPS.DBF, and it would have the structure described in Table 16.4.

Table 16.4 *Structure of the Generic Tips Table*

Name	Size/Type	Source	Comments
*TIP_CATID	1 Character	Data Sheets**	Unique ID for each category
TIP_CATNAM	20 Characters	Data Sheets**	Name of this category
TIP_DESC	Memo	Data Sheets**	Generic troubleshooting info for this product category

*Indicates the indexed field(s). Values in indexed fields must be unique.

**Categories have been decided upon based on review of the data sheets.

TIP_CATID would be a single uppercase alphabetic character that would serve as an index into the table. This would give me 26 possible product categories. Obviously, the index must be unique.

TIP_CATNAM would contain a descriptive name for the category, such as "Projection Devices." It would not need to be indexed.

TIP_DESC is the memo that would hold the generic instructions for this type of product. Couldn't index on a memo field to save my life.

Table 5: The Products Table

This would be the King of Tables in this application, containing all pertinent data for the five example products used in the demo. Most of the information would be taken directly from product data sheets, but a few items would have to be gleaned from the Vendors table and from vendors' catalogs, information fabricated for the demo. One additional field would specify whether or not a product was subject to state sales tax when sold—I'd fake this info as well.

I have always been known for my imagination in making up file names. I decided to call this file PRODUCTS.DBF. The field list appears in Table 16.5.

PRD_STKNUM would contain a unique stock number for each product. This will be the field used to rapidly look up all the information for a specific product, so it must be indexed. Since each stock number is unique, the index must be unique also.

PRD_NAME will contain the descriptive name of the product. No indexing to be done here.

PRD_DESC is a memo field that will hold the complete description of the product, taken from its data sheet. No indexing, of course.

Table 16.5 *Structure of the Products Table*

Name	Size/Type	Source	Comments
*PRD_STKNUM	20 Characters	Data Sheets**	Unique stock number for each product
PRD_NAME	25 Characters	Data Sheets**	The product's nomenclature
PRD_DESC	Memo	Data Sheets**	Description of the main product
PRD_SPECS	Memo	Data Sheets**	Product specifications
PRD_PICT	BLOB	Data Sheets**	A photo of the product
PRD_CATGRY	1 Character	Data Sheets***	Category type of product
PRD_TIPS	Memo	Data Sheets**	Specific product usage/ troubleshooting tips
PRD_VENDID	12 Characters	Vendors Table	Unique ID for vendor of product
PRD_VENDPN	20 Characters	Vendor Catalog	Vendor's part number for this product
PRD_WARNTY	12 Characters	Vendor Catalog	Vendor's warranty period for this product
PRD_ACCESS	Memo	Data Sheets**	Accessories available for this product
PRD_PRICE	Number:8:2	Data Sheets**	Current Boxlight price for this product
PRD_TAXABL	Logical		Accounting System. If sold at retail, is this product taxable?

*Indicates the indexed field(s). Values in indexed fields must be unique.

**Information entered directly from Boxlight product data sheets.

***This item serves as an index into the Generic Tips table.

PRD_SPECS is another memo field, this one containing the product's technical specifications. This info will also be taken from the data sheet. Again, no indexing.

PRD_PICT is a BLOB (Binary Large Object) field that will hold a bitmap graphic. The graphic will be a photograph, scanned from the product data sheet. Index on a picture? No way.

PRD_CATGRY will be a single character that will correspond to the TIP_CATID field in the Generic Tips table. For the demo, every product gets an "A" here.

PRD_TIPS is yet another memo. This one will hold the detailed troubleshooting information for each product.

PRD_VENDID will contain the unique identification code for the vendor that provides this product to Boxlight. It corresponds to the VEN_ID field in the Vendors table. I considered indexing on this field. It would come in handy if

I wanted a response to the command, "Show me all the products provided to Boxlight by this particular vendor." For the demo, at least, I decided I didn't need this capability—but it could be added without much difficulty.

PRD_VENDPN will contain the unique part number given to a product by its vendor. This is the number Boxlight uses when it orders the product. I couldn't see a reason to index on it.

PRD_WARNTY will hold a phrase that will describe the warranty period specified by the product's vendor. Boxlight may or may not give the same warranty to its customers. Definitely not indexing material.

PRD_ACCESS is a memo field that will describe the various accessories available for a product. The information would be taken from the data sheets. No possible reason to index on this.

PRD_PRICE would hold Boxlight's current price for a product. The field was formatted as a number with a maximum length of 8 characters, which includes 2 decimal places. Not indexed.

PRD_TAXABL is a logical field that will be used to specify whether a product is subject to Washington State sales tax if the product is sold at retail. Can't index on it, and I wouldn't know what to do with it if I could.

I didn't remember eating any of the soufflé, but nevertheless, it was gone. I decided to nuke the veggie patty after all, so I popped the plate in the microwave and set it for one minute at Power Level 5. I hit the Start button.

The resulting racket sounded like rebel forces conducting a strafing attack on Comatose 7. I hurriedly punched the Stop button, removed the fork, keyed in 1-0-0-0 and hit Start again. This time the oven started without complaint. While I was waiting, I reviewed my situation.

I had just described all the information the demo application would have to know about people and products. Now it was time to add information from the sales invoices. This is the data the technician would use to generate an RMA. Knowing the exact invoice number, the tech could easily locate the specific product (right down to the serial number) to reference on the RMA. Having the information included on the invoice, the technician could verify that the customer requesting the RMA did indeed purchase the product, and whether or not the product was still under warranty.

An invoice is an interesting document, I mused. It is unique, containing its own individual serial number. It ties a single company to a single purchase, but there can be any number of items included in that purchase. It is the classic example of what is called a *master-detail relationship*.

Since a data table must always be made up of records having an identical format, it makes sense to represent invoices as two tables that have a relationship with each other. The first table, called the *master table*, contains overall information about invoices—the stuff that appears at the top of the form, such as the invoice number, customer, address, payment terms, and so on. The second table, called the *detail table*, contains information on each item purchased on an invoice—stock number, quantity, serial number, and so forth. To link the two tables, the entry for each item in the detail table must also contain the invoice number the item appeared on. Given an item, it's easy to locate the invoice. Starting with the invoice, it's a slam dunk to locate all the items on it.

A bell went off. Master-detail. That's how I'll handle the invoices, I thought. Of course. A child could do it.

When the bell went off three more times, I realized it was the timer on the microwave oven. I pulled out the smoking mass of carbonized vegetable matter and just stood there staring at it. What had happened to my veggie burger? Reading back a few paragraphs, I realized I had accidentally punched in an extra zero, giving it *ten minutes* instead of the one minute I had intended. At least I *almost* had it right. I scraped what now resembled a smoldering hockey puck into the garbage can and flipped the lid down to give it a respectful burial. I guess I wasn't all that hungry, anyway. With a sigh, I slipped the plate and fork into the sink and headed back to my desk to resume my note taking.

Table 6: The Invoices Table

This would be the master table that would hold the basic information on each invoice. Normally, this data would be readily available from Boxlight's accounting system, but for the demo I was on my own to develop a ration of bogus data. I decided to call the file INVOICES.DBF. Its structure is detailed in Table 16.6.

INV_NUM would contain the serialized invoice number printed on the physical invoice. This is one of two fields I decided to use as an index. Knowing the invoice number, I could rapidly retrieve the rest of the header information on that invoice. Since no two invoices can have the same number, the invoice number would also serve well as a unique index.

Table 16.6 *Structure of the Invoices Table*

Name	Size/Type	Source	Comments
*INV_NUM	12 Characters	Accounting System	Unique invoice number for each record
INV_DATE	Date	Accounting System	Date of invoice
INV_CUSTID	12 Characters	Accounting System	Customer's ID
*INV_PONUM	20 Characters	Accounting System	Customer's PO reference number
INV_TERMS	20 Characters	Accounting System	Payment terms listed on invoice
INV_SALEID	12 Characters	Accounting System	Salesperson's employee ID
INV_TXRATE	Number:8:2	Accounting System	Sales tax rate for this invoice
INV_SHMODE	12 Characters	Accounting System	Shipping mode information
INV_SHCOST	Number:8:2	Accounting System	Shipping charge

*Indicates the indexed field(s). Invoice number index is unique.

INV_DATE would simply hold the date the invoice was created. I didn't see any reason to try to index on it.

INV_CUSTID would contain Boxlight's ID for the customer specified on the invoice. This field would be analogous to the CST_ID field in the Customers table. In a more advanced version of this demo, I might have decided to index on this field, so I could rapidly gather all of the invoices written against a specific customer. That would be a handy way to locate an item if the customer didn't know the invoice number. If used for that purpose, it would not be used as a unique index. I decided not to index on it at this time.

INV_PONUM would hold the purchase order number, if any, supplied by the customer. I decided to index on this field, just in case I wanted to provide an alternate way of retrieving the invoice, given a purchase order number. Since a purchase order can possibly apply to more than one invoice, I did not make the index unique.

INV_TERMS would contain the terms of payment listed on the invoice. No reason to index on it.

INV_SALEID would store the salesperson's employee ID. The content of this field is identical to EMP_ID in the Employees table. Given the contents of INV_SALEID, it would be a simple matter to use it as an index into the Employees table to get the salesperson's name and initials. No need to index it again here.

INV_TXRATE would tell me the rate of state sales tax that was applied to this invoice. Orders from out of state are not normally charged sales tax. The true rate would be taken from Boxlight's accounting system. No conceivable reason to index on this.

INV SHMODE would describe how the order was shipped—U.P.S., FedEx, or whatever. Not indexed.

INV_SHCOST is the numeric field that would contain the total amount charged for shipping. No reason to index on it.

Table 7: The Invoice Items Table

The Invoice Items table would be a detail table that would include a record of every product ever ordered by any customer. Normally, this information would be taken from Boxlight's accounting system. I would have to fake it. I decided to call the table INVITEMS.DBF. I developed the structure in Table 16.7.

ITM_INVNUM would specify the number of the invoice on which the item appeared. This field would be identical to the INV_NUM field in the Invoices table. Looking at a specific item, it is a no-brainer to locate the invoice information that is associated with that item. This field is indexed, but because more than one item can appear on an invoice, the index is not unique.

ITM_STKNUM would store the item's stock number. This field's contents would come right out of the PRD_STKNUM field in the Products table. Knowing the value of ITM_STKNUM, it would be a snap to locate any information about the item in the Products table. Since a specific stock number can appear more than once on a single invoice (they may have the same stock number, but each must have a different serial number), the index could not be unique.

Table 16.7   *Structure of the Invoice Items Table*

Name	Size/Type	Source	Comments
*ITM_INVNUM	12 Characters	Accounting System	Invoice on which this item appeared
*ITM_STKNUM	20 Characters	Accounting System	This item's Boxlight stock number
ITM_SERNUM	12 Characters	Accounting System	This item's serial number
ITM_QTY**	Number:6:0	Accounting System	Quantity of this item

*Indicates the indexed field(s). None of the indexes is unique.

**Assumed to be equal to 1, unless no serial number is entered.

ITM_SERNUM would hold the item's serial number. Not all items have serial numbers (especially the less expensive ones), so this field may sometimes be blank. It was not a candidate for indexing.

ITM_QTY would be a numeric field that would specify the quantity of an item that was ordered. The value of this field would be assumed to be "1", as long as the ITM_SERNUM field is not blank. If that field is blank, ITM_QTY could take on other values. No reason to index on it.

I rubbed my eyes. They had become irritated, I guessed, because I had been staring at the screen for so long. I was probably getting dehydrated to boot. I drained the last bit of coffee from my cup and proceeded with my notes.

Table 8: The RMA Table

Thus far, all the tables had been constructed from information already existing in Boxlight's accounting, personnel, and contact management systems, or from their product data sheets. The other seven tables contain reference information that would not be changed. The RMA table would be a different animal. Although about half of the information contained in this table would come directly from other tables, this puppy would be maintained by the demo application. This file I would call RMA.DBF. The structure is described in Table 16.8.

Table 16.8 *Structure of the RMA Table*

Name	Size/Type	Source	Comments
*RMA_ID	12 Characters	RMA App	Unique ID for each RMA
RMA_DATE	Date	RMA App	The date of issue of the RMA
*RMA_INVNUM	12 Characters	Invoices Table	The Boxlight invoice number the item was ordered on
*RMA_STKNUM	12 Characters	Invoices Table	The stock number of the item
RMA_SERNUM	12 Characters	Items Table	The serial number of the item
RMA_CUSTID	12 Characters	Invoices Table	The customer's ID code
RMA_STATUS	20 Characters	RMA App	The status of the RMA
RMA_DESC	Memo	RMA App	Description of the problem
RMA_INITS	3 Characters	Employee Table	Initials of employee entering the RMA
RMA_UPDATE	Date	RMA App	Date of last change made to this RMA entry

*Indicates the indexed field(s). Only the ID index is unique.

RMA_ID would contain a unique identifier assigned to each RMA entry. The field would be formatted in a specific way, according to the way Boxlight assigns its RMA numbers: BXNNN-YY, where *NNN* is a 3-digit, leading-zero-filled sequence number ("003" for instance), and *YY* are the last 2 digits of the current year (again, leading zero filled). Because RMA_ID would be unique, it will be used as a unique index, making it easy to locate a specified RMA.

RMA_DATE would simply be the date the RMA is generated. It will be automatically assigned the value of the current date at the time the record is added. Not indexed.

RMA_INVNUM will contain the number of the invoice on which the item was purchased. Its contents will be identical to the contents of the INV_NUM field in the Invoices table, making it very fast to pull up invoice information. This field will be indexed, but it will not be a unique index, because more than one item on an invoice can become the subject of an RMA.

RMA_STKNUM is another field that will be indexed to quickly reference other information. Its contents will be identical to those in the PRD_STKNUM field in the Products table, which will give direct access to any information about the product. The index will not be unique, since more than one item on an invoice can have the same stock number, and the same stock number can be involved in more than one RMA.

RMA_SERNUM will contain the serial number of the item, taken directly from the Invoice Items table. Together, RMA_STKNUM and RMA_SERNUM will identify one and only one item. I couldn't see a reason for indexing on this field at this time.

RMA_CUSTID would hold the Boxlight customer ID, identical to the one contained in the CST_ID field of the Customers table. I could have relied on getting the same information by using RMA_INVNUM to locate the invoice and then using INV_CUSTID. It was a judgment call, and I decided to store it here, too. It didn't need to be an index.

RMA_STATUS is the numeric field that would hold one of several standard status levels, starting at zero. The application would use the value stored here as an index into a string array containing standard status messages. I didn't see any reason to index this field.

RMA_DESC is a memo that would hold some detailed notes about the problem or its potential resolution. No indexing, no way.

RMA_INITS would provide a path to the name of the technician generating the RMA, by recording their initials. The contents of this field would be identical to the EMP_INITS field of the Employees table. Since I saw no need to answer the query, "Show me all the RMAs generated by a certain employee," I chose not to index on this field.

RMA_UPDATE would contain a date that would automatically be updated by the demo application whenever the RMA information was edited. Initially, it would be assigned the date the RMA was generated. No reason to index on it.

I sat back and examined my work. Each of the tables met the criteria I had set up. Each was a tightly integrated collection of information dedicated to that table's purpose. Each had been set up to provide the relational links that would provide quick and easy access for the needs of the demo program. Perhaps *more* than it needed. I wasn't sure.

I had been staring intensely at my computer screen for a long time, oblivious to everything around me. My irritated eyes were now burning worse than ever. Tears were streaming down my face. I looked up, and suddenly realized I was quite literally engulfed in a thick, murky fog.

It was at that moment the smoke alarm went off.

Apparently the smoldering veggie patty hadn't been as dead as I had thought, and had landed on some flammable material in the garbage can. Smoke was billowing out profusely around the lid. I stood up and nearly choked on the acrid smoke that was hugging the ceiling. Stumbling my way over to the can, I flipped open its lid, which then released a dense cloud that obscured what little vision I had left. Sweeping my hand across the counter, I groped blindly for the yet half full bottle of Purely Poulsbo mineral water I had opened earlier. Finding the bottle, I dumped its entire contents into the garbage can.

It was then I realized I had mistakenly grabbed the bottle of *Glad Nordman* Chardonnay I had used in making the spinach soufflé.

• • •

"Good-bye. And thanks again!" I waved to the last firefighter as he disappeared in the torrential downpour and the black void beyond the porch light at the front door of my office. As the engine lumbered away, I walked back inside, leaving the door open for ventilation. I guessed that I really wouldn't miss my eyebrows and eyelashes that much. Anyway, they would grow back with time. In the meantime, if I needed them for some special occasion, I could probably borrow an eyebrow pencil from Mellow.

But I had lost much more than facial hair. My ill-timed improvisation had cost me precious moments. I glanced at my watch—already 10:18, and I only had a *specification* for the tables needed by my application. The firefighters' efforts had saved the building and my computer, but left water and debris everywhere. I'd have to mop up the mess later, however. Now, I needed to create the tables and fill them with data. I cautiously waded back to my desk.

CREATING AND POPULATING THE DATA TABLES

Creating the tables was an easy task. First, I used the Windows File Manager to make a new directory called C:\BOXLIGHT\TEMP. This would be the place I would create all my tables and indexes. I would later copy them to the data directory I would designate for the application.

I brought up Delphi and launched the Database Desktop from the Tools menu. From DBD's File menu I chose New|Table and selected dBASE for Windows from the types of files offered. I then filled in the Create Table dialog with the field specifications. The dialog for the Customers table is shown in Figure 16.1.

To create an index on a field within a table, I clicked the Define button (see Figure 16.1), which brought up a Define Index dialog. From the list of fields, I selected the index field by double-clicking on it, then checked the Unique box if it was to be a unique index (see Figure 16.2 for an example of defining the CST_COMPNM index for the Customers table). Some of my tables had more than one index; in those instances I would just continue to add the indexes to the table, in the order they appeared on my structure specification.

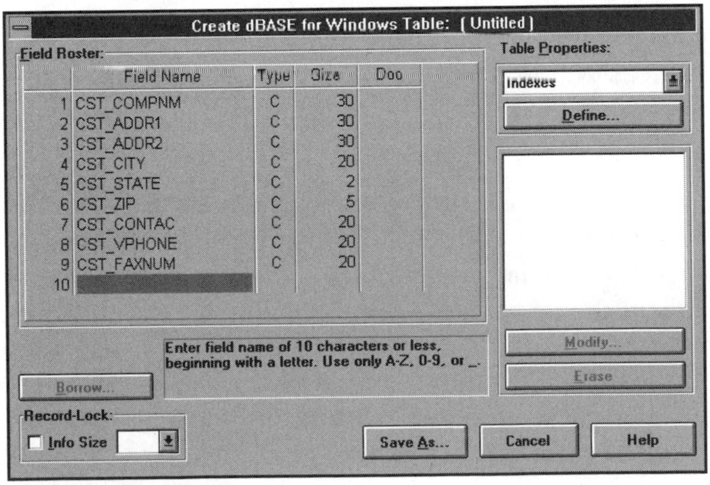

Figure 16.1　*Creating a new table.*

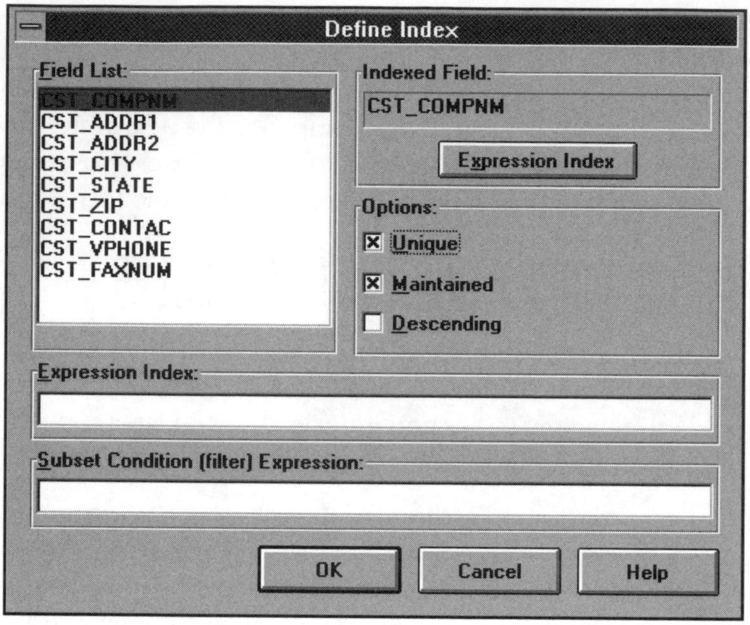

Figure 16.2 Defining a table index.

Once I had fully specified all the fields and indexes, I clicked the Save As button on the Create Table dialog, and I saved the file in C:\BOXLIGHT\TEMP.

For the most part, it was a straightforward exercise. I concocted some data, making certain that the data in the relational fields would be consistent. I made sure the invoices and the items on them tracked between their respective tables. But half an hour later I found myself at an impasse.

The DBD was great for creating databases and entering numbers, dates, and short text fields. But how was I going to enter data in the memo and BLOB fields in the Products table—and how was I going to cram data into the memo field in the Generic Tips table?

I decided I would have to create two quick and dirty tools with Delphi. Very quick. And *very* dirty. One utility would contain a DBMemo object that I would link to one of the memo fields. I would enter the data into that field for all the records in the table, then I would recompile the utility, changing the DBMemo to work with a different memo field. After four passes I would have entered all the textual information into the Products table. Then I could switch over to the Generic Tips table and work with the memo field there.

The second utility would contain a DBImage object, which I would link to the BLOB field in the Products table. I would then bring in the bitmap graphics, one at a time, through the clipboard and paste them into the DBImage.

Creating Quick and Dirty Utility 1

I whipped out the first utility in no time flat, using a single form. On it I placed a DBMemo and a DBNavigator component. I would only need to access one table at a time, so I dropped in a single TTable/DataSource component pair. I also added a DBText component that I would connect to PRD_NAME when working with the Products table, so I could see which product I was working with. I immediately modified the **VisibleButtons** property of the DBNavigator so I would see only the first four buttons. There is a picture of the form in Figure 16.3.

With everything in place, I modified some of the properties of the objects to work with the Products table. I clicked on Table1 and set its **DatabaseName** property (in this case, the *path* to the database directory containing the tables) to C:\BOXLIGHT\TEMP, the place where I had created the tables with DBD. I then clicked on Table1's **TableName** property and selected PRODUCTS.DBF, and then clicked on **IndexName** and selected PRD_STKNUM. I connected the DataSource to the Table, and then I connected the DBNavigator, DBText, and DBMemo to the DataSource. For the DBText, I chose PRD_NAME as the **DataField** property. My initial choice for the DBMemo's **DataField** was PRD_DESC. Table 16.9 contains the list of all the properties I changed from their default values.

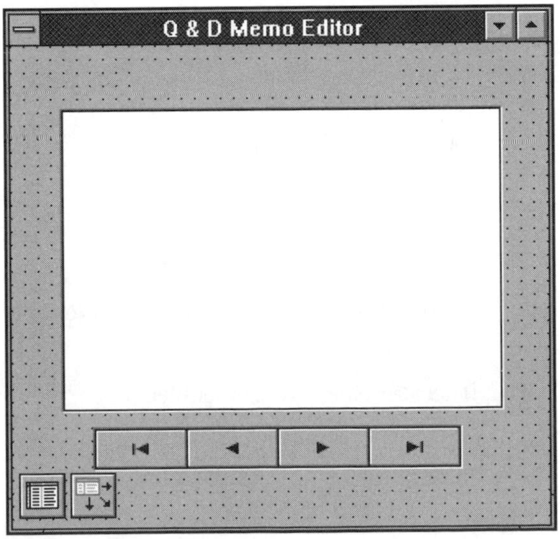

Figure 16.3 *My quick and dirty memo editor.*

Table 16.9   *Changed Properties for the Memo Editor (Products Table)*

Name	Property	Value
Form1	Left	200
	Top	99
	Width	337
	Height	321
	Caption	Q & D Memo Editor
DBText1	Left	75
	Top	11
	Width	162
	Height	17
	DataField	PRD_NAME
	DataSource	DataSource1
DBMemo1	Left	31
	Top	39
	Width	270
	Height	183
	DataField	PRD_DESC
	DataSource	DataSource1
DBNavigator1	Left	50
	Top	233
	Width	225
	Height	25
	DataSource	DataSource1
	VisibleButtons	[nbFirst, nbPrior, nbNext, nbLast]
Table1	DatabaseName	c:\boxlight\temp
	IndexName	PRD_STKNUM
	TableName	PRODUCTS.DBF
DataSource1	DataSet	Table1

After setting all the properties, I double-clicked on Table1's **Active** property to connect it to PRODUCTS.DBF. "ColorShow 1200" appeared in DBText1; because the default on all data-aware objects permits direct editing of fields, I was set. I ran the program and simply entered the descriptive information for each product, moving between product records with the navigator buttons.

When I finished entering that data, I left the program, changed DBMemo1's **DataField** property to PRD_SPECS, and compiled and ran the utility again, this time entering the technical specifications from the data sheets. I repeated the process for the PRD_TIPS and PRD_ACCESS fields.

Next, I switched to the Generic Tips table to edit its single memo field. I would change DBMemo1 to link it to the memo field, and I would modify the DBText component to display the category name. Other than that, all I had to do was change Table1's **TableName** and **IndexName** properties, and then set its **Active** property to **True**. The modifications appear in Table 16.10.

Creating Quick and Dirty Utility 2

With one utility already under my belt, the second was a snap. I basically duplicated what I had done for the first utility, this time substituting a DBImage component for the DBMemo. The new utility's form is shown in Figure 16.4.

The property settings were pretty much the same, too. Other than the caption of the main form, the only real differences were the settings for the DBImage component. The modified properties are listed in Table 16.11.

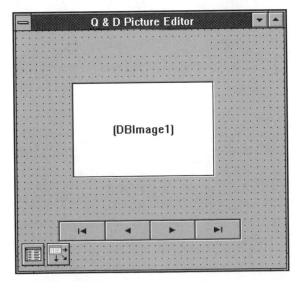

Figure 16.4 *My quick and dirty picture editor.*

Table 16.10 *Additional Changes for the Memo Editor (Generic Tips Table)*

Name	Property	Value
DBText1	DataField	TIP_CATNAM
DBMemo1	DataField	TIP_DESC
Table1	IndexName	TIP_CATID
	TableName	GENTIPS.DBF

Table 16.11 *Changed Properties for the Picture Editor*

Name	Property	Value
Form1	Left	200
	Top	99
	Width	337
	Height	321
	Caption	Q & D Picture Editor
DBText1	Left	75
	Top	11
	Width	162
	Height	17
	DataField	PRD_NAME
	DataSource	DataSource1
DBImage1	Left	68
	Top	64
	Width	174
	Height	115
	DataField	PRD_PICT
	DataSource	DataSource1

continued on next page

Table 16.11 *Changed Properties for the Picture Editor*

continued from previous page

Name	Property	Value
DBNavigator1	Left	50
	Top	233
	Width	225
	Height	25
	DataSource	DataSource1
	VisibleButtons	[nbFirst, nbPrior, nbNext, nbLast]
Table1	DatabaseName	c:\boxlight\temp
	IndexName	PRD_STKNUM
	TableName	PRODUCTS.DBF
DataSource1	DataSet	Table1

I set Table1's **Active** property to **True**, and then I compiled and ran the utility. Sure enough, I was able to navigate through each of the five product records. In each case, the image was blank. I suppose I could have used the Delphi Image Editor to copy the images, but old habits die hard. Instead, I launched a copy of Windows Paintbrush. One at a time, I loaded the bitmap graphics into Paintbrush, copied them to the clipboard, and then hot-keyed back to my utility, where I pasted them into DBImage1. It worked like gangbusters.

I looked up at the clock. It was exactly 11:30. I had managed to create all of my tables and fill all but the RMA table with example data. That particular table would be the responsibility of the demo application, once it was completed sometime later tonight.

I poured five scoops of Guatemalan Dark Roast beans into the grinder and then shook the precious powder into the filtered cup in the coffee maker. I filled it with water and flipped on the switch.

It was a good start, but I still had a long way to go. A *very* long way.

It Happened in the Library

Don Taylor

The night is young, but getting older fast, and Ace hunkers down to belt out a UI for the demo app.

With the database portion of the job completed, I was impatient to create the demo application. I recalled the well-known picture of two vultures sitting on a limb. "Patience my eye," one bird says to the other. "I'm going to *kill something!*" I understood perfectly. Having done all the work developing the data, I was anxious to sit down and start *writing code*. But that's not the way visual programming works: First you envision what your program will be, from the top down. Then you create it.

I wanted to have this first Delphi application completely finished within 24 hours of starting. But before I could proceed, I needed some guidelines, if I was to make the best use of the little time I had left. I decided to fall back on some logic that had served me well in the past: First Things First. First I would first make the application work. Once it was working, *then* I would try to make it pretty. Furthermore, I would develop the application using a process called *stepwise refinement*, using some specific guidelines:

1. Decide what the application is to do, and what its limitations are to be.
2. Divide the application's functionality into pieces that will be represented by forms.
3. Develop a rough layout of the application—all its forms and components.
4. Set the properties of each component, customizing it for the specific purpose it will fulfill.
5. Create the event handlers necessary to implement the dynamic operation of the components.
6. Add any special code required beyond simple event handling.
7. Smooth the application by repeating Steps 4, 5, and 6, refining the operation of the components with each pass.

I can do that, I thought. I poured the last of the pot of Guatemalan Dark Roast into my cup. It was time to begin the process.

STEP 1: DETERMINE THE SCOPE OF THE APPLICATION

It was obvious that the demo application was to serve two related but quite distinct purposes: (1) Provide product and troubleshooting information to marketing people, and (2) Operate a Return Material Authorization (RMA) system that will be used by technicians.

The Product Information portion would need to place a variety of data in its users' hands, including the name and stock number of the product; a photograph; a product description; technical specifications; general tips; and specific troubleshooting procedures. Data for a product should be accessed by specifying the stock number (probably picking it from a combo box). None of the data would need to be altered. No printed reports would be required.

The RMA portion was a skunk of a different stripe. Although it, too, would reference several other tables on a read-only basis, it would also be required to manage a table of its own. To create a new RMA, a technician must be able to locate an item that has been shipped, based on the customer supplying the Boxlight invoice number. At that time the RMA record would be created, and particulars of the problem and status of the authorization would be keyed in. A tech must be able to search the RMA table to determine the current status of a given RMA. The demo should also be capable of printing a status report of all active RMAs.

In addition to all this stuff, the application must also have a simple Windows Help capability, giving information on help file contents and supporting topic searches. And, of course, there must be an About box.

Whew! I took another gulp of the black elixir. I was ready for the next step.

STEP 2: DIVIDE THE APPLICATION INTO FUNCTIONAL PIECES

Under ordinary circumstances, the two primary purposes of the demo application might well be accomplished with two separate applications. The requirement here was for a single application, so that's the way it would be. It seemed to make the most sense to create an overall "administrative" window, from which the user could choose either function—perhaps by using a menu.

Each of the two major functions would have its own form. With the Main form and the About box, that brought the total to four forms. Depending on how the adding and editing of RMAs would be handled, there could be more.

It occurred to me there is a tradeoff in using forms. Each time you create a new form, you also create an accompanying Object Pascal unit. This is a natural, if the form is general-purpose enough to be used in another project, because the unit (the form) can easily be pulled into another project with Delphi's Project Manager. On the down side, it's slightly more work to pass information between units than between components on a single unit.

So when should I use a different form—and when should I try to cram as much on one form as possible? When I looked at how Borland had laid out the Delphi Integrated Development Environment, I got some clues. When they are working with separate data or functions related to the program (the Project and Environment options, for example), they use different forms (dialogs). But when they are working with *different aspects of the same data or functions* (either the Project or Environment option), they use tabbed notebooks to offer several groups of related items.

Using that same logic for the demo application, that meant using separate forms for the Product Information and RMA Management functions. For the large amount of textual data that would be displayed as Product Information, I would use a tabbed notebook.

I tilted my head upward as I drained the last bit of coffee from my cup, inhaling deeply, to capture the last whiff of the full-bodied aroma. I glanced over the notes I had made to this point. The first two steps had been completed. I was ready to start creating the application.

 ### Building the Boxlight Demo

From this point on, Ace will be developing the application, step by step. You are encouraged to follow along with him. All the files you will need can be found on the source code disk accompanying this book, in the directory \BOXLIGHT and its subdirectories. All data for the project—including tables, bitmaps and icons—can be found in \BOXLIGHT\FINAL. If you would rather follow along with the text and compile and run Ace's work as it develops, you can do that instead. Several versions of the project files are located in subdirectories named for the chapters in this book (for example, \BOXLIGHT\CHAP17). Each version of the project represents the state of the application at the end of the referenced chapter. We suggest you copy the entire \BOXLIGHT directory, along with its subdirectories, to your hard disk before you start.

STEP 3: DEVELOP A ROUGH LAYOUT OF THE APPLICATION

Before I could get started in earnest, I would have to do four things:

- Select a directory for the project.
- Add the name of the designated data subdirectory to my list of aliases.
- Create a new project.
- Make another large pot of coffee. (I decided to do this last item first, and opened the can of Double Dutch Mocha that Helen had given me three months ago for my birthday.)

Selecting the Project Directory

Earlier tonight I had created a subdirectory named \BOXLIGHT on my hard disk. Now I added two subdirectories beneath it: APP and DATA. Then I made a copy of the entire database I had created in the \BOXLIGHT\TEMP directory with DBD, including the table, index, and memo files. I placed the copies of the files in BOXLIGHT\DATA.

While I was waiting for the coffee to perk, I used Delphi's Image Editor to create an icon and a small graphic for the project. I saved them in the DATA subdirectory as well.

The coffee and the directories were both ready. Two tasks complete. I poured some Mocha in my cup and set three miniature marshmallows afloat on the steaming black sea.

Changing the Names to Protect the Innocent

As a Private Investigator, I was used to assuming an alias when I was working undercover. I especially remember a case in Dallas, where the client thought his wife was spending far too much time at the circus. As it turned out.... Well, that's another story entirely.

When I switched to the programming trade, I found out that an alias in the database world is a horse of a different color—it basically enables you to declare a system-wide variable and then assign a path name to it. With Delphi, you can then tell Table components to accept the alias as the path where data tables are located. If those tables are later moved to another location (a server, for instance), you just have to go to a single place and change the alias to point to the new location. Pretty slick. And you don't have to sit in a gorilla costume and do nothing for hours.

For the demo application, I would create a new alias named BOXLIGHT and assign to it the location where I had located the data—C:\BOXLIGHT\DATA.

From Delphi, I selected Database Desktop from the Tools menu. From there, I chose Aliases on DBD's File menu. I clicked the New button, entered "BOXLIGHT" in the Database Alias box, entered the path name ("C:\BOXLIGHT\DATA") in the Path box, and then clicked on Keep New. What I saw is depicted in Figure 17.1.

I clicked the OK button. I was shown the dialog in Figure 17.2 and asked if I wanted to save the new alias permanently, so it would be available to any

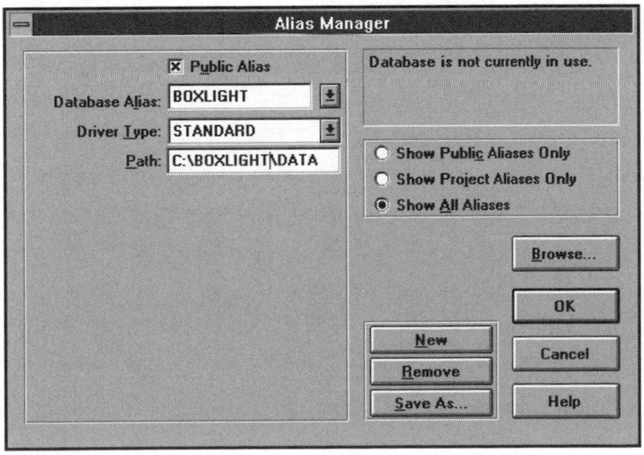

Figure 17.1 *Entering a new alias.*

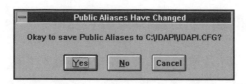

Figure 17.2 *Making an alias permanent.*

program that used IDAPI (also known as the Borland Database Engine, or BDE). I clicked on Yes, then I closed DBD. Another task complete. One more to go.

Creating the New Project

Now I could create a fresh project and get on my way. From Delphi's File menu, I chose File|New Project and then File|Save Project As to save the new project. I saved the unit file in the \BOXLIGHT\APP subdirectory as MAINUNIT.PAS, and saved the project in the same directory as BOXLIGHT.DPR.

My purpose was to create a "rough draft" of the forms, leaving the setting of component properties until later. The only modification I would make to the main form at this time was the addition of a menu. I clicked on the MainMenu button on the speedbar and then dropped a Menu object onto the form. What I saw appears in Figure 17.3.

Building a Rough Product Information Form

I decided the best way to write a visual program was by first creating a set of rough sketches of each form. I could then use each sketch as a "blueprint" from which I could build a more detailed form.

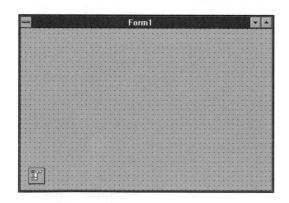

Figure 17.3 *A rough version of the main form.*

I spent the next few minutes envisioning what the Product Information form should look like. There should be a way the users could select the stock number of the product they wanted info on. Radio buttons would be nice, but they take up a lot of space—and the number of choices would be limited to the number of buttons. That would mean each time Boxlight added a new product, the program would have to be modified. Yikes! Better to have a list the user could select from. To save space, I would use a combo box.

There needed to be a picture of the selected product on the form, and I would use a DBImage component for that. The information to be presented would be contained in four memo fields. I decided it would be best to create a four-page tabbed notebook, placing one DBMemo on each page. Lastly, I needed a button somewhere on the form that the users could click when they were through using the form.

I sat down with my pencil and ruler, and in my spiral notebook I drew the sketch in Figure 17.4.

It was time to build a rough version of the Product Information form. I chose New Form from the File menu, and selected a blank form from the Gallery. I would be using a tabbed notebook, and although the Gallery offered a form that included one, the components on the form were so highly customized

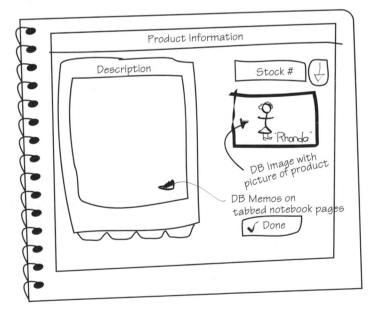

Figure 17.4   Ace's sketch of the Product Information form.

that it seemed easier to start from scratch. I saved the new form (automatically labeled "Form2") as PRODINFO.PAS.

I stretched the form both horizontally and vertically to give myself more room to work. Then I added a Notebook near the left side of the form. I also stretched it, so it took up about two-thirds of the form. The notebook would later be expanded to several pages that would each play host to DBMemo objects that would contain the product description, specifications, tips, and troubleshooting information. For now, I placed a single DBMemo (which would later contain the product description from the Products table) and a Label on the default Notebook page.

 ### Size Your Forms for the End User

Visual programmers like lots of screen space to spread out in, and Ace is no exception. Ace uses a high-resolution VGA, but he has the sense to know that his users might have screens of all different resolutions. There's nothing quite so callous as forcing an end user to frantically scroll-bar an oversized form in and out of view while filling it out. There goes that legendary Windows productivity.... In short, make sure as you design a form that it will fit comfortably on a 640×480 resolution display. Few, if any, current Windows machines have screen resolutions smaller than that, but it might pay to ask at your end user site if anyone is still running a 350-line EGA. If so, it might make sense to deliver a cheap VGA card with your application!

Beneath the Notebook, I placed a TabSet component, and then stretched it so that it was as long as the notebook was wide. To the right of the Notebook I placed a Panel, which I stretched to take up most of the remaining space on the right side of the form. On the Panel I plopped the combo box for the stock number, the DBImage, and the button. (I decided I wanted one of those geegaw buttons with a green check mark on it.)

One last thing to do—add the data access components. I would need a Table and a DataSource for each table I wanted to access from the form. But which tables would I need? I could come up with only two: the Products table (for the stock number, description, picture, specs, etc.) and the Generic Tips table (for the generic troubleshooting information). I dropped two Table components and two DataSource components on the form, not paying any particular attention where, since they become invisible when the application runs. I saved the file as PRODINFO.PAS.

The rough draft of the Product Information form is shown in Figure 17.5.

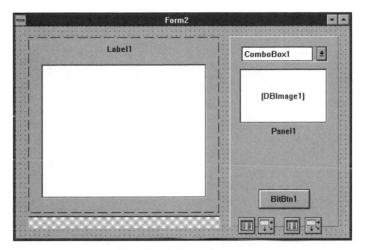

Figure 17.5 *A rough version of the Product Information form.*

Building a Rough RMA Management Form

Pretty easy so far. But now I faced a more difficult task. The RMA Management form would have to display considerably more information than the Product Information form. Thankfully, most of this information would come from a single source, the RMA table, and none of it would require any editing. That meant I would be making heavy use of DBText objects.

I took stock of the information I would need to display: the RMA number; the issue date; the initials of the technician who logged the RMA; the date the RMA was last updated; the status; the invoice number; the stock number of the item; and its serial number. All of these would be available from the RMA table, and all but one (the status) was a direct readout of a field value. DBText objects would do fine for them. For the status, an ordinary Label would suffice. One more piece of information would come directly from the RMA table—the description of the problem. That would require a DBMemo.

I wanted three more pieces of information on the form: the customer's name, phone number, and the name of the product. The name and phone number would come directly from the Customers table into DBText objects. The product's name would come into a third DBText from the Products table.

The technician would need a way to navigate through the RMAs, and to find a particular RMA to display. He or she would also need to add new RMAs, edit existing ones, and even delete one from time to time. I would take care of this with a DBNavigator and several buttons.

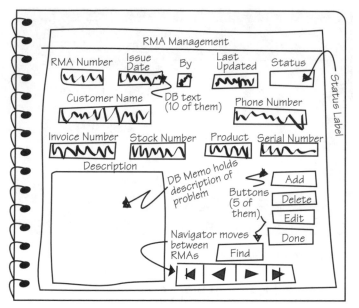

Figure 17.6 *Sketch of the RMA Management form.*

I grabbed my pencil and ruler, and I sketched a rough version of what I had in mind. The drawing appears in Figure 17.6.

I added a blank form to the project (Delphi called it Form3). This form would be holding a lot of objects, so I resized it to occupy a large part of my screen, while staying within least-common denominator VGA 640×480 pixel limits. I placed 11 Labels in the top half of the form. Under what would be the Status label, I placed one additional Label that would display the status message. Under each of the remaining labels I placed a DBText. I added the DBMemo, five buttons, and a DBNavigator. I put one more Label above the DBMemo.

If my count was correct, I had three tables to access, so I added that many Table/DataSource pairs to the form. The resulting form is shown in Figure 17.7. I saved the file as RMAMGMT.PAS.

Daddy, Where Do RMAs Come From?

Until now, I had been deftly avoiding how I would handle the mechanics of entering new RMAs and editing existing ones. I was now at a point where I would have to make some hard and fast decisions.

I needed to clear my head. I stood up and stretched, and waded over to the corner of the office where I keep my exercise equipment. I climbed onto the ski machine and started striding and pulling on the ropes.

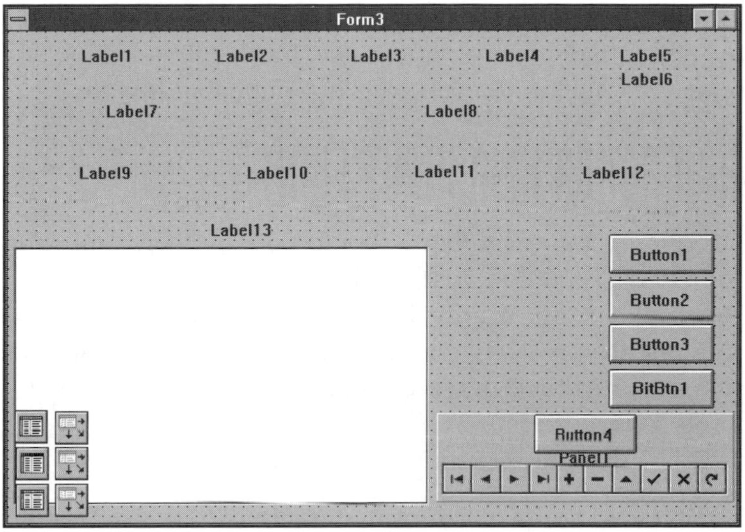

Figure 17.7 *A rough version of the RMA Management form.*

Under ordinary circumstances, I probably would have done the adding and editing of RMAs on the same form that displayed them. But this situation was different, right from the get-go. My intuition had told me to use DBText components, which would only display the information, rather than DBEdits that would allow me to directly edit the data.

I mounted the stationary bicycle. As I pedaled, I began to see what made this situation so unique. Most of the time, data entry consists of keying information into fields—names, addresses and the like. In this application, I was picking out data that already existed in other systems—invoice numbers, stock numbers, and so forth. Even the RMA numbers and dates would be generated automatically. In fact, the only information to be keyed in would be the problem description! That means the bulk of editing an RMA record would be done with combo boxes. Using combo boxes to display information when you're not editing seems unnatural somehow. It feels clunky.

I moved to the stair climber and further considered the situation. There was another reason not to perform edits while on the RMA Management form. When the form is in display mode, the Find button and navigational controls would be used to move through records in the RMA table. But when users are appending or editing an RMA, they need to navigate through the *invoices* to find the particular item in question. That would mean either adding another set of navigational controls (there wasn't enough room for that), or using the existing controls to navigate through RMAs or invoices, depending on whether the user is displaying or editing. Naw—too confusing.

I stepped up to the punching bag, and started doing the old "Hackensack Shuffle." My timing had gotten a little rusty, but I still had some steam left in my fists. I quickly fell into an even left-right punching rhythm.

BUILDING A ROUGH RMA INPUT FORM

I had come to the conclusion that I should add another form to handle the addition and editing of RMAs. That would mean one more unit, and that both the RMA Management form and the new form—I'd call it the RMA Input form—would need a little bit of communication between them. (Table objects connected to the same data table operate independently. To get Tables on different forms to point to the same record, you have to pass index keys back and forth.) This would be something to be dealt with later.

I was just beginning to visualize the contents of the new form when my cellular phone began to *deedle*. Without missing a beat, I switched to my left jab as I reached into my open briefcase and grabbed the cell phone with my right hand. The clock in the phone's LCD display read 1:04.

"Ace Breakpoint. How may I empower you?"

"Ace—it's Biff. What's going on over there?"

"I'm pulling an all-nighter on a hot project. Why?"

"It's just that... Wait a minute..."

In the background I could hear the sounds of pouring rain and a car's engine idling, and I knew instantly that he was calling from work. Biff had majored in Business Ethics at our alma mater, and upon graduation went directly into private enterprise. Some two years later, he was still working at the same place—Buck McGawk's Norwegian Fried Chicken House. He'd managed to work himself up to Counter Person. Tonight I surmised he was working the takeout window.

"I'm back," he said. "Had to take care of a customer."

"So, old buddy, how's life in the fast food lane?" I asked, a little impatiently.

"Pretty good until five minutes ago. Bohacker was just here."

"That could ruin anybody's day. Something I should know?"

"He wanted me to give you a message."

I had no idea what I was about to hear, but my blood pressure shot up five points, just in sheer anticipation.

"Just what did *Old Binary Breath* have to say?" I asked.

"I don't know if I should tell you. I get the feeling there's some pretty bad blood between you two right now. What he said wasn't too affirming or edifying."

"Try me."

Biff hesitated for a moment, then apparently decided I could handle it.

"Bohacker said, 'Tell your friend the *Soufflé King* I'm going to beat him *double time* on this one. He doesn't have a clue. I'm holding a little advance victory celebration tonight, in his honor.' He ordered a double portion of Extra Greasy with Norse fries and slaw, and then he tore out of here like a barber heading for Woodstock. I'm telling you, Ace, he had a crazy look in his eyes. I think maybe he was on dextrose."

"That's it?"

"There was one other thing. He said he was going to send you the cleaning bill for his jacket."

"Gotta go, Biff. I'll talk to you tomorrow. And don't worry."

"Okay, Ace." He hung up his receiver. I touched the Hangup button on the cell phone and stuffed it in my hip pocket.

All through the conversation I had maintained a constant, even rhythm on the speed bag with my left hand. I had remained calm. But now I felt something welling up inside of me. An inexplicable rage that came from deep within my gut, probably due to rejection I had suffered during my infant years. As I watched the bag, I began to see Bohacker's face on it as it danced just beyond the knuckles on my left hand. The image became more and more vivid, until I could no longer tell fantasy from reality. He was right there in front of me. Taunting me. Daring me to make the first move.

At last, I could stand it no more. "Take *this*, pal!" I shouted, as I lashed out with the full power of my right arm. I threw my shoulder into the blow as I lunged toward the target. My fist struck paydirt, and the leather orb nearly exploded as it hurtled away from me at breakneck speed. At once my rage began to dissipate. I experienced an instant release. I watched the bag as it reached the end of its travel and then, in a perfect exhibition of physics, rebounded back with nearly the same power and speed with which it had left. Now it seemed to be moving in slow motion, coming closer and closer, until it completely filled my vision....

• • •

I gingerly smoothed down the edges of the adhesive tape that had pulled my lower lip back together. My snoot had almost stopped bleeding, and the ice pack had pretty much halted the progression of swelling. It would be okay. My mug would gradually heal with time. As near as I could tell, I had been out cold for about 15 minutes. For the second time tonight, I had lost precious time because I had been the victim of a situation totally beyond my control. I retreated to my desk.

BACK TO THE RMA INPUT FORM

I toyed with my pencil as I considered my next move. This form would be the most complex yet, because it had to access data from several tables. The form would automatically assign serial numbers and issue dates to new RMAs, and it would display both of these items on the form (directly from the RMA table). This could be handled by a DBText. The initials field would be perfectly served by a combo box containing all the initials in the Employees table. The status message would use the value in the RMA_STATUS field of the RMA table to select an item in a string list, which would work well with a combo box. Of course, the description of the problem would be placed in a DBMemo.

Now for the tricky part. I needed a way to search for a specific invoice or just navigate through the Invoices table. Once a particular invoice was located, several pieces of information would become directly or indirectly available to me. The stock numbers and serial numbers on the invoice could be obtained from the Invoice Items table. By viewing a list of the items on the invoice (I decided a DBGrid would be good for that purpose), the Tech could pick the one the customer specified. The invoice would also provide the customer ID, so I could get the customer's name from the Customers table.

I would need the same navigation equipment provided on the RMA Management form—a DBNavigator and a Find button. In addition, I would need OK and Cancel buttons. For the third time, I put pencil to paper and drew a sketch in my notebook. That sketch appears in Figure 17.8.

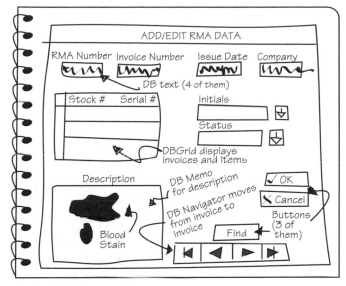

Figure 17.8 *Sketch of the RMA Input form.*

Again I created a new form (Form4) and enlarged it. In a horizontal row across the top, I placed four Labels. Beneath each Label I placed a DBText. Then I plopped all the remaining components in my sketch onto the new form.

If I counted right, I needed five Table/DataSource pairs for the tables—RMA, Invoices, Invoice Items, Customers, and Employees. But wait! How was I going to handle the sequence number portion of the RMA number? That number would have to be maintained and somehow incremented each time a new RMA was added. I could have stored the value in a special data file, but I decided instead to create one more table—a table that would have but one field and one record. The number in that field would be assigned to the next RMA.

I called up the DBD again, and I created the Next RMA table as a dBASE for Windows table, and I saved it as RMANXT.DBF. Its structure is shown in Table 17.1. I assigned RXT_RMANUM an initial value of 1.

With that out of the way, I plunked six Table/DataSource pairs on the RMA Input form and saved the file as RMAADD.PAS. A shot of the rough form is shown in Figure 17.9. I had completed the rough design of all my forms.

Table 17.1 *Database Structure for the Next RMA Table*

Name	Size/Type	Source	Comments
RXT_RMANUM	Number:8:0	–	Number assigned to the next RMA Not indexed.

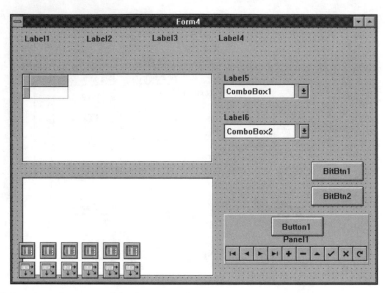

Figure 17.9 *A rough version of the RMA Input form.*

FURTHER RUMINATIONS

In creating the RMA Management and RMA Input forms, I realized I would at some point be forced to create two more forms. The first would be a dialog that would accept an RMA number to search for. The second would collect an invoice number to search for. It occurred to me that by manipulating component properties, I just might be able to make a single form do the work of two.

I was also aware that I still had yet another form to create—the About Box form. I decided to put that one off as long as possible. I would make it the "finishing touch" on tonight's work.

I rocked back in my chair and took a deep breath. The clock applet on my Windows screen read 1:42. It had been almost exactly 12 hours since I had walked into the Boxlight offices. In that many hours I had completed the first three major steps toward reaching my goal: (1) Deciding exactly what the application was going to do; (2) Dividing the application's functionality into forms; and (3) Developing a rough layout of the forms and components.

I dipped a plain rice cake into my cup of Mocha and cautiously put it to my lips. I had scoped out the territory. I'd built the foundation. Now I was going to perform some *serious* property management.

Staking Out Some Hot Properties

CHAPTER 18

Don Taylor

Time's running out, but after some furious detail work on the application's properties, Ace finally begins to see some results.

I hit Off on the TV's remote control. I had taken a short break and caught the last few minutes of The Hair/Brain Connection, one of those late-night cable infomercials. Tonight's featured product: Hair Apparent, a totally natural hair replacement system. Helen always chided me for watching these shows, because she said I had absolutely no sales resistance. Ridiculous, of course—the only reason I watched was for the entertainment value.

Slipping my credit card back into my wallet, I recalled that, having ordered tonight, I'd receive the eyebrow implantation attachment—at no extra cost.

The break was over. Time to get my bearings. I had completed Step 3 of the design, creating a "rough draft" of the application with all its forms and components. I had determined the overall *shape* of the application. In the next hours, I would be changing properties on the four forms I'd designed, molding each piece of the application into a specialized device whose operation would be consistent with the overall design. Then I would compile and run the program for the first time.

STEP 4: SET THE PROPERTIES OF EACH COMPONENT

I dunked the last bit of rice cake into the Mocha and tossed it into my mouth. I would work on one form at a time, starting with the Main form. But first, I needed to assign meaningful names to all the components, so when I got to writing event handlers and supplemental code, I wouldn't be trying to figure out which data item "DBText14" related to. My M.O. would be to assign to each component a name that would combine the type of the component and the function it served in the program. Later, I would be able to tell at a glance which piece of data a component related to, as well as its relevant properties and events. I took on the Main form first, which was a piece of cake. Then I moved to the Product Information form. The old and new component names are summarized in Table 18.1.

Looking at the entries in the table, I could see how giving more meaningful names to components would save me a lot of time and thrashing later. I moved on to the RMA Management form and worked some more magic. The results are included in Table 18.2.

Table 18.1 *New Component Names — Main and Product Info Forms*

Form	Old Name	New Name
MainForm	Menu1	MainMenu
ProdInfoForm	Notebook1	ProductNotebook
	TabSet1	ProductTabSet
	DBMemo1	DescDBMemo
	Label1	DescLabel
	Panel1	ProductPanel
	ComboBox1	StkNumComboBox
	DBImage1	PictDBImage
	BitBtn1	DoneBtn
	Table1	ProductsTable
	Table2	GenTipsTable
	DataSource1	ProductsSource
	DataSource2	GenTipsSource

Table 18.2 *New Component Names — RMA Management Form*

Form	Old Name	New Name
RMAMgmtForm	Label1	RMALabel
	Label2	IssueDateLabel
	Label3	ByLabel
	Label4	UpdateLabel
	Label5	StatusLabel
	Label6	StatusMsgLabel
	Label7	CustNameLabel
	Label8	PhoneLabel
	Label9	InvNumLabel
	Label10	StkNumLabel
	Label11	NameLabel
	Label12	SNLabel
	Label13	DescLabel
	DBText1	RMADBText
	DBText2	IssueDBText
	DBText3	ByDBText
	DBText4	UpdatedDBText
	DBText5	CustNameDBText
	DBText6	CustPhoneDBText
	DBText7	InvNumDBText
	DBText8	StkNumDBText
	DBText9	ProductDBText
	DBText10	SNDBText
	Button1	AddBtn
	Button2	DeleteBtn
	Button3	EditBtn
	Button4	FindBtn
	BitBtn1	DoneBtn

continued on next page

Table 18.2 *New Component Names — RMA Management Form*

continued from previous page

Form	Old Name	New Name
	Panel1	NavPanel
	DBNavigator1	RMANavigator
	DBMemo1	DescDBMemo
	Table1	RMATable
	Table2	CustomerTable
	Table3	ProductsTable
	DataSource1	RMASource
	DataSource2	CustomerSource
	DataSource3	ProductsSource

One last form to process. Within a few minutes I had it done. The names for the RMA Input form's components are listed in Table 18.3.

UPDATING THE MAIN FORM

I was now ready to begin updating each of the forms, starting with the Main form. I figured that was an easy place to start, since the only component on the Main form was the Menu object. I would just have to readjust the form a bit, and then set up a quick-and-dirty menu based on the requirements I had come up with in Step 2. The changes to the Main form's properties are specified in Table 18.4.

Table 18.3 *New Component Names — RMA Input Form*

Form	Old Name	New Name
RMAAddForm	Label1	RMALabel
	Label2	InvoiceLabel
	Label3	IssueDateLabel
	Label4	CompanyLabel
	Label5	InitLabel
	Label6	StatusLabel

continued on next page

Table 18.3   *New Component Names — RMA Input Form*

continued from previous page

Form	Old Name	New Name
	DBText1	RMADBText
	DBText2	InvoiceDBText
	DBText3	IssueDBText
	DBText4	CustomerDBText
	ComboBox1	InitComboBox
	ComboBox2	StatusComboBox
	Panel1	NavPanel
	Button1	FindBtn
	BitBtn1	OKBtn
	BitBtn2	CancelBtn
	DBGrid1	ItemsDBGrid
	DBMemo1	DescDBMemo
	DBNavigator1	InvoiceNav
	Table1	RMATable
	Table2	InvoiceTable
	Table3	ItemsTable
	Table4	EmployeeTable
	Table5	CustomerTable
	Table6	NextRMATable
	DataSource1	RMASource
	DataSource2	InvoiceSource
	DataSource3	ItemsSource
	DataSource4	EmployeeSource
	DataSource5	CustomerSource
	DataSource6	NextRMASource

I could now edit the properties of MainMenu, using Delphi's Menu Designer. I decided to have three items on the menu: File, System, and Help. Under File, I would offer only one option, exiting the program. Under System, I would have two options—One would bring up the Product Information form, the other would call up the RMA Management form. Each form would be modal,

Table 18.4 *Changed Properties for the Main Form*

Name	Property	Value
MainForm	Left	209
	Top	142
	Width	435
	Height	300
	Caption	'Support System Demo'
	Menu	MainMenu

meaning the users couldn't use any other part of the application until they had clicked the Done button on the form to put it away.

The Help menu would offer three choices. The first would be the usual Contents option. The second would be a standard Topic Search. The last would be the About dialog. I would divide the last two options with a separator line. The contents of the Menu (called **MainMenu**) are described in Table 18.5.

I had no sooner saved the changes to my file than the phone rang again. *Another interruption*, I thought. *Doesn't anyone realize I'm busy?* I reluctantly picked up the receiver.

"Ace Breakpoint. How may I empower you?"

"Yeah, we'd like a Monumental Montezuma to go, with a super size carton of Inca Drink."

Table 18.5 *MainForm's Menu Properties*

Name	Menu	Caption
MainMenu	MainMenuFile	&File
	FileMenuExit	E&xit
	MainMenuSystem	&System
	SystemMenuProduct	&Product Info...
	SystemMenuRMA	&RMA Management...
	MainMenuHelp	&Help
	HelpMenuContents	&Contents
	HelpMenuTopic	&Topic Search
	N1	- (separator)
	HelpMenuAbout	&About...

He hadn't heard a word I had said, of course. They never did. My number was just one digit off the phone number of the local Chichen Itza Pizza Store, and I got at least one call like this every night. For the first month or so I had considered getting my number changed, but decided instead I could have a little fun with it at no expense—to *me*, that is.

"You want any anchovies on that?" I asked.

"Like, no way, man."

"How about a bag of Ancient Aztec whole-grain crusts? No extra charge." I always offered the best deal in town.

"Surely, Dude. We'll be down there to pick it up in 20 minutes."

"Make it so," I said.

I hung up the receiver. Then I picked it up again, and punched in the code that would forward any further calls to my voice mail box. I was getting far too many interruptions. If anyone really wanted to reach me, they could just leave a message.

UPDATING THE PRODUCT INFORMATION FORM

Of the three forms that remained, the Product Information form appeared to be the least complex. The overall design still looked good to me, so I just changed a few appropriate properties. To get the green doohickey (I think it's called a "glyph") on the button, I just set its **Kind** property to **bkOK**. Then I changed the caption to "Done". The **StkNumComboBox** is set by default to **csDropDown**. This enables the user to enter a value by typing it into the box. Since I would be working with data that couldn't be modified, I chose **csDropDownList** instead.

The Table and DataSource components were a snap to set up. I worked with the Tables first, so the DataSources would recognize them. Since none of the data on this form was to be modified by the end user, I set each Table's **ReadOnly** property to **True**. I chose the proper index for each table, based on the options offered. Then I connected the sources. I was definitely clicking and grinning. The results are shown in Table 18.6.

So far, so good. My biggest challenge with the Product Information form was the Notebook component. I needed to create several pages, placing a DBMemo and a descriptive label on each page. Later I would connect the Notebook pages to the TabSet by modifying their event handlers.

Table 18.6 *Initial Changes to the Product Info Form*

Name	Property	Value
ProdInfoForm	Left	152
	Top	121
	Width	636
	Height	385
	Caption	Product Information
ProductNotebook	Left	6
	Top	13
	Width	397
	Height	301
ProductTabSet	Left	6
	Top	314
	Width	398
	Height	21
ProductPanel	Left	413
	Top	12
	Width	206
	Height	321
	Caption	(blank)
StkNumComboBox	Left	23
	Top	18
	Width	160
	Height	24
	Style	csDropDownList
	Text	(blank)
PictDBImage	Left	23
	Top	60
	Width	161
	Height	114
	DataField	PRD_PICT
	DataSource	ProductsSource

continued on next page

Table 18.6 *Initial Changes to the Product Info Form*

continued from previous page

Name	Property	Value
DoneBtn	Left	65
	Top	268
	Width	78
	Height	26
	Caption	Done
	Kind	bkOK
ProductsTable	DatabaseName	BOXLIGHT
	IndexName	PRD_STKNUM
	ReadOnly True	
	TableName	PRODUCTS.DBF
GenTipsTable	DatabaseName	BOXLIGHT
	IndexName	TIP_CATID
	ReadOnly True	
	TableName	GENTIPS.DBF
ProductsSource	DataSet	ProductsTable
GenTipsSource	DataSet	GenTipsTable

Creating the pages was easier than I thought. I clicked on the **ProductNotebook** object, and then clicked on the **Pages** property, then on the "..." button to bring up the Notebook Editor. I simply typed in the names of the pages, as I wanted them to appear later on the tabs below the Notebook. Just as with the other components, I didn't bother to change the Help context of any of the pages; I just wouldn't have time to build that much detailed help into the demo application. I snapped a photo of the editor while I was working. (The result can be seen in Figure 18.1.)

I could now move between pages in the Object Inspector by changing **ProductNotebook**'s **ActivePage** property. Each page had the same name I had given it in the editor, and all but the Description page were blank. I decided to spiff that page up a bit. The properties I modified are listed in Table 18.7.

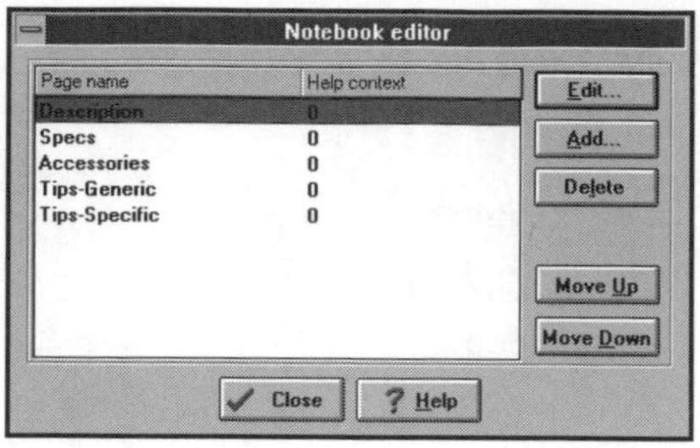

Figure 18.1   *Creating pages with the Notebook editor.*

Now I needed to populate the other pages of **ProductNotebook**. I selected
DescMemo and **DescLabel** from the Description page, copied them to the
Clipboard, and then pasted the Clipboard contents to each of the other four
pages. Once pasted, I modified their properties. I copied down the detailed
properties of the pages and put them in Tables 18.8 through 18.11.

Table 18.7   *Description Page Properties*

Name	Property	Value
	Left	0
	Top	0
	Caption	Description
DescMemo	Left	10
	Top	45
	Width	378
	Height	237
	DataField	PRD_DESC
	DataSource	ProductsSource
	ScrollBars	ssVertical
DescLabel	Left	161
	Top	17
	Width	74
	Height	16
	Caption	Description

Table 18.8 *Specifications Page Properties*

Name	Property	Value
	Left	0
	Top	0
	Caption	Specs
SpecsDBMemo	Left	10
	Top	45
	Width	378
	Height	237
	DataField	PRD_SPECS
	DataSource	ProductsSource
	ScrollBars	ssVertical
SpecsLabel	Left	153
	Top	14
	Width	91
	Height	16
	Alignment	taCenter
	Caption	Specifications

Table 18.9 *Accessories Page Properties*

Name	Property	Value
	Left	0
	Top	0
	Caption	Accessories
AccessDBMemo	Left	10
	Top	45
	Width	378
	Height	237
	DataField	PRD_ACCESS
	DataSource	ProductsSource
	ScrollBars	ssVertical

continued on next page

Table 18.9 *Accessories Page Properties*

continued from previous page

Name	Property	Value
AccessLabel	Left	160
	Top	18
	Width	79
	Height	16
	Caption	Accessories

Table 18.10 *Generic Tips Page Properties*

Name	Property	Value
	Left	0
	Top	0
	Caption	Tips-Generic
GenTipsDBMemo	Left	10
	Top	45
	Width	378
	Height	237
	DataField	TIP_DESC
	DataSource	GenTipsSource
	ScrollBars	ssVertical
GenTipsLabel	Left	159
	Top	16
	Width	82
	Height	16
	Caption	Generic Tips

I now changed **ProductNotebook**'s **ActivePage** property back to Description, my default page.

One last little detail. **StkNumComboBox** would need the stock numbers of the Boxlight products stored in its StringList, so it could offer the list of choices to the user. Creating that list was essentially the same as creating the pages for

Table 18.11   *Specific Tips Page Properties*

Name	Property	Value
	Left	0
	Top	0
	Caption	Tips-Specific
TipsDBMemo	Left	10
	Top	45
	Width	378
	Height	237
	DataField	PRD_TIPS
	DataSource	ProductsSource
	ScrollBars	ssVertical
TipsLabel	Left	158
	Top	16
	Width	83
	Height	16
	Caption	Specific Tips

the Notebook. I just clicked on the **Items** property of **StkNumComboBox**, then on the "..." button. That brought up the StringList Editor. Then I simply entered the five stock numbers, in numerical order. A snapshot of my work appears in Figure 18.2.

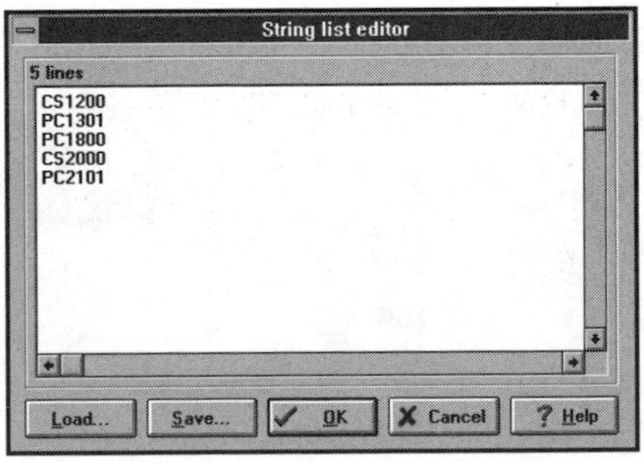

Figure 18.2   *Adding stock numbers to StkNumComboBox.*

With everything hooked up, I was ready to turn this puppy on. (In writing this application, I would assume that all tables are already open and active whenever the program runs.) I double-clicked on each Table's **Active** property to set it to **True**. To my delight, text appeared in **DescMemo**—and a picture popped up in **PictDBImage**!

As nice as it looked, there was something missing. I pondered for a moment, then realized what it was. To determine which product I was looking at, I either had to recognize the photo, or I had to read the text in the description. I decided to add two more DBText components to the form—one that would display the product name and another that would display the price. Since both of these pieces of information are available in the **Products** table I already had open, it proved a simple task.

I dropped two more DBTexts on the **ProductPanel**, just below **PictDBImage**. Then I set their properties as shown in Table 18.12. The product's name and price instantly appeared. *I was getting the hang of this Delphi thing.*

I took a look at my work on the Product Information form. All in all, it looked pretty good. A picture of it is included as Figure 18.3.

Table 18.12 *Some Last-Minute Additions to the Product Info Form*

Name	Property	Value
ProductNameDBText	Left	20
	Top	182
	Width	167
	Height	17
	Alignment	taCenter
	DataField	PRD_NAME
	DataSource	ProductsSource
PriceDBText	Left	20
	Top	205
	Width	164
	Height	17
	Alignment	taCenter
	DataField	PRD_PRICE
	DataSource	ProductsSource

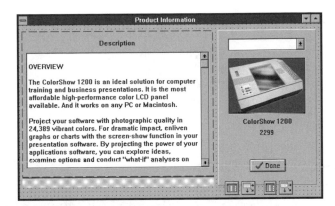

Figure 18.3 *The updated Product Information form.*

UPDATING THE RMA MANAGEMENT FORM

My wristwatch told me it was 2:05 a.m. I was making excellent progress. I was about to proceed to the RMA Management form, when I heard an eerie knocking coming from the sliding glass door that connected my office to the small portico outside. Through the glass I could see a familiar face. I slid the door open and he slipped in, not saying a word. It was obvious he was waiting for me to start a conversation.

"Haven't seen you for a while. Where've you been?" I asked.

Silence. He just stared at me. I pressed harder.

"You look like you haven't eaten. Is there something I can get you?"

His green eyes bored steadily into mine for several seconds. Then he finally broke his silence.

"Meow," he said.

Mewnix was a tiny, eight-week-old kitten when Helen had given him to me at Christmas time, three years ago. He has since grown into a 22-pound, long-haired calico with a predilection to wander at night, looking for fisticuffs and female companionship. I guess that's why we got along so well—we were kindred spirits.

I was wondering where he had been. Apparently the commotion with the fire engines earlier this evening had scared him away. Now he was back, and he was making his presence known. He was as hungry as he was wet, and he was demanding his dish be filled. I fumbled through the refrigerator until I found an open can of *Cat-a-Leana* Diet Turkey and dumped the rest of it into his dish. He was quite unimpressed.

"Hey, pal," I told him. "This is Ace you're dealing with—not Helen. I know she gives you anything your heart desires. But she isn't here—and you're sticking to your low-fat diet."

"*Meow.*" It wasn't *what* he said, it was the *way* he said it that showed his disdain. Apparently he decided this was all he was going to get, though, because he began to pick at the contents of his dish. The mocha was history, so I put on a pot of *Seattle Sleepless* and headed back to my keyboard.

Even though the RMA Management form contained a lot of components, it presented no real challenges. I decided to limit the buttons on **RMANavigator** to four—first record, previous record, next record, and last record. The rest of the buttons didn't make sense here, because there was nothing to be edited or posted. I connected the Table components to their corresponding tables, setting each to **ReadOnly** status. I selected the obvious index for each of them.

Looking at the form, I decided it needed a little rearranging to make it more pleasing to the eye. I changed the position of the buttons, and I resized and relocated the navigator panel and its associated controls. A summary of all the changes is contained in Table 18.13.

Table 18.13 *Changes to the RMA Management Form*

Name	Property	Value
RMAMgmtForm	Left	162
	Top	99
	Width	627
	Height	441
	Caption	RMA Management
RMALabel	Left	16
	Top	11
	Width	83
	Height	16
	Caption	RMA number

continued on next page

Table 18.13   *Changes to the RMA Management Form*

continued from previous page

Name	Property	Value
IssueDateLabel	Left	137
	Top	11
	Width	68
	Height	16
	Caption	Issue date
ByLabel	Left	263
	Top	11
	Width	18
	Height	16
	Caption	By
UpdateLabel	Left	340
	Top	11
	Width	84
	Height	16
	Caption	Last updated
StatusLabel	Left	464
	Top	11
	Width	41
	Height	16
	Caption	Status
StatusMsgLabel	Left	464
	Top	31
	Width	105
	Height	16
	Caption	(blank)
CustNameLabel	Left	17
	Top	59
	Width	102
	Height	16
	Caption	Customer name

continued on next page

Table 18.13 *Changes to the RMA Management Form*

continued from previous page

Name	Property	Value
PhoneLabel	Left	355
	Top	59
	Width	94
	Height	16
	Caption	Phone number
InvNumLabel	Left	17
	Top	109
	Width	100
	Height	16
	Caption	Invoice number
StkNumLabel	Left	164
	Top	109
	Width	88
	Height	16
	Caption	Stock number
NameLabel	Left	289
	Top	109
	Width	49
	Height	16
	Caption	Product
SNLabel	Left	465
	Top	109
	Width	91
	Height	16
	Caption	Serial number
DescLabel	Left	141
	Top	158
	Width	74
	Height	16
	Caption	Description

continued on next page

Table 18.13 *Changes to the RMA Management Form*

continued from previous page

Name	Property	Value
RMADBText	Left	16
	Top	30
	Width	92
	Height	17
	DataField	RMA_ID
	DataSource	RMASource
IssueDBText	Left	137
	Top	28
	Width	88
	Height	17
	DataField	RMA_DATE
	DataSource	RMASource
ByDBText	Left	263
	Top	30
	Width	65
	Height	17
	DataField	RMA_INITS
	DataSource	RMASource
UpdatedDBText	Left	340
	Top	30
	Width	102
	Height	17
	DataField	RMA_UPDATE
	DataSource	RMASource
CustNameDBText	Left	17
	Top	79
	Width	297
	Height	17
	DataField	CST_COMPNM
	DataSource	CustomerSource

continued on next page

Table 18.13 *Changes to the RMA Management Form*

continued from previous page

Name	Property	Value
CustPhoneDBText	Left	355
	Top	79
	Width	189
	Height	17
	DataField	CST_VPHONE
	DataSource	CustomerSource
InvNumDBText	Left	17
	Top	129
	Width	100
	Height	17
	DataField	RMA_INVNUM
	DataSource	RMASource
StkNumDBText	Left	164
	Top	129
	Width	104
	Height	17
	DataField	RMA_STKNUM
	DataSource	RMASource
ProductDBText	Left	289
	Top	129
	Width	152
	Height	17
	DataField	PRD_NAME
	DataSource	ProductsSource
SNDBText	Left	465
	Top	129
	Width	83
	Height	17
	DataField	RMA_SERNUM
	DataSource	RMASource

continued on next page

Table 18.13 *Changes to the RMA Management Form*

continued from previous page

Name	Property	Value
AddBtn	Left	530
	Top	192
	Width	73
	Height	25
	Caption	&Add
DeleteBtn	Left	530
	Top	236
	Width	73
	Height	24
	Caption	&Delete
EditBtn	Left	530
	Top	280
	Width	73
	Height	24
	Caption	&Edit
FindBtn	Left	20
	Top	26
	Width	133
	Height	24
	Caption	&Find RMA
DoneBtn	Left	530
	Top	349
	Width	73
	Height	24
	Caption	Done
	Kind	bkOK
NavPanel	Left	338
	Top	193
	Width	171
	Height	111

continued on next page

Table 18.13 *Changes to the RMA Management Form*

continued from previous page

Name	Property	Value
RMANavigator	Left	20
	Top	61
	Width	133
	Height	25
	DataSource	RMASource
	VisibleButtons	[nbFirst, nbPrior, nbNext, nbLast]
DescDBMemo	Left	6
	Top	183
	Width	320
	Height	215
	DataField	RMA_DESC
	DataSource	RMASource
	ScrollBars	ssVertical
RMATable	DatabaseName	BOXLIGHT
	IndexName	RMA_ID
	TableName	RMA.DBF
CustomerTable	DatabaseName	BOXLIGHT
	IndexName	CST_ID
	ReadOnly	True
	TableName	CUSTOMER.DBF
ProductsTable	DatabaseName	BOXLIGHT
	IndexName	PRD_STKNUM
	ReadOnly	True
	TableName	PRODUCTS.DBF
RMASource	AutoEdit	False
	DataSet	RMATable
CustomerSource	AutoEdit	False
	DataSet	CustomerTable
ProductsSource	AutoEdit	False
	DataSet	ProductsTable

I went through each of the Table components, setting their **Active** properties to **True**. I didn't witness the spectacular effect I had seen in the Product Info table, but there were definitely some changes to the display. Figure 18.4 shows what the revised RMA Management form looked like.

I don't know if I had ever seen as many figures and tables in one place as I had created tonight—and I wasn't done yet. My only solace came in that, although it was a pain to document all my work for future reference, at least no one else would ever have to read any of this stuff.

It had been a long day, and it was getting more and more difficult for me to concentrate. Mewnix interrupted my daydreaming by scratching on the sliding glass door. He had apparently decided it was drier outside in the storm that it was here in the office, and he may well have been right. I got up and let him out.

Helen really does dote on that cat, I thought. My thoughts drifted back to earlier times. Helen and I had been together for four years now. When I first met her, she had a lot going for her. Good looking. Nice personality. Wealthy family. But she was always wanting to take care of me. She was continually taking in stray animals, and I sometimes felt like one of them. There were times I thought she cared *too much*. But just lately, she had been very aloof. Very unlike herself.

Then, there was Rhonda...

The rush of steam from the coffee maker broke my trance, telling me the batch of *Sleepless* was ready for duty. I wandered over to the cupboard and picked out the biggest mug on the shelf. Then I filled it with hot coffee and sat back down in front of my CRT.

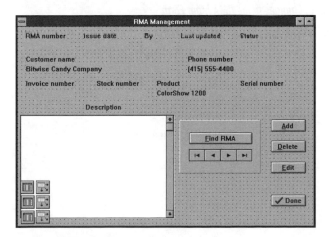

Figure 18.4 *The updated RMA Management form.*

UPDATING THE RMA INPUT FORM

Back at my computer, I began to consider what I would need to change on the RMA Input form. Much would be similar to what I had done on the previous two forms: I would fill the ComboBoxes with strings that could be selected. I would limit the DBNavigator to the same four buttons as before. I would do some rearranging and resizing of the components.

Beyond that, there were two considerations. First, the DBGrid. These things have scads of options to choose from, and I would need to select those that would make the DBGrid an appropriate device for displaying and selecting items found on invoices. I decided on several. I wanted to show titles, so users would know what they were looking at. I wanted them to be able to resize the columns to their taste. I thought it would look best to show lines between both rows and columns. And I wanted the little arrow that pointed to the selected row.

As for the Tables and DataSources, much was the same, but there were two exceptions: This time, both **RMATable** and **NextRMATable** would *not* be set to **ReadOnly** status. The Input form would be adding and modifying records in the RMA table, and when it was adding records, it would also be updating the number in the Next RMA Number table.

One last addition. I thought it would be nice to add a label over **DescDBMemo**, so I dropped a Label there and named it **DescLabel**. Table 18.14 details all the changes I made to the form.

Table 18.14   *Initial Changes to the RMA Input Form*

Name	Property	Value
AddRMAForm	Left	169
	Top	93
	Width	606
	Height	451
	Caption	Add RMA Record

continued on next page

Table 18.14 *Initial Changes to the RMA Input Form*

continued from previous page

Name	Property	Value
RMALabel	Left	21
	Top	10
	Width	83
	Height	16
	Caption	RMA number
InvoiceLabel	Left	134
	Top	10
	Width	100
	Height	16
	Caption	Invoice number
IssueDateLabel	Left	284
	Top	10
	Width	68
	Height	16
	Caption	Issue date
CompanyLabel	Left	396
	Top	10
	Width	61
	Height	16
	Caption	Company
InitLabel	Left	365
	Top	78
	Width	44
	Height	16
	Caption	Initials

continued on next page

Table 18.14   *Initial Changes to the RMA Input Form*

continued from previous page

Name	Property	Value
StatusLabel	Left	365
	Top	145
	Width	41
	Height	16
	Caption	Status
DescLabel	Left	138
	Top	227
	Width	74
	Height	16
	Caption	Description
RMADBText	Left	21
	Top	31
	Width	89
	Height	17
	DataField	RMA_ID
	DataSource	RMASource
InvoiceDBText	Left	134
	Top	31
	Width	115
	Height	17
	DataField	INV_NUM
	DataSource	InvoiceSource
IssueDBText	Left	284
	Top	31
	Width	88
	Height	17
	DataField	RMA_DATE
	DataSource	RMASource

continued on next page

Table 18.14   *Initial Changes to the RMA Input Form*

continued from previous page

Name	Property	Value
CustomerDBText	Left	396
	Top	31
	Width	188
	Height	17
	DataField	CST_COMPNM
	DataSource	CustomerSource
InitComboBox	Left	365
	Top	99
	Width	81
	Height	24
	Style	csDropDownLIst
	ItemHeight	16
StatusComboBox	Left	365
	Top	164
	Width	172
	Height	24
	Style	csDropDownList
	ItemHeight	16
NavPanel	Left	361
	Top	254
	Width	211
	Height	92
FindBtn	Left	36
	Top	13
	Width	139
	Height	27
	Caption	&Find Invoice

continued on next page

Table 18.14 *Initial Changes to the RMA Input Form*

continued from previous page

Name	Property	Value
OKBtn	Left	407
	Top	376
	Width	76
	Height	27
	Kind	bkOK
CancelBtn	Left	497
	Top	375
	Width	77
	Height	28
	Kind	bkCancel
ItemsDBGrid	Left	17
	Top	64
	Width	322
	Height	149
	DataSource	ItemsSource
	Options	[dgTitles, dgIndicator, dgColumnResize, dgColLines, dgRowLines, dgRowSelect]
DescDBMemo	Left	18
	Top	248
	Width	322
	Height	155
	DataField	RMA_DESC
	DataSource	RMASource
InvoiceNav	Left	35
	Top	48
	Width	141
	Height	25
	DataSource	InvoiceSource
	VisibleButtons	[nbFirst, nbPrior, nbNext, nbLast]

continued on next page

Table 18.14   *Initial Changes to the RMA Input Form*

continued from previous page

Name	Property	Value
RMATable	DatabaseName	BOXLIGHT
	IndexName	RMA_ID
	TableName	RMA.DBF
InvoiceTable	DatabaseName	BOXLIGHT
	IndexName	INV_NUM
	ReadOnly	True
	TableName	INVOICES.DBF
ItemsTable	DatabaseName	BOXLIGHT
	IndexName	ITM_INVNUM
	ReadOnly	True
	TableName	INVITEMS.DBF
EmployeeTable	DatabaseName	BOXLIGHT
	IndexName	EMP_INITS
	ReadOnly	True
	TableName	EMPLOYEE.DBF
CustomerTable	DatabaseName	BOXLIGHT
	IndexName	CST_ID
	ReadOnly	True
	TableName	CUSTOMER.DBF
NextRMATable	DatabaseName	BOXLIGHT
	TableName	RMANXT.DBF
RMASource	AutoEdit	False
	DataSet	RMATable
InvoiceSource	AutoEdit	False
	DataSet	InvoiceTable

continued on next page

Table 18.14 *Initial Changes to the RMA Input Form*

continued from previous page

Name	Property	Value
ItemsSource	AutoEdit	False
	DataSet	ItemsTable
EmployeeSource	AutoEdit	False
	DataSet	EmployeeTable
CustomerSource	AutoEdit	False
	DataSet	CustomerTable
NextRMASource	AutoEdit	False
	DataSet	NextRMATable

I had forgotten to fill the lists in the two ComboBoxes. A simple matter of using the StringList editor again. I decided that for testing purposes, I would enter the initials of five of the employees into the InitComboBox **Items** list, placing them in no particular order. I also made up four status messages for the **StatusComboBox** list. The exact data I entered is shown in Table 18.15.

Once again, I set the **Active** property for all the Table components to **True**. This time I got a pleasant surprise, as **InvoiceDBText** showed the number of the first invoice, and **ItemsDBGrid** showed a list of items. Of course, the name that appeared in **CustomerDBText** was incorrect—since there were no entries in the RMA table, it was merely displaying the first entry in the **Company** table.

These two-way controls are pretty cool, I thought. It's great when you can see real data appearing on your forms during the design phase. Then it occurred

Table 18.15 *Initial Data for the ComboBox String Lists*

InitComboBox	StatusComboBox
CMF	Awaiting return
WJM	Awaiting replacmt
SRL	Completed
BDB	Deleted
BLT	

to me that I was seeing far too much data in **ItemsDBGrid**. When I took a closer look, I could see that every item on every invoice was listed!

Dang! I broke out in a sweat. I examined the properties of **ItemsTable**. Yes, it was connected to the **Invoice** Items table. Yes, it was using its invoice number index. Then I saw the problem: *I had forgotten to set up the master-detail relationship.*

As I had it configured, **ItemsTable** was looking at *every* entry in the Invoice Items table, and displaying them in order by invoice number. I needed to define a master source and a master field, to limit the entries **ItemsTable** would display. I entered the information in Table 18.16.

Dang! No difference. *Why didn't this thing work?* I wondered. Then it hit me. What if the information that Delphi displays in its data-aware controls isn't really "live"—but only a snapshot of what the control saw when the table was made active? I cycled **ItemsTable**'s **Active** property to **False** and back to **True**. The display flashed. Sure enough, now I was seeing only one entry in **ItemsDBGrid**—and its invoice number matched the one in **InvoiceDBText**. I snapped a photograph. It can be seen in Figure 18.5.

Table 18.16   *Additional Changes to the RMA Input Form*

Name	Property	Value
ItemsTable	MasterFields	INV_NUM
	MasterSource	InvoiceSource

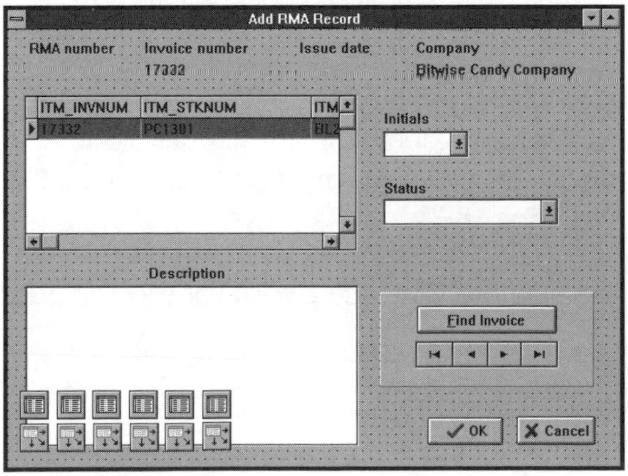

Figure 18.5   *The updated RMA Input form.*

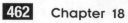

COMPILING AND RUNNING FOR THE FIRST TIME

I caught myself daydreaming about Rhonda. She had been on my mind off and on, ever since I met her yesterday afternoon. So cool. So uncaring. She was unlike any woman I had ever known...

I shook my head in an attempt to clear the cobwebs from my brain. The long night's work was beginning to take its toll. I had to get my mind back on the project at hand.

Right now, I really needed to see the fruits of my labor. I had to see the demo run. Yes, it would be pretty crippled, but I wanted to get the "feel" of the program I had been creating for the last several hours.

To accomplish that feat, I would have to write a couple of simple event handlers, so the Product Information and RMA Management forms could be selected from **MainMenu**, and so the RMA Input form could be activated from the RMA Management form. I would also have to make sure that when one form called up another, the second form was made known to the first by including its unit name in the calling form's **uses** clause.

I switched to Delphi's code editor and brought up the **MainForm** unit file, called MAINUNIT.PAS. To its **uses** clause I added the names of the units for the Product Information and RMA Management forms. The result is shown in Listing 18.1.

LISTING 18.1   The modified uses declaration for MAINUNIT.PAS

```
uses
  SysUtils, WinTypes, WinProcs, Messages, Classes, Graphics, Controls,
  Forms, Dialogs, Menus, ProdInfo, RMAMgmt;
```

Looking at the menu on the Main form, I clicked on *System* and then clicked on *Product Info* to reveal the default event handler code. I simply wanted to bring up the Product Information form as a modal dialog. The event handler I wrote appears in Listing 18.2.

LISTING 18.2   The simple OnClick event for the Product Info choice

```
procedure TMainForm.SystemMenuProductClick(Sender: TObject);
begin
  ProdInfoForm.ShowModal;
end;
```

I did the same for the RMA Management choice, this time selecting System and then RMA Management from the menu. The event handler for that one is shown in Listing 18.3.

LISTING 18.3   The simple OnClick event for the RMA Management choice

```
procedure TMainForm.SystemMenuRMAClick(Sender: TObject);
begin
 RMAMgmtForm.ShowModal;
end;
```

To launch the RMA Input form from the RMA Management form, I would first have to make the RMA Management form aware of the other's existence. I modified the **uses** clause in RMAMGMT.PAS to that shown in Listing 18.4.

LISTING 18.4   The modified uses declaration for RMAMGMT.PAS

```
uses
 SysUtils, WinTypes, WinProcs, Messages, Classes, Graphics, Controls,
 Forms, Dialogs, DBCtrls, StdCtrls, Buttons, ExtCtrls, DB, DBTables,
 RMAAdd;
```

One last little chore. I needed to write a simple OnClick event handler for the Add button on the RMA Management form, so I could activate the RMA Input form. I double-clicked on the **AddBtn** component and wrote the event handler code in Listing 18.5.

LISTING 18.5   The simple OnClick event for AddBtn

```
procedure TRMAMgmtForm.AddBtnClick(Sender: TObject);
begin
 AddRMAForm.ShowModal;
end;
```

Great—now I should be able to activate all the forms as modal dialogs. But how would I terminate them? As it turns out, BitBtn objects that have their **Kind** properties set to **bkOK** or **bkCancel** will, by default, always terminate a modal dialog when clicked. The OK and Cancel buttons I had placed on the RMA Input form automatically did this, and because I had set the **Kind** property on the Done buttons on the other forms to **bkOK**, I was covered there, too. I was ready for take-off.

I compiled and ran my first version of the demo. Many of the controls didn't work properly yet, but I did get a feel of the program's operation. The forms came up when I selected them from the menu or clicked the Add button. They went away when I clicked OK, Cancel, or Done. **InvoiceNav** was working nicely on the RMA Input form. When I clicked on its buttons, the invoice number changed in **InvoiceDBText**—and the correct item (or items) for the selected invoice showed up in **ItemsDBGrid**. I liked it. I liked it a *lot*.

The wind had kicked up, and I could hear the sliding glass door rattling in its tracks. Torrents of rain were now smashing themselves against the glass with each gust of wind. I thought of poor Mewnix out there, making his way in that raging storm. But he's the one who asked to go out. And we must all live with our own decisions.

If all went well, by sometime this afternoon I would be delivering a finished demo to Dave Carson at Boxlight. I wondered what the weather would be like then. I switched on the radio and hunted along the dial, looking for a current weather report. I finally found it: "Rain, turning to rain with wind, switching to rain with showers by afternoon."

I should have just stuck with the only proven system for forecasting the weather in Western Washington. It had been revealed to me a couple of years ago, while talking to an age-challenged native Washingtonian, a man with a scraggly gray beard and a dishpan face.

"Funny weather you have around here," I said to him.

"Yep. Some folks seem to think so."

" I mean it changes. A *lot*. It's unpredictable." I pursued.

"It's only unpredictable to those what don't know the signs," he countered.

"So tell me," I asked, pulling up close to him. "What are they? How can I tell what the weather is going to do?"

He looked me up and down for several seconds, as if deciding whether I was trustworthy enough to share his secret. He took a couple of puffs on the Meerschaum that had been resting in his palm. Then he turned back to me.

"Well, if you can see Mount Rainier, it's gonna rain."

"And what if I *can't* see Mount Rainier?" I asked, leaning forward to catch his every word.

"Well, then," he said, "it's *already raining.*"

I snapped off the radio. Its clock read 3:07. I knew the next couple of hours would be eventful.

But I didn't have the slightest idea how eventful they were going to be.

A Strange Turn of Events

Don Taylor

And now, the Main Event: Creating the code that ties all of the far-flung forms together. Can Ace do it before dawn—or his heart—breaks?

Whether or not I could see Mount Rainier, one thing was for sure: It was already raining. As I stood at the window, peering through the slit between the curtains, I could barely make out the street light that stood not more than 50 feet away.

The coffeemaker was empty again, so I rummaged through the refrigerator, hoping to find some beans I had previously overlooked. As luck would have it, I found one remaining bag of Kona Volcanic Blend in the freezer. This was the last of the specialty coffees I bought when Helen and I visited Hawaii last year, and it was really great stuff. I tossed some of the beans in the grinder and then put on a pot on to brew.

Step 4 of the design process had been completed. I had made the major property settings for the forms and components, and the application now had a degree of functionality. I would now create event handlers that would increase that functionality by providing interaction between some of the components themselves, and between components and the information in the database.

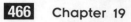

STEP 5: CREATE THE EVENT HANDLERS

Each of the forms would require some event handling. The Main form would only need the ability to exit the program without having to use its control box or the Alt-F4 hot key. The Product Information form's additions would be minimal as well—I just needed to hook the TabSet and the Notebook together, and connect the ComboBox so it could select product records.

The RMA Management and RMA Input forms would be somewhat more demanding. I knew for certain I would have to "wire" the Add, Edit, and Delete buttons. Beyond that, I wasn't exactly sure what would be required. I would just have to take it one step at a time.

Adding Event Handling to the Main Form

I first looked at the two routines I had already added to the Main form, **SystemMenuProductClick** and **SystemMenuRMAClick**. In each case, all I wanted was to call up a form as a modal dialog. Since I didn't need to make any decisions based on what happened while it was active, I decided those two very simple event handlers were exactly what was needed.

All that remained was to provide a means for the user to shut down the application by selecting Exit from the menu. I clicked on that item on the main form's menu, and then I created the handler in Listing 19.1.

Listing 19.1   The simple OnClick handler for the Exit menu choice

```
procedure TMainForm.FileMenuExitClick(Sender: TObject);
begin
 Close;
end;
```

Adding Event Handling to the Product Information Form

I decided my first goal was to get the Notebook pages working with the TabSet component. That's what I call *The What*. Making it happen is simply a matter of coordinating the tab captions with the page captions, and the tab index with the page index. That's *The How*. I was to discover that in Delphi programming, there is one more very important principle: *The When*. When something gets done—and how often it gets done—is determined by which event you tap into to accomplish *The What*.

When in the Course of Human Events...

Each component has its own mixture of events to select from, and that includes forms. Among the nearly two dozen events that apply to forms, the two most frequently used are OnCreate and OnActivate.

OnCreate normally gets called only once during the execution of a program—when the form is first created. Naturally, this is the event to use when you want to initialize a component on a form (or the form itself) as the program starts.

OnActivate, on the other hand, gets called when the application gives the focus to the form. This event doesn't occur if the user is shifting back and forth between Windows applications. It only happens when focus is shifted around within the Delphi application. One example of this is when one form calls the **ShowModal** method of another form.

It was fairly obvious to me that the link between the Notebook and the TabSet would only need to be established once, and that task should therefore be taken care of by the OnCreate event for the Product Information form. The handler I wrote appears in Listing 19.2.

Setting the Default Page...

When you're working with a tabbed Notebook, it's convenient to use the Object Inspector to switch between Notebook pages to work with the components on them. When Delphi compiles and runs a program, however, it uses the current property values—which means it may select a page other than the one you had planned. It's a good idea to always include a line such as

```
Notebook1.PageIndex := 0;
```

in the OnCreate event handler for the form containing a Notebook.

Listing 19.2 The simple OnCreate handler for the Product Information form

```
procedure TProdInfoForm.FormCreate(Sender: TObject);
begin
  { Hook the Notebook pages to the Tabs }
  ProductNotebook.PageIndex := 0;
  ProductTabSet.Tabs := ProductNotebook.Pages;
  ProductNotebook.PageIndex := ProductTabSet.TabIndex;
end;
```

Once the link is made, it will have to be maintained. Each time one of the tabs was clicked, the Notebook would have to synchronize its pages with the tabs. Obviously, this would be a job related to the OnClick event for the TabSet. The handler code I created is shown in Listing 19.3.

Listing 19.3   The simple OnClick handler for the TabSet

```
procedure TProdInfoForm.ProductTabSetClick(Sender: TObject);
begin
  { Make the Notebook's page index follow the selected tab }
  ProductNotebook.PageIndex := ProductTabSet.TabIndex;
end;
```

I figured the code I had written would fully take care of the Notebook and the TabSet. Now for the stock number ComboBox. I had my choice of several events, but I chose the OnChange event. When the contents of **StkNumComboBox** changed, I wanted to move to the record in the Products table that corresponded to the new selection. That entailed a classic search for an exact match between a table index and the stock number selected from the ComboBox string list. The process requires several steps. First, you disable all the table's controls (so the user doesn't see any thrashing in any linked controls while the search is taking place). Then you move to the first record in the table, so you'll always find the first possible match in the table. Then you put the table in search mode with SetKey, set the field to search on to the value you want to match, and go for it. When the process is through and the new record is selected, you re-enable the table controls. The code I wrote for the stock number ComboBox is shown in Listing 19.4.

Listing 19.4   The OnChange handler for the stock number ComboBox

```
procedure TProdInfoForm.StkNumComboBoxChange(Sender: TObject);
begin
  with ProductsTable do
    begin
      DisableControls;
      First;
      SetKey;
      FieldByName('PRD_STKNUM').AsString := StkNumComboBox.Text;
      GoToKey;
      EnableControls;
    end; { with }
end;
```

Everything appeared to work, except for one thing—although the defaults picked up the first item on the list (the CS1200), nothing showed up in **StkNumComboBox** until a selection was made. I decided it was another one of those situations where the ComboBox needed to be forced into synchronization, so I added the following line at the end of the OnCreate handler for the Product Information form:

```
StkNumComboBox.ItemIndex := 0;
```

I compiled and ran the application again. This time everything on the Product Information form worked.

There was one bit of housekeeping I needed to take care of. When I set the properties on **StkNumComboBox** earlier this evening, I had hard coded in some values using the StringList editor, so I would be able to test my work while keeping things as simple as possible. But I'm certain that Professor Carruthers wouldn't approve of such a practice outside of a troubleshooting situation, even for a demo like this.

As a former P.I., I know that data is a lot like evidence in a murder case. You never want to disturb it, unless you can avoid it. That's why I enabled the **ReadOnly** property on the reference tables. And as any mouthpiece will tell you, the best testimony in a court of law comes not from hearsay, but from an actual eyewitness. That's why you always compare stuff directly with the contents of a table, whenever possible, due to the effects of Ace's First Law: *Reality will change when you least expect it.*

Take the situation with Boxlight, for instance. If I hard coded in the stock numbers for their product line, I would have to go in and change the program every time they added a new product. The smart thing to do here was to read in the stock numbers from the Product table, in indexed order, and then store them directly in the ComboBox's StringList. That sounded to me like it should be done only once, at program startup, and that meant using the Product Information form's OnCreate handler. The code I added to that handler appears in Listing 19.5.

Listing 19.5 Additional code for the form's OnCreate handler

```
with ProductTable do
  begin
    StkNumComboBox.Items.Clear;
    First;
```

```
    while not EOF do
      begin
      StkNumComboBox.Items.Add(FieldByName('PRD_STKNUM').AsString);
      Next;
    end; { while }
  end; { with }
```

Now then. I'm not generally noted for my photographic memory, and that's why I relentlessly document details. So I'll make a record here in my casebook of what the code in Listing 19.5 really does.

It first erases whatever is already in the list—the stuff that may be lurking in the list as a result of prior testing. That's accomplished by using the **Clear** method of the ComboBox's **Items** list. The next part of the code points the table to its first record, because I'm going to access every record, from start to finish. The **while** loop accomplishes that, pointing the table to its next record each time through the loop, until an EOF (End of File) is detected. Each time through the loop, **Items**' **Add** method is called to append the current product stock number to the list. All in all, pretty simple (or as we professional programmers say, "elegant"). Oh, one more thing: I also added a line near the end of the handler that would force the Product table back to its first record. That way the program would always start by displaying the first item in the catalog.

I compiled and ran the demo again. This time everything on the Product Information form performed flawlessly. Clicking on the ComboBox showed all five of the products, listed in ascending alphanumeric order, just as it is indexed. I was finished with this form for the time being. A snapshot of the "running" form is shown in Figure 19.1. The complete listing of the unit appears in Listing 19.6.

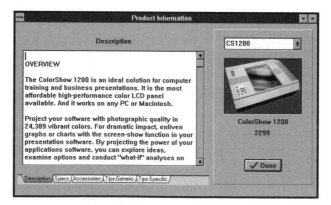

Figure 19.1 *The Product Information form in operation.*

Listing 19.6   Complete version of the Product Information form

```
{————————————————————————————————}
{                  The Boxlight Demo                     }
{        PRODINFO.PAS : Product Information Form         }
{              By Ace Breakpoint, N.T.P.                 }
{                 Assisted by Don Taylor                 }
{                                                        }
{ Chapter 19 version of the form that displays           }
{ information about selected products from the           }
{ Boxlight Corporation's catalog.                        }
{ Written for *Delphi Programming Explorer*              }
{ Copyright (c) 1995 The Coriolis Group, Inc.            }
{                 Last Updated 3/30/95                   }
{————————————————————————————————}

unit Prodinfo;

interface

uses
    SysUtils, WinTypes, WinProcs, Messages, Classes, Graphics, Controls,
    Forms, Dialogs, StdCtrls, DBCtrls, ExtCtrls, Tabs, Buttons, DB, DBTables,
    DBLookup;

type
    TProdInfoForm = class(TForm)
       ProductNotebook: TNotebook;
       ProductTabSet: TTabSet;
       ProductPanel: TPanel;
       DescLabel: TLabel;
       DescMemo: TDBMemo;
       PictDBImage: TDBImage;
       DoneBtn: TBitBtn;
       ProductsTable: TTable;
       ProductsSource: TDataSource;
       SpecsLabel: TLabel;
       SpecsDBMemo: TDBMemo;
       AccessLabel: TLabel;
       AccessDBMemo: TDBMemo;
       GenTipsLabel: TLabel;
       GenTipsDBMemo: TDBMemo;
       GenTipsTable: TTable;
       GenTipsSource: TDataSource;
       TipsLabel: TLabel;
       TipsDBMemo: TDBMemo;
       ProductNameDBText: TDBText;
       PriceDBText: TDBText;
       StkNumComboBox: TComboBox;
       procedure FormCreate(Sender: TObject);
       procedure ProductTabSetClick(Sender: TObject);
       procedure StkNumComboBoxChange(Sender: TObject);
    private
       { Private declarations }
    public
```

```
      { Public declarations }
    end;

var
   ProdInfoForm: TProdInfoForm;

implementation

{$R *.DFM}

procedure TProdInfoForm.FormCreate(Sender: TObject);
begin
 { Hook the Notebook pages to the Tabs }
 ProductNotebook.PageIndex := 0;
 ProductTabSet.Tabs := ProductNotebook.Pages;
 ProductNotebook.PageIndex := ProductTabSet.TabIndex;

 { Load the Stock Number ComboBox }
 with ProductsTable do
   begin
    StkNumComboBox.Items.Clear;
    First;
    while not EOF do
      begin
       StkNumComboBox.Items.Add(FieldByName('PRD_STKNUM').AsString);
       Next;
      end; { while }
   end; { with }

 { Make sure the combo box and table are at the beginning }
 StkNumComboBox.ItemIndex := 0;
 ProductsTable.First;
end;

procedure TProdInfoForm.ProductTabSetClick(Sender: TObject);
begin
 { Make the Notebook's page index follow the selected tab }
 ProductNotebook.PageIndex := ProductTabSet.TabIndex;
end;

procedure TProdInfoForm.StkNumComboBoxChange(Sender: TObject);
begin
 with ProductsTable do
   begin
    DisableControls;
    First;
    SetKey;
    FieldByName('PRD_STKNUM').AsString := StkNumComboBox.Text;
    GoToKey;
    EnableControls;
   end; { with }
end;

end.
```

My First Shot at the RMA Forms

With the simple work out of the way, I proceeded to higher ground. I figured that, due to the interaction that would be required between the RMA Management and RMA Input forms, I would need to make a couple of runs at them.

The Kona had been steeping for almost half an hour, and I had been so absorbed that I hadn't even taken time to get some of it. I stood up and waded back over to the kitchenette, filling my mug with the powerfully caffeinated brew. It had been several hours since I had eaten anything, so I began searching through the cupboards for something to eat. To my dismay, I discovered that the high-pressure fire hoses had forced water into all the cupboards and drawers, soaking just about everything in sight. I did manage to find a large tin partially full of animal cookies. These were the same cookies I had bought several years ago, when I would sometimes baby-sit Rodney while Deucey was attending the Hackensack Beautician's School. The tin was a little rusty, making it difficult to remove the lid. I finally pried it off and got at the contents. The cookies were stale. *Very* stale. Like Mewnix, I would have to accept what was available. I grabbed the tin and the coffee and brought them back to my desk.

I was planning to use the RMA Input form for both appending new records and editing existing ones. To do that, I declared a public variable on the Input form that would tell the Input form whether it was editing or appending. The variable would be set by the Management form, just before it called up the Input form.

I would also need to provide a mechanism that would keep the Management and Input forms in lockstep with each other. Each would have a Table object that would be connected to RMA.DBF. It would be my job to make sure that when a user selected an RMA to edit from the Management form, the Input form would grab the same record. As with controlling the editing/appending operation, I could achieve control of RMA table synchronization through the use of a public variable on the Input form. The Management form would set it before calling the Input form to edit the data. Appending new records would work in reverse: The Input form would set the variable when the form had completed its work, so the Management form could automatically move to the new record on the return.

But what types of variables were these to be? It didn't take a rocket scientist to figure out that the variable controlling the editing/appending process should be a **Boolean** type. And what of the variable that would synchronize tables on a record— should that be a **Word** or **Longint**, pointing to the proper record number?

Sorry, wrong answer. In the old days, before client/server databases, it was very common to work with records by referring to their physical numbers. Nowadays, more than one person on a network can be looking at records in the same table. In fact, it's possible for more than one person to be adding or editing records in a table at the same time! That means if I were editing record number 100, and someone at another networked computer inserted a new record between, say, 59 and 60, then the actual number of my record would become 101. If I were to finish editing my record and tell the table to store it back at position 100, I would be wreaking some serious havoc with the table's integrity!

Instead, modern systems let you access tables with an index. When you finish editing your record, the system puts the record in its proper place, even if the table has changed.

The variable I would need to synchronize the tables, then, must be one that will contain the *value found in the indexed field*—in this case, RMA_ID. I decided to use a string data type.

The Input form would also be responsible for managing the next RMA sequence number used when appending new RMA records. This variable would hold the number assigned to the next RMA, and it would be used to update the Next RMA table when the appending process was completed successfully. I decided to use an integer. Since its purpose was solely limited to the operation of the Input form, I declared it to be **private**. Listing 19.7 is a snapshot of the public and private declarations I added to the RMA Input form.

Listing 19.7 Public and private declarations on the RMA Input form

```
private
   { Private declarations }
   RMANum : Integer;
public
   { Public declarations }
   RMAIndexStr : String;
   Editing : Boolean;
end;
```

With the declarations in place, I would now make sure the new variables got properly initialized each time the program was run. If I initialized them each time the form was activated, I would be overriding the settings made from the Management form. The logical choice was to initialize them in the OnCreate handler. That piece of work is highlighted in Listing 19.8.

Listing 19.8   OnCreate handler for the RMA Input form

```
procedure TAddRMAForm.FormCreate(Sender: TObject);
begin
 RMANum := 0;
 RMAIndexStr := '';
 Editing := False;
end;
```

I took a gulp of Java and absent-mindedly reached for the tin to grab another handful of cookies. I accidentally knocked the can over. I attempted to recover, but when my arm shot out to catch the can, my fingertips hit the side of the can, causing it to fly upward with a spinning motion, spraying the remainder of its contents in every possible direction onto the wet floor.

Dang! I said to myself. *That was the last bit of food in my apart—er, office.* I consoled myself that I would be going out for breakfast in the Next Chapter. I forged onward.

I decided to set up a minimal mechanism, to test my initializations and to demonstrate whether or not the Add and Edit buttons on the Management form were operational. When either button was clicked, I would first want to set the edit/append control variable, and then I would store the value of the current index in the Management form's RMA table to the Input form's index string variable. At that point, all I would have to do is call up the Input form as a modal dialog. The OnClick handlers I wrote are detailed in Listing 19.9.

Listing 19.9   OnClick handlers for the RMA Management Add and Edit buttons

```
procedure TRMAMgmtForm.AddBtnClick(Sender: TObject);
begin
 { Tell the Add/Edit form we're appending }
 AddRMAForm.Editing := False;
 AddRMAForm.RMAIndexStr := RMATable.FieldByName('RMA_ID').AsString;
 AddRMAForm.ShowModal;
end;

procedure TRMAMgmtForm.EditBtnClick(Sender: TObject);
begin
 { Tell the Add/Edit form we're editing }
 AddRMAForm.Editing := True;
 AddRMAForm.RMAIndexStr := RMATable.FieldByName('RMA_ID').AsString;
 AddRMAForm.ShowModal;
end;
```

I had to perform one more task before I could make my first test. I needed the routine that would be called when the Input form was activated by the Management form. This time around, I would just place a different caption on the Input form, based on whether I was supposed to be appending or editing a record. This simple handler is shown in Listing 19.10.

Listing 19.10   Simple OnActivate handler for the RMA Input form

```
procedure TAddRMAForm.FormActivate(Sender: TObject);
begin
 if Editing
   then begin { Edit the specified record }
         Caption := 'Edit RMA Record';
        end
   else begin { Append a new record }
         Caption := 'Add RMA Record';
        end;
end;
```

I compiled and ran the demo, this time selecting the RMA Management form from the Main form's menu. Sure enough, it seemed to work. If I clicked the Add button on the Management form, the Input form came up with the caption 'Add RMA Record'; if I clicked Edit, the caption said 'Edit RMA Record'. I was hot!

I had barely made a dent in what had to be done, but I had some fundamental concepts in place. I stood up and stretched, trying to clear my brain. I was pleased to see that most of the water had drained away, perhaps into the office below mine. I walked over to the phone.

I had heard the soft buzz of the phone several times during the past hour or so, which meant it had probably survived the onslaught of water. I might even have several messages waiting for me. When I checked, I found I had only one. It was a mysterious message from Helen.

"Ace. I've been trying to call you for more than an hour. I know you're there, and just not answering your phone. So I'm going to leave you this message, in hope that you get it in time: *Something we both treasured has died, and we need to make arrangements to bury it.* I'll be waiting for you at Sonja's, but only until 4 am. Please come. For old time's sake."

I hadn't heard from her in nearly two weeks, and now I get this bizarre message. What on earth could it mean? I didn't have a clue, but it sounded like Life and Death. My watch told me I had only 10 minutes to get to Sonja's, so I grabbed my car keys and sailed toward the door.

The porch light flashed brightly and then burned out when I flipped the switch. I didn't want to take time to replace it right now, so I groped my way through the dark and the rain to get to the car. In the process I managed to trip over a hunk of curbing, which sent me flying headlong onto the asphalt, tearing my pants and twisting my ankle. I picked myself up and limped to the driver's door and climbed in. After all, I thought, my ankle would gradually heal with time. Right now, I had to make it to that appointment with Helen. I dropped the lever into Drive and punched the accelerator.

• • •

It was 4:03 when I wheeled into Sonja's Trucker Cafe and Service Station. It was one of those typical 24-hour "All you can stand" buffet restaurants, and the only place in town where you could get gas while you ate. I drove past the pumps and pulled my car into the first open space.

Once inside, I headed for the dining room, hoping that Helen would still be there. I spotted her at a table in the far corner, just as she was getting up to leave.

"I thought maybe you weren't coming," she said. She laid her purse on the table and sat down again. I pulled up a chair and sat facing her.

"I just got your message a few minutes ago."

"How's Mewnix?" She was obviously distraught about something. Her eyes darted back and forth, never meeting mine.

"He's doing pretty good. He misses you." She didn't respond, so I followed up. "How have you been?"

"Just fine." She was lying. I didn't know why, but she was as nervous as a cat in a room full of rocking chairs. She seemed to be on the verge of tears. She looked at my face and gave a small start.

"Oh—how did *this* happen?" she asked, automatically reaching out to touch my bandaged lip. She took a closer look. "Do you know you don't have any eyebrows?"

"Just hum a few bars," I replied. "Hey, you ought to see the other guy."

"I see." She suddenly became withdrawn. She stared at the table for several seconds, and I got the distinct impression she was trying to compose herself.

Then she lifted her soft brown peepers, making full eye contact with me for the first time. Her hands were visibly shaking.

"I guess I should get right to the point," she said hesitantly. "Did you get a call from someone today, asking you to meet him for coffee?"

Who could forget that crazy meeting with Mellow, I thought to myself. "Yes, I did. Why do you ask?"

"Well, I suppose you probably thought it was a little strange and all, right out of the blue."

"Strange doesn't begin to describe it, Baby," I said, chuckling to myself.

"I told him I should be the one to tell you first, but for some reason he just insisted." She seemed a little bit relieved. "Anyway, I'm glad you understand," she said, forcing a smile. "You and I had some pretty good times together, didn't we?"

Something was very, very wrong. I didn't understand what she was saying, and I was going to get to the bottom of this, fast.

"What do you mean, '*had* some good times'," I demanded.

I could see panic building in her eyes. "You mean he didn't tell you about *us*— about the new relationship?" She could see by the look on my face I had no idea what she was talking about. "That's why he was supposed to meet with you." She struck her fist on the table in dismay. "Oh, I just *knew* I should have told you personally. After all these years I felt I owed you that much. But Mel—"

"What?!" I gasped, cutting her off. Suddenly it all came rushing back like a paisley tie to a department store. *So that's what Mellow was leading up to with his lecture on relationships*, I thought. *And why he said it was going to affect our futures*. I finally found my voice.

"Are you honestly trying to tell me you're dumping me for that—*that 'Mellow' guy?*" I asked incredulously. "He's nothing but a plastic character—he isn't even for real!"

"I suppose you could look at it that way," she replied, a bit defensively. "He *is* a bit unusual, and not at all like you."

Now I was really distraught. "He's not at all like *anybody*," I countered. "Don't you understand? His bits have shifted into the overflow register. He doesn't even know who he is!"

"Apparently neither do *you*." Suddenly she was steamed. "Ace Breakpoint, when I first met you, I thought you were one of the most stubborn, hard-headed people in the world. You were a tough-minded, no nonsense kind of guy with a bad suit and an attitude to match. But I loved you for it. A girl like me needs someone like that—someone she can take care of. Someone she can love so much that it hurts just to think of letting go."

"I'm still that same guy," I argued.

"No, Ace. Ever since you started hanging around with that crowd at school, you've changed. Little by little, you've become someone I no longer know. You won't communicate honestly with me. You can't even own your own feelings any more. You don't know how that hurts me."

"I feel your pain," I said.

"You may have been stubborn, but at least you had your principles and you stuck to them. I liked that. I *needed* that. But you've gone completely wishy-washy. I want a man who stands up for what he believes."

"Whatever works for you." I couldn't understand where she was going with this.

"You were your own man, strong and independent," she said. "Now look at you. You can't even accept responsibility for your own actions."

"Hey, that's where you're wrong," I protested. "I accept full responsibility as a victim of our society and my environment."

She sighed deeply, and then stood up. "I guess there's nothing more to say, Ace." Mascara-stained tears were flowing down her cheeks. She looked me straight in the eye one last time. "Here's looking at *you*, Kid," she said, bravely wiping the tears from her face. She grabbed her purse and strode briskly across the dining room.

"Helen—wait!" I tried to catch her, but by the time I hobbled to the door, she was nowhere in sight.

"Too bad about the girl," said a gravelly voice from behind me.

I turned to see who had made the remark. It was Sonja, who was manning the cash register. She was a 240-pound ex-pro wrestler with wayward teeth and hair best combed with a spaghetti fork. Some of the truck drivers said she looked like the runner-up in a Marjorie Main lookalike contest. I preferred to think of her as *femininely challenged*.

"What did you say?" I asked confusedly.

"I said, too bad about the girl, Dearie. She not only broke your heart, she also left you the check. That'll be five bucks, even."

I reached in my pocket and pulled out my money clip. "Keep the change," I said, peeling off a five-spot and tossing it on the counter. I reached into the fish bowl and grabbed a complimentary book of matches. Then I limped over to the door.

When it rains, it pours, I thought to myself. *But every cloud has a silver lining. And things are always darkest before the dawn.* I decided I would go back to the office to make hay while the sun shines. I slipped out into the dark and stormy night.

• • •

MY SECOND SHOT AT THE RMA FORMS

I walked back into the office in a daze. Through no fault of my own, tonight I had lost my girlfriend of four years. My honey. My *squeeze.* It would be the most natural thing in the world for me to slip into a whirling cesspool of self-analysis. But I couldn't let that happen to me. I decided to lose myself totally in the project I was working on. I refilled my mug and resumed my work on the RMA forms.

I decided to focus my efforts on the OnActivate handler for the Input form. It was here that much of the mechanics of preparing the form for its appending and editing tasks would take place. Until I had some records in the RMA table, I had no way of testing any routines I might write for editing. So I zeroed in on the portion of the handler that would add records to the RMA table.

Several things must take place in order to append a new record. One of the most important is to fill the record with acceptable data. This prevents the user from unwittingly appending a record with invalid data (including blank fields) in it. I thought a few moments, then I wrote down this laundry list of steps that must be performed:

1. Append a blank record to the RMA table.
2. Get the next available RMA number and put it in the record.
3. Put today's date in the Issued and Updated date fields.

4. Get the very first item on the first invoice and store it in the record.

5. Get the Customer ID on that first invoice and put it in the record.

6. Get the first set of initials from the Employee list and stuff them in the record.

7. Finally, store the default status level code in the record.

The first task was the easiest. I simply added the line

```
RMATable.Append;
```

to the code, to put the table in its append mode.

Getting the Next RMA Number and Dates

To do the work of creating the RMA number string, I needed a working string variable, so I created a **var** declaration for the handler. I added the lines

```
var
 s : String;
```

The procedure would be to set the form's **RMANum** variable from the **NextRMA** table, then turn it into some sort of string I could use for testing purposes (I would come up with the exact form sometime later). Next, I would store today's date in the appropriate fields in the new RMA record. The code is shown in Listing 19.11.

Listing 19.11 Adding an RMA number and dates to the new record

```
{ Set up the RMA number and the issue and update dates }
RMANum := NextRMATable.FieldByName('RXT_RMANUM').AsInteger;
Str(RMANum, s);
s := 'XXX' + s; { I'll create a proper RMA string later... }
RMATable.FieldByName('RMA_ID').AsString := s;
RMATable.FieldByName('RMA_DATE').AsString := DateToStr(Date);
RMATable.FieldByName('RMA_UPDATE').AsString := DateToStr(Date);
```

Getting Invoice-Related Stuff into the Record

Once again, this was a pretty straightforward task. It amounted to making sure the Invoices and Invoice Items tables were pointing to their first records, and then copying information from those tables to the RMA table. The code I wrote is shown in Listing 19.12.

Listing 19.12 Adding invoice data to the new record

```
{ Set the invoice and items tables to their first records }
InvoiceTable.First;
ItemsTable.First;

{ Set up the default values }
RMATable.FieldByName('RMA_INVNUM').AsString
   := InvoiceTable.FieldByName('INV_NUM').AsString;
RMATable.FieldByName('RMA_STKNUM').AsString
   := ItemsTable.FieldByName('ITM_STKNUM').AsString;
RMATable.FieldByName('RMA_SERNUM').AsString
   := ItemsTable.FieldByName('ITM_SERNUM').AsString;
RMATable.FieldByName('RMA_CUSTID').AsString
   := InvoiceTable.FieldByName('INV_CUSTID').AsString;
```

Adding the Info from the ComboBoxes

Getting the employee initials and the status level was a snap. As a general rule, though, I wouldn't know what state those controls were in. So I first had to initialize them. The code appears in Listing 19.13.

Listing 19.13 Gathering default data from the ComboBoxes

```
{ Get the default employee initials }
InitComboBox.ItemIndex := 0;
RMATable.FieldByName('RMA_INITS').AsString
   := InitComboBox.Text;

{ Get the default status information }
StatusComboBox.ItemIndex := 0;
RMATable.FieldByName('RMA_STATUS').AsInteger := 0;
```

Before I could test my new routine, I needed to provide a way to post the new record to the RMA table, and to advance the Next RMA number—if I was actually appending and not editing. The logical place for this would be in the OnClick event handler for the OK button. The code was easy to write. It's shown in Listing 19.14.

Listing 19.14 Initial OnClick handler for the OK button

```
procedure TAddRMAForm.OKBtnClick(Sender: TObject);
begin
 RMATable.Post;

 if not Editing
   then begin { We must have appended a new RMA }

          { Increment the RMA next-number counter }
          Inc(RMANum);
```

```
        { Stuff the new number in the Next RMA Table }
        with NextRMATable do
         begin
           Edit;
           FieldByName('RXT_RMANUM').AsInteger := RMANum;
           Post;
         end; { with }
       end;
end;
```

I compiled and ran the demo again, clicking the Add button on the RMA Management form. My default data showed up perfectly on the Input form. I was able to navigate my way through invoices. The ComboBoxes worked fine. I clicked the OK button and returned to the Management form. I expected to see the data appear there, but I was in for a surprise. The fields were just as they were when I left—and the Navigator control was still disabled, indicating there were still no records in the RMA table.

What had gone wrong? I wondered. I was *sure* I had added a record. I clicked on Add again, then on OK. Same result. I quit the application and examined my code, but I still couldn't see anything wrong. I ran the demo again. This time, both the records were there! Just as I had expected, the fields contained the data I had initialized them with. The only difference between the two records was the RMA number, which meant my RMA numbering routine was working. Of course, the customer information and the product name were incorrect, because I had done nothing to the Management form to make it locate the proper records in the Customer and Product tables. And the status message label was still blank, because I had not assigned any value to it.

Why were the two records missing? I was convinced it had something to do with the way the Management form was updating its display. I would keep that in mind for later. Right now, it was time to work on the editing portion of the Input form's OnActivate handler.

Professor Carruthers taught us one valuable lesson: Editing data is like watching the ocean waves roll in and out. When you begin an edit, data rolls into the form. When you complete the edit, data rolls back out again.

In this case, that meant to edit the data in a specified record, I would need to fill the components on the form with the data from the tables. When the editing (or appending of a new record) is complete, the data in the controls is rolled into the record and posted to the tables. I worked out a list of tasks that I would need to accomplish to initialize the Input form for the editing of a record:

1. Go to the specified RMA record.
2. Go to the specified invoice record.
3. Go to the specified item record.
4. Put the RMA table into its editing mode.
5. Put the initials in their ComboBox.
6. Put the status message in its ComboBox.

Moving to the Specified RMA and Invoice Records

The RMA table has to locate the record that matches the index passed to the Input form by the Management form through the string variable **RMAIndexStr**. Once this record is found, it's an easy matter to find the corresponding invoice record by looking for a match with the RMA_INVNUM field in the RMA table. My code for this appears in Listing 19.15.

Listing 19.15 Locating the RMA and Invoice records

```
{ Go to the specified RMA record }
RMATable.DisableControls;
RMATable.First;
RMATable.SetKey;
RMATable.FieldByName('RMA_ID').AsString := RMAIndexStr;
RMATable.GotoKey;
RMATable.EnableControls;

{ Go to appropriate invoice record }
InvoiceTable.DisableControls;
InvoiceTable.First;
InvoiceTable.SetKey;
InvoiceTable.FieldByName('INV_NUM').AsString
   := RMATable.FieldByName('RMA_INVNUM').AsString;
InvoiceTable.GotoKey;
InvoiceTable.EnableControls;
```

Moving to the Specified Item Record and Enabling the Edit

This would be a little trickier. Because the Items table is in a master-detail relationship with the Invoices table, the only items seen by the Items table are those that match the invoice number in the record currently selected in the Invoices table. The Items table, when subjected to a master-detail relationship, becomes in effect a tiny, filtered table that contains at most only a handful of records. In fact, in many cases (where there is but one item on an invoice) there is only a single record in the filtered Items table.

The master-detail link guaranteed there was already a match on the invoice number. Now all I had to do was find a match on the item's product ID number *and* its serial number. I would have to begin at the start of the Items table (actually, the first item in the filtered version of the Items table) and step through each item, until a match is found on both RMA_STKNUM and RMA_SERNUM. The first one to match wins. Once I had my item, I would initiate the editing process. Listing 19.16 contains the code.

Listing 19.16   Locating the Item record

```
{ Go to the appropriate item record that matches
  the stock number AND the serial number }
ItemsTable.DisableControls;
ItemsTable.First;

while not ItemsTable.EOF
    and ((ItemsTable.FieldByName('ITM_STKNUM').AsString
            <> RMATable.FieldByName('RMA_STKNUM').AsString)
    or (ItemsTable.FieldByName('ITM_SERNUM').AsString
            <> RMATable.FieldByName('RMA_SERNUM').AsString))
    do ItemsTable.Next;

ItemsTable.EnableControls;

RMATable.Edit;
```

Putting the Initials in Their ComboBox

This was probably the trickiest code of the night. The idea was to search through the list of initials in the ComboBox's string list, looking for a match with the RMA_INITS field in the RMA table. If a match was found, the ComboBox's **ItemIndex** property would be set to correspond to the item in the list. To pull this off, I had to add three more variables to the **var** declaration of the OnActivate handler. The full declaration was now:

```
var
 s : String;
 Idx : Integer;
 Count : Integer;
 Match : Boolean;
```

To accomplish my goal, I set the string variable **s** equal to the initials field in the table, set the index counter (**Idx**) to correspond to the first item in the list, and got the number of items in the list into **Count**. Then I stepped through the list looking for a match. If I found one, I set **ItemIndex** and bailed out. If no match was found, I set **ItemIndex** to -1, which tells a ComboBox that no item in the list is selected. My code for this is in Listing 19.17.

Listing 19.17   Getting the initials into the ComboBox

```
{ Put the initials in the ComboBox }
with InitComboBox do
begin
 Idx := 0;
 s := RMATable.FieldByName('RMA_INITS').AsString;
 Count := Items.Count;

 { Search through the list of initials. If a
   match is found, update the ComboBox. }
 if Count > 0 then
  repeat
   Match := s = Items[Idx];
   if Match
     then ItemIndex := Idx
     else Inc(Idx);
  until Match or (Idx = Count);
 if not Match or (Count = 0) then ItemIndex := -1; { Unselected }
end; { with }
```

Putting the Status in its ComboBox

This one was straightforward; Set the index to the value in the RMA_STATUS field. If that value is valid (there is an item in the string list at that index position), set **ItemIndex** to point to the string. Otherwise, put **ItemIndex** in an unselected state. The code appears in Listing 19.18.

Listing 19.18   Getting the status message into the ComboBox

```
{ Put the status in the ComboBox }
with StatusComboBox do
 begin
  Idx := RMATable.FieldByName('RMA_STATUS').AsInteger;
  if (Idx >= 0) and (Idx < Items.Count)
   then ItemIndex := Idx
   else ItemIndex := -1;  { Unselected }
 end; { with }
```

Finishing the RMA Input Form

I now had a form that was nearly self-sufficient. It could append and edit records, and it could accept the changes. There were only three things to do to complete the Input form for now:

1. Add a procedure to update the record, copying data from the components to the record.

2. Add the updating procedure to the Input form's private declarations list, and then call it from other event handlers, as appropriate.

3. Create an event handler for the Cancel button.

I created a procedure I called **UpdateRMARecord** that moved all the information from other data tables—invoice number, item stock and serial numbers, employee initials and company information—into the RMA table record being appended or edited. This routine would need to be called whenever the user ended an edit or append operation by clicking the OK button. I added the procedure's name to the private section of the Input form's declaration list.

Obviously, **UpdateRMARecord** would be called in the OnClick handler for the OK button—by clicking on this button, the user would be signaling acceptance of any changes that had been made. But as I was to find out, the routine also needed to be called whenever the DBNavigator changed the selected invoice number. Otherwise, it wouldn't catch the invoice and item changes. So I created an OnClick handler for the Navigator, and put in a call to **UpdateRMARecord**.

Finally, I created an OnClick handler for the Cancel button. It simply called the **Cancel** method of the **RMATable** component.

That finished the RMA Input form for the time being. I spiffed the code a little, using **with** statements to make things a bit more readable. A picture of the form, taken while the demo was running, is shown in Figure 19.2. A complete listing appears in Listing 19.19.

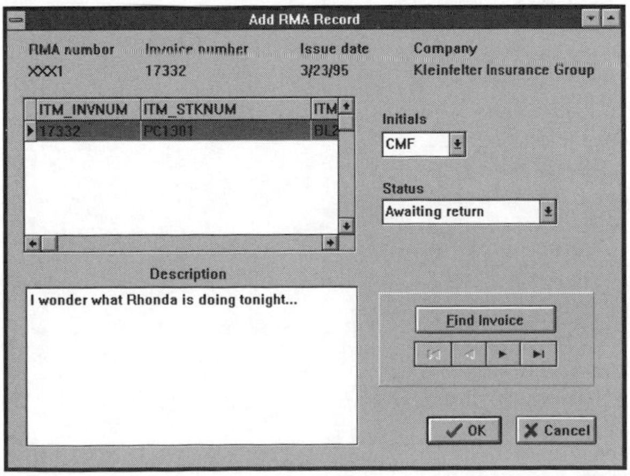

Figure 19.2 *A 'running' version of the RMA Input form.*

Listing 19.19   Complete version of the RMA Input form

```
{————————————————————————————————————————————}
{                    The Boxlight Demo                       }
{             RMAADD.PAS : RMA Input Form                    }
{              By Ace Breakpoint, N.T.P.                     }
{                 Assisted by Don Taylor                     }
{                                                            }
{ Chapter 19 version of the form that supports the           }
{ appending and editing of records in the RMA               }
{ table.                                                     }
{ Written for *Delphi Programming Explorer*                  }
{ Copyright (c) 1995 The Coriolis Group, Inc.                }
{                 Last Updated 3/30/95                       }
{————————————————————————————————————————————}

unit Rmaadd;

interface

uses
    SysUtils, WinTypes, WinProcs, Messages, Classes, Graphics, Controls,
    Forms, Dialogs, DBCtrls, StdCtrls, Buttons, ExtCtrls, DBLookup, Grids,
    DBGrids, DB, DBTables;

type
    TAddRMAForm = class(TForm)
        RMALabel: TLabel;
        InvoiceLabel: TLabel;
        IssueDateLabel: TLabel;
        ItemsDBGrid: TDBGrid;
        DescDBMemo: TDBMemo;
        NavPanel: TPanel;
        InvoiceNav: TDBNavigator;
        RMATable: TTable;
        InvoiceTable: TTable;
        ItemsTable: TTable;
        EmployeeTable: TTable;
        CustomerTable: TTable;
        RMASource: TDataSource;
        InvoiceSource: TDataSource;
        ItemsSource: TDataSource;
        EmployeeSource: TDataSource;
        CustomerSource: TDataSource;
        InitLabel: TLabel;
        StatusLabel: TLabel;
        FindBtn: TButton;
        RMADBText: TDBText;
        InvoiceDBText: TDBText;
        IssueDBText: TDBText;
        InitComboBox: TComboBox;
        StatusComboBox: TComboBox;
        DescLabel: TLabel;
```

```pascal
        CompanyLabel: TLabel;
        CustomerDBText: TDBText;
        OKBtn: TBitBtn;
        CancelBtn: TBitBtn;
        NextRMATable: TTable;
        NextRMASource: TDataSource;
        procedure FormCreate(Sender: TObject);
        procedure FormActivate(Sender: TObject);
        procedure OKBtnClick(Sender: TObject);
        procedure CancelBtnClick(Sender: TObject);
        procedure InvoiceNavClick(Sender: TObject; Button: TNavigateBtn);
        procedure StatusComboBoxChange(Sender: TObject);
private
        { Private declarations }
        RMANum : Integer;
        procedure UpdateRMARecord;
    public
        { Public declarations }
        RMAIndexStr : String;
        Editing : Boolean;
    end;

var
    AddRMAForm: TAddRMAForm;

implementation

{$R *.DFM}

procedure TAddRMAForm.FormCreate(Sender: TObject);
begin
 RMANum := 0;
 RMAIndexStr := '';
 Editing := False;
end;

procedure TAddRMAForm.FormActivate(Sender: TObject);
var
 s : String;
 Idx : Integer;
 Count : Integer;
 Match : Boolean;

begin
 if Editing
   then begin { Edit the specified record }
          Caption := 'Edit RMA Record';

          { Go to the specified RMA record }
          with RMATable do
           begin
             DisableControls;
             First;
```

```
    SetKey;
    FieldByName('RMA_ID').AsString := RMAIndexStr;
    GotoKey;
    EnableControls;
  end; { with }

{ Go to appropriate invoice record }
with InvoiceTable do
 begin
    DisableControls;
    First;
    SetKey;
    FieldByName('INV_NUM').AsString
      := RMATable.FieldByName('RMA_INVNUM').AsString;
    GotoKey;
    EnableControls;
  end; { with }

{ Go to the appropriate item record that matches
   the stock number AND the serial number }
with ItemsTable do
 begin
    DisableControls;
    First;

    while not EOF
      and ((FieldByName('ITM_STKNUM').AsString
            <> RMATable.FieldByName('RMA_STKNUM').AsString)
      or (FieldByName('ITM_SERNUM').AsString
            <> RMATable.FieldByName('RMA_SERNUM').AsString))
     do Next;

    EnableControls;
  end; { with }

RMATable.Edit;

{ Put the initials in the ComboBox }
with InitComboBox do
 begin
    Idx := 0;
    s := RMATable.FieldByName('RMA_INITS').AsString;
    Count := Items.Count;

    { Search through the list of initials. If a
      match is found, update the ComboBox. }
    if Count > 0 then
     repeat
       Match := s = Items[Idx];
       if Match
        then ItemIndex := Idx
        else Inc(Idx);
     until Match or (Idx = Count);
```

```
                  if not Match or (Count = 0) then ItemIndex := -1; { Unselected }
                end; { with }

                { Put the status in the ComboBox }
                with StatusComboBox do
                  begin
                    Idx := RMATable.FieldByName('RMA_STATUS').AsInteger;
                    if (Idx >= 0) and (Idx < Items.Count)
                      then ItemIndex := Idx
                      else ItemIndex := -1; { Unselected }
                  end; { with }
           end
      else begin { Append a new record }
             Caption := 'Add RMA Record';
             with RMATable do
               begin
                 Append;

                 { Set up the RMA number and the issue and update dates }
                 RMANum := NextRMATable.FieldByName('RXT_RMANUM').AsInteger;
                 Str(RMANum, s);
                 s := 'XXX' + s; { I'll create a proper RMA string later... }
                 FieldByName('RMA_ID').AsString := s;
                 FieldByName('RMA_DATE').AsString := DateToStr(Date);
                 FieldByName('RMA_UPDATE').AsString := DateToStr(Date);

                 { Set the invoice and items tables to their first records }
                 InvoiceTable.First;
                 ItemsTable.First;

                 { Set up the default values }
                 FieldByName('RMA_INVNUM').AsString
                    := InvoiceTable.FieldByName('INV_NUM').AsString;
                 FieldByName('RMA_STKNUM').AsString
                    := ItemsTable.FieldByName('ITM_STKNUM').AsString;
                 FieldByName('RMA_SERNUM').AsString
                    := ItemsTable.FieldByName('ITM_SERNUM').AsString;
                 FieldByName('RMA_CUSTID').AsString
                    := InvoiceTable.FieldByName('INV_CUSTID').AsString;

                 { Get the default employee initials }
                 InitComboBox.ItemIndex := 0;
                 FieldByName('RMA_INITS').AsString
                    := InitComboBox.Text;

                 { Get the default status information }
                 StatusComboBox.ItemIndex := 0;
                 FieldByName('RMA_STATUS').AsInteger := 0;
               end; { with }
           end;
    end;
```

```
procedure TAddRMAForm.OKBtnClick(Sender: TObject);
begin
 UpdateRMARecord;
 RMATable.Post;

 { Pass back the current record's index }
 RMAIndexStr := RMATable.FieldByName('RMA_ID').AsString;

 if not Editing
   then begin { We must have appended a new RMA }

           { Increment the RMA next-number counter }
           Inc(RMANum);

           { Stuff the new number in the Next RMA Table }
           with NextRMATable do
            begin
              Edit;
              FieldByName('RXT_RMANUM').AsInteger := RMANum;
              Post;
            end; { with }
         end;
end;

procedure TAddRMAForm.CancelBtnClick(Sender: TObject);
begin
 RMATable.Cancel;
end;

procedure TAddRMAForm.UpdateRMARecord;
begin
 with RMATable do
   begin

    { Update only if we are in the Insert or Edit mode }
    if (State = dsInsert) or (State = dsEdit)
      then begin
              { Get the invoice number and customer ID from the Invoice Table }
              FieldByName('RMA_INVNUM').AsString
                := InvoiceTable.FieldByName('INV_NUM').AsString;
              FieldByName('RMA_CUSTID').AsString
                := InvoiceTable.FieldByName('INV_CUSTID').AsString;

              { Get the stock number and serial number from the Items Table }
              FieldByName('RMA_STKNUM').AsString
                := ItemsTable.FieldByName('ITM_STKNUM').AsString;
              FieldByName('RMA_SERNUM').AsString
                := ItemsTable.FieldByName('ITM_SERNUM').AsString;

              { Get the initials from the ComboBox }
              FieldByName('RMA_INITS').AsString
                := InitComboBox.Text;
```

```
                { Get the status information from the ComboBox }
                FieldByName('RMA_STATUS').AsInteger
                   := StatusComboBox.ItemIndex;
                end;
     end; { with }
  end;

procedure TAddRMAForm.InvoiceNavClick(Sender: TObject;
   Button: TNavigateBtn);
begin
  UpdateRMARecord;
end;

procedure TAddRMAForm.StatusComboBoxChange(Sender: TObject);
begin
  RMATable.FieldByName('RMA_STATUS').AsInteger
     := StatusComboBox.ItemIndex;
end;

end.
```

Finishing the RMA Management Form

I used the last bit of Kona in the pot to top off my mug. It was then I finally noticed I was not using just any mug—it was my fave. I suppose it was supreme irony that the cup I would pick was the one Helen had made especially for me in Pottery Physics 103. After carefully "throwing" the cup by hand on the pottery wheel, she attached the handle and then used an industrial laser to blast a simple message on the side: *Ace of Hearts*.

It was too much to bear. I turned the engraving away from me, determined that if I must, I would forevermore drink with my other hand. I took a big sip, clumsily spilling almost half the cup down the front of my shirt. It would be okay. The burn would eventually heal. Right now, I would concentrate on finishing the RMA Management form.

It looked almost too simple to be true. As near as I could figure, I needed to do only three things to finish the Management form for the time being:

1. Create and call a routine that would update all the components on the form.

2. Develop a routine that would keep the RMA records in synchronization between the Input and Management forms.

3. Write an event handler for the Delete button.

Two New Routines

I elected to call the first routine **RefreshForm** and the second **Synchronize**. The purpose of **RefreshForm** would be similar to the routine I had written to update the components on the Input form, except this one was simpler. Its first task was to move the Products table to the record specified by the stock number in the RMA table's record. Next, it was to move the Customers table to the record that matched the customer ID in the RMA record. Finally, I used a **case** statement to pick the proper status message, based on the status level in—yep—the RMA record.

Synchronize was easy to write, too. It had bothered me earlier that, following the addition of the first record in the RMA table, the Management form didn't have a clue there was a record in the table. When the demo was restarted, all of a sudden the DBNavigator on the Management form indicated there was at least one record. As it turns out, some other quirky things were happening. Most of the time when a new record was added or edited and I returned to the Management table, I wouldn't come back to the same record. It was wonky.

It soon became obvious what was happening. I had set up the **RMATable** component on the Input form always to seek the record specified by the index key (**RMAIndexStr**) passed to it by the Management form. I had even forced the Input form to update the value of **RMAIndexStr** if the OK button was clicked, so it was correct whether the operation was an edit or an append. What I hadn't done was make sure the corresponding **RMATable** component on the Management form synchronized itself to the record specified by **RMAIndexStr** whenever the table's state was in question.

The synchronization process, then, was simple: Just move the RMA table to the index specified by the variable **RMAIndexStr** on the Input form. And since moving to another record could potentially screw up the display, I called **RefreshForm** for good measure.

Now my problem was when to call these two new routines. It seemed logical to call **Synchronize** whenever I was returning from adding or editing, so I modified the event handlers for the Add and Edit buttons to add the call to **Synchronize**.

As for **RefreshForm**, it needed to be called whenever the RMA table moved to another record. As near as I could tell, there were only two ways to make that happen. The first was returning from the Input form after adding a record. I had taken care of this situation when I added the call to **RefreshForm** in the **Synchronization** procedure. The second mechanism that would select another RMA record was pressing any of the DBNavigator buttons. So I added an OnClick event handler for the DBNavigator, and placed a call to **RefreshForm** in it.

One more bit of housekeeping—I added **RefreshForm** and **Synchronize** to the list in the private section of the Management form's declarations.

The Delete Button Event Handler

Getting the Delete button to work was a dream. All I had to do was create an OnClick handler for the button, and include one line that called the RMA table's **Delete** method.

That finished the RMA Management form—at least for now. I compiled and ran the demo yet another time. It felt a lot more solid. Figure 19.3 is a picture of what the RMA Management form looked like while the demo was running. Listing 19.20 is the complete listing for the Management form, including **RefreshForm**, **Synchronize**, and the event handler for the Delete button.

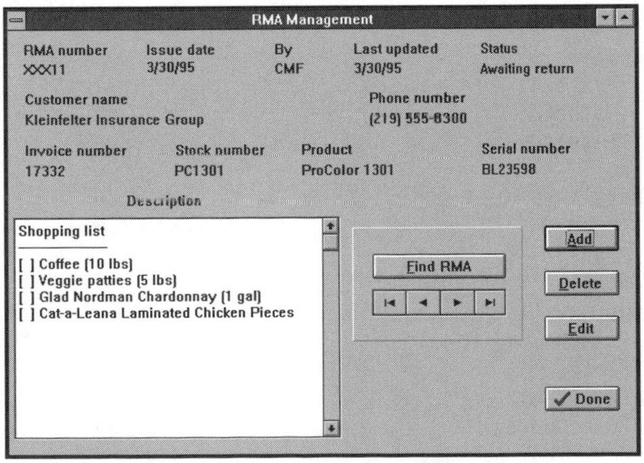

Figure 19.3 *A 'running' version of the RMA Management form.*

Listing 19.20   Complete version of the RMA Management form

```
{---------------------------------------------------------------}
{                     The Boxlight Demo                          }
{              RMAMGMT.PAS : RMA Input Form                      }
{                 By Ace Breakpoint, N.T.P.                      }
{                  Assisted by Don Taylor                        }
{                                                                }
{ Chapter 19 version of the form that displays RMA              }
{ information and navigates through the RMA table.              }
{ Written for *Delphi Programming Explorer*                     }
{ Copyright (c) 1995 The Coriolis Group, Inc.                   }
{                  Last Updated 3/30/95                          }
{---------------------------------------------------------------}

unit Rmamgmt;

interface

uses
   SysUtils, WinTypes, WinProcs, Messages, Classes, Graphics, Controls,
   Forms, Dialogs, DBCtrls, StdCtrls, Buttons, ExtCtrls, DB, DBTables,
   RMAAdd;

type
   TRMAMgmtForm = class(TForm)
      RMALabel: TLabel;
      IssueDateLabel: TLabel;
      ByLabel: TLabel;
      UpdateLabel: TLabel;
      StatusLabel: TLabel;
      CustNameLabel: TLabel;
      PhoneLabel: TLabel;
      InvNumLabel: TLabel;
      StkNumLabel: TLabel;
      NameLabel: TLabel;
      SNLabel: TLabel;
      ProductDBText: TDBText;
      DescDBMemo: TDBMemo;
      DescLabel: TLabel;
      NavPanel: TPanel;
      FindBtn: TButton;
      RMANavigator: TDBNavigator;
      RMATable: TTable;
      CustomerTable: TTable;
      RMASource: TDataSource;
      CustomerSource: TDataSource;
      CustNameDBText: TDBText;
      CustPhoneDBText: TDBText;
      ProductsTable: TTable;
      ProductsSource: TDataSource;
      RMADBText: TDBText;
      IssueDBText: TDBText;
```

```
      ByDBText: TDBText;
      UpdatedDBText: TDBText;
      InvNumDBText: TDBText;
      StkNumDBText: TDBText;
      SNDBText: TDBText;
      AddBtn: TButton;
      DeleteBtn: TButton;
      EditBtn: TButton;
      DoneBtn: TBitBtn;
      StatusMsgLabel: TLabel;
      procedure AddBtnClick(Sender: TObject);
      procedure EditBtnClick(Sender: TObject);
      procedure RMANavigatorClick(Sender: TObject; Button: TNavigateBtn);
      procedure DeleteBtnClick(Sender: TObject);
   private
      { Private declarations }
      procedure RefreshForm;
      procedure Synchronize;
   public
      { Public declarations }
   end;

var
   RMAMgmtForm: TRMAMgmtForm;

implementation

{$R *.DFM}

procedure TRMAMgmtForm.AddBtnClick(Sender: TObject);
begin
 { Tell the Add/Edit form we're appending }
 AddRMAForm.Editing := False;
 AddRMAForm.RMAIndexStr := RMATable.FieldByName('RMA_ID').AsString;
 AddRMAForm.ShowModal;
 Synchronize;
end;

procedure TRMAMgmtForm.EditBtnClick(Sender: TObject);
begin
 { Tell the Add/Edit form we're editing }
 AddRMAForm.Editing := True;
 AddRMAForm.RMAIndexStr := RMATable.FieldByName('RMA_ID').AsString;
 AddRMAForm.ShowModal;
 Synchronize;
end;

procedure TRMAMgmtForm.Synchronize;
begin
 { Force the RMA table to the record indicated  by
    RMAIndexStr, and then refresh the form }
 with RMATable do
   begin { Do it only if the index isn't blank }
```

```
    if AddRMAForm.RMAIndexStr <> ''
      then begin
             Cancel;
             DisableControls;
             First;
             SetKey;
             FieldByName('RMA_ID').AsString := AddRMAForm.RMAIndexStr;
             GotoKey;
             EnableControls;
           end
      else First;
  end; { with }
 RefreshForm;
end;

procedure TRMAMgmtForm.RefreshForm;
begin
 { Go to appropriate product record }
 with ProductsTable do
   begin
    DisableControls;
    First;
    SetKey;
    FieldByName('PRD_STKNUM').AsString
      := RMATable.FieldByName('RMA_STKNUM').AsString;
    GotoKey;
    EnableControls;
   end; { with }

 { Go to appropriate customer record }
 with CustomerTable do
   begin
    DisableControls;
    First;
    SetKey;
    FieldByName('CST_ID').AsString
      := RMATable.FieldByName('RMA_CUSTID').AsString;
    GotoKey;
    EnableControls;
   end; { with }

 { Refresh the Status }
 case RMATable.FieldByName('RMA_STATUS').AsInteger of
   0 : StatusMsgLabel.Caption := 'Awaiting return';
   1 : StatusMsgLabel.Caption := 'Awaiting replacmt';
   2 : StatusMsgLabel.Caption := 'Completed';
   3 : StatusMsgLabel.Caption := 'Deleted';
 else
   StatusMsgLabel.Caption := 'Error!';
 end; { case }
end;
```

```
procedure TRMAMgmtForm.RMANavigatorClick(Sender: TObject;
   Button: TNavigateBtn);
begin
 RefreshForm;
end;

procedure TRMAMgmtForm.DeleteBtnClick(Sender: TObject);
begin
 RMATable.Delete;
end;

end.
```

A PERSONAL CONFESSION

I had to admit that at first, suddenly losing my girlfriend of four years was quite a shock. I had been a victim of Ace's First Law. In an odd sort of way, I was now beginning to enjoy my new status. It was like a new-found freedom. I could go out with other women if I wanted. Who needed Helen, anyway?

In the past hour, between test runs I had taken a few moments to compose a short poem to Rhonda. Professor Drivelmeister used to tell me that when it came to poetry, I had no talent for it. (In fact, both he and Professor Bristlebender, my personal painting coach, told me I was "right-brain dead.") But I thought this poem was one of my better efforts. Unfortunately, it had disappeared somewhere in the pile of papers and files. Perhaps if I could find it, I thought, I might even share it with Rhonda when I stopped by the Boxlight offices this afternoon.

But that visit was still several hours away. It was 6:26, and although I had gotten the basics of the demo application working—complete with event handling   I still had quite a bit of polishing to do. I started by polishing off the rest of the Kona.

Returning to the Scene

Don Taylor

A new day dawns, and the project hurtles toward conclusion. Ace begins tying up loose ends and putting the final touches on his forms.

I could hear Mewnix scratching at the door, demanding to be let inside. I got up and stretched, and eventually wandered over to the slider, pulled back the drape and let him in. He headed straight for the couch, not even looking at his dish as he staggered by. He was soaking wet, and looked like he had been dragged through a knothole sideways.

As his kindred spirit, I knew how he felt. I had experienced many things during this night. I had been injured and nearly killed several times. I had lost the love of my life. Most important of all, I had taken a concept for an application and turned it into a functional program. I had completed the first five steps of my process, having scoped out the application, divided it into functional pieces, performed the rough layout, configured the properties of its components, and written event handlers to enhance its dynamic operation.

Next would come the addition of some extra code that would perform some core operations. I would also be tweaking some of the components, and generally refining the program's performance.

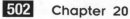

I felt in need of improving my own performance as well. The long night's experiences had certainly taken its toll on my ability to concentrate. I don't know how many gallons of designer coffee I had consumed, but it had ceased to have any affect on me. In spite of the excitement of the competition, I was catching myself drifting off every few minutes. I reckoned the solution might lie in achieving a certain *blend* of coffees. I ground up a mixture of equal portions of Lithuanian Extra Dark, Oro de Burkina Faso, and Wailin' Venezuelan. I filled the coffeemaker with water and poured about half a pound of the amalgam into the filter cup. Then I staggered back to my computer.

STEPS 6 AND 7: ADD THE SPECIAL CODE AND SMOOTH THE DEMO

It seemed to me that finishing the Product Information form would be a good place to start. Two things bugged me about this form. First, it was still a little plain, a little blocky. Second, I wanted the price formatted in dollars and cents.

As I expected, the solutions to both of these picayune problems were simple ones. To spiff up the form, I decided first to put a bevel around the photograph and include the price and product name DBTexts within that bevel. I popped a bevel on top of **ProductPanel**, called the bevel **ProductBevel**, and stretched it to encompass the DBTexts. The contents of the panel now needed some readjusting, but I couldn't seem to select anything inside the bevel! Of course—this stuff is in layers, with ProductPanel as the bottom surface. I selected the bevel, then picked Send to Back from Delphi's Edit menu—the problem was solved.

I adjusted the positions of **PictDBImage**, **ProductNameDBText**, and **PriceDBText** until everything on the panel looked in balance.

Next, I took on the formatting of the price displayed by **PriceDBText**. I double-clicked on the **ProductsTable** component on the form, which brought up the Fields editor, as shown in the snapshot in Figure 20.1. I clicked the Add button, which brought up the Add Fields dialog with all fields in the Products table highlighted, as shown in Figure 20.2. Then I clicked on OK to select all the fields shown. I was returned to the Fields editor, which I then put away.

I had just created intermediate (field) components that would tie the actual columns in the data table to the data-aware components on my form. I could now control several aspects of how data could be limited on input, or how it

Figure 20.1   *Using the Fields Editor on the Products table.*

Figure 20.2   *Selecting table columns for field components.*

could be formatted for display. My next step was to edit the properties of the field component (which Delphi had by default named **ProductsTablePRD_PRICE**) that corresponded to the PRD_PRICE field (column) in the Products table. I simply selected the field component from the Object Inspector, then clicked to set its **Currency** property to **True**. **PriceDBText** instantly reformatted to display dollars and cents.

Excited by the changes I had already been able to make so easily, I determined to change the font in the title labels on each of the pages in **ProductNotebook**. I have always believed that when displaying data, the data should be more prominent that the labels describing it. The font and size used as the default by Delphi were very prominent—perhaps *too* prominent. My first step was to lighten the look of the text in the DBMemos on all the Notebook pages. The easiest thing was to change the font for **ProductNotebook** itself. I decided on the Arial Regular font (not bold, not italic). My next goal on this form (and the others that would follow) was to change the emphasis on the labels.

I started with the labels on each of the **ProductNotebook** pages. For each label, I modified the Font-related properties to make the font Arial Bold, set the size to 9 point and change the color to navy blue. I noticed immediately that the careful work I had done to center the labels over the DBMemos was

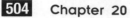

now out the window. To combat this, I set the labels' **Autosize** property to **False**, and I lengthened each label horizontally until it just fit inside the page borders. Then I set its **Alignment** property to **taCenter**. Now the labels would be properly positioned, no matter which font and point size I might choose.

I compiled and ran the demo to check my work. It looked a lot better, but one thing still bothered me. The TabSet had a definite border around it, but the page it was tied to didn't. I placed a bevel around the Notebook, just outside its perimeter, being careful to click on the form itself, so the bevel wouldn't become an object belonging to the Notebook, and thus limited to its physical boundaries. Then I pulled the bottom of the bevel downward until it just exactly encompassed the TabSet.

This would provide a definite border around the pages, I thought. And it did— almost. The lowered box looked a bit strange next to the panel on its right. So I changed the bevel's **Shape** property to **bsFrame**, so only the border line was lowered. Then I made some slight adjustments to the TabSet and to **ProductPanel** and its components, so everything would be in alignment.

I ran the demo again. This time I tried pressing keys and using the Tab key to move between controls, instead of using the mouse. I discovered that I needed to change which components had their **TabStop** properties set, and I also needed to perform an overhaul on the tabbing order of all the components. I went back to the Delphi environment, and edited **ProductNotebook** and **DBImage** to modify their **TabStop** properties. Then I used a right-button mouse click on the form to bring up a speed menu, from which I picked Tab Order. I set the order as shown in Figure 20.3.

I noticed that **ProductPanel** appeared on the list, but the items located on it did not. Then I remembered that Panel components "own" anything placed on them. To see **PictDBImage** and **DoneBtn**, I would have to adjust the tab order of the Panel. I right-clicked on **ProductPanel**, and then selected Tab

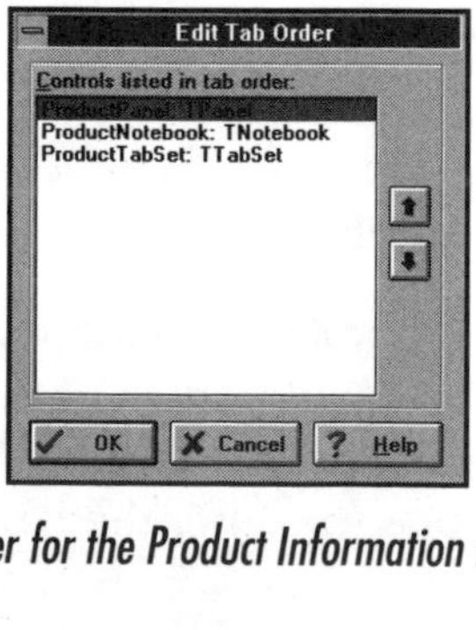

Figure 20.3 *Choosing the tab order for the Product Information form.*

Figure 20.4 *Adjusting the tab order of ProductPanel.*

Order. Bingo—there were the missing components. I adjusted their tab order as shown in Figure 20.4. The latest changes to components on the Product Information form are detailed in Table 20.1.

Table 20.1 *Final Changes to the Product Info Form*

Name	Property	Value
ProductNotebookBevel	Left	5
	Top	9
	Width	404
	Height	332
	Shape	bsFrame
ProductNotebook	Font.Name	Arial
	Font.Style	[ ]
	TabOrder	1
DescLabel	Left	3
	Top	18
	Width	390
	Height	5
	Alignment	taCenter
	Caption	Description
	Font.Color	clNavy
	Font.Height	-12
	Font.Name	Arial
	Font.Style	[fsBold]

continued on next page

Table 20.1 *Final Changes to the Product Info Form*

continued from previous page

Name	Property	Value
SpecsLabel	Left	3
	Top	18
	Width	389
	Height	15
	Alignment	taCenter
	AutoSize	False
	Caption	Specifications
	Font.Color	clNavy
	Font.Height	-12
	Font.Name	Arial
	Font.Style	[fsBold]
AccessLabel	Left	4
	Top	18
	Width	390
	Height	15
	Alignment	taCenter
	AutoSize	False
	Caption	Accessories
	Font.Color	clNavy
	Font.Height	-12
	Font.Name	Arial
	Font.Style	[fsBold]
GenTipsLabel	Left	3
	Top	18
	Width	391
	Height	15
	Alignment	taCenter
	AutoSize	False
	Caption	Generic Tips
	Font.Color	clNavy
	Font.Height	-12
	Font.Name	Arial
	Font.Style	[fsBold]

continued on next page

Table 20.1 *Final Changes to the Product Info Form*

continued from previous page

Name	Property	Value
TipsLabel	Left	3
	Top	18
	Width	391
	Height	16
	Alignment	taCenter
	AutoSize	False
	Caption	Specific Tips
	Font.Color	clNavy
	Font.Height	-12
	Font.Name	Arial
	Font.Style	[fsBold]
ProductTabSet	Left	6
	Top	318
	Width	402
	Height	21
ProductPanel	Left	413
	Top	9
	Width	206
	Height	333
	TabOrder	0
ProductBevel	Left	13
	Top	54
	Width	181
	Height	199
StkNumComboBox	TabOrder	0

continued on next page

Table 20.1   *Final Changes to the Product Info Form*

continued from previous page

Name	Property	Value
ProductNameDBText	Left	19
	Top	194
	Width	167
	Height	17
PriceDBText	Left	20
	Top	217
	Width	164
	Height	17
PictDBImage	Left	23
	Top	68
	Width	161
	Height	114
DoneBtn	Left	66
	Top	286
	Width	78
	Height	26
	TabOrder	1
ProductsTable	PRD_PRICEFieldName	PRD_PRICE
	Currency	True

I ran the demo one more time, pulling up the Product Information form for inspection. It worked for me. I had managed to improve both the looks and the operation of the form without having to write a single line of code. A picture of the form appears in Figure 20.5. As far as I was concerned, this part of the job was complete.

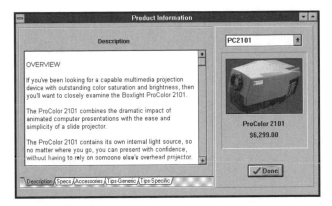

Figure 20.5 *The final version of the Product Information form.*

Finishing the RMA Input Form

I awoke with a start. I had apparently drifted off for about 10 minutes. As I struggled to regain consciousness, I slowly became aware once again of the sights and sounds of my office. But there was one thing missing—the *smell of coffee in the air*. In a near panic, I raced to the kitchenette, only to find I had forgotten to turn on Mr. CoffeeMaker's switch. I did that now, and immediately got on the exercise bike for the 5 minutes it took to complete the brewing process. I filled my mug to the brim, and then returned to my desk to ponder how I would approach changing the RMA Input form.

I would be fine-tuning the look of this form, in much the same way I did with the Product Information form. There were other details I had to consider first, however: Updating the date a record is changed; the loading into the ComboBox of employee initials from the Employees table; adding the capability of searching for invoices; and creating a "proper" format for RMA numbers. I also needed to figure out what I would do to eliminate multiple instances of status message strings in the program.

Updating the Date

This was exceedingly simple. All I had to do was add a single line to freshen the update field. I inserted that line in the code right after the line that put the RMA table into its editing mode:

```
RMATable.Edit;
RMATable.FieldByName('RMA_UPDATE').AsString := DateToStr(Date);
```

Adding the Initials to the Combo Box

I chose the loading of initials as my first target. This situation was virtually identical to the one I had faced earlier, when loading the product stock numbers into a ComboBox. I needed only to load the initials once, when the Input form was created. I merely had to extend the Input form's OnCreate event handler I had previously written. The additional code I wrote appears in Listing 20.1.

Listing 20.1 Additional code for the RMA Input form's OnCreate handler

```
{ Fill the Initials ComboBox string list }
 with EmployeeTable do
   begin
    InitComboBox.Items.Clear;
    First;
    while not EOF do
      begin
       InitComboBox.Items.Add(FieldByName('EMP_INITS').AsString);
       Next;
      end; { while }
    First;
   end; { with }
```

Searching for Invoices

Next, I decided to add the capability to search for a specific invoice. I knew that whatever I did here would probably be duplicated to a large degree on the RMA Management form, where I would be searching for an RMA number.

Basically, I would bring up a dialog that would ask for an invoice number, which would be entered as a string. That should be that easy, right? Well, almost.

I recalled there are two types of searches provided for Delphi's data tables. The first (which uses the **GoToKey** method) is a search for an exact match on a specified key, and the second (which uses the **GoToNearest** method) is a search where a partial match on a key is acceptable. In the **GoToKey** search, the process examines the current record and then each succeeding record, looking for an exact match with the key. If a match is found, the process stops, leaving the matched record as the current one. If an exact match is not found, the search fails and the current record does not change.

The **GoToNearest** search also starts at the current record, and it attempts to locate the first match with the key provided. But this time, it will consider it a match if the characters in the key match the corresponding characters in the designated field. Let's say I were to pick "Bo" as the key. In a **GoToNearest** situation, the search would stop on "Bohacker." (It would also consider it a match with "Bogus", "Boor", and "Borborygmus", which I consider appropriate.) If a partial match is not found, the current record moves to the first record with an ASCII value *greater* than the partial key. In other words, if nothing beginning with "Bo" were present in the database, the first record past where "Bo" would fall would get the pointer—probably something beginning with "Br".

I settled on the **GoToNearest** search. If the customer could only provide the support tech with an approximate invoice number, it just might get him or her close enough to find the exact one by stepping through invoices with the DBNavigator.

Now I needed a way to request a search string from the user. A dialog, of course. From the Delphi File menu, I selected New Form, and then from the Browse Gallery dialog, I selected the Standard Dialog Box with the three buttons along the bottom. The new blank form is shown in Figure 20.6.

I immediately removed the Help button, because I wouldn't be providing help capabilities beyond the simple offerings on the Main form's menu. I rearranged the OK and Cancel buttons, and added a Label component and an Edit component, and resized the bevel and the **FindRecordDlg** form itself. I then rearranged the tab order, and I set the Edit as the form's **ActiveControl**, so it would receive the focus when the form was activated—meaning it would be ready to accept an invoice number as soon as it became visible.

This would be the first form in the project that didn't require even one line of code. Table 20.2 contains the detail of the special component settings for the new dialog.

Figure 20.6 *A Standard Dialog ready for modification.*

Table 20.2 *Component Properties for the Find Record Dialog*

Name	Property	Value
FindRecordDlg	Left	263
	Top	115
	ActiveControl	SearchStrEdit
	BorderStyle	bsDialog
	Caption	Find Record
	ClientHeight	184
	ClientWidth	317
	Position	poScreenCenter
FindBevel	Left	8
	Top	8
	Width	300
	Height	127
	Shape	bsFrame
	IsControl	True
SearchStrLabel	Left	46
	Top	29
	Width	5
	Height	13
OKBtn	Left	147
	Top	149
	Width	77
	Height	27
	TabOrder	1
	Kind	bkOK
	Margin	2
	Spacing	-1
	IsControl	True

continued on next page

Table 20.2 *Component Properties for the Find Record Dialog*

continued from previous page

Name	Property	Value
CancelBtn	Left	230
	Top	149
	Width	77
	Height	27
	TabOrder	2
	Kind	bkCancel
	Margin	2
	Spacing	-1
	IsControl	True
SearchStrEdit	Left	46
	Top	50
	Width	142
	Height	20
	TabOrder	0
	Text	[blank]

After adding a reference to **FindRec** in the **uses** declaration of the RMAAdd unit, I was able to write an OnClick handler for the Find button. The handler appears in Listing 20.2.

Listing 20.2 OnClick handler for the RMA Input form's Find button

```
procedure TAddRMAForm.FindBtnClick(Sender: TObject);
begin
 with FindRecordDlg do
   begin
    Caption := 'Find Invoice';
    SearchStrLabel.Caption := 'Invoice number';
    SearchStrEdit.Text := '';
    if (ShowModal = mrCancel)
      or (SearchStrEdit.Text = '') then Exit;
   end; { with }
```

```
with InvoiceTable do
  begin
    Cancel;
    First;
    SetKey;
    FieldByName('INV_NUM').AsString
      := FindRecordDlg.SearchStrEdit.Text;
    GotoNearest;
  end; { with }
end;
```

The first part of the code in Listing 20.2 sets up the dialog for invoice searching (when used later for searching for an RMA number, I would have to change the captions). By making the string blank before executing the dialog, I would force the user to enter a new value each time the dialog is displayed. I also checked to see if they clicked the Cancel button. If so (or if they didn't enter a search string), I just took it on the lam. Otherwise, I took the text they entered and performed a search on it. A picture of the dialog in action can be seen in Figure 20.7.

In the second part of Listing 20.2, I took the string entered in the dialog and used it as the key to perform the partial-match search on the Invoices table. The code worked like a champ.

FORMATTING RMA NUMBERS

It was time to get down to the business of creating RMA numbers in the Boxlight format, just as soon as I refilled my mug. The added kick from the blend I had prepared did seem to be doing some good, even if the flavor was a bit strange.

I dove in to the RMA formatting. Although this would have been an easy task, I had bypassed it earlier, so I could quickly create some data for testing purposes.

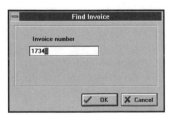

Figure 20.7 *The Find Invoice dialog.*

I consulted my notes. Each RMA number had to be a string of exactly 8 characters, in the form BXNNN-YY, where *NNN* is a 3-digit, zero-filled sequence number and *YY* are the last 2 digits of the current year. I immediately noticed that this format does not lend itself well to indexing. The first two characters never change, meaning they are dead weight as far as indexing goes. The remainder of the string will force a table to first order the RMA records by sequence number and then by year. Navigating through records indexed this way for 1995 and 1996 would give you the first RMA of 1995, followed by the first one in 1996, followed by the second in 1995, and so on. Not exceptionally useful. As Boxlight grows, they may find a need to log more than 999 RMAs in a year. I would have to speak to them about changing this part of their existing system.

Unfortunately, I couldn't do that right now. So as Professor Bristlebender used to say, "Sometimes, when life hands you a bowl of lemons, you have to paint their picture." A few minutes later I had replaced the original code in the Input form's OnActivate handler with that in Listing 20.3. The code required adding an another string variable (**s1**) to the declarations for the handler. Other than that, it was just a process of converting the RMA sequence number from an integer to a string, zero-filling it from the left so it is 3 digits long, converting today's date to a string, getting the last 2 digits and zero filling, and then putting the whole thing together in the specified format.

Listing 20.3 Creating a proper RMA number

```
RMANum := NextRMATable.FieldByName('RXT_RMANUM').AsInteger;
Str(RMANum, s);        { The sequence number }
while Length(s) < 3 do s := '0' + s;     { Zero fill it }
s1 := DateToStr(Date);        { The date }
s1 := copy(s1, Length(s1)-1, 2);     { Just the year }
while Length(s) < 2 do s := '0' + s;       { Zero fill it }
s := 'BX' + s + '-' + s1;        { Put it all together }
```

IMPROVING STATUS MESSAGES

I found it was redundant to include the text of the status message strings in both the Input and Management forms. If the project were to be expanded, and other forms added, the problem might well get worse. If the messages ever changed, I would be looking in nooks and crannies for all the places I had hidden them. This was clearly a violation of the Prime Directive—to keep reference data in only one place, if possible.

What about putting the messages in a dedicated data table, as I had done with the next RMA sequence number? That would certainly keep the messages in one place, where they could easily be changed. But how often would they change, really? It sure seemed like these messages were purely constants, rather than variables. That being the case, how could I put constants in one place, so they would not only be available to the forms I had now, but others I might create in the future?

The answer: *Put them in a unit.* Hey, why not? From the Delphi File menu, I selected New Unit. I saved the file as RMACONST.PAS. I then coded the new unit to specify the number of messages, and then I created an array of string constants that contained the text of the messages. The result appears in Listing 20.4.

Listing 20.4   A unit for RMA message string constants

```
{————————————————————————————————————————}
{                  The Boxlight Demo                }
{            RMACONST.PAS : RMA Constants Unit      }
{                By Ace Breakpoint, N.T.P.          }
{                 Assisted by Don Taylor            }
{                                                   }
{ Chapter 20 version of a unit containing constants }
{ used by the RMA forms in the Boxlight Demo        }
{ application.                                       }
{ Written for *Delphi Programming Explorer*         }
{ Copyright (c) 1995 The Coriolis Group, Inc.       }
{                 Last Updated 3/30/95              }
{————————————————————————————————————————}

unit Rmaconst;

interface
const
 NumStatusMessages = 4;
 StatusMessages : array [0..NumStatusMessages - 1] of string =
   ('Awaiting return',
    'Awaiting replacmt',
    'Completed',
    'Deleted');

implementation

end.
```

Initializing the **StatusComboBox**'s string list would now be done in a different manner, to incorporate the RMAConst unit. First of all, that meant adding a reference to **RMAConst** in the RMA Input form's **uses** declaration. Then it was simply a matter of adding an integer variable (**i**) and a few lines of code to the Input form's OnCreate handler. The additional code appears in Listing 20.5.

Listing 20.5   Additional code to load the RMA status messages

```
{ Fill the Status Message ComboBox string list }
 with StatusComboBox do
   begin
    Items.Clear;
    for i := 1 to NumStatusMessages do
      Items.Add(StatusMessages[i]);
   end; { with }
```

IMPROVING THE VIEW

It was time to spiff up the look of the form, as I had done with the Product Information form. I started by changing the font on all the labels to 9-point Arial Regular, in navy blue. Then I changed the **TitleFont** property on **ItemsDBGrid** to 8-point Arial Regular, this time in purple. I ran the demo again, and found these simple changes had made a dramatic difference, which could easily be seen by comparing the Input and Management forms.

Even though the appearance had improved, the titles on the DBGrid were still aesthetically challenged. The field names I had chosen had served me well, in terms of telling me which field in which table I was viewing. But as titles, they left a lot to be desired. I would now assign Field objects to each of the fields in the Items table, so I could control their display in data-aware components.

I right-clicked on the **ItemsTable** component, called up the Fields Editor, and added all the fields. The Field Editor, with all fields listed for **ItemsTable**, is shown in Figure 20.8.

Once I had added the Field components, I merely had to edit their properties to change the titles. After changing titles, I decided to make the Quantity

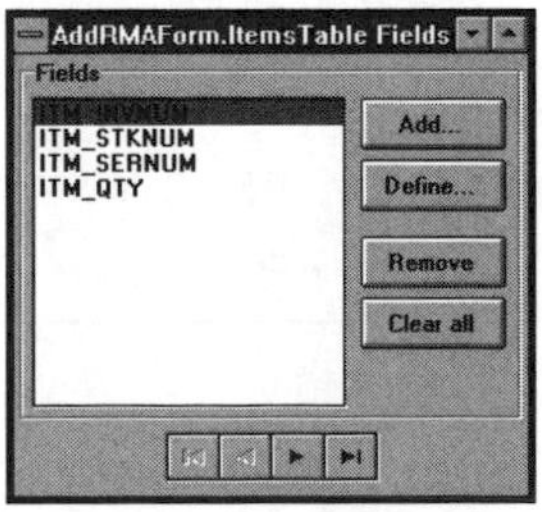

Figure 20.8   *Adding Field components for the Items table.*

column invisible, since quantity had no bearing on selecting an item by serial number. And since the invoice number was already being displayed in a DBText above the DBGrid (and the invoices and items had proven they were tracking reliably), I decided to made the Invoice Number column invisible as well. Then I readjusted the DBGrid's column widths by clicking on the column lines and dragging them left and right. The changes I made are detailed in Table 20.3.

One last bit of housekeeping: I redefined the tab order of the controls on the form, to give what I thought would be a natural progression of input. Then I ran the demo and selected the RMA Input form one last time. It looked good to me. It is shown in Figure 20.9. The complete listing for the form appears in Listing 20.6.

Table 20.3 *Changes to the Items Table's Field Properties*

Name	Property	Value
ItemsTableITM_INVNUM	DisplayLabel	Invoice
	DisplayWidth	7
	FieldName	ITM_INVNUM
	Visible	False
ItemsTableITM_STKNUM	DisplayLabel	Stock number
	DisplayWidth	13
	FieldName	ITM_STKNUM
ItemsTableITM_SERNUM	DisplayLabel	Serial number
	DisplayWidth	22
	FieldName	ITM_SERNUM
ItemsTableITM_QTY	DisplayLabel	Qty
	DisplayWidth	4
	FieldName	ITM_QTY
	Visible	False

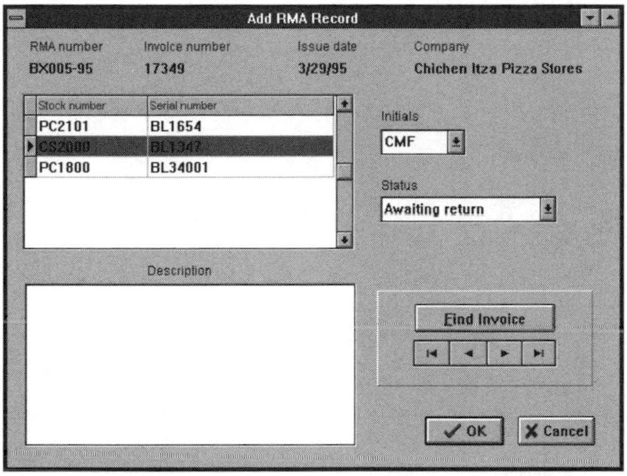

Figure 20.9 *Final version of the RMA Input form.*

Listing 20.6   Complete code for the final version of the RMA Input form

```
{————————————————————————————————}
{                 The Boxlight Demo                    }
{          RMAADD.PAS : RMA Input Form                 }
{              By Ace Breakpoint, N.T.P.               }
{              Assisted by Don Taylor                  }
{                                                      }
{ Chapter 20 version of the form that supports the     }
{ appending and editing of records in the RMA          }
{ table.                                               }
{ Written for *Delphi Programming Explorer*       }
{ Copyright (c) 1995 The Coriolis Group, Inc.          }
{              Last Updated 3/30/95                    }
{————————————————————————————————}

unit Rmaadd;

interface

uses
   SysUtils, WinTypes, WinProcs, Messages, Classes, Graphics, Controls,
   Forms, Dialogs, DBCtrls, StdCtrls, Buttons, ExtCtrls, DBLookup, Grids,
   DBGrids, DB, DBTables, FindRec, RMAConst;

type
   TAddRMAForm = class(TForm)
      RMALabel: TLabel;
      InvoiceLabel: TLabel;
      IssueDateLabel: TLabel;
      ItemsDBGrid: TDBGrid;
      DescDBMemo: TDBMemo;
```

```
      NavPanel: TPanel;
      InvoiceNav: TDBNavigator;
      RMATable: TTable;
      InvoiceTable: TTable;
      ItemsTable: TTable;
      EmployeeTable: TTable;
      CustomerTable: TTable;
      RMASource: TDataSource;
      InvoiceSource: TDataSource;
      ItemsSource: TDataSource;
      EmployeeSource: TDataSource;
      CustomerSource: TDataSource;
      InitLabel: TLabel;
      StatusLabel: TLabel;
      FindBtn: TButton;
      RMADBText: TDBText;
      InvoiceDBText: TDBText;
      IssueDBText: TDBText;
      InitComboBox: TComboBox;
      StatusComboBox: TComboBox;
      DescLabel: TLabel;
      CompanyLabel: TLabel;
      CustomerDBText: TDBText;
      OKBtn: TBitBtn;
      CancelBtn: TBitBtn;
      NextRMATable: TTable;
      NextRMASource: TDataSource;
      ItemsTableITM_INVNUM: TStringField;
      ItemsTableITM_STKNUM: TStringField;
      ItemsTableITM_SERNUM: TStringField;
      ItemsTableITM_QTY: TFloatField;
      procedure FormCreate(Sender: TObject);
      procedure FormActivate(Sender: TObject);
      procedure OKBtnClick(Sender: TObject);
      procedure CancelBtnClick(Sender: TObject);
      procedure InvoiceNavClick(Sender: TObject; Button: TNavigateBtn);
      procedure StatusComboBoxChange(Sender: TObject);
      procedure FindBtnClick(Sender: TObject);
    private
      { Private declarations }
      RMANum : Integer;
      procedure UpdateRMARecord;
    public
      { Public declarations }
      RMAIndexStr : String;
      Editing : Boolean;
    end;

var
  AddRMAForm: TAddRMAForm;

implementation

{$R *.DFM}
```

```
procedure TAddRMAForm.FormCreate(Sender: TObject);
var
 i : Integer;
begin
 RMANum := 0;
 RMAIndexStr := '';
 Editing := False;

 { Fill the Initials ComboBox string list }
 with EmployeeTable do
   begin
    InitComboBox.Items.Clear;
    First;
    while not EOF do
      begin
       InitComboBox.Items.Add(FieldByName('EMP_INITS').AsString);
       Next;
      end; { while }
    First;
   end; { with }

 { Fill the Status Message ComboBox string list }
 with StatusComboBox do
   begin
    Items.Clear;
    for i := 0 to NumStatusMessages - 1 do
      Items.Add(StatusMessages[i]);
   end; { with }
end;

procedure TAddRMAForm.FormActivate(Sender: TObject);
var
 s : String;
 s1 : String;
 Idx : Integer;
 Count : Integer;
 Match : Boolean;

begin
 if Editing
   then begin { Edit the specified record }
          Caption := 'Edit RMA Record';

          { Go to the specified RMA record }
          with RMATable do
           begin
             DisableControls;
             First;
             SetKey;
             FieldByName('RMA_ID').AsString := RMAIndexStr;
             GotoKey;
             EnableControls;
           end; { with }
```

```
{ Go to appropriate invoice record }
with InvoiceTable do
 begin
   DisableControls;
   First;
   SetKey;
   FieldByName('INV_NUM').AsString
     := RMATable.FieldByName('RMA_INVNUM').AsString;
   GotoKey;
   EnableControls;
 end; { with }

{ Go to the appropriate item record that matches
   the stock number AND the serial number }
with ItemsTable do
 begin
   DisableControls;
   First;

   while not EOF
     and ((FieldByName('ITM_STKNUM').AsString
           <> RMATable.FieldByName('RMA_STKNUM').AsString)
     or (FieldByName('ITM_SERNUM').AsString
           <> RMATable.FieldByName('RMA_SERNUM').AsString))
    do Next;

   EnableControls;
 end; { with }

RMATable.Edit;
RMATable.FieldByName('RMA_UPDATE').AsString := DateToStr(Date);

{ Put the initials in the ComboBox }
with InitComboBox do
 begin
   Idx := 0;
   s := RMATable.FieldByName('RMA_INITS').AsString;
   Count := Items.Count;

   { Search through the list of initials. If a
     match is found, update the ComboBox. }
   if Count > 0 then
    repeat
      Match := s = Items[Idx];
      if Match
        then ItemIndex := Idx
        else Inc(Idx);
    until Match or (Idx = Count);
   if not Match or (Count = 0) then ItemIndex := -1; { Unselected }
 end; { with }

{ Put the status in the ComboBox }
with StatusComboBox do
```

```
                  begin
                    Idx := RMATable.FieldByName('RMA_STATUS').AsInteger;
                    if (Idx >= 0) and (Idx < Items.Count)
                      then ItemIndex := Idx
                      else ItemIndex := -1; { Unselected }
                  end; { with }
              end
        else begin { Append a new record }
              Caption := 'Add RMA Record';
              with RMATable do
               begin
                 Append;

                 { Set up the RMA number and the issue and update dates }
                 RMANum := NextRMATable.FieldByName('RXT_RMANUM').AsInteger;
                 Str(RMANum, s);                          { The sequence number
}
                 while Length(s) < 3 do s := '0' + s;   { Zero fill it }
                 s1 := DateToStr(Date);                      { The date }
                 s1 := copy(s1, Length(s1)-1, 2);       { Just the year }
                 while Length(s) < 2 do s := '0' + s;   { Zero fill it }
                 s := 'BX' + s + '-' + s1;                  { Put it all together }

                 FieldByName('RMA_ID').AsString := s;
                 FieldByName('RMA_DATE').AsString := DateToStr(Date);
                 FieldByName('RMA_UPDATE').AsString := DateToStr(Date);

                 { Set the invoice and items tables to their first records }
                 InvoiceTable.First;
                 ItemsTable.First;

                 { Set up the default values }
                 FieldByName('RMA_INVNUM').AsString
                    := InvoiceTable.FieldByName('INV_NUM').AsString;
                 FieldByName('RMA_STKNUM').AsString
                    := ItemsTable.FieldByName('ITM_STKNUM').AsString;
                 FieldByName('RMA_SERNUM').AsString
                    := ItemsTable.FieldByName('ITM_SERNUM').AsString;
                 FieldByName('RMA_CUSTID').AsString
                    := InvoiceTable.FieldByName('INV_CUSTID').AsString;

                 { Get the default employee initials }
                 InitComboBox.ItemIndex := 0;
                 FieldByName('RMA_INITS').AsString
                    := InitComboBox.Text;

                 { Get the default status information }
                 StatusComboBox.ItemIndex := 0;
                 FieldByName('RMA_STATUS').AsInteger := 0;
               end; { with }
            end;
     end;
```

```
procedure TAddRMAForm.OKBtnClick(Sender: TObject);
begin
 UpdateRMARecord;
 RMATable.Post;

 { Pass back the current record's index }
 RMAIndexStr := RMATable.FieldByName('RMA_ID').AsString;

 if not Editing
   then begin { We must have appended a new RMA }

           { Increment the RMA next-number counter }
           Inc(RMANum);

           { Stuff the new number in the Next RMA Table }
           with NextRMATable do
            begin
              Edit;
              FieldByName('RXT_RMANUM').AsInteger := RMANum;
              Post;
            end; { with }
         end;
end;

procedure TAddRMAForm.CancelBtnClick(Sender: TObject);
begin
 RMATable.Cancel;
end;

procedure TAddRMAForm.UpdateRMARecord;
begin
 with RMATable do
   begin
     { Update only if we are in the Insert or Edit mode }
     if (State = dsInsert) or (State = dsEdit)
       then begin
               { Get the invoice number and customer ID from the Invoice Table }
               FieldByName('RMA_INVNUM').AsString
                  := InvoiceTable.FieldByName('INV_NUM').AsString;
               FieldByName('RMA_CUSTID').AsString
                  := InvoiceTable.FieldByName('INV_CUSTID').AsString;

               { Get the stock number and serial number from the Items Table }
               FieldByName('RMA_STKNUM').AsString
                  := ItemsTable.FieldByName('ITM_STKNUM').AsString;
               FieldByName('RMA_SERNUM').AsString
                  := ItemsTable.FieldByName('ITM_SERNUM').AsString;

               { Get the initials from the ComboBox }
               FieldByName('RMA_INITS').AsString
                  := InitComboBox.Text;

               { Get the status information from the ComboBox }
```

```
              FieldByName('RMA_STATUS').AsInteger
                  := StatusComboBox.ItemIndex;
              end;
    end; { with }
  end;

procedure TAddRMAForm.InvoiceNavClick(Sender: TObject;
    Button: TNavigateBtn);
begin
  UpdateRMARecord;
end;

procedure TAddRMAForm.StatusComboBoxChange(Sender: TObject);
begin
  RMATable.FieldByName('RMA_STATUS').AsInteger
      := StatusComboBox.ItemIndex;
end;

procedure TAddRMAForm.FindBtnClick(Sender: TObject);
begin
  with FindRecordDlg do
    begin
      Caption := 'Find Invoice';
      SearchStrLabel.Caption := 'Invoice number';
      SearchStrEdit.Text := '';
      if (ShowModal = mrCancel)
        or (SearchStrEdit.Text = '') then Exit;
    end; { with }

  with InvoiceTable do
    begin
      Cancel;
      First;
      SetKey;
      FieldByName('INV_NUM').AsString := FindRecordDlg.SearchStrEdit.Text;
      GotoNearest;
    end; { with }
end;

end.
```

That Empty Feeling

I stood up and stretched again. Mewnix was sawing logs on the couch. I limped to the window and pulled back the drape. It had become daylight. I could tell, because I could *see* the rain as well as hear it. My watch told me it was 8:14, but my stomach was transmitting an even more important message.

I put on my coat and hat, and reached for my keys. I was ready for adventure. I was ready for danger. I was ready for *breakfast*.

• • •

"Hi ya, Ace. Eatin' alone today?"

When it came to waitresses, Shirley was one of the best, if not the most brilliant. She was a pretty brunette of medium height, with corrective lenses and shoes to match. As always, she was wearing a starched, peach-colored uniform with her name embroidered on the front. The curves it revealed wouldn't have challenged a beginning Driver's Ed student.

"Yeah. I've already tried it the other way," I responded.

"What'll it be, Sweetie—the usual?" she asked, drawing the order pad from her hip like a gunfighter pulling a Colt 45. "Our special today is the Spotted Owl Lumberjack Breakfast."

"Sure. Why not? Give me the special," I said.

"Okay. That's two soy flour pancakes, two pieces of turkey ham, and two slices of rice toast with fat-free cream cheese and sugarless jam on the side. How'd you like your Egg Beaters?"

"Scrambled."

"Coffee?"

"What's the Café du Jour?"

"Antediluvian Mist. You'll just go mad for it." She popped her gum in waltz time as she continued. "It comes from high in the Antediluvian Mountains, where the beans are hand-picked by native non-smokers, and then carried down the mountainside in recyclable, hand-woven bags on the backs of miniature burros..."

"I'll take a cup," I interrupted. It was evident that Sven the Coffee Salesman had been through town again. I won't say that Shirley is gullible, but last week she bought a home study course called "Speak Esperanto Like a Native."

She nodded her assent, then disappeared into the kitchen. A few minutes later she presented me with a steaming platter and a mug of black brew.

Helen and I had met frequently for breakfast here at Arnor's Espresso Cafe and Endangered Species Museum. It was the one place in town where "the elite meet to eat." The kind of place where a person could enjoy some intellectually stimulating conversation with his or her meal. Today I didn't feel like talking to anyone, so as I ate I contemplated Arnor's renowned exhibit of color posters depicting some of the world's most endangered species. The great egret. The hognose snake. The roseate spoonbill. My eyes swept to the right, to another group of posters. The white rhinoceros. The sandhill crane. And the snow leopard. Then a shiver ran up my spine, as on the facing wall, my eyes became riveted on what were perhaps the three most endangered of all—Products made in America, Two-Parent Families, and High School Graduates who can read and write.

I had been so engrossed I hadn't noticed that Shirley had returned to my table.

"Anything else, Hon?" she asked.

"Nothing," I said. "Just the check."

"You're almost outta coffee," she said, motioning with one of the two glass pots she held. "How 'bout a warm-up?"

"No thanks," I said, tossing the last couple of ounces down my gullet. "I like my coffee the way I like my women—plain, cold and totally devoid of sweetness." A glance at Shirley told me instantly that she knew my words were as empty as my cup.

"Ya know, it really is too bad about you and Helen," she said, tearing off a slip of paper from her pad and handing it to me. "She's really a nice kid. Who'da figured after all this time it'd be her and that big guy. Kinda crazy, ain't it? I wonder what they'll have in common."

The nice thing about living in a small town is that everybody knows everybody else's business. Sometimes even before it happens.

"Probably half their clothes closet," I replied bitterly. "Of course, if they coordinate, they can probably save a bundle on their wardrobe."

"Oh, well. Live and let live. That's what I always say." She bent down, bringing her face close to mine. She gave me a puzzled look, and said "Ya know, there's something a little odd about your face, but I can't quite put my finger on it."

"Shirley, you must have noticed I had no eyebrows the minute I walked in here," I said.

"Naw, that ain't it. But then again, you may be right. Go figure." She turned and marched back toward the kitchen, the clicking of her heels on the linoleum perfectly syncopated with the popping of her gum.

I tossed a five-spot on the table and ambled to the door. I badly needed to do some grocery shopping, but the food hitting my stomach was already causing my metabolism to drop like a rock. If I wasn't careful, I would wind up somewhere just south of Dreamland. If I was to survive this day, I would have to keep my mind off anything having to do with sleep.

Through the window I could see the rain coming down in sheets, covering everything like a blanket. It was a tough job I still had to do. But I'd made my bed. Now I would have to lie in it.

I headed for my car.

IMPROVING THE RMA MANAGEMENT FORM

I walked back into the office with renewed determination and two sacks full of groceries. I was ready to work the same magic on the RMA Management form as I had on the RMA Input form. I had six goals to accomplish:

1. Add the capability of searching for RMAs by number.
2. Ask for confirmation from the user before deleting RMAs.
3. Enable and disable buttons, depending on the state of the RMA table.
4. Incorporate the status message constants.
5. Adjust the size, color, and fonts of the form's labels.
6. Put away the groceries. (I decided to accomplish this task first, so the frozen tofu wouldn't thaw.)

To a large degree, I would be repeating the operations I had performed on the Input form.

Searching for RMAs by the Number

In trying to retrieve an RMA, I would be looking at the same type of partial-match search I had used for locating invoices on the Input form. The largest difference would be the captions on the labels on the Find Record form, and the name of the table and field I would be searching. I literally did a cut-and-paste of the routine from the Input form, and I made my changes to the copy.

While running a few tests, I discovered that the search is case-sensitive, which means typing in "bx006" won't find a match with "BX006". There are a couple ways of handling this situation. One is to use a MaskEdit component instead of an Edit on the Find Record dialog. By manipulating the MaskEdit's mask, the entry could be limited to numerals when used to accept invoice numbers, and it could be set to automatically uppercase letters when entered as part of the RMA number. Too complicated for this demo—I just uppercased the entry before I assigned it to the field to search. The resulting OnClick handler is shown in Listing 20.7.

Listing 20.7   OnClick handler for the RMA Management form's Find button

```
procedure TRMAMgmtForm.FindBtnClick(Sender: TObject);
begin
 with FindRecordDlg do
   begin
    Caption := 'Find RMA Record';
    SearchStrLabel.Caption := 'RMA number';
    SearchStrEdit.Text := '';
    if (ShowModal = mrCancel)
      or (SearchStrEdit.Text = '') then Exit;
   end; { with }

 with RMATable do
   begin
    Cancel;
    First;
    SetKey;
    FieldByName('RMA_ID').AsString
       := UpperCase(FindRecordDlg.SearchStrEdit.Text);
    GotoNearest;
   end; { with }

end;
```

Confirming Deletions

It's much too easy for a user to hit a wrong button. When that action allows something to be deleted with no recourse, problems are guaranteed to arise. I wanted to provide a little "safety net" when deleting RMA records.

The approach was simple: Use the **MessageDlg** function to display the current RMA number and request a confirmation. This function returns a value that corresponds to the button pressed. By checking this value I would know if the user confirmed the deletion. If so, I would present them with a

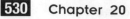

ShowMessage dialog that notified them that the deletion really did take place. The code for this appears in Listing 20.8.

Listing 20.8   Revised OnClick handler for the Management form's Delete button

```
procedure TRMAMgmtForm.DeleteBtnClick(Sender: TObject);
var
 s : string;
begin
 s := 'Delete RMA #' + RMATable.FieldByName('RMA_ID').AsString + '?';
 if MessageDlg(s, mtConfirmation, [mbYes, mbNo], 0)
   = mrYes
   then begin
           RMATable.Delete;
           ShowMessage('Record deleted.');
         end;
end;
```

Enabling and Disabling Buttons

It's easy to get into a heap of trouble when you try to delete or edit a record, but there are no records in the table. Other strange anomalies can crop up when operating a form on which the components make implicit assumptions about the state of one or more tables.

One way to approach the challenge of enabling and disabling controls is to try to anticipate every possible condition, and then write code for every one of those conditions. Code written that way can be very efficient if it is perfectly correct. If it is not, it is guaranteed to come back to haunt you. I decided on a second approach: Writing a generalized routine that would appraise the state of the table and set the component states accordingly. I would then call that routine any time something could *possibly* change.

The **RefreshComponents** procedure (see Listing 20.9) examines the state of the RMA table. If **RMATable**'s Beginning Of File (**BOF**) and End Of File (**EOF**) properties are both **True**, the table must be empty. Under those conditions, several controls should be either disabled or hidden. If the table is not empty, the reverse is true.

Now, when should this be called? I decided to add it near the end of the **Synchronize** routine. That meant it would automatically be called as part of handling a click on the Add or Edit button. Of course, I added it to the **DeleteBtn** handler. The only thing that remained was to make sure everything was jake when the form first appeared. I created the simple OnActivate handler shown in Listing 20.10. The call to **RefreshForm** was included to ensure all data on the form would be correctly displayed when the form was activated.

Listing 20.9   Enabling and disabling the Management form's buttons

```
procedure TRMAMgmtForm.RefreshComponents;
begin
 if RMATable.BOF and RMATable.EOF { The table is empty }
   then begin
           { Disable the Delete, Edit, and Find buttons }
           DeleteBtn.Enabled := False;
           EditBtn.Enabled := False;
           FindBtn.Enabled := False;

           { Hide the Customer name and phone, and Product name }
           CustNameDBText.Visible := False;
           CustPhoneDBText.Visible := False;
           ProductDBText.Visible := False;

           { Hide the status message }
           StatusMsgLabel.Visible := False;
         end
   else begin
           { Enable the Delete, Edit, and Find buttons }
           DeleteBtn.Enabled := True;
           EditBtn.Enabled := True;
           FindBtn.Enabled := True;

           { Show the Customer name and phone, and Product name }
           CustNameDBText.Visible := True;
           CustPhoneDBText.Visible := True;
           ProductDBText.Visible := True;

           { Show the status message }
           StatusMsgLabel.Visible := True;
         end;
end;
```

Listing 20.10   OnActivate handler for the RMA Management form

```
procedure TRMAMgmtForm.FormActivate(Sender: TObject);
begin
 RefreshForm;
 RefreshComponents;
end;
```

Incorporating the Status Message Constants

To make use of the string constants I had added in the RMAConst unit, all I had to do was to declare the unit in the Management form's uses list, and to replace the case statement used to create the caption for **StatusMsgLabel**. The modified code that replaces the case statement appears in Listing 20.11.

Listing 20.11 Modified code for captioning the status message label

```
{ Refresh the Status }
StatusMsgLabel.Caption :=
  StatusMessages[RMATable.FieldByName('RMA_STATUS').AsInteger];
```

Spiffing the Form

Time for a little plastic surgery. By changing a few properties, I could quickly improve the look of the form, just as I had with the RMA Input form.

I changed the fonts on all of the labels (except **StatusMsgLabel**, of course) to 9-point Arial Regular, in navy blue. I grouped the labels and DBTexts a little closer vertically, and I surrounded the information display in the upper part of the form with a frame-style bevel.

While testing, I discovered I had forgotten to set **DescDBMemo** to **ReadOnly** status. I remedied that situation, and set its **TabStop** property **False** so that it couldn't get the focus. Then I rearranged the tab order to provide what I considered a natural progression through the form. A "running" version of the RMA Management form, including all my changes, is shown in Figure 20.10.

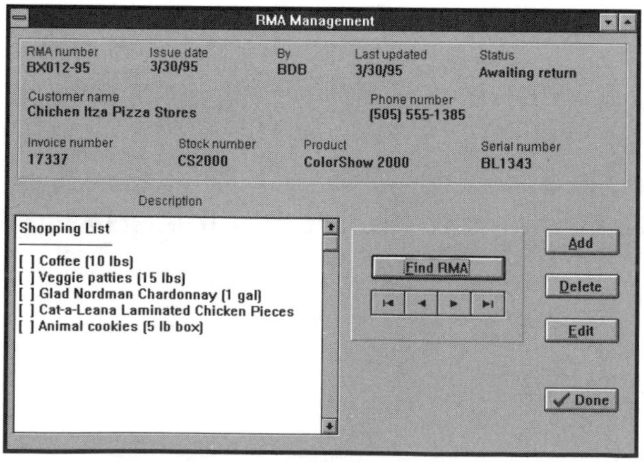

Figure 20.10 *Latest version of the RMA Management form.*

At first I was tempted to call this the "final" version of the Management form. Then I started thinking about the next step, where I would be adding a printed report. I had not yet provided a means to generate that report, and it seemed to me now the most logical place to offer a report was from this form. I decided to keep an open mind on this.

Updating the Main Form

I glanced at my watch. It said it was 9:11. I think I was beginning to hallucinate. Out the front window, in the gray downpour, I could almost swear I saw a very large boat float by, with animals sticking their heads out the portholes. I got up and poured another mug full of my special mixture.

All the other forms had gone through an overhaul, so I figured I could invest a few minutes spiffing the Main form as well. I knew that this would not be the final version of the Main form, because I would later add a tie-in to the Windows help system, as well as adding an About dialog.

I had long since grown tired of the button-gray look of the Main form, and I thought it would be nice to give it a little color. I changed the form's color to Windows' application work space color. Then I changed its position on the screen to be centered when it came up.

The demo needed a little pizzazz. What I really wanted was to pop the Boxlight logo on the screen, and then make it disappear when the user moved the mouse or pressed a key. I figured that would be pretty easy. I didn't realize I was in for a mini-adventure.

I had created a bitmap logo earlier this evening, so that was available. All I needed now, I thought, was an Image component to hold the bitmap. That much was true. But I found out that the application was "seeing" the mouse movements and responding to them before the form became visible on the screen. The result was disappointing, to say the least: the Main form became visible, and the logo immediately disappeared.

Then a thought struck me. What if I were to add a timer to the form, and use it to mask out any mouse movements and keystrokes for a specified period of time? I came up with a 3-step plan:

1. Use the Main form's OnCreate event to initiate and enable the timer for a period of 10 seconds.

2. Write a handler for the timer's OnTimer event. When the timer "fires," have it disable itself.

3. Create a monitoring routine that tests the logo to see if it is visible. If it is visible, the routine should then test the timer to see if it is disabled. If it is disabled, the masking time is over, and it's okay to make the logo invisible.

The approach worked like a charm. I discovered a thing or two about placing images on forms, too. If the form is left with its default properties, then maximizing or resizing the form really messes up the balance—the image that was intended to be centered suddenly appears in the upper left corner. I changed the Main form's **BorderIcons** and **BorderStyle** properties to give me a form that could not be resized or maximized.

The changes I made to the properties are listed in Table 20.4. A snapshot of the form in action is included in Figure 20.11. The complete listing appears in Listing 20.12.

Table 20.4   *Changes to the Main Form's Properties*

Name	Property	Value
MainForm	BorderIcons	[biSystemMenu, biMinimize]
	BorderStyle	bsSingle
	Color	clAppWorkSpace
	Position	poScreenCenter
	OnClick	FormClick
	OnCreate	FormCreate
	OnKeyPress	FormKeyPress
	OnMouseMove	FormMouseMove
LogoImage	Left	111
	Top	75
	Width	201
	Height	65
LogoTimer	OnTimer	LogoTimerTimer

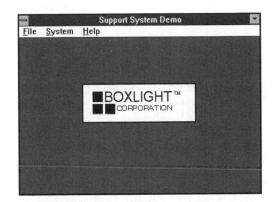

Figure 20.11 *Latest version of the Main form.*

Listing 20.12   Complete listing of the Main form

```
{————————————————————————————————————————————————————}
{                    The Boxlight Demo                 }
{              MAINUNIT.PAS : Main Form                }
{              By Ace Breakpoint, N.T.P.               }
{                Assisted by Don Taylor                }
{                                                      }
{ Chapter 20 version of the Main unit of the           }
{ Boxlight Demo application.                            }
{ Written for *Delphi Programming Explorer*            }
{ Copyright (c) 1995 The Coriolis Group, Inc.          }
{                Last Updated 3/30/95                  }
{————————————————————————————————————————————————————}

unit Mainunit;

interface

uses
   SysUtils, WinTypes, WinProcs, Messages, Classes, Graphics, Controls,
   Forms, Dialogs, Menus, ProdInfo, RMAMgmt, ExtCtrls;

type
   TMainForm = class(TForm)
      MainMenu: TMainMenu;
      MainMenuFile: TMenuItem;
      FileMenuExit: TMenuItem;
      MainMenuSystem: TMenuItem;
      SystemMenuProduct: TMenuItem;
      SystemMenuRMA: TMenuItem;
      MainMenuHelp: TMenuItem;
      HelpMenuContents: TMenuItem;
      HelpMenuTopic: TMenuItem;
      N1: TMenuItem;
      HelpMenuAbout: TMenuItem;
```

```
      LogoImage: TImage;
      LogoTimer: TTimer;
      procedure FileMenuExitClick(Sender: TObject);
      procedure SystemMenuProductClick(Sender: TObject);
      procedure SystemMenuRMAClick(Sender: TObject);
      procedure LogoTimerTimer(Sender: TObject);
      procedure FormKeyPress(Sender: TObject; var Key: Char);
      procedure FormMouseMove(Sender: TObject; Shift: TShiftState; X,
        Y: Integer);
      procedure FormClick(Sender: TObject);
      procedure FormCreate(Sender: TObject);
    private
      { Private declarations }
      procedure MonitorLogo;
    public
      { Public declarations }
    end;

var
   MainForm: TMainForm;

implementation

{$R *.DFM}

procedure TMainForm.FileMenuExitClick(Sender: TObject);
begin
 Close;
end;

procedure TMainForm.SystemMenuProductClick(Sender: TObject);
begin
 ProdInfoForm.ShowModal;
end;

procedure TMainForm.SystemMenuRMAClick(Sender: TObject);
begin
 RMAMgmtForm.ShowModal;
end;

procedure TMainForm.LogoTimerTimer(Sender: TObject);
begin
 LogoTimer.Enabled := False;
end;

procedure TMainForm.FormKeyPress(Sender: TObject; var Key: Char);
begin
 MonitorLogo;
end;

procedure TMainForm.FormMouseMove(Sender: TObject; Shift: TShiftState; X,
   Y: Integer);
begin
```

```
  MonitorLogo;
end;

procedure TMainForm.FormClick(Sender: TObject);
begin
 MonitorLogo;
end;

procedure TMainForm.FormCreate(Sender: TObject);
begin
 LogoTimer.Interval := 10000;
 LogoTimer.Enabled := True;
end;

procedure TMainForm.MonitorLogo;
begin
 if LogoImage.Visible and not LogoTimer.Enabled
   then LogoImage.Visible := False;
end;

end.
```

MAKING THE DECISION

Whew! I stopped to catch my breath. In the span of a few hours, I had gone from a stack of papers and disks that described a company's operation to a nearly complete demo application.

There were still two areas to cover. First, I would need to create a printed report that would list all of the currently active RMAs, and then I would have to modify the application so it could generate the report. Then I would add some fairly simple help capabilities to the application.

I reached into my pocket, fishing for my roller pen to take some notes. Instead, I found the business card Dave Carson had given me. My thoughts instantly turned to Rhonda, and her face unspoiled by the artifice of makeup. Had she found me appealing? Would she consider going out with me?

The clock told me it was 9:38, but the real question was, *would Rhonda give me the time of day?* It was now or never. I picked up the phone and started dialing the number on the card. To anyone else, it would have been merely a local phone number. For me, it was seven digits that would change my life forever.

A Matter of Hard Evidence

Don Taylor

Ace's long night's journey into Delphi heads into the stretch, as he adds output reporting capabilities to the demo app—and discovers a secret ally.

I carefully laid the phone back in its cradle.

At first Rhonda had been very cool, very standoffish. But when I reminded her I was the consultant she had met at Boxlight yesterday, she warmed right up to me. We talked for a couple of minutes, and then she had to get back to work. Before she hung up, though, I asked her for a date tonight— and she said "yes."

The trouble with Helen was that she always wanted to do the same things. Movies. Baseball games. Hiking. Bicycle riding. Ordinary stuff. But tonight Rhonda and I would go places and do things Helen and I never had. We'll start the evening with a quiet dinner at the Sons of Norway lodge. (Dutch treat, of course.) Then for the evening's entertainment, we'll be off to the Art School for the first lecture in the series, "The Rise of Receptionism in the 20th Century." Following that, some deep conversation over a cup of cappuccino at the Poulsbohemian Coffee House. And if we're in the mood for a nightcap, afterwards we can stroll down Front Street to the Ruptured Duck Tavern.

There's just no substitute for fine culture.

With a night like that in the offing, I knew it would be a challenge to keep my mind focused on the work at hand. I would need an *edge*. Perhaps it had not been the quality of the coffee blend I had put together earlier, but the *sheer quantity* I was drinking that had had a positive effect. If that were true, I reasoned, then consuming *even more* might yield improved results. I rummaged in the cupboards under the sink until I found the 50-cup urn Rodney had given me for graduation. I poured 5 pounds of my ground coffee mixture into the basket, and then filled the tank with the garden hose. I plugged in the stainless steel behemoth and stood back. The light came on, it shook a little, and then it started perking away. I walked over to the answering machine and flipped its switch, so I could screen my calls.

It was time to get back to work. This time out, I had two tasks ahead of me. First, I would create a report using the full-blown version of ReportSmith. Once that task was complete, I would modify the demo so it would use the runtime version of ReportSmith to print the report. It didn't sound all that difficult.

WHY REPORTSMITH?

My first question was why I needed to use ReportSmith in the first place. Delphi offers such depth, it seemed strange that I would have to use a separate report generator to print a document from my program.

As it turns out, I didn't *have* to use ReportSmith. I had access to all my data tables through my Delphi components. I could step through tables and read records, and I could print a custom report.

But ReportSmith made it much faster and easier to create a good-looking report. As with Delphi, I would be able to design a report and see right on my screen what I would get on my printer. I would be able to work with visual objects that I could move around at will.

And, ReportSmith is a powerful tool that doesn't rely on Delphi itself in any way. Its interface is directly with the data tables, either locally or (in the advanced version of ReportSmith) on remote servers. There are only two ties between Delphi and ReportSmith: the runtime version of ReportSmith, which enables Delphi programs to display or print existing reports without requiring the full ReportSmith product; and the Report component, which provides the interface between ReportSmith runtime and programs written with Delphi.

Planning the Report

Before I could create a report, I figured I should have an idea of what it would look like. It was to be a simple report that would list all of the "active" RMAs (those not completed or deleted), including some appropriate level of detail. I decided on a straight columnar report, with columns containing the RMA number, issue date, technician's initials, customer ID, invoice number, stock number, serial number, and status.

With all that information, it would probably be a good idea to print the report sideways—in landscape format. Come to think of it, just how would printed copies of the report be stored? Most likely in a 3-ring binder, so the pages would need to be formatted with enough room at the top to allow for the punched holes.

Of course, it would be nice to include the same Boxlight logo I had used on the demo's "splash screen." And perhaps a divider line or two. Some nice fonts. I had to remind myself once again of the priorities: First get it working, and *then* make it pretty.

Making Connections

As soon as I launched ReportSmith, I realized I had stepped into a whole new world. It was obvious this was not an extension of the Delphi environment. I got the feeling I was in for several new experiences. It started with aliases.

Like the DBD, ReportSmith permits an "alias" for the names of paths used to locate tables. In ReportSmith, however, the term *alias* is used to describe an alternate name for tables and fields. For variables that represent data paths or server names, ReportSmith uses the term *connection*s instead.

Before getting started on the report, I needed to set up a connection to the directory where the Boxlight data was kept. From Delphi's Tools menu, I launched ReportSmith. From ReportSmith, I selected File|Connections, and got the Connection dialog shown in Figure 21.1.

Besides the variations in the alias concept, there turned out to be another significant difference between the way Delphi and the DBD handled data, and the way it was treated by ReportSmith. While DBD uses IDAPI drivers, ReportSmith prefers the ODBC flavor. (It's possible to use the IDAPI driver with ReportSmith, but it seems to have only minimal support for Structured Query Language when used with dBASE and Paradox tables.) That's why I selected RS_dBase [ODBC] as the type of connection, as shown in Figure 21.1.

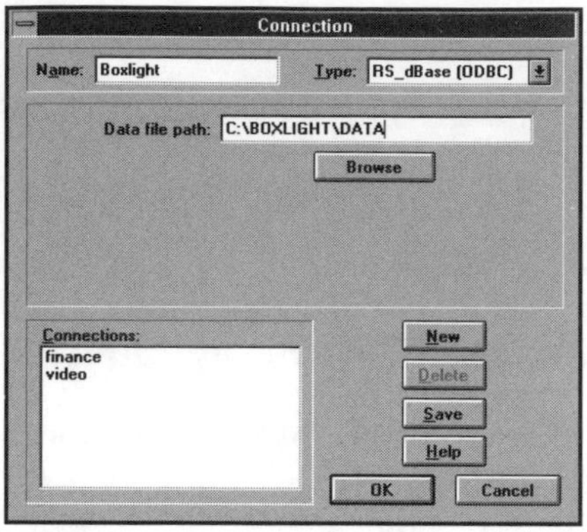

Figure 21.1   *ReportSmith's Connection dialog.*

When I had entered everything as shown in the figure, I clicked the OK button to save the connection and put the dialog away.

Populating the RMA Table

To have some meaningful data for the report, I needed to expand the number of entries in the RMA table. I closed the Delphi project file, and then ran Database Desktop. From DBD, I opened the RMA table. I then clicked on the Edit Data speed button, and I deleted every record in the table. Next, I selected Table | Restructure Table from the menu, marked the Pack Table checkbox, and then clicked on the Save button. I now had a pristine RMA table.

From that point, I loaded and ran the demo from the Delphi IDE, adding several bogus RMA entries to the table. With that data under my belt, I could build the report with ReportSmith.

CREATING THE REPORT

From the outset, it was important that I should understand exactly what a "report" is: *A report is the result of a query on one or more data tables, arranged in a pre-defined format for display.* I reached for my roller pen, and scratched down the following "formula":

```
Report = Database + Report Query + Report Format
```

It seemed true enough to me. A report was, in effect, the sum total of these three elements. If any of those elements changed, the report would change also.

I had already taken care of the Database portion of my quasi-formula by populating the RMA table. It was now time to create the Report Query, using a default columnar-style format to get started. Once the query portion was complete, I would work on the format of the report.

I selected File|New from the ReportSmith menu, and got the Create a New Report dialog shown in Figure 21.2. I selected the Columnar report (and the Columnar style as well) and then clicked OK to close the dialog.

The Report Queries dialog then came up with its Tables page automatically selected. To fully define the query portion of the report, I would have to specify several things—starting with the tables to include in the query.

I clicked on the "Add table" button and got the Select Table to be Added dialog (see Figure 21.3). I selected "Boxlight" as the connection, and I was shown the names of all the tables in the demo's data directory. I selected the RMA table and then clicked on OK.

I was returned to the Tables page of the Report Query dialog, as shown in Figure 21.4. It was pretty evident there were fields in the RMA table that I

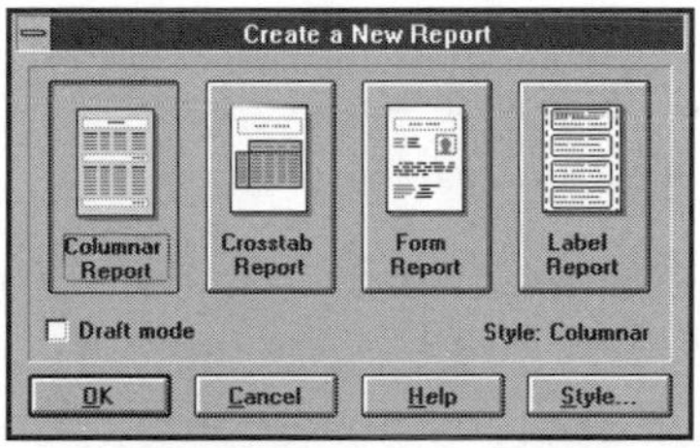

Figure 21.2 *Selecting the type of a new report.*

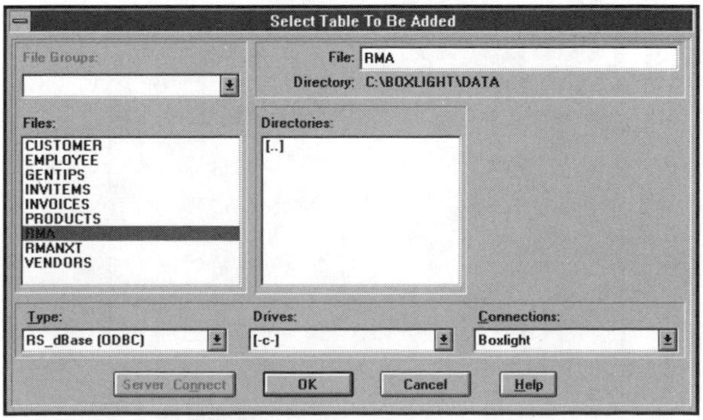

Figure 21.3 *Adding the RMA table to the report.*

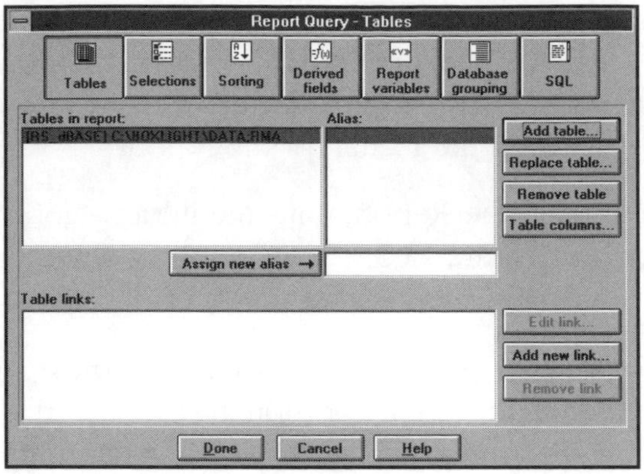

Figure 21.4 *The Tables page of the Report Query dialog.*

didn't want printed on the report. That is taken care of by individually select-ing the table columns that are to be included as part of the report. I clicked on the "Table columns" button and was presented with the Table Columns dialog of Figure 21.5.

It is assumed that every column in the table will be included in the report. I clicked on RMA_CUSTID, and then "control-clicked" to select RMA_UPDATE as well. Then I clicked the "Exclude from report" radio button to eliminate the two fields from further consideration.

A note to myself: I had the opportunity on the Tables page of the Report Query dialog to define an alias for the RMA table. Here on the Table Columns dialog, I had a chance to assign an alias to any of the columns. I had taken pains to create table and field (column) names that were easily recognized, so I decided not to assign any aliases.

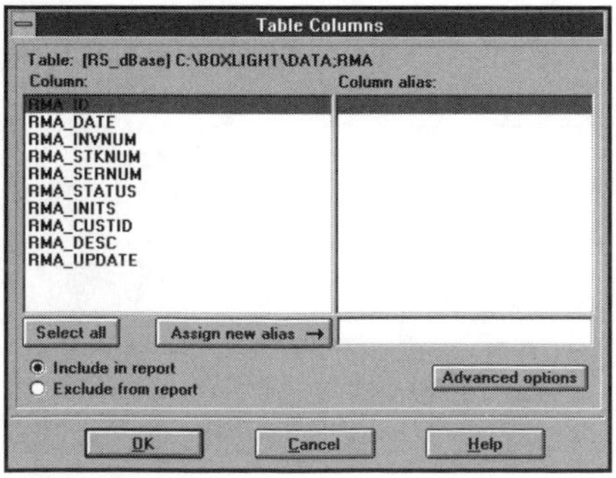

Figure 21.5 *Selecting the columns for the report.*

I clicked the OK button to put away the Table Columns dialog and return to the Tables page of the Report Query dialog.

I was ready to choose how I would order the records that would appear in the report. Since there would be no duplicate RMA numbers, the only thing I had to tell ReportSmith was that I wanted the records in order by ascending RMA number. I clicked on the "Sorting" button and got the Sort page, with the RMA_ID field already highlighted in the "Report fields" box. I simply clicked the "Insert into sort list" button to add that field to the "Sort list" box at the top. The result is shown in Figure 21.6.

That's all I needed to do here. I'd made a rough definition of the query that would be answered by the data that would appear in the report. I clicked the Done button to close the Report Query dialog.

My hard disk thrashed for several seconds, and to my amazement, the default columnar report appeared on my screen. It was very rough—and the Customer ID column didn't even fit on the page on the screen—but it was a report nevertheless. (A picture of it appears in Figure 21.7.) I saved the report as ACTIVRMA.RPT in the \BOXLIGHT\APP directory.

The new report needed to be rotated so it would fit on an 8-1/2 by 11-inch sheet in landscape mode. I selected File | Page Setup from the menu, which brought up the Page Setup dialog. I clicked on the "Size and orientation" radio button, which brought up a page that allowed me to select landscape orientation. I clicked the "Margins" radio button to return to the original page, and then I filled in the margins as shown in Figure 21.8. I clicked on the OK button to close the dialog, and then I was asked if I wanted to resize the report sections to fit the new margins. I gave it the go-ahead.

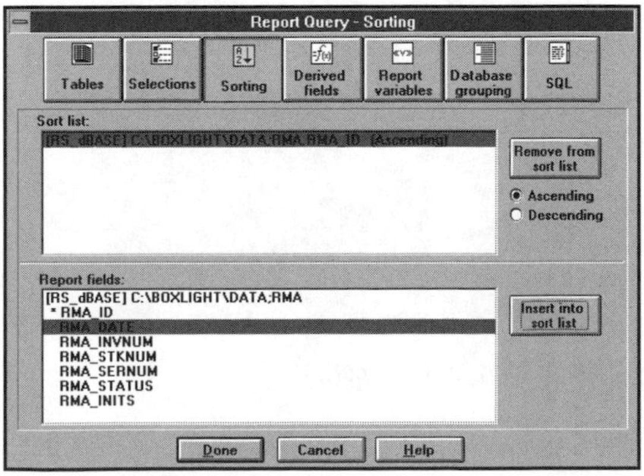

Figure 21.6 _Sorting the report on the RMA number._

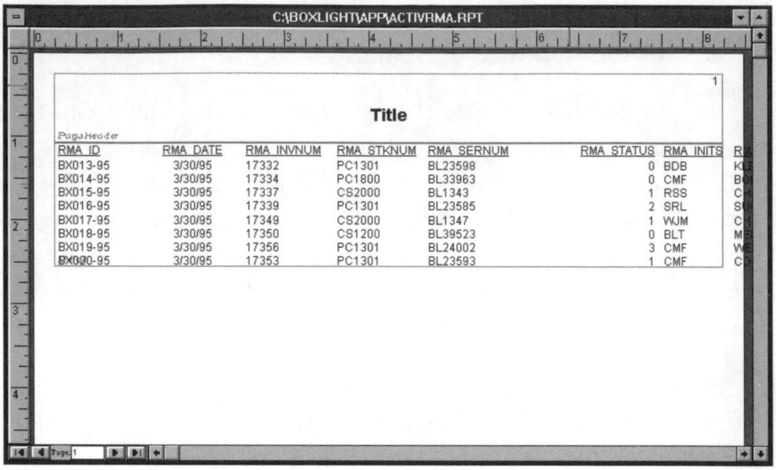

Figure 21.7 *First version of the Active RMA report.*

Although the width of the page was now wider than my screen, at least all of the fields fit on the page. I saved the report again.

Limiting the Report to Active RMAs

The report on my screen included every record in the RMA table. But the goal was to list only the "active" RMAs—those with status codes of 0 (awaiting return) or 1 (awaiting replacement parts or units). I reasoned that ReportSmith must somewhere include a mechanism for narrowing down the number of records used in the report.

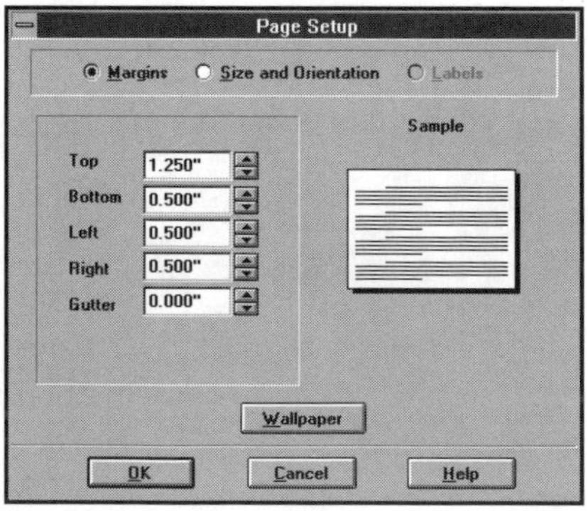

Figure 21.8 *Selecting page margins for the report.*

Under the Tools option on ReportSmith's menu, I noticed that the first item was the Report Query dialog, and several of the options beneath it referred to the pages offered on that dialog, providing a direct way to get to those pages. I chose Tools|Selections, which brought up the Selections page. On that page, I clicked on the square with the numeral "1" in it, and then chose "Add selection criteria" from the listbox that was presented. The following line appeared:

```
[1] data field   RMA.RMA_ID   is equal to   text   ___
```

I could now create an expression that would tell ReportSmith which records should be included in the report—those with a status value of 0 or 1. Starting at the left side of the expression on the screen, I clicked on each item and selected from the choices offered. For the last item I typed in the numeral "2". When I was through, the expression looked like:

```
[1] data field   RMA.RMA_STATUS is less than   number   _2__
```

I clicked the Done button. After a few seconds of thrashing, the report appeared again, this time including only records for which the status field had a value of 0 or 1. I was definitely making progress. Next, I would…

My thought was interrupted by a short knock at the door. It was my pal, Muffy, who bounded into the office with her usual enthusiastic aura.

"Hi ya, Ace. Just thought I'd drop by and—Whoa! This place is really a mess!"

"Yeah," I said. "I had a little altercation with a waste basket last night. There was a tiny little fire that had to be taken care of."

"I knew that," Muffy replied. She put her hands in the back pockets of her western-style jeans and sidled toward the sink.

"The standing water was left by the firefighters," I explained, following her to the kitchenette. "That thick black stuff all over the walls and ceiling is just a little smoke deposit. It will wash off with a sponge and some water," I continued. "And that kitchen wall isn't gutted nearly as bad as it appears. It's those exposed pipes and the wiring hanging out of the wall, and that 3-foot hole into the bathroom that makes the wall appear to be damaged."

"I knew that," she said, turning to face me. She crossed her arms in front of her, leaned against the counter, and gave me *The Look*. It wasn't a look, really—it was more of a *stare*. As if she were looking right through me. I knew there simply was no way I could conceal anything from her.

"Helen and I broke up last night," I confessed.

"I knew that."

There wasn't much you could tell Muffy that she didn't already know. She was a professional part-time psychic who worked for one of those 900-number "Call a Live Psychic" companies. After changing her major five times, she finally graduated last year with a degree in Fashion Therapy. Today her long brown hair was tied in back, and she was wearing designer jeans, a designer blouse and designer sneakers. She called it her "Early Ellie Mae Clampett" statement.

"I've been meaning for several days to come over and talk to you about your break-up," she said.

"You mean you knew it was going to happen?" I asked.

"Well, sort of. I mean, I guess a lot of people did. I think it was inevitable."

I supposed the separation *was* inevitable. Helen and I had begun separating the day we met. I held fond memories of that day at the Recycling Center. I was separating my office paper from my newsprint. She was separating her green glass from the brown.

"I'm always the last to know," I replied. "So what did you want to tell me?"

"I'm getting some funny 'vibes' about this whole thing. Some confusion. Like there's someone else involved."

"There *is* someone else involved," I said. "She didn't just break up with me—she left me for another guy. And for your information, there's someone else in my life, too—I'm going out with another woman," I added, a little defensively.

"I knew that. But I really..." she trailed off. She was giving me *The Look* again. This time she was staring directly at my face. After several seconds, she said, "Ace, are you aware that—"

"I don't have any eyebrows?" I broke in to finish her question. I could tell she was impressed.

"Yeah, I knew that. But how did *you* know? Hey—are you psychic, too?"

"If so, it's hereditary," I said. "Sometimes my mother could predict the future. Whenever I did anything bad, she could always tell me what was going to happen when my dad got home."

"Maybe that's it, all right," she said. "Anyway, what I wanted to say—"

Beep-beep! Beep-beep!

The intellectual void had suddenly been invaded by the diamond-studded designer pager on Muffy's designer belt.

"Oops—gotta go," she said. "I'm on call this morning, and it looks like somebody wants to know about their love life. I'll phone you later," she called out over her shoulder as she headed through the pouring rain to the parking lot. She jumped into her Beamer 735 and turned its key, setting the powerful engine in motion. The car backed out of its parking place and then suddenly stopped. Rolling down her window, Muffy pointed to my car and yelled, "I *love* the new bumper sticker!"

"Thanks! Got it at Sonja's," I yelled back.

A bolt of lightning momentarily lit up the entire sky. Muffy yelled something I couldn't quite make out over the explosion of the ensuing thunder, but I think it may have been "I knew that." Then she slammed the accelerator to the floor. I waved, but she was already out of sight.

I stood there for a moment, wondering why a professional psychic would need a pager. Wouldn't they already know someone was calling them?

Using Real Customer Names

I had no time or answers for rhetorical questions. The report I had created had a long way to go to be acceptable. I shut the door and ambled back to the computer. I filled my mug again from the now half-empty coffee urn.

I suppose customer ID codes are fine for some, but providing the actual name of the customer conveys a lot more information. On one level, I knew the mechanism for making this happen: Use the customer ID that appears here as the index to select the name from the Customer table. But how would I accomplish that?

A little reading gave me the answer. I would need to add the Customer table to the report, then exclude every column except the one I wanted—CST_COMPNM. Then I would have to establish a link between the RMA table and the Customer table, based on the customer ID field in each of those tables.

From the menu, I selected Tools | Table to get the Tables page of the Report Query dialog. From there, I clicked on the "Add table" button, then I selected the Customer table from the list offered to me. I clicked on OK to accept my choice.

I had to limit the fields, so I clicked the "Table columns" button. Since I only wanted two fields available to the report (CST_ID for the link and CST_COMPNM for the name), I clicked the "Select all" button, then I clicked the "Exclude from report" radio button. To add back the two fields I wanted, I clicked on each of their names, following that action in each case with a click on the "Include in report" button. Once again, I clicked the OK button to return to the Tables page.

I clicked the Done button, and I was surprised to see a dialog warning me that I might be creating a huge bunch of records. I didn't understand why, so I clicked "No," meaning I didn't want to change what I had done. A few seconds later, I appreciated the warning I had received. The report was suddenly overflowing with entries!

Dang! By forgetting to establish the link, I had implicitly asked ReportSmith to perform an *outer join*, which means that for each record in Table A, a duplicate will be created for each record in Table B. If Table A has x records and Table B has y records, the resulting join will have x *times* y records. That can mount up in a hurry!

I quickly selected Tools | Tables again. Next, I clicked the "Add new link" button on the Tables page, which brought up the Create New Table Link dialog (see Figure 21.9). The upper-left box showed the RMA table as se-

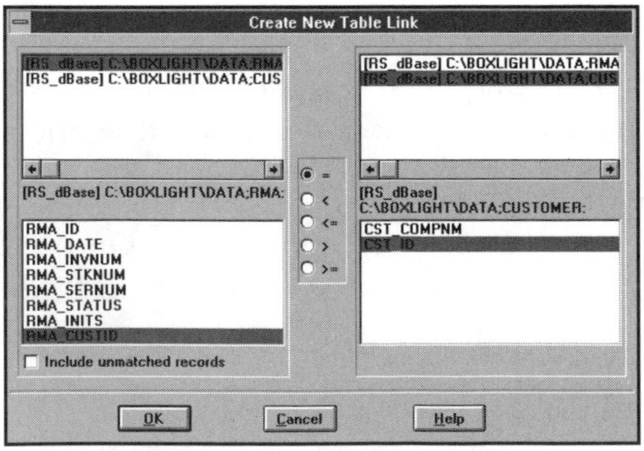

Figure 21.9 *Creating a link between the RMA and Customer tables.*

lected, and the box below it listed all the fields I had chosen to include in the report. On the right side were identical boxes that showed the Customer table as selected, and the two fields available from it. In the lower left box I clicked on RMA_CUSTID, and in the lower right box I selected CST_ID. The relational operator in the center panel was already set to establish a link where the two fields were equal, so my job was complete. Figure 21.9 shows the criteria I chose for the link. I clicked the OK button to return to the Tables page, then clicked Done to return to the report.

This time there was no warning, and the report came back with only six line items. Sure enough, each line included the name of the customer (although it was pushed off the right side of the page). In fact, I now had *three* versions of the customer information, provided by RMA_CUSTID, CST_ID, and CST_COMPNM! Then a small revelation hit me: Although you may have to include a field in a report to be able to perform computations, establish links, or make decisions, *you don't necessarily have to display it.*

I clicked on the column of data below the RMA_CUSTID label, and a box complete with black "handles" (similar to those on Delphi components) appeared, showing me the column was selected. I held my breath and tapped the Delete key. The column—including its label—disappeared. Wow! I did the same thing with the CST_ID column, and suddenly all the data once again fit within the width of the page. I saved my work.

Adding the Status Messages

Displaying the company name had been almost too easy. Now I wanted to get rid of the numbers for the status level, and replace them with the status messages I had used in the demo. But first things first. My mug was empty again, and I needed to increase my efficiency. At first I considered looking for a bigger mug, until I remembered I was already using the largest mug I owned. I toyed with the idea of using two mugs, which would cut my number of trips to the urn in half. Then the obvious solution struck me: *I would bring the Mountain Grown to Mohammed.* I removed my TV from its roll-around cart, and put the urn in its place. Then I rolled the cart right up beside my chair and plugged it in. Now there would be no wasted motion.

To replace the numerical status levels with their corresponding message strings, I would have to create what ReportSmith calls a *derived field.* A derived field is one that doesn't exist in any of the tables, but is instead synthesized by combining fields from one or more tables, or by manufacturing a custom field from data, by way of calculations or string manipulations. Once created, it can be treated like any other field.

There are two methods available to create a derived field. One uses SQL, the other relies on the use of "macros" (short program segments) written by the programmer. The latter method seemed the logical one here.

I suspected that because ReportSmith is included with Delphi but not totally integrated with it, I would probably not be able to use the RMAConst unit I had created earlier for the demo. That suspicion turned out to be correct. In fact, I would be writing routines in an entirely different context, in a different Integrated Development Environment, and with an entirely different language—ReportBasic.

After a short study, I was ready to proceed. I selected Tools|Derived fields, which brought up the Derived Fields page of the Report Query dialog, a picture of which is shown in Figure 21.10. As can be seen in the figure, I named the new field **StatusMessage**, and I declared it to be defined by a ReportBasic macro. I clicked the Add button to proceed.

I was now presented with the Choose a Macro dialog. As shown in Figure 21.11, I named the new macro **MakeStatusMsg**, and then clicked the New button.

Clicking the New button brought up the Edit Macro dialog, as shown in Figure 21.12. This was where I would create the code for the new macro, and there appeared to be several convenient ways to accomplish that task. I chose to hold the ReportSmith manual in one hand, while I typed with the other.

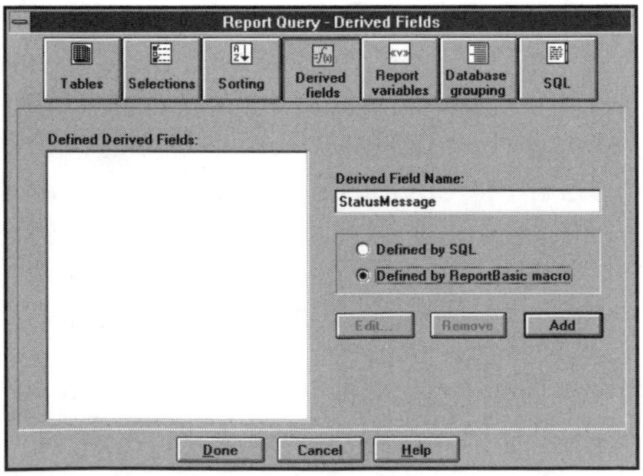

Figure 21.10   *Creating a derived field called StatusMessage.*

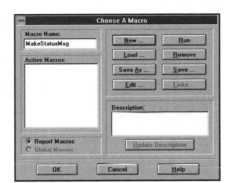

Figure 21.11 *Declaring the MakeStatusMsg macro.*

After several failed tries (it took a while to get the syntax exactly right), I wrote the macro that appears in Listing 21.1. Basically (no pun intended) it's a **case** statement similar to those I had used earlier in Object Pascal. If the status value in the table indicates the RMA is still active, the macro simply returns a string with a status message identical to one of those in my RMAConst unit. Otherwise, it returns with an error message.

I clicked the OK button in order to return to the Choose a Macro dialog, then I clicked the OK button on that dialog to take me back to the Derived Fields page, where I was able to click the Done button to return to the report.

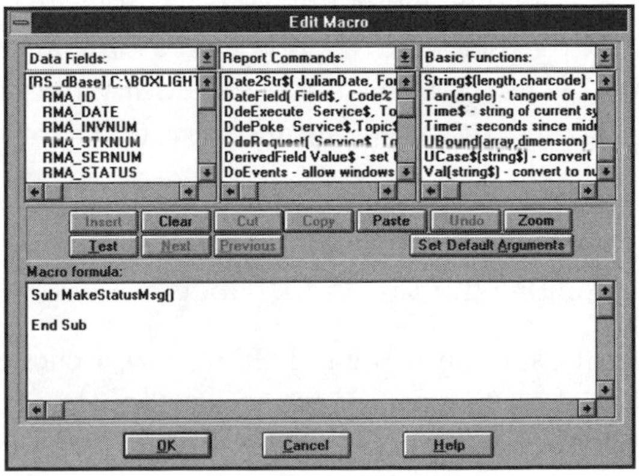

Figure 21.12 *Entering the code for the MakeStatusMsg macro.*

Listing 21.1 The MakeStatusMsg macro in ReportBasic

```
Sub MakeStatusMsg()
 Select Case Field$("RMA_STATUS")
   Case is = "0"
     DerivedField "Awaiting return"
   Case is = "1"
     DerivedField "Awaiting replacmt"
   Case Else
     DerivedField "** Undefined **"
 End Select
End Sub
```

I was back at the report, and after a few seconds, the **StatusMessage** field appeared off the right end of the page. Everything looked great—the messages matched the status codes.

Having accomplished my goal, there was no longer a need to display the RMA_STATUS data on the report. I clicked on that column to select it, and then I tapped the Delete key to make it disappear.

Spiffing the Body of the Report

Although I had prepared the Database portion of my formula and the Report Query was now finished, I still had to complete the Report Formatting portion. I had managed to get all the information in the body of the report to fit within the margins. Now it was time to perform a little body and fender work.

As I reviewed at the report, I thought it might look a little better if the RMA_INITS and CST_COMPNM columns were reversed. As before, I clicked on the CST_COMPNM column to select it. Then I clicked on it and dragged it just to the left of the RMA_INITS column. When I lifted my finger from the mouse button, the screen flashed and the columns relocated.

Pretty cool, I thought. The only other thing I wanted to do to the body of the report was to improve the appearance of the titles. The first step was to change the titles by editing the text in the labels at the top of each column.

Starting with the leftmost column's label (RMA_ID), I clicked on the label to select it, and then clicked a second time to get the I-bar cursor, indicating I could edit the text. I gave each label a new title, as listed in Table 21.1.

Now, to change the font on the titles. I moved my cursor to the left of the row of titles, until it turned into a heavy, right-pointing arrow. When I clicked, the entire row of labels containing the titles became selected. While they were

Table 21.1 *Changes to the Column Labels*

Old Title	New Title
RMA_ID	RMA number
RMA_DATE	Issue date
RMA_INVNUM	Invoice #
RMA_STKNUM	Stock #
RMA_SERNUM	Serial #
RMA_INITS	Tech
CST_COMPNM	Customer
StatusMessage	Status

still selected, I chose Format | Character from the menu, and then set the font to 8-point Arial Bold. Zowie! Figure 21.13 illustrates what the report looked like at this point.

Spiffing the Page Header

With the formatting of the body of the report finished, I was ready to move on to the page header. First, I wanted to pop the Boxlight logo onto the form. I selected Insert | Picture from the menu, and then selected the logo file (I had called it LOGO.BMP). My cursor turned into a box the size of the graphic, and I placed the cursor in the upper left corner of the page header and then clicked to complete the insertion. The logo appeared right where I had placed it.

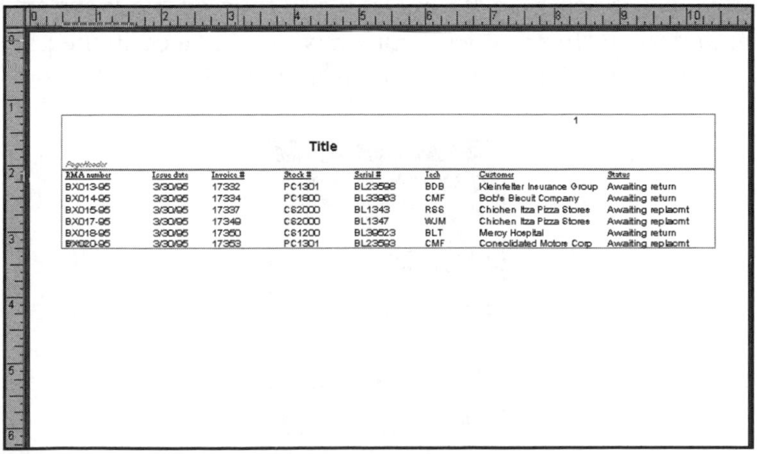

Figure 21.13 *Rough version of the active RMA Status Report.*

I could see I was going to want a little more elbow room in the page header, so I clicked inside of it to select it, and then I dragged the bottom of it downward (by grabbing the handle in the middle) until the indicator on the ruler was at 2 3/8 inches.

Next, I clicked on the label titled "Title" to select it, and then clicked on it again to edit it. Its title changed to "Active RMA Report". When I had finished editing, I clicked on the label again so it was once again selected, and then I chose Format|Character and changed its font size to 24 point. I put off trying to find an exact place for it right now. I decided instead to wait until I had created all of the pieces. Then I would work with all of them to achieve the balance I wanted.

A page-number label had automatically been created with the report. I wanted to add another label that simply said "Page" to go with it. I clicked on the Text speed button (just to the right of the % button), and then moved the I-beam cursor into the page header and clicked the mouse to get a flashing text entry cursor. I typed the word "Page" and then clicked outside the header. Next, I clicked on the label I had just created to select it, and then moved it near the upper right corner of the header.

I wanted two more labels that would display the current date and time on the report. ReportSmith has some pre-defined labels called "System Fields" that do this. I selected Insert|Field from the menu, which brought up the Insert Field dialog (see Figure 21.14). From the ComboBox, I selected the System Fields list as shown.

My next move was to click on "Print Date" and then on the Insert button. The cursor changed to an "Insert object" cursor, which I placed in the page header and clicked. A single field with the date appeared. Next, I chose a "Print

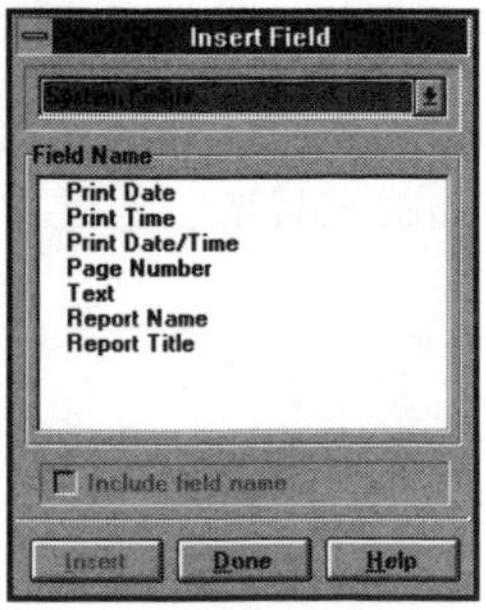

Figure 21.14   Choosing a System Field for the report.

Time" system field and repeated the process. Once the two fields were on the page header, I clicked the Insert Field dialog's Done button to put it away.

I wasn't really crazy about the format of either of the fields I had just placed. I selected the date field and then chose Format | Field Formats from the menu. Up popped the Format Field dialog (see Figure 21.15). As seen in the figure, I selected the "d-mmm-yy" format. I clicked the OK button to accept it. Using the same process, I set the time field's format to "h:mm AM/PM".

I took another big gulp from the mug. Now I was ready to finish the job. I changed the font on both the "Page" label and the page number system field to 12-point Arial bold, and then located them in the upper right corner. Below them, I placed the date field, and below that, the time field. Then I readjusted the position of the title label.

One more finishing touch: a single line to separate the page header from the body of the report. From the menu, I selected Tools | Drawing to get the palette of drawing tools (Figure 21.16). Since these tools were similar to those used in other programs, I had no trouble selecting the line tool and drawing a horizontal line from left to right, margin to margin, just at the top of the words "Page Header". Then I clicked on the arrow (pick) tool to deselect the line tool.

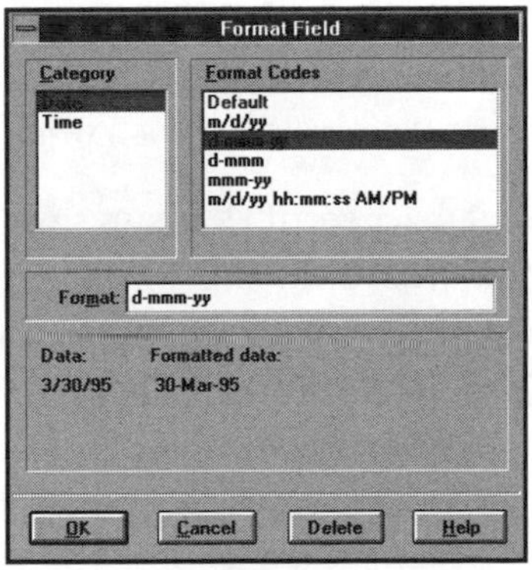

Figure 21.15   *Altering the format of System Fields.*

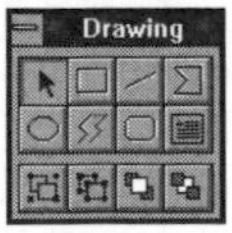

Figure 21.16   *ReportSmith's palette of drawing tools.*

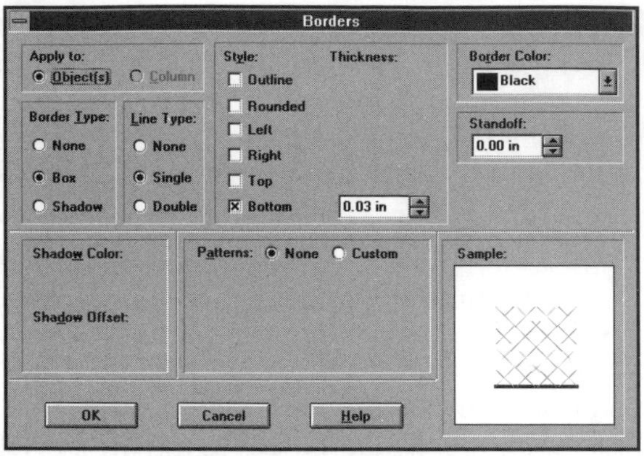

Figure 21.17   *Selecting the width of the separator line.*

Next, I clicked on the line I had just drawn to select it, and then chose Format | Border from the menu, which gave me the Borders dialog. I selected "Bottom" as the style, and then 0.03 inch width, as shown in Figure 21.17. I clicked the OK button and the thickness of the line instantly changed.

I printed a copy of the final report and gave it the once-over. It looked pretty good, but I wouldn't consider it a "keeper" until I had safely printed it from the demo application.

The report was finished. I saved it and exited ReportSmith. Now all I had to do was connect it to the demo, then add the help capability. The project was rapidly drawing to a close, and I could almost *smell* the victory.

Suddenly, the phone rang. I had set the answering machine to screen calls, and now I was glad I did. It was Bohacker on the line.

"Hey, Breakpoint! It's your old buddy, Bo! How ya comin' on the demo? Just thought I'd let you know I finished it already. Hey—I know you're there. Pick up the phone, Loser! Hahahahaha! I've got some *really* bad news for you—" I cycled the power switch to hang up on him.

The only thing that had been holding me together was nervous energy. Now even that was gone, and depression flooded over me in waves.

During this night I had been burned, battered, and bedraggled. I had lost my best girl and most of my facial hair. I had twisted my ankle and nearly ruined my face. The only thing that was keeping me awake was my body shaking from a bad case of coffee jitters. Now I found out that, in spite of my best efforts, Bohacker had beaten me again.

I slumped down into my chair. A blue funk hung over me like wet pantyhose on a shower rod, and suddenly I felt like a cheap character in a forty-dollar technical book. *It's hard to be a fictional character*, I thought. *You have no life of your own.* I stared at the pile of stuff on the top of my desk for several minutes. In sheer desperation, I picked up the copy of *Delphi Programming Explorer* I had laid there earlier. I began to skim through it. *And then my eyes caught something that sent an electric charge up my spine.*

The Author—it says in the notes that he lives right here in town!

I snatched the phone directory from the bottom drawer. Sure enough—there was his number. My fingers flew across the keys on my desk phone. Then I waited for what seemed like an eternity—hoping beyond hope that he would be there—as I listened to the soft purr of the ringing signal.

Ker-chunk! Then I heard a voice. "Hello..."

"Hello, this is Ace Breakpoint," I said. My heart was pounding.

"What a coincidence. I was just writing you, Ace. I'll bet you want to know about that call from Bohacker."

"Yes. And I want to know what else is going to happen to me. I'm lost here."

"Well, it's not good for any character to know too much about his future. But at least I can tell you this—Bohacker is putting you on. He hasn't really finished the demo. It's purely a ruse to get you discouraged, so you'll quit."

"Well, it's working," I said. "I *am* discouraged. And I'm not at all sure I'm going to make it."

"Listen, Ace," said the voice. "I'm in charge of character development, and right now I want you to develop a little more character. You've been through a lot, but have yet to face your biggest challenge. That will come later in the story."

"You mean it's going to get even *tougher*?" I asked in dismay.

"Ace, I created you expressly for the role you're to play in this story. No other fictional character could possibly accomplish what you can." He paused. "It wouldn't work with Phil Marlowe."

"Nick Charles couldn't do it?" I asked tentatively.

"*Not even Sam Spade*. Yes, it will get tougher. Just remember this, Ace: I'm in charge, and everything comes out okay in the end. Trust me on this. Got to go now. I'm working on the Next Chapter. Bye." Click.

I hung up the phone. The depression was gone. I suddenly felt recharged. Now I *knew* I could do it.

CONNECTING THE REPORT TO THE DEMO APP

I slugged down the remaining coffee in my cup and jumped back into my work with the determination of a Chihuahua chasing a truck tire. I reloaded the project, brought up the RMA Management form, and dropped a Report component on it. I entered the name of the report and the directory where I had located it. I didn't think the Active RMA Status Report would be printed very frequently (probably not more than once a day), so I set **AutoUnload** to **True**.

On the right side of the form, I added a button to print the report. Table 21.2 details the property values I assigned. I double-clicked on the new button and wrote the simple OnClick handler that appears in Listing 21.2.

Listing 21.2   Simple OnClick handler for the report button

```
procedure TRMAMgmtForm.ReportBtnClick(Sender: TObject);
begin
 RMAStatusReport.Run;
end;
```

I held my breath for what seemed like a long time, while the runtime version of ReportSmith loaded and printed the report. The transition to the runtime

---

Table 21.2   *Property Changes to the RMA Management form*

Name	Property	Value
RMAStatusReport	ReportName	activrma.rpt
	ReportDir	c:\boxlight\app\
	AutoUnload	True
ReportBtn	Left	337
	Top	348
	Width	172
	Height	25
	Caption	"Status Report"

certainly wasn't seamless, and there were times I wondered if anything besides disk thrashing was going on. But the results were worth the wait. There was my report, just as I had designed it, complete with the current date and time. I've included a reproduction of the report in Figure 21.18. While I was at it, I took a snapshot of what was now the final version of the RMA Management form. It appears in Figure 21.19. And the complete listing of the form is contained in Listing 21.3.

Listing 21.3 Complete code for the final version of the RMA Management form

```
{———————————————————————————————————}
{                    The Boxlight Demo                      }
{              RMAMGMT.PAS : RMA Input Form                 }
{                 By Ace Breakpoint, N.T.P.                 }
{                   Assisted by Don Taylor                  }
{                                                           }
{ Chapter 21 version of the form that displays             }
{ RMA information and navigates through the RMA            }
{ table.                                                    )
{ Written for *Delphi Programming Explorer*                }
{ Copyright (c) 1995 The Coriolis Group, Inc.              }
{                 Last Updated 3/30/95                      }
{———————————————————————————————————}
```

| | | | | | | | | Page 1 |
| BOXLIGHT™ CORPORATION | | **Active RMA Report** | | | | | | 30-Mar-95 11:56 am |

RMA number	Issue Date	Invoice #	Stock #	Serial #	Tech	Customer	Status
BX013-95	3/30/95	17332	PC1301	BL23598	BDB	Kleinfelter Insurance group	Awaiting return
BX014-95	3/30/95	17334	PC1800	BL33963	CMF	Rob's Biscuit Company	Awaiting return
BX015-95	3/30/95	17337	CS2000	BL1343	RSS	Chichen Itza Pizza Stores	Awaiting replacmt
BX017-95	3/30/95	17349	CS2000	BL1347	WJM	Chichen Itza Pizza Stpres	Awaiting replacmt
BX018-95	3/30/95	17350	CS1200	BL39523	BLT	Marcy Hospital	Awaiting return
BX020-95	3/30/95	17353	PC1301	BL23593	CMF	Consolidated Motors Corp	Awaiting replacmt

Figure 21.18   *Printed version of the final Active RMA Report.*

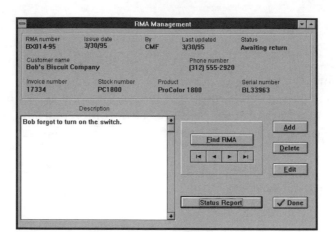

Figure 21.19   *Final version of the RMA Management form.*

```
unit Rmamgmt;

interface

uses
   SysUtils, WinTypes, WinProcs, Messages, Classes, Graphics, Controls,
   Forms, Dialogs, DBCtrls, StdCtrls, Buttons, ExtCtrls, DB, DBTables,
   RMAAdd, FindRec, RMAConst, Report;

type
   TRMAMgmtForm = class(TForm)
      RMALabel: TLabel;
      IssueDateLabel: TLabel;
      ByLabel: TLabel;
      UpdateLabel: TLabel;
      StatusLabel: TLabel;
      CustNameLabel: TLabel;
      PhoneLabel: TLabel;
      InvNumLabel: TLabel;
      StkNumLabel: TLabel;
      NameLabel: TLabel;
      SNLabel: TLabel;
      ProductDBText: TDBText;
      DescDBMemo: TDBMemo;
      DescLabel: TLabel;
      NavPanel: TPanel;
      FindBtn: TButton;
      RMANavigator: TDBNavigator;
      RMATable: TTable;
      CustomerTable: TTable;
      RMASource: TDataSource;
      CustomerSource: TDataSource;
      CustNameDBText: TDBText;
```

```
          CustPhoneDBText: TDBText;
          ProductsTable: TTable;
          ProductsSource: TDataSource;
          RMADBText: TDBText;
          IssueDBText: TDBText;
          ByDBText: TDBText;
          UpdatedDBText: TDBText;
          InvNumDBText: TDBText;
          StkNumDBText: TDBText;
          SNDBText: TDBText;
          AddBtn: TButton;
          DeleteBtn: TButton;
          EditBtn: TButton;
          DoneBtn: TBitBtn;
          StatusMsgLabel: TLabel;
          InfoBevel: TBevel;
          RMAStatusReport: TReport;
          ReportBtn: TButton;
          procedure AddBtnClick(Sender: TObject);
          procedure EditBtnClick(Sender: TObject);
          procedure RMANavigatorClick(Sender: TObject; Button: TNavigateBtn);
          procedure DeleteBtnClick(Sender: TObject);
          procedure FindBtnClick(Sender: TObject);
          procedure FormActivate(Sender: TObject);
          procedure ReportBtnClick(Sender: TObject);
        private
          { Private declarations }
          procedure RefreshComponents;
          procedure RefreshForm;
          procedure Synchronize;
        public
          { Public declarations }
        end;

var
   RMAMgmtForm: TRMAMgmtForm;

implementation

{$R *.DFM}

procedure TRMAMgmtForm.AddBtnClick(Sender: TObject);
begin
 { Tell the Add/Edit form we're appending }
 AddRMAForm.Editing := False;
 AddRMAForm.RMAIndexStr := RMATable.FieldByName('RMA_ID').AsString;
 AddRMAForm.ShowModal;
 Synchronize;
end;

procedure TRMAMgmtForm.EditBtnClick(Sender: TObject);
begin
 { Tell the Add/Edit form we're editing }
```

```
 AddRMAForm.Editing := True;
 AddRMAForm.RMAIndexStr := RMATable.FieldByName('RMA_ID').AsString;
 AddRMAForm.ShowModal;
 Synchronize;
end;

{
"Ode to Rhonda"
by Ace Breakpoint, N.T.P.

Oh, Rhonda, Rhonda, my beautiful Rhonda,
It's not Jane, but you I'm fonda,
We'll not be bored
And be in one Accord
As we ride through life in my Honda.
}


procedure TRMAMgmtForm.Synchronize;
begin
 { Force the RMA table to the record indicated  by
   RMAIndexStr, and then refresh the form }
 with RMATable do
   begin { Do it only if the index isn't blank }
     if AddRMAForm.RMAIndexStr <> ''
       then begin
               Cancel;
               DisableControls;
               First;
               SetKey;
               FieldByName('RMA_ID').AsString := AddRMAForm.RMAIndexStr;
               GotoKey;
               EnableControls;
             end
       else First;
   end; { with }
 RefreshComponents;
 RefreshForm;
end;

procedure TRMAMgmtForm.RefreshComponents;
begin
 if RMATable.BOF and RMATable.EOF { The table is empty }
   then begin
           { Disable the Delete, Edit, and Find buttons }
           DeleteBtn.Enabled := False;
           EditBtn.Enabled := False;
           FindBtn.Enabled := False;

           { Hide the Customer name and phone, and Product name }
           CustNameDBText.Visible := False;
           CustPhoneDBText.Visible := False;
           ProductDBText.Visible := False;
```

```
            { Hide the status message }
            StatusMsgLabel.Visible := False;
          end
  else begin
            { Enable the Delete, Edit, and Find buttons }
            DeleteBtn.Enabled := True;
            EditBtn.Enabled := True;
            FindBtn.Enabled := True;

            { Show the Customer name and phone, and Product name }
            CustNameDBText.Visible := True;
            CustPhoneDBText.Visible := True;
            ProductDBText.Visible := True;

            { Show the status message }
            StatusMsgLabel.Visible := True;
          end;
end;

procedure TRMAMgmtForm.RefreshForm;
begin
 { Go to appropriate product record }
 with ProductsTable do
   begin
    DisableControls;
    First;
    SetKey;
    FieldByName('PRD_STKNUM').AsString
      := RMATable.FieldByName('RMA_STKNUM').AsString;
    GotoKey;
    EnableControls;
   end; { with }

 { Go to appropriate customer record }
 with CustomerTable do
   begin
    DisableControls;
    First;
    SetKey;
    FieldByName('CST_ID').AsString
      := RMATable.FieldByName('RMA_CUSTID').AsString;
    GotoKey;
    EnableControls;
   end; { with }

 { Refresh the Status }
 StatusMsgLabel.Caption :=
   StatusMessages[RMATable.FieldByName('RMA_STATUS').AsInteger];
end;

procedure TRMAMgmtForm.RMANavigatorClick(Sender: TObject;
```

```
      Button: TNavigateBtn);
begin
 RefreshForm;
end;

procedure TRMAMgmtForm.DeleteBtnClick(Sender: TObject);
var
 s : string;
begin
 s := 'Delete RMA #' + RMATable.FieldByName('RMA_ID').AsString + '?';
 if MessageDlg(s, mtConfirmation, [mbYes, mbNo], 0)
   = mrYes
   then begin
           RMATable.Delete;
           RefreshComponents;
           ShowMessage('Record deleted.');
         end;
end;

procedure TRMAMgmtForm.FindBtnClick(Sender: TObject);
begin
 with FindRecordDlg do
   begin
    Caption := 'Find RMA Record';
    SearchStrLabel.Caption := 'RMA number';
    SearchStrEdit.Text := '';
    if (ShowModal = mrCancel)
      or (SearchStrEdit.Text = '') then Exit;
   end; { with }

 with RMATable do
   begin
    Cancel;
    First;
    SetKey;
    FieldByName('RMA_ID').AsString
       := UpperCase(FindRecordDlg.SearchStrEdit.Text);
    GotoNearest;
   end; { with }

end;

procedure TRMAMgmtForm.FormActivate(Sender: TObject);
begin
 RefreshForm;
 RefreshComponents;
end;

procedure TRMAMgmtForm.ReportBtnClick(Sender: TObject);
begin
 RMAStatusReport.Run;
end;

end.
```

A STATUS REPORT OF MY OWN

I glanced at my screen as I drained the last few drops from the coffee urn into my waiting cup. The Windows Clock applet now read 12:02 p.m. It had been a hard day's night. Or a long day's journey into night. I wasn't quite sure which. But one thing I did know: I had developed a demo application that looked good and did what Dave Carson had asked for. It displayed product data, and it performed the operations expected of a simple RMA management system. And now, it had the capability of printing a status report on the active RMAs. There was but one step to go, the addition of functional online help.

Today I had started a new life with Rhonda. But something kept haunting me. Somehow I couldn't get Helen out of my mind.

I stood at the window, sipping my coffee and watching the never-ending deluge. The parking lot looked like a sound stage for "Singing in the Rain," choreographed with intermittent bursts of chain lightning. In the distance I could hear the dull rumble of thunder, as it rolled along the Olympic Mountain range.

I found myself staring at the back of my car, parked as always in spot number 132. From here I could just make out the message on my new Delphi bumper sticker. It read: *Visualize Windows Apps.*

HELP ARRIVES IN THE NICK OF TIME

Don Taylor

With a Help system and an About box, the demo is done! Ace packs up his laptop and heads for Boxlight HQ—but stops long enough for the surprise of his life.

I turned from the window and stared at the now empty coffee urn, which was standing next to my computer like some sort of stainless steel tribute to the wakefulness of mankind. I was drifting in and out of bad metaphors, and I needed an extra boost. The blend wasn't working any more, and I just couldn't consume coffee any faster than I had during the past couple of hours. The only variable I had left was the strength of the coffee beans.

I had tried everything else, and now I was down to the last resort. Reluctantly, I would have to use *the ultimate weapon*.

I slipped over to the couch, being careful not to awaken Mewnix, who was still sleeping peacefully. I kneeled down in front of the floor safe I used as an end table, and spun the dial. The massive safe door swung open, revealing the contents at the front of the safe. I pushed the collection of papers out of the way, looking for the precious package I had long ago slid into the deepest recesses.

As I gazed into the coal black cavern, I caught a glimpse of something in the back. The light reflecting off the gold foil on the package gave the impression that it was glowing in the dark. My hand shaking, I reached in and pulled out the paper bag containing the strongest coffee beans known to mankind. The label read:

Maltese Falcon Brand
Denatured Thermonuclear Espresso
Handle with Extreme Care

I poured the entire bag into the grinder, and soon had the 50-cup vessel perking away. I would probably need the entire boatload to see me through the next couple hours.

Adding a help capability to the demo would entail a two-step process. First, I would need to create the help file that would be fully compatible with WINHELP.EXE (WinHelp), the Windows hypertext reader. Second, I would have to modify the Main form on the demo application to connect it to both WinHelp and my help file.

Then, of course, there would be the About box. By comparison, creating that should be child's play.

ANATOMY OF A HELP FILE

Before proceeding, I needed to perform a quick mental review of the overall structure of the hypertext system upon which Windows help is built.

A hypertext document is made up of one or more "pages." A page can actually be as long as you want it to be—the equivalent of several printed pages. Each hypertext page dedicates itself to a "topic" that can consist of text, references to other topics, or any number of things. What differentiates a hypertext document from a book is how it is organized; a hypertext document is *nonlinear*. With a book, you read from one page to the next. In a hypertext document, you can randomly jump from one topic to another, and you can perform fast searches on keywords to locate a particular topic.

I took out my pencil and made a sketch of a symbolic hypertext "page" in my spiral notebook. That sketch is included as Figure 22.1. Although the diagram was highly oversimplified and technically not totally accurate, it would serve the purpose.

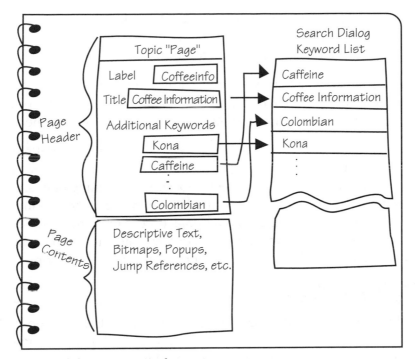

Figure 22.1 *Symbolic representation of a topic page.*

The page actually consists of two parts. The *header*, which appears in the upper portion of the figure, contains locator information. Because hypertext is a non-linear system, there must be a way to jump from one topic page to another—in other words, each page must have an "address" where the hypertext system can find it. This address is provided in the form of a unique label assigned to each topic page.

The next item in the header is the page's *title*. This title appears at the top of the page when the page is displayed in the Help window, and the same title is also automatically included in the keyword list available to the help system's Search dialog.

The final item in the header is a list containing zero or more keywords. These keywords are also made available to the Search dialog (which, as the diagram shows, always displays items in alphabetical order). Instead of limiting a search to exact topic titles, providing keywords related to topics gives readers a much greater chance of finding what interests them. It is also possible to assign the same keyword to more than one topic. If I wanted to have another topic page dedicated to Hawaii, for example, I might attach the keyword

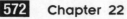

"Kona" to it as well. When the reader selected that keyword from the Search dialog and clicked on the Show Topics button, both "Coffee Information" and "Hawaii" would appear in the dialog's topics list.

The Page Contents, which appears in the lower portion of Figure 22.1, contains the topic message. That may be any combination of descriptive text, bitmaps, references to popup messages, or jump references to other topics.

Popup messages are usually used to display a box containing a definition of a term that is highlighted in text. Jump references are the most interesting of all. They provide a means to relate a screen "hot spot" containing highlighted text to the address (that is, the label) of another topic page. By clicking on the highlighted text, the hypertext system brings up the referenced topic. This is the method I would use in my Table of Contents page, to jump to the topics I would list there. I might also use it to jump directly between topics.

Help File Creation Process

All this thinking about coffee had made me thirsty. I filled my cup with the nearly radioactive brew. As I sipped the steaming hot liquid, I reviewed the process used to create the .HLP files used by WinHelp.

Compatible help files are created by compiling Rich Text Format (RTF) files with a utility provided by Microsoft (for Windows 3.1, this utility is called HC31.EXE, a copy of which is provided with Delphi). Developing the RTF file is no picnic. First, it normally requires a word processor capable of editing— or at least exporting—RTF files. Second, the RTF file must contain special codes that describe the structure and interrelationship of all the topic pages that make up the hypertext document.

In addition to the RTF file, the help compiler requires a project file that contains entries specifying settings for the compiler's options.

Much too complex. Once again, I needed an edge—something that would simplify the process for me. I was aware of several third-party products for creating Help files—RoboHelp, Help Magician, and Visual Help, just to name a few. I thought I had remembered hearing that Borland was also offering a new product called ForeHelp. But right now, there was no time to order a product and wait for it to arrive. There wasn't even time to visit the local software store!

What was I going to do?

Deja Vu, All Over Again

I remembered seeing something about a help file generator while I was thumbing through my copy of *Delphi Programming Explorer* an hour or so earlier. I picked it up and read the back cover. Sure enough, it said the disk included with the book included a shareware utility called HelpGen that would simplify the development of help files.

I anxiously ripped the disk from inside the back cover, slipped it into Drive A:, and ran a directory listing on it. The ZIP file containing the program was there, all right. But what I saw gave me the biggest shock of my life.

On that disk was the complete demo I had been working on—*including the portions I hadn't even finished yet!*

I was stunned. Had I been wasting my time on this project? Had the whole thing been some sort of ugly dream? Was this the ultimate challenge The Author had promised?

My first instinct was to load the project files onto my computer and check them out. But something told me that it would be a mistake to use those files. Perhaps it would be like cheating on a test. Then again, it might cause an irreparable rift in the space-time continuum.

It may have been my fear of reprisal that stopped me from examining those files. Or perhaps I was beginning to develop some character. In either case, I decided to copy only the file HPGN12.ZIP onto my hard disk and unzip it.

INSTALLING HELPGEN

Installing the utility was very simple. I just created a new directory called \HELPGEN, and unzipped HPGN12.ZIP there. All that remained was to create a new program item from the Windows Program Manager, giving it the command line C:\HELPGEN\HLPGEN.EXE.

It wasn't too surprising to discover that HelpGen's documentation comes completely in the form of a Windows help file.

HelpGen Overview

After spending a few minutes navigating through that help file, I had a pretty good grasp on how the utility helps automate the help file generation process. You start a project by creating a macro file that HelpGen will later use to prepare the RTF file for submission to the help compiler. As created, the macro file is an ASCII text file that contains some very basic commands that describe a very simple help file. By editing this file with a text editor (HelpGen automatically launches Notepad), a person writing a document can add topic pages, cross-references, popups, and even bitmaps to that document.

At your request, HelpGen will also create a default project file. This file can also be easily edited by simply selecting a menu item.

Creating the actual help file is a two-step process. First, you ask HelpGen to create the RTF file, using the macro file as the specification. Second, you direct HelpGen to call the help compiler. It will automatically hand the compiler the project file it needs to turn the RTF file into the help file. Completed help files can be tested by selecting Test from the HelpGen menu. (Speed buttons are also provided for the most-used tasks.)

Defining the Project

My first step was to create a macro file for the demo project. I launched HelpGen, and noted that the entire file generation process is summarized in a flow diagram that appears in the HelpGen window (see Figure 22.2).

From the menu I selected the File | Open Macro File option. To create a new file, I simply typed its name, including the path. I decided to call it BOXLIGHT.MAC, and locate it in the \HELPGEN directory. When I clicked the OK button, I was asked to approve the creation of the new default macro file. I gave the go-ahead signal.

From the menu, I selected Edit | Macro File. HelpGen called Notebook and loaded in the file. It appears in Listing 22.1.

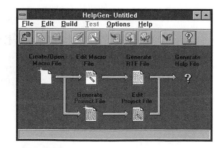

Figure 22.2 *The HelpGen main window.*

Listing 22.1   Default macro file for the Boxlight project

```
.rem(===========================================================)
.rem(BOXLIGHT.MAC)
.rem( )
.rem(Created by the HelpGen Help Generator, version 1.21)
.rem(Copyright © 1994 by Rimrock Software)
.rem(All rights reserved.)
.rem(===========================================================)

.start(main,Contents,Hlpgen.BMP,xxxx)
.top(Help)
.top(Table of Contents)

.s
Put your table of contents topics here.

 NOTE: You should replace the bitmap name and 'xxxx' field in the
       start macro.
.end

.ent(1con,Information,Icon )
This icon topic .b(MUST) be present. It is activated by clicking
on the icon in the Table of Contents. You may place your own
text here.
.end

.end_file
```

Creating a Default Project File

I couldn't resist. I had to compile the default file, just to step through the process and to make sure this whole thing was going to work. I had a macro file. Now I needed a project file to go with it.

I simply selected Build|Project File from the menu. HelpGen automatically created the file for me. The file's contents are shown in Listing 22.2.

Listing 22.2   Default project file for the Boxlight project

```
;===========================================================
; Project File for BOXLIGHT.MAC
;
; Created by the HelpGen Help Generator, version 1.21
; Copyright © 1994 by Rimrock Software
; All rights reserved.
;===========================================================
```

```
[OPTIONS]
; This section specifies various options that control how a help file
; is built. This is an optional section, but must be placed first if
; it is used. To enable one of the options, remove the semicolon from
; the beginning of the option and complete the option.
;
; BMROOT designates the directory used to store bitmap files, if they
; are not in the current directory. Syntax: BMROOT=D:\PATH
;BMROOT=

; COMPRESS specifies what type of compression is used when building
; the help file.   Syntax: COMPRESS=xxx where xxx is 0 for no
; compression, Medium for 40% compression and High for 50%
; compression.
COMPRESS=0

; COPYRIGHT adds a copyright message to the help file's About dialog
; box. It can be up to 35 characters in length. NOTE: for the copy-
; right symbol, use Alt-1-6-9.
COPYRIGHT=© 1994 Rimrock Software.

; ERRORLOG will route all the help compiler's error messages to a
; file, instead of being displayed on the screen.
;  Syntax: ERRORLOG=D:\PATH\FILENAME.EXT
ERRORLOG=ERRORLOG.TXT

; ICON specifies the icon to be used when the help file is minimized.
; This will override the default question mark icon.
;  Syntax: ICON=D:\PATH\FILENAME.BMP
;ICON=

; REPORT determines the type of error messages that are displayed
; during help file compilation.
REPORT=ON

; WARNING determines the level of error messages the help compiler
; displays during compilation. 1 is only the most severe, 2 is medium
; and 3 is all messages.
WARNING=3

; TITLE determines the text that appears on the help file title bar.
TITLE=BOXLIGHT Help

[FILES]
; This section specifies the topic files (RTF files) that are to be
; included in the help file. Initally, there will be one file in this
; list. Add new files as needed.
BOXLIGHT.RTF

[BITMAPS]
; This section specifies bitmap files included in the help file. If
; your help file includes any bitmaps, they should be listed here,
; unless you've listed a path for them using BMROOT in the OPTIONS
; section.
```

```
[WINDOWS]
; This section controls the appearance of the main help window. It is
; required if you want to customize the appearance of the help window.
;
; The following statement controls the size, color and position of the
; main help window.   Syntax is
;    main=caption,(horpos,verpos,width,height),state,bkgnd_color,
;                nonscrll_bkgnd,on_top
; bkgnd_color and nonscrll_bkgnd are RGB triplets in the form
; (Red,Green,Blue)
;
; If any fields are missing, the commas must still be there. The
; following line sets the non-scrolling background to a light green.
main=,,0,,(0,128,64)
```

Taking a Test Drive

I was ready for a dry run. I chose Build|RTF File from the menu, and almost instantly I was informed that the file had successfully been generated. Now the Windows help compiler had everything it needed to perform its job—the RTF file and the project file.

From the HelpGen menu, I selected Build|HLP File. My screen suddenly turned black, and I realized that the help compiler is actually a DOS application! It processed the project file, giving me several status messages along the way. When it finished, my Windows screen was returned to me, and I was looking at the HelpGen main window again. I did a little snooping with File Manager, and discovered the help compiler had produced the files BOXLIGHT.RTF and BOXLIGHT.HLP, both of which it had placed in the \HELPGEN directory.

At this point, I clicked on the Test menu item—and up came the document. I was looking at the Table of Contents. It was pretty sparse, but at least I knew the process worked. It was time to figure out how I could create my own Table of Contents, and then add my own topics and whatnot.

Examining the Macro Syntax

So much for theory. Now it was time for serious study. I pored over HelpGen's own help file, examining the syntax of the various commands that could be embedded within a macro file. I discovered that in its simplest form, a hypertext help document consists of only one topic page (the Table of Contents), and it is created as follows:

```
.start(main,Contents,LOGO.BMP,Coffee Anyone?)
.end
.end_file
```

The **.start** command signals the beginning of a new document, and its Contents topic page. The word "main" is the label for the page, "Contents" is the keyword supplied to the Search dialog, "LOGO.BMP" is the name of the file containing the bitmap that will be displayed on the Contents page, and "Coffee Anyone?" is the string that will be displayed in the header of the Contents page. The **.end** command marks the end of the Contents topic, and **.end_file** marks the end of the document.

Creating additional topics requires only a handful of lines:

```
.ent(coffeeinfo,Coffee Information,)
.top(Coffee)
This topic discusses the merits of drinking coffee.
.end
```

The **.ent** command creates a new topic page entry, with the address label "coffeeinfo" and the title "Coffee Information". (The comma at the end of the parameter list of the **.ent** command needs to be there. There can be another "prefix" parameter attached to the topic's title, but I wouldn't be using it.)

The second line contains an optional command (**.top**) that adds a keyword to the topic page. The next line is the text that will appear on the page when it is displayed. This text could go on for many lines. The end of the text is signaled by the **.end** command.

The process for adding a popup, I discovered, is nearly identical to that of adding a topic page. The only difference is the command: **.pent** instead of **.ent**.

There were two other mechanisms I would need: Calling up a popup from highlighted text, and jumping to another page from a highlighted reference. Both turned out to be straightforward. I scratched out an example:

```
.ent(worldcoffee,Coffees of the World,)
The world's most popular adult drink might
 be .p(coffeedef,coffee).
.s
See also: .j(coffeeinfo,More information about coffee)
.end
```

Within this new topic page, I had incorporated an example of each of the techniques. The phrase **.p(coffeedef, coffee)** would include the word "coffee" (but not the label "coffeedef") in the text. The word "coffee" would be highlighted. If the reader clicks on that word, a popup with the label "coffeedef" would appear.

In the second part of this example, I used a jump reference. Here, the words "More information about coffee" would be highlighted. If the reader clicks on that phrase in the text, the topic will jump to my "Coffee Information" topic—the one with the label "coffeeinfo."

The **.s** command simply created a blank line. Since help windows can be resized, the hypertext system has the added burden of word wrapping the text found on topic pages. When performing its word wrapping, it will totally ignore "hard" carriage returns in the text. To force the end of a line, the **.n** command is used. To create a blank line, it's the **.s** command. And to make sure there's a space between words when a hard carriage return is used (as in the example above), lines following line breaks are preceded with a space.

Putting the Whole Thing Together

Okay, I had the basics down. Time to roll up the sleeves on my trenchcoat and go to work. The first thing would be to construct my Table of Contents. I wanted to offer three topics to choose from—looking up product information, looking up an existing RMA, and adding a new RMA to the system. I knocked out the macro definition in Listing 22.3.

Listing 22.3   Initial macro for the Table of Contents page

```
.rem(===============================)
.rem( Table of Contents definitions )
.rem(===============================)

.start(main,Contents,LOGO.BMP,Boxlight Demo)
.top(Table of Contents)
.s
\qc
.b(Table of Contents)
.s
\ql
.in
##.j(prodlookup,Getting information on products).n
##.j(rmalookup,Looking up an RMA).n
##.j(rmaentry,Entering a new RMA).n
.un
.end
```

I had used a few more of the commands provided in HelpGen. The **.b** command boldfaced the text enclosed in the parentheses. **\qc** and **\ql** were RTF commands that shifted the formatting to centered and back to left justified. The command pair **.in** and **.un** indented the lines between them. And the **##** command at the beginning of the three jump references would place a bullet in front of those lines when they were displayed.

I took another gulp of coffee. I was ready to create an entire help file, albeit a simple one. Using **.ent**, I created topic pages for each of the topics I had planned, plus one more—printing the RMA Status Report. (I placed a jump reference to that one in the topic on looking up existing RMAs.) Then I went wild. I created jumps between topics. I used **.pent** to create popups that provided definitions for terms used in the topics. I edited the topic text, to create hot spots that would activate the popups.

When the smoke cleared, I had created a macro file that would more than do the job for now. The file's contents are detailed in Listing 22.4.

Listing 22.4 Complete help macro file for the Boxlight demo

```
.rem(===============================================)
.rem(BOXLIGHT.MAC)
.rem( )
.rem(Created by the HelpGen Help Generator, version 1.21)
.rem(Copyright © 1994 by Rimrock Software)
.rem(All rights reserved.)
.rem(===============================================)
.rem(              Help macro file for Boxlight demo              )
.rem(                   By Ace Breakpoint, N.T.P.                  )
.rem(                    Assisted by Don Taylor                    )
.rem(          Written for *Delphi Programming Explorer*          )
.rem(         Copyright [c] 1995 The Coriolis Group, Inc.         )
.rem(                   Last updated 3/30/95                       )
.rem(===============================================)


.rem(===============================)
.rem( Table of Contents definitions )
.rem(===============================)

.start(main,Contents,LOGO.BMP,Boxlight Demo)
.top(Table of Contents)
.s
\qc
.b(Table of Contents)
.s
\ql
.in
##.j(prodlookup,Getting information on products).n
```

```
##.j(rmalookup,Looking up an RMA).n
##.j(rmaentry,Entering a new RMA).n
.un
.end


.rem(==============================)
.rem( Topic definitions           )
.rem(==============================)

.rem(==============================)
.rem( Topic: Corporate Background  )

.ent(icon,Corporate Background,    )
.bmpl(LOGO.BMP)
.s
Boxlight Corporation is a provider of high-tech display
 products, including projection panels, overhead projectors,
 laser pointers — just about everything anyone could
 possibly need to put across a presentation.
.s
In less than 10 years, Boxlight Corporation has grown from its
 humble beginnings as a home-based business into one of the fastest
 growing companies in the United States — and one of the recognized
 leaders in the projection display industry, offering a catalog
 of nearly 100 products to professionals.
.s
For a free catalog, call 1-800-762-5757.
.end

.rem(==============================)
.rem( Topic: Product Information   )

.ent(prodlookup,Looking up Product Information,)
If you would like to view product information on five of Boxlight's
 most popular .p(panel,display panels) and video projectors, simply
 select "System|Product Info" from this demo's menu.
.s
Along with a photograph of each product, you will get information
 on product usage and application, technical specifications, tips
 and troubleshooting, and current pricing.
.end

.rem(==============================)
.rem( Topic: Existing RMAs         )

.ent(rmalookup,Looking up an Existing RMA,)
It's easy to look up a specified .pl(RMA) (or even to navigate
 your way through all listed .p(RMA,RMAs)).  Simply select "System|RMA
 Management" from this demo's menu.
.s
Use the navigator controls to step through the .pl(RMA) list, or
 click on the "Find RMA" button to bring up a dialog that will
 let you specify the .p(rmanum,RMA Number) you're looking for.
.s
```

Once you've selected the .p1(RMA) you want, you will see complete
 information on it, including the date issued, item, invoice, customer,
 status, and the description of the problem.
.s
See also:.n
.in
##.j(rmaentry,Entering a New RMA).n
##.j(rmaprint,Printing an RMA Status Report).n
.un
.end

.rem(==============================)
.rem(Topic: Entering RMAs   )

.ent(rmaentry,Entering a New RMA,)
Entering a new .p1(RMA) record is a snap. From the demo's menu, choose
 "System|RMA Management". Then from the RMA Management dialog, click
 on the Add button to get the Add New RMA dialog.
.s
On the Add New RMA dialog, use the navigator controls to step through
 the list of invoices on file, or click on "Find Invoice" to bring up
 a dialog that will let you specify the exact invoice number you are
 looking for. Once the invoice is selected, the items on that invoice
 (both stock # and serial #) will be displayed. Simply click on the
 item you want to include in the .p1(RMA).
.s
Next, select the item's status from the Status combo box, and then
 pick your initials from the Initials combo box. Finally, click on
 the Description memo field, and enter a description of the problem.
 When you're all finished, click the OK button.
.s
See also:.n
.in
##.j(rmalookup,Looking up an Existing RMA).n
.un
.end

.rem(==============================)
.rem(Topic: Printing Status Reports)

.ent(rmaprint,Printing an RMA Status Report,)
To print a report detailing the status of all active .p(RMA,RMAs),
 first select "System|RMA Management" from the demo's menu. This
 will bring up the RMA Management dialog. To generate the report,
 simply click on the Status Report button.
.s
See also:.n
.in
##.j(rmalookup,Looking up an Existing RMA).n
.un
.end

```
.rem(==============================)
.rem( Popup definitions            )
.rem(==============================)

.pent(rma,RMA,)
.top(Return Materials Authorization)
A Return Materials Authorization (RMA) is a document issued
 by Boxlight that authorizes a customer to return a specified
 piece of equipment for warranty repair or replacement.
.end

.pent(rmanum,RMA Number,)
An RMA Number is a unique, sequential identifier assigned to a
 Boxlight RMA.  It is in the format BXNNN-YY, where "NNN" is
 the sequential number (000-999) and "YY" are the last two
 digits of the year ("95" for 1995).
.end

.pent(panel,Display Panel,)
A Display Panel is a device that connects to a computer's
 video output and displays the image on a translucent screen.
 By passing light through the panel, the computer video image
 can be projected on a large surface, such as a screen.
.end_file
```

There was one change I wanted to make: I didn't like the default title that HelpGen had created for me. I needed to modify the string displayed in the title bar of the help window. I selected Edit|Project File from the menu, and then replaced the line that read

```
TITLE=BOXLIGHT Help
```

with

```
TITLE=Boxlight Demo Help
```

I recompiled the file and tested it one last time. I was very happy with it. The Table of Contents can be seen in Figure 22.3. The Search dialog, showing the topic keywords, appears in Figure 22.4. I finally stopped admiring my work and exited Windows Help, and then HelpGen. I copied the BOXLIGHT.HLP file to my \BOXLIGHT\APP subdirectory.

MAKING CONNECTIONS WITH THE DEMO

I fired up Delphi again and loaded the Boxlight demo project. I had my help file; now all I had to do was connect it to the demo application. I spent several minutes searching through the manuals, and I found how to associate

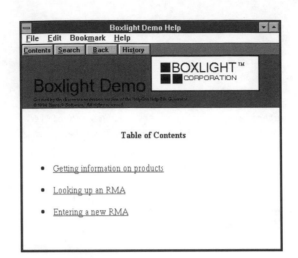

Figure 22.3   *The Table of Contents page.*

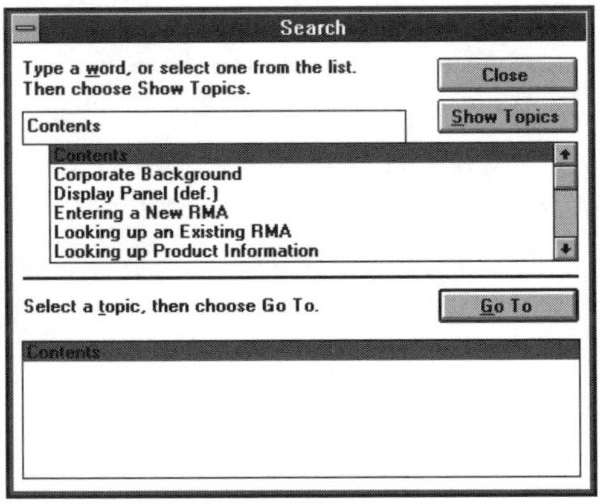

Figure 22.4   *Search dialog for the Boxlight demo.*

a Delphi program with its help file. But I couldn't see how to call the WinHelp functions from my Help menu selections.

Temporarily stymied, I reached for the stack of cards that lay in a disheveled pile on the corner of my desk. Perhaps they would help change my perspective.

I had been an inveterate collector of things since I was a kid. Over the years I had collected all kinds of things, including matchbooks, hotel guest soaps, and bad debts. My latest treasure was a set of Famous Programming Author trading cards.

As I pondered the problem at hand, I thumbed through the cards, seeking inspiration from my heroes. On the top of the stack were my two Jeff Duntemann cards, one picture with a hat, the other without. The next card was Jim Mischel. And then Keith Weiskamp. I continued to shuffle cards from one hand to the other. Ah, yes—there was Michael Abrash. Tom Swan. And Bruce Eckel. I got to the last card. With every new pack of cards, you invariably got some rookie writers. The card on the bottom was for some guy named Taylor.

Suddenly I had an inspiration. I tossed the cards back on the desk, and I called up Delphi help and performed a Search All on the topic "Help." Among the many entries was one called "HelpCommand." *I had struck gold.* It turned out that once I had specified the help file to be used with my program, I could send specific commands to WinHelp through the **HelpCommand** method that was part and parcel of every Delphi application.

From Delphi's menu, I selected Options | Project, and then from the Project Options dialog, I clicked on the tab marked "Application." Aha! Here was the place I could specify not only the help file that my application would use—I could also choose the icon that would be shown when the app was minimized, along with the label that would be displayed with that icon.

I had already moved the .HLP file into the subdirectory with my application. Now I would have to enter the name of that file (including the path), so it could be passed from my application to WinHelp when it was called. (It would become a consideration again, though, if I were to distribute the application. I would then have to make sure WinHelp could find its file, wherever the user happened to install it.) As for the icon and the title, no sweat: they would both be incorporated directly into the program file. I used the icon I had created yesterday afternoon: BOXLIGHT.ICO.

I took my chances, and I made my choices. They can be seen in Figure 22.5.

Now, about those commands I needed to send to WinHelp. I brought up the Main form, and on its menu, I clicked on Help | Contents so I could enter an event handler for that selection. Next, I clicked on Help | Topic Search and created a handler for that. This one was a little trickier. To fool WinHelp into

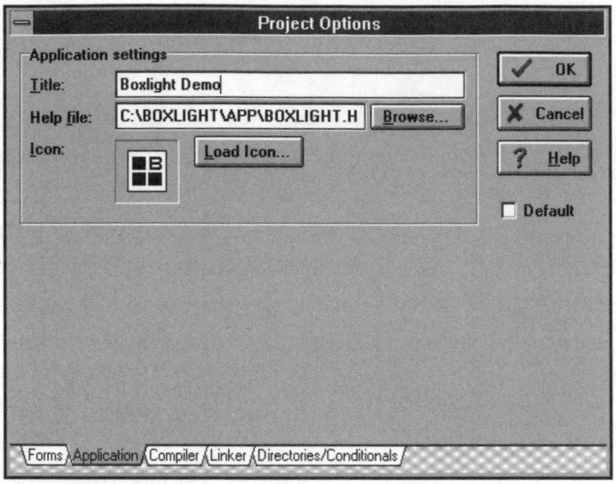

Figure 22.5 *Setting project options for the Boxlight demo.*

displaying a Search dialog with no topic selected, I had to pass it a long integer that was actually a pointer to an empty string. The code for the two handlers is shown in Listing 22.5.

Listing 22.5   Event handlers that call WinHelp functions

```
procedure TMainForm.HelpMenuContentsClick(Sender: TObject);
begin
 Application.HelpCommand(Help_Contents, 0);
end;

procedure TMainForm.HelpMenuTopicClick(Sender: TObject);
var
 s : Array[0..79] of Char;
begin
 StrCopy(s, '');
 Application.HelpCommand(Help_PartialKey, Longint(@s));
end;
```

ADDING THE ABOUT BOX

I had but one task left to complete the demo—creating an About box. Once again, I had reached the bottom of the enormous urn of coffee. I held the spout open and tilted the massive structure forward, to drain the last bit of the concoction into my waiting cup. I unplugged the device and sat back down, to accomplish what was to be the *coup de grâce* of the entire project.

From Delphi's menu, I clicked on File|New Form, and selected the generic About box from the Gallery. After saving the new form as ABOUT.PAS, I first set out to change the graphic. I clicked on the Image component containing the standard Delphi icon, then clicked on its Picture property, and finally on the button marked "..." to bring up the Picture Editor dialog, as shown in Figure 22.6.

I clicked the Load button, and then selected the BOXLIGHT.ICO file. Then I clicked OK to accept the new icon and return to my work on the form. I resized the Image to fit my new graphic. I changed the captions on the labels, and added one more label. I added a bevel and slipped it underneath the graphic. It all looked pretty snazzy. The relevant property values are listed in Table 22.1.

Figure 22.6 *Loading a new icon with the Picture Editor.*

Table 22.1 *Property Changes to the AboutBox form*

Name	Property	Value
ProductName	Left	88
	Top	16
	Width	152
	Height	20
	Caption	"The Boxlight Demo"
	Font.Name	MS Sans Serif
	Font.Style	[fsBold]

continued on next page

Table 22.1 *Property Changes to the AboutBox form*

continued from previous page

Name	Property	Value
Version	Left	88
	Top	40
	Width	65
	Height	13
	Caption	"Version 1.0"
	Font.Name	MS Sans Serif
	Font.Style	[fsBold]
Copyright	Left	8
	Top	80
	Width	263
	Height	13
	Alignment	taCenter
	Caption	"Programming by Ace Breakpoint, N.T.P."
	Font.Name	MS Sans Serif
	Font.Style	[fsBold]
Comments	Left	8
	Top	98
	Width	264
	Height	18
	Alignment	taCenter
	Caption	"Assisted by Don Taylor"
	Font.Name	MS Sans Serif
	Font.Style	[fsBold]

continued on next page

Table 22.1   *Property Changes to the AboutBox form*

continued from previous page

Name	Property	Value
Dedication	Left	10
	Top	130
	Width	260
	Height	14
	Alignment	taCenter
	Caption	"Dedicated to my dad, Jack Breakpoint"
	Font.Height	-11
	Font.Name	Arial
	Font.Style	[]
OKButton	Left	48
	Top	179
	Width	197
	Height	27
	Caption	"Here'#39's clicking at you, Kid..."

All that remained was to connect **AboutBox** to the menu on the Main form. I added About to the Main form's **uses** statement, and then I clicked on Help|About to create the handler that would call it up as a modal dialog. I saved my work, which can be seen in Listing 22.6.

Listing 22.6   Final version of the Main form

```
{------------------------------------------------------}
{                 The Boxlight Demo                    }
{             MAINUNIT.PAS : Main Form                 }
{             By Ace Breakpoint, N.T.P.                }
{               Assisted by Don Taylor                 }
{                                                      }
{ Chapter 22 version of the Main unit of the           }
{ Boxlight Demo application.                            }
{ Written for *Delphi Programming Explorer*             }
```

```
{ Copyright (c) 1995 The Coriolis Group, Inc.                }
{                      Last Updated 3/30/95                  }
{————————————————————————————————————————————————————————————}

unit Mainunit;

interface

uses
    SysUtils, WinTypes, WinProcs, Messages, Classes, Graphics, Controls,
    Forms, Dialogs, Menus, ProdInfo, RMAMgmt, ExtCtrls, About;

type
    TMainForm = class(TForm)
        MainMenu: TMainMenu;
        MainMenuFile: TMenuItem;
        FileMenuExit: TMenuItem;
        MainMenuSystem: TMenuItem;
        SystemMenuProduct: TMenuItem;
        SystemMenuRMA: TMenuItem;
        MainMenuHelp: TMenuItem;
        HelpMenuContents: TMenuItem;
        HelpMenuTopic: TMenuItem;
        N1: TMenuItem;
        HelpMenuAbout: TMenuItem;
        LogoImage: TImage;
        LogoTimer: TTimer;
        procedure FileMenuExitClick(Sender: TObject);
        procedure SystemMenuProductClick(Sender: TObject);
        procedure SystemMenuRMAClick(Sender: TObject);
        procedure LogoTimerTimer(Sender: TObject);
        procedure FormKeyPress(Sender: TObject; var Key: Char);
        procedure FormMouseMove(Sender: TObject; Shift: TShiftState; X,
            Y: Integer);
        procedure FormClick(Sender: TObject);
        procedure FormCreate(Sender: TObject);
        procedure HelpMenuContentsClick(Sender: TObject);
        procedure HelpMenuTopicClick(Sender: TObject);
        procedure HelpMenuAboutClick(Sender: TObject);
    private
        { Private declarations }
        procedure MonitorLogo;
    public
        { Public declarations }
    end;

var
    MainForm: TMainForm;

implementation

{$R *.DFM}
```

```
procedure TMainForm.FileMenuExitClick(Sender: TObject);
begin
 Close;
end;

procedure TMainForm.SystemMenuProductClick(Sender: TObject);
begin
 ProdInfoForm.ShowModal;
end;

procedure TMainForm.SystemMenuRMAClick(Sender: TObject);
begin
 RMAMgmtForm.ShowModal;
end;

procedure TMainForm.LogoTimerTimer(Sender: TObject);
begin
 LogoTimer.Enabled := False;
end;

procedure TMainForm.FormKeyPress(Sender: TObject; var Key: Char);
begin
 MonitorLogo;
end;

procedure TMainForm.FormMouseMove(Sender: TObject; Shift: TShiftState; X,
   Y: Integer);
begin
 MonitorLogo;
end;

procedure TMainForm.FormClick(Sender: TObject);
begin
 MonitorLogo;
end;

procedure TMainForm.FormCreate(Sender: TObject);
begin
 LogoTimer.Interval := 10000;
 LogoTimer.Enabled := True;
end;

procedure TMainForm.MonitorLogo;
begin
 if LogoImage.Visible and not LogoTimer.Enabled
   then LogoImage.Visible := False;
end;

procedure TMainForm.HelpMenuContentsClick(Sender: TObject);
begin
 Application.HelpCommand(Help_Contents, 0);
end;
```

```
procedure TMainForm.HelpMenuTopicClick(Sender: TObject);
var
 s : Array[0..79] of Char;
begin
 StrCopy(s, '');
 Application.HelpCommand(Help_PartialKey, Longint(@s));
end;

procedure TMainForm.HelpMenuAboutClick(Sender: TObject);
begin
 AboutBox.ShowModal;
end;

end.
```

I compiled and ran the demo one last time. The "running" version of the About box is shown in Figure 22.7.

FINAL APPROACH

It all worked. Hooray! I was finally done! *Almost*. I still had to deliver the whole enchilada to Boxlight. I looked at my watch. It was 1:42. I picked up the phone and called Dave Carson at Boxlight to make an appointment to show off the demo. No, he hadn't heard a peep out of Bohacker. Yes, he would be pleased to meet with me at 2:00. I asked him if Rhonda was back from lunch. He said yes—and then told me even the president of the company would be there to see it. We both hung up.

I couldn't lug my computer down to the Boxlight office, so I decided to transfer everything to my notebook computer. As I was lashing up the connection between the two computers, I chuckled to myself as I thought of demonstrating the program in Boxlight's conference room. I would be able to hook the notebook to one of their projectors, so everyone could see the demo. I wondered what it would look like, when the RMA Management form popped on the screen—four feet high!

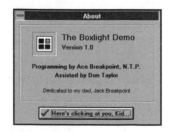

Figure 22.7 *"Running" version of the About box.*

The upload had started, and in my mind I was running through various scenarios of what I would say to Rhonda when I saw her.

Just then, the phone began to ring. After the attack from Bohacker, I had decided to continue screening my calls. Besides, I was extremely pressed for time. Whatever it was, it could wait. But this time a woman's voice came over the speaker. It was Helen.

"Ace, I know you're there, and I'm hoping you'll pick up the phone..."

Before she could finish her sentence, I had leaped across the room and hit the answer button.

"I'm here, Helen," I said expectantly.

"Hi, Ace. Listen, I know this is really bad timing, and I'm sorry." I could detect genuine compassion in her voice. "It's just that—well, there's a couple of things that need taking care of."

I guessed she wanted to make arrangements to return my audio CD library containing the complete works of Yanni. Instead she pitched me a curve I couldn't have stopped with a baseball strike.

"Ace, it's Bruiser. Something terrible has happened. I'm really worried about him."

Oh, so it's "Bruiser" now, is it? I thought. Whatever happened to "Mellow"?

Several moments of silence. "Are you still there?" she asked.

"Yes, Helen. I'm still here."

"I know it's awkward for both of us. But I thought you would want to know, because after all, he's your friend, too."

I'd have to say that one took the cake. After giving her the best four years of my life, she runs off with a guy, and then calls *me* to help *him*! It was all I could do to keep my cool.

"So what's the problem?" I asked through clenched teeth.

"Bruiser called me this morning and asked me to meet him for breakfast. When I got to Lute's, he was already there. He was wearing a purple bathrobe, a crown made from a salad strainer, and he was using a serving spoon as a scepter. He called himself 'Benevolence', and he asked me if I would vote

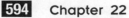

for him if he ran for King of the World." She hesitated a moment. I could tell she was almost in tears. "Ace, I think he's in serious trouble."

"What else is new?" I asked nonchalantly. "You must have known that already."

She suddenly came unglued. "What in the world is wrong with you, Ace? This is our dear friend from school days—a man we haven't seen or heard from in two whole years. Then this morning, he turns up out of the blue, living in some sort of fantasy world. Where is your compassion? I just don't understand—"

 "What?" I interrupted. "Neither of us has seen him for *two years*? Just who did you leave me for?"

She paused for several seconds.

"Now that you've brought it up, that's something else I'm puzzled about," she said slowly. "When Mel stopped by with some fried chicken late last night, he implied he had talked with you yesterday about the new relationship. That's also what you led me to believe when we met last night at Sonja's. But it didn't sit right somehow. So I called Mel this morning and pressed him on the subject, and he said he had *meant* to tell you, but hadn't. He promised he would call you just as soon as he finishes the project he's working on."

She paused, and then asked, "So if *he* hadn't told you, how on earth did *you* know I'd been going out with Melvin Bohacker?"

It was as if someone had shoved a searing, red-hot poker into my brain. And then started twisting it. Back and forth. My mouth was moving, but no sounds were coming out. My brain temporarily went numb, and I couldn't think. Then it all became as clear as the stands at a Major League game: I had lost the woman I loved to my arch nemesis—a man who should be committed to an institution for the digitally challenged. I went ballistic.

"You left me for Bohacker?!" I yelled. "You are willing to throw away everything we had, to walk off into the sunset with 'Bits for Brains'? Aaaaaaarrrrrrgggghhh!! How could you do this to me?"

She seemed totally taken aback. "Then you really didn't know after all," she said.

"How *could* I have known," I wailed. "And what could you possibly see in him, anyway?"

"I'd say it was more what he saw in *me*," she replied, a little defensively. "He thought my companionship was worthwhile. He paid attention to me. Like *you* used to do, when we first started going together."

"Are you saying I don't appreciate you any more?" I demanded.

"I'm just saying that when I needed someone, he was there, and you weren't. He looked out for me, Ace. He protected me. That's all."

"Believe me, Helen, I can tell you from experience that Bohacker doesn't have a thoughtful bone in his body," I argued.

"That's not true. Why, he even insisted that he should be the one to tell you about us, so I would be spared the pain. I just don't understand why he hasn't done it yet. I guess he's just been under the gun. He was rather distracted the entire time he was here last night. Kept mentioning some woman he met yesterday at a business conference. I suppose it all has to do with this big competition he's involved in right now." She paused. "Oh, I guess I'm just confused," she said in disgust.

I struggled to get my wits about me. Finding none, I took my second-best shot. I put the whole thing on hold.

"Listen, Baby. We need to get together and talk about this situation at length. How about if I call you in a day or two, after things have calmed down a little? Maybe we can have coffee."

"That sounds good to me," she said. "Just give me a call."

Click. She hung up.

I put down the phone. My hands were white and shaking, and beads of cold sweat poured down my forehead. *So this is what The Author was talking about,* I thought. *The biggest challenge I would face in this story.* Even though I had known it was coming, I was still devastated by it. I still didn't have the slightest idea what to do.

The uploading process had finished while I was on the phone, so I started packing up my gear. My life was a total shambles. My brain had been folded, spindled, and mutilated. My emotions were twisted as tight as a pair of cotton shorts during a wrestling match. But the experts say that everyone is dysfunctional to some degree. And my psyche would gradually heal with time. Right now, my entire career was on the line, and I had serious business to take care of at Boxlight. I slugged down the last few drops of coffee and slipped my notebook computer into my briefcase. I picked up my car keys, and I headed for the door.

Nothing was going to stop me now. I had an *Appointment with Destiny.*

Epilogue: Ace Looks to the Future

Don Taylor

Ace won the competition—but how could he lose with Delphi? And the first prize, it seems, wasn't money after all.

I tapped the Hangup button on my cell phone and sucked in a lungful of invigorating salt air. I was standing on the pier at the Marina, just outside the Boxlight offices. The rain had finally let up, and the skies had turned a lighter shade of gray. A dense fog had rolled in to replace the rain, and as I looked over at the Boxlight building, it almost seemed to dissolve into the murky cloud, making it appear dreamlike.

There certainly were times during the past 24 hours I had felt like I was living in a dream—a *bad* dream. But as usual, The Author had been right. In the long run, everything had turned out for the best.

I won the competition, of course. Carson loved the demo and hired me on the spot to create a suite of custom business applications for Boxlight. We made an appointment for next week to talk over the details. When they called Bohacker to give him the bad news, I found out he hadn't even gotten past the point of designing some screen layouts. He had foolishly assumed that I was using the same old development tools I al-

597

ways had. It was the Tortoise and the Hare all over again. But this time, *the Tortoise was driving a Maserati.*

I broke off the date with Rhonda. I guess I finally realized I was just a guy on the rebound, someone desperate for human companionship. Funny thing, though. She seemed a little taken aback when I introduced myself. In fact, she was more than a little flustered. But I let her down easy, and she almost seemed relieved to have the date canceled.

I slipped the cell phone back into my coat pocket. I had just finished a long conversation with Helen, and I had gotten some really good news: Our relationship was back on again. In spades. My victory in the competition had seemed hollow without her, so I had given her a call right after I left Boxlight...

• • •

"Bohacker lied to you, Baby," I told her. "He didn't really care about you."

"I know that now," Helen confessed. "I thought he was trying to spare my feelings. Now I realize he was just using me to try to hurt you. I feel so ashamed."

"Don't be," I said. "It happens to all of us at one time or another. It's all a part of experiencing *relationships.*"

"What do you mean?"

"Well, Sweetheart, each of us is an individual, made up of his or her unique characteristics. We each have our strengths and weaknesses, but we must also be able to stand, alone and proud. As we share a part of ourselves with others, we become connected in a way that makes each person stronger than they could possibly be by themselves. That's called *relationships.*" That was the second time today I had been able to use that rap to my advantage. I definitely owed Bruiser a debt of gratitude.

"Oh, Ace," Helen cooed. "You've grown so much in the last two weeks. I think maybe you finally understand."

"Count on it," I said.

"And you're right. We all have to be connected, and yet we have to be strong and stand on our own. You and I both."

"Right you are," I confirmed.

"Just to show you how much I really care about you, Ace, I'm going to let you stand on your own. I'm going to let you do your own laundry from now on. And I won't cook your meals, either. Or clean that tiny apartment you call your office."

"Uh, we can talk more about that later. The main thing is that we're back together again."

"Oh, Ace," she said tearfully, "this time I just *know* it will be different."

"Count on it," I said. "Stick with me, Baby, and you'll have Road Apples as big as diamonds."

● ● ●

I had also managed to talk her into letting me be the one to break the Bad News to Bohacker. Perhaps he and I could do lunch, I thought. I would be more than willing to treat him to a double portion of Knuckle Sandwich.

With my right hand I touched the lapel of my trenchcoat. I could feel the satisfying bulge of the envelope in my inside pocket—the envelope containing the $1,000 check given to me by Dave Carson. I planned to use that dough for several things.

I would pay the deductible on my fire insurance and hire someone to come in and clean up my office. I would send a $30 check to Rimrock Software, to register the copy of HelpGen I had used in creating the demo. I was even considering buying an hour or two of professional counseling for Bruiser. After all, I did owe the big lug a favor.

But the biggest chunk of the wad would be spent tomorrow evening. When I phoned, Helen had agreed to go out with me, as long as we could be "real" together. Like the old days. This afternoon I was going to find out how long a human being can sleep at one stretch. But tomorrow night is a Friday night, and weekends were made for celebrations. Helen and I would be dining and dancing at *Cholesterol's*, Seattle's chic new supper club. I had to admit I was looking forward to wolfing down a big, juicy two-inch-thick steak. Medium rare. With sautéed mushrooms. Clam chowder. Salad, smothered with bleu cheese dressing. And a big slab of New York style cheesecake for dessert. And then, who knows what would happen. Hmm. Maybe I would even wear my *formal* trenchcoat for the occasion.

As I started walking down the pier, I reviewed my most recent adventure. I had learned three important lessons in the past 24 hours:

1. *Delphi is an awesome tool for rapidly developing Windows applications.* In a single day, I had been able to turn a concept into a more-or-less complete application, complete with printed report and limited help capabilities. In the past, that would have taken me at least a week of hard work. And all things considered, the job had been pretty easy. Hey—if *I* can do this Delphi thing, I guess just about *anybody can.* Even Bohacker. So I'm not going to tell him about it.

2. *You don't miss your porch light until it burns out.* Even though Helen was the light of my life, in the four years we had known one another I had begun to take her for granted. And until you stumble and experience the Twisted Ankles of Life, you really have no appreciation of the good things you already have. (*Note to myself:* Replace that bulb before it gets dark tonight.)

3. *Nobody can be yourself the way YOU can.* I suppose it was the lecture Helen gave me at Sonja's that finally made me realize I had drifted far from my goals and ideals. She was right: I wasn't the "real" Ace any more—the one The Author had intended me to be. I guess it's always good to be open to new concepts and ideas. But if you get into the position of borrowing too much of something that doesn't really belong to you, you can eventually find yourself bankrupt.

I had reached the end of the pier. A fog horn sounded from somewhere in the distance. I pulled off my hat and raked back my hair with my fingers. Yes, this adventure had come to an end. But even greater ones lay ahead.

I carefully slipped the Fedora back on my head, grabbing the brim to snug it down tight. The fog had begun to lift, and shafts of sunlight were already piercing the mass of gray cotton candy. Looking out over Liberty Bay, I could just make out the silhouette of Mount Rainier through the swirling mist. As I rested my foot on the pier railing, a gratified smile spread across my face.

What an absolutely gorgeous day, I thought. Looks like it's gonna rain.

Appendix: A Delphi Perspective for VB Users

If you've been through the earlier parts of this book, by now you're familiar with many of the new features that Delphi offers. This chapter will put a different spin on looking at Delphi by contrasting it to Visual Basic. For existing Visual Basic developers this should provide an understanding of Delphi from a common knowledge base as well as a point of comparison between the two products. After that, we'll show you how to move your existing VB applications into Delphi with some provided tools so you can continue working with Delphi in your current projects.

DELPHI VS. VISUAL BASIC

The methodology for RAD design consists of creating forms that contain reusable components (or controls), creating specific event code for these controls, generating an executable and debugging to produce the final application. Both Visual Basic and Delphi subscribe to this methodology, which makes the products appear deceptively similar. However, there are several key enhancements that have been added to the process by Delphi:

- Two-way code development

- More built-in controls

- Enhanced icon array organization for access to controls

- Enhanced object placement

- Enhanced modification of property lists

- More powerful underlying programming language

- Incorporation of OOP programming methodology

601

- Shared event functions

- Debugger and object inspection

An obvious difference between Visual Basic and Delphi is the underlying programming languages, Basic and Object Pascal, respectively. The availability of Object Pascal for code development has several important repercussions.

- Pascal is, by nature, a more powerful language than Basic.

- Object Pascal is an object-oriented language allowing full capability for class architectures, inheritance, virtual functions, and polymorphism. Note that although the developer need not be familiar with object-oriented concepts to create programs using Delphi, the experienced user can enjoy the benefit of these capabilities.

- Pascal is compiled instead of interpreted (as is Visual Basic) for higher performance executables.

- The organization of files as DCU's provides a clean mechanism for creating libraries and reusable code.

- Object Pascal utilizes the world's fastest compiler.

One final point to note about the usage of Object Pascal with Delphi. In Visual Basic, all code files must be specifically associated with a form except for a global .BAS file. In other words, a function must be global to the *entire project* unless associated with a specific form. In Delphi, however, code files and therefore classes and functions can be disassociated with any form. This allows proper scoping of functions and variables without loss of functionality.

RAD TOOL EVALUATION CRITERIA

To accomplish a complete comparison of the merits of Delphi and Visual Basic, the developer should consider several factors. First and foremost, the development environment must enhance the productivity of the developer. This can be accomplished simply by the ease of use of the environment itself, as well as the repertoire of reusable components that are available for the developer's use. Since development environments like Visual Basic and Delphi are frequently used for database applications, database readiness has to be a significant point of evaluation. And finally, for those applications intended for the mass market, high performance is key to maintaining a competitive edge. Therefore, the following four issues are significant to a comparitive look at Visual Basic and Delphi:

- Performance

- Rapid Application Development

- Component Reuse

- Database Scalability

Performance

With the evolution of large, distributed client-server applications, any lack of executable speed becomes so much more apparent due to the higher system demands. Delphi's performance is significantly enhanced simply because it produces compiled code executables, whereas Visual Basic produces semi-interpreted code. Also, Delphi uses an optimizing native code compiler instead of the slower interpreted p-code used by competing products, giving Delphi a 10 to 20 times performance edge. Additionally, the optimizing linker enables segment optimization, reducing executable size up to 30 percent. This generates code that will load faster, further improving performance.

A common objection to choosing to work with a compiled language is that the development time is slowed by waiting for repeated compilations. In reality, the compiler for Delphi's Object Pascal is so fast that the developer will see little or no difference in the productivity between Delphi compilation and the Visual Basic interpreter.

In addition to creating standalone .EXE's, Delphi can also be used to create reusable DLL's. These DLL's do not require a runtime interpreter further enhancing overall performance.

Rapid Application Development

There are several aspects of Visual Basic and Delphi that contribute to their degree of developer productivity. One of the more significant differences between the two is Delphi's concept of *two-way code development*. Delphi creates a code window that synchronizes all visual design work with actual code. In other words, as the application is constructed by dropping objects into a form, the corresponding source code is created simultaneously in an adjoining code window. There are no limitations, because the code is always accessible. Further, modifications to the code are instantly reflected visually within the visual form under development. Work can alternate between the code window and the visual design windows to allow the developer to select the most efficient mode of operation for each part of the development task. In contrast, Visual Basic development is primarily restricted to the visual tools. Access to specific event code is only available via the form itself.

Some of the other issues that affect the efficiency of design methodology are these:

Control Palette

The Visual Basic control palette is just that: An array of icons whose pictorial representations may not always be a sufficient clue to decipher the nature of the associated control. The Delphi tabbed palette provides a more self-explanatory solution with its "fly by" hints to identify icons. Additionally, the tabbed palette saves screen real estate while providing an effective organization of all design components. Many more drop-in components can be made available to the developer in the same screen space as Visual Basic.

Templates and Experts

Delphi includes form template galleries that make it easy to develop standard applications or application elements such as MDI, database forms, tables, about boxes, multi-page dialogs, and dual list boxes. The architecture is completely open, allowing the developer to easily register his or her own custom templates and experts into the gallery.

Object placement

Delphi speeds object placement with features such as automatic object alignment, sizing, and scaling. Built-in Visual Basic functionality includes raw placement only. Delphi's automatic alignment capabilities significantly speed the creation of balanced, visually pleasing forms.

Property Lists

A subtle yet significant distinction between the two systems can be seen in the implementation of component property lists. Using Visual Basic, the developer can access a pulldown selection of options for a particular property via an entry bar at the top of the list. Thus, when changing several property items, the developer must click on the item, then click on the entry bar to make the change, then click on the next item, and so on. In Delphi, pulldown lists can be accessed directly at the property value, making for more rapid and intuitive property management.

Debugging And Object Inspection

Visual Basic provides program debug capability including variable watches and a modal call stack. However, the functionality is limited in two ways: 1) it is not able to break on a condition, and 2) the call stack is modal; that is, it is not viewable throughout the entire debug session. Delphi's close coupling to Object Pascal includes a full-featured debugger with conditional breakpoints and a modeless call stack viewer. In addition, the debug window and viewers can be saved from session to session, allowing the developer to create a comfortable and highly customized environment. Additionally, Delphi includes the powerful object browser that is also found in Borland C++. The browser provides a comprehensive display of code objects and classes including the capability to trace object lineage (inheritance) and virtual procedures.

Component Reuse

One of the most significant advances in RAD methodology is the concept of creating an application from high level components rather than lines of traditional, low-level source code. By "hooking up" predefined building blocks, the developer need only define the glue between objects that specifies the unique qualities of his application. Fully exploiting this paradigm has the potential for enormous gains in productivity. Both Delphi and Visual Basic provide various ways to reuse and share components and code. However, Delphi again proves to be the cleaner and simpler solution.

The issue of reusability can be discussed from three perspectives:

- Shared event functions

- Reusable functions

- Reusable building blocks (Controls, for example)

Shared Event Functions

A common problem encountered in Windows programming is how to share a function that is executed upon the occurrence of Windows events. Although the solution is similar in both Delphi and Visual Basic, the Delphi solution has some obvious advantages. In Visual Basic, shared functions must be placed in the local code file or, in the case that the function is to be shared across files, it must be placed in a global .BAS file. The problem with this is that the function is now global to the entire project. In contrast, Delphi allows placement of the function within the local file or in a .DCU (Object Pascal unit file) which is explicitly referenced only by the files that use it.

Reusable Functions and Libraries

As discussed above, shared libraries can be in the form of a global .BAS file in Visual Basic or within .DCU precompiled Pascal units. Additionally, both Visual Basic and Delphi can take advantage of functions organized within DLLs. Delphi can both use and create high performance Windows DLLs. Furthermore, through the use of Object Pascal, the developer can reuse and customize functionality within a class by simply subclassing and modifying the desired functionality (see OOP methodology, below).

Custom Components

Custom control components called VBXs can be written for Visual Basic that contain functionality usable across projects. A disadvantage to custom VBXs is the high degree of low-level Windows expertise required to create them. Controls in Delphi are called VCLs, and are easily created. Unlike Visual Basic, where controls must be created with an external C/C++ compiler, VCL's are created from within the Delphi development environment itself, in the same Object Pascal language used in all Delphi development. Delphi adds one more big advantage with its use of VCLs: The developer can easily subclass the functionality of a VCL in order to create a slightly modified and therefore customized version of the control. This feature gives the developer significantly more power than with the use of VBX components, which are not readily subclasses.

Database Scalability and Support

In Visual Basic, the developer can place a data control object into a form. Using the data control as a conduit, a GUI object (edit box, grid, combo box, and the like) within the form can be associated with an ODBC database allowing bi-directional communication. The data control can also be used as a crude mechanism to navigate through the data base using arrows representing first, next, previous, last. Other database tasks like SQL queries, reports and even setup of the database are accomplished through a fairly tedious process within the design environment. Several third party tools have evolved to facilitate this process.

On the other hand, Delphi includes extensive database support including built-in support for queries, reports, and database creation. The **TQuery** (query component) provides the ability to perform SQL queries to generate subset datasets. Delphi includes the powerful ReportSmith for PC and SQL databases to provide an intuitive interface for report creation, using live data on the screen. ReportSmith supports queries, crosstabs, templates, calculations, and unlimited report sizes. Additionally, Delphi includes "experts" that facilitate rapid design and implementation of databases and the corresponding user interface. The DataSet designer that comes with Delphi allows you to rapidly create table or query data for the database accessed through the forms. You can specify which set of fields from the database you want to incorporate into the table or query.

Delphi ships with several controls for data entry and display including tables and grids. Delphi also comes with the DBEdit control to allow a consolidated control to handle this task of designing the grid database. Grid-aware, specialized versions of the control are available for labels, lists, combo boxes, images, memo (multi-line editors), check and radio buttons, lookup lists, and lookup combo lists.

Database access is supported through the Borland Database Engine and middleware layers that support local and remote data sources. The Borland database architecture provides the developer with high performance access to a variety of data sources including ODBC. Delphi includes both data-access components as well as data-aware user interface components to provide a complete database solution.

MAKING THE SWITCH TO DELPHI

So—you want to start using Delphi, but you don't want to redo all your work already completed in Visual Basic. The process of migrating your existing Visual Basic applications over to Delphi is easy, thanks to the Conversion Assistant from EarthTrek. An evaluation copy of Conversion Assistant is available on the listings disk for this book.

What Needs to Be Translated

There are four major aspects of an application to be translated:

- Project files (.MAK to .DPR)

- Form files (.FRM to .DFM)

- Translation of the Basic to Pascal code (.BAS to .PAS)

- Import of controls

The first step is to run the application through The Conversion Assistant, which will provide an 80 to 100 percent mapping of project files, form files (including object placement and sizing, colors, and fonts), and code files (including control arrays and event code mapping). An evaluation version of The Conversion Assistant is available on this book's companion disk. You can use the evaluation copy to get a feel for how to import projects and what the output looks like.

Installing the Conversion Assistant

The Conversion Assistant evaluation unit is a Windows application, and a SETUP.EXE program has been provided for it. The best approach to installing the evaluation unit is to copy the Conversion Assistant self-extracting archive CA.EXE from the diskette to a temporary directory somewhere on your hard disk. We'll use C:\TEMP as an example. Once CA.EXE is in the temporary directory, execute CA.EXE. This can be done from the Windows File|Run dialog, or by viewing the temporary subdirectory in File manager and double-clicking on the file entry for CA.EXE. The self-extracting archive will expand to the various files in the Conversion Assistant install set.

Once CA.EXE has extracted itself, run SETUP.EXE. You'll see a screen similar to Figure A.1.

Decide where you want the install to place Conversion Assistant, and alter the displayed directories by clicking on the Change buttons to the right of each

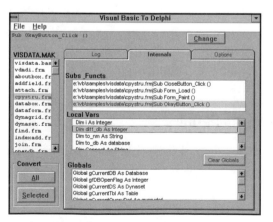

Figure A.1 *Conversion Assistant's Install Screen.*

directory path display. When the directories are the way you want them, click on the Install button to begin the install.

The installation process is automatic and doesn't take much time. When it's done, the Conversion Assistant evaluation unit is ready to use.

Using the Conversion Assistant

As a preliminary step, save your Visual Basic application (.FRM and .MAK files) "As Text". The Visual Basic project can be loaded into the Conversion Assistant using File | Open (or click on the "No file open" message). Select the VB project by loading its .MAK file. You will immediately see the individual components of the project in the view pane. More details about each file can be seen in the Internals tabbed pane by clicking on any of the VB files in the view pane list. See Figure A.2.

The Output Path defaults to the same as the VB .MAK directory and since the file extensions are different, the converted files will not overwrite your Visual Basic source. You have the option of setting the Output Path by clicking the Change button.

You can either choose to convert the entire project by clicking the All button within the "Convert" button group or you can click on an individual file within the list box and convert it only by clicking on Selected. The resulting output is a Delphi project (.DPR) with the same name as the Visual Basic .MAK file prefixed with the letter "p".

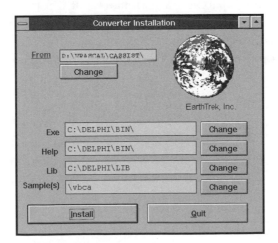

Figure A.2 *The Conversion Assistant Screen.*

There are just a few options that can be set in the Conversion Assistant that primarily affect how much information is displayed or logged as the conversion is progressing. Shut all of these options off if you want to speed up the conversion process.

After you exit the converter, you can immediately load the new project into Delphi. Press F9 to compile the project within Delphi. In most cases you will need to make several manual modifications to your projects to complete the conversion process. More on that a little later.

To facilitate customization of the conversion process, a map file is provided to indicate specific translation between VB objects and Delphi objects. The user can add to the default map file which includes all of the common translations.

When you load your converted project into Delphi, you may see the messages "Invalid Property" or "Error Reading Form". The main reason that this occurs is that the Conversion Assistant has attempted to convert a VB property to a non-existent Delphi property. To resolve these errors, simply click on *Ignore All* as the project is being loaded. Once the project is within Delphi, you can manually correct the discrepancies within the object's property window.

Importing VBX Controls

The Conversion Assistant will automatically translate to Pascal the Visual Basic code relating to your external VBXs, and place those VBXs within the Delphi forms that are created. However, the actual import of the VBXs occurs using Delphi's import capability. This means that if a third party VBX is not currently supported by Delphi, then the Conversion Assistant *will not* be able to complete translation of this object. To import the VBX into Delphi, choose Options I Install Components I VBX from the Delphi main menu. You will then see the icon of your VBX available under the VBX tab in the toolbar. Note that all imports of VBXs must be done *before* loading the converted Delphi project.

Other Conversion Issues

There are several areas that are a straightforward manual process but are very difficult to implement as an automatic process. For this reason, the Conversion Assistant was designed to give you a strong push toward a complete translation. Most of the items not translated can be identified easily by simply compiling the project and noting any syntax errors. A list of the most common discrepancies are noted along with their corresponding remedy.

Boolean type declaration

There is no type **Boolean** in Visual Basic. In Visual Basic, a Boolean variable is represented as an **INT**. These declaration must be changed to **Boolean** in the Delphi program.

Implied property reference

Visual Basic allows you to set a label's **Caption** property implicitly, without specifying the "Caption" property keyword in the expression. Delphi requires explicit property specifications. For example, you need to change:

```
Label1 := 'Hello';
```

to

```
Label1.Caption := 'Hello';
```

Similarly, for Visual Basic Edit controls, you need to change:

```
Edit1 := 'Hello';
```

to

```
Edit1.Text := 'Hello';
```

Automatic type conversion

Visual Basic provides automatic type conversion (for example, from integer to string) as needed. In Delphi, these conversions must be explicit. Several functions are provided with the Conversion Assistant to mimic the Visual Basic functions **VAL**, **STR**, and **LEFT**. The letters "VB" are prefixed to the functions. These functions are provided in the file VB.DCU.

For example, assuming **x** was defined as type **Integer**;

```
x := Label1.Caption
```

would need to be modified, for Delphi, to

```
x := vbVAL(Label1.Caption);
```

And

```
Label1.Caption := x;
```

would need to be modified to

```
Label1.Caption := vbSTR(x);
```

Array Dimensions

Array dimensions with array designators are not converted to Pascal. Thus

```
Dim ar(5) As Integer
```

would become, in Delphi:

```
Var ar: array[1..5] of integer;
```

Chars and pChars

Strings greater than 256 chars in length must be of type **pchar,** which closely resembles the null-terminated string types in C. The Conversion Assistant converts all strings declared in Visual Basic to **char** arrays in Delphi. If you know that your string needs to be longer than 256 characters, change its type declaration to **pchar**. Be sure to use the proper **pchar** functions to manipulate the string—and remember that memory for a non-constant **pchar** must be dynamically allocated. A final note: In DLL function declarations, *all* strings must be referenced as **pchar** strings, done automatically by the Conversion Assistant.

The Variant type

The Conversion Assistant does not translate VB variants. One workaround in Delphi is to translate your variant to a general-purpose pointer. Then, you can dereference it after it is passed as a parameter to the actual type needed.

Redim and Resize

Visual Basic allows dynamic memory allocation through the **REDIM** and **RESIZE** statements. Since Delphi offers several means of memory allocation, the developer will need to determine which one is applicable in each specific case. For example, the functions **New** and **Dispose** allocate space for an object; **GetMem** and **FreeMem** get and release a block of memory of a specific size without assigning it to any particular object; and **NewStr** and **AssignStr** handle memory allocation for strings.

.FRX files

The .FRX file most commonly contains references to image files (.BMP) within the form. Typically you would have set a **Picture** property in a VB application by clicking on the property and selecting your desired .BMP file. The Conversion Assistant places and sizes the image control containing the image; however the same procedure should be followed within Delphi to reference the image files themselves.

DDE/OLE calls

In Visual Basic, such calls are accomplished with properties. However, the Delphi approach is to drop a control into the form and use it as a DDE/OLE conduit, much as you would use the VB data control.

CONVERSION EXAMPLE

The example discussed here converts to Delphi the CALC.MAK sample project that ships with Visual Basic. (Note that the converted file is available with the Conversion Assistant evaluation package on your disk.) After running the project through the Conversion Assistant, the following items will cause syntax errors and therefore need to be changed manually:

Modification 1 line 52

```
Op1,Op2: integer { possible unknown, or user type };
DecimalFlag: boolean;
NumOps: integer;
LastInput: string { possible unknown, or user type };
OpFlag: char { possible unknown, or user type };
TempReadout: string { possible unknown, or user type };
```

Comments: *The types of the variables can require manual intervention. In VB, a Boolean is defined as an Integer. A Variant VB type can be used as any of several different types and the corresponding Pascal type must be deduced from the variable's context. The "OpFlag" may appear to be a string, but inspection of the code (in the* **Select Case** *statement) shows it to really be a* **Char** *type.*

Modification 2

Change all "ReadOut" to "ReadOut.Caption" (whole words only)

Comments: *VB allows you to access/set an EditBox's* **Text** *or Label's* **Caption** *property without specifying them. A single Search/Replace will solve this problem.*

Modification 3 line 81

Old: **Form_Load**;
New: **Form_Load(Sender);**

Comments: *Add the Delphi required parameter.*

Modification 4 line 158

```
Op2 := vbVAL(TempReadout);
```

Modification 5 line 161

Old: **Op1 := VBval(Op1) + VBval(op2);**
New: **Op2 := Op1 + Op2;**

Comments: *Although this did pass in VB, it is inconsistent because there is no reason to convert **Op1** or **Op2** to a "val" since they already are integers.*

Modification 6 line 186

Old: **ReadOut.Caption := Op1;**
New: **ReadOut.Caption := VBstr(Op1);**

Comments: *Cannot assign an integer to a string, so we must convert.*

Modification 7 line 193

Old: **OpFlag := Operator(VBIndex(Sender)).Caption;**
New: **OpFlag := Operator(VBIndex(Sender)).Caption[1];**

Comments: *Since **OpFlag** is a **Char**, we want to assign it to the first character of the **.Caption** property.*

Modification 8 line 198

Old: **ReadOut.Caption := ReadOut.Caption div 100;**
New: **ReadOut.Caption := VBstr(VBval(ReadOut.Caption div 100);**

Comments: *Convert strings to numbers, calculate and convert back to a string.*

INDEX

—C—

—D—

—R—

The Coriolis Group Home Page!

➡ You'll be able to browse our wide selection of books and order them directly online, get a sneak preview of upcoming titles, and check out the latest issue of **PC TECHNIQUES** Magazine. Just set your Web browser to:
http://www.coriolis.com/coriolis

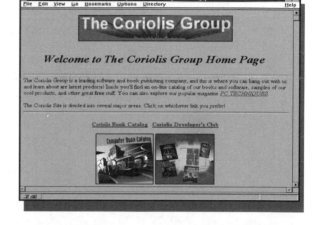

➡ And don't forget to stop by the FREE $TUFF Web site where you'll get access to the bestselling **FREE $TUFF from the Internet**—absolutely free. And if you want to cruise on over into the paid area, you'll get the hypertext links that will take you directly to all the FREE $TUFF you could ever want!! Set your Web browser to:
http://power.globalnews.com/freestuff

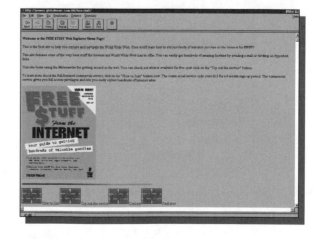

READ THE MAGAZINE OF TECHNICAL EXPERTISE!

Published by The Coriolis Group

For years, Jeff Duntemann has been known for his crystal-clear, slightly-bemused explanations of programming technology. He's one of the few in computer publishing who has never forgotten that English is the one language we all have in common. Now he's teamed up with author Keith Weiskamp and created a magazine that brings you a selection of readable, practical technical articles six times a year, written by himself and a crew of the very best technical writers working today. Michael Abrash, Tom Swan, Jim Mischel, Keith Weiskamp, David Gerrold, Brett Glass, Michael Covington, Peter Aitken, Marty Franz, Jim Kyle, and many others will perform their magic before your eyes, and then explain how *you* can do it too, in language that you can understand.

If you program under DOS or Windows in C, C++, Pascal, Visual Basic, or assembly language, you'll find code you can use in every issue. You'll also find essential debugging and optimization techniques, programming tricks and tips, detailed product reviews, and practical advice on how to get your programming product finished, polished and ready to roll.

Don't miss another issue—subscribe today!

☐ 1 Year $21.95   ☐ 2 Years $37.95

☐ $29.95 Canada; $39.95 Foreign   ☐ $53.95 Canada; $73.95 Foreign

Total for subscription: _____
Arizona orders please add 6% sales tax: _____
Total due, in US funds:_____

Send to:
PC TECHNIQUES
7339 E. AcomaDr., Suite 7
Scottsdale AZ 85260

Name _____
Company _____
Address _____
City/State/Zip _____
Phone _____

Phone
(602) 483-0192
Fax
(602) 483-0193

VISA/MC # _____ Expires: _____

Signature for charge orders: _____

ABOUT THE AUTHORS

Jeff Duntemann has been writing about microcomputing since 1977. He worked as a programmer for Xerox Corporation until 1985, when he became Technical Editor of *PC Tech Journal*. He left in 1987 to found Borland's programmers' magazine *Turbo Technix*. His book *Complete Turbo Pascal* sold over 100,000 copies in four editions for almost ten years, and his *Assembly Language Step By Step*, with almost 100,000 copies in print, may well be the best selling book on PC assembly language ever published. He now works as Editorial Director of The Coriolis Group, Inc., publishers of *PC TECHNIQUES* magazine and Coriolis Group Books. Jeff lives in the high desert north of Scottsdale, Arizona, with his wife Carol. He operates amateur radio station KG7JF, restores antique radios and amateur gear, and drives a near-mint 1969 Chevelle.

Jim Mischel began his career writing software for the banking and financial services industry, and has been a microcomputing enthusiast since 1978. Jim began writing on programming in 1989, and published his first book, *Macro Magic with Turbo Assembler*, in 1992. More recently, Jim's book *The Developer's Guide to WINHELP.EXE* has been the core around which Jim has developed a seminar series on developing online Help content for Windows. Jim is a regular writer for *PC TECHNIQUES* and Windows/DOS Developer's Journal, and develops leading edge 3-D game software for Cinematronics in Austin, Texas. Jim lives outside Austin with his wife Debra and operates amateur radio station KB7UQD when he isn't out chasing armadillos through the bluebonnets.

Don Taylor is well known to the Borland Pascal community as the founder of Turbo User Group and editor of its newsletter, *TUG Lines*. Don was also the coordinator of the much-enjoyed Get-TUG-Gether, an annual party/seminar series held in Silverdale, Washington, for users of the Borland languages. Don has written extensively for *PC TECHNIQUES* and other magazines in recent years. Don is currently an independent software consultant and president of Turbo Communications, a generalist audiovisual and copyrighting agency specializing in technical writing, technical presentations, and advertising copy. He lives in the hills above Poulsbo, Washington, with his wife Carol.

Notes on the Companion Software

This book may be packaged with either a high-density diskette or CD-ROM. (The CD-ROM version comes only as part of the *Delphi Starter Kit* published by The Coriolis Group.)

Using the Delphi Diskette

All of the Delphi form, code, and data files you'll need to compile and run all the projects in this book are present on the companion diskette. They're not just pointless demo programs, either. Some of the highlights:

- A software stopwatch that really works, with separate time and lap counters.

- A file viewer that automatically displays either text files or bitmapped images.

- A Windows implementation of that old SpiroGraph toy that drew elaborate cycloid curves using plastic gears running around a toothed track. With Delphi, you don't need no steenking plastic gears! And with a high-resolution laser printer, you can print cycloid patterns of a complexity that no plastic SpiroGraph could ever equal.

- A mortgage calculator program that will allow you to generate and display the amortization table for any type of mortgage loan.

- A sophisticated database system for tracking products and repair product authorizations. The database demonstrates most of Delphi's desktop database power, and includes bitmapped photos of the products stored right in the database.

We've included a shareware version of HelpGen, a simple Windows Help authoring utility that will save you an enormous amount of time creating Windows Help files for your Delphi applications.

Finally, on the diskette is an evaluation version of EarthTrek's Conversion Assistant, a way-cool utility for translating your Visual Basic applications to Dephi. Conversion Assistant looks at your VB apps and gets you about 85 percent of the way there. Once it's done, all you need to do is tough up some of the "rough spots" (see the Appendix for more details) and you're up and running with Delphi!

Using the Delphi CD-ROM

All of the above software is available on the CD-ROM. In additon, it features the commercial version of Conversion Assistant, Delphi custom controls, and other Delphi-related material. To use the CD-ROM, see the readme file on the CD-ROM.